Royal Courts
of the Ancient Maya,
Volume Two:
Data and Case Studies

Royal Courts of the Ancient Maya,

Volume Two: Data and Case Studies

EDITED BY

Takeshi Inomata
University of Arizona

AND

Stephen D. Houston
Brigham Young University

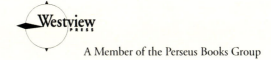

A Member of the Perseus Books Group

All rights reserved. Printed in the United States of America. No part of this publication may be reproduced or transmitted in any form or by any means, electronic or mechanical, including photocopy, recording, or any information storage and retrieval system, without permission in writing from the publisher.

Copyright © 2001 by Westview Press, A Member of the Perseus Books Group

Published in 2001 in the United States of America by Westview Press, 5500 Central Avenue, Boulder, Colorado 80301–2877, and in the United Kingdom by Westview Press, 12 Hid's Copse Road, Cumnor Hill, Oxford OX2 9JJ

Find us on the World Wide Web at www.westviewpress.com

Library of Congress Cataloging-in-Publication Data
  Royal courts of the ancient Maya / edited by Takeshi Inomata and Stephen D. Houston.
    p. cm.
  Includes bibliographical references and index.
  Contents: v. 2. Data and case studies
  ISBN 0-8133-3880-8 (pbk)
  1. Mayas—Kings and rulers. 2. Maya architecture. 3. Mayas—Antiquities.
4. Inscriptions, Mayan. 5. Royal houses—Mexico. 6. Royal houses—Central America.
7. Mexico—Antiquities. 8. Central America—Antiquities. I. Inomata, Takeshi, Ph. D.
II. Houston, Stephen D.

F1435.3.K55 R69 2000
972.81'016—dc21

00-063306

The paper used in this publication meets the requirements of the American National Standard for Permanence of Paper for Printed Library Materials Z39.48–1984.

10   9   8   7   6   5   4   3   2   1

*To the memory of
Floyd Lounsbury*

Contents

List of Tables and Illustrations ix
Preface xix

1 The Architecture of Early Kingship: Comparative
  Perspectives on the Origins of the Maya Royal Court,
  John E. Clark and Richard D. Hansen 1

2 The Royal Court of Early Classic Copan, *Loa P. Traxler* 46

3 Thrones and Throne Structures in the Central Acropolis of
  Tikal as an Expression of the Royal Court, *Peter D. Harrison* 74

4 The Royal Court of Caracol, Belize: Its Palaces and People,
  Arlen F. Chase and Diane Z. Chase 102

5 Palaces and Thrones Tied to the Destiny of the Royal Courts
  in the Maya Lowlands, *Juan Antonio Valdés* 138

6 The Buenavista-Cahal Pech Royal Court: Multi-Palace
  Court Mobility and Usage in a Petty Lowland Maya Kingdom,
  Joseph W. Ball and Jennifer T. Taschek 165

7 Life at Court: The View from Bonampak, *Mary Miller* 201

8 Triadic Temples, Central Plazas and Dynastic Palaces:
  A Diachronic Analysis of the Royal Court Complex,
  Calakmul, Campeche, Mexico, *William J. Folan, Joel D. Gunn,
  María del Rosario Domínguez Carrasco* 223

9 Post-Classic and Terminal Classic Courts of the Northern Maya
   Lowlands, *William M. Ringle and George J. Bey III*   266

10 Post-Classic Maya Courts of the Guatemalan Highlands:
   Archaeological and Ethnohistorical Approaches,
   Geoffrey E. Braswell   308

11 The People of the Patio: Ethnohistorical Evidence of
   Yucatec Maya Royal Courts, *Matthew Restall*   335

List of Contributors   391
Index   395

Tables and Illustrations

Tables

5.1 Dimensions of Palace H-Sub 2 of Uaxactun (in meters)
5.2 Dimensions of Palace H-Sub 5 of Uaxactun (in meters)

8.1 Chronological Sequence of Calakmul, Campeche, Mexico

11.1 Courtly Meetings in Conquest Times: Some Examples of Maya Summits, circa 1530–1600
11.2 Yucatan's Ruling Dynasties at the Time of the Spanish Conquest, circa 1520–1570
11.3 The Officers of the Court: Political Offices in Yucatan, circa 1400–1800
11.4 Some Examples of Maya Courtly Retinues, circa 1440–1700
11.5 The Yaxakumche Branch of the Xiu Lineage
11.6 Maya Origin Myth References in the Ethnohistorical Sources

Figures

1.1 Map of Middle Pre-Classic centers showing the locations of sites mentioned in the text (circles) and those built on the MFC pattern (squares).
1.2 Site plan of early La Venta, Tabasco, Mexico (adapted from González Lauck 1996:Figure 1).
1.3 Site plan of early Chiapa de Corzo, Chiapas, Mexico.
1.4 Site plan of Mirador, Chiapas.
1.5 Site plan of La Libertad, Chiapas.
1.6 Site plan of early Nakbe, Peten, Guatemala.
1.7 Group 18 at Nakbe, a possible royal compound (redrawn from Martínez and Hansen 1993:Figure 8).
1.8 Early E-Group at Tikal (redrawn from Fialko 1988: Figure 3).
1.9 Plaza E at Uaxactun during the Pre-Classic (redrawn from Rosal et al. 1993:Figure 34).
1.10 Site plan of the ceremonial center of Protoclassic Chiapa de Corzo.

1.11 Plan of the Mound 5, A.D. 100 palace at Chiapa de Corzo (redrawn from Lowe 1962:Figure 46).
1.12 Reconstruction of the Mound 5 palace at Chiapa de Corzo (by Ayax Moreno).
1.13 Pottery assemblage from Cache 17–1, Mound 17, Chiapa de Corzo, which has the same vessel forms and proportions as those from Mound 5, chamber B (from Lowe 1962:Figure 34).

2.1 Motmot Marker (drawing by Barbara Fash).
2.2 Detail from carved peccary skull found in Tomb 1 (drawing by Barbara Fash).
2.3 Plan of Main Group at the site of Copan, Honduras (based on Fash 1991:Figure 1).
2.4 ECAP preliminary plan of Yune Platform and early structures of the royal compound (Traxler).
2.5 ECAP preliminary plan of Witik Platform and structures of the royal compound during the reign of Ruler 2 (Traxler).
2.6 ECAP preliminary plan of royal compound late in the reign of Ruler 2 showing initial masonry palace structures that replaced adobe predecessors (Traxler).
2.7 ECAP preliminary plan of royal compound with masonry palace groups (Traxler).

3.1 Map of Central Tikal. The Central Acropolis is located at the center of the city, adjacent to Temples I and II.
3.2 Detail of the ceremonial center of the city with the religious temples to the north and the more secular palaces of the Central Acropolis in close proximity to the south.
3.3 Painted scene on a burial vessel from Tikal showing presentation of a jaguar skin (Kerr, File No. 2697). Note also the livery of the tribute-givers and the fringed cover of the throne (courtesy of Kerr Associates).
3.4 This simple reception scene from Burial 116 (Hasaw Chan K'awil) illustrates a throne type that has not been found at Tikal, unless the decoration is assumed painted (from Tikal Report No. 25, Part A, Culbert, Figure 69A; courtesy of the University of Pennsylvania Museum).
3.5 Drawing of a segment of the Carved Lintel 2 of Temple III showing Nu Bak Chak II in front of his portable throne. Details from the right end of the throne are clear (after Tikal Report No. 33, Part A, Jones and Satterthwaite, Figure 72; courtesy of the University of Pennsylvania Museum).
3.6 Artist's conception of a reconstruction of the portable throne shown on three lintels at Tikal (drawn by T.W. Rutledge; scale figure based on Lintel 2 of Temple III).

3.7 Reconstruction of the opulence and drama of a typical throne room at Tikal, based upon the archaeological remains. Many examples of this type were uncovered in the Central Acropolis (drawing by Amalia Kenward).
3.8 Structure 5D–46 in its final form. The central core and stair were built by Jaguar Claw the Great who may have founded the royal court in the Central Acropolis in the middle fourth century. The cache vessel in Figure 3.7 was recovered from beneath this stair (photo by Harrison 1969).
3.9 Drawing of the carved dedicatory cache vessel from Structure 5D–46, identifying the building as the "House" (*na*) of Jaguar Claw the Great. The "*na*" glyph is highlighted (courtesy of the University of Pennsylvania Museum).
3.10 Part of the map of the Central Acropolis highlighting four throne structures: from left, 5D–118, 5D–61 (addition), 5D–59 and 5D–123. Structures in question are hatched.
3.11 Drawing of the masonry baffles that restricted traffic from Court 2 to Court 3, immediately adjacent to the throne structure of 5D–59 on the right.
3.12 Reconstruction drawing of Structure 5D–123 showing the throne bench with seated *ajaw*.
3.13 Structure 5D–118 on the right is the building with almost no front wall; Maler's Palace is on the far left (photo by Harrison 1967).
3.14 The addition to Structure 5D–61 in the foreground contains a throne facing left (north). Another throne is located in the room beyond the open door (photo by Harrison 1969).
3.15 Structure 5D–65 (Maler's Palace) is a multiroomed structure with several throne rooms on both stories.
3.16 Artist's reconstruction of the royal court in action on the north side of Structure 5D–65. The iconography of the upper zone is based on recorded fact but is mostly the artist's conception by T.W. Rutledge.
3.17 The multiple stairs that connect different levels and structures between Courts 4 (below) and 3 (above) demonstrate the structural complexity of the Central Acropolis and the restriction of access to throne structures and rooms (photo by Harrison 1966).

4.1 Map of the central portion of Caracol showing the location of many of the palace compounds discussed within this paper; architectural features, reservoirs, and terraces are suppressed; Figure 4.15 positions this central portion of Caracol relative to the site's inner ring of termini.
4.2 Restricted entrances in Caracol palaces: (a) upper front building, Caana (see Figure 4.3); (b) western building, Barrio (see Figure

4.9); (c) mid–level front building, Caana (see Figure (4.3); (d) northern building, South Acropolis (see Figure 4.8).
4.3 Plan of Caana, Caracol's most elaborate palace compound.
4.4 Detail of eastern inner room of Caana mid–range palace looking south; lower "bar" equals 1 meter (drawing by J. Ballay, Caracol Archaeological Project).
4.5 Slate axe found in collapse associated with Caana; it records the name of Caracol lord K'an II (drawing by J. Ballay, Caracol Archaeological Project); maximum width of the axe is 8.2 centimeters.
4.6 Plan of Structures B4, B5, and B6 palace compound.
4.7 Plan of Central Acropolis (after D. Chase and A. Chase 1996:Figure 2).
4.8 Plan of South Acropolis.
4.9 Plan of Barrio palace compound.
4.10 Hypothetical plan of C Group palace compound.
4.11 Caracol Ballcourt Marker 3; the "Second Sul" glyph is located at position D5 (drawing by N. Grube, Caracol Archaeological Project); monument averages 51.2 centimeters in width.
4.12 Graffiti incised in Structure B20–2nd (from A. Chase and D. Chase 1987b:20); human figure to the left is 13 centimeters in height.
4.13 Court scene recorded on a vessel from an interment recovered within the Structure B5 stair fill; height of the vase is 25.6 centimeters.
4.14 Caracol stable isotope data showing "palace diet." Higher levels of 15N Collagen indicates the consumption of more protein. Lower levels of 13C Collagen indicates higher levels of maize consumption. "★" indicate individuals in epicentral tombs, including those associated with palace compounds. "◆" indicate individuals with a "palace diet" who are not buried in palace compounds. "■" indicate other Caracol burials that were sampled.
4.15 Spatial distribution of Caracol interments evincing the epicentral "palace diet" (those individuals shown by "★" and "◆" on Figure 4.14); the outer ring of Caracol termini is not shown on this map.

5.1 Drawing of the limestone model discovered in the Lost World Group at Tikal (Proyecto Nacional Tikal).
5.2 Reconstruction of the acropolis of Group H at Uaxactun during the Late Pre-Classic period (redrawn by F. Luin from Hansen 1998).
5.3 The royal palace of Uaxactun Sub–2C at the beginning of the Early Classic period (redrawn by F. Luin).
5.4 The royal palace of Tikal, built by Ruler Toh Chak Ich'ak (photograph by J.A. Valdés).

5.5 North-south profile of Palace A–18, residence of the ruler of Uaxactun during the last part of the Early Classic period (drawn by Raúl Anguiano).
5.6 Buildings of the palace type at Tikal, built during the final part of the Early Classic period over low platforms (Laporte 1989).
5.7 Aguateca Structure M7–35, showing the throne in the central room (photograph by J.A. Valdés).
5.8 Polychrome vase from the Ik Site discovered at Tamarindito (drawn by F. Luin).
5.9 Copan Structure 10L–18 (photograph by J.A. Valdés).
5.10 Drawing of the throne discovered in the Lost World Group at Tikal (redrawn by F. Luin from Laporte and Fialko 1995).
5.11 Detail of the throne of the Lost World Group at Tikal (photograph by J. A. Valdés).
5.12 Detail of the incisions on the western lateral wall of the throne from Tikal (photograph by J. A. Valdés).
5.13 Drawing of the throne from Aguateca, attached to the exterior of the palace M7–32 (drawn by M. Urquizú).
5.14 View from the Aguateca throne during the work of restoration in 1999 (photograph by J.A. Valdés).
5.15 Female and male members of the court of Aguateca represented in the figurines and musical instruments from this site.

6.1 Map of greater lower Mopan-Macal drainage zone showing select major and minor centers.
6.2 Map of Buenavista del Cayo site with significant referenced features identified.
6.3 Map of Cahal Pech site with significant referenced features identified.
6.4 Set of bowls in the Buenavista del Cayo "palace school" style.
6.5 (a) Principal interior courtyard, Buenavista del Cayo royal palace, from the northwest; Structure 31 in right background; (b) innermost residential courtyard, Cahal Pech royal palace, from the southwest; Structure 13 in background.
6.6 Comparison plans of the royal residential inner sancta at Buenavista del Cayo and Cahal Pech in the middle eighth and early ninth centuries.
6.7 Late Pre-Classic–Terminal Classic ceramic-phase chronology and regal burial-ballcourt distributions for Buenavista and Cahal Pech.
6.8 Schematic ballcourt histories, Buenavista del Cayo and Cahal Pech.
6.9 Center-point cache, North Ballcourt, Buenavista del Cayo.
6.10 Center-point playing field cache pit, North Ballcourt, Buenavista del Cayo.

6.11 East-west topographic cross-section of the lower Mopan-Macal Triangle through Buenavista and Cahal Pech (vertical exaggeration 5:1).
6.12 Axonometric reconstruction of the North Plaza Group at Buenavista seen from the southeast.

7.1 Palenque Palace (redrawn by Gillett Griffin; used by permission).
7.2 Bonampak Structure 1, plan and section (drawing by Regan Huff; courtesy Bonampak Documentation Project).
7.3 Bonampak murals, Room 1, view of bench and lintel (copy by Antonio Tejeda after Ruppert, Thompson, and Proskouriakoff 1955).
7.4 Detail of Stela 1, Bonampak (rawing by Peter Mathews; used by permission).
7.5 Bonampak Structure 1, elevation (drawing by Regan Huff; courtesy Bonampak Documentation Project).
7.6 Uaxactun painting (copy by Antonio Tejeda after Smith 1950).
7.7 Bonampak murals, Room 1, upper southern wall (digital enhancements by Doug Stern to photographs of Enrico Ferrorelli, copyright National Geographic Society; used by permission.
7.8 Bonampak murals, Room 1, north wall (copy by Felipe Dávalos; courtesy Florida State Museum).
7.9 Infrared detail of dressing scene, Room 1, northern wall (courtesy Bonampak Documentation Project).
7.10 Infrared detail of drummer, Room 1 (courtesy Bonampak Documentation Project).
7.11 Bonampak murals, Room 1, northeastern corner (copy by Felipe Dávalos; courtesy Florida State Museum).
7.12 Yaxchilan Hieroglyphic Stairs 2, Step X (drawing by Ian Graham, CMHI 3:163; copyright 1982 by the President and Fellows of Harvard College).
7.13 Bonampak murals, Room 2, northern wall (copy by Antonio Tejeda after Ruppert, Thompson, and Proskouriakoff 1955).
7.14 Bonampak murals, Room 3, eastern, southern, and western walls (copy by Antonio Tejeda after Ruppert, Thompson, and Proskouriakoff 1955).
7.15 Bonampak murals, Room 3, upper eastern wall (digital enhancements by Doug Stern to photographs of Enrico Ferrorelli, copyright National Geographic Society; used by permission).

8.1 The Calakmul Basin showing the location of Calakmul and related sites, settlements, bajos, hills, arroyos, and rivers (INEGI with additions by Joel D. Gunn; drawn by Juan José Cosgaya M.).

8.2 Map of Calakmul, Campeche, México, 30 square kilometers (Jacinto May Hau, Rogerio Couoh Muñoz, Raymundo González Heredia, William J. Folan (1990), Centro de Investigaciones Históricas y Sociales, Universidad Autónoma de Campeche).
8.3 The upper southern facade of the triadic Temple VII suggesting its first known construction period during the Pre-Classic period (reconstruction drawing by María del Rosario Domínguez Carrasco and Aida Amine Casanova Rosado).
8.4 Reconstruction rendition of the main plaza of Calakmul during the Terminal Classic period with Structure I in the upper-right background and Structure II to the right; Structure III is to the immediate left (or northeast) of Structure II (painting by Ernesto Tamay Segovia; photo by Eldon Leiter).
8.5 Section drawing of Structure II acropolis showing the locations of Stelae 114, 115, 116, various buildings, and the room at the rear (south) of Building IIA. Note location of the tunnel to the south where the Late Pre-Classic nature of Structure II was determined (architectural reconstruction by Abel Morales L. and Ernesto Tamay S.; redrawn by Aida Amine Casanova R. and Fabian Pérez J.). Also present is Building II-B-sub showing its associated tombs and their location below building II-B (redrawn from Carrasco et al. 1999:Figure 5).
8.6 Artist's rendition of a section drawing of Structure III during the Terminal Classic showing the location of Early Classic Tomb 1 (drawing by Sophia Pincemin 1994).
8.7 Structure III activity areas (Domínguez, Gunn, and Folan 1997:Figure 7 [revised rendition]).
8.8 The lower facade of Structure II showing the location of activity areas based on the analyses of ceramics and lithics registered during excavation (Domínguez C. et al. 1997; drawing by Raymundo González H. and Juan José Cosgaya M.).
8.9 Lower facade of Structure II showing the location of skeletal material mainly located among collapsed masonry (Tiesler et al. 1997). Location of skeletal material by Abel Morales Lopez (drawing by Raymundo González H.).
8.10 Cycle 8, Stela 114 at Calakmul located in a partially vaulted niche. A round miniature altar supported by a layer of ash was found at its fire-blackened base (Pincemin et al. 1998; original drawing by Juan José Cosgaya M.).
8.11 Tool kits from the rooms in Structures II and III. The combinations of tools were extracted by factor analysis from the presence or absence of tool types in rooms (Gunn et al. 1999). See text for discussion of tool-kit functions. Tool-kit probabilities, that is, the probability that they occurred by chance, were calculated by

Fischer's Exact Probability method (1 p=.005, 2a p=.006, 2b p<.001, 3a not calculated, 3b p=.005, 4 p=.004, 5 p=.06, 6 p=.001).

8.12 Structure II, Calakmul, Campeche. Quantitative distribution of figurines, effigy whistles, ocarinas, and flutes.

8.13 Structure III, Calakmul, Campeche. Quantitative distribution of figurines, effigy whistles, ocarinas, and flutes.

8.14 Noh Cah Santa Cruz and vicinity circa 1860 (drawn from a photograph, courtesy of Alfredo Barrera Vasquez, Dumond 1997:Figure 1; reprinted from the *Machete and the Cross: Campesino Rebellion in Yucatan* by Don E. Dumond by permission of the University of Nebraska Press © 1997).

8.15 Building II-B palace at Calakmul (Folan, Folan, and Cauich Mex 1990; drawing by Abel Morales L. and Sophia Pincemin D.).

8.16 The Pre-Classic acropolis organized around pyramid Structure II crowned with a triadic architectural symbol. These structures reflected the royal court. The increased population and administrative responsibilities of the Early Classic dynastic period, not to mention increased ceremonial demands, precipitated construction of Palace Structure III down pyramid to the left.

9.1 Genealogy of the Pech family in the *Crónica de Chacxulubchen*.

9.2 Location of chacmools, sculpted benches, and jaguar thrones at Chichen Itza (map from Ruppert 1943:Figure 1).

9.3 Plan of the central precinct of Ek Balam; temple assemblages are shaded.

9.4 Dunning's Puuc site core architectural patterns (after Dunning 1992:Figures 5–19, 5–20).

9.5 Uxmal: Plan of the structures within the enclosure wall (Graham 1992).

9.6 Two Puuc arched entryways. (a) El Arco, Labna (Pollock 1980:Figure 79); (b) central section of the central south facade, Las Monjas, Uxmal (Schele and Mathews 1998:Figure 7.11).

9.7 Mayapan: Plan of the main group of ruins (Proskouriakoff 1962).

9.8 House "dedication" texts from Chichen Itza. (a) Monjas Lintel 4: D5-E4 (Bolles 1977:271[drawing by I. Graham]); (b) Four Lintels 2:B3-B7 (Krochock 1989); (c) Three Lintels B2-I2 (Krochock 1989).

11.1 (a) Plaza and patio as courtly centers: the example of Calkini in 1541; (b) A Maya map of Yucatan, centered on Tiho (Merida) (drawing by the author from the original in the *Book of Chilam Balam of Chumayel*). Key to (a): (1) territorial Calkini *cah*; (2) residential Calkini *cah*; (3) the ceiba tree; (4) Napot Canche's patio. Sources: (a) based on text in TC: 11–17 (Restall 1998a:86–90); (b) facsimile in CBC (Edmonson 1986:195).

11.2 The Ceiba at the Center of the World: Stela 5, Izapa, Chiapas (drawing by the author after Gareth Lowe in Lowe et al. 1982:30, 93, 298; and Pons 1997).

11.3 The patio of the Cocom Palace, Sotuta (photograph courtesy of Tsubasa Okoshi Harada).

11.4 "Royal" hands: the signatures of don Pablo Paxbolon, *batab* of Tixchel, 1567; don Miguel Pech, *batab* of Mococha, 1567; Gaspar Antonio Chi, interpreter general, Merida, 1578 (onetime *batab* of Mani); don Juan Xiu, nobleman and petitioner, Yaxakumche/Oxkutzcab, 1640 (onetime *batab* of Oxkutzcab and Maxcanú); don Bentura Uicab, *batab* and notary, Citilcum, 1669. Sources: AGI-*México* 367:68r; AGI-*México* 367:71v; AGN-*Inquisición*, 69, 5:158; XC: 13; AGI-*Escribanía* 317c, 2:312.

11.5 The Mani Map version in the Xiu papers, showing the Mani region in the late sixteenth century (from XC, courtesy of the Tozzer Library, Harvard University).

11.6 The Xiu Family Tree (ca. 1560 with ca. 1685 additions; from XC, courtesy of the Tozzer Library, Harvard University).

11.7 A Family of rulers: the Canche of sixteenth-century Calkini. Note: The names in bold served as *batab* (governor) of Calkini or another *cah* in the region; the elder Namay was part of the departure from Mayapan in the 1440s and a member of the Canul court; the younger Namay won through warfare the *batabil* (governorship) of Dzitbalche; he died before the Spanish invasion; his son Napot was confirmed as *batab* of Calkini in 1541, when Spanish officials also confirmed the eligibility (and possibly gubernatorial positions in the region) of two of his brothers and his son-in-law; a grandson of Napot, Nachan Couoh, was *batab* of Calkini in the late-sixteenth century; Alonso Canche served as *alcalde* (see Table 11.1) in Calkini in the 1570s and was still alive in 1595. Source: TC: 13–18 (Restall 1998: 88–91).

11.8 The memorial to the massacre at Otzmal (drawing by the author after the seventeenth-century etching in Cogolludo 1867–68, 3:VI).

11.9 Imagining kings: Colonial Maya depictions of Maya rulers (drawings by the author after originals in *The Book of Chilam Balam of Chumayel*). Source: CBC (drawings in Roys 1933:150, 153, 158, 161; facsimiles in Edmonson 1986:128, 150, 218, 66).

Preface

This constitutes the second volume of *Royal Courts of the Ancient Maya*. Volume 1 (*Theory, Comparison, and Synthesis*) contains chapters addressing theoretical issues related to royal courts, as well as a comparative study (by Susan Evans) and a set of concluding remarks (by Michael Coe). The objectives of the book and problems pertaining to definitions of the royal court were discussed in the introductory chapter of that volume.

Volume 2 charges directly into a series of meticulous case studies, rich with data. Here the authors discuss courts at specific centers and areas, presenting data from major research projects, including some that are still ongoing. The chapters are organized in rough chronological order. The first chapter by Clark and Hansen targets the early development of courts during the Pre-Classic period, dissecting the nature of foreign influence as illuminated by their data from the Mirador Basin of northern Peten and from Chiapas. Traxler examines the beginning of the Copan dynasty and the possibility of its foreign origin. The court as de novo construction, in both symbolic and material senses, underscores the role of rupture and innovation in the emergence of courts.

The next three chapters address some of the largest Classic centers in the lowlands. Harrison analyzes the functions of throne rooms in the Central Acropolis of Tikal. Another large center, Caracol, is described by Arlen and Diane Chase, who present evidence of "palace diets" as a unique tool for identifying court members. Their study of multiple courts in this densely settled Maya city points to a complex pattern of courtly organization. In the following chapter, Valdés also addresses the functions and meanings of thrones, referring primarily to archaeological data from Uaxactun. Ball and Taschek, who have been working at the minor centers of Buenavista and Cahal Pech, direct themselves to the questions of dual-palace systems and court mobility. Miller then turns to iconography and texts in mural paintings at Bonampak, using images enhanced through new technologies. Finally, Folan, Gunn, and Domínguez scrutinize data from excavations at Calakmul and argue for a temple-based economy at that and other sites. These chapters fill a half-full vessel and complete our experiment in accessing the structure, ambitions, machinations, and participants of Maya courtly societies.

Two editorial matters deserve mention: First, Inomata thanks Erin McCracken for her timely help in the editorial process. Second, readers should note that the Press preferred "Pre-Classic" to " Preclassic" and "Post-Classic" to "Postclassic," and so on. We follow that style here, with some reluctance, mindful that it runs counter to current practice in Maya studies.

Takeshi Inomata and Stephen Houston

1

The Architecture of Early Kingship: Comparative Perspectives on the Origins of the Maya Royal Court

JOHN E. CLARK AND RICHARD D. HANSEN

The historic roots of Classic Maya kingship and royal court life can be traced back to between 600 to 400 B.C. in the Mirador Basin of northern Peten, Guatemala, the likely location of the first Maya state (ca. 300 B.C.). In this essay we examine one aspect of the early Maya royal court—its residential compounds—and compare them to earlier developments in the Olmec heartland, Chiapas, and Oaxaca. Courtly life, royal residence, and ritual architecture can be traced back even centuries earlier to San Lorenzo (see Cyphers 1996, 1999), but evidence of royal residences and compounds there is not yet fully published. The evolution of the royal compound has significant implications for the composition of Mesoamerica's earliest royal courts, their day-to-day functioning, and their origins. From a broad spatial and diachronic perspective, it appears clear that the Middle Pre-Classic Maya of the Mirador Basin and northern Peten were influenced in many ways by venerable, regal institutions of their western Olmec, Zoque, and Zapotec neighbors and that they developed these further into the institution that became the Classic Maya royal court.

Because of the limited available data that can be brought to bear on questions of early courtly life, our discussion must necessarily emphasize physical remains of the royal court as a material, architectural entity rather than the sociality of royal networks of kings, courtiers, and their servants and dependents. These attendants would also leave some archaeologically detectable material evidence of their activities, but they remain to be investigated. We must rely on speculation more than we would like to build a plausible case for the evolution of the Maya royal court.[1] Our principal interest in this chapter is a better understanding of

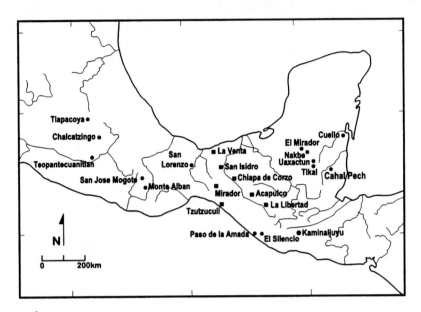

FIGURE 1.1 Map of Middle Pre-Classic centers showing the locations of sites mentioned in the text (circles) and those built on the MFC pattern (squares).

this institution. We consider briefly evidence from partially contemporaneous capitals in Mesoamerica, namely, La Venta (Tabasco, Mexico), Chiapa de Corzo, Mirador, La Libertad (Chiapas, Mexico), San José Mogote, Monte Alban (Oaxaca, Mexico), and Nakbe, Tikal, and Uaxactun (Peten, Guatemala); see Figure 1.1.

The point of departure for our discussion is the identification and dating of royal compounds or palaces at the sites mentioned. By "royal compound" we refer to the residential precinct of the king or ruling elite at each center. The legitimate concerns about how these royal residences were distinguished from elite and commoner houses and other structures are critical to the plausibility of our argument but cannot be addressed here. We consider identifications provided by others as likely correct, and we proceed with our descriptions and analyses on this charitable presumption.

In the following discussion, we first describe briefly the meager data available for royal compounds and ceremonial architecture at the Middle Pre-Classic sites mentioned. The remainder of the essay addresses implications of the spatial and temporal patterns in the data concerning the ancient conduct of courtly life, its origins, and its promulgation throughout Mesoamerica. Indicators of public architecture, royal compounds, and courtly life at the six non-Maya sites predate those known in the Mirador Basin by one to five centuries but appear similar to it in a broad range of criteria. Consequently, we argue that the Pre-Classic Maya adopted their royal institutions and court from western cultures, principally those known archaeologically as the Olmec and ethnically as Zoques. The appearance of royal life in the Maya lowlands is attributable to a combination of local developments and cultural borrowing.

Early Middle Pre-Classic Royal Compounds, 850–600 B.C.

Formal patterns of ceremonial architecture date at least to the beginnings of the Middle Pre-Classic period at La Venta, Tabasco, the easternmost Olmec capital.[2] This ancient city plan later became the blueprint for founding and building a network of early capitals in central Chiapas, of which Chiapa de Corzo, Mirador, and La Libertad are the best-known examples. The similarities in these plans may signal identity in functions of the various pyramids and platform complexes built at these centers. The early Middle Pre-Classic period presents an analytical opportunity in this respect as no pyramid centers were constructed prior to this time, and all cities of this era started from scratch. (In this chapter we consider data both from Mirador, Chiapas, and El Mirador, Guatemala. These are both referred to as "El Mirador" in their own regions. To avoid confusion, we refer to the Chiapas site as *Mirador* and the larger and later Guatemalan site as *El Mirador* and to this region as the *Mirador Basin*.)

La Venta

The founding of La Venta required clearing and minor leveling of the central portion of the low island on which it was erected, establishing the central axis of the site, and then deciding the locations and sizes of the various platform constructions. Labor was then mobilized to heap up earth and clay in the spots indicated and to the heights desired. The main axis and northern part of La Venta was built by at least 850–800 B.C. (Drucker et al. 1959; Lowe 1989), and the southernmost sector was constructed by at least by 500 B.C. (Gallegos 1990). Chiapa de Corzo and Mirador were constructed at least by 750 B.C. and La Libertad by 650 B.C. (see Lowe 1977). La Libertad was the most distant capital from La Venta built on its linear pattern. It is of special interest that all known sites aping the La Venta pattern are in Chiapas in what was Zoque territory. John Clark thinks that La Venta was a Zoque city and that all of these planned cities and regional centers were part of a complex interaction and trade network of Zoque imprimatur (this argument will be developed elsewhere).

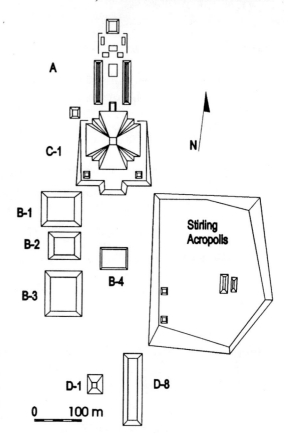

FIGURE 1.2 Site plan of early La Venta, Tabasco, Mexico (adapted from González Lauck 1996:Figure 1).

Similarities in city layout can be best appreciated by comparing the early plans of La Venta, Chiapa de Corzo, Mirador, and La Libertad shown in Figures 1.2–1.5. It is noteworthy that another half-dozen contemporaneous centers in Chiapas shared this general site plan (Figure 1.2; see Lowe 1977), which we will designate here as the Middle Formative Chiapas (MFC) pattern.[3] As we conceive it, the MFC pattern or complex consists of a north-to-south axial arrangement of regularly spaced pyramidal platforms and plazas. The tallest platform or pyramid is located to the north, and in the south is a paired arrangement of a long, low mound flanked on the west by a tall pyramid. This latter arrangement has long been known as an "E-Group" in Maya studies because it was first identified in the 1930s at Group E at Uaxactun (see below). Nearly equidistantly placed between the principal northern and southern mounds of MFC sites is a smaller platform located near the center of a large, central plaza measuring about 160 by 320 meters. Of special interest for this chapter is the large acropolis to the east of this central mound. We believe the limited evidence from all the early centers mentioned indicates that the adjacent acropolis was probably the location of a royal compound or precinct, as recently argued by Reilly (1999). Other low mounds delimit the plaza on the west and may have also served residential functions. The stereotypic placements of acropoli with regard to the principal mounds and plaza argue for an identity of function at La Venta and the early Chiapas capitals. This assumption is our point of departure in the following descriptions and analyses.

The available evidence adequately demonstrates that the principal platforms along the central axis served ceremonial functions. At La Venta, the central axis has long been demonstrated as the principal line of ceremonial offerings and sculptures (see Drucker et al. 1959), almost as if the ancients placed their offerings for the convenience of future discovery. Little data, however, are available for the large acropolis located just southeast of the principal mound. Limited excavations there in 1968 suffered nearly every conceivable setback, and so the excavation data are admittedly inadequate (Heizer et al. 1968). The most unusual reported features of this acropolis are the presence of five stone drains, some of which run east-west and others north-south; given the limited investigations it is probable that others will also be found. Associated with some of the drains were large stone basins. The excavators speculated that these water-control devices could have been used in various rituals, as has been postulated for the earlier Olmec center of San Lorenzo, where similar covered drains of *U*-shaped, volcanic stones have been found (Coe and Diehl 1980). Recent explorations at San Lorenzo, however, demonstrate that some of these elaborate drains were associated with elite residences and really did serve as drains (Cyphers 1996, 1999). If they served a similar function at La Venta, the number and orientation of drains provide vital clues to the number of buildings atop the acropolis and their orientations. The orientations are parallel and perpendicular to the main axis of the site. The excavators did note a small clay structure associated with one drain, but they did not know what to make of it (Heizer et al. 1968:146). This "low clay mound structure" may have been a basal platform for a residence. Acropoli from Chiapas centers show that numerous small platforms were placed atop them, with the largest generally toward the southern edge, as is the case at La Venta (see Figure 1.2). The limited radiocarbon dates from the La Venta acropolis demonstrate that it was occupied during the full duration of the site, or about 900–850 to 400 B.C. (Heizer et al. 1968:152).

One critical difference between sites, however, may be the special precinct (Group A) constructed at La Venta, north of the principal mound. This unique area of special offerings distinguishes La Venta from all the contemporaneous Chiapas centers and probably signaled conceptual differences of sacred status to the people themselves. There may have been further differences in the southern sector, but not enough is known of this sector at La Venta to make an informed comparison (see Gallegos 1990).

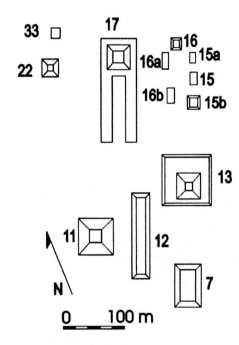

FIGURE 1.3 Site plan of early Chiapa de Corzo, Chiapas, Mexico.

Chiapa de Corzo

Located in the center of the state of Chiapas, Mexico, along the Grijalva River and prime levee land, Chiapa de Corzo is the oldest continuously occupied city in the Western Hemisphere. Its earliest attested occupation dates to about 1200 B.C., and the place has been occupied by one group or another ever since. Chiapa de Corzo became a bona fide, planned city with civic and ceremonial architecture by at least 750 B.C. As noted, it was constructed as a near copy of the earlier city of La Venta (cf. Figures 1.2 and 1.3). The overall arrangement of the central mounds at both sites is similar, with mounds of the same size and general orientation placed at the same distances from each other. We cannot yet tell the precise degree of similarity between these early cities because the original sizes of the earliest buildings that lie beneath later constructions at both sites has not been determined.

Most of the buildings shown in Figure 1.3 have been tested archaeologically and shown to date to 750 to 650 B.C., or earlier (Chiapa II and III phases). The earliest documented mound is a low, broad platform beneath

Mound 36, the northernmost mound. The pyramid erected on this mound reached its final 9 meter height about 450 B.C., and it is known to cover an earlier pyramid dating to about 700 B.C., but excavations did not reach deep enough in this structure to determine whether there is an earlier pyramid (Lowe 1962:58). The basal platform dates to about 800–750 B.C. and duplicates the middle Olmec style of large stone slabs and alternating stone cobbles (Lowe 1962:57–59, Figure 37, Plate 29h) known for Chalcatzingo and Teopantecuanitlan in highland Mexico (see Martínez Donjuan 1994; Grove 1989). At Chiapa de Corzo, the horizontal sandstone slabs set in dark clay mortar bracket a double row of river cobbles. David Grove (1989:144) has made a case that this architectural style is a highland Olmec characteristic. We suggest that the practice of making designs in walls by alternating horizontal and vertical stone slabs with cobble insets mimics the more elaborate stone facings known from early La Venta, in which shaped, serpentine slabs were placed in alternating horizontal and vertical patterns, sometimes capped with basalt pillars placed horizontally to create a *talud-tablero* look (see Drucker et al. 1959: plates 7, 10–13).

Elaborate burials of royal personages at Chiapa de Corzo have been recovered from Mound 17 (Lee 1969). The lowermost interment, a woman, dates to the end of the Chiapa II phase, about 750–700 B.C. (Gareth W. Lowe, personal communication). The twin, 100 meter long, low platforms adjoining Mound 17 and extending southward date to the Chiapa II phase, or about 900–700 B.C. (Lowe 1962:56) and may have been an early ballcourt or open-ended courtyard. These structures would have been just north and west of the royal compound at Mound 13. This latter structure has not been extensively explored. Its initial construction date is not known, but one of the earlier buildings in Mound 13, a stepped earthen platform, was 6.2 meters high and dates to the Chiapa III times, or about 700 B.C. Evidence of an even earlier structure was found inside of this pyramid (Hicks and Rozaire 1960:5). Limited excavations in the terrace to the north and west of the pyramid showed the construction of the low basal platform—the candidate for a royal compound—to date to the Chiapa II and III phases. The Chiapa III platform was 1.75 meters high and was erected over an earlier, lower structure (Mason 1960b:2).

Mounds 11 and 12 form the E-Group complex in the southern part of the formal Chiapa de Corzo center. At the time the site was investigated, Mound 11, the tallest mound at the site, served as a base for a water tower and could not be excavated. Limited investigations in its companion structure, Mound 12, uncovered an earlier platform about 3.5 meters high that dates to Chiapa III times (Mason 1960a:2, 3). The original length of this early structure was not determined. Based upon the overall site pattern, a strong inference can be made that Mound 11 also dates at least to the Chiapa III phase. Sherds collected from its surface indicate a Middle and Late Pre-Classic date.

Mound 7 also dates at least to this same time period. The 700 B.C. mound discovered in its interior was about 1.3 meters high and of earth and clay. This structure had steps at least on the western and northern sides. Excavations were limited, but they demonstrated that the structure was at least 15 by 15 meters in basal dimensions. It was resurfaced at least four times during the Chiapa III phase, thereby raising its height to 2 meters and expanding its horizontal dimensions. In the subsequent Chiapa IV phase, the platform continued to be elaborated, raised, and expanded until by 450 B.C. it was a broad platform 3.4 meters in height. Plaster had replaced clay as the preferred flooring material by this time (Lowe 1962:45–46).

All of the available data indicate that the core of the MFC complex (i.e., Mounds 36, 17, 11, 12, and 7) was in place at Chiapa de Corzo by 700 B.C. or earlier. The sizes of all the various structures at this time have not yet been determined, but most seem to have been broad platforms, some of which supported modest pyramids. This would seem to signal a significant difference with the massive size of La Venta, and it may well do. It is important to remember, however, that the monumentality evident at La Venta (and at Chiapa de Corzo) results largely from subsequent additions made to earlier, more modest structures. Data are lacking from La Venta for detailed construction histories. The outer veneers of some La Venta buildings, such as the "great mound" at C–1, date to about 500–400 B.C. (González Lauck 1997:93), but earlier buildings in their interiors, if they exist, have not yet been explored. The buildings at both sites appear in homologous positions and presumably served homologous functions. In some cases, they may also have followed parallel construction histories.

Chiapa de Corzo was planned, measured, and marked out about 750 B.C. by someone with intimate knowledge of the layout of La Venta. The pyramid at Mound 13, Chiapa de Corzo, does not seem to have an obvious counterpart at La Venta, but this may be due to divergence in subsequent histories after initial construction. The primary, early construction of Mound 13 appears to have been a broad platform that supported a low mound. We speculate that early usage of this platform may have been as a royal compound and that its function was subsequently superceded by the placement of a temple platform, perhaps a mortuary shrine to an interred royal person. At this time the royal compound may have been moved south to Mound 7. At an even later date we think that the royal compound was moved to the palace at Mound 5 (see below). All of this would suggest modifications to an original adopted concept of a city plan at Chiapa de Corzo through time. The difficulties of excavating at Chiapa de Corzo prevented an extensive look at either of these candidates for royal compounds, but such data are available from two of its sister cities—Mirador and La Libertad.

The Architecture of Early Kingship

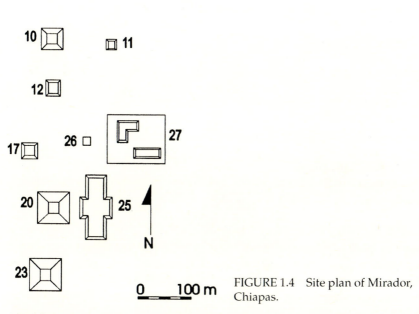

FIGURE 1.4 Site plan of Mirador, Chiapas.

Mirador

Mirador is located west of Chiapa de Corzo in the Cintalapa Valley, a particularly advantageous spot to control trade routes west to the Isthmus of Tehuantepec, southward to the Pacific Coast, and northward to the Olmec heartland (see Agrinier 1984). The principal mounds at Mirador were contemporaneous with those at Chiapa de Corzo and La Venta. The MFC complex at Mirador is constituted by Mounds 10, 12, 20, 25, 27, and 33 (see Figure 1.4). All but Mound 33 have been tested and found to date at least to Chiapas III times (Quequepac phase), or 700–500 B.C. (Agrinier 1970, 1975, 2000). The large acropolis east of the site's axial line, Mound 27, was intensively tested by Pierre Agrinier in 1965–1973 with three large trenches, seven small trenches, and 10 test pits (Agrinier 2000).

The E-Group at Mirador consists of the long Mound 25 flanked on the west by Mound 20, a 15-meter-high mound. During the Chiapa III phase, Mound 20 was a 5-meter-high clay mound with stairs on the eastern side, facing Mound 25; it supported a wattle-and-daub "superstructure with a stone base" (Agrinier 1970:9). During the subsequent period (Chiapa IV), this mound was elevated to 12 meters in height. The long mound, Mound 25, was tested only with one test pit through its center. This low platform is 100 meters long, 20 meters wide, and 4 meters high and appears to have been constructed in Chiapa III times. "The contour of the mound suggests two buried stairways: a main one to the east side and a rear one on the west side facing Mound 20" (Agrinier 2000:4).

The large northern mound on the main north-south axis is Mound 10. During Chiapa III times, this was a very low mound or platform only 70 centimeters high (Agrinier 1975:6). Although it eventually became the second tallest mound at the site, it does not appear to have been significant in Chiapa III times. The more modest Mounds 12 and 33 may have been the original small platforms associated with the MFC pattern at Mirador. These are nearly equally spaced from the short, intersecting axial line of the E-Group. Mound 33 has not been investigated, but Mound 12 was investigated with an exploratory trench. This mound is only 2 meters high and 28 meters in diameter. The nine superimposed floors recovered in this area show that most date to the early Chiapa III phase (ca. 700–650 B.C.); this mound represented a small platform about 1.5 meters high at the time that Mound 20 was 5 meters high and Mound 25 was 4 meters high (Agrinier 2000).

Mound 27 is the Mirador acropolis located to the east of the main north-south axis of the site. The extensive explorations of this mound revealed a complex construction history, with platform-building being limited to Chiapa III times. This is the most thoroughly explored royal compound of any of the Chiapas sites considered here. Agrinier (2000) recorded at least six construction episodes for some of the buildings discovered inside the mound. Several features are noteworthy. First, the mound grew by accretion and the coalesence of several small platforms over earlier floors and domestic features. All of the various structures are associated with domestic activity, evident from the presence of trash pits, hearths, caches, and subfloor burials. Second, multiple buildings and platforms were involved until Mound 27 achieved its final L shape and measured 105 by 125 meters and 5 meters in height (Agrinier 2000:4). The original arrangement of early buildings has not been determined, but they were made using puddled adobe, similar to the other buildings at the site. Agrinier (2000:6) notes that many architectural innovations were already evident by early Chiapa III times. These included "apron-molding, a combination of basal- and apron-moldings, stepped balustrades with double corners, molded projections, and rounded corners." Toward the end of the phase, uncut stones were used as outer facing stones on walls. Fragments of burned daub indicate that perishable superstructures were placed atop the low platforms.

Of particular interest is a 57.5 meter (or longer) stone drain located 1.5 meters below the surface. It is oriented 15 degrees east of magnetic north (Agrinier 2000:21). Portions of another, parallel drain were also recovered. It parallels a wall of one of the low platforms. Agrinier suggests that the water drained from the Mound 27 complex ran off to the north into a prepared reservoir. Such reservoirs or reflecting pools may have been part of the MFC complex, but this has not yet been verified at other sites.

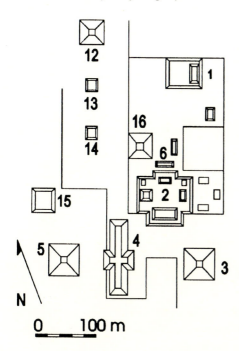

FIGURE 1.5   Site plan of La Libertad, Chiapas.

Agrinier (2000) reports a wide variety of figurines and other artifacts from his Mound 27 excavations. Some of these came from primary deposits and trash pits, but most are domestic refuse incorporated into platform fill. Nonetheless, there is ample evidence for domestic functions at the complex of subplatforms at Mound 27, including hearths and millings stones. The high frequency of figurines from these structures may signal some other special activities as well. Artifact inventories from compounds at other Chiapas sites appear to be mostly from incorporated domestic refuse used in mound fill rather than primary refuse.

La Libertad

La Libertad was founded and constructed in a previously unoccupied riverine zone about 700–650 B.C. in the southeastern edge of the central river valley of Chiapas. It appears to have served, among other things, as a control center for items traded from highland Guatemala, in particular obsidian and jade (Clark 1988). Reconstruction of early Middle Pre-Classic trade patterns suggests that the main route from highland Guatemala to La Venta followed the central valley of Chiapas (Clark and Lee 1984). The principal capitals and way stations along this route were Kaminaljuyu, La Libertad, Chiapa de Corzo, San Isidro, and La Venta, with many smaller centers being strategically placed between these largest centers (see Figure 1.1). To our knowledge, La Libertad is the most distant outpost of the MFC pattern (Figure 1.5). The contemporaneous portion of Kaminaljuyu,

Guatemala, appears to have been organized somewhat differently, with no obvious E-Group complex in its aligned mounds and plazas (see Michels 1979). The principal difference between the layout of La Libertad and its sister cities is the additional tall mound to the east of the E-Group complex at the southern edge of the site.

The central acropolis at La Libertad was extensively tested in 1976 by Donald Miller under the direction of Gareth Lowe. As evident in Figure 1.5, this broad, elevated platform supported four large and two small mounds, located along the sides of the acropolis, thereby defining a large, central plaza. Although stairways to the lower plazas were found on three sides of the acropolis, we suspect that the buildings on the small platforms were oriented inward toward the central plaza of the acropolis. The most impressive structure excavated was a stone-veneer base of a building (Mound 2A) that measured 15 by 21 meters (Miller 1976). It may have been a residence of someone from the ruling class. Two elite house mounds excavated at the southern edge of the site were about the same size, measuring 24 by 18 meters and 15 by 18 meters (Clark 1988; Miller 1979). The significant differences among houses of the elite would have been the central location and elevation of the buildings on the acropolis rather than their size and elaboration. No obvious differences in the types of artifacts associated with the various buildings were noted. One jade-encumbered male burial was exhumed from the summit of the adjacent pyramidal mound of the E-Group (Miller 1976), so it is certain that highly prestigious ruling elites, presumably kings, resided at the site.

The compounds at Chiapa de Corzo and La Libertad measure about 80 meters square at their bases and are about 3 meters high. In contrast to later patterns (see below), the striking features of the compounds are the numerous separate buildings and their probable separate functions or associated functionaries. Presumably, palaces constructed in subsequent periods represent a consolidation of the multiple rooms, buildings, and functions of earlier royal compounds. The good state of preservation at La Libertad gives us the best evidence of the arrangement of one of these compounds (see Figure 1.5). Essentially, the complex looks like a large, elevated courtyard group. The orderly mounds arranged around the periphery of the acropolis were probably platforms for pole and thatch superstructures. Of particular interest at La Libertad are the other buildings adjacent to the compound that may have constituted part of it or have been buildings for attached personnel. Also of interest, just to the north of the compound, is a small ballcourt formed by one wall of the compound and an addition mound.

San José Mogote and Monte Alban

Although the Valley of Oaxaca is much farther afield than the regions just considered, it merits brief attention given the claims made for the early sites of San José Mogote and Monte Alban. Richard Blanton et al. (1999:57) argue that Monte Alban was the first urban center in Mesoamerica, as well as the first state—an opinion clearly at odds with that expressed above concerning the early Olmecs at San Lorenzo and La Venta and the Maya in the Mirador Basin. Founded about 500 B.C., Monte Alban is thought to have been the logical consequence of largely indigenous processes occurring in the Valley of Oaxaca and its immediate environs.

Joyce Marcus and Kent Flannery (1996:168) also make a case for an early Zapotec state at Monte Alban, arising in the Late Formative period (ca. 100 B.C.–A.D. 200). This date would make the major events at Monte Alban posterior to those in the Mirador Basin (see below). The long and well-documented history of public buildings and elite residences in Oaxaca starts with Early Formative San José Mogote. The small public buildings there, dating from 1350 to 1000 B.C., are well publicized. These special buildings are the first evidence in Mesoamerica for the use of lime plaster in public buildings and of special buildings oriented 8 degrees west of north. Marcus and Flannery (1996:87) argue that these small buildings, measuring about 4 by 6 meters, served as "initiates temples" or "lineage houses" (Marcus 1999:69), a function analogous to men's houses in New Guinea. About 1000 B.C. these small structures were replaced by larger and more elaborate public buildings that probably served the needs of more than just the community of San José Mogote (Marcus 1999:86). These later basal platforms evince several architectural innovations of interest that occur later in the Maya and Chiapas regions, including the use of bun-shaped adobe bricks for retaining walls and cells for constructing basal platforms, dry-laid stone facing masonry, inset stone stairways, megalithic stone blocks (up to half a ton), and lime plaster. The superstructures of these buildings were probably wattle and daub constructions.

Not enough is known of early Mesoamerica to determine whether these architectural innovations indeed started in Oaxaca or from some other adjacent area. Contemporaneous large mounds with stone facings are known for the site of Tlapacoya in the Basin of Mexico (Niederberger 1996), Chalcatzingo, Morelos (Grove 1989, 1999), and Teopantecuanitlan, Guerrero (Grove 1989; Martínez Donjuan 1994). At the moment, all of these stone-facade buildings appear to be earlier than anything in Chiapas or the Maya area. In terms of the spatial organization of early centers, however, the Oaxaca data are still of limited use because no map of early San José Mogote has yet been published, and all of the early buildings at Monte Alban lie buried beneath later constructions. Marcus and Flannery (1996:87) note that the small public buildings at San José Mogote were in the westernmost residential area of that community. Later, San José Mogote was modified to copy Monte Alban, with its long, central plaza flanked by northern and southern mound complexes and temples, with other buildings along the east and west sides of the plaza. The general orientation of these two sites conforms to that of the MFC pattern described above, with the size of the main plazas of the Chiapas and Oaxaca sites being nearly equal. However, at Monte Alban there is no obvious parallel to the acropolis east of the main plaza that we posit as the locus of the royal compound. Rather, the evidence is of early elite residences east of the North Plaza (Arthur Joyce, personal communication, 1999; see also Winter 1994). Marcus and Flannery (1996:168; cf. Flannery 1998) argue that there were no true palaces at Monte Alban until after 100 B.C.; the local precursors of palaces are unknown. In sum, on the basis of current data there appears to be little direct influence from Oaxaca on the development of the MFC pattern or early Maya palaces, but several architectural innovations known in the Maya area, such as the use of large cut stone blocks, may have come from Oaxaca.

Some Observations of Capitals

Returning to La Venta, it is noteworthy that the acropolis at this site is more than twice the size of those at Chiapa de Corzo, Mirador, La Libertad, and other Chiapas centers. This may reflect a deliberate difference to signal disparities in political hierarchy; alternatively, the whole eastern edge of the central core of a site, and not just its acropolis, may have been reserved for domestic functions associated with the royal court. As noted for Mirador–Mound 27, and Chiapa de Corzo–Mound 7, the first building episode of some of these compounds was at ground level, with the acropolis representing the cumulative effect of multiple rebuilding episodes. One implication of the hypothesis of La Venta's temporal priority and the changes to the city plan through time is that at later sites, such as La Libertad and Nakbe, the basal platforms may have been constructed in a single episode rather than representing accumulations of different constructions, with all of the small platforms built on top of the broad, basal platform rather than this being built over earlier platforms (this has not been verified). One implication of the differences in sizes of acropoli is that the various sites had different numbers of royal functionaries. If this functional logic is correct, and assuming the synchronic use of all the structures, La Venta may have had many more royal functionaries than its rival Chiapas centers. This would fit general expectations based upon other lines of evidence, such as the types and frequencies of offerings and sculptures found at the different capitals.

With the exception of the largest pyramid at La Venta, the near identicality of layout, spacing, and platform sizes between Chiapa de Corzo and La Venta is remarkable (cf. Figures 1.2 and 1.3). The placement of royal compounds was such as to allow ready access for the elite to a site's primary sacred space and suggests that the personnel living in these compounds were involved in the ritual activities carried out in that space. It is of interest that these early centers also have a complementary series of facing, smaller mound groups located west of the north-south axial line, perhaps signaling symbolic and functional complementarity with the personnel of the main acropolis. Some of these patterns of royal compounds persisted into the Late Pre-Classic period and are found at the earliest centers in the Maya lowlands.

Later Pre-Classic and Protoclassic Patterns, 600 B.C.–A.D. 100

The patterns of site arrangement and royal compounds evident at Middle Pre-Classic Zoque centers underwent modifications in later centuries. The earliest Maya centers at Nakbe, Uaxactun, and Tikal show some influence from these centers in certain key elements and independence in others. Chiapa de Corzo is particularly interesting because, over the course of its occupation, it shifted from an initial MFC pattern to the early Maya pattern. We consider each site in turn here before addressing some of the implications of the patterns described.

Nakbe

Nakbe is located in the Mirador Basin of northern Peten in an area of abundant bajo land and swamps. Its initial occupation may predate 800 B.C., but the first clear evidence of strong occupation dates to this period.[4] By 600 B.C., Nakbe was a thriving community about 50 hectares in extent, with simple plazas, stone platforms 2–3 meters high, wattle-and-daub constructions, and houses of rough stone covered with crude stucco. There is evidence of complex architecture and possible status distinctions between elites and less fortunates. Evidence of cranial deformation and dental inlays are known for this period, both of which may suggest significant status differences (Mata Amado and Hansen 1992); however, others see dental inlays and cranial deformation as evidence for individual "beautification" rather than status differences (see Hammond 1999, Joyce 1999, and Hendon 1999). A recent analysis (Krejci and Culbert 1995) demonstrates that there is no correlation between early evidence of cranial deformation, filed or inlaid teeth, and high-status burial in the Maya lowlands. One Nakbe figurine may depict a three-pronged jester image of the symbol of kingship (Hansen 1994b:30). Strong foreign exchange programs were established by this period, with imports of strombus shells from the Caribbean, obsidian from highland Guatemala, and jade (including a single blue-green bead) from Guatemala and other areas.

The latter half of the Middle Pre-Classic (Middle Ox phase, 600–350 B.C.) witnessed Nakbe's rise to preeminence. Numerous woven-mat mo-

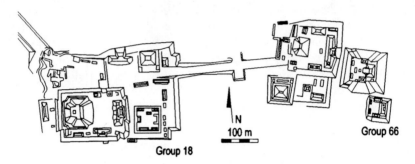

FIGURE 1.6 Site plan of early Nakbe, Peten, Guatemala.

tifs were incised on the bodies of ceramic vessels of this period, suggesting an emphasis on elements that were known in subsequent Maya periods as symbols of kingship. Similar symbols are known on carved bone from Cuello, Belize, for this time period (Hammond 1995:55, 1999:58) and even earlier on pottery from San José Mogote, Oaxaca, for the late San José phase (Marcus and Flannery 1996:96).

Large-scale constructions at Nakbe, dating to the end of the Mamom horizon (ca. 400 B.C.), included platforms, causeways, and pyramids up to 18 meters in height. The first consistent ritual architectural form in the Maya lowlands, the E-Group, also appears at this time at Nakbe, Wakna, and possibly El Mirador (see Figure 1.6). The consistency of this architectural form, also found at numerous other sites in the Maya lowlands (see below), suggests a pervasive and stable ritual pattern all across this region. One innovation of this period of interest, perhaps deriving from Oaxaca, concerns advances in specialist masonry. Rather than the crude stone of the earlier era, skilled artisans began quarrying large limestone blocks (ca. 45 x 45 x 90 centimeters) to be used in public constructions, platforms, elite residences, and possibly palaces (Hansen 1998).

A possible royal compound at Nakbe (Group 66) is located just east and south of the E-Group at the site (Figure 1.6). This compound, and others, were on elevated platforms about 3 meters high and measuring about 80 meters square at the base. They are remarkably similar to the earlier compounds at La Libertad and other Chiapas sites. Atop each platform is an orderly series of small mounds (presumably building foundations for perishable superstructures) placed near the edges of the platform so as to create a large, open courtyard between them (see Figure 1.7). Possible palace/residence structures dating to the Middle and Late Pre-Classic periods at Nakbe are Structures 4, 13, 31, 502, and 512 and Groups 18 and 66. The presence of multiple royal compounds at one site

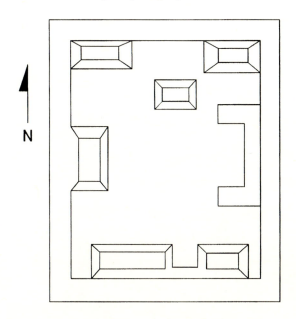

FIGURE 1.7 Group 18 at Nakbe, a possible royal compound (redrawn from Martínez and Hansen 1993:Figure 8).

perhaps indicates the periodic relocation of the royal residence, for whatever reason, as suggested for Chiapa de Corzo. Alternatively, it is more probable that these compounds were also made for other high nobles and not just for kings. Some may have housed noble priests who maintained and functioned at the temples. The number of such compounds at a site may be a good indicator of the size of its royal population. The nearly stereotypic arrangement of royal compounds vis-à-vis the standard E-Group arrangement of temples is particularly interesting. This relationship appears to have been superceded during the Late Pre-Classic when triadic temple architecture became the dominant form (Clark et al. 2000; Hansen 1990, 1992a, 1992b, 1998).

Although royal compounds have been tested archaeologically, there is still not much to go on for inferring past activities of royal courts. Limited information available from nearby El Mirador provides two observations of interest. First, domestic debris recovered from the El Mirador structures did not appear to differ in any obvious ways from that found in ordinary households of the same center. All residents appear to have had access to the same sorts of pots, stone tools, figurines, and so on. Second, *manos* and *metates* and inside hearths were not found, suggesting that the menial tasks of grinding corn and cooking food took place outside the proposed palace area and that food was brought in already prepared (Hansen 1990). Excavations at possible royal compounds in Nakbe (Groups 18 and 66) evince the same pattern noted at El Mirador

(Martínez and Hansen 1993:77). This pattern contrasts that noted for Mirador, Chiapas, in which hearths, trash pits, and grinding stones were recovered in the compound.

Group 18 of the West Group at Nakbe, measuring 80 by 78 meters at its base (Figure 1.7), shows six mounds around the open court and central mound of the compound, and Group 66 measures 80 by 73 meters at its base. If these were residential structures or sleeping quarters, they would have accommodated 20–50 individuals. Presumably, the royal retainers, craftsmen, and others attached to this royal "house" would have lived in other buildings off the platform but perhaps nearby. The occupants of this compound had immediate and ready access to the temple platforms as well as large plazas, a pattern noted at all other capital centers contemporaneous with Nakbe. The large carved stone monuments dating to this time period were placed on axial alignments associated with sacred structures rather than proximate to the residential compounds (Hansen 1991a, 1991b, 1995). At the moment, no royal burials have been recovered from the Mirador Basin for this time period, but they are well known at contemporary capitals in the Chiapas and Tabasco area as well as in highland Guatemala (see Clark et al. 1999) and slightly later for Tikal (see Krejci and Culbert 1995).

At first glance, the late Middle Pre-Classic site arrangement at Nakbe appears strikingly different from those at the earlier sites described above. Maya sites such as Nakbe, El Mirador, and Tintal are oriented roughly east-west rather than north-south, as was the norm for Zoque centers. However, other early sites such as Wakna are oriented on a north-south axis. Rather than the long, linear arrangement of mounds known for La Venta, early Maya ceremonial architecture is compressed and, as far as we can tell, consists of an elevated E-Group and its adjacent compound. As described above, this paired arrangement of mounds constituted the southern sector of the MFC complex.

If we have correctly identified early Maya royal compounds, they are remarkably similar to those in Chiapas in size, orientation, composition, and layout. Many of the large platforms at Nakbe, for example, are about 78–80 meters square at their bases and 3 meters high. They support an ordered series of small building platforms around the periphery of a central courtyard. One major difference is in the placement of these royal compounds south and/or east of their respective E-Groups or ceremonial buildings. Zoque sites have acropoli north and east of their E-Groups (Figures 1.2–1.5), as do early Maya sites such as Wakna. If one grants, however, that the early Maya E-Group was a simplification or modification of an older MFC pattern, as was the royal compound/acropolis, then the apparent orientation shift may make sense in terms of earlier logics of placing the royal compound south and east of the main ceremonial mounds.[5] Since the Maya pattern corresponds to the southerly mounds of the MFC complex, a corresponding shift of the royal compound may have been necessary to maintain the critical spatial relationship between royal residences and the principal temples and plazas. The shift to a different cardinal orientation for the ceremonial center as a whole, however, does represent a significant departure from neighboring patterns. This is good evidence that with the late Middle Pre-Classic Maya we are dealing with a syncretic situation in which borrowed elements from the west were integrated with older norms of the Maya's own tradition.

Tikal

The earliest known occupation of Peten has been found at Tikal, located southeast of the Mirador Basin. Recent excavations in the Mundo Perdido complex recovered two large deposits of Eb-phase ceramics as well as the earliest evidence of an E-Group in the Maya lowlands (Laporte and Fialko 1995; Laporte and Valdés 1993). The early ceramics and associated artifacts come from refuse deposits from large *chultuns* (cavities) in the bedrock sealed by the earliest plaza floors (Early Tzec; formerly Late Eb) at the Mundo Perdido. These were thought to date to about 800–700 B.C. (Harrison 1999:47; Laporte and Fialko 1993a, 1995:44–45), but recent reexamination of these materials demonstrates that they are strikingly similar to late Cunil phase ceramics from Cahal Pech, Belize, (David Cheetham, personal communication) and must date to about 900–750 B.C. (cf. Cheetham 1998). This means that the earliest occupation at Tikal predates the earliest extant evidence from Nakbe and the Mirador Basin by at least a century, all other things being equal (see Forsyth 1999; Laporte and Alvarado 1999).

Not much is known of Tikal's earliest occupants other than that they got there early and favored high ground with good drainage (Laporte and Valdés 1993b) and good vantage for observing the sun (Harrison 1999:48). The recently noted tight ceramic correspondences with the Cunil ceramic complex suggests that the early agriculturalists had (or retained) strong connections to Belize and perhaps colonized the Tikal area from the east, perhaps coming up the Belize and Mopan Rivers (see Laporte and Alvarado 1999). The artifacts sealed in the refuse deposits provide some insight into their domestic activities, but nothing about their architecture or arrangement of the early community is known (see Harrison 1999; cf. Hendon 1999 for Uaxactun). The recent excavations at Tikal, however, provide excellent data on the development of ritual architecture and space. The E-Group located in the Mundo Perdido was first built in the Middle Pre-Classic period (Late Eb–Early Tzec phases) and was rebuilt four times during the Pre-Classic and two times during the

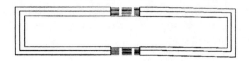

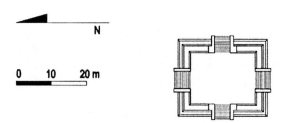

FIGURE 1.8   Early E-Group at Tikal (redrawn from Fialko 1988:Figure 3).

Classic period (Fialko 1988; Laporte and Fialko 1993b, 1995). The earliest evidence suggests a prototype of this ritual complex as early as the late Eb phase (published as 700–600 B.C.) (Laporte and Fialko 1993b:18–19; 1995:45) with a very clear E-Group being built during the Early Tzec phase (see Figure 1.8).

The dating of these early complexes is based on associated ceramics. Given the recent reappraisal of the Eb ceramic complex, it might appear logical to assume that this earliest E-Group is even earlier than originally suggested. Such a reassessment, however, does not necessarily follow. The same reappraisal of the Eb ceramics noted above suggests that late Eb ceramics are more appropriately considered as Early Tzec (see Hermes 1999:11; David Cheetham and Donald Forsyth, personal communications) and would date to 750–500 B.C. This suggests an earliest date for the first E-Group at the Mundo Perdido of about 700 B.C., with a more probable date being toward the end of the phase (ca. 600–500 B.C.), as originally published (Fialko 1988:13), rather than the beginning. Based solely on the ranges of the dated ceramic complexes, the early buildings at Tikal must, for the time being, be seen as technically contemporaneous with those in Chiapas. The different construction histories, however, suggest that there was a significant temporal lag, with the Chiapas mounds being built at the beginning of the phase and the Tikal structure toward the end of the same phase. If true, this would place the Mundo Perdido E-Group at least a century after the E-Group complexes in Chiapas and Tabasco, Mexico. These possibilities need to be checked with better dating techniques.

As with the Chiapas examples, the early E-Group at Tikal was a rather modest affair. The Late Eb–Early Tzec E-Group at Tikal consisted of a small, 3-meter-high pyramid (Mound 5C–54–1), measuring 23 meters square at the base, located to the west of a low, long mound. This latter mound (5D–84/88–2) was about 42 meters long, 11 meters wide, and located about 42 meters to the east of the pyramid (see Figure 1.8) (Laporte and Fialko 1993b:18–19;1995:46–47). No clear antecedents to this pattern are currently known in the Maya lowlands.[6] At earlier sites in Belize and at Uaxactun (see below), small circular platforms preceded the E-Group complexes.

Uaxactun

Evidence of Pre-Classic occupation in the Maya region was first discovered at the site of Uaxactun in 1926 in what was the first formal excavation of a plaza of a Maya city. The extensive excavations undertaken there from 1926 to 1937 remain today the best evidence we have of early Maya centers (see O. Ricketson 1932, 1937). As noted, the E-Group was first identified at Uaxactun, and the exploration of what was thought to be a solar observatory was one of the primary reasons that the site was selected for excavation by the Carnegie Institution, the other reason being that the site had the earliest dated stone monument known at the time— and its cycle-8 long-count date provided the rational for naming the site Uaxactun, or "eight stone" (O. Ricketson 1928a, 1928b).

Early explorations at Uaxactun centered around the possible solar observatory constituted by Mound E-VII and the long mound with its three small summit temples (Mounds E-I, E-II, and E-III) located directly to the east (O. Ricketson 1928a, 1928b, 1932). Extensive trench excavations were carried out in the plaza in order to reconstruct the building sequence of the complex (O. Ricketson 1937). The most spectacular find was the early stucco and masked pyramid (E-VII-sub), dating to the Late Pre-Classic period, entombed within the Classic-period temple mound E-VII. A possible earlier building was detected within this pyramid (O. Ricketson 1937:91–92). The trench excavations of the plaza revealed the presence of at least two episodes of occupation prior to the construction of the first E-Group, which is thought to date to the Late Mamom phase (O. Ricketson 1937:117–123; Rosal et al. 1993:70–72). Recent excavations at Uaxactun during 1983–1985 (see Rosal et al. 1993) supplement some of the details available from Ricketson's (1937) early work.

The earliest occupation at Uaxactun corresponds to the redefined Eb phase at Tikal. There is no pure deposit of this material yet known for Uaxactun, but early sherds are mixed with the earliest Mamom deposits found in a sealed *chultun* beneath the plaza floor in the northeastern part of the Group E plaza (E. Ricketson 1937; Smith 1955). Above the earliest occupation (*chultuns* and fragments of one-course walls) are four circular platforms (A, B, C, and D) about 30–40 centimeters high, each measuring 5.5–5.8 meters in diameter; these date to the early part of the Mamom phase and predate the earliest construction of the Group E plaza and complex (O. Ricketson 1937:114–117). Whether these early platforms served an analogous function to the later E-Group remains to be determined. It is of interest to note that the earliest ritual buildings in Cahal Pech, Belize, are low, circular structures that are probably contemporaneous with those at Uaxactun (see Powis 1996). A contemporaneous (i.e., Rosario phase, 700–500 B.C.), circular platform, 50–60 centimeters high and 6 meters in diameter, is also known for San José Mogote in the Valley of Oaxaca (Marcus and Flannery 1996:130), but such structures are rare in Oaxaca. In the Maya lowlands, they appear to represent an early ritual complex. About 500–400 B.C., these early structures were replaced at Uaxactun by the more formal, monumental E-Group arrangements. The two complexes appear to have been coeval at Cahal Pech, Belize (David Cheetham, personal communication, 1999). As noted, E-Groups continued to be used and refurbished well into the Classic period (see Aveni and Hartung 1989; Chase 1985; Chase and Chase 1995). Data from the Mirador Basin suggest that the heyday of the E-Group was the Middle and Late Pre-Classic periods and that the formal arrangement of triadic temples became prominent during the Late Pre-Classic (see Hansen 1998). The earliest example of a triadic arrangement at Uaxactun is the sunken patio complex on the southern edge of the Group E plaza (Rosal et al. 1993:72).

In terms of our concern with the origins and development of the Maya royal court, of particular interest at Uaxactun are data on the sequence of ritual structures dating to the Middle and Late Pre-Classic periods and the evidence for the organization of an early plaza group. At the time of the earliest E-Group, Plaza E was organized as shown in Figure 1.9, having a complex of buildings on the south and another mound along its northern edge. A similar arrangement is clear in the poorly investigated Group D at Uaxactun. Unreported excavations there revealed that it, too, dates to the Mamom phase (Renaldo Acevedo, personal communication to R. Hansen). Both Groups D and E appear to be oriented north-south, having northern and southern mounds in a pattern roughly similar to that of the MFC pattern described above. There is no obvious acropolis known for either Uaxactun or Tikal, but perhaps the complex of buildings in the sunken patio in the southern portion of Group E served an

The Architecture of Early Kingship

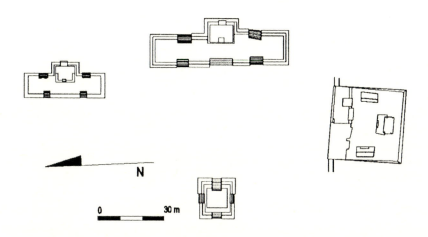

FIGURE 1.9 Plaza E at Uaxactun during the Pre-Classic (redrawn from Rosal et al. 1993:Figure 34).

analogous function. One acropolis at Nakbe is located just south of the E-Group. Each plaza group at Uaxactun is smaller than those at the Chiapas sites. When considered together, the overall site of Uaxactun is oriented east-west rather than north-south, similar to the site pattern known for Nakbe. The reasons for these similarities and differences with earlier sites in Chiapas remain to be determined. It is of interest that organizational changes in the site of Chiapa de Corzo represent a divergence from the La Venta pattern and a convergence with the early Maya pattern (see below).

The past function of the E-Group arrangement of mounds is potentially critical for deciding issues of the origins and spread of the Maya court. Unfortunately, these issues cannot be resolved with extant data. For purposes of discussion it is sufficient to repeat the generality that this special arrangement of mounds served ritual purposes, perhaps connected with observations of the sun's passage and with calendrical rites (see Chase and Chase 1995 for discussion). Clark supposes that the E-Group arrangement of mounds in the Maya lowlands was borrowed from the MFC pattern as part of a package that also included the royal compound. Hansen argues that the E-Group may have originated in the Maya region and spread to the Chiapas area. As noted, precise data for the dates for the groups in each area are too ambiguous to decide the matter at the moment. It is worth pointing out, however, that assessments of past function might eventually be critical in deciding the matter. If the complex was originally designed to take solar observations of solstices and equinoxes, then the earliest examples should be of such a size and orientation to do so. In contrast, later variants of this architectural form may have copied the form and proportions but not adapted them astronomically to local conditions as functioning observatories. The diversity of orientations among the known E-Groups suggests this latter possibility (see Aveni and Hartung 1989; Chase and Chase 1995; Ruppert 1940). The orientations of the early E-Groups outside of the Maya area remain to be evaluated, but recent evaluations of the early Maya E-Groups show that they could not have functioned as solar observatories in the manner originally imagined.[7] For the moment, then, this conclusion weakens any functional argument for a Maya origin of this ritual complex. This ritual architecture appears to have been adopted from the Olmec/Zoque area to the west and to have included, perhaps at a later date, the royal compound and the institution of kingship.

Chiapa de Corzo

The data for royal compounds at Chiapa de Corzo are best for the early Middle Pre-Classic period, as discussed above, and the Protoclassic. During this latter time Chiapa de Corzo experienced a dramatic change of fortunes and construction of other royal compounds. Figure 1.10 shows the plan of later Chiapa de Corzo and the succession and southward migration of possible royal compounds. The first platform constructed at the site was soon modified to add a pyramidal platform near its southern edge about 650 B.C., and a smaller, low platform was constructed to the south. By about 550 B.C. this had been expanded into a broad platform roughly 3 meters high and 80 meters square at the base. Investigation of this platform is difficult because of the presence of a modern house on top, but limited excavations revealed some of its construction history. The upper surface has a thick plaster floor, but the limited test excavations did not reveal any evidence of superstructures. What is remarkable here is that the shift of the acropolis south of the E-Group of the site anticipates or replicates the Maya pattern noted for Nakbe and Uaxactun. With current evidence, it appears that the arrangement at Chiapa de Corzo may have been a century earlier than its appearance in the Mirador Basin. Of particular interest, this platform structure appears to have remained unmodified during the first phase of intense interaction with the lowland Maya (ca. 250–50 B.C.), so its similarities to Maya architectural complexes cannot be attributed to these later trade contacts. It is important to note that Middle Pre-Classic innovations, such as the E-Group complex, may not have been used during this period as ritual compounds in the same manner as in the lowland centers (e.g., the stairways on the long mounds in Chiapas have different orientations than those in the Maya area).

Chiapa de Corzo appears to have started as an Olmec city, but the Olmec system fell apart by about 400 B.C., with both La Venta and La Libertad being abandoned about this time (see Clark et al. 2000). Chiapa de Corzo, however, continued on as viable as ever. About 1 B.C. a small, multiroom

The Architecture of Early Kingship

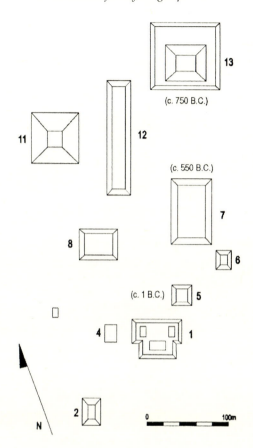

FIGURE 1.10 Site plan of the ceremonial center of Protoclassic Chiapa de Corzo.

palace was constructed at Chiapa de Corzo. This followed a period of intense interaction with communities in the Maya lowlands, as evident in imported pottery and changes in masonry techniques and building styles. Architectural norms and techniques shifted at Chiapa de Corzo from the puddled clay constructions typical of the Pre-Classic period to dressed limestone and plaster masonry, ideas and techniques that most likely came from the Maya lowlands—the Maya being the great innovators of stone masonry in Mesoamerica. The active core of the Chiapa de Corzo ceremonial center appears to have shifted southward at this time. The previously open plaza south of Chiapa de Corzo's E-Group became the locus of the construction of a new temple and palace complex (Figure 1.10).

This southernmost temple at Chiapa de Corzo began as a long, low residential platform and was associated with the small mounds that were later rebuilt into a palace (Lowe 1960). Under the sway of Maya canons of civilized life, the Zoques at Chiapa de Corzo constructed what was essentially a new royal compound consisting of separate buildings, south of the acropolis that may have formerly served this function. A king was interred below the floor of one of these modest structures (Tomb 7 of

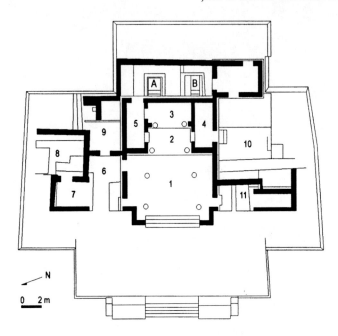

FIGURE 1.11 Plan of the Mound 5, A.D. 100 palace at Chiapa de Corzo (redrawn from Lowe 1962:Figure 46).

Mound 1), and following this event the entombing building was converted into a temple that saw the interment of four more royal individuals over the next century (Lowe 1960). Both the temple and adjacent palace (Mound 5) underwent numerous expansions and renovations during the first century A.D. The timing of these developments corresponds to the heyday of El Mirador as the preeminent Maya capital of southern Mesoamerica. It is not yet clear what developments of royal compounds took place at El Mirador at this time, but deep pits into the Central Acropolis at El Mirador by Matheny revealed an extensive sequence of floors going back to Middle Pre-Classic times (Hansen, personal observation; R. Matheny, personal communication). The transition from royal compounds to palaces noted at Chiapa de Corzo probably occurred earlier at El Mirador. The plan of the rather modest palace at Chiapa de Corzo is shown in Figure 1.11 and its reconstruction in Figure 1.12.

This small platform structure had thirteen rooms and passageways (the following details are from Lowe 1962). Other than two small, open passage ways, all the rooms were roofed. The central rooms were covered with a massive, flat adobe-and-stucco roof supported by large, 60-centimeter-diameter wooden posts and smaller beams. Side rooms to the north and at the back of the palace were roofed with thatch. The basal platform of the A.D. 100 palace was 2 meters high and 20 by 28 meters in extent. It was cross-shaped, with broad stairs leading up from the central

The Architecture of Early Kingship

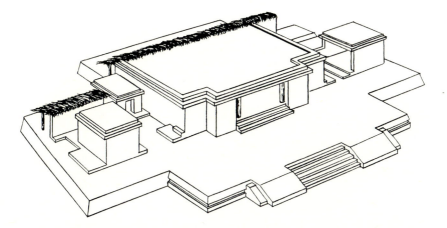

FIGURE 1.12   Reconstruction of the Mound 5 palace at Chiapa de Corzo (by Ayax Moreno).

plaza to an open forecourt in front of the palace. A further broad stairway led to the central receiving area of the palace. This room was probably curtained off. Curtains could also have been opened to reveal two successively higher and smaller rooms that extended to the back of the palace, depending on the occasion. Lowe argues that these were reception and presentation areas. Rooms were separated by thick stone walls of dressed stone and mud mortar covered with a thin layer of stucco. All of the rooms were rather small.

There are not many clues to the past functions of the various rooms other than the floorplan and location of doorways. If we consider the largest central room as principally reserved for public functions and display, the four smaller rooms behind the curtains would probably have been the main living and sleeping quarters. Their number and limited floor space indicate a rather small group of primary occupants in this palace, perhaps less than ten. Presumably, they would have used hammocks or wooden beds for sleeping, as permanent benches are absent. The two side rooms to the north of the central room lacked the well-prepared stucco floor of the rest of the palace, or its lime-covered adobe roof and drains. Lowe suggests that these may have been food preparation rooms. At the back of the palace were two large, subterranean chambers that were probably used for storing food and drink. They had to be entered by a ladder. A circular, covered shaft about 45 centimeters in diameter and 3 meters deep was also discovered on the north side of the palace; it is thought to have been used to keep stored liquids cool.

The remarkable state of preservation of this early palace is due to the fortuitous circumstance of its deliberate destruction about A.D. 100. At this time the palace was razed. Noteworthy are the hundreds of pottery vessels found on the floor and in the storage chambers. Lowe (1962) suggests that this may have been a deliberate termination ritual provoked by civil strife that saw the departure from the site of its ruling elite. They are thought to have destroyed the palace in a scorched-earth move that anticipated coming changes. Lowe further suggests that the vessels on the floors represent most of the inventory of the palace and the other buildings within the southern courtyard of the site and that these were all placed as a final termination ritual. The subsequent rebuilding of the palace is attributed to a new ethnic group, as signaled by a radical change in pottery preferences and masonry standards. Other than the presence of more than 700 crushed pots under the baked roof and wall remains from the burned structure, Lowe remarks on the "clean" nature of the rooms and the absence of any special debris that would signal past room functions. As noted above, this may be a general feature of palaces under normal circumstances—that they were kept clean and were not places where mundane domestic activities were carried out.

The number of pottery vessels left on the palace floor present an interpretive challenge. In contrast to Lowe's ideas about imported terminal offerings, we are intrigued by the possibility that all the vessels found crushed on the floors of this palace may actually have been associated with it. Given the presence of special storage areas, it may be that the extraordinarily large ceramic inventory indicates past feasting activities at this palace. Large caches of pottery were found in each of the two chambers at the back of the palace, and they are rather different in form and assemblage composition, suggesting a complementarity of functions. Chamber B (Cache 5–6) contained rather mundane pottery. Of the recovered 136 whole or nearly whole vessels, four were deep, wide-mouthed basins, five were special bridge-spout pots for serving liquids, and the remaining 127 were rather plain brown, small, shallow bowls or dishes appropriate for individual servings (Figure 1.13). Most of these vessels were stacked or nested and, to us, appear to have been in a primary storage location rather than placed as a special termination offering. Many of the bowls and plates in the other chamber were also carefully stacked (Cache 5–7, Chamber A). The principal difference is that these represented finer "table" wares and serving vessels. A total of 101 restorable whole vessels was recovered, but none of the small bowls predominating in the companion chamber was found among them. "It is as if one category of pottery, or of pottery-related contents, went into one chamber and a quite different category into another. It is perhaps equally, or more, probable simply that pottery types associated with one group or class of persons went into the one chamber, and of another group or class in the second" (Lowe 1962:25). The majority of the other 500 vessels found on the floors of the palace came from two rooms, the main room and the northern "preparation" area.[8] It is significant that no *manos* or *metates* were found in this structure; neither were there any clear cooking areas. In regard to this last observation, it is important to stress that numerous three-

FIGURE 1.13 Pottery assemblage from Cache 17-1, Mound 17, Chiapa de Corzo, which has the same vessel forms and proportions as those from Mound 5, chamber B (from Lowe 1962:Figure 34).

pronged incense burners were found; some of these could have been braziers for cooking rather than for burning incense. However, the overall evidence for food preparation at Mound 5 is not compelling, and many basic services appear to have been provided for the occupants of this palace by servile personnel who lived and performed basic palace tasks elsewhere.

The assemblages of vessels in the other rooms differ from those in the two stone-lined chambers. Following Lowe's hypothesis, these would signal status differences of the people who brought them to the palace as offerings. We find it more plausible to believe that most or all of the vessels were actually associated with the palace and were stored in the northern wing or in the rear chambers until needed. The strong clues that the vessels in the two storage chambers were in their primary storage locations suggests several important things about the functioning of the Chiapa de Corzo royal court. First, the number of vessels belonging to the royal house, whether 700 or merely 300, far exceeded the needs of the few individuals who could have lived there. Certainly the elites of this building used the same types of pottery as commoners—but in astronomical quantities, perhaps on special occasions. Second, several classes of vessels are evident in the different stashes. The mundane pottery and serving vessels of the one chamber look like serving vessels for prosaic occasions, perhaps for low-status groups or work crews. Other pottery would have served for higher-status groups. With this ceramic inventory, the ruler could fete several hundred people at a time; many of these could probably crowd onto the open forecourt (8 by 20 meters) in the front of the palace (see Figure 1.11), with others in the adjacent plaza. More select occasions of 30–50 persons could have been celebrated in the central room. Third, the more utilitarian northern rooms may indeed have been for food preparation on special occasions but not on a daily basis. Many serving vessels could have been stored there when not in use. Fourth, within the ceramic inventory were several very special effigy pots and carved vessels that would probably not have been available to commoners.

A remarkable feature of the small palace on Mound 5 at Chiapa de Corzo is that so much of its limited space appears to have been devoted to public functions, with only a few closet-sized rooms reserved for privacy. The royals at this site appear to have been readily accessible to the populace at large and, if our speculations about feasting are correct, had good public relations. It is important to reiterate that the large temple on the south of this plaza was just kiddie-corner from the palace, and the palace royals could have conducted some of the rituals there. What is not clear at Chiapa de Corzo—and at the other sites considered here—is where the priests lived. More problematic, it is not clear that there was a separate priest class at all, as is believed to have existed among the lowland Maya. It may well be that the kings were actually priest-kings and conducted themselves accordingly. The data considered here cannot resolve this question. It would be better addressed by examining mortuary remains that would allow one to derive strong inferences of past social roles.

Spatial Implications: Serving God and Mammon

The spatial dimension of royal compounds can be evaluated at a series of increasing scales, from individual residences to regional settlement patterns. In doing so it becomes apparent that the royal compound was both a centralizing and mediating institution at ancient capital centers. This is most clearly seen in the MFC pattern where the royal acropolis was immediately east of the principal temple structures and opened on its own eastern margin to one of the residential wards of the city. Based upon the limited information presented above for various compounds and the Chiapa de Corzo palace, it is probable that the various structures of the royal compound, or the rooms of the palace, served specialized functions, as seen in the incomplete inventory of domestic artifacts at most compounds (i.e., absence of corn-processing equipment). At all of the sites mentioned, it is also fairly clear that the ruling elite sponsored and controlled a variety of economic activities, such as craft specialties, trade of special goods, and public works projects (Clark 1988, 1997; Hansen

1992a, 1992b, 1992c, 1994a, 1994b). For lack of space, we do not discuss these here, but they are important for understanding the ebb and flow of activity at royal compounds. The intermediary position of these compounds between secular and sacred space at these early centers is patent and signals the rulers' dual functioning in at least two spatially and conceptually distinct spheres of power: god and mammon.

The proximity of royal compounds to primary temples implies that kings and other royal members of the court, including priests, were involved in rituals associated with these edifices. At La Libertad and Chiapa de Corzo, burials of kings accompanied in death by human sacrificial victims (see Lee 1969) have been exhumed from the largest pyramids closest to the royal compounds, and their burials there signal the kings' intimate association with the sacred rites that took place at summit temples. Temple burial of kings and queens becomes a common Maya pattern during the Classic period and does not require further justification here. Still, the royals of these same sites were adept at political economy and foreign relations. The large open courtyards (ca. 50 by 50 meters) within the royal compounds could have been used to host large gatherings for less sacred functions that perhaps frequently involved provision of food and refreshment. The large stores of serving vessels found at Chiapa de Corzo palace–Mound 5 provide some interesting data here on feasting and the size and composition of various groups. Several hundred people could have been served with the available serviceware.

Without elaborating the point, the actual activities of the ruling elite would have involved them in secular as well as sacred functions, and in each sphere they may have represented the other sphere. Kings as supreme mediators between the heavens and earth, between the gods and the people, marked their pivotal positions in the locations of their royal residences, balanced as they were between the two worlds of the sacred and profane.

In a literal sense, the location of the royal compound fits with Fray Diego de Landa's brief description of Maya towns (Tozzer 1941), with the most important individuals living closest to the temples, the lesser individuals living farther away from the center. The royal compounds are central to the sites in which they are found (the site as it was during the time the compound was in use). And, we have argued, they were also medial between the pedestrian world and the sacred center. The actual size of these buildings and the measured spaces between them may eventually prove to be significant, but not enough precise information is available concerning the size or orientation of early buildings to evaluate this idea.

The distribution of royal palaces within regions and macroregions still has to be worked out. Implicit in all our arguments is the notion that the presence of these compounds and acropoli mark a site as a regional capital. Moreover, it appears probable that some of these capitals may have exercised hegemony over others within their immediate regions. Of the dozen or so regional capitals strung along the Grijalva River Valley of central Chiapas during the Middle Pre-Classic, five stand out as exceptional: La Libertad, Acapulco, Chiapa de Corzo, Mirador, and San Isidro. Subsidiary centers in the immediate vicinity of each capital were privileged to have several small pyramids in axial alignment, but they lacked the central acropolis or other manifestations of permanent royal presence (see Clark 1988). If our inference is correct, sufficient excavations at centers with supposed royal compounds should reveal burials of bona fide kings, all other things being equal. A strong case can be made for the presence of kings at La Venta (Clark 1997; Reilly 1999), even though conditions of preservation there are such that none has been absolutely attested with osteological remains. Middle and Late Pre-Classic royal burials have been recovered from both Chiapa de Corzo and La Libertad (Clark et al. 2000; Lee 1969), with royal burials for the Mirador Basin currently known only from Late Pre-Classic contexts (Hansen 1998:88–95; cf. Krejcí and Culbert 1995). We suspect that with more excavation, their presence at Mirador Basin sites will be confirmed.

Temporal Implications: Old Gods and Royal Ancestors

Most of our arguments for the temporal succession of the various royal compounds have been summarized in conjunction with discussions of site patterns. We argue that the appearance of kingship and royal courts among the Pre-Classic Maya is a case of stimulus diffusion of a high-status institution from one region to another. Many investigators are particularly sensitive to such claims these days, so our claim merits more formal presentation here. The argument for regional diffusion or borrowing relies on three presumptions: (1) Close similarities of institutions in adjacent regions, such as E-Groups or royal compounds, indicate a common origin or historic connection; (2) temporal priority of an institution or artifact form (such as an elite acropolis) in one area and its later occurrence in another suggests the direction of the borrowing, all other things being equal; and (3) the extant archaeological sample is an accurate reflection of large, as yet untested regions. With regard to this last presumption, we recognize that Chiapas, unlike the Maya lowlands, has received modest archaeological study for nearly fifty years and that viewing conditions in this semiarid, well-populated region favor the discovery of pyramid sites. In contrast, most of the large sites in the Maya lowlands, particularly in western Peten, remain to be investigated.

Clark claims that ceremonial and royal architecture is earlier in the Olmec and Chiapas regions—those closest to the Maya lowlands. These are aspects of early Maya developments that had appeared until now to be independent of any Olmec or Zoque influence. Others have already demonstrated historic connections with other classes of artifacts, symbols, and concepts. In contrast, Richard Hansen argues, on the basis of ceramics and carbon-14 dates, that much of the touted influence could have gone in the other direction, from the Maya to the Olmec and Zoques.

Despite these differences, we think it clear that borrowing and cultural interaction were critical for the passage of notions of kingship from earlier societies to the Maya, but making this claim falls far short of a satisfying or adequate explanation. Rather, it is better taken as an important clue as to where to search for a fuller explanation. If one grants the temporal priority of Olmec kingship to Maya kingship, and a historic transmission from one to the other, what was the nature of the historic connection and how did it occur? We have argued that numerous Chiapas sites were part of the Middle Pre-Classic Olmec pattern. This raises a serious problem for any historic explanation, as it multiplies the options and opportunities for cultural borrowing and lending. Who borrowed what from whom and why? We have alluded to the stereotypic MFC siteplans and royal compounds as "La Venta" and "Olmec" patterns because they may be earlier there than elsewhere. It does not follow, however, that the Maya of Nakbe borrowed from the La Ventans. In addition to their own cultural practices, they could have interacted with peoples at secondary centers such as Chiapa de Corzo or La Libertad. Having opened the Pandora's box of diffusion and historic connections, we must admit that the data available cannot take one much beyond assertions of historic connections and some minor content. But these can be narrowed down in time and space.

One of the important implications of the rather full documentation of early Maya developments in the Mirador Basin is that they allow one to pinpoint with some precision the critical century of transition. The appearance of monumental, formalized architectural programs were clearly extant in the fifth century B.C. at Nakbe,[9] Tikal, and possibly Uaxactun. Subsequent developments at Nakbe were a logical progression from an initial stage of interaction with foreign kingdoms and adoption and adaption of their regal institutions. The documented absence of these activities in the Mirador Basin at an earlier date is compelling evidence that they were borrowed from neighboring groups who had them at an earlier time.

Considering a broader range of data, the few clues to the possible historic process become clearer. Some of the cultural elements that appear to be earlier in the Olmec and Zoque areas than in the Maya lowlands are the following: (1) pyramids, (2) royal compounds, (3) axial placement of offerings, (4) royal tombs and crypts, (5) acropoli measuring about 80 meters square, (6) E-Groups, (7) formal, patterned plazas, (8) arrangements of four god masks on pyramid facades (see González Lauck 1997), (9) temples, (10) ballcourts, (11) stone sculptures (altars and stelae), (12) thrones, (13) regal vestments and jewelry, (14) jester-god crowns, (15) snake scepters, (16) special headdresses and capes, (17) memorial monuments to kings, and (18) representations of gods. Other elements that appear earlier in the Maya lowlands than in the Olmec region are even earlier in the Valley of Oaxaca and the Mexican Plateau. These include (1) megalithic architecture, (2) internal cell wall construction, and (3) vertical walled platforms (see Marcus and Flannery 1996; Marcus 1999). This partial list does not deal with specific symbols, royal insignia, and special paraphernalia. On all counts, the Maya appear to have borrowed from institutions of Olmec kingship and sacred space. But many of these elements they quickly changed and modified to suit their own tastes and circumstances, as noted in our discussion of site orientations.

Many aspects of Maya culture can be traced back in the Maya area to pre-Olmec times, and so invoking the Olmecs as the source for these cultural phenomena would clearly be an inappropriate and unhelpful exaggeration of cultural process (see Clark et al. 2000). When it comes to kingship and royal court life, however, the borrowed elements listed above suggest a strong and important connection. This is one area where an historic connection is particularly difficult to deny or ignore. As has been shown, the early Maya themselves referred to their Olmec heritage, and many of the earliest Maya inscriptions are found on the backsides of heirloom jades that depict Olmec gods or elite protagonists (Schele and Freidel 1990; see also Freidel and Suhler 1995; Schele 1995). This suggests that the Maya borrowed portions of the Olmec royal complex, including gods, props, and sundry paraphernalia. And in the end, the Pre-Classic Maya may have even adopted Olmec royal ancestors and grafted themselves into the Olmec's royal line, as suggested in a Late Classic text referring to tenth-century B.C. kings (Schele and Freidel 1990). Of course, if the genealogical claims to the "foreign" system were not fictive, then things get even more interesting.

Whatever the specific origins of the borrowed elements of kingship and courtly life, the Maya gave them their own cast. If we are correct in our surmise about shifts during the Late Pre-Classic period at El Mirador (i.e., the reduced size of sculpture, the ascendency of triadic temples, monumental architectural art, and the elaboration of the first stone palaces), then transformations in the material trappings of courtly life in the Maya lowlands were rather rapid and significant (for details, see Clark et al. 2000 and Hansen 1998). These modifications constituted dramatic change and, in their own right, had a significant impact on neighboring cultures, as shifts in the royal compounds and architecture at Chiapa de Corzo clearly attest. Their most profound impact, however, was probably in their own backyard and the propagation of kingship across the Maya lowlands. This would have been basically the same historic process of diffusion just described from the Olmecs or Zoques to the Maya at Nakbe and other towns in the Mirador Basin. The differences in the loaning and borrowing cultures involved are relatively minor in terms of appreciating the general cultural process. Multilingualism was probably common in ancient Mesoamerica, at least at cultural boundaries, so language differences were probably not a barrier to cultural interaction between neighbors.

It is possible that the first kings in the Mirador Basin were connected to foreign powers from the Maya western frontier, meaning that these first kings would have been enticed into the swampy Mirador region from elsewhere. If so, genealogical claims to the older system by subsequent Maya kings would have had a biological and not merely a fictive basis. It is worth emphasizing, however, that there is currently no evidence for foreign kings in the Maya lowlands—but given the limited evidence for anything regal in the Mirador Basin during the Middle Pre-Classic, the extant information is not yet fatal to this idea, or for any of its alternatives. Historically, establishment of cadet royal lines on the edges of one's domain is a rather common way to promulgate kingship and to have it slip out of control, the result being new upstart kingdoms, much like suckers around the roots of a tree. Clark would not be surprised if the eventual recovery of early royal tombs in the Mirador Basin showed their occupants to have had strong connections to the western frontier. Hansen proposes an autochthonous origin, and so we wait and see. The problem of the origins of the royal court is clear; it remains to do the arduous research to resolve it.

Conclusion

Our focus here has concerned what we call "royal compounds" and some of the implications that follow if their identifications and historic sequence are correct. Perhaps the most significant implication is that it would point to the origins of early Maya kingship as a cultural borrowing from the Zoques or Olmecs to the west. Given the meager data upon which we built this argument, it is not worth pushing farther at this time. We intend to subject these ideas to rigorous field testing in future research at most of the sites mentioned. The most obvious place to start is with intensive and extensive excavations in the supposed royal compounds discussed. Also, it will be important to recover the remains and offerings of the surmised early Maya kings in the Mirador Basin before looters mutilate and sell the evidence. We expect the discovery and analysis of such remains to demonstrate some cultural borrowing from the Zoque or Olmec regions and to recover clear clues on the nature of courtly life.

The analytical problem of demonstrating a clear historic connection between early Maya kings and their predecessors is actually more serious than portrayed because the early history of kingship is so poorly known in all of its aspects. Almost nothing is known about early Olmec kingship, for example, other than what various interpreters think they can infer from monuments and offerings (see Reilly 1999). Our speculative exercise here of trying to trace the origins of the Maya royal court suggests that critical resources still essentially untapped are the royal compounds and residences themselves. Even in the tropical Gulf Coast lowlands, where human remains do not preserve, it is possible to recover royal residences and compounds, as well as their artifacts and features (see Cyphers 1996, 1999). It should further be possible to divine their general position within a site vis-à-vis other structures of known function and to make simple inferences about relationships. In short, the early royal court as a physical entity has the potential to be the key for understanding the earliest history of Mesoamerican kingship and of the royal court as a sociological phenomenon.

References

Agrinier, Pierre. 1970. *Mound 20, Mirador, Chiapas, Mexico*. Papers of the New World Archaeological Foundation, No. 28. Provo: Brigham Young University.

_____. 1975. *Mounds 9 and 10 at Mirador, Chiapas, Mexico*. Papers of the New World Archaeological Foundation, No. 39. Provo: Brigham Young University.

_____. 1984. *The Early Olmec Horizon at Mirador, Chiapas, Mexico*. Papers of the New World Archaeological Foundation, No. 48. Provo: Brigham Young University.

_____. 2000. *Mound 27 and the Middle Preclassic Period at Mirador, Chiapas, Mexico*. Papers of the New World Archaeological Foundation, No. 58. Provo: Brigham Young University.

Aveni, Anthony F., and Horst Hartung. 1989. "Uaxactun, Guatemala; Group E and Similar Assemblages: An Archaeo-astronomical Reconsideration." In Anthony E. Aveni, ed., *World Archaeoastronomy*, pp. 441–461. Cambridge: Cambridge University Press.

Blanton, Richard E., Gary M. Feinman, Stephen A. Kowaleski, and Linda M. Nichols. 1999. *Ancient Oaxaca*. Cambridge: Cambridge University Press.

Chase, Arlen F. 1985. "Archaeology in the Maya Heartland." *Archaeology* 38: 32–39.

Chase, Arlen, R., and Diane Z. Chase. 1995. "External Impetus, Internal Synthesis, and Standardization: E Group Assemblages and the Crystallization of Classic Maya Society in the Southern Lowlands." In Nikolai Grube, ed., *The Emergence of Lowland Maya Civilization: The Transition from the Pre-Classic to the Early Classic*, pp. 87–101. Möckmühl, Germany: Verlag Anton Saurwein.

Cheetham, David. 1998. "Interregional Interaction, Symbol Emulation, and the Emergence of Socio-political Inequality in the Central Maya Lowlands." Master's Thesis, University of British Columbia.

Clark, John E. 1988. *The Lithic Artifacts of La Libertad, Chiapas, Mexico: An Economic Perspective*. Papers of the New World Archaeological Foundation, No. 52. Provo: Brigham Young University.

———. 1997. "The Arts of Government in Early Mesoamerica." *Annual Review of Anthropology* 26: 211–234.

Clark, John E., Richard D. Hansen, and Tomas Perez. 2000. "La zona maya en el preclásico." In Linda Manzanilla and Leonardo Lopez Luján, eds., *Historia antigua de Mexico*, 2d ed., pp. 437–510. Mexico, D.F.: Universidad Nacional Autónoma de México.

Clark, John E., and Thomas A. Lee Jr. 1984. "Formative Obsidian Exchange and the Emergence of Public Economies in Chiapas, Mexico." In Kenneth G. Hirth, ed., *Trade and Exchange in Early Mesoamerica*, pp. 235–274. Albuquerque: University of New Mexico Press.

Coe, Michael D., and Richard A. Diehl. 1980. *In the Land of the Olmec: The Archaeology of San Lorenzo Tenochtitlan*. Austin: University of Texas Press.

Cyphers, Ann. 1996. "Reconstructing Olmec Life at San Lorenzo." In Elizabeth P. Benson and Beatriz de la Fuente, eds., *Olmec Art of Ancient Mexico*, pp. 60–71. Washington, DC: National Gallery of Art.

———. 1999. "From Stone to Symbols: Olmec Art in Social Context at San Lorenzo Tenochtitlán." In David C. Grove and Rosemary A. Joyce, eds., *Social Patterns in Pre-Classic Mesoamerica*, pp. 155–181. Washington, DC: Dumbarton Oaks Research Library and Collection.

Drucker, Philip, Robert F. Heizer, and Robert Squier. 1959. *Excavations at La Venta, Tabasco, 1955*. Bureau of American Ethnology Bulletin 170. Washington, DC.

Fialko, Vilma. 1988. "Mundo Perdido, Tikal: Un ejemplo de complejos de conmemoración astronómica." *Mayab* 4: 13–21.

Flannery, Kent V. 1998. "The Ground Plan of Archaic States." In Gary M. Feinman and Joyce Marcus, eds., *Archaic States*, pp. 15–58. Santa Fe: School of American Research.

Freidel, David, and Charles Suhler. 1995. "Crown of Creation: The Development of the Maya Royal Diadems in the Late Preclassic and Early Classic Periods." In Nikolai Grube, ed., *The Emergence of Lowland Maya Civilization: The Transition from the Preclassic to the Early Classic*, pp. 137–150. Möckmühl, Germany: Verlag Anton Saurwein.

Forsyth, Donald W. 1999. "La cerámica preclásica y el desarrollo de la complejidad cultural durante el preclásico." In Juan Pedro Laporte and Héctor L. Escobedo, eds., *XII Simposio de Investigaciones Arqueológicas en Guatemala*, pp. 51–63. Guatemala: Ministerio de Cultura y Deportes, Instituto de Antropología e Historia, Asociación Tikal.

Gallegos Gómora, M. Judith. 1990. "Excavaciones en la Estructura D-7 en La Venta, Tabasco." *Arqueología* 3: 17–24.

González Lauck, Rebecca B. 1996. "La Venta: An Olmec Capital." In Elizabeth P. Benson and Beatriz de la Fuente, eds., *Olmec Art of Ancient Mexico*, pp. 73–81. Washington, DC: National Gallery of Art.

———. 1997. "Acerca de Pirámides de tierra y seres sobrenaturales: observaciones preliminares en torno al edificio C–1, La Venta, Tabasco." *Arqueología* (enero-junio): 79–97.

Grove, David C. 1989. "Chalcatzingo and Its Olmec Connection." In Robert J. Sharer and David C. Grove, eds., *Regional Perspectives on the Olmec*, pp. 122–147. Cambridge: Cambridge University Press.

———. 1999. "Public Monuments and Sacred Mountains: Observations on Three Formative Period Sacred Landscapes." In David C. Grove and Rosemary A. Joyce, eds., *Social Patterns in Pre-Classic Mesoamerica*, pp. 255–299. Washington, DC: Dumbarton Oaks Research Library and Collection.

Hammond, Norman. 1995. "Ceremony and Society at Cuello: Pre-Classic Ritual Behavior and Social Differentiation." In Nikolai Grube, ed., *The Emergence of Lowland Maya Civilization: The Transition from the Pre-Classic to the Early Classic*, pp. 49–59. Möckmühl, Germany: Verlag Anton Saurwein.

———. 1999. "The Genesis of Hierarchy: Mortuary and Offertory Ritual in the Pre-Classic at Cuello, Belize." In David C. Grove and Rosemary A. Joyce, eds., *Social Patterns in Pre-Classic Mesoamerica*, pp. 49–66. Washington, DC: Dumbarton Oaks Research Library and Collection.

Hansen, Richard D. 1990. *Excavations in the Tigre Complex, El Mirador, Petén, Guatemala*. Papers of the New World Archaeological Foundation, No. 62. Provo: Brigham Young University.

———. 1991a. "An Early Maya Text from El Mirador, Guatemala." *Research Reports on Ancient Maya Writing*, No. 37: 19–32. Washington, DC: Center for Maya Research.

———. 1991b. "The Ancient Maya Rediscovered: The Road to Nakbe." *Natural History* (May): 8–14.

———. 1992a. "The Archaeology of Ideology: A Study of Maya Pre-Classic Architectural Sculpture at Nakbe, Petén, Guatemala." Ph.D. diss., University of California–Los Angeles.

———. 1992b. "Proyecto Regional de Investigaciones Arqueológicas del Norte de Petén, Guatemala: Temporada 1990." In Juan Pedro Laporte, Héctor L. Escobedo, and Sandra Villagrán de Brady, eds., *IV Simposio de Arqueología Guatemalateca*, pp. 1–36. Guatemala: Ministerio de Cultura y Deportes, Instituto de Antropología e Historia, Asociación Tikal.

———. 1992c. "El proceso cultural de Nakbe y el área del Petén nor-central: Las épocas tempranas." In Juan Pedro Laporte, Héctor L. Escobedo A., and Sandra Villagrán de Brady, eds., *V Simposio de Investigaciones en Guatemala*, pp. 81–96. Guatemala: Ministerio de Cultura y Deportes, Instituto de Antropología e Historia, Asociación Tikal.

———. 1994a. "Investigaciones arqueológicas en el norte del Petén, Guatemala: Una mirada diacrónica del los origines mayas." In William J. Folan, ed., *Campeche Maya Colonial*, pp. 14–54. Universidad Antónoma del Sureste, Campeche, Mexico.

———. 1994b. "Las dinámicas culturales y ambientales de los orígines mayas: Estudios recientes del sitio arqueológico Nakbe." In Juan Pedro Laporte and Héctor L. Escobedo, eds., *VII Simposio de Investigaciones Arqueológicas en Guatemala*, pp. 369–387. Guatemala: Ministerio de Cultura y Deportes, Instituto de Antropología e Historia, Asociación Tikal.

———. 1995. "Yax Te Tun: The Incipient Development, Context, and Cultural Implications of Early Monuments in the Maya Lowlands." *Abstracts of the 94th Annual Meetings* 75, American Anthropological Association. Washington, DC.

———. 1998. "Continuity and Disjunction: The Pre-Classic Antecedents of Classic Maya Architecture." In Stephen D. Houston, ed., *Function and Meaning in Classic Maya Architecture*, pp. 49–122. Washington, DC: Dumbarton Oaks Research Library and Collection.

Harrison, Peter D. 1999. *The Lords of Tikal: Rulers of an Ancient Maya City*. London: Thames and Hudson.

Hendon, Julia A. 1999. "The Pre-Classic Maya Compound as the Focus of Social Identity." In David C. Grove and Rosemary A. Joyce, eds., *Social Patterns in Pre-Classic Mesoamerica*, pp. 95–125. Washington, DC: Dumbarton Oaks Research Library and Collection.

Hermes, Bernard. 1999. "La cerámica y otro tipo de evidencia anterior al período clásico en Topoxte, Petén." In Juan Pedro Laporte and Héctor L. Escobedo, eds., *XII Simposio de Investigaciones Arqueológicas en Guatemala*, pp. 3–49. Guatemala: Ministerio de Cultura y Deportes, Instituto de Antropología e Historia, Asociación Tikal.

Hicks, Frederick, and Charles E. Rozaire. 1960. *Mound 13, Chiapa de Corzo, Chiapas, Mexico*. Papers of the New World Archaeological Foundation, No. 10. Provo: Brigham Young University.

Heizer, Robert F., John A. Graham, and L. K. Napton. 1968. "The 1968 Excavations at La Venta." *Contributions of the University of California Archaeological Research Facility*, No. 5: 127–154.

Joyce, Rosemary A. 1999. "Social Dimensions of Pre-Classic Burials." In David C. Grove and Rosemary A. Joyce, eds., *Social Patterns in Pre-Classic Mesoamerica*, pp. 15–47. Washington, DC: Dumbarton Oaks Research Library and Collection.

Krejci, Estella, and T. Patrick Culbert. 1995. "Preclassic and Classic Burials and Caches in the Maya Lowlands." In Nikolai Grube, ed., *The Emergence of Lowland Maya Civilization: The Transition from the Preclassic to the Early Classic*, pp. 103–116. Möckmühl, Germany: Verlag Anton Saurwein.

Laporte, Juan Pedro, and Marco Tulio Alvarado. 1999. "El período preclásico en el sureste de Petén: Asentamiento, arquitectura, cerámica." In Juan Pedro Laporte and Héctor L. Escobedo, eds., *XII Simposio de Investigaciones Arqueológicas en Guatemala*, pp. 79–98. Guatemala: Ministerio de Cultura y Deportes, Instituto de Antropología e Historia, Asociación Tikal.

Laporte, Juan Pedro, and Vilma Fialko. 1993a. "Análisis cerámico de tres depósitos problemáticos de fase Eb, Mundo Perdido, Tikal." In Juan Pedro Laporte and Juan Antonio Valdés, *Tikal y Uaxactún en el Preclásico*, pp. 53–69. Mexico, D.F.: Universidad Nacional Autónoma de México.

Laporte, Juan Pedro, and Vilma Fialko. 1993b. "El preclásico de Mundo Perdido: Algunos aportes sobre los orígenes de Tikal." In Juan Pedro Laporte and Juan Antonio Valdés, *Tikal y Uaxactún en el Preclásico*, pp. 9–46. Mexico, D.F.: Universidad Nacional Autónoma de México.

———. 1995. "Un reencuentro con Mundo Perdido, Tikal, Guatemala." *Ancient Mesoamerica* 6: 41–94.

Laporte, Juan Pedro, and Juan Antonio Valdés. 1993. *Tikal y Uaxactún en el preclásico*. Mexico, D.F.: Universidad Nacional Autónoma de México.

Lee, Thomas A. Jr. 1969. "Salvamento Arqueológico en Chiapa de Corzo." *Boletin INAH* 38 (dec.): 17–22.

Lowe, Gareth W. 1960. *Mound 1, Chiapa de Corzo, Chiapas, Mexico*. Papers of the New World Archaeological Foundation, No. 8. Provo: Brigham Young University.

_____. 1962. *Mound 5 and Minor Excavations, Chiapa de Corzo, Chiapas, Mexico*. Papers of the New World Archaeological Foundation, No. 12. Provo: Brigham Young University.

_____. 1977. "The Mixe-Zoque as Competing Neighbors of the Early Lowland Maya." In R.E.W. Adams, ed., *The Origins of Maya Civilization*, pp. 197–248. Albuquerque: University of New Mexico Press.

_____. 1989. "The Heartland Olmec: Evolution of Material Culture." In Robert J. Sharer and David C. Grove, eds., *Regional Perspectives on the Olmec*, pp. 33–67. Cambridge: Cambridge University Press.

Marcus, Joyce. 1999. "Men's and Women's Ritual in Formative Oaxaca." In David C. Grove and Rosemary A. Joyce, eds., *Social Patterns in Pre-Classic Mesoamerica*, pp. 67–96. Washington, DC: Dumbarton Oaks Research Library and Collection.

Marcus, Joyce, and Kent V. Flannery. 1996. *Zapotec Civilization: How Urban Society Evolved in Mexico's Oaxaca Valley*. London: Thames and Hudson.

Martínez Donjuan, Guadalupe. 1994. "Los Olmecas en el Estado de Guerrero." In John E. Clark, ed., *Los Olmecas en Mesoamérica*, pp. 143–163. Madrid: Editorial Equilibrista.

Martínez, Gustavo, and Richard D. Hansen. 1993. "Excavaciones en el Complejo 59, Grupo 66 y Grupo 18, Nakbé, Petén." In Juan Pedro Laporte, Héctor L. Escobedo, and Sandra Villagrán de Brady, eds., *III Simposio de Arqueología Guatemalteca*, pp. 73–85. Guatemala: Ministerio de Cultura y Deportes, Instituto de Antropología e Historia, Asociación Tikal.

Mason, J. Alden. 1960a. *Mound 12, Chiapa de Corzo, Chiapas, Mexico*. Papers of the New World Archaeological Foundation, No. 9. Provo: Brigham Young University.

_____. 1960b. *The Terrace to North of Mound 13, Chiapa de Corzo, Chiapas, Mexico*. Papers of the New World Archaeological Foundation, No. 11. Provo: Brigham Young University.

Mata Amado, Guillero, and Richard D. Hansen. 1992. "El diente incrustado temprano de Nakbe." In Juan Pedro Laporte, Héctor L. Escobedo, and Sandra Villagrán de Brady, eds., *V Simposio de Investigaciones Arqueológicas en Guatemala*, pp. 115–118. Guatemala: Ministerio de Cultura y Deportes, Instituto de Antropología e Historia, Asociación Tikal.

Michels, Joseph W. 1979. "A History of Settlement at Kaminaljuyu." In Joseph W. Michels, ed., *Settlement Pattern Excavations at Kaminaljuyu, Guatemala*, ed., pp. 277–305. University Park: Pennsylvania State University.

Miller, Donald E. 1976. "La Libertad, a Major Middle and Late Pre-Classic Ceremonial Center in Chiapas, Mexico: A Preliminary Report." Manuscript. New World Archaeological Foundation, San Cristobal de las Casas, Chiapas, Mexico.

_____. 1979. "Elite Domestic Structures at La Libertad, Chiapas, Mexico." Paper presented at the forty-third International Congress of Americanists, Vancouver.

Niederberger, Christine. 1996. "The Basin of Mexico: A Multimillenial Development Toward Cultural Complexity." In Elizabeth P. Benson and Beatriz de la

Fuente, eds., *Olmec Art of Ancient Mexico*, pp. 95–103. Washington, DC: National Gallery of Art.

Powis, Terry G. 1996. "Excavations of Middle Formative Period Round Structures at the Tolok Group, Cahal Pech, Belize." Master's Thesis, Trent University.

Reilly, F. Kent III. 1999. "Mountains of Creation and Underworld Portals: The Ritual Function of Olmec Architecture at La Venta, Tabasco." In Jeff K. Kowalski, ed., *Mesoamerican Architecture as a Cultural Symbol*, pp. 15–39. Oxford: Oxford University Press.

Ricketson, Edith Bayles. 1937. *Uaxactun, Guatemala: Group E—1926–1931. Part II: The Artifacts*. Carnegie Institution of Washington, No. 477. Washington, DC.

Ricketson, Oliver G. Jr. 1928a. "Astronomical Observatories in the Maya Area." *Geographic Review* 18(2): 215–225.

———. 1928b. "Notes on Two Maya Astronomic Observatories." *American Anthropologist* 30: 434–444.

———. 1930. "The Excavations at Uaxactun." *Proceedings of the Twenty-third International Congress of Americanists*, New York, September 17–22, 1928.

———. 1932. "Las Excavaciones en Uaxactun." *Anales de la Sociedad de Geografia e Historia, Guatemala* 9: 34–57.

———. 1937. *Uaxactun, Guatemala: Group E—1926–1931. Part I: The Excavations*. Carnegie Institution of Washington, No. 477. Washington, DC.

Rosal, Marco Antonio, Juan Antonio Valdés, and Juan Pedro Laporte. 1993. "Nuevas exploraciones en el Grupo E, Uaxactún." In Juan Pedro Laporte and Juan Antonio Valdés, *Tikal y Uaxactún en el Preclásico*, pp. 70–91. Mexico, D.F.: Universidad Nacional Autónoma de México.

Ruppert, Karl. 1940. "A Special Assemblage of Maya Structures." In C. Hay, R. Linton, S. Lothrop, and H. Shapiro eds., *The Maya and Their Neighbors*, pp. 222–231. New York: Appleton-Century.

Schele, Linda. 1995. "Sprouts and the Early Symbolism of Rulers in Mesoamerica." In Nikolai Grube, ed., *The Emergence of Lowland Maya Civilization: The Transition from the Preclassic to the Early Classic*, pp. 117–135. Möckmühl, Germany: Verlag Anton Saurwein.

Schele, Linda, and David Freidel. 1990. *A Forest of Kings: The Untold Story of the Ancient Maya*. New York: William Morrow.

Tozzer, Alfred M. 1941. *Landa's Relacion de las cosas de Yucatan*. Papers of the Peabody Museum of American Archaeology and Ethnology, vol. 18. Cambridge: Harvard University.

Smith, Robert E. 1955. *Ceramic Sequence of Uaxactun, Guatemala*. Middle America Research Institute Publication 20. New Orleans: Tulane University.

Winter, Marcus. 1994. "El Proyecto Especial Monte Albán: Antecedentes, intervenciones y perspectivas." In Marcus Winter, ed., *Monte Albán: Estudios Recientes*, pp. 1–24. Oaxaca: Proyecto Especial Monte Albán, 1992–1994.

Notes

1. As authors we are engaged in a continuing debate about the quality of the available data (especially the dating of the various mounds and buildings at the sites considered), their significance, and the scholarly limits of acceptable speculation without better evidence. As our intent here is to advance a new hypothesis

that on the basis of extant evidence can be sustained but not proved, we continue to argue evidential issues of proof while cooperating in the current inductive exercise of discovery and hypothesis formulation. This chapter should be considered an exploratory effort to think about issues and to expose avenues for future research rather than a final argument for the origins of the Maya royal court. Ambiguities in the data are huge and can be squeezed in various ways. The current squeezing largely represents Clark's bias that La Venta, as a planned ceremonial center, is at least a century earlier than those at the other sites considered, and culturally dominant; Hansen views Nakbe and vicinity as coeval with La Venta and as engaged in some generic, pan-Mesoamerican phenomenon. However, neither possibility can be proved beyond reasonable doubt at the moment because of the contradictory interpretations given to the absence of concrete evidence. Clark's hypothesis that La Venta antedates Nakbe and its neighbors and was culturally influential makes more sense of a greater amount of data (especially that from Chiapas) with the fewest number of assumptions, and so we argue from an appreciation of broad patterns of Middle Formative sites. It is worth stressing, however, that the dating of most non-Maya sites considered in this chapter comes from Clark's appraisal of the ceramic types and assemblages at all the sites considered. Few of these claims would stand up in court on the basis of radiocarbon dates or ceramic phase lengths; thus, the chronological case is circumstantial at this point and will remain so until better data are forthcoming. Consequently, we avoid tedious descriptive details of ceramic associations and limited carbon-14 dates because these would only convey a false sense of precision unwarranted by the data. At this point, plain assertions about dating of sites and buildings suffice to raise the possibilities explored here. At present, the data cannot resolve current ambiguities in chronologies one way or the other. Taken as a whole, however, the ceramic data provide a strong circumstantial case of the general historic process of cultural borrowing described in this chapter. Having raised these possibilities, basic ethics of scholarly speculation commit us to the future testing of all the ideas outlined here.

2. Earlier monumental architecture is known from San Lorenzo (Veracruz), Paso de la Amada and El Silencio (Chiapas), San José Mogote (Oaxaca), Chalcatzingo (Morelos), Teopantecuanitlan (Guerrero), and Tlapacoya (Mexico), but none has been published in sufficient detail to determine relationships, if any, between site organization and alignments to the pattern seen at La Venta and other Middle Pre-Classic centers.

3. Creating labels for cultural patterns that will aid rather than hinder understanding is especially problematic if the pattern's derivation, function, and history are not well understood, as it usually cannot be in the beginning stages of investigation. We have considered calling this site pattern the "La Venta pattern," or the "Olmec pattern," but the full antiquity of this pattern remains to be attested in most of the cities where it occurs. Here we choose to call it the "Middle Formative Chiapas" (MFC) pattern to signal the geographic area in which it predominates. We prefer "Formative" to "Pre-Classic" for developments outside of the Maya area. The "Chiapas" label is not meant to make any claim of temporal priority. We suspect that the total configuration of mounds and alignments that constitute this pattern first came together at La Venta about 850 B.C. and spread

quickly to Chiapas, but this remains to be determined. Its antiquity in Chiapas has been established as far back as 750–700 B.C., but it may be even earlier.

4. A series of radiocarbon dates taken from primary deposits suggests a beginning date for Nakbe of 1000–800 B.C. These dates, however, do not accord well with the expected ages of the associated ceramics, and so as authors we disagree strongly on the usefulness of these dates and their significance. The discrepancy between the dates and the associated ceramics will be subjected to further tests in future research.

5. The origin of the E-Group arrangement of a long mound flanked on the west by a tall pyramid remains to be determined. Most of those from Chiapas date at least to the early part of the Chiapa III phase (ca. 700–650 B.C.) but may be earlier. At La Venta, these buildings have not been dated; Clark's presumption of their early date relies on the logic of the overall configuration of the MFC pattern and dates based upon ceramic associations with Chiapas sites. It is important to stress that the Chiapas data provide a terminal date rather than a beginning date. The E-Group was popular in the central Maya lowlands (see Chase and Chase 1995 for distribution of E-Groups), but the earliest known examples there appear to postdate the sixth century B.C. (see below). On the basis of current evidence, the E-Group complex appears to have been earlier in the Olmec and Zoque areas and to have diffused to the Maya area, perhaps beginning in the northern Peten. An early prototype (ca. 950–850 BC) for the E-Group is known from El Silencio in the Soconusco region of Chiapas, Mexico (Figure 1.1).

6. An early E-Group (dating to the Jenny Creek phase, about 700 B.C.) may be present at Cahal Pech, Belize. A convincing case can be currently made for an early long-mound structure and plaza, but the presence of a paired pyramid to the west of the long mound has not been verified. A small pyramid could lie concealed beneath the later range structure built in the appropriate location (David Cheetham, personal communication). The possibility of an E-Group in Belize at such an early date would alter some of the arguments presented here. It would be the oldest formal plaza arrangement of public ritual structures known for the Maya Lowlands, and it would be contemporaneous with those in Chiapas.

7. Aveni and Hartung (1989) evaluate twenty-seven E-Groups for the Peten region and note that the complex at Uaxactun is the only one that may have functioned as a solstice observatory. They refer to the Classic-period E-Group and not its predecessors. As argued, the E-Group at Tikal is the earliest currently known in the region; therefore, any functional assessments with historic ramifications must deal with this complex. Vilma Fialko (1988:18) argues that this early E-Group, because of its orientation and size, could not have functioned in the manner described for the later complex at Uaxactun:

> The complex identified at Mundo Perdido, Tikal, has a deviation that exceeds 6° East of true North, making it difficult, for this reason, to have functioned as an astronomical observatory. The place is characterized by its lack of an ample horizon to the East, although with respect to the West there was the option of observing the points of the setting sun throughout the year.
>
> For now it is difficult to determine what purpose induced the Eb builders at Tikal to orient the first version of the complex with such a deviation and why they always maintained this alignment when they could have corrected it to true north, imitating

[sic] the complex located in Group E at Uaxactun. The fact that this latter example is the exception, prompts one to consider that the principal purpose of these groups was not linked to the exact solstice and equinox positions but that they represented a deep allegory of the same. (Clark's translation)

It is important to emphasize that the latest manifestation of the E-Group at Uaxactun remains exceptional and that it is derivative from earlier examples. The excavations in the substructures of the E-Group mounds demonstrate a consistent orientation through time of the earlier structures (Rosal et al. 1993). In terms of function, it is important to recognize that the triple temple arrangement was a later innovation (see Chase and Chase 1995) and that stone or wooden markers may have been set on top of the long mound to mark the alignments (see Lowe 1989). Sockets for such monuments have not been detected. It is of interest to note for both Tikal and Uaxactun that the length of the long mound was augmented considerably through time. This suggests an extension of the two possible lines of sight at the termini of the long mound. These changes, in and of themselves, suggest a shift in the observational phenomena through time at these complexes.

Originally, the orientation of the two mounds of the E-Group at Uaxactun were thought to constitute a solar observatory for solstices and equinoxes (O. Ricketson 1928a, 1928b; Ruppert 1940). Recent study has shown that the complex could indeed have been used to make observations of the solstices (Aveni and Hartung 1989) but that the other groups could not have done so. An alternative, proposed by O. Ricketson (1928b:440, 1930:185), is that the E-Group was for geomancy rather than astronomy. He suggested that the "buildings were erected in their respective positions as temples dedicated to the four seasons, or the four most significant positions of the sun in the course of the solar year, and that their erection is to be more closely associated with geomancy than with astronomy" (O. Ricketson 1928b:440).

It is worth emphasizing that the functions of these groups need to be evaluated with their earliest manifestations rather than later copies. If the early E-Group at Uaxactun proves to be earlier than those at Tikal and Nakbe, then this would alter the functional argument. A functioning ritual complex of buildings at one place could be copied and rebuilt elsewhere in such a way that form might have been emphasized over function. The lack of correspondence between the majority of E-Groups in the Maya lowlands and their ancient horizons may derive from an emulation of ritual form without function. A better place to evaluate the ritual significance of these complexes would be with the group at La Venta or those in Chiapas. This has not been done.

8. One of the reasons that Lowe interpreted the numerous vessels in the chambers as special offerings is that some of the vessels were fragmentary. But the presence of large sherds and broken vessels does not necessarily signal an offering context as large fragments of vessels are known to be useful for a variety of reasons. The likelihood that the vessel assemblages found in each chamber were of pots that dribbled in as ad hoc offerings and segregated according to the class of persons offering them is almost nil. The absolute numbers and proportions of the Chamber B vessels, for example, appear to be significant and to duplicate those of other contemporaneous offerings found elsewhere at Chiapa de Corzo

(see Figure 1.13). The fact that the proportions of vessels duplicate those of other offerings suggests a functional assemblage of containers rather than a random collection of donated pots. The occurrence of this particular set of vessels in dedicatory caches lends credence to Lowe's conjecture that the pots in the Mound 5 rear chambers were offerings but undermines the logic of his argument. Yet the hypothesis of a functional complex of vessels used in rituals, sometimes placed in dedicatory caches, is compatible with the idea that ritual vessels were stored in the palace for periodic use and do not represent a formal cache in this instance.

9. The East Group at Nakbe (Strs. 47-53), as currently visible on the surface, dates to this period, but the confirmed presence of earlier buildings inside these structures argues for a greater antiquity for the group. It is not yet known, however, whether these interior buildings were an earlier version of the E-Group complex as currently defined.

2

The Royal Court of Early Classic Copan

LOA P. TRAXLER*

The royal court during the Classic period (A.D. 250–900) was the political core of the Maya polity, composed of individuals in different social roles, holding offices or stations, representing lineages and other groups in the community. These courtiers were powerful in their own regard yet ultimately were subordinate to the ruler. Although scholars recognize court figures in ancient society through hieroglyphic texts and artistic representations, relatively little about Classic Maya courtiers has been documented archaeologically. Fundamental questions await investigation: Who were the members of the court? Were they primarily royal kin, heads of noble families, or specialists perhaps of religious or military orders? And in comparison to the ruler, how powerful were these individuals and the court as a group?

To reconstruct the social world of a Classic Maya court involves reasoned interpretation, drawing upon excavated remains in all forms, imagery, and deciphered inscriptions. Any reconstruction also involves a

---

*I would like to thank the editors, Takeshi Inomata and Stephen Houston, for their efforts that resulted in both an engaging conference and publication. Thanks also go to Jeffrey Quilter, Robert Sharer, Joyce Marcus, and William Fash for their comments on earlier versions of this chapter. The Copan research is conducted under the auspices of the Instituto Hondureño de Antropología e Historia. William Fash directed the Copan Acropolis Archaeological Project (PAAC) and orchestrated the work of its many codirectors. The Early Copan Acropolis Program continues under the direction of Robert Sharer, supported by the University of Pennsylvania Museum. Funding for this research has been provided by the National Geographic Society, National Science Foundation, Foundation for the Advancement of Mesoamerican Studies, the Selz Foundation, the Maya Workshop Foundation, and several private donors. The efforts of many colleagues involved in the various programs of the PAAC form the basis of this chapter. Responsibility for any errors or misrepresentation of their work belongs to the author.

measure of speculation, drawing on comparisons with models of court life from other cultures and other times. This brief discussion focuses on some of the evidence for a royal court during the Early Classic period (ca. A.D. 400–600) at the site of Copan. This evidence comes from several research programs that formed the Copan Acropolis Archaeological Project, directed by William Fash. In particular, this chapter draws on excavations conducted by the Early Copan Acropolis Program, directed by Robert Sharer. This discussion includes comment on possible motives of Copan's rulers in the architectural design of the polity center during the Early Classic.[1]

The Court and Royal Household

A few terms deserve attention at the outset. In this chapter the term "court" refers to a subgroup of the community that included the royalty and other individuals who possessed a large measure of political power. Their power derived from personal histories, control of economic resources, religious authority, and access to resources of physical coercion or persuasion. These individuals exercised their political power in a social arena focused on the ruler. Furthermore, the term as used here implies a cluster of individuals, the majority of whom had named positions, stations, and roles recognized in the community. These positions, held by men and women, likely had an explicit ranking within the court, specialized duties, and protocols of behavior. This proposed structure within a court does not deny competition, negotiation, and usurpation of power among the court personnel; rather, court protocol set the formal context in which those efforts had meaning.

One readily suspects that the character of Maya courts varied over time and in different polities. The history and personality of the ruler, those of the individual courtiers, their number, and their community's history all influenced the social context of political action. For Classic period polities such as Tikal or Caracol, architectural and epigraphic data suggest a rather sizable court existed at times, including the seniors of established lineages, other individuals with subordinate political titles, noble scribes, and other identified specialists. Polities of smaller scale and fewer settlements such as Copan likely had courts with proportionally fewer members. It is unclear at present, however, whether the composition of the courts varied in relation to scale. It seems possible that the court of a smaller polity had similar positions and specialists represented among its personnel as the court of a large center. It could hold that the composition of a court was more significantly related to broadly held cultural ideals than the scale of the polity, but this is a matter for future investigation.

Equally difficult to generalize is the influence of a court within a polity. Its influence could vary greatly depending on the historical context subsuming the people, past events, and longer-range forces impinging on any current situation. For example, one need only consider the potential differences between the influence of the court of the twelfth ruler of the Copan polity, who reigned during a time of expansion and prosperity in the Late Classic period, and the court of the fourteenth ruler, who came to power in the wake of his immediate predecessor's defeat at the hands of the once-subordinate ruler of Quirigua.

The court as introduced above is distinct from, yet overlapped with, another subgroup important to this discussion: the royal household. Generally considered to include the ruler, his spouse and additional wives, the designated heir, and other children, this royal domestic unit also included other relatives living as part of the household, various attendants, specialist retainers, and slaves. This domestic group included persons who were not likely considered members of the court, such as lesser wives, young children and kin, prisoners, and slaves, who did not necessarily possess or wield political power. This distinction of the royal household from the royal court, particularly for large-scale Maya polities, allows research to explore what may be a more complex organization than an elite domestic unit writ large.

The activities of these two social groups—the royal court and the royal household—loosely associate with architectural settings. For most members of the royal household, the royal residence, including multiple houses, storage, and other specialized structures within a compound, was the setting for most of their daily activities. It is somewhat more difficult to recognize discrete settings associated with the activities of the royal court. Multiple and diverse settings were likely important for the different administrative and ritual activities in which the members participated. Court activities unfolded in the public, nonresidential facilities of the polity center, including temple structures, ball courts, and plaza spaces. Court activities could be situated at other locales outside the polity center, such as other subordinate communities, shrines, and pilgrimage sites. However, primary among these diverse spatial settings, one could argue, were the formal areas of the royal residence. The royal palaces and courtyards represent the architectural settings where the activities of the royal court and royal household spatially overlapped.

The royal palace was the most formal architecture of the royal residence, designed to convey wealth, power, order, and heritage. In most Classic centers, the royal palace is recognizable as the most elaborate of the large, multiroom range structures, and its central or prominent location in the architectural design of the polity center reinforced the dominant position of the ruler within the community (see Houston 1998). The architecture of the royal palace was designed to separate the royalty from the populace both physically and symbolically. The design and manipulation of space reinforced social distinction and control, typically situating the ruler and the court as central, elevated in society, and circumscribed.

The royal palace was the setting where the court and domestic life of the ruler overlapped. The palace was designed as a residence of power, decorated with symbols of rulership, divine sanction, and ancestry. It could be considered an ideal home presented to elite society. This architecture manifested the highest status and investment of wealth in a polity, and one suspects that rulers put those impressive qualities to use. Based on scenes in Classic Maya art, the royal palace was a setting to welcome dignitaries, conduct the business of the polity, and celebrate special events. It could accommodate activities of court personnel, receiving guests as well as goods. The royal palace was the backdrop for the political enterprise (see Flannery 1998).

Information from Inscriptions on the Copan Court

Hieroglyphic inscriptions provide some of the most explicit information about Maya royalty and the court. Historical details of individual lives and events as well as indirect information about social groups, roles, and relations form the base of any reconstruction of the royal court. At present the only people mentioned in the deciphered texts from the Early Classic at Copan are rulers.

The historical record of the Classic period dynasty begins with the career of a man who reigned in the early fifth century A.D. and who was recognized as first in a succession of sixteen rulers continuing through the early ninth century. Preserved hieroglyphic texts referring to Early Classic times at Copan and the nearby site of Quirigua record an event in the year A.D. 426 in which K'uk' Mo' Ajaw received the symbols of rulership and, three days later, arrived in Copan as K'inich Yax K'uk' Mo' (Schele and Grube 1992; Stuart and Schele 1986). His successors referred to him as "the founder," using his formal appellation, and noted their ordinal relation to him. Other poorly preserved retrospective texts indicate, however, that K'inich Yax K'uk' Mo' was not the first ruler of Copan. Fragmentary remains of carved monuments such as Stela 24 and sections of texts on Stela I and E name two other individuals who ruled the polity at some time before K'inich Yax K'uk' Mo's arrival (Stuart 1989, 1992). At present no further details are known about these two rulers, but continued research with the texts and future excavations may provide more information about the time before the events of 426.

During his reign K'inich Yax K'uk' Mo' celebrated the completion of the eighth Bak'tun cycle of the Long Count calendar. This date of 9.0.0.0.0 (December 11, 435) figures prominently in the inscriptions throughout the history of Copan, as it does at many Classic sites. K'inich Yax K'uk'

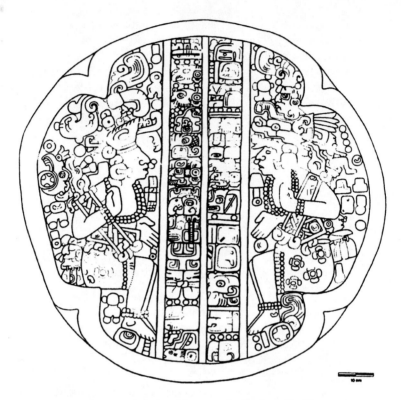

FIGURE 2.1 Motmot Marker (drawing by Barbara Fash).

Mo' died within two years after this date and was succeeded by Ruler 2, who came to power in A.D. 437 and reigned for perhaps as long as thirty-five years (Schele et al. 1994a; Schele and Grube 1994). Until recently, little was known of him, but excavations beneath the Acropolis have uncovered hieroglyphic inscriptions as well as architecture and other remains dating to his reign. Three carved texts—the Xukpi stone, the Motmot marker, and Stela 63—relate Ruler 2 to K'inich Yax K'uk' Mo' as his son and direct successor.[2]

The Xukpi stone records the dedication of a mortuary structure by Ruler 2 in 9.0.2.0.0 (A.D. 437) (Schele et al. 1994b; Sedat and Sharer 1994), but the original architectural context of the sculpted block was later destroyed, and it was reused as part of a burial vault (see below). The Motmot marker (Figure 2.1) was set in a courtyard floor in front of the structure called Motmot and covered ritual offerings and an elaborate burial within a circular stone crypt (Stuart 1997; Williamson 1996). Its inscription refers to the 9.0.0.0.0 period ending and a ritual by the founder. The text continues with reference to a second ritual involving Ruler 2 (Schele et al. 1994a).

Stela 63 was erected within a structure called Papagayo built later by Ruler 2 (W. Fash et al. 1992), covering the Motmot structure and its marker. The stela commemorates the period ending and states that Ruler 2 was the son of K'inich Yax K'uk' Mo'. A later renovation of Papagayo involved the addition of a carved step in front of the stela. This carved step bears an inscription naming the fourth ruler of the dynasty, Cu-Ix. Small carved fragments of a destroyed monument may indicate that Cu-Ix was the son of Ruler 2, leading some epigraphers to link the third ruler and Cu-Ix as grandsons of K'inich Yax K'uk' Mo' (Schele and Grube 1994).

These texts relate the events of the founding of the dynasty, the celebration of the period ending, and the dedication of later structures as well as the rulers in power during these events. These texts and comparisons made with others to support their decipherment suggest some details of the ritual events—actions and materials involved—but these are thin details in light of the social reconstruction of the royal court that we are pursuing.

Representations of the Copan Court

Representational art provides emic, stylized scenes of social groupings that in some cases represent court activity. The famous Late Classic murals from Bonampak (Miller 1986) are elaborate examples, but more limited scenes are found on painted pottery vessels and stone carvings. Men and women are shown in groupings, some of which convey social ranking and hierarchy based on the spatial arrangement and gestures of those portrayed. Other scenes present individuals in more complex groupings of social roles, including royal and noble men and women, subordinate elite, dwarves, captives, porters, military figures, musicians, and so forth. Texts associated with pictorial scenes often substantiate the interpretation of relations among the individuals portrayed and may identify courtiers by name or role.

At Copan, there are few representational scenes that relate to court activity. Although sculpted monuments such as Altar Q (from the Acropolis) or Altar T (from the site covered by the modern town) spring readily to mind as group portraits, these monuments present historical composites of rulers and supernatural figures and do not represent scenes of contemporaries involved in court activity. Another example discussed by Miller (1988) is the carved bench from the final phase of Str. 11 (Schele and Miller 1986: plate 36). This sculpture shows twenty individual figures facing a central text that includes the accession date of the sixteenth ruler, Yax Pasah. On the bench, as on Altar Q, which Yax Pasah also commissioned, the figures are recognizable as individuals. All are men, each shown with slightly different costume elements and headdresses. The men face the central text panel, and most gesture in that direction with their hands or the varied objects they hold. All but two of the figures are seated on hieroglyphs that at present are only partially deciphered (Schele and Freidel 1990:490).

FIGURE 2.2   Detail from carved peccary skull found in Tomb 1 (drawing by Barbara Fash).

Miller initially suggested this scene represents a gathering of the royal court of Yax Pasah. Later work with Linda Schele led to a revision of this interpretation, reassigning the bench to the category of historical composite images of the dynastic line (Schele and Freidel 1990:327). Recently, Viel (1999) has proposed a variation of this idea and suggests that the carved scene presents a historical composite of selected rulers (similar to Altar Q) as well as members of Yax Pasah's court surrounding the central figures of K'inich Yax K'uk' Mo' and Yax Pasah himself. These proposals have yet to be fully explored and tested against the archaeological record.

Another potential view of contemporary members of Copan's royal court is the facade decoration of Str. 22A (B. Fash 1992:Figure 11), which has been recently excavated and restored.[3] Current interpretation of this structure's sculpted mosaic decoration suggests nine seated human figures of the upper facade were leaders of the dominant lineages and settlements of the Copan polity during the reign of the fourteenth ruler, known as Smoke Monkey. This structure may have served as a *popol nah* (council house) during the reign of Smoke Monkey (A.D. 738–749) and later kings (Fash 1991; B. Fash et al. 1992; Stomper 1996).

From Early Classic times, representations of royal courtiers are very limited. The carved peccary skull (Longyear 1952:Figure 107o) found in

Tomb 1 shows two elaborately dressed figures engaged in activity centered on an altar and stela between them (Figure 2.2). One figure may be identified in the very short text in the scene and is shown seated on a jaguar skin. The carved date on this piece, 8.17.0.0.0 (A.D. 376) (Fash 1991), may be retrospective, although it was found within a burial of Early Classic date. Unfortunately, as Stuart (1992) has pointed out, because the skull is a portable object, the carved scene may have no connection to the history of Copan.

The recently uncovered floor marker associated with Str. Motmot (Williamson 1996) shows the seated figures of K'inich Yax K'uk' Mo' and his son Ruler 2 facing each other with two columns of text between them. Both royal figures may have taken part in period-ending rituals referred to on the initial date in the text and be shown on the marker together in real time. However, the two were also sequential rulers, and the reference to a second event in the text, which may have occurred after the death of K'inich Yax K'uk' Mo', may indicate the scene is a historical composite like Altar Q and the Str. 11 bench.

Other sculpture from Copan may yet prove to show contemporary groups of figures. The Four-Lobed disk found by Gustav Strömsvik (see Baudez 1994:Figure 72), the sets of ballcourt markers (see Baudez 1994:Figure 76; Fash 1991:Figure 69), and the carved bench from the Sepulturas Str. 9N–82 (Webster 1989:Figure 13) deserve further analysis along these lines. At present there are no known Early Classic scenes of human figures in groups larger than two, and the examples discussed all seemingly represent a ruler with another elite individual. The overwhelming majority of representational art at Copan relates to the ruler, supernatural figures, and their interaction. These images at the moment, therefore, provide slim information about the Early Classic royal court, and our discussion must draw on other types of information.

Architecture of the Early Classic Court at Copan

Although the founding narrative of a Classic period dynasty is not unique to Copan, the archaeological record of the founding era at Copan certainly is. Buried deep beneath its center lie the remains of a restricted architectural group associated through multiple lines of evidence with the Early Classic founder, K'inich Yax K'uk' Mo'. Dated inscriptions, stratigraphic sequences, and ceramic associations place the construction of this group to around the time of the founder's "arrival," recorded to have occurred in A.D. 426. This group is interpreted as the first royal residential compound beneath the Acropolis, and it provides a focus to our discussion of the Early Classic royal court.

Initial work by the Peabody Museum (Gordon 1896) and the Carnegie Institution of Washington (Strömsvik 1952) had provided hints to the development of the polity center (Figure 2.3) and the mass of superimposed

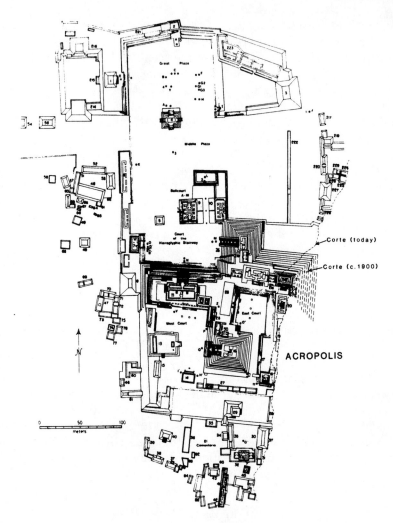

FIGURE 2.3 Plan of Main Group at the site of Copan, Honduras (based on Fash 1991:Figure 1).

construction that was dubbed the Acropolis. The work of the Copan Archaeological Project (PAC), initiated by the Honduran government during the mid-1970s and directed first by Baudez (1983) and later by Sanders (1986), made the first significant progress on the chronological history of the Acropolis. Building on the ceramic analysis of Longyear (1952), excavations by Cheek (1983) and Becker (1983) established an outline for the major construction phases as recognized to that point.

The Copan Acropolis Archaeological Project continued some of the lines of research begun during the first and second phases of the PAC. The Early Copan Acropolis Program (ECAP) set out in 1989 to define the architectural evolution of the Acropolis. The recent and extensive tunnel excavations into the Acropolis by these projects (Agurcia 1996; Fash 1998; Fash and Sharer 1991; W. Fash et al. 1992; Sharer et al. 1992, 1999a, 1999b) have provided additional radiocarbon dates, revised ceramic-phase associations, and uncovered new hieroglyphic texts that allow us to reconstruct the Acropolis evolution in greater detail than before.

The Acropolis was the center of political and religious power during the Classic period at Copan from around A.D. 425 to 825. This impressive complex situated near the river in the bottomland of the Copan Valley was created by layer upon layer of architecture built over the centuries by Copan's rulers. The excavations within its Early Classic levels have revealed several contemporary architectural groups. These groups reflect subdivisions of royal architectural space and served as the foundation of the architectural design of the polity center for generations.

Royal Compound of K'inich Yax K'uk' Mo'

The royal compound is dominated by a formal patio group; its structures of masonry and of adobe share an extensive plaster patio bounded by perimeter walls. The compound also includes other adjacent patio groups of adobe that do not share the initial formal plaster surface of the primary group but do share some of the perimeter walls. This multipatio compound is part of an entire complex that, based on new stratigraphic information, is argued to have been established around this time (Traxler n.d.a). This Early Classic complex included the royal compound just introduced, the ceremonial structures associated with the completion of the eighth Bak'tun, and the entire expanse of the public plaza. This revises earlier reconstructions of the development of the main plaza based largely on the work by Cheek and the Carnegie team before him (Traxler n.d.b). The sum of this extensive construction program created a new center of political power for Copan. This complex set the overall design of the polity center for the next 400 years (Sharer et al. 1992, 1999a).

The royal compound includes structures of varied form and construction (Figure 2.4). Perimeter walls and terrace faces of cobble construction define the limits of the compound and divisions within it. Puddled adobe substructures with adobe and perishable superstructures represent the majority of initial buildings. However, masonry structures appear early in the subsequent development of the compound, still during the reign of K'inich Yax K'uk' Mo'.

The primary patio group, explored in excavations supervised by David Sedat, initially comprised adobe structures arranged around a plastered patio that was serviced by stone-lined drains to channel water. The eastern structure was first built of adobe with posts supporting its roof (Sharer et al. 1998). It was replaced by a masonry structure built atop a

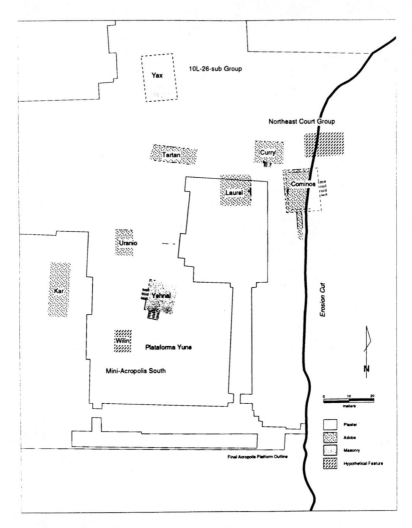

FIGURE 2.4 ECAP preliminary plan of Yune Platform and early structures of the royal compound (Traxler).

talud-tablero masonry substructure known as Hunal with an outset stairs providing access on the north side. The remains of the superstructure indicate it had at least two rooms, defined by an east-west interior wall and an offset doorway with curtain holders near its eastern end (Sedat 1997a). The evidence of interior rooms that could be closed for privacy suggests this structure was a residence (Sharer 1997a), although diverse activities could have unfolded here. Plaster adhering to masonry debris found covering the remains of Hunal suggests it had elaborate, polychrome-painted murals.

Sedat (1997b) interprets another masonry substructure as a residence that was constructed early in the sequence occupying the southern position in this patio. Excavations did not penetrate the remains of this structure to determine if an adobe predecessor existed or to investigate possible remains of a masonry superstructure. The western structure of the group was built of adobe and remained in use with modifications through the entire time span of the group.

Occupying the northern position in the patio, an adobe platform initiated a sequence of specialized adobe structures. The first platform, named Uranio, rose just 1 meter high but covered a burial of a seated adult with jade-inlayed teeth. This platform was later buried by the construction of a higher, two-terraced platform, named Cobalto, that was associated with extensive ceremonial deposits of carbon, shattered jade, and carved jade objects, suggesting it was a more specialized, ritual facility.

Contemporary with the primary group, other adobe patio groups were built that cluster along the eastern limit of the royal compound. The best-documented of these lies to the northeast of the primary group, although evidence was encountered in the eroded edge of the Acropolis for adobe structures to the southeast as well. These groups also include specialized structures and share some of the perimeter walls delimiting the compound. They stand on a terrace artificially leveling the terrain that sloped downward to the river farther east. These adobe platforms define at least four patio areas to the northeast of the primary group. These patio areas were surfaced with various materials, including flat paving stones, cobble surfaces, and gravel layers. Some structures were initially surrounded by a skirting floor of coarse plaster.

The primary group along with the other nearby adobe patio groups are interpreted as the royal palace compound of K'inich Yax K'uk' Mo' (Traxler 1998). This compound is proposed as the main setting for court life and activities during his reign and that of his son, Ruler 2. The architectural remains preserved several burials and ritual deposits that provide direct information about some activities and individuals of the time. Details from burials allow researchers to propose identities of these individuals, and it is likely that several were court members in their day. Evidence forcefully suggests that a burial chamber early in the development of the primary group holds the remains of the founder of the Classic period dynasty, K'inich Yax K'uk' Mo'.

The analysis of skeletal remains from elite burials within these groups shows local and nonlocal distinctions in bone chemistry between individuals of contemporary periods. Based on the work of Jane Buikstra and her colleagues (Buikstra et al., n.d.), some individuals were of local residence from childhood through adult life while others were of nonlocal residence during most of their lives before being interred at Copan. There is evidence that both local and nonlocal individuals were given special and respectful tomb burials. Yet there is also evidence for sacrificial burial of local as well as nonlocal individuals. The analysis of the burial furnishings also reveals local and nonlocal traditions of costuming, pottery, and styles of its decoration.

The Early Classic architectural remains also preserved elaborate building decoration, details of architectural style, and rich iconography. The iconographic evidence indicates that facade decorations of several of the earliest buildings beneath the Acropolis reflect ties with the Peten region. At the same time, the architectural style of the Hunal structure in the primary group derived from contemporary architecture of central Mexico. This style is also expressed in construction at other sites with connections to central Mexico such as Tikal in the Peten and Kaminaljuyu in the southern highlands during this time. Other contacts to central Mexico are found in the painting style on early tomb vessels, as well as in the ornaments and burial furnishings of elite burials. One buried male wore a costume different from other burials and was interred with darts and other objects associated with warrior figures in pictorial art from central Mexico.

Royal Household of K'inich Yax K'uk' Mo'

The primary patio group is interpreted as the home for the royal household. The low platforms of the group did not preserve clear evidence of domestic activity associated with residences, but the lack of ceremonial remains associated with these structures, in contrast to the specific case of Uranio and its successors, tends to support the interpretation of their use as residential facilities. Nowhere in the Early Classic strata of the Acropolis does one find in situ domestic refuse that might lend support to interpretations of residential use.

A tomb constructed in the base of Hunal is believed to contain the remains of K'inich Yax K'uk' Mo' (Sharer 1997b, 1997c). The elderly male buried within the chamber was adorned with several emblems of royalty, including a jade-bar pectoral, jade earflares, shell-spangle headdress, and leg ornaments of jaguar teeth (Sharer et al. 1998). Preliminary analysis by Buikstra of his skeletal remains indicates his adult life was not care-free. This man sustained a blow to the center of his right forearm, breaking both bones, which never properly healed. In addition to this parry injury, the man suffered a broken left shoulder that likewise did not heal, undoubtedly leaving him dependent on assistance for many activities (Buikstra et al., n.d.). Sharer has pointed out the similarities between this buried individual (including his ornaments and skeletal clues) and the portrait of K'inich Yax K'uk' Mo' shown on Altar Q, carved three centuries later. The portrait shows K'inich Yax K'uk' Mo' with similar ornaments and a shield held in his right hand, covering his right forearm. The varied evidence within the chamber is persuasive that the burial is in-

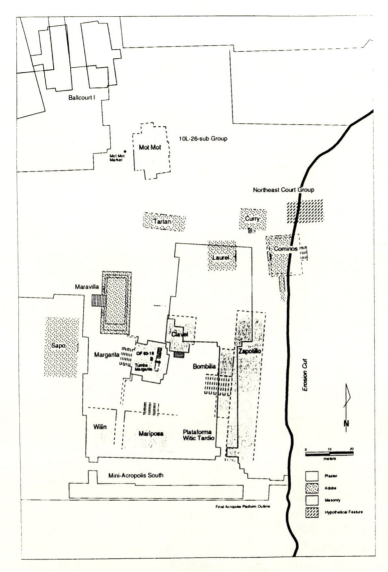

FIGURE 2.5   ECAP preliminary plan of Witik Platform and structures of the royal compound during the reign of Ruler 2 (Traxler).

deed that of K'inich Yax K'uk' Mo', and the vertical sequence of structures (see Stuart 1997) that covers this location, each displaying his name in varied iconographic forms, makes this case all the more convincing.

The skeletal remains within the Hunal tomb reveal additional biographical information that is significant. Preliminary results from strontium isotope analysis of bone samples indicate this man lived much of his life somewhere other than the Copan Valley (Buikstra et al., n.d.).

Samples that track his skeletal development through time indicate he lived most of his life in an area with different geology where groundwater produced a different isotope profile in his developing bones. Ongoing research directed by Buikstra will hopefully provide some indication of where his native land might have been if sufficient comparative material from other populations can be analyzed.

These same analyses of bone chemistry indicate that the female occupant of a second tomb was a local resident throughout her life. This second tomb was constructed as part of the building called Yehnal that immediately covered the remains of Hunal and the tomb of K'inich Yax K'uk' Mo'. This tomb exhibits a complex architectural design because it was not finished until a subsequent structure, called Margarita, was built covering Hunal and Yehnal (Figure 2.5). The construction allowed repeated entry to the burial chamber, and there is ample evidence for such reentry and continued reverence of the body (Sharer et al. 1999b). This woman, who died at an advance age and was buried with lavish funerary goods, was perhaps the wife of K'inich Yax K'uk' Mo' and mother of Ruler 2. This current interpretation is based on her burial in this location and in such close proximity to the earlier tomb, the repeated acts of veneration, and the skeletal indications that she bore at least one child during her life (Buikstra et al., n.d). The final construction of the upper vault of her tomb chamber incorporated the Xukpi stone (Sedat and Sharer 1994), which names K'inich Yax K'uk' Mo' and Ruler 2 (Harris 1997; Schele et al. 1994b) as its foundation.

Based on the skeletal evidence and the historical details from inscribed monuments, we can state that K'inich Yax K'uk' Mo' came from foreign lands to Copan. His royal household would have included his wife, who may have been a local woman, and perhaps secondary wives, who may have been local or foreign. The household included his heir, Ruler 2, and probably other children and perhaps included other relatives who also made the journey to Copan. The household may also have included relatives from his wife's local family. Household retainers and servants likewise could represent a mix of local and outside origin. At present the architectural remains suggest ample space for household members and activities. At least three large structures are thought to have served as residences within the primary group.

The Court of K'inich Yax K'uk' Mo'

Based on the varied cultural traditions reflected in the material culture, the court of K'inich Yax K'uk' Mo' probably included people of varied backgrounds and positions. It is unclear how K'inich Yax K'uk' Mo' came to rule Copan—by conquest, coercion, or alliance?—but in any scenario it seems unlikely that he traveled and arrived alone. After coming to power, his court would seemingly have included some who came to Copan with him. These may have been companions of his family, trusted assistants, religious officials, and military captains. The list could go on. Unfortunately, at present little direct evidence of these various sorts of people exists.

After establishing his rule in Copan, K'inich Yax K'uk' Mo' may also have assembled trusted nobles of the local community in his court. Perhaps there were lineages with whom K'inich Yax K'uk' Mo' found support, or with whom he established ties through marriage, as may be indicated by the local woman buried with such extravagance so near to him. Religious figures along with scribes and artisans of local or foreign origins may have held court positions as well. The mastery of foreign decorative styles seen in the architecture and burial furnishings suggests artists from outside the southeastern region were active at Copan. These individuals may have been members of the court or the royal household.

Of the other burials outside the royal residence that date to this time (during the reign of K'inich Yax K'uk' Mo' or very early in the reign of Ruler 2), only one could be sampled for bone-chemistry analysis. This burial was a that of a nonlocal female placed in the circular chamber beneath the Motmot marker (Buikstra et al., n.d.; Williamson 1996). Her identity is not known, and it is unclear if she was buried with the ceremony befitting a noblewoman or was an elaborate offering as part of the period-ending rituals referred to on the marker that covered her burial. Was she related to K'inich Yax K'uk' Mo'? Was she a foreign wife? Or was she sent to be part of the ceremonies of 435 A.D.? There are more questions than answers at present, but continuing research will hopefully shed more light on this enigmatic woman.

The household and court of K'inich Yax K'uk' Mo' seems to have occupied the new compound at the southern end of the axis of the polity center complex. The close proximity of the adobe patio groups to the northeast of the primary group may indicate K'inich Yax K'uk' Mo' had daily interaction with members of his court beyond his family. These groups of structures integrate with the perimeter wall defining the eastern limit of the compound. Several appear most likely to have been residences, and at least one special-purpose structure is recognized. In combination, this royal compound provided for the activities and residences of his inner circle of court personnel.

A larger grouping of court members, including prominent lineage heads, probably were convened less frequently. One imagines they had access to the ruler to address questions, resolve disputes, and arrange activities and resources. It seems premature to envision a large number of functionaries in the court of K'inich Yax K'uk' Mo'. The start-up character of his enterprise may have established positions with special and long-term responsibilities, such as ones relating to the Bak'tun structure, for example. However, the relatively short time of his reign, the lack of dramatic contrast in elevation between patio spaces in the royal compound, and the relative accessibility between the various groups of his new complex, I believe, would argue against an elaborate bureaucratic structure within his royal court.

Royal Compound of Ruler 2

After a relatively brief reign of some eleven years (A.D. 426–437), K'inich Yax K'uk' Mo' was succeeded by his son. The further architectural development of the royal compound into the Acropolis by Ruler 2 is discussed in detail elsewhere (Sedat and Lopez 1999; Sharer 1999; Sharer et al. 1999a). I will briefly outline this development, focusing on the northeastern patio groups, as they were probably closely associated with the court personnel of Ruler 2 and later rulers.

The founder's compound was quickly built up during the reign of Ruler 2 with constructions of masonry architecture in monumental proportions, becoming the initial version of the towering Acropolis. He built Yehnal, the first memorial structure to his father, which covered the remains of Hunal and included the lower chamber of the elaborate Margarita tomb. Later construction produced Str. Margarita emblazoned with his father's name on its elaborately sculpted facade panels (see Stuart 1997). Ultimately, this structure would be destroyed and the tomb chamber closed, occupied by the woman thought to be his mother.

Ruler 2 also commissioned a three-terrace adobe platform covering the two terraced Cobalto structure described earlier. This monumental adobe structure, called Maravilla, remained in use for a great length of time, even though the expanding masonry terraces of the early Acropolis surrounded and encroached upon it. The continued renewal of this ritual facility in adobe suggests this material had symbolic importance in architecture that endured for several generations (Sharer et al. 1999a).

The royal compound of Ruler 2 continued to be set apart in the site complex, as was his father's, but it was set apart by elevation rather than by perimeter walls. The architectural symbolism continued to distinguish the royal household while high masonry platforms introduced a more emphatic statement of literally higher status for this group. At the same time, Ruler 2 connected himself to his father through public monuments, creating a founder image for K'inich Yax K'uk' Mo' and connecting them both to the completion of the eighth Bak'tun cycle and the beginning of the new era.

Court Architecture of Ruler 2

The northeastern residential groups continued as adobe architecture alongside the masonry Acropolis until they were rebuilt as masonry courtyard groups, elevated on masonry terraces extending the Acropolis to the north (Traxler 1996, n.d.a). These courtyard groups are interpreted

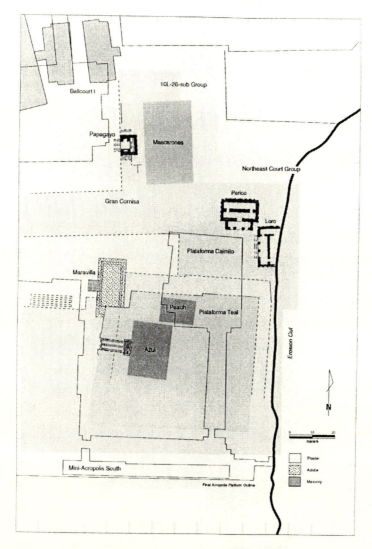

FIGURE 2.6 ECAP preliminary plan of royal compound late in the reign of Ruler 2 showing initial masonry palace structures that replaced adobe predecessors (Traxler).

as a residential compound for the court personnel who served Ruler 2 and his successors (Ruler 3 and Cu-Ix).

When the earthen patio groups were replaced by masonry construction, the adobe buildings of the two highest structures on the northern and eastern sides of the central patio were left standing atop a new 3.5-meter-high masonry platform, extending out from a preexisting terrace of the Acropolis. How long these old buildings were used after their substructures were buried is difficult to quantify. However, the fact that they were maintained for a period of time, then replaced with masonry buildings directly over them (Figure 2.6), leads one to believe that there was a continuity of activities and personnel associated with this group as it changed from an earthen to masonry facility.

These masonry structures are clear evidence of what are traditionally called "palace" structures in Classic lowland Maya architecture. They exhibit the characteristics of residential buildings of highest elite construction. They sit on low substructure platforms with broad stairway access; they are organized around formal courtyard areas, defining a series of courts aligned east to west. The easternmost courtyard group identified was mostly destroyed by river erosion at the edge of the Acropolis.

These courtyard groups continue the trend seen in the earlier adobe patio groups. The large masonry buildings found on the western and eastern sides of the central court are the main residential structures. These have spacious interiors, divided into long, tandem rooms making up the core of the structure with transverse rooms on the northern and southern ends. The wide interior spaces of these buildings, with rooms measuring up to 5.5 meters in width, and their rather narrow walls; about 1 meter in width, suggest they were not vaulted structures; some probably had plaster and timber roofs behind masonry facades. Their exteriors displayed sculpted and brightly painted plaster decoration.

These buildings have direct access from the court surface into their first rooms but restricted access to their innermost room. Most interior doorways have cordholders on either side. These Early Classic palaces do not have interior benches or other construction features common in Late Classic palace architecture. One presumes removable furniture was used in these rooms, perhaps similar to stone benches used as burial platforms in Early Classic royal tombs (Traxler 1996). Later in the Acropolis sequence, vaulted roofs were more prevalent; rooms were more narrow; and integral benches were common interior features.

The initial masonry platform was later expanded, and new buildings were added that completed the quadrangle (Figure 2.7), perhaps during the reign of Cu-Ix. In time this version grew with additional rooms, ultimately consuming most of the open space between the original buildings. The masonry courtyard groups as a unit were even more spatially distinct than the adobe predecessors. They stood in a newly elevated precinct between the summit of the early Acropolis (Sharer et al. 1999a) and the ballcourt group with Papagayo located to the north (W. Fash et al. 1992; Fash 1998). Terraces and anciently destroyed stairways would have clearly defined its limits and the access between these areas. This expansion may have accommodated an expanding royal court. Ultimately, the masonry courtyard groups were moved beyond the Acropolis, probably during the reign of the seventh ruler.

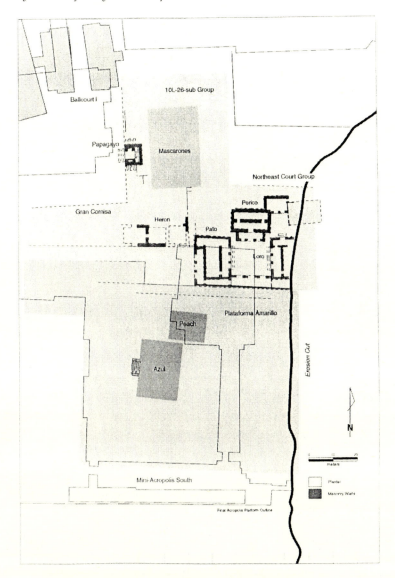

FIGURE 2.7   ECAP preliminary plan of royal compound with masonry palace groups (Traxler).

Court of Ruler 2

The court of Ruler 2 would seem to include those who were associated with the adobe patio groups. These patio groups were maintained during the early part of his reign and grew in modest terms alongside the monumental platforms of the Acropolis, until they were incorporated as elevated courtyard groups on platform extensions from it.

The court of Ruler 2 likely evolved from his father's court, particularly because Ruler 2 may have come to power at a young age. If he was in fact the son of K'inich Yax K'uk' Mo' and a local woman, he may have been only eleven when his father died. Sharer (1997c) has speculated that his mother served as regent for some time, for she probably lived many years after her husband's death, based on her skeletal remains and the stratigraphic sequence of the primary group. Ruler 2's court may have included his mother, uncles (brothers of K'inich Yax K'uk' Mo' or his mother), and perhaps other relatives such as cousins. It would have included his trusted assistants, war captains, and nobles who may have been courtiers during his father's time. He may have included others who were excluded from the court during his father's reign because of conflicts upon his arrival. The court would have seemingly been rounded out by religious figures, scribes, and artisans whose work was in great demand.

The reign of Ruler 2 may have brought the opportunity for expansion of the court with the stability of a longer reign, generational growth of the number of his immediate kin, and the efforts to solidify his power. However, it would seem, based on the architecture, that early in his reign his court was still characterized by a close subset whose activities involved daily interaction with the ruler and close proximity to his most exclusive precinct of the Acropolis summit. The later replacement of the original adobe patio groups with masonry courtyard groups and their expansion of those court groups in time may correlate with an expanding royal court.

Polity Center Architecture and Politics

From the archaeological evidence, I interpret an evolving scenario of court politics in the Early Classic period. It seems clear that K'inich Yax K'uk' Mo' was not of local royalty, and his claim to power and Copan resources was not based on inheritance. His power may have come through rights of conquest, establishing a new ruling lineage by force or decree, or by adding a new level of political domination over the existing nobility. His power may have been built by alliance through marriage to a local noble family (Marcus 1992; Sharer 1997c).

To distinguish his power from that of previous rulers, K'inich Yax K'uk' Mo' established a new architectural design for the center of Copan. Although the original terrain along the western bank of the Copan River can only be described in general terms, during his reign a low terrace construction along the bank and leveling fill farther to the west created extensive area for new buildings. His architectural program laid out a new royal residence group, nearby facilities for some members of his royal court, a new public plaza, and a ritual group that was the setting for the Bak'tun completion of 9.0.0.0.0.

These constructions are juxtaposed to a complex that may have been the center of the previous rulers located at the northwestern corner of the Main Group. Test excavations directed by William Fash and additional excavations by Jay Hall and Rene Viel suggest that the initial construction of this large platform, Plt. 10L–1, may date to a time prior to K'inich Yax K'uk' Mo'. This complex however, based on current evidence, was not used by K'inich Yax K'uk' Mo' as a location of new construction or as a focus in his new design for the polity center. There seems to have been a purposeful separation of his royal compound away from this area. If indeed Plt. 10L–1 predates the reign of K'inich Yax K'uk' Mo', the new plaza that he created left the earlier complex standing at the western limit of the plaza's northern end. Occupying the central focus of the northern end of the new plaza was a new adobe platform, Str. 10L–2–3rd, constructed of the same material used as the leveling fill in the plaza (Traxler n.d.b; cf. Cheek and Kennedy Embree 1983).

One interpretation of this design shift might conclude that by positioning his new compound to the south of Plt. 10L–1, K'inich Yax K'uk' Mo' relegated the previous royal works to the past and to ancestral associations of northern locations (Ashmore 1992; Coggins 1980). However, rather than center his new plaza and royal compound on an axis based on the previous complex, the design axis was shifted to the east with a long plaza expanse anchored on the south, center, and north by a series of new constructions.

The accession of Ruler 2 likely brought changes to the political dynamic of the court, for he probably represented the foreign ancestry of his father as well as the local prestige of his mother. His changes to the architectural complex that K'inich Yax K'uk' Mo' created were ones of monumental development and elaboration of the royal residence. Str. 10L-sub–2 (Cheek 1983:Figure C–6) was built around this time as a long, low structure that extended northwest from the ritual group toward the Plt. 10L–1 complex. The structure's unusual orientation may have been designed to visually connect the predynastic Plt. 10L–1 to the royal compound of K'inich Yax K'uk' Mo'. As such it may represent an architectural statement of rapprochement or reconciliation between the new dynasty and the nobles who were alienated with the shift of political power. Ruler 2, as the offspring of K'inich Yax K'uk' Mo' and the local noble woman, could represent a resolution of the conflict between the foreign usurper and the local elite.

If the motivation for the construction of Str. 10L-sub–2 was to consolidate power, its effectiveness may be indicated by the tremendous architectural program that followed. Adjacent to it, the first ballcourt was built along with Motmot structure renewing and expanding the ritual group. As described above, Ruler 2 constructed building upon building in the royal residential group. His efforts to consecrate the locations associated with his father may reflect efforts to hold together alliances and solidify his legitimate claim to power in opposition to other claims. Ruler 2's efforts created the Cult of the Founder through construction in the royal compound, the ballcourt group, and the numerous inscribed monuments that he set in place. He also ensured the continuation of the kingdom by solidifying ties to Quirigua and other communities under Copan's control (Looper and Schele 1994).

Ruler 2 maintained the adobe residential facilities that may have housed court members with renovations and additional structures. These groups remained modest in comparison to the upward expansion of the platforms the royal compound. Significant investment in the masonry facilities for the court would seem to date to later in the reign of Ruler 2, perhaps forced by increased numbers of people in this group or their desire for new structures. The result was elevated courtyard groups of residential buildings connected to the terraces of the Early Classic Acropolis. These courtyard groups were further elaborated during the reign of the third and fourth rulers of the dynasty. They were later relocated but continued as courtyard groups for another generation or more into the early sixth century A.D. At that time it would appear the court facilities were relocated beyond the limits of the preserved Acropolis, possibly resettled to the south in the area of Group 10L–2 (Andrews n.d.; Andrews and Fash 1992).

Conclusion

Archaeologists are able to document the remains of buildings, unearth the residues of daily life and ritual ceremonies, and recover the fragmentary remains of individuals from the past. These documented remains provide the basis for reconstructions of lives, activities, and cultural trends. The hieroglyphic inscriptions provide specific details of individual people and events that archaeologists compare to remains to reconstruct the ancient social context. The inscriptions at Copan emphasize key historical events of the reign of K'inich Yax K'uk' Mo'. The recently excavated material contemporary with the reign of this dynastic founder provides the information from which the reconstruction of the social context emerges.

In A.D. 426 K'inich Yax K'uk' Mo' ruled Copan, having arrived from foreign lands. He and his entourage seem to have brought with them many cultural signatures typical of the Early Classic, including decorative styles and goods from central Mexico. Architectural traditions from the Peten lowlands as well as the southern highlands and central Mexico were represented within his royal residential group, which was the most elaborate residence at Copan during this time. His royal compound, with ample space for the residences and activities of a new or "restructured" royal court, was situated by K'inich Yax K'uk' Mo' to the south and east of an apparently earlier royal complex. The new royal compound was designed with direct access to the river farther east for commerce and communications throughout the region.

This new royal group was rapidly transformed into the monumental early Acropolis by K'inich Yax K'uk' Mo's son and successor, Ruler 2. At the same time, nearby elite groups of adobe were maintained in close proximity to the royal residential and ceremonial areas. These groups were rebuilt in time as masonry courtyard groups (by A.D. 480) and probably served as the palace compound for the royal court late in the reign of Ruler 2 and succeeding Ruler 3 and Cu-Ix. This masonry palace compound was expanded over time, and the latest version preserved beneath the Acropolis integrated multiple platform levels, situated between the highest and most private Acropolis precinct and the more accessible Ballcourt complex and public plaza.

The challenge to archaeologists is to interpret the activities within these varied architectural settings. The analysis of the spatial organization and architecture of the polity center holds promise for revealing decisions about access, hierarchy, and distance, particularly in sites where the contemporary architecture of a complex can be examined. At Copan, the recent programs of excavation allow this form of analysis to begin.

Productive discussion of a Maya court is one that reconstructs this social group as it might have existed in a specific historical context. Many questions concerning the dynamics and influence of a Maya court remain unresolved and, indeed, may lie beyond the scope of archaeological study. The sources of information from Copan on the Early Classic royal court are by and large indirect, mostly drawn from the architectural data of recent excavations. Although we have direct evidence in the form of buried individuals and inscriptions, these critical sources are few and limited for the most part to the ruler and his immediate family. The social station of other burials (some mentioned in this discussion) are ambiguous or clearly sacrificial burials, and so the direct data on Copan courtiers remain rather slim.

Our interpretations and speculations are bound to evolve with continuing analysis of the archaeological material and inscriptions. What can be stated at present is that the royal court during the Early Classic period included people of varied backgrounds. Some were clearly foreign elite, whereas others were from local and probably noble families. The architectural evidence suggests a dynamic political scene with the demotion of former royalty with the arrival of K'inich Yax K'uk' Mo', changes toward greater emphasis on the ruler during the reign of Ruler 2, and possible efforts by him to reintegrate the older nobility into his political agenda.

References

Agurcia Fasquelle, Ricardo. 1996. "Rosalila, el corazón de la Acrópolis: el templo del rey-sol." *Yaxkin* 14: 5–18.

Andrews, E. Wyllys V. n.d. "The Organization of a Royal Maya Residential Compound at the Center of Copan." In William Fash and E. Wyllys Andrews, V, eds., *Copan: The Rise and Fall of a Classic Maya Kingdom*. Santa Fe: School of American Research Press.

Andrews, E. Wyllys, V, and Barbara W. Fash. 1992. "Continuity and Change in a Royal Maya Residential Complex at Copan." *Ancient Mesoamerica* 3: 63–88.

Ashmore, Wendy. 1992. "Deciphering Maya Architectural Plans." In Elin Danien and Robert J. Sharer, eds., *New Theories on the Ancient Maya*, pp. 173–184. Philadelphia: University Museum, University of Pennsylvania.

Baudez, Claude, ed. 1983. *Introducción a la arqueología de Copán, Honduras*. Tegucigalpa: Secretaria de Estado en el Despacho de Cultura y Turismo, y Instituto Hondureño de Antropología e Historia.

Baudez, Claude-François. 1994. *Maya Sculpture of Copán: The Iconography*. Norman: University of Oklahoma Press.

Becker, Marshall J. 1983. "Excavaciones en el corte de la Acropolis." In Claude Baudez, ed., *Introducción a la arqueología de Copán, Honduras*, pp. 349–379. Tegucigalpa: Secretaria de Estado en el Despacho de Cultura y Turismo, y Instituto Hondureño de Antropología e Historia.

Buikstra, Jane, Douglas Price, James Burton, and Lori Wright. N.d. "The Early Classic Royal Burials at Copan: A Bioarchaeological Perspective." In Ellen E. Bell, Marcello Andrea Canuto, and Robert J. Sharer, eds., *Understanding Early Classic Copan*. Philadelphia: University of Pennsylvania Museum.

Cheek, Charles D. 1983. "Las excavaciones en la Plaza Principal, resumen y conclusiones." In Claude Baudez, ed., *Introducción a la arqueología de Copán, Honduras, Tomo I*, pp. 319–348. Tegucigalpa: Secretaria de Estado en el Despacho de Cultura y Turismo, y Instituto Hondureño de Antropología e Historia.

Cheek, Charles D. and Veronica Kennedy Embree. 1983. "La Estructura 10L-2." In Claude Baudez, ed., *Introducción a la arqueología de Copán, Honduras, Tomo II*, pp. 93–141. Tegucigalpa: Secretaria de Estado en el Despacho de Cultura y Turismo, y Instituto Hondureño de Antropolgía e Historia.

Coggins, Clemency. 1980. "The Shape of Time: Some Political Implications of a Four-part Figure." *American Antiquity* 45: 729–739.

Fash, Barbara W. 1992. "Late Classic Architectural Sculpture Themes at Copan." *Ancient Mesoamerica* 3: 89–102.

Fash, Barbara W., William L. Fash, Sheree Lane, Rudy Larios, Linda Schele, Jeffrey Stomper, and David S. Stuart. 1992. "Investigations at a Classic Maya Council House at Copan, Honduras." *Journal of Field Archaeology* 19: 419–442.

Fash, William L. 1991. *Scribes, Warriors, and Kings: The City of Copan and the Ancient Maya*. London: Thames and Hudson.

―――. 1998. "Dynastic Architectural Programs: Intention and Design in Classic Maya Buildings at Copan and Other Sites." In Stephen D. Houston, ed., *Function and Meaning in Classic Maya Architecture*, pp. 223–270. Washington, DC: Dumbarton Oaks Research Library and Collection.

Fash, William L., and Robert J. Sharer. 1991. "Sociopolitical Developments and Methodological Issues at Copan, Honduras: A Conjunctive Perspective." *Latin American Antiquity* 2: 166–187.

Fash, William L., Richard V. Williamson, Carlos Rudy Larios, and Joel Palka. 1992. "The Hieroglyphic Stairway and Its Ancestors: Investigations of Copan Structure 10L-26." *Ancient Mesoamerica* 3: 105–116.

Flannery, Kent V. 1998. "The Ground Plans of Archaic States." In Gary M. Feinman and Joyce Marcus, eds., *Archaic States*, pp. 15–57. Santa Fe: School of American Research Press.

Gordon, George B. 1896. *Prehistoric Ruins of Copan, Honduras: A Preliminary Report of the Explorations by The Museum 1891–93.* Peabody Museum Memoirs I. Cambridge: Harvard University.

Harris, John. 1997. "The Xucpi Stone Text." ECAP Papers No. 12. Philadelphia: Early Copan Acropolis Program and Instituto Hondureño de Antropología e Historia.

Houston, Stephen D., ed. 1998. *Function and Meaning in Classic Maya Architecture.* Washington, DC: Dumbarton Oaks Research Library and Collection.

Looper, Matthew G., and Linda Schele. 1994. "The Founder of Quiriguá, Tutum-Yol-K'inich." Copan Note 119. Copan, Honduras: Copan Acropolis Archaeological Project and Instituto Hondureño de Antropología e Historia.

Longyear, John. M., III. 1952. *Copan Ceramics: A Study of Southeastern Maya Pottery.* Carnegie Institution of Washington Publication 597. Washington, DC.

Marcus, Joyce. 1992. *Mesoamerican Writing Systems: Propaganda, Myth, and History in Four Ancient Civilizations.* Princeton: Princeton University Press.

Miller, Mary Ellen. 1986. *The Murals of Bonampak.* Princeton: Princeton University Press.

_____. 1988. "The Meaning and Function of the Main Acropolis." In Elizabeth Boone and Gordon Willey, eds., *The Southeast Maya Zone*, pp. 149–194. Washington, DC: Dumbarton Oaks Research Library and Collection.

Sanders, William T., ed. 1986. *Excavaciones en el Area Urbana de Copán,* vol. 1. Tegucigalpa: Secretaria de Cultura y Turismo, Instituto Hondureño de Antropología e Historia.

Schele, Linda, Federico Fahsen and Nikolai Grube. 1994a. "The Floor Marker from Motmot." Copan Note 117. Copan, Honduras: Copan Acropolis Archaeological Project and Instituto Hondureño de Antropología e Historia.

_____. 1994b. "The Xukpi Stone: A Newly Discovered Early Classic Inscription from the Copan Acropolis-Part II: Commentary on the Text (Version 2)." Copan Note 114. Copan, Honduras: Copan Acropolis Archaeological Project and Instituto Hondureño de Antropología e Historia.

Schele, Linda, and David A. Freidel. 1990. *A Forest of Kings.* New York: William Morrow.

Schele, Linda, and Nikolai Grube. 1992. "The Founding Events at Copan." Copan Note 107. Copan, Honduras: Copan Acropolis Archaeological Project and Instituto Hondureño de Antropología e Historia.

_____. 1994. "Who Was Popol-K'inich?" Copan Note 116. Copan, Honduras: Copan Acropolis Archaeological Project and Instituto Hondureño de Antropología e Historia.

Schele, Linda, and Mary Ellen Miller. 1986. *The Blood of Kings: Dynasty and Ritual in Maya Art*. Fort Worth, TX: Kimball Art Museum.

Sedat, David W. 1997a. "The Earliest Ancestor to Copan Str. 10L–16." ECAP Papers No. 3. Philadelphia: Early Copan Acropolis Program and Instituto Hondureño de Antropología e Historia.

———. 1997b. "The Founding Stage of the Copan Acropolis." ECAP Papers No. 2. Philadelphia: Early Copan Acropolis Program and Instituto Hondureño de Antropología e Historia.

Sedat, David, and Fernando Lopez. 1999. "Tunneling into the Heart of the Copan Acropolis." *Expedition* 41(2):16–21.

Sedat, David, and Robert J. Sharer. 1994. "The Xukpi Stone: A Newly Discovered Early Classic Inscription from the Copan Acropolis." Copan Note 113. Copan, Honduras: Copan Acropolis Archaeological Project and Instituto Hondureño de Antropología e Historia.

Sharer, Robert J. 1997a. "Formation of Sacred Space by the First Kings of Copan." ECAP Papers No. 10. Philadelphia: Early Copan Acropolis Program and Instituto Hondureño de Antropología e Historia.

———. 1997b. "Initial Research and Preliminary Findings from the Hunal Tomb." ECAP Papers No. 5. Philadelphia: Early Copan Acropolis Program and Instituto Hondureño de Antropología e Historia.

———. 1997c. "K'inich K'inich Yax K'uk' Mo' and the Genesis of the Copan Acropolis." Paper presented at the symposium Tale of Two Cities: Copan and Teotihuacan. Harvard University, Cambridge, MA.

———. 1999. "Archaeology and History in the Royal Acropolis, Copan, Honduras." *Expedition*. 41(2): 8–15

Sharer, Robert J., William L. Fash, David W. Sedat, Loa P. Traxler, and Richard Williamson. 1999a. "Continuities and Contrasts in Early Classic Architecture of Central Copan." In Jeff Karl Kowalski, ed., *Mesoamerican Arcitecture as a Cultural Symbol*, pp. 220–249. New York: Oxford University Press.

Sharer, Robert J., Julia C. Miller, and Loa P. Traxler. 1992. "Evolution of Classic Period Architecture in the Eastern Acropolis, Copán: A Progress Report." *Ancient Mesoamerica* 3: 145–159.

Sharer, Robert J., David W. Sedat, Loa P. Traxler, Ellen E. Bell, Christine Carrelli, Fernando Lopez, and Christian Wells. 1998. "PIAT Informe de la Temporada de 1998." Manuscript on file with Instituto Hondureño de Antropología e Historia.

Sharer, Robert J., Loa P. Traxler, David W. Sedat, Ellen E. Bell, Marcello A. Canuto, and Christopher Powell. 1999b. "Early Classic Architecture Beneath the Copan Acropolis: A Research Update." *Ancient Mesoamerica* 10:3–23.

Stomper, Jeffrey. 1996. "The Popol Na: A Model for Ancient Maya Community Structure at Copán, Honduras." Ph.D. diss., Yale University.

Strömsvik, Gustav. 1952. *The Ball Courts at Copan, with Notes on Courts at La Unión, Quirigua, San Pedro Pinula, and Asunción Mita*. Carnegie Institution of Washington Publication 596. Washington, DC.

Stuart, David. 1989. "The 'First Ruler' on Stela 24. Copan." Copan Note 7. Copan, Honduras: Copan Acropolis Archaeological Project and Instituto Hondureño de Antropología e Historia.

_____. 1992. "Hieroglyphics and Archaeology at Copan." *Ancient Mesoamerica* 3: 169–184.

Stuart, David, and Linda Schele. 1986. "Yax K'uk' Mo', the Founder of the Lineage of Copan." Copan Note 6. Copan, Honduras: Copan Mosaics Project and Instituto Hondureño de Antropología e Historia.

Stuart, George. 1997. "The Royal Crypts of Copan." *National Geographic Magazine* 192(6): 68–93.

Traxler, Loa P. 1996. "Los grupos de patios tempranos de la Acrópolis de Copán." *Yaxkin* 14: 35–54.

_____. 1998. "At Court in Copan: Palace Groups of the Early Classic." Paper presented at the sixty-third annual meeting of the Society for American Archaeology, Seattle, Washington.

_____. N.d.a. "Evolution and Social Meaning of Court Group Architecture of the Early Classic Acropolis, Copan, Honduras." Ph.D. diss., University of Pennsylvania.

_____. N.d.b. "Redesigning Copan: Early Architecture of the Polity Center." In Ellen E. Bell, Marcello Andrea Canuto, and Robert J. Sharer, eds., *Understanding Early Classic Copan*. Philadelphia: University of Pennsylvania Museum.

Webster, David L.. ed. 1989. *The House of the Bacabs, Copan, Honduras*. Washington, DC: Dumbarton Oaks Research Library and Collection.

Williamson, Richard V. 1996. "Excavations, Interpretations, and Implications of the Earliest Structures Beneath Structure 10L–26 at Copan, Honduras." In Merle Greene Robertson, Martha J. Macri, and Jan McHargue, eds., *Eighth Palenque Round Table*, pp. 169–175. San Francisco: Pre-Columbian Art Research Institute.

Notes

1. This research involves fieldwork and analyses by numerous colleagues; their work is ongoing, and therefore interpretations of the material presented here should be considered preliminary.

2. These carved monuments were uncovered in excavations conducted by the Copan Acropolis Archaeological Project. Stela 63 and the Motmot marker were encountered in excavations supervised by Joel Palka and Richard Williamson and directed by William Fash (Fash 1991; Fash et al. 1992; Williamson 1996). The Xukpi stone was uncovered in excavations supervised by David Sedat and directed by Robert Sharer (Sedat and Sharer 1994; Sharer et al. 1999a).

3. The Copan Mosaics Project began in 1985 and became part of the Copan Acropolis Archaeological Project in 1988. The excavations of Str. 22A were directed by William Fash and supervised by Sheree Lane and later by Jeffrey Stomper (B. Fash et al. 1992; Stomper 1996). The sculptural analysis and building restoration were directed by Barbara Fash and Rudy Larios respectively (B. Fash 1992).

3

Thrones and Throne Structures in the Central Acropolis of Tikal as an Expression of the Royal Court

PETER D. HARRISON

This chapter addresses several topics relevant to the identification of the presence of a royal court at Tikal, the physical markers of such a court, and some specific examples of the bench type (identified herein as a "throne") as a marker of courtly activity. The importance of the throne as an identifier of the presence of the royal court is discussed with specific examples from the Central Acropolis of Tikal, including several separate structures that served as throne rooms.

The relationship of the Central Acropolis to the ceremonial center of Tikal is illustrated in Figures 3.1 and 3.2. Although the hard data invoked in this chapter are drawn mainly from this one architectural complex, a broader range of the throne concept is reviewed along with thoughts on the variety in form of this courtly marker. The Central Acropolis at Tikal represents a grouping of palace structures from which a multiplicity of evidence (Harrison 1970) indicates a focus of the royal court of this city. Although the primary concern of this chapter is to examine the variety of reception thrones as evidence of court function, a few other related topics are discussed. These include consideration of some markers that identify a royal court (with a focus upon the throne), acknowledging that the term "throne" is borrowed from the European base; the role of such a court at Tikal in particular; and identification of rooms and/or structures where royal functions took place in the Central Acropolis at Tikal (with thrones serving as the primary indicator). A general definition of the royal court is provided in the Introduction (Chapter 1) by Inomata and Houston in Volume 1 of this series.

At Tikal the seat of the royal court moved over time from one locale to another. Although the court per se consisted of the people who occupied the positions—political and religious—upon which it depended as part of the sociopolitical structure of the society (see Inomata and Houston,

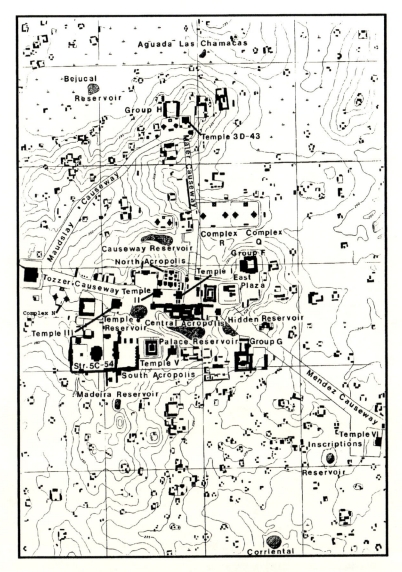

FIGURE 3.1 Map of Central Tikal. The Central Acropolis is located at the center of the city, adjacent to Temples I and II.

Chapter 1 in Volume 1), these people required a physical setting and associated features of architecture that enabled the performance of their duties. This setting has been perceived, at Tikal, as well as at other sites, to be located indoors within the structures called "palaces." The palace grouping closest to the ceremonial center of Tikal is the Central Acropolis, the base data source for this chapter.

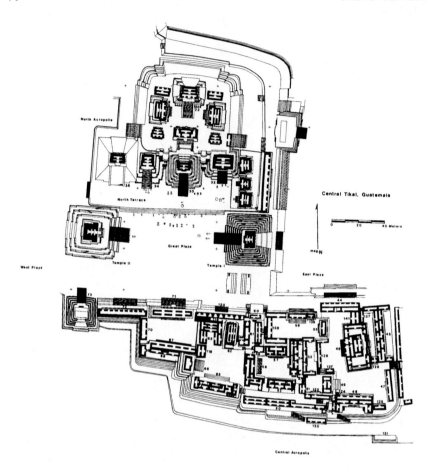

FIGURE 3.2 Detail of the ceremonial center of the city with the religious temples to the north and the more secular palaces of the Central Acropolis in close proximity to the south.

However, we know from archaeology (Laporte 1993) that temple and palace complexes also were active in the region of the Lost World complex at Tikal. Furthermore, other palace groupings occur, identified as Group F, Group G, and the Bat Palace, which likely served as seats of the royal court. As palace groupings, these sets of architecture are also candidates for royal court activities (Harrison 1999). Fewer excavation data are available from these locales, although I have favored their use as seats of the royal court elsewhere (Harrison and Andrews 1998).

Cross-cultural comparisons with several markers of other recognized royal courts were examined (Harrison 1996, 1998, 1999), including the court of Louis XIV in France and the royal Inka court of Cuzco. The markers examined in that study included the use of livery, the use of thrones, and the association of church and state. The conclusion was that such markers compared favorably with the features of Classic Maya culture, such that the existence of a royal court could be accepted for the ancient Maya and that its purposes and functions were similar to those of other cultures. This chapter focuses upon the specific role of thrones and buildings used exclusively for throne-reception. To proceed, it is necessary first to examine the functions of a royal court before analyzing the thrones at Tikal. The next steps are to compare the situation at Tikal with the use and form of thrones at other sites; the epigraphy that distinguishes throne qualities of spirituality; the source material for the construction of thrones as a variable; and decoration (or lack of it) and the reasons for it. The role of the portable throne will then be discussed, with particular importance at Tikal and relevance to source material. Finally, we focus on the throne at Tikal, its distribution in residential structures, the separate throne building, and thrones in nonfamily residences followed by conclusions.

The Functions of a Royal Court

Aside from the basic function of validating and consolidating the society (as described in the definition provided in Chapter 1 of Volume 1), the pertinent official appeared in his various roles seated upon the seat of office—the "throne." The variety of functions dispensed from this royal seat are best found depicted on painted vessels from the Late Classic period (A.D. 650–900). The largest repository of data for this type of scene is found in the *Maya Vase Book* (five volumes, published by Justin Kerr 1989–1997). This source is particularly useful, as the images have been photographed using a special roll-out technique that allows the viewer to observe the whole scene that had been painted cylindrically. The one drawback of this source is that many of the vessels are unprovenienced, which limits their usefulness. Most of the vessels cited here are from Tikal or other known sites. The breadth of subject and richness of detail allow comparisons with archaeological situations. Some of the functions that are depicted in architectural settings, including both indoors and outdoors, include: the reception of tribute goods (Figure 3.3); reception of prisoners involving the presence of military guards (File 680 in Kerr 1977); reception of visiting dignitaries displaying personal livery (Figure 3.3); apparent scenes of ritual divination (File 1453 in Kerr 1981); possible scenes of accession ritual (File 2695 [from Tikal] in Kerr 1985); and domestic family scenes (File K5421, Kerr 1997).

Benches, Thrones, and their Forms in the Lowlands Compared to Tikal

The topic of benches in general and thrones in particular as one bench "type" is not a simple subject. Benches represent a dataset that has enormous variety in form and context, as well as changes over time. For

FIGURE 3.3   Painted scene on a burial vessel from Tikal showing presentation of a jaguar skin (Kerr, File No. 2697). Note also the livery of the tribute-givers and the fringed cover of the throne (courtesy of Kerr Associates).

benches, the function has a very broad range, from completely unknown to specified interpretive functions such as sleeping platforms and thrones. Within the category of thrones, the single unifying element is that a ruler (or other high official) sat upon them. The range of functions served by a throne is as broad as its forms, although the relationship between these two variables is not known. The throne serves to seat a personage in a symbolically elevated position at a higher level than those who are being received. The range of this function has already been discussed by several scholars (Coe and Kerr 1998; Harrison 1996; Houston 1996; Inomata, Chapter 2 in Volume 1) and is summarized above.

The throne form is likewise diverse throughout the Maya lowlands, and it is appropriate to cite some of the better-known examples here. Probably the most straightforward statement that can be made here about Tikal's contribution to the field of throne construction is that they are the simplest, plainest, least-decorated thrones in the lowlands. Highly decorated thrones have been uncovered at numerous sites, many of them much smaller and presumably less powerful than Tikal. Among these are examples from La Milpa, in northern Belize (Hammond 1998), where a finely decorated throne with a carved front panel was uncovered in a palace setting. At Dos Pilas, another example was excavated under the auspices of Arthur Demarest; the throne had sun deities as armrests and duck-billed (crocodilian?) figures supporting the seat in pseudo-Atlantean fashion.

Furthermore, we have the entire class of throne-benches that are decorated on the seat rim by a sky-band, as on the bench in Structure 66C at Copan. This form of decoration provides yet another level of distinction in the function of thrones (Webster et al. 1998). This particular type of decoration sets the supported personage above the sky-band, suggesting a cosmological element of both celestial location and attributes to the seated individual. Benches of this type are most commonly associated with the site of Copan but are also known at Palenque. They are unknown at Tikal. The difference between the celestial throne and more mundane varieties is discussed below with reference to the epigraphic terminology.

Perhaps the most celebrated example of decoration is that exhibited on Throne 3 of Piedras Negras (Baudez and Bequilin 1984: plate 61), with its intricately carved backscreen and legs using three-dimensional stone-carving techniques. More recently, the newly discovered Early Classic throne in the Cross Group (Temple XIX) at Palenque (Robertson et al. 1999) is made of carved limestone and depicts a succession of lords. Its intricacy may rival Throne 3 of Piedras Negras for decorative indulgence, a feature utterly absent at Tikal apart from exterior monumental building decoration. Why was such a large city with prolonged political influence and wealth also the location of the plainest thrones to seat its highest officials? The answer is related in part to the austerity of style that prevailed at Tikal and is reflected in the architecture as well. Despite having introduced the so-called central Peten style of architecture (probably more accurately the "Tikal style"), the primary features of this style are height with emphasis on metric tonnage of fill. Apart from the use of alternating horizontal and vertical planes to create a boxlike series of shadows, the architectural style is almost as plain as the benches. None of this commentary reflects upon the complexity of variety of form and context of the Tikal thrones, only upon the apparent absence of decoration.

The Epigraphy of Thrones

Steve Houston has pointed out the known existence of two different terms in the epigraphy of hieroglyphic texts, both of which refer to thrones (Houston, personal communication, 1999). One is *te:m*, which although rare has turned up at several locations including Palenque (File 1524 in Kerr 1989; Robertson 1985:Figure 227). The second term has not yet been translated but is found on an image of an enthroned figurine (pictured in Coe and Kerr 1998). This same rare glyph occurs in the Tablet of 96 Glyphs from Palenque. Houston suggests that the first term (*te:m*) is a reference to an informal type of throne for the "high seat," a socially honored position, whereas the untranslated term is more cosmological in concept, as described above, invoking the axis mundi on behalf of the exalted, seated subject. This concept champions an opposition of the celestial versus the mundane in the function of thrones.

One conclusion at this point is that thrones not only have a horizontal variation in form with variables such as regional style and specific, practical, situational functions but also reflect an important culturally vertical variable related to mundane versus celestial roles of the seated person.

Source Material and Time Variables

The time variable that is observable at Tikal in the Central Acropolis is relevant here because it provokes a consideration of the nature of source materials in the construction of benches in general and thrones in the specific. It is known from other sites (Palenque, Copan) that decorated thrones carved in stone were manufactured during the Early Classic period. This was not so at Tikal on the basis of admittedly one prominent piece of evidence from the Central Acropolis. Structure 5D-52-2nd was an Early Classic palace that was partially razed and wholly buried by the construction of it successor, 5D-52-1st, built by the lord of Tikal named Yik'in Chan K'awil (Ruler B) in the year A.D. 741. The earlier buried palace (known as the Palace of the Red Dado) exhibited the most complex room pattern that was recorded in the Central Acropolis, the tandem-transverse pattern. In the original analysis (Harrison 1970), this pattern qualified the structure as residential in nature, although the type of residence depended upon other attributes. This Early Classic building contained no masonry benches whatsoever, let alone thrones. Despite being a single instance, 5D-52-2nd does represent a moment frozen in time, and the inference made possible is that at Tikal masonry-constructed benches in general were a Late Classic phenomenon. No Early Classic example exists in the Central Acropolis. Therefore, it can be argued that masonry benches did not exist at Tikal prior to the Late Classic period. It is not reasonable to argue that neither benches nor thrones were utilized prior to the Late Classic at Tikal when they are known to be such an important cultural item at so many other cities in the lowlands. The more acceptable argument is that benches and royal seats were manufactured of a material other than stone or masonry, and in support of this theory we can look to the source materials for the respective sites in question.

At Palenque and other sites along the Usumacinta drainage, such as Yaxchilan and Piedras Negras, native stone with high tensile strength is locally available, such that it can be utilized as lintels spanning wide openings and as seats for thrones, such as the prime example from Piedras Negras. The native stone at Tikal did not offer this characteristic. Stone slabs carved from local quarries at Tikal were used only for the manufacture of altars and stela; neither form had to sustain high tensile strength when placed in a vertical or horizontally ground-based position and had to be cut at three or four times the thickness that is required for a lintel or throne seat in order to avoid breaking. Rather, the tradition at Tikal for spanning wide spaces requiring tensile strength was to use the medium of wood. The wooden lintels of Tikal are famous for the intricacy of their carving and also for the availability of the source materials in the immediate environment: *Chico zapote* and logwood from the adjacent wetlands and its borders were readily available and have been long established as the source of Tikal's lintel material sources (Lundell 1937). There is a source-material difference, then, between Tikal and its contemporary cities in all directions. Stone suitable for carving as lintels or thrones was not available at Tikal, and its absence is particularly notable in the Early Classic period, when, apparently, no furniture was made of carved stone or masonry. During the Late Classic period we have the supreme examples of wood carving in the form of the lintels from the Great Temples, with all the intricacy and subtle artistic delicacy that is noted in the decorated benches of other contemporary sites elsewhere but rendered in lapidary-quality stone.

Below I discuss the use of portable thrones based upon images that appear in no less than three of the surviving carved wooden Late Classic lintels. These images strongly indicate the presence at Tikal of a woodcarving industry that served the furniture needs of the royal court, supplanting the absence of suitable stone for such furniture.

The point here is that the very plainness of Tikal's thrones may well be an expression of medium availability at the site. Wood, rather than stone, was the material utilized for thrones and other furniture such as beds up through the Early Classic period and continuing where necessary into the Late Classic as well.

It may well be that a long tradition of wood carving imposed by necessity led to reluctance to switch to another medium in the Late Classic period. The Maya of Tikal were adept at stucco decoration on the facades of their architecture, especially palaces. This medium of decoration could have been adapted for use on thrones, but it was not. There are no known examples of stucco decoration on thrones at Tikal.

Sources of Knowledge for Throne Decoration at Tikal

Before leaving this topic, it is useful to consider some other forms of decoration for which only secondary evidence now exists. There are painted vessels retrieved from burials at Tikal and there is no reason to interpret them as imports from other cities. Specific examples from a burial recovered by Juan Pedro Laporte in Structure 5C–49 (Figure 3.3) and from Burial 116, the burial of Hasaw Chan K'awil under Temple I (Figure 3.4), both show lords seated upon thrones that exhibited certain decoration. The idea that Tikal's thrones were utterly undecorated would fly in the face of what we know of Maya culture. The difference lies in the manner and medium that was employed and how ingenious we, as archaeologists, can be in making the proper and appropriate interpretations. In the case of the vessel showing a presentation scene excavated by Laporte (Figure 3.3), the throne appears to be covered by a material of textile with a fringe that hangs over the throne's edge in the form of a European bedspread. On the vessel (or, rather, several similar vessels) from Burial 116,

FIGURE 3.4   This simple reception scene from Burial 116 (Hasaw Chan K'awil) illustrates a throne type that has not been found at Tikal, unless the decoration is assumed painted (from Tikal Report No. 25, Part A, Culbert, Figure 69A; courtesy of the University of Pennsylvania Museum).

the throne is shown as having corner supports that appear to be made of separate stone. These supports could well be painted to replicate the style of support that was known from the western Peten regions, such as Piedras Negras and along the Usumacinta. These styles of adornment, by textile and by paint, would not leave traces of their presence today.

When benches and thrones were introduced in solid masonry form at Tikal, the norm was a plain, solid platform, adorned, in the case of a throne, with side-arms, also of masonry and occasionally with a backscreen of solid but plain masonry. There are a few rare exceptions at Tikal. The most frequent but still rare adornment was the use of an overhanging lip on the seat, and this does not correlate perfectly with the additional features of a throne (the presence of side-arms is the identity marker used here). There is a single example of a bench (not a throne) that is hollow, that is, constructed of masonry but having a thin masonry seat and a small, enigmatic opening at the center of the front of the bench. This occurred in the extreme southern endroom of 5D–54–1st in the Central Acropolis. The interior of the open space was plastered and showed no signs of interior burning. We remain at a loss for an explanation of this unique example of a nonthrone bench.

Although the variation in bench-throne form around Tikal is limited to known excavations, one other unusual example is worth mentioning. This is the presence in one structure (5E–51) west of Group G, a palace group, of a series of benches of unusually high dimension. Teobert Maler, who was the only individual to perform an investigation here, deemed the structure the Palace of the Great Sone Benches (Maler 1911:13–15).

FIGURE 3.5 Drawing of a segment of the Carved Lintel 2 of Temple III showing Nu Bak Chak II in front of his portable throne. Details from the right end of the throne are clear (after Tikal Report No. 33, Part A, Jones and Satterthwaite, Figure 72; courtesy of the University of Pennsylvania Museum).

These benches also exhibited overhanging lips on the platform seat but do not otherwise conform to the features of a throne. They all face south.

Portable Thrones

Before proceeding to the discussion of specific throne structures, a few observations are in order with reference to the perishable variety of throne referred to above in conjunction with Tikal's tradition of fine wood carving. Thus far, only nonperishable examples of masonry or stone thrones that survive in the archaeological record have been considered. The use in ancient times of perishable versions is well-documented and is relevant to our earlier discussion of the source materials available

FIGURE 3.6 Artist's conception of a reconstruction of the portable throne shown on three lintels at Tikal (drawn by T.W. Rutledge; scale figure based on Lintel 2 of Temple III).

at Tikal. The primary examples at Tikal are royal seats depicted on the wooden lintels from Temples I, III, and IV (see Tikal Report 33, Part A, 1982; Figure 3.5).

These seats are depicted as resting upon the greater structure of a portable palanquin and have been described by others as portable thrones. The detail of the preserved carving in the wooden lintels invokes an interpretation that these portable thrones were also of perishable material, presumably wood. In each case there is a cushioned seat atop the elaborately carved base. On three examples (two from Temple I and one from Temple III) the view is of the side of the royal seat. The one example from Temple IV, which shows a front view of the same class of seat, indicates that it was proportionately much wider across the front than the side. From this moderately well preserved glimpse into the royal paraphernalia, we cannot know the proportion of royal seats that were made of perishable materials known only from secondary sources, such as these lintel depictions. Such carved seats may have outnumbered the masonry ones that have survived. Figure 3.6 shows an artist's reconstruction of the portable royal seat of Tikal.

Close examination of the designs of decoration and form of the portable thrones in the Tikal sample suggest that the same, or at least very similar, seats are depicted on all of the lintels despite a time span estimated at seventy-eight years. The decoration includes repetitions of the royal mat design, human heads, and a more complex, less decipherable design on the front. The similarity of the end views provided on the lintels of Temples I and III is most compelling. Shown from the viewpoint of the sitter, we see the right end of the throne on Lintel 2 of Temple I, and the left end on Lintel 2 of Temple III. Because of poor preservation, the view of the front of this type of throne is limited on Lintel 3 of Temple IV. However, this corpus of iconography provides a good idea of the shape, size, and decoration of the portable throne. It is a long, narrow bench with a padded seat and heavily carved base. The likelihood that the same actual seat is shown on the lintels of Temples I and IV must be allowed. There is only a time span of about nine years between the two carvings. In the subject matter of the text of Temple IV, Y'ikin Chan K'awil imitates the tale of his father Hasaw Chan K'awil as told on the lintels of Temple I. He may actually be using the same portable throne in the telling of his own, similar story of conquest and the capture of palanquins. The portable seat shown on the lintel of Temple III is similar but somewhat different. A span of sixty-nine years separates this carving from that of Temple IV (seventy-eight years from Temple I). There may be a new royal portable throne depicted, or it may merely be a remembered image of a view differently rendered, or even a recarved version of the same seat. Yet the similarity of style and form is undeniable. The date for the Temple III lintel is derived (by association) with Stela 24 at the base of the temple at A.D. 810. If the same seat were indeed being passed on as a treasured family heirloom, it would have had to survive only seventy-eight years compared to the 1,200-year preservation of the lintels. In the texts of both the lintels of Temples I and IV, mention is made of the seizing of the palanquins of the opponent, but the thrones themselves are not mentioned. Thus, the possibility is real that the original of the portable throne already belonged to Hasaw Chan K'awil *before* his famous conflict with Calakmul in A.D. 692. Use of his own throne atop the captured palanquin could be the crowning symbol of dominance: "his" throne resting on "their" palanquin. The perpetuity of this symbolism on Temple IV is clear. The reappearance of a similar (or same) throne on Temple III is intriguing.

Examination of the royal reception scenes published by Justin Kerr in the *Ceramic Vase* series (see also Coe and Kerr 1998), reveals that the type of simple, solid, undecorated bench found archaeologically in the Central Acropolis is *not* depicted on these painted vessels, not even on those from Tikal. What this likely tells us is that the variety of throne seats is quite broad and that this variety may reflect regional (or site) distribution as well as function. The role of medium, stone seats versus wood, is relevant to this discussion, as we have argued that wood was the accessible medium at Tikal and that wood replaced stone for the use of furniture at least during the Early Classic period and likely to a large extent also in the Late Classic as evidenced by the portable thrones shown on Late classic lintels.

The Throne at Tikal

Benches abound in number in the Central Acropolis; they served as the primary data source for this chapter even though they seldom resemble those depicted on the painted vases for lack of decoration. Analysis of bench features (Harrison 1970) revealed that there are thirteen different forms of masonry bench in the Central Acropolis displaying the three variables: (1) number of walls contacted by the bench; (2) presence or absence of masonry elements, such as side-arms or backscreens; and (3) the proportional shape of the bench. Of these, the types that correlate best with the function of thrones are those that abut only one wall at the rear of the bench and possess added side-arms. Scenes on the painted vessels tell us that very plain benches with no side-arms were also used for formal functions; these are also numerously present in the Central Acropolis.

There is a significant difference between benches illustrated in Kerr and those found archaeologically in the Central Acropolis. The differences lie in the degree of decoration as well as the apparent nature of construction. In the Central Acropolis, all benches were constructed secondarily to the plastering of the floor and walls, and all but one are of solid masonry. An overhanging lip separating the seat from the base is a rare occurrence (but is present, as noted above). Because even painted ceramic vessels of Tikal provenience demonstrate a considerably higher degree of decoration (Figure 3.3), we must assume that much of this depicted decoration was either painted on the masonry or represents some form of perishable cover. Certainly, the perishable elements that would make the royal receiving seat comfortable are convincingly invoked by the painted scenes. Cushions, cloth, and skin covers, as well as hangings to the side, front, and rear of the royal throne, are repeatedly depicted (Figure 3.7).

Archaeologically, the evidence for a support system of the drapes and curtains is found in the presence of sub–spring beam holes placed around the masonry benches in such a way that could have easily suspended either curtains or the ropes and strings that manipulated them. The emphasis in the iconography of the painted vessels published by Kerr draws heavily on drama and theatricality and on the difference of absolute elevation that separates the lord from his audience and attendants.

Distribution of Benches:
Residential Structures in the Central Acropolis

In the Central Acropolis, there are forty-six structures of the type called palaces (more recently redefined as "range-type" structures for greater objectivity). Earlier analysis (Harrison 1970) of the floor plans of these buildings, compared with a variety of other features, indicated that only

FIGURE 3.7 Reconstruction of the opulence and drama of a typical throne room at Tikal, based upon the archaeological remains. Many examples of this type were uncovered in the Central Acropolis (drawing by Amalia Kenward).

one form suggested familial residence. Of the excavated buildings, only Structure 5D–46 fulfilled all the requirements of this function (Figure 3.8), a conclusion later confirmed by the translation of a text incised on the lid of a cache vessel buried by inclusion beneath the western stair. This text indicated that the structure (*na* in the text) belonged to the fourteenth lord of Tikal, Great Jaguar Claw (Figure 3.9). It must be noted that this interpretation (i.e., that the *na* and *ot ot* glyphs refer to the building rather than the vessel on which it is carved) remains this author's interpretive insistence (on the basis of archaeological logic) despite disagreement from several epigraphers. Just as this same glyph carved on a lintel at Yaxchilan refers to the building by extension, not to the lintel itself, I interpret the glyph on the lidded vessel to refer to the staired structure under which it was included as an archaeological dedicatory cache. An alternative explanation could be that the cache vessel encapsulates the "spirit" of the structure together with the tangible sacred objects that represent the blessing of the cache itself. In this sense, the vessel itself could be referred to as the "house" (*na* or *ot ot*) for the spirit.

This building (5D–46) contains at least one throne bench on the eastern side of the structure, facing east. Thrones in rooms that are part of a complex structure are common in the Central Acropolis and, most commonly, face east, north, or south. Exceptions to the rule are discussed below.

FIGURE 3.8 Structure 5D–46 in its final form. The central core and stair were built by Jaguar Claw the Great who may have founded the royal court in the Central Acropolis in the middle fourth century. The cache vessel in Figure 3.7 was recovered from beneath this stair (photo by Harrison 1969).

FIGURE 3.9 Drawing of the carved dedicatory cache vessel from Structure 5D–46, identifying the building as the "House" (*na*) of Jaguar Claw the Great. The "*na*" glyph is highlighted (courtesy of the University of Pennsylvania Museum).

During the original analysis of structure function (e.g., family residence versus specialized forms of residence), it did not seem that any other building in the group was in fact a family residence due to lack of excavation. New knowledge and retrospect allow us to admit one other building as a likely family residence: Structure 5D–57. This building was excavated only on three of its exterior facades. The western, southern, and eastern outer walls were fully exposed to the extent of their survival. The interior was not excavated and even today awaits to reveal its secrets. The reason for believing it served a residential function is twofold: The wall plan is visible and reveals the signature tandem-transverse room pattern that is basic to residences; and the sculptures on the exterior and accompanying text inform us that the building (house) glorifies Hasaw Chan K'awil, the twenty-sixth ruler of Tikal and is dedicated in conjunction with his most famous military conquest. The combined signature of the structure's builder with the residential plan and the convenient location close to Temple I argue that this could also have been Hasaw's permanent place of residence.

Separate Throne Structures

I also seek to identify separate structures that are devoted to the functions of the royal enthroned reception. The type of throne-bench accepted here to identify a throne structure is manifested by the solid-masonry bench with masonry side-arms described above (see Figure 3.7), usually accompanied by other features that allow for royal adornment and the drapery of theatrical presentation.

Because of the frequency of so-called throne rooms contained within greater palace structures in the Central Acropolis, the possibility of separate throne structures had not been considered prior to comparison with Group 10L2 at Copan (Harrison and Andrews 1989). In the latter residential zone, throne structures as separate units *do* occur, adjoined to residential buildings, which apparently always face *south*, a consistency not found in the Central Acropolis at Tikal. Reexamination of the Central Acropolis data revealed three free-standing structures that apparently served as comparable separate throne structures. They are 5D–59, located immediately west of Structure 5D–57; 5D–123, located to the eastern side of the five-story palace (5D–52); and 5D–118 in Maler's Court. Additionally, one example of an added room as an architectural accretion is described in the throne-structure category. This is the appended west addition of Structure 5D–61 (Figure 3.10).

Structure 5D–59

The location and stratigraphic position of this structure are highly suggestive of its royal function. Immediately adjacent to the east, Structure

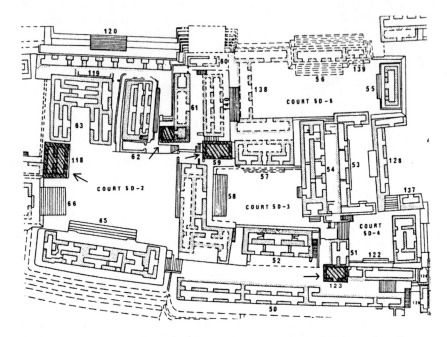

FIGURE 3.10 Part of the map of the Central Acropolis highlighting four throne structures: from left, 5D–118, 5D–61 (addition), 5D–59 and 5D–123. Structures in question are hatched.

5D–57 has been suggested to be a house, in the sense of residence, of Hasaw Chan K'awil, the twenty-sixth ruler of Tikal and restorer to power of the clan of Jaguar Claw. Such restoration was manifest by the raising of the first major architectural monuments and inscriptions since the Tikal hiatus (A.D. 557–692).

Structure 5D–57 bears this hero's image in two known places, together with an inscription that verifies his identity, showing the act of capture of a lord of Calakmul depicted on the eastern upper zone of the building. In the latter sculpted carving, Hasaw shows himself in the garb of Teotihuacan, holding the captive prince of Calakmul on a rope. At the other end of the building Hasaw again shows himself in the same highly formalized and stylized apparel in a rare occurrence of a lower-zone orthostat, once again carved in stone and stucco. This structure, 5D–57, had to have been constructed shortly after the well-documented conquest of Calakmul by Hasaw Chan K'awil in A.D. 692.

Close to the western end of the house, a separate building was constructed at a later date—just how much later is not known. However, the stratigraphy of the connecting floors establishes a notable time gap. A narrow alley separated this adjacent throne structure from 5D–57, barely leaving room for human passage (see Figure 3.10). This separation is in con-

Thrones and Throne Structures in the Central Acropolis of Tikal 91

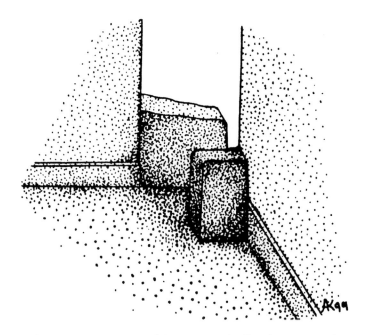

FIGURE 3.11 Drawing of the masonry baffles that restricted traffic from Court 2 to Court 3, immediately adjacent to the throne structure of 5D-59 on the right.

trast to the more common practice of direct-contact addition as a means of increasing the interior space of structures in the Central Acropolis. However, in this case the separation of the two buildings preserved access to the image of the orthostat of Hasaw Chan K'awil, keeping the image visible, rather than burying it as a simple addition would have done. The throne structure, 5D-59, sits just inside the confines of Court 5D-3 at its northwestern corner, adjacent to a highly restricted access from Court 5D-2 on the same vertical level. The baffle walls that restrict the access are a Late Classic addition, partially blocking the easy passage from Court 2 to Court 3 (Figure 3.11 ; see also Figure 3.10). The effect is to make Court 3 more defensible where the throne structure and house of Hasaw were located, occupying the northern side of the court. The structure of 5D-59 is unusually large in proportion for a single-room building, that is, a nontandem-nontransverse building, which in the nomenclature of the Central Acropolis is, by definition, *not* a residence. The spacious, single-room form fits well for such a specialized function as a throne structure. The room interior measures 3.56 meters wide by 6.6 meters long. It contains three benches, a plain one centered on the northern wall facing the doorway and measuring 2.32 meters in length; a plain bench centered on the western wall measuring only 2.5 meters in length; and a larger bench with side-arms filling the entire eastern wall (3.56 meters in length). This latter is the throne bench. It is assumed that this was one of perhaps several throne structures utilized by Hasaw Chan K'awil; given the time span that separates the construction of his house (5D–57) and the throne structure (5D–59), it must be assumed that other locales, such as throne rooms within other buildings, likely even 5D–57 itself, were used prior to construction of 5D–59. It should be noted that the throne is positioned in this case so that the seated figure would not be visible from the exterior, and even though the throne faces west there is no view outside of the room in that direction. The structure was vaulted and had collapsed. Both sculptures at the western and eastern ends of 5D–57 were buried by deliberate construction, at later dates, filling the gaps between 5D–57 and its adjacent buildings.

The multiplicity of throne rooms (as opposed to separate throne structures) in a palace complex as large as the Central Acropolis suggests that they were utilized for different types of court function, that is, a variety of internal and external administrative functions as described earlier.

Structure 5D–123

Another structure parallel in form and orientation is 5D–123, perched partly on the roofs of 5D–51 and 5D–128 (see Figure 3.10). This structure has no route of access to either of the structures on which it is perched but rather pertains to, and is adjacent to, the space that fronts 5D–52, on its immediate western side. The latter is a three-story structure in its final phase of construction. Stratigraphy places the small building later than the stair to the second story of 5D–52. We know that the first story of this complex building was commissioned by Y'ikin Chan K'awil, the son of Hasaw Chan K'awil, in A.D. 741. The distance dates for the second and even later third stories are not known. Therefore, the throne structure, 5D–123, could pertain either to Y'ikin or one of his descendants. The architectural setting of 5D–123 differs from that of 5D–59 in two ways. It is positioned to the eastern instead of the western side of the principally associated building (5D–52). Second, 5D–59 was raised adjacent to a building (5D–57) that bears the attributes of a probable permanent residence, whereas this is not the case with 5D–123. The nearest and only adjacent building (5D–52) does not bear attributes of a permanent residence. Rather, it has been interpreted as a building of ceremonial retreat or, more specifically, a men's retreat house (Harrison 1970). Nonetheless, the location provides this small building with an unobstructed, splendid view of the palace reservoir toward Temple V on the southern side of the reservoir ravine. Given the known chronology, it is probable that Temple V had not yet been built when this particular candidate for a throne structure was built.

Structure 5D–123 is very similar to the size and proportions of 5D–59. It measures 6.01 meters in interior length and 3.00 meters in width. The

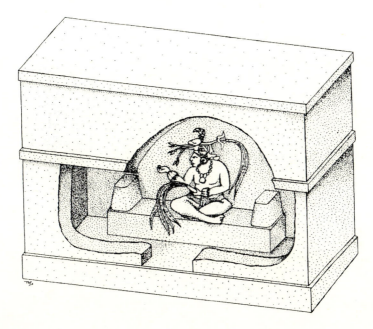

FIGURE 3.12 Reconstruction drawing of Structure 5D–123 showing the throne bench with seated *ajaw*.

throne bench with side-arms occupies the northern wall facing the doorway, that is, facing south, and measures 4.32 meters in length. No other benches occupy the room (Figure 3.12). The structure had been vaulted but was badly deteriorated, possibly due to lack of reinforcement, having been attached only at the rear to an earlier structure. The uniformly collapsed vaulting on these structures will be discussed below.

The multiple functions suggested by the iconography to be associated with throne benches also suggest that their precincts were not limited to the presence of elite individuals only. If the function of reception thrones includes the judiciary role, as believed, then nonroyal individuals would have to be admitted into these areas. This might explain the use of art on the exterior walls of 5D–57 of fierce warrior images of Hasaw. This type of image is consistent with the tradition of other publicly placed and politically oriented monuments at Tikal, specifically the stelae and decorated roof combs of temples in open public locations that display warrior versions of the ruler. Such presentations in public places, presumably accessible to all social levels of the populace, are in contrast to the more revealing and intimate scenes depicted on the painted vessels—objects presumably not meant to be for public observation. The ruler, as shown on painted vessels, is not only the judge but also and almost always the scholar, in addition to his other roles (Coe and Kerr 1998). This softer,

FIGURE 3.13   Structure 5D–118 on the right is the building with almost no front wall; Maler's Palace is on the far left (photo by Harrison 1967).

more intellectual role is most frequently presented on the painted vessels. The point is that although the open spaces around these structures in the Central Acropolis containing thrones are highly controlled with restricted access, we nevertheless expect that members of a variety of social levels could have access to view these images of the victorious warrior. They are not there just for the consumption of the ruler's fellow elite, whereas the painted vessels are presumed to carry such a restriction.

Structure 5D–118

There remains one other structure in the Central Acropolis that may have served the function of a separate throne structure. This is 5D–118 (Figure 3.13; see also Figure 3.10), a late building situated in Court 2 between structures 5D–63 on the northern side of the court and Structure 5D–60, an oratorio on the western side of the same court. The two flanking structures differ widely in their form and undoubtedly in their function. Structure 5D–60 has the shape of a very small temple with a single room well elevated above the court. The room proportion is unusual, as it is extremely wide for a stone vault. However, the presence of a vault was demonstrated in the remains. The fact that this vault collapsed readily is not surprising given the span of the room. In contrast, 5D–63 is a complex palace building with many rooms formed in a U shape. The high proportion of bed-benches contained in this unique building suggests a very specialized, and probably temporary and ritual, form of residence. I have suggested elsewhere that this building functioned as temporary housing for a team of ballplayers residing in separated and holy isolation above the ballcourt in the Great Plaza below (Harrison and Andrews 1998).

Structure 5D–118 also has specialized architectural features, like the two flanking buildings, their disparate functions distinguishing this architectural environment from those of the other proposed throne structures already discussed. The first two buildings described face south, but 5D–118 faces east. This orientation makes the building comparable to many throne rooms in the Central Acropolis, which are contained in larger buildings with multiple functions. Most such rooms face east (e.g., in 5D–65, 5D–49, 5D–46, and 5D–54), suggesting that an eastern orientation for this function is at least an alternative to facing south. This structure (5D–118) contains tandem rooms rather than the usual single room, and the throne bench is in the rear. In compensation, there is an exceptionally wide front doorway, with virtually no front wall at all, such that an enthroned *ajaw* in the back room would be quite visible from the exterior courtyard. Given all the factors—orientation, association with a specialized residence, presence of a throne bench—it is concluded that this structure also may well have served the function of a free-standing throne structure.

Stratigraphy confirms that 5D–118 could not have been built before the time of Yax Ain II, the twenty-ninth ruler, who is the interpreted builder of Maler's Palace in the same courtyard (Harrison 1999). Therefore, use of this building was very late in the sequence of Tikal rulers.

Yet another conclusion emerges. A succession of kings appears to have built throne structures in the Central Acropolis even if they did not maintain private households in the same complex. I have interpreted elsewhere that the rulers Y'ikin Chan K'awil and Yax Ain II did indeed build their own separate households in the form of palace complexes outside of the Central Acropolis (Harrison 1999). These were, respectively, Groups G and F. If this interpretation is correct, then Hasaw was likely the last king to hold residence in the Central Acropolis, but not the last to maintain some of the many court functions within this group. The suggestion is that there was an increasing trend to separate the functions of private residence from those of the court. Such separation late in the history of Tikal (after A.D. 734) may have been motivated by needs of personal security or merely the desire and ability to achieve family privacy. Not all wives and children would be pleased to have troops of suppliants, diplomats, and even criminals or captives parading through parts of their house and undoubtedly sneaking peeks into the off-limits apartments. The luxury of royal privacy may not have been possible (or practical) until the well-manifested wealth had been achieved that is evident

FIGURE 3.14 The addition to Structure 5D–61 in the foreground contains a throne facing left (north). Another throne is located in the room beyond the open door (photo by Harrison 1969).

after the reign of Hasaw Chan K'awil. This wealth and general prosperity, which was enjoyed in the latter decades of Tikal's glory, can be attributed to the success of his campaigns.

Structure 5D–61 Addition

There is one further architectural element relevant to this discussion. This is the room that had been added to the western side, that is, at the southern end of Structure 5D–61 on the northern side of Court 2. The original building was quite early in the Acropolis sequence. A date close to the beginning of the Late Classic period is a guess, and the original building had a solitary room at the southern end with a single doorway facing west, possibly serving as an oratorio. The addition (Figure 3.14) was made at an unknown but considerably later date, as attested by the stratigraphy; it faces north.

Inside is a single, room-spanning throne bench with side-arms facing out the doorway to the north and toward a view of Temple I (assuming that Temple was already built at this time). The Great Plaza and North Acropolis were certainly in place when this addition was raised. The access is awkward, gained from a narrow alley between Structures 5D–61 and 5D–62. The interior room that was enclosed by the addition also contains a throne bench against the eastern wall, facing west. Because all benches were constructed secondarily at Tikal, there is often no way to determine if the time span between the construction of the building and that of the bench is significant or not. In its current state, the throne of the older interior room has a view only into the addition, whereas the outer throne freely faces an outdoor view to the north. The sequence of construction of the two thrones is not known; neither is the date of the addition. To the knowledge of this investigator, no thrones had a free and open view to the west in their final configuration, and it is argued here that this restriction was chosen for cultural reasons, namely ,that this view toward the dying sun was reserved, by taboo, for sacerdotal functions.

There are several possible explanations for the unusual arrangement found in the southern end of 5D–61. One is that the north-facing throne could be the earlier of the two, so that when the west-facing interior bench was constructed it enjoyed only the interior view of the later addition. Conversely, the west-facing throne could have been installed by an intrusive ruler unfamiliar with the Tikal conventions that otherwise pertained in the Central Acropolis.

Throne Rooms in Buildings

Rooms that contain benches with backscreens and side-arm screens marking the throne function are also found in multiroomed, multifunction buildings. Most frequently these are found preserved on the ground floor, although a few examples of such thrones in second stories do occur. This latter distribution raises an interesting question of access, if individuals and groups from outside of the family household were to be received. From the point of view of our culture, there is a conflict. On the one hand, the occupants of the Central Acropolis, be they familial or not, did gradually move toward increasing restriction of access to the interior courtyards. Second stories, even third stories in a few cases, represent a change in the demographic configuration of the complex, and they are of necessity later in time. To build a late upper story (say, after A.D. 710)—one that automatically embodied a highly restricted route of access and then to build within it a reception room—appears to be a conflict of purpose. Once again, this may be accounted for in terms of increasing diversity and complexity of function in reception rooms. Some functions may benefit from extreme remoteness and restriction of access. Scenes of conjuring, involving the use of smoke and mirrors, are depicted on painted

FIGURE 3.15 Structure 5D–65 (Maler's Palace) is a multiroomed structure with several throne rooms on both stories.

vessels with a setting that clearly is within a palace. Such scenes may be taking place in the limited-access throne rooms found in upper stories. Private divinatory ceremonies or the reception of trusted diplomats come to mind as benefiting from such remote venues. One example in the Central Acropolis is in the second-story east-end room of Maler's Palace (5D–65; see Figures 3.15 and 3.16).

There are several things that we do not know from excavation or even from extrapolation from other sources of data. What actually happened in those upper stories? After half a millennium or more of growth, the Central Acropolis came to have the look of a Middle Eastern city, or *tell*, in its own right. This is largely due to the varied levels of the courtyards determined originally by the contours of the bedrock of the hilltop that the Central Acropolis shares with the North Acropolis and the Great Plaza. The highest courtyard, Court 2, is the product of aggressive artificial construction, mostly achieved during the reign of Y'ikin Chan K'awil. The changes in descending level from Court 2 through Courts 3, 4, and 6 resulted in the necessity for multiple stairways to provide access routes (Figure 3.17). The configuration of these stairs and their associated access baffles tells us a lot about the contemporary concepts of allowed and denied access.

FIGURE 3.16 Artist's reconstruction of the royal court in action on the north side of Structure 5D–65. The iconography of the upper zone is based on recorded fact but is mostly the artist's conception by T.W. Rutledge.

FIGURE 3.17 The multiple stairs that connect different levels and structures between Courts 4 (below) and 3 (above) demonstrate the structural complexity of the Central Acropolis and the restriction of access to throne structures and rooms (photo by Harrison 1966).

Although the directions of south and east seem to have been preferred for a free-standing building or rooms in complex palaces, both containing thrones, we have already seen that in one of these buildings, 5D-59, the throne itself faced west but had no exterior view in that direction. It is my position that doorways opening to the west were related to functions of religion and afterlife, even where they occur in palaces, at least for the Central Acropolis at Tikal.

Conclusion

In conclusion, the royal seat, as a throne, serves as a major marker of the royal court at Tikal and has been considered in a variety of venues in this chapter. Portable thrones allow mobility to certain functions of the ruler, and an argument has been presented here that such objects were sufficiently revered to be passed through the generations representing the wood-carving tradition of Tikal. Examples have been examined of throne benches in a variety of differing architectural environments in the Central Acropolis, including in separate, free-standing buildings and in multiroom buildings.

Thrones were found facing all four cardinal directions, although the west-facing ones have no open view to that direction in their final state. East is statistically the most preferred direction, with south a close second. There is indication that the courtly functions of the throne room were at first associated with the residence of the ruler and that this gradually changed in two ways. First, the throne function was moved into a separate building which was close to the residential structure; second, residences moved out of the Acropolis entirely, but the court functions of the throne rooms and buildings continued in the Central Acropolis. A final observation is that the Acropolis was not by any means the exclusive location of courtly functions as identified by throne benches. These occur in other complexes around the city. However, the Central Acropolis does seem to have remained a focal point for such activities for at least five centuries.

It has been suggested that different decoration styles on thrones have an association with two different levels of presentation of the seated human. One of these is celestial, or liturgical, in nature, marked by the presence of the decorative sky-band. Although also decorated at other cities in the lowlands, other thrones may be categorized as having served the more mundane ceremonial functions such as judiciary, military, and tribute reception events. The kinds of events that would require the form of the celestial throne, such as accession to power, are surely more religious or momentous in the life of the lord involved. Due to the current plainness of the Tikal thrones, whose only decoration consists of rare use of an overhanging seat lip, it must be assumed that such decoration was perishable, painted, or made of textile, drawing limits to assignment of specific function from the database in the Central Acropolis. Despite these limitations, some insights into the role of thrones and throne rooms have been offered.

References

Baudez, Claude F., and Pierre Becquelin. 1984. *Les Mayas*. Paris: Editions Gallimard.

Coe, Michael D., and Justin Kerr. 1998. *The Art of the Maya Scribe*. New York: Harry N. Abrams.

Hammond, Norman, and Ben Thomas. 1998. "Another Maya Throne Room at at La Milpa." *Context* 14(1): 15–16.

Harrison, Peter D. 1970. "The Central Acropolis, Tikal, Guatemala: A Preliminary Study of the Functions of its Structural Components During the Late Classic Period." Ph.D. diss., University of Pennsylvania.

———. 1996. "Court of Courts: Ceremonial, Legal, and Hierarchical Functions in Maya Elite Society." Paper presented at the annual meeting of the American Anthropological Association, San Francisco.

———. 1999a. *The Lords of Tikal*. London: Thames and Hudson.

———. 1999b. "Palaces of the Royal Court at Tikal, Guatemala." In Jessica Christie, ed., *Maya Palaces and Elite Residences: An Interdisciplinary Approach*. Austin: University of Texas Press. In press.

Harrison, Peter D., and E. Wyllys Andrews V. 1998. "The Palaces of Tikal and Copan." Paper presented at symposium Ancient Palaces of the New World: Form, Function, and Meaning, Dumbarton Oaks Research Library and Collection, Washington, DC.

Jones, Christopher, and Linton Satterthwaite. 1982. *The Monuments and Inscriptions of Tikal: The Carved Monuments, Tikal Report No. 33, Part A*. Philadelphia: University Museum, University of Pennsylvania.

Kerr, Justin. 1989–97. *The Maya Vase Book: A Corpus of Rollout Photographs of Maya Vases*. Vols. 1–5. New York: Kerr Associates.

Laporte, Juan Pedro. 1993. "Architecture and Social Chance in Late Classic Maya Society: The Evidence from Mundo Perdido, Tikal." In Jeremy A. Sabloff and John S. Henderson,eds., *Lowland Maya Civilization in the Eighth Century A.D.*, pp. 299–317. Washington, DC: Dumbarton Oaks Research Library and Collection.

Lundell, Cyrus L. 1937. *The Vegetation of the Peten*. Carnegie Institution of Washington Publication No. 478. Washington, DC.

Maler, Teobert. 1911. *Explorations in the Department of Peten, Guatemala: Tikal*. Memoirs of the Peabody Museum of American Archaeology and Ethnology, vol. 5, no. 1. Cambridge: Harvard University.

Robertson, Merle Greene. 1985. *The Sculpture of Palenque*, vol. 2. Princeton: Princeton University Press.

Robertson, Merle Greene, Alfonso Morales, and David Stuart. 1999. "Cross Group Project Discovers, Tomb, Throne, and Limestone Panel in Palenque." *Precolumbian Art Research Institute Newsletter* 28: 1–4.

Webster, David, Barbara Fash, Randolph Widmer, and Scott Zeleznik. 1998. "The Skyband Group: Excavations of a Classic Maya Elite Residential Complex at Copán, Honduras." *Journal of Field Archaeology* 25: 319–444.

4

The Royal Court of Caracol, Belize: Its Palaces and People

ARLEN F. CHASE AND DIANE Z. CHASE*

Although it is true that activities and actors in ancient Maya courts can no longer be directly viewed and examined, they can be interpreted from archaeological, epigraphic, and iconographic data in combination with careful analogy. If one assumes that Maya courts were palace-based, then architectural form can provide significant clues as to their structure and

---

*A portion of this chapter derives from a presentation made at the sixty-third annual meeting of the Society for American Archaeology in March 1998. The authors would like to thank Stephen Houston, Takeshi Inomata, and two anonymous reviewers for their comments on earlier versions of this chapter. The stable isotope data were provided by Christine White of Western Ontario University. The University of Central Florida Caracol Archaeological Project has been assisted by many individuals, institutions, and foundations over the course of its existence. At the University of Central Florida the Trevor Colbourn Endowment has been critical to the continuation of the Caracol Archaeological Project. The government of Belize and certain of its representatives—particularly the Department of Archeology and its Archaeological Commissioners Harriot Topsey, Allan Moore, John Morris, and Brian Woodye as well as the Department of Forestry—also have been particularly instrumental in ensuring the success of the project. Over the years funding for the project has been obtained from numerous sources: private donations to the University of Central Florida, the Harry Frank Guggenheim Foundation, the U.S. Agency for International Development, the government of Belize, the National Science Foundation (Grants Nos. BNS–8619996, SBR–9311773, and SBR–9708637), the Miami Institute for Maya Studies, the Dart Foundation, the Foundation for the Advancement of Mesoamerican Studies, the Stans Foundation, the Ahau Foundation, and the J.I. Kislak Foundation. Special thanks are also due to Robert Schyberg and Winifred Clive. Members of the Caracol Archaeological Project have contributed greatly through their labor and perseverance; a formal staff listing and end-of-season photographs of these individuals may be found on our website, located at [www.caracol.org].

organization. Just as there are different kinds of palaces, there may well have been differences among courts. When found in association with palaces, numerous kinds of residues—ranging from in situ artifactual materials to stable isotope analyses of human bone—can help flesh out the activities that were carried out as well as identify the people who were integrated into a given court. Iconographic details found on buildings, painted and modeled pottery vessels, and other artifacts can also help elucidate what transpired in these ancient settings; in some cases, hieroglyphic records are also relevant.

Like others before us (see Adams 1974), we define a "Classic period Maya palace" as an elite or royal dwelling place, usually constructed using stone walls and a vaulted roof. We differentiate such a structure type from a purely ritual building, such as a temple or shrine (also often of stone construction), and from more humble residences, largely made of perishable materials. However, a Maya palace was not only a residence, as it probably also had administrative functions. The conjoining of functions in a single building is noted by Landa (Tozzer 1943:118, 124, 171, 306) for the sixteenth-century Yucatec Maya. Although some may identify a single-room building as a palace (cf. Valdés 1997), we agree with Peter Harrison (1986:55–56) that the term "palace" implies more than one room.

There is great variation in the kinds of structures that have been called palaces archaeologically, presumably due to a constellation of factors. First, there is temporal variation in the form of palaces: Classic period palaces are generally sited on elevated substructures and use stone construction; however, Post-Classic Maya palaces may rest directly on their associated plaza levels and use perishable materials. Second, even within the temporal span of the Late Classic period, a single building might have had several different uses and been extensively modified, thereby resulting in great variation in form. Finally, given the diversity among groups that we lump together as "the Maya," there was likely regional variation in the form that palaces might take. It is important to note at the outset that the presence of a palace in and of itself does not imply the existence of a specific form of social, political, or economic organization. Palaces, as a kind of building, cut across a variety of political and economic forms.

In this chapter we seek to examine the "royal court" at the Classic period Maya city of Caracol, Belize. Although similar tenets and beliefs may have been shared among the ancient Maya, particularly among the ancient elite, at many Maya sites, as represented by a shared writing system, this does not mean that all Late Classic Maya royal courts were similarly structured and organized. Caracol exhibits great differences from its Late Classic Maya neighbors. Elsewhere, we (A. Chase and D. Chase 1996a, 1996b, 1996c; D. Chase 1994, 1998; D. Chase and A. Chase forthcoming) have suggested that a specific cultural identity was cultivated among the site's populace in order to foster the expansionist goals of its various sovereigns. We have also commented on Caracol's centralized organization (A. Chase and D. Chase 1994a, 1996c, 1998), its administered economy (A. Chase 1998; A. Chase and D. Chase 1994a; A. Chase et al., 2001), and its expansive midlevel society (A. Chase 1992; A. Chase and D. Chase 1996a; Jaeger Liepins 1994). Thus, Caracol's palaces and courts may not reflect the structure and organization of these units in the Maya lowlands at large.

Interpreting Maya Courts

The archaeological data for reconstructing the social aspects of a Maya court come in various forms. For example, architectural plans and the features of palaces can be studied both from the standpoint of traffic flow and architectural configuration to suggest how a given building could have been used. Remains of ancient activities can be found on palace floors or buried within their construction fills. Painted scenes on pottery vases can suggest aspects of palace life. Carved stelae can also provide information on at least some of the individuals who lived in palaces. The bones of the individuals buried throughout a site can be compared to assess social relations and diet.

Yet each class of data has its limitations. Stone buildings can be easily and quickly modified; and perishable modifications, such as wooden benches and wall partitions, which could have substantially altered traffic flow or how a given building or room was utilized, are not generally recovered in the archaeological record. The latest artifactual materials left on a floor do provide some sense of how a given building was utilized immediately prior to abandonment (Inomata 1997; Inomata and Triadan 2000; A. Chase and D. Chase 2001; D. Chase and A. Chase 2000), but again many subsidiary considerations must be weighed in making interpretations of function. Were any materials removed prior to abandonment? How and why did items end up on a floor or bench? Do the remains accurately reflect how a given building was used throughout its life span, or are the materials simply the reflection of the terminal use of a building within a changed social context?

Monument portraits and texts provide only very limited information on court life. Palaces themselves are also often devoid of human skeletal remains. It thus becomes more difficult to talk about the people who may have lived in these buildings. Iconographic images that may be related to palaces (and that show individuals) are sometimes painted on pottery vessels, but these usually consist of highly standardized poses and, even though they may show activities taking place near thrones or benches, are generally difficult to correlate with specific buildings. Architectural

The Royal Court of Caracol

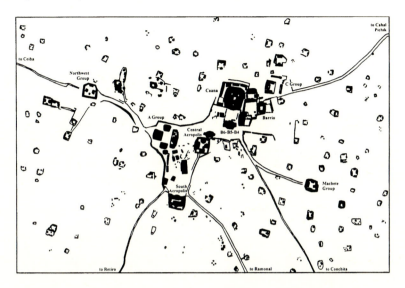

FIGURE 4.1   Map of the central portion of Caracol showing the location of many of the palace compounds discussed within this paper; architectural features, reservoirs, and terraces are suppressed; Figure 4.15 positions this central portion of Caracol relative to the site's inner ring of termini.

decoration often includes facades with images and texts, but—with some potential exceptions in the western part of the Maya world (Schele and Mathews 1998:100, 108)—these features are more likely to contain symbolic information or dynastic history than to directly inform us as to building function.

In spite of the difficulties involved in the archaeological interpretation of Maya courts and their use, we feel that substantial archaeological data exist at Caracol (Figure 4.1) for inferring how various buildings and compounds were used in antiquity. These same data also can inform us about the people who were interacting within these palaces and complexes as part of the royal court. Rather than having to look at general models of court organization elsewhere in the world or constructing a priori models of royal courts, the combined archaeological, iconographic, and epigraphic data from a Maya site like Caracol can effectively provide useful insight into some of its past social constructions.

Caracol's Royal Court

By saying that Caracol had a "royal court," one is implying that Caracol had a sovereign. It is generally agreed and assumed that such sovereigns are the individuals portrayed on the carved stone monuments that grace most Classic Maya sites (e.g., Proskouriakoff 1960). At Caracol, portraits of these sovereigns are presented in essentially public spaces, specifically the central plaza areas. These portraits do not correlate clearly with specific palaces or palace compounds. Although stone portraits of Caracol's past sovereigns are found in the site's epicenter, they do not directly indicate where these individuals lived or held court. Other data classes, however, do imply that the site's sovereigns and royalty were associated with epicentral palaces. In particular, the iconographic decoration that is found in the upper facades of Caracol's epicentral palaces includes stuccoed indications of elite costuming and dress as well as the use of royal symbols and cosmology. And the epigraphic texts that are found on these same buildings record historic information relevant to the royal dynasty, including the names of several individuals who are directly associated with Caracol's emblem glyph and who are also represented in the epigraphic texts that are carved on the stone monuments. Additionally, one of the artifacts found in association with an epicentral palace complex was a carved slate axe, upon which was inscribed the name of a Caracol sovereign. Thus, it can be inferred from the associated epigraphy, iconography, and artifactual remains that the epicentral palace buildings were used by Caracol's sovereign and the royal court.

The site of Caracol has many palace compounds. However, the synchronic and diachronic relationships of these compounds need to be considered in assessing their functions. In addition, a series of questions needs to be addressed. Were palace compounds time successive at any given Maya site, with each sovereign constructing and living in his own building complex, perhaps similar to the situation postulated for Chan-Chan, Peru, by Michael Moseley (1990:13)? Was more than one palace compound used simultaneously by the royal court? Were palace compounds built and utilized by individuals who were not part of the royal court?

Archaeological data from Caracol would appear to indicate that most epicentral palace compounds were used coevally throughout the Late Classic period. All, additionally, have evidence that they were contemporaneously occupied at the time of site abandonment. Whether specific palace compounds were constructed or refurbished in association with a particular ruler is unclear. Most were modified over time and continued in use after their initial construction. There is also substantial evidence at Caracol for the engulfment of previously used palace compounds within the platforms of later palace constructions. In some cases, similar building plans are in evidence, and in other cases building orientation shifted 180 degrees or building types changed. Thus, even though the construction or refurbishing of specific palace compounds can be correlated with specific sovereigns, it cannot be proven at this point.

If one considers the royal court to have been localized in the Caracol epicenter, then a further question arises over the function of outlying, nonepicentral, palace compounds. Such palace compounds, many of which are located in residential groups linked by their own vias or causeways to the plazas of Caracol's causeway termini, may have been representative of social and political factions at the site; however, some of their members were clearly integrated into the royal court (see below). In our estimation, these outlying palace compounds were occupied by both royal (not the sovereign per se, but rather members of his extended family) and nonroyal (secondary elite) family groups, all of whom were ultimately subject to the centrally based royal court and were presumably instrumental in carrying out administrative matters. With more than 115,000 inhabitants (A. Chase and D. Chase 1994a:5), Caracol had more than enough population to sustain the multiple palace compounds that have been recorded.

Caracol's Palaces

Over the course of sixteen consecutive field seasons, a wealth of architectural information has been gathered on the structures that occupy the 177 square kilometers that make up the site of Caracol. Although much of the larger stone-constructed architecture is found in the site epicenter, equivalent stone buildings also occur in the site core and are especially associated with Caracol's causeway termini (at distances from less than 1 kilometer to roughly 8 kilometers from the site epicenter). However, not all stone constructions at Caracol with more than one room are palaces. There are a number of multiroom stone constructions that are not considered to be palaces, largely because they do not appear to have any residential function. Perhaps the most common of these structures are buildings that have features suggesting a predominantly ritual function and that are elsewhere referred to as "temples" (Andrews 1975:39–43). At Caracol, temples are often indicated by rounded substructure "corners" (A. Chase and D. Chase 1994a:7) and by ritual deposits of incense burners (D. Chase 1988).

The Caracol Palace Sample

The Caracol sample of known palaces consists of minimally nine epicentral and twelve core palace compounds. As standing architecture and room configuration are generally not visible at Caracol prior to excavation, the actual number of palaces is likely greater. Each area identified as a palace compound may contain several palaces, and each palace may contain varying numbers of rooms and different building plans.

Different Kinds of Palaces at Caracol. Two very different kinds of palace compounds are in evidence in epicentral Caracol. One kind of palace compound includes pyramidal temples within the courtyard groups. These temple-palace groups appear to overlap in use with east-focused residential groups found throughout Caracol's epicenter and core areas in that they combine domestic architecture with ritual constructions that contain the remains of mortuary activity (A. Chase and D. Chase 1994b). Unlike Palenque, Uaxactun, and most of Tikal (except for the Tikal South Acropolis), where palaces and temples are not integrated into the same architectural courtyards, four areas within the Caracol epicenter effectively demonstrate the conjunction of palace compounds and temples: the Central Acropolis, the Northwest Acropolis, the summit of Caana, and the B Plaza; the South Acropolis may be yet a fifth example. A second kind of epicentral palace compound does not exhibit these tall, squarish, pyramidal temples and also lacks the distinctive burial and ritual component generally found in association with Caracol's residential groups. Two palace compounds in the eastern part of the Caracol epicenter, Barrio and the C Group, are architectural examples of this kind of complex; both had a residential function. It may be that such nonpyramid palace compounds formed a supplementary unit to nonresidential buildings and plazas in the epicenter. For instance, impressive tombs and caches are found in the pyramidal temples that surround the A Plaza, but this architectural unit is neither directly associated with any palace buildings or compounds, nor does it contain evidence of any Late Classic residential debris.

Special Palace Compound Entryways. In two extensively excavated palace compounds at Caracol, a formal architectural plan that permitted entryway to the palace courtyard can be identified (Figure 4.2). Full versions of this specialized entryway occur in association with the Caana summit and with the Barrio group; an abbreviated version occurs in association with the South Acropolis. The standard architectural plan occurs as the central element in tandem-room buildings. A long room with three exterior doorways forms the front room of the building. No architectural features such as benches occur in this first room. A single central doorway permits passage into the "rear" room and then from there to an enclosed courtyard. However, the rear room consists of small inset side benches or small inset side rooms that are entirely raised to form benches. The constricted plan of these rear rooms or benches clearly controlled and reduced traffic into and out of the associated enclosed courtyards and contrasts greatly with the open expansiveness of the front rooms of these architectural units. This formal architectural entry plan is not restricted to Caracol; it is also evident in the great palace Structure A-V at Uaxactun (Smith 1950: Figure 69).

Variability in Caracol Benches. Benches are an especially important and integral part of Caracol's palaces. Virtually all of Caracol's presumed palaces contain benches that may have been used for sleeping (e.g.,

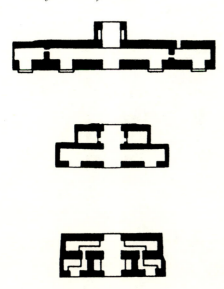

FIGURE 4.2 Restricted entrances in Caracol palaces: (a) upper front building, Caana (see Figure 4.3); (b) western building, Barrio (see Figure 4.9); (c) mid–level front building, Caana (see Figure (4.3); (d) northern building, South Acropolis (see Figure 4.8).

Adams 1974; Harrison 1986) or as throne, display, guard, or reception areas. As Harrison (1986) has noted for Tikal, their number and kind varies substantially. Some palaces have one or two benches, whereas others have much larger numbers. Some benches have armrests (also referred to as "side screens" [Harrison 1986]); some have borders; others are decorated with paint. They vary in form from square to rectangular to U-shaped to L-shaped. Some benches are attached to only one wall; others are attached to three or four walls and may take up most of a room. The central banks of Caracol benches vary in height from 22 to 80 centimeters. They may be located immediately opposite entryways or within enclosed rooms. The kinds of benches present and their location provide architectural clues as to how a given building was utilized. At Caracol, at least two functional variants are apparent. Benches with arms are most likely used in formal throne, reception, or display areas; the area bounded by the arms generally indicates that this kind of bench is ill-suited for sleeping. "Unarmed," or "simple," benches were more likely used for a wider variety of purposes. The largest surface area occurs on L-shaped benches; because such benches are also often tucked into side rooms, it is suggested that this kind of bench lent itself well to sleeping. Other simple benches at Caracol probably served multiple purposes that were context-dependent and ranged from guard areas to reception locales to domestic sleeping areas. In addition to architectural variation,

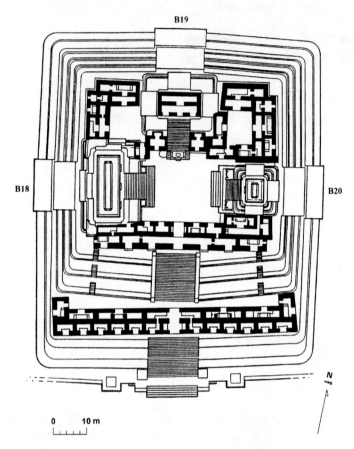

FIGURE 4.3 Plan of Caana, Caracol's most elaborate palace compound.

many of the excavated palace compounds have on-floor artifactual remains as well as special deposits (caches and burials) located within adjacent nonresidential buildings that offer other detailed functional information. Thus, a comprehensive study of Caracol palaces requires a consideration of palace and group configuration, architectural details, and contextual associations.

Caana

Caana forms by far the most elaborate palace compound at Caracol (Figure 4.3). It contains minimally sixty-six contemporaneously used rooms in four palace units integrated with three temples. These rooms contain at least forty-five and most likely forty-eight benches (several rooms are not completely excavated). There is clear stratigraphic evidence for the longevity of this palace compound and for substantial rebuilding efforts.

FIGURE 4.4   Detail of eastern inner room of Caana mid-range palace looking south; lower "bar" equals 1 meter (drawing by J. Ballay, Caracol Archaeological Project).

Midrange Palace. Twenty-four rooms are located in a single building placed halfway up the southern face of Caana. Thirteen rooms span the front of this generally tandem-plan building, each with a central door; two transverse rooms occupy the western and eastern ends of the structure. The only rooms without benches occur in the two lateral rooms of one of the rear three-room suites. The benches facing the front plaza are generally *U*-shaped. Each of the four main rooms in the alley contain benches with arms. Many rooms were decorated with red floors, with red wall stripes, or with red wall blocks that were used to further define bench areas (Figure 4.4).

We can speculate as to how this central building was utilized by Caracol's court. Based on spatial relationships, it probably was paired with Structures B4, B5, and B6 to the south of B Plaza (see Figure 4.6). There is redundancy in bench form in each of the south-facing rooms. The benches are positioned so that an individual would be clearly visible through the door of each of the rooms, and it is suspected that this suite of twelve rooms functioned as part of a public display for the royal court. Only two of the southern rooms on this range building contained on-floor artifactual materials: One contained three vessels—two jars and a large platter; another contained a tripod plate and portions of a *metate*. Although the vessels are likely indicative of either domestic or ritual food serving or consumption, the partial nature of the *metate* and the documentation that *metates* can be used for other than food processing (e.g., Sharer 1977) in combination with a lack of any ash or hearth areas precludes any identification of food preparation in association with this

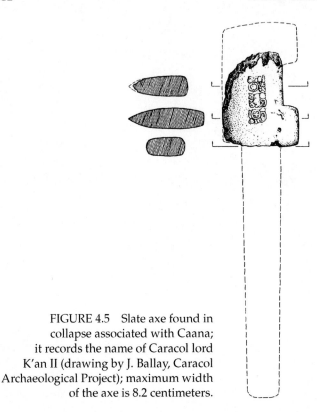

FIGURE 4.5 Slate axe found in collapse associated with Caana; it records the name of Caracol lord K'an II (drawing by J. Ballay, Caracol Archaeological Project); maximum width of the axe is 8.2 centimeters.

building. The central front room had benches to either side, and we suspect that these smaller seats held individuals, or guards, who controlled the flow of traffic going farther into Caana. In contrast to the southern exposure, a good amount of refuse was recovered from the eastern part of the north-facing alley. The suite of rooms adjacent to the eastern alley exhibits the greatest variability in terms of benches and additions to benches. In combination with the trash (ceramic tripod plates, two large ceramic barrels, and a bone tool), this area seems most likely to have seen residential use, although these materials could have been the result of some specific rite or ritual. Each of the four north-facing doors fronting the alley exhibits an "armed" bench. The dimensions and placement of these benches make it unlikely that they were used for sleeping. Instead, they appear to have functioned more like thrones; the walls behind these areas are also decorated to emphasize these architectural features (e.g., Figure 4.4). They thus give the appearance of audience rooms, and we suspect that part of the administrative efforts of Caracol's royal court were carried out from these locales.

Trenching the central axis of the midrange palace revealed no deposits but recovered earlier construction activity and both Late and Terminal

Classic ceramics. On-floor debris is exclusively Terminal Classic in date. A stone axe, hieroglyphically name-tagged with Caracol's ruler K'an II, was also found in collapse within the inner alleyway (Figure 4.5). Glyphic texts from the stucco facade of the building record historical events for a period of time in which there are no known stone monuments (late Late Classic—9.16.0.0.0), indicating that the building was decorated after A.D. 760. The construction of this palace, then, likely took place at the beginning of the Terminal Classic period.

Upper-Range Palace. The frontal palace on Canna's summit functioned to shield the upper main court from public view. Like the midrange palace, it consisted of a tandem row of rooms with direct central passage. Seven doors, leading to five rooms, faced the B Plaza. The central three rooms, accounting for five doors, had no benches and formed a single, interiorly connected suite. Each of the two end rooms had armed benches; neither bench would have formed a comfortable sleeping area, suggesting that these areas functioned as audience/administrative rooms. Artifacts on the floor of the outer western chamber included nonutilitarian items—part of a broken bone artifact inscribed with hieroglyphs and part of a ceramic flute. Also at the western end of the frontal summit palace, a blocked inner door led to an in-filled rear room; excavation demonstrated that this engulfed room had a large L-shaped bench and crude red *ahaws* painted on one of its white plastered walls, indicating that this room may have once served a more combined residential/administrative function.

Besides its central access, Caana's main summit court could also be entered through a door that connected two tandem rooms; the in-filled western end room (completely engulfed by the latest version of Structure B18) also at one point permitted lateral passage into the summit court. To gain central access to Caana one passed first through a broad room with three doors into a small room with side benches and then stepped-down into the summit court. Like the front room of the midrange palace, this rear central room with its side benches presumably was used by individuals or guards who monitored and controlled those who entered Caana's main court.

Main Court. Like the B Plaza, the upper summit plaza was delimited on its northern and southern sides by suites of rooms. One of the southern rooms facing the court held an armed bench and was presumably used as a reception area. Another of the southern rooms faced the court but was tucked into the corner at the base of Structure B18; it had a simple, L-shaped bench and was possibly used as a sleeping area. The other two rooms on the southern side of the summit court were devoid of such obvious architectural features. Little in the way of artifactual material was recovered from the floors of any of these rooms, with the exception of a human long bone.

Separated from this upper court, yet connected to it, was a more private building compound located immediately south of Structure B20. This area was accessed from a raised alleyway immediately south of Structure B20. Entrance was through a presumably roofed hallway into a small, open-air court that had a western stairway to the roof of the upper frontal summit palace. Two suites of rooms faced this private courtyard. The northern suite consisted of three rooms with an armed central bench and with a substantially elevated bench in the eastern room; the floors and central bench were painted entirely red. An inset niche was set behind the central bench, and a window opened into the complex's accessway from the eastern room. A two-room building suite occupied the eastern side of this private court; most of this building had collapsed off the side of Caana. Artifactual materials associated with the red-room suite included a complete spiked and pedestaled incense burner with its lid as well as a deep bowl with an effigy-lid. Deep penetration in multiple places revealed no special deposits but did find a buried palace directly beneath the current one. This earlier palace had its eastern roof facade intact; this facade was elaborately decorated and associated with a stucco hieroglyphic text describing important Late Classic Caracol events and names. The dates included in this text indicate that the building was engulfed within a raised Caana summit sometime after A.D. 680.

On the northern side of the summit plaza, to either side of the central stairway for Structure B19, a set of tandem rooms was set into the lower terrace of the temple. A rear bench had been ripped out of the western rear room set. An oval, benchlike dais—stuccoed with a mat fringe and set against an oval backing painted with jaguar spots—was situated at plaza level to the west of the central stair and in front of the inset rooms.

In addition to the architectural details already described above, the summit plaza was fronted by three temples to the west, north, and east (Structures B18, B19, and B20), and the entrances to two additional palace compounds that were situated on the northwestern and northeastern corners of Caana's summit. Surface indications show that the western temple, Structure B18, supported a tandem-room building with three frontal doors. It had a wide frontal stair with two side masks. An enormous amount of stucco was associated with the building. In addition to a mat design on the building's northern substructure, there were several fallen life-size and larger human figures, the largest of which (three times life-size) is female.

Currently rising some 43.5 meters above the B Plaza, Structure B19 is the tallest temple at Caana and at Caracol. It supported a tandem-room building with one inner and three outer doors. Latest remains include in situ Terminal Classic ceramics and an unsealed cache of four vessels. The partial and unarticulated skeletal remains of at least two children were also found on the building floor. At the base of Structure B19, and associated with Altar 17, was a deposit of two incense burners, a bowl, a human skullcap, and several hundred chert drills. The building was penetrated to a depth of over 20 meters below the building summit and revealed a series of caches, a simple burial, and an elaborate, presumably royal, tomb dating to A.D. 634 (associated with an earlier version of Structure B19; see A. Chase and D. Chase 1987a).

The summit of the eastern temple, Structure B20, was approached by a frontal stair flanked by balustrades and stuccoed masks. An earlier version of Structure B20 exhibited a tandem-room plan and a rear bench. It had been painted black and contained graffiti in its front room showing a person being carried in a litter or palanquin (Figure 4.12). A central basal mask was set into the stair of this earlier building, and a body had been left in the hollow mouth of this mask when it was covered over by later construction. Four elaborate tombs and one crypt were recovered in association with various construction episodes for Structure B20. Two painted dates are known from these tombs: A.D. 537 and A.D. 576.

Northeastern Court. The northeastern palace quadrangle was completely excavated. It attached directly to the eastern side of Structure B19, but a narrow alleyway ran between this compound and Structure B20. Formal access to the enclosed plaza formed by this quadrangular palace was through a room containing an *L*-shaped bench that attached to the southeastern corner of Structure B19. Two-room suites defined the east, west, and south sides of this enclosed plaza; a three-room suite bounded the northern part of this court. At least one room in each suite had a bench (five out of nine rooms). Overall, benches occur in nine of thirteen rooms. No buildings were penetrated by excavation. However, there were extensive on-floor remains. Large storage vessels were found in three rooms. Three almost complete *metates*, several *manos*, animal bone, and part of an effigy pedestal drum were found in the plaza. No cooking areas or cooking vessels were encountered anywhere in the northeastern court. The two-room suite that abutted Structure B19 had been sealed in antiquity and contained twelve relatively complete tripod plates, four incised deep bowls, and one large storage jar. A small child, five or six years old, was found unburied in the inner doorway of the southern suite of rooms.

The combination of armed and *L*-shaped benches in the rooms around the northeastern courtyard would indicate that residential and administrative space was combined. The *L*-shaped bench in the western room suite was long and spacious. In the northern suite, an *L*-shaped bench dominated the rear room. In the southern suite, a central bench was set opposite the entranceway, and a large *L*-shaped bench occupied most of the space in the inner room. On the eastern side of this courtyard, a central armed bench occupied the inner room of the two-room suite.

Two exteriorly facing rooms, not connected to the inner plaza, were also set within the eastern building. These rooms were probably approached by means of the alley between the northeastern court and Structure B20. The southernmost eastern room contained an armed bench, which would have held a seated figure of the Caracol court. The northern side door led to a two-room suite, the inner room of which contained a U-shaped bench. In our estimation, and in contrast to the rooms set about the more private courtyard, both of these exteriorly facing rooms were nonresidential.

Northwestern Court. The northwestern quad was entered through a single room with an armed bench. This room had been inserted into an earlier palace building that had been engulfed by the latest construction efforts directed at Structure B18. In this latest manifestation, it is likely that an individual positioned in this locale closely monitored (presided over) access to the private northwestern court. Hieroglyphic cartouches were associated with this entrance. Unlike the northeastern court, there were no multiple-room suites on the southern or eastern sides of this court. The interior plaza was defined to the south and east by Structures B18 and B19. Structure B18's substructure exhibited a huge stuccoed mat design.

The entire northwestern palace compound was not excavated. Only the front rooms of the northern and western buildings were completely cleared. Interior corners for other rooms were visible, however, on the surface. The buildings in this courtyard exhibited finer construction technique than was found in the northeastern summit court. The northern building was also entirely painted red on its interior floor. Compared with other palace areas, there was little on-floor debris. If one were to predict where the royal sovereign was housed, however, the seclusion, spatial arrangement, and architectural detail would suggest this court.

Caana Summary. Overall, a wealth of archaeological information is known about the Caana palace compounds. Food-serving vessels and large storage containers are found in various palace rooms, but there is no indication that cooking took place within any of the Caana palace compounds. The combined architectural plans, stucco texts, in-situ artifactual remains, and tombs all suggest that Caana was the residential compound for the sovereign and played a major role in the royal court.

Structures B4, B5, and B6

Structures B4, B5, and B6 together form a palace-temple compound (Figure 4.6) that is directly opposite Caana and that commands the southern side of the B Plaza. Structures B4 and B6, both "palaces," were initially added to the sides of Structure B5, a temple, in the Early Classic period

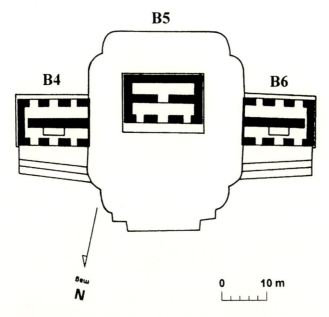

FIGURE 4.6 Plan of Structures B4, B5, and B6 palace compound.

and underwent extensive modifications during the Late Classic period. Three doors are set into both the front and rear facades of Structures B4 and B6. Each of these buildings contains two tandem rooms, connected interiorly by a single lateral door. Both buildings also have a simple bench centrally located in the front rooms.

In addition, both structures had substantial in situ floor refuse and burning. Both buildings were associated with high-status trash that included jadeite (a partial earflare in Structure B4) and shell jewelry and Terminal Classic fineware vessels; both also contained smashed domestic pottery in their rear rooms and substantial deposits of animal bone throughout their loci (D. Chase and A. Chase 2000); both were also associated with more chert points (mostly atlatl) than were normally recovered in other palace contexts (ten atlatl points for Structure B6 and six for Structure B4). Structure B6 also had a mace head in its southern (rear) room. Trenching of Structure B6 in two places revealed no special deposits but did recover portions of an earlier underlying palace construction, presumably of Early Classic date.

Structure B5 rests on a substructure with rounded corners and is associated with two summit burials as well as one dating to the Terminal Classic period that was placed within the axial stairway. It is considered to be a temple. No on-floor refuse was recovered from the summit building.

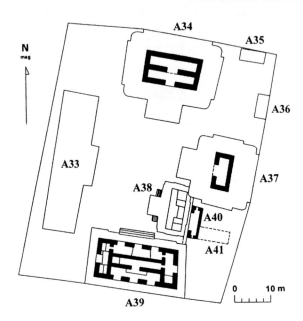

FIGURE 4.7 Plan of Central Acropolis (after D. Chase and A. Chase 1996:Figure 2).

At least in their latest use, Structures B4, B5, and B6 served as an elite residential compound, although the simple tandem plan and presence of weapons may suggest a somewhat variant, perhaps military, function. Evidence exists for food serving, but not food cooking. The in situ burning appears to be coincident with the final abandonment of the compound. Buildings of similar form have been designated as "temporary residences" at Tikal (Harrison 1986:55).

Central Acropolis

Two palace buildings occur in the Central Acropolis (Figure 4.7). They are located on the southern and western sides of this plaza group. Only the southern palace has been excavated. It has five rooms and evidence of extensive modification. Three tandem rooms are bounded by two transverse end rooms. Each outer tandem room has three doors. The central room is connected only to the southern and eastern rooms. Simple benches occur in the northern and the two lateral rooms; evidence of a ripped-out bench was found in the western end of the central room. Axial excavation of this southern palace revealed no special deposits but did uncover an earlier version of this palace. On-floor debris inside the structure and to its north in an alleyway produced Terminal Classic finewares (including Sacaba Modeled-Carved), large storage jars, a three-pronged pedestal *incensario*, animal bone, and several smaller artifacts.

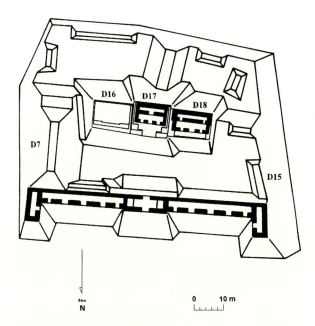

FIGURE 4.8 Plan of South Acropolis.

Other excavations into the Central Acropolis demonstrate that the northern building, Structure A34, was a temple. This building housed two tombs, one at its summit and one at its base. The basal one was certainly royal (D. Chase and A. Chase 1996). Both eastern buildings also housed tombs. Excavations into Structure A37 yielded one early Late Classic tomb, one burial, and two caches—indicating the edifice's function as a mortuary shrine. Investigation of Structure A38 similarly produced one tomb, one burial, and one cache—proving the building to be a shrine that was temporally later than Structure A37.

Excavation data demonstrate that the Central Acropolis was a royal residential compound that was in use from the beginning to the end of the Late Classic period. Given the large size of Caracol, the site's royal family was probably quite large and certainly occupied several palace compounds simultaneously. A similar, albeit factionalized, use of multiple royal residential compounds has been demonstrated for Tikal (Haviland 1981; Laporte and Fialko 1990).

South Acropolis

Excavation has shown that the South Acropolis (Figure 4.8) has been extensively modified over time. Based on its spatial layout and the single-room depth on its northern range building, it is suspected that much of this palace compound may have been largely nonresidential and functioned only within specific settings related to the royal court. However, some of the unexcavated buildings within the compound will certainly prove to be residential upon investigation, and the three recovered tombs from the South Acropolis were all likely royal, so this complex is considered to be part of Caracol's royal court.

In terms of compound layout, a long single-room range building faced the A Group reservoir. The very identifiable central unit of this range building was excavated and produced a single room through which all traffic into the South Acropolis must have passed. Like the central passage areas in the frontal Caana range palaces, the central elevated unit of the South Acropolis range building exhibits two lateral benches, and this architectural unit presumably served a similar guard function; unlike the small Caana benches, each of the South Acropolis lateral benches is quite expansive and could have accommodated multiple individuals. No in situ refuse was recovered on the floors of this central building, but the cremated remains of several individuals were placed exteriorly to the northwestern corner of the central unit. Axial penetration of the range structure revealed an earlier building platform that faced south, the opposite direction of the current range building.

A series of three distinct stone buildings occupies the central east-west platform in the interior court of the South Acropolis. Each of these buildings has produced a high-status tomb (Anderson 1958, 1959; A. Chase 1994:167–169). Based on structure plans and building features, it is doubtful that any of these central buildings served a residential function. Little in situ trash was found with any of these buildings; the only object of any note was a Terminal Classic pottery tripod cylindrical vase recovered in the alleyway between Structures D17 and D18. None of the other buildings in the rest of the South Acropolis was excavated.

Barrio

Extensive stripping excavations were undertaken in the Barrio palace compound (Figure 4.9), resulting in the definition of three separate palaces and a raised northern substructure with rounded corners. The southern building was entirely excavated, revealing eight rooms. A central four-room suite was laid out in a *T* shape. Its front room, which had no benches and had its floors painted entirely red, permitted access to a raised tandem room; its floors were also painted entirely red. This rear tandem room had a simple bench centrally situated on its rear wall and lateral access to benched side rooms. The other four rooms in the southern palace were self-contained units, each with its own exterior door and bench (both transverse rooms had *L*-shaped benches). A deep axial trench revealed no special deposits. Only one of the rooms in Barrio's

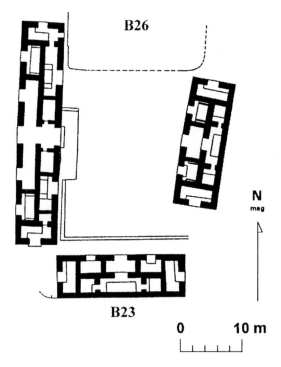

FIGURE 4.9 Plan of Barrio palace compound.

southern palace was associated with in situ debris; the western transverse room had been extensively burned and had in situ shell beads and other refuse on its floor.

Barrio's eastern palace is almost a mirror image of the southern building. Six of its eight rooms were excavated, and the form of the remaining rooms can be easily inferred. Like the southern palace, the eastern palace also had four single rooms with exterior access and benches as well as a central T-shaped four-room suite. The benches in the eastern building are more elaborate than those in the south, with the two that directly face the interior plaza both exhibiting arms. In situ trash, which included a partial jadeite pendent, was found on the plaza floor in front of the eastern palace. All three rooms facing the interior court were axially trenched; no special deposits were recovered.

The western building differs from both the southern and eastern palaces. It shows extensive interior and exterior modifications with at least four blocked doorways, suggesting great variation in its use over time. Approximately 65 percent of this building was excavated. Six of its estimated ten rooms were exposed. Like the other two palaces, there is a central four-room suite; however, unlike the other two palaces, the three conjoined rooms (with benches in the lateral rooms) face the private courtyard with a single doorway connecting the central room to the interior court; the rear western tandem room has a greater total length than the three linear front rooms combined, as well as three doorways to the plaza west of Barrio. Thus, direct passage was permitted through this palace from the interior Barrio plaza to the western plaza. However, the interior central door of this four-room suite was ultimately blocked, preventing access through the building and effectively dividing the function of this western palace between two different plazas. Excavated single rooms that face both the interior and exterior plazas exhibit armed "display," or "reception," benches, thus suggesting a nonresidential function for these quarters. One of these interior rooms contained the remains of a large drum on its floor. An excavated transverse room on the southern end of this palace has an L-shaped bench. Red and green stucco painting and modeled stucco medallions were recovered in structure collapse. A deep axial trench revealed no special deposits. An east-facing platform was added to the latest building version in the interior plaza. Material associated with the protruding platform included Terminal Classic finewares and debris that indicates that manufacturing was undertaken on *Oliva* shell.

Barrio's northern building may have been a low nonpyramidal temple, based on both its elevation and its rounded substructure corners. Basal excavations uncovered a simple burial with a stingray spine in the fill beneath its stair.

Excavation data, therefore, indicate that Barrio was an elaborate Late Classic to Terminal Classic residential compound that was integrated with formal display and reception areas. However, these data vary from the general residential plaza group pattern at Caracol in that there was no eastern mausoleum and no eastern interments. The existence of coeval palace compounds within the Caracol epicenter indicates how large the royal court must have been at the site, as well as perhaps some functional differences with the different compounds. The lack of eastern "family" temples or mausoleums at Barrio suggests that the inhabitants, even though the group was clearly residential, differed from those who occupied Caana and the Central Acropolis in that none of their honored dead were placed within the Barrio compound.

C Group

The C Group contains a U-shaped complex of palaces containing tandem and transverse rooms (Figure 4.10). Excavations have been undertaken both in the western (central) and southern palace buildings of this compound. These excavations (as well as surface mapping) suggest that the northern and southern C Group palaces each consisted of six rooms; in the excavated sample, no passage was permitted between the tandem rooms. Unlike the other palaces at Caracol, no bench occurs in the exca-

The Royal Court of Caracol

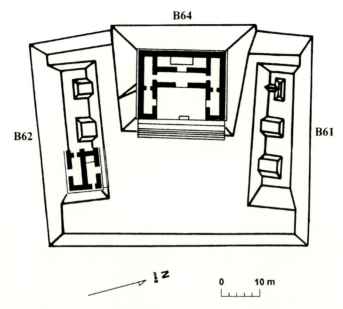

FIGURE 4.10   Hypothetical plan of C Group palace compound.

vated rear room of the southern palace. A low flat bench, however, was set across the western side of the front room.

Excavations were undertaken in the central elevated western building in the C Group. This structure forms a smaller U-shaped unit within the larger U-shaped complex. An axial east-west trench was placed through the central doors of the central tandem rooms of this palace, encountering a bench in the rear room. None of the other rooms was investigated; earlier interior floors for the building were also not penetrated, even though the axial trench was dug deep into the courtyard plaza. This central C Group palace occupied its own elevated plaza area. The U-shaped central palace defines three of the sides of this raised court with a small altar or shrine occurring on the eastern side. Excavation within this small eastern construction recovered two Terminal Classic burials. An extension of the axial trench to this shrine recovered a cache beneath the plaza floor sealed within an earlier construction. An extensive trash deposit recovered on the floor of the elevated courtyard associated with this central palace contained fineware and domestic ceramics, animal bone, lithics, and carved bone pins. Parts of an elaborate stucco facade from the palace building, which had fallen into the central court, were also recovered. It contained a partially reconstructible hieroglyphic text referring to the birth of a previously unknown Caracol lord. The combined textual and artifactual remains suggest that this palace compound was used by high-status occupants—possibly members of the ruling family—until its abandonment around A.D. 890 (see also A. Chase and D. Chase 2001).

Other Caracol Palaces

Other largely unexcavated palace areas are located throughout the site. Some of these are located in the epicenter (Northeast Acropolis, Northwest Acropolis) and may have been directly associated with the royal court. At least thirteen other palaces or palace compounds have been identified as a result of surface mapping. Most are concentrated at or in the vicinity of causeway termini (Pajaro, Royal, Tulakatuhebe, Retiro, Ceiba, Sage, Dos Tumbas, Cohune, and Machete). In some cases members of the extended royal family may have resided in these outlying palace compounds; this may be directly indicated by the painted tomb chambers that are known from Machete (A. Chase and D. Chase 1987a:43), Royal (A. Chase and D. Chase 1987a:46), and Retiro (D. Chase and A. Chase 1996). These outlying palaces, however, were not homes to the sovereigns of Caracol but probably housed the wealthy and elite personages (both nonroyal and members of the extended royal family) who formed a part of Caracol's extended administrative bureaucracy. Thus, it is conceivable that they could be considered part of the court, regardless of their status and distance from the epicenter. Multiroom stone buildings, probably small palaces, are also found scattered throughout the settlement that makes up Caracol's residential core (Northwest Group, South Group, Monterey 2); even though located in nonfocal parts of Caracol, such buildings likely housed wealthy, possibly even elite, personages. However, we suspect that the use and construction of such palace buildings were independent of any central administrative or court function.

The People in Caracol's Royal Court

Although it may never be possible to fully reconstruct the vibrant actions and intrigue of ancient Maya court life, the people in Caracol's royal court can be identified and described through iconographic, epigraphic, and archaeological data. However, these data are not always simple to interpret. For example, although they can identify individuals, epigraphic statements and iconographic portrayals serve specific purposes that must be considered. History can be rewritten. Individuals can be made to appear more important than they really were; titles and offices can accrue, perhaps not mirroring reality. Iconography can be similarly employed to create alternative meanings and realities, projecting what one hopes a given situation or cosmic setting will be, rather than reflecting what it actually is. Other archaeological remains are not completely unambiguous. Thus, epigraphy and archaeology are data classes that should be reviewed carefully—and conjunctively—in relation to Maya courts.

FIGURE 4.11 Caracol Ballcourt Marker 3; the "Second Sul" glyph is located at position D5 (drawing by N. Grube, Caracol Archaeological Project); monument averages 51.2 centimeters in width.

History and Epigraphy in Caracol's Royal Court

The hieroglyphic texts at Caracol, whether from stone monuments or stucco facades, provide information on Caracol's history and sovereigns but only limited information on other members of the site's royal court. Epigraphic texts indicate that Caracol had a sequence of at least twenty-eight sovereigns, beginning with the initial founding of the dynasty in 8.14.13.10.4 or A.D. 331 (Chase, Grube, and Chase 1991). The relationships between sovereigns is sometimes explicit in the hieroglyphic texts, as in the parentage statements made by the two sons of Lord Yahaw Te. In other cases, succession is less clear, and in some cases, such as after Lord Hok Pol in the Late Classic period, direct succession lines may have been broken. Caracol's hieroglyphic texts include the usual information on birth, accession, warfare, and captives found at most other Classic period sites. However, there are also indications of individuals besides the sovereigns. For instance, Caracol Ballcourt Marker 3 contains reference to a "Second Sul" (Figure 4.11:D5), presumably a titled member of the royal court (Chase, Grube, and Chase 1991:7). And Caracol Altar 23 names an individual who is associated with the Caracol Glyph but who is surely not the sovereign;

again, presumably this person was a member of the royal court. Although limited, these data suggest that members of the royal court other than the sovereign may have had formal titles or held named offices. Based on the iconographic and dietary data (discussed below), it would appear that they also could live in an area outside of the Caracol epicenter.

Iconography and the Royal Court at Caracol

Iconography provides some additional information on the Caracol royal court. The site's stone monuments predominantly portray only one or two individuals that are usually some combination of sovereigns, captives, or dwarves. Although the carved stone monuments are expectedly not replete with court scenes, their locations and associations suggest that Caracol's royal court included individuals who lived outside the site epicenter. In the Terminal Classic period, this is specifically seen in the positioning of carved stone monuments containing the Caracol emblem in the Plaza of the Two Stelae (Chase, Grube, and Chase 1991), 1 kilometer distant from the epicenter, and presumably in the Machete Group, 500 meters distant from the epicenter. Another carved monument is located in the Sage Group, which is attached to the Puchituk terminus and is more than 3 kilometers distant from the epicenter.

Iconography from stucco facades is replete with images of male and female individuals, presumably ancestors or past sovereigns in combination with representations of deities. The iconographic images in stucco facades, however, serve more to set the sovereign's (or other individual's) place in the universe than to define the activities of the royal court. Iconographic scenes portrayed in other nonmodeled mediums, however, may provide at least some insight into court activities.

Structure B20, the eastern temple at the summit of Caana, was rebuilt several times. The blackened stucco interior wall of the front room of Structure B20–2nd, just south of its door jamb, was incised with graffiti that formed an elaborate scene (Figure 4.12). This graffiti depicts what may have been a Late Classic event that occurred in the plaza associated with Caana's summit. Retainers support a litter that contains what surely must have been a royal individual based on the elaborate headdress iconography. To the front of the palanquin stands a figure with his arms bound behind his back. Facing the litter and prisoner are three individuals, whose headgear seemingly denotes differences in status. It is suspected that this scene reflects formal negotiations between the individual in the palanquin and the three other individuals over the future of the prisoner—an activity that could have appropriately occurred in the royal court at the summit of Caana.

A collapsed crypt uncovered within the frontal stair of Structure B5, the central building of the palace compound that brackets the southern

FIGURE 4.12 Graffiti incised in Structure B20–2nd (from A. Chase and D. Chase 1987b:20); human figure to the left is 13 centimeters in height.

side of the B Plaza, provides further iconographic information. This interment, which dates to the Terminal Classic period, contained the remains of a single individual and three pottery vessels. The diet of this individual, as indicated by isotopic analysis, matches that of others who constituted part of the royal court (see below); his placement within a formal burial in the central temple unit of a palace compound also suggests court membership. Ronald L. Bishop's (personal communication, 1998) neutron activation study of Caracol pottery indicates that the elaborately painted Joyac cream polychrome cylinder (A. Chase 1994:177) included with this individual was locally made. The cylinder shows a court scene that likely was representative of court activities at Caracol (Figure 4.13).

The scene on this vase portrays six individuals and takes place within and at the doorway of a room with a bench. The primary individual is seated on the bench and holds a broad, perhaps feather, fan. Five other individuals face him, two kneeling and three standing; all have their arms crossed over their chests. The three standing individuals all wear the same kind of frontally elongated headdress, probably indicating their similar (lower) rank. Identical headgear is worn by secondary figures on a miniature wall panel from Palenque Temple 21 (Stuart 1998:Figure 31); similar forward-swept (or bound) hair occurs on secondary figures on Lintel 2 from Tikal Temple 3 (Jones and Satterthwaite 1982:Figure 72) and from Panels C and D from X'telhu in the northern lowlands (Robertson 1986: figs. 8 and 11). Both individuals who are kneeling on the vase have different headgear and directly face the individual on the bench, one within and one outside the room. The kneeling individual outside the

FIGURE 4.13   Court scene recorded on a vessel from an interment recovered within the Structure B5 stair fill; height of the vase is 25.6 centimeters.

room has headgear similar to the individual on the bench. Although the scene is one of supplication and consultation, it is suspected that the kneeling individuals are of higher rank than those individuals with the frontally elongated headgear, who are probably courtiers of the primary figure. Given its architectural location, the scene indicates the formal use of palace buildings and benches and also shows the interaction of individuals of different rank within the court.

Archaeology and the People of Caracol's Royal Court

Archaeological data permit special insight into the people of Caracol's royal court. Perhaps the most revealing information derives from burials that are sited within palace compounds and from stable isotope analysis of human bone that demonstrates the existence of different diets. At Caracol, burials that occur within palace compounds are associated with temples rather than with the palaces themselves. And the burials that are associated with these epicentral temples may be further broken down into tomb and nontomb interments. Tombs are usually situated directly in the core of a given temple. In the epicenter, these chambers tend to be quite large, in some cases encompassing over 20 square meters of space (A. Chase 1992:38). In general the epicentral tombs hold from one to five individuals of both sexes, the majority of which are adults between the ages of twenty-five and forty-five at the time of their death (see D. Chase 1994). These individuals are sometimes accompanied by large numbers of ceramic vessels and a wide variety of shell, bone, and stone artifacts, as well as unique faunal material that includes, in some cases, complete birds and jaguar paws (see D. Chase 1998).

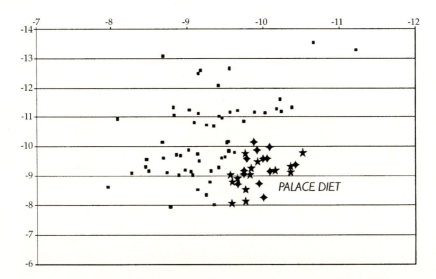

FIGURE 4.14 Caracol stable isotope data showing "palace diet." Higher levels of 15N Collagen indicates the consumption of more protein. Lower levels of 13C Collagen indicates higher levels of maize consumption. "★" indicate individuals in epicentral tombs, including those associated with palace compounds. "◆" indicate individuals with a "palace diet" who are not buried in palace compounds. "■" indicate other Caracol burials that were sampled.

It is possible to identify royal tombs at Caracol (A. Chase 1992, 1994; D. Chase 1994; A. Chase and D. Chase 1996b). These chambers contain hieroglyphic texts on their walls or capstones. In one case, the individual's name precedes a Caracol emblem; in another, the text indicates that the Caracol ruler witnessed the tomb consecration. Royal tombs are among the largest at the site, and with one exception (Machete's Structure L3) all of these royal tombs are located within epicentral constructions. Most of these tombs are located within epicentral palace compounds. Thus, we can easily identify at least some of the royal members of Caracol's court.

Stable isotope analysis of the skeletal remains of individuals buried within both painted and nonpainted Classic period tombs located in Caracol's epicentral palace compounds confirms that these individuals shared a similar diet, which remained relatively consistent over time (Figure 4.14). This so-called palace diet was uniformly higher both in protein and in maize than any diet consumed by other segments of Caracol's population. A number of simple, nontomb epicentral burials, particularly those located within the fill of stairway additions or placed in the plaza to the front of a given temple, have been identified as sacrifices. They include children and adults, often in association with perforators or obsidian eccentrics. Stable isotope analysis of the diet of these individuals indicates that they did not share in the palace diet; these people consumed lower levels of both protein and maize (A. Chase et al. 2001; D. Chase et al. 1998). Thus, location, associated artifacts, and dietary information indicates that minimally some (if not all) of these nontomb burials were placed within private palace compounds as part of ritual or sacrificial practices.

It is also interesting to note certain other dietary patterns that can be found in the stable isotope evidence of Caracol's ancient Classic period inhabitants. Most of the individuals associated with Caracol's causeway termini and their associated residential groups did not share in the same diet as the royal court, as they appear to have eaten significantly more maize but less protein. However, stable isotope analysis indicates that the occasional individual from these locales manifests the same diet as that seen in the royal court, confirming linkages that would have been inferred based on the archaeological data alone. Structure L3 produced the only tomb with a painted capstone that has thus far been found outside of the site epicenter. Stable isotope analysis confirms that the individual in this chamber had the same general diet as the individuals that came from other royal tombs. Thus, the high status accorded to this tomb based on archaeological data is confirmed by stable isotope analysis.

Residential groups adjacent to Caracol's epicenter exhibit some of the worst dietary regimens known at the site and are especially different from the diet found in the epicentral palaces and the epicenter in general (A. Chase et al. 2001; D. Chase et al. 1998). However, specific individuals within the clearly nonroyal residential groups that ring the epicenter exhibit anomalous diets compared to the other individuals interred within their residential groups. Interestingly, these seemingly anomalous diets—usually confined to a single individual per group—match the values for the epicentral palace diet. Given the proximity of these groups to the epicenter or to direct causeway linkage with the epicenter, we believe that these individuals provided services that made them a functional part of the royal court. They would not have maintained a permanent residence or burial place in the epicentral palace groups; rather, they likely traveled from their outlying residential complexes to the epicentral palaces on a regular basis. They did not eat the majority of their meals in their own residential units but apparently were fed from the same kitchens that fed the Caracol royalty. Thus, by looking at stable isotope analysis relating to diet, we are able to see individuals who were seemingly part of the royal court and to examine the spatial distribution of its attendants and lesser members (Figure 4.15).

Economics, Administration, and Infrastructure

The archaeological data also permit discussion of the functions of palaces and the relationships between palaces and other areas and units of the

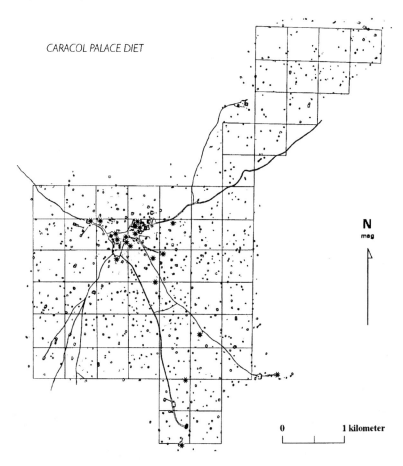

FIGURE 4.15 Spatial distribution of Caracol interments evincing the epicentral "palace diet" (those individuals shown by "★" and "◆" on Figure 4.14); the outer ring of Caracol termini is not shown on this map.

site. These data reflect day-to-day activities, economies, administration, and infrastructure.

Extensive on-floor remains have been recovered from the latest use of Caracol's palaces (A. Chase and D. Chase 2001; D. Chase and A. Chase 2000). As indicated previously, these remains may be taken to indicate that the palaces, and by extension their respective plazas, had a domestic component. Well-made ceramic vessels used for serving food and cruder storage vessels are found in various palace rooms. Other items that would have been useful in food preparation, such as complete or almost complete *manos* and *metates* as well as grater bowls, have also been recovered in limited numbers. However, thus far no hearths or burned cooking vessels have been recovered in association with Caracol's excavated palaces, suggesting that the majority of food preparation and cooking likely took place in areas outside the formal stone palaces.

Other tools—specifically awls, needles, and antler tines—have also been recovered from the floors of Caracol's palaces. These strongly suggest that specialized domestic activities were taking place within these buildings. Although these kinds of bone artifacts are found in outlying burials, they generally are not recovered from nonpalace floor contexts. With the exception of *Oliva* shell being worked in the Barrio group (Cobos, personal communication, 1999), manufacturing debris related to shell, lithics, or other items does not occur in association with Caracol's palace floors or plazas. However, such debris is sometimes secreted in specialized contexts within palace compounds (particularly in association with temples), such as in caches or above tombs (e.g., Moholy-Nagy 1997).

In contrast, residential *plazuela* groups outside the Caracol epicenter contain far more evidence of manufacturing activities, especially in terms of lithic and shell debris (e.g., A. Chase and D. Chase 1994a; Cobos 1994; Pope 1994). These artifactual residues clearly indicate that production at Caracol was household-based. Adjacent core households focused on the manufacture of different products. Conch shell was worked in three known households, all located more than 1 kilometer distant from the epicenter in different parts of the site. *Spondylus* shell was worked in a residential group more than 1 kilometer distant from the site epicenter. Yet another residential group, 4 kilometers from the epicenter, focused intensively on lithic production; the resultant debris was visible on the plaza surface of this group. A dozen other residential groups, all widely separated from one another and located anywhere from 1 to 4 kilometers distant from the Caracol epicenter, exhibited large numbers of lithic chips and drills, presumably indicative of extensive woodworking (Pope 1994).

In contrast to the household-based production of a wide variety of products, distribution appears to have been more centrally controlled in Caracol's administered economy (A. Chase 1998). Caracol's extensive causeway system was likely utilized to administer and integrate its people and resources. As Caracol's most impressive palaces occur in the epicenter, which is also the central hub for all of the site's roads, as well as in association with high-status residential groups, which are attached to the site's causeway termini, it can be inferred that the individuals who occupied and used these buildings and compounds were instrumental to the functioning of the overall urban center. Thus, just as Caracol's economic, sociopolitical, and religious organizations were integrated via the site's extensive causeway system, so, too, were Caracol's many palaces and, by extension, the royal court.

Conclusion

The Caracol investigations provide information on the physical form of a royal Maya court, on the people that were part of that court, and on some of the activities that took place there. For these reasons, the Late Classic to Terminal Classic palaces at Caracol are of interest on several levels, ranging from definitional to interpretative. The palaces have been identified as a functional unit based on a conjunction of architectural features with on-floor deposits of trash. Most—if not all—of the defined palaces contain more than two rooms, associated benches, and a configuration that does not allow a simple interior access into all of the rooms in the building or compound. Armed benches, thought to have been used for nondomestic purposes, often but not always face toward open plazas. The smallest identified Caracol palace compound consists of four rooms; the largest contains sixty-six or more. More usual is the fact there are five to ten rooms per palace. Epicentral palaces generally contain two or more palace buildings within a single compound.

There are generally no caches or burials within the physical palace buildings at Caracol, although special deposits may be found in temples or shrines located within the palace compound. The latest refuse on palace floors is generally distinctive from debris found in the vast majority of residential groups that do not include palaces (A. Chase and D. Chase 2001). These same on-floor items indicate continued access to trade items by Caracol's final elite.

There are a large number of palaces at Caracol. They cluster in the epicenter and causeway termini but may also be located at some distance from major architectural nodes and causeways within the core settlement. We suspect that, were Caracol completely mapped (and excavated), approximately 1 percent of all groups (estimated at ninety groups) would be classified as having palaces. Not all palaces at Caracol were royal, although all were likely elite. Thus, palaces may be a more discriminating status indicator than features such as tombs, which are present in over 60 percent of Caracol's residential groups. Finally, the large number of palaces at Caracol undoubtedly reflects the site's Late Classic size and prosperity.

The evidence for the people utilizing palaces at Caracol comes from a variety of data classes. Significantly, this combined information indicates that there was a distinctive palace diet. Members of the court included high-status individuals, presumably maintaining residence in a palace, as well as lower-status individuals (i.e., nonroyals), who presumably performed services in the court but had their burial rites within their outlying residential groups. For the most part, such secondary members of the court resided within residential groups ringing the epicenter. The sovereign's immediate royal family does not appear to have moved to outlying causeway termini. Termini residences were likely occupied by lesser nobility (such as Tulakatuhebe individuals) or alternative elite factions, all of whom were integrated into the epicentrally based royal court. Some of these people were likely attendant in the epicentral court (based on consumption of a palace diet) but were interred in their own outlying palace compounds. Nonkin, nonroyal burials within the court appear to represent sacrificial victims.

Activities taking place within the Caracol palaces probably included the production of a limited number of items needed for or related to the court. However, only minimal evidence of anything related to food preparation has been recovered within the site's palace compounds, and it is suspected that food was carried to these palace groups from one or more central kitchens. Within and around palaces there is also no evidence of manufacturing at the scale that is present within many of the site's residential groups. The fact that the palaces had a domestic component, however, is apparent in the on-floor debris, especially the presence of serving vessels. The fact that they were also used for administrative purposes is suggested both in overall architectural design and in iconographic details.

The administrative system housed in the royal court at Caracol was a functional entity, a fact that is seen especially in the growth and prosperity of Caracol during the Late Classic period. It has been suggested that this success was due in some part to a sitewide focus on shared identity (D. Chase 1998; A. Chase and D. Chase 1994b, 1996b), effective systems for communication and transportation (A. Chase 1998; A. Chase and D. Chase 1996a, 1996c), and an intensive agricultural system based on terrace farming (A. Chase and D. Chase 1987a, 1998). The strategy of shared identity is apparent not only from the distribution of items such as tombs at Caracol but also from the site's relatively widespread palaces and in the shared similarity of items found on palace floors. Thus, investigations at Caracol provide substantial insights into the relationships among the royal court and the political, social, and economic activities of one key political unit within the Late Classic Maya landscape.

References

Adams, Richard E.W. 1974. "A Trial Estimation of Classic Maya Palace Populations at Uaxactun." In Norman Hammond, ed., *Mesoamerican Archaeology: New Approaches*, pp. 285–296. Austin: University of Texas Press.

Anderson, A. Hamilton. 1958. "Recent Discoveries at Caracol Site, British Honduras." *Proceedings of the 32nd International Congress of Americanists*, pp. 494–499, Copenhagen, Denmark.

———. 1959. "More Discoveries at Caracol, British Honduras." *Actas del 33 Congreso Internacional de Americanistas*, pp. 211–218. San Jose, Costa Rica.

Andrews, George F. 1975. *Maya Cities: Placemaking and Urbanization*. Norman: University of Oklahoma Press.

Chase, Arlen F. 1992. "Elites and the Changing Organization of Classic Maya Society." In Diane Chase and Arlen Chase, eds., *Mesoamerican Elites: An Archaeological Assessment*, pp. 30–49. Norman: University of Oklahoma Press.

_____. 1994. "A Contextual Approach to the Ceramics of Caracol, Belize." In Diane Chase and Arlen Chase, eds., *Studies in the Archaeology of Caracol, Belize*, pp. 157–182. Monograph 7. San Francisco: Pre-Columbian Art Research Institute.

_____. 1998. "Planeación cívica e íntegración de sitio en Caracol, Belice: Definiendo una economía administrada del período clásico maya," *Los Investigadores de la Cultura Maya* 6: 26–44. Campeche: Universidad Autónoma de Campeche.

Chase, Arlen F., and Diane Z. Chase. 1987a. *Investigations at the Classic Maya City of Caracol, Belize: 1985–1987*. Monograph 3. San Francisco: Pre-Columbian Art Research Insitute.

_____. 1987b. *Glimmers of a Forgotten Realm: Maya Archaeology at Caracol, Belize*. Orlando: University of Central Florida.

_____. 1994a. "Details in the Archaeology of Caracol, Belize: An Introduction." In Diane Chase and Arlen Chase, eds., *Studies in the Archaeology of Caracol, Belize*, pp. 1–11. Monograph 7. San Francisco: Pre-Columbian Art Research Institute.

_____. 1994b. "Maya Veneration of the Dead at Caracol, Belize." In Merle G. Robertson and Virginia M. Fields, eds., *Seventh Palenque Round Table, 1989*, pp. 55–62. San Francisco: Pre-Columbian Art Research Institute.

_____. 1996a. "The Organization and Composition of Classic Lowland Maya Society: The View from Caracol, Belize." In Merle Robertson, Martha Macri, and Jan McHargue, eds., *Eighth Palenque Round Table, 1993*, pp. 213–222. San Francisco: Pre-Columbian Art Research Institute.

_____. 1996b. "A Mighty Maya Nation: How Caracol Built an Empire by Cultivating its 'Middle Class.'" *Archaeology* 49(5): 66–72.

_____. 1996c. "More than Kin and King: Centralized Political Organization Among the Ancient Maya." *Current Anthropology* 37: 803–810.

_____. 1998. "Scale and Intensity in Classic Period Maya Agriculture: Terracing and Settlement at the 'Garden City' of Caracol, Belize." *Culture and Agriculture* 20(2/3): 60–77.

_____. 2001. "Terminal Classic Status-Linked Ceramics and the Maya 'Collapse': *De Facto* Refuse at Caracol, Belize," In Don Rice, Prudence Rice, and Arthur Demarest, eds., *The Terminal Classic in the Maya Lowlands: Collapse, Transition, and Transformation*. Boulder: Westview Press. In Press.

Chase, Arlen F., Diane Z. Chase, and Christine D. White. 2001. "El paisaje urbano maya: La integración de los espacios construidos y la estructura social en Caracol, Belice." In A. Ciudad, M.J. Iglesias, and C. Martines, eds., *La Ciudad Antigua: Espacios, Conjuntos e Integración Sociocultural en la Civilización Maya*. Madrid: Sociedad Española de Estudios Mayas. At Press.

Chase, Arlen F., Nikolai Grube, and Diane Z. Chase. 1991. "Three Terminal Classic Monuments from Caracol, Belize." *Research Reports on Ancient Maya Writing*, No. 36. Washington, DC: Center for Maya Research.

Chase, Diane Z. 1988 "Caches and Censerwares: Meaning from Maya Pottery." In Luanna Lackey and Charles Kolb, eds., *A Pot for All Reasons: Ceramic Ecology Revisited*, pp. 81–104. Philadelphia: Temple University, Laboratory of Anthropology.

———. 1994. "Human Osteology, Pathology, and Demography as Represented in the Burials of Caracol, Belize." In Diane Chase and Arlen Chase, eds., *Studies in the Archaeology of Caracol, Belize*, pp. 123–138. Monograph 7. San Francisco: Pre-Columbian Art Research Institute.

———. 1998. "Albergando a los muertos en Caracol, Belice." *Los Investigadores de la Cultura Maya* 6: 9–25. Campeche: Universidad Autónoma de Campeche.

Chase, Diane Z., and Arlen F. Chase. 1996. "Maya Multiples: Individuals, Entries, and Tombs in Structure A34 of Caracol, Belize." *Latin American Antiquity* 7: 61–79.

———. 2000. "Inferences about Abandonment: Maya Household Archaeology and Caracol, Belize." *Mayab* 13: 67–77.

———. 2001. "What the Glyphs Don't Tell You: Archaeology and History at Caracol, Belize." Manuscript in preparation for *Latin American Antiquity*.

Chase, Diane Z., Arlen F. Chase, Christine White, and Wendy Giddens. 1998. "Human Skeletal Remains in Archaeological Context: Status, Diet, and Household at Caracol, Belize." Paper presented at the fourteenth International Congress of Anthropological and Ethnological Sciences, Williamsburg, Virginia.

Cobos, Rafael. 1994. "Preliminary Report on the Archaeological Mollusca and Shell Ornaments of Caracol, Belize." In Diane Chase and Arlen Chase, eds., *Studies in the Archaeology of Caracol, Belize*, pp. 139–147. Monograph 7. San Francisco: Pre-Columbian Art Research Institute.

Harrison, Peter D. 1986. "Tikal: Selected Topics." In Elizabeth Benson, ed., *City-States of the Maya: Art and Architecture*, pp. 45–71. Denver: Rocky Mountain Institute for Pre-Columbian Studies.

Haviland, William A. 1981. "Dower Houses and Minor Centers at Tikal, Guatemala: An Investigation into the Identification of Valid Units in Settlement Hierarchies." In Wendy Ashmore, ed., *Lowland Maya Settlement Patterns*, pp. 89–120. Albuquerque: University of New Mexico Press.

Inomata, Takeshi. 1997. "The Last Day of a Fortified Classic Maya Center: Archaeological Investigations at Aguateca, Guatemala." *Ancient Mesoamerica* 8: 337–351.

Inomata, Takeshi, and Daniela Triadan. 2000. "Craft Production by Classic Maya Elites in Domestic Settings: Data from Rapidly Abandoned Structures at Aguateca, Guatemala." *Mayab* 13: 57–66.

Jaeger Liepins, Susan. 1994. "The Conchita Causeway Settlement Subprogram." In Diane Chase and Arlen Chase, eds., *Studies in the Archaeology of Caracol, Belize*, pp. 47–63. Monograph 7. San Francisco: Pre-Columbian Art Research Institute.

Jones, Christopher, and Linton Satterthwaite. 1982. *The Monuments and Inscriptions of Tikal: The Carved Monuments*. University Museum Monograph 44. Philadelphia: University of Pennsylvania.

Laporte, Juan Pedro, and Vilma Fialko C. 1990. "New Perspectives on Old Problems: Dynastic References for the Early Classic at Tikal." In F.S. Clancy and P.D. Harrison, eds., *Vision and Revision in Maya Studies*, pp. 33–66. Albuquerque: University of New Mexico Press.

Moholy-Nagy, Hattula. 1997. "Middens, Construction Fill, and Offerings: Evidence for the Organization of Classic Period Craft Production at Tikal, Guatemala." *Journal of Field Archaeology* 24(3): 293–313.

Moseley, Michael E. 1990. "Structure and History in the Dynastic Lore of Chimor." In Michael Moseley and Alana Cordy-Collins, eds., *The Northern Dynasties: Kingship and Statecraft in Chimor*, pp. 1–41. Washington, DC: Dumbarton Oaks Research Library and Collection.

Pope, Cynthia. 1994. "Preliminary Analysis of Small Chert Tools and Related Debitage at Caracol, Belize." In Diane Chase and Arlen Chase, eds., *Studies in the Archaeology of Caracol, Belize*, pp. 148–156. Monograph 7. San Francisco: Pre-Columbian Art Research Institute.

Proskouriakoff, Tatiana. 1960. "Historical Implications of a Pattern of Dates at Piedras Negras, Guatemala." *American Antiquity* 25: 454–475.

Robertson, Merle Greene. 1986. "Some Observations on the X'telhu Panels at Yaxcaba, Yucatan." In E. Wyllys Andrews V, ed., *Research and Reflections in Archaeology and History: Essays in Honor of Doris Stone*, pp. 87–111. Middle American Research Institute Publication No. 57. New Orleans: Tulane University.

Schele, Linda, and Peter Mathews. 1998. *The Code of Kings: The Language of Seven Sacred Maya Temples and Tombs*. New York: Scribner.

Sharer, Robert J. 1977. "The Maya Collapse Revisited: Internal and External Perspectives." In Norman Hammond, ed., *Social Process in Maya Prehistory*, pp. 531–552. New York: Academic Press.

Smith, A. Ledyard. 1950. *Uaxactun, Guatemala: Excavations of 1931–1937*. Publication 588. Washington, DC: Carnegie Institution of Washington.

Stuart, David. 1998. "'The Fire Enters His House': Architecture and Ritual in Classic Maya Texts." In Stephen D. Houston, ed., *Function and Meaning in Classic Maya Architecture*, pp. 373–425. Washington, DC: Dumbarton Oaks Research Library and Collection.

Tozzer, Alfred M. 1941. *Landa's Relacion de las Cosas de Yucatan*. Papers of the Peabody Museum, vol. 18. Cambridge: Harvard University.

Valdés, Juan Antonio. 1997. "Tamarindito: Archaeology and Regional Politics in the Petexbatun Region." *Ancient Mesoamerica* 8: 321–335.

5

Palaces and Thrones Tied to the Destiny of the Royal Courts in the Maya Lowlands

JUAN ANTONIO VALDÉS*

Discoveries at the end of the twentieth century have shown that Maya religious and political ideology, from the Pre-Classic period on, was centered in a place of great prestige and inexhaustible abundance. Cities were conceived as the fifth cardinal direction, marked generally by the main plaza or the acropolis, which functioned as axis mundi, allowing individuals congregated there to travel between different levels of the sacred world (Eliade 1991; Freidel et al. 1993; McAnany 1995; Schele and Freidel 1990). For this reason, the vanguard architecture that exalted the king and his divine powers were constructed in these locations, so that the rulers could receive the benediction of the gods as well as the praise of humankind.

From the first century B.C., the political system was strengthened and centralized under one person who surrounded himself with a retinue of nobles, sages, and priests. This group was the beginning of the royal court that acquired prestige, power, and distinguished members through the centuries, augmenting its reputation through the continuous use of ideological and technological concepts. Monumental works were built by the sovereign and his court to patent their power and that of the gods, ordering the construction of sumptuous pyramids that emulated the cosmos, from where public messages were transmitted to an illiterate populace that was faithful to the principle of loyalty to their leaders.

The competition had begun. The great cities of that moment in time became entangled in rivalries, reaching for the ideal of becoming the center of the world, in the axis of the cosmos, in the place favored most by the gods. Tikal and Uaxactun competed in the central area; Nakbe, Wakna,

---

*Translated from Spanish by Antonia Foias and emended by Stephen D. Houston.

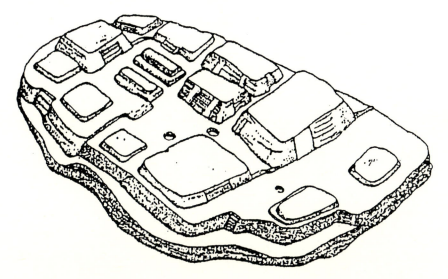

FIGURE 5.1 Drawing of the limestone model discovered in the Lost World Group at Tikal (Proyecto Nacional Tikal).

Tintal, El Mirador, and Calakmul in northern Peten; Cerros and Lamanai in Belize responded with novel projects. A limestone scale model discovered in the Lost World Group in Tikal (Figure 5.1) serves as proof of the construction plans for a large-scale project with fourteen edifices, including pyramidal terraces, rectangular platforms, ballcourt, *chultuns*, plazas of different levels, and stairways for entering and exiting the complex. The grand scale of this construction project reflects the progress and prosperity of the leading group of Tikal.

Nevertheless, after satisfying the gods with the construction of pyramids, ever higher and higher, it was necessary to satisfy the demands of the sovereign who, as a rising divinity, also required his "sacred space." His architects employed their genius to conceive a new concept of sacred place that was worthy of receiving the king and his court. This is when the first vaulted multiroomed structures were constructed, representing a distinct organization of internal space. The oldest examples of this new architecture date to the Late Pre-Classic period and have been discovered at Tikal, Uaxactun, El Mirador, and Nakbe (Coe 1967; Hansen 1992, 1998; Valdés 1992a). However, it is in the second of these cities where the most complete and best-preserved examples were found, most dating to the first century B.C. (Valdés 1989, 1992a, 1992b). Taking into account their context and external decoration, those with one room have been identified as temples, whereas those with several rooms were proposed as palaces used by the rulers for the functions required to govern their kingdom.

During the Early Classic period, the growing number of nobles needed the construction of new palaces in other areas apart from the central precinct of each site. Meanwhile, the royal palaces that had different functions were rebuilt to larger dimensions, with wider doorways, more rooms, and even more superimposed levels. For the Late Classic period, during the seventh and eighth centuries A.D., these royal palaces became intricate complexes of structures with multiple rooms, long chambers with private space, internal corridors, semi–hidden doors, internal and external stairways, and three or more levels. The Central Acropolis of Tikal is the best example of this architectural transformation (Harrison 1970, 1986).

To demonstrate the power of the rulers, elaborate ceremonial paraphernalia was created, which included the use of stationary and portable thrones. The fixed stone thrones were incorporated as an element of palatial architecture starting from the latter part of the Early Classic period. Their use became more frequent in the first chamber of the palace during the Late Classic, so that the rulers could see the exterior and at the same time be seen by people attending important events. Stone thrones built outside the edifices are less frequent; these were without a doubt covered by awnings or textile tarpaulins to protect the king and his court from the heat and sun (Valdés 1997). Nevertheless, the art and hieroglyphic inscriptions have shown us the prevalent use of thrones and portable palanquins, not only for the king but also for other members of the court who enjoyed the same elevated status (Reents-Budet 1994).

Vaulted Structures of the Late Pre-Classic Period

The first vaulted edifices were built in the most important sectors of the cities, taking advantage of the technological advances and innovations of the time. Perhaps the most significant of these advances was the unification of sculpture and painting with architecture, creating an integrated visual system used to transmit to the public the new social and ideological order emanating from the leading group. They thus emphasized the image of the sovereign and his protective deities as means of strengthening his power.

The cities with active and growing populations during the Late Pre-Classic period revealed architecture that used limestone walls and roofs, as in the North Acropolis at Tikal where excavations unearthed small edifices (Structures [Strs.] 5D-Sub 1–1a and 5D-Sub 10–1a) from the early half of the first century B.C., in which the first overhanging stones of the vaults could still be observed (Coe 1967). Stone roofs were also reported from El Mirador (Str. 34) and Nakbe (Str. 27) (Hansen 1998), but perhaps the best documented case is from Strs. H-Sub 2, H-Sub 4 and H-Sub 5 in the Group H at Uaxactun, as these were buried almost intact so that valu-

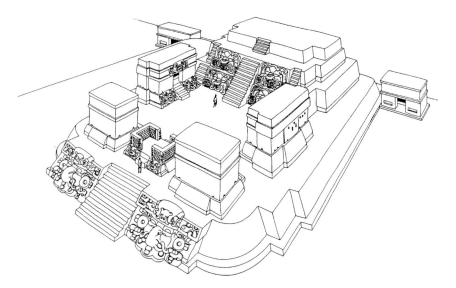

FIGURE 5.2   Reconstruction of the acropolis of Group H at Uaxactun during the Late Pre-Classic period (redrawn by F. Luin from Hansen 1998).

able information and evidence about their plan and architecture could be gleaned during excavation (Valdés 1989, 1992a).

These vaulted edifices from Uaxactun are rectangular in form and consist of two longitudinal chambers, constructed on basal platforms that included innovative and varied architectural elements. These basal platforms showed for the first time the introduction of polychrome stucco masks representing deities placed on both sides of the access stairway, a low bench on the frontal part, a molding on the lower part of the lateral and back walls, as well as an apron in the center of the posterior section (Figure 5.2). The vaulted buildings also included a new architectural design: an ample but low entrance doorway in front, narrow chambers of rectangular shape connected by an off-center door, openings in the walls for air and light access, the use of cornices, wood crossbeams to give strength to the stone vaults, as well as lintels of *chicozapote* wood over the doors. Thrones, benches, or niches were not discovered in the interior of any of these buildings.

To soften the roughly finished surface of the walls, the stonework was covered with thick layers of stucco and painted preferably with the color red in the exterior and white in the interior. In the higher parts of the structure exteriors, friezes were placed on all four sides, upon which mythological personages were modeled in stucco. Likewise, evidence of mural paintings using the colors red and white were found during excavations of the exterior walls.

It should be remarked that all the elements just mentioned were integrated into Maya architecture of the central lowlands from an early date, being used in the large basal platforms that supported temples and palaces during all the centuries through which Maya civilization lasted.

Palaces During the Late Pre-Classic Period?

As previously explained, from their origins the vaulted edifices included all the elements of the monumental architecture known from the Classic period: a basal platform to support the vaulted structure, access stairways, walls and vaults of stone covered by stucco, large but narrow chambers, wood lintels, and decorative elements including masks, friezes, cornices, moldings, and aprons in the posterior parts. Nevertheless, we should use a great deal of caution in using the term "palace" for the vaulted edifices of the Pre-Classic period. We simply do not have unambiguous evidence that these were used as residences—a function that the majority of authors attributed previously to the vaulted structures with multiple rooms of the Classic period—although the recent tendency is to recognize that they served a variety of functions from residential to administrative and other public uses (Harrison 1970, 1986; Houston 1998; Schele and Mathews 1998).

I believe that the term "palace" can be applied to these Pre-Classic structures, provided we understand that these were the "sacred residences" of the kings; and although it is unknown how long the rulers spent inside them, it must have been sufficient to accomplish the duties required by governance and its sumptuous paraphernalia. The majority of these palaces consist of two or three chambers and one door off the center axis connecting them, permitting the creation of spaces with more privacy in the rear room. Taking into consideration the hypothesis in the case of Str. 5C–2a at Cerros (Schele and Freidel 1990), the rooms served during the Pre-Classic period to complete rituals in which the ruler reproduced the trajectory of the sun over the universe, which culminated in the deepest extreme of the rear room, emulating the position of the kingly star at the end of the afternoon. This hypothesis supports the idea that in the internal rooms the king undertook the acts that required most privacy, including bloodletting as well as the prayers, meditation, and dreams used to reach the trances needed in these ceremonies. We cannot forget at any time that these palaces were built to harbor the king as a divine figure and the offspring of the gods. For these reasons, I consider it useful to interpret these palaces as "sacred houses" for the sovereign chosen by the gods.

It is not surprising that the Pre-Classic vaulted palaces, as the oldest examples, do not have the dimensions observed in the Classic examples; neither do they have as many rooms. It is obvious that the number of

TABLE 5.1   Dimensions of Palace H-Sub 2 of Uaxactun (in meters)

	Length	Width	Height	Wall Thickness	Stairs
Base	13.25	9.25	2.45	--	3.00 x 2.15
Palace	10.70	5.40	2.90	0.90	--
Room 1	8.40	1.45	2.70	0.90	--
Room 2	9.10	1.58	2.70	0.90	--
Entrance	?	?	?	0.90	--
Doorway b/w Rooms 1 and 2	--	1.30	1.30	0.7	0.30

chambers present in palaces increased over time as a response to the growing responsibilities attributed to the rulers, who supervised activities both ritual and administrative in nature.

In the case of Uaxactun, it is known that Group H was abandoned in a premeditated manner, and its inhabitants took their household implements, pottery, and all other goods with them; thus, when excavated, the rooms lacked all such remains. The function of palaces for these vaulted structures (H-Sub 2, H-Sub 4, and H-Sub 5) has been assigned based on the context of the interaction between the king and his court with the populace, extracted from the characteristics of each building, as well as from the iconographic analysis of the figures that decorated the facades. These stucco friezes contained elements that defined the attributes of political power, especially in the representations of the ruler (Valdés 1992c). With respect to this last element of the friezes, at the entrance to Group H we found the *popol nah* (council house) with its walls covered with stucco modeled with the royal symbol of the mat, interlaced with the portraits of the king decorating the doors and corners of the structure. Furthermore, a limestone sculpture was discovered in the plaza fill. This sculpture must be the image of the sovereign in full, as it shows a personage seated with his legs crossed. A similar analysis (Michelet and Becquelin 1996) was performed to identify the edifices that represented the seat of political power in the western Puuc region during the Classic period.

Because of the interest in these earliest palaces using stone vaults, their architectural features are summarized in Tables 5.1 and 5.2.

Palaces of the Early Classic Period

The most characteristic features of Maya civilization crystallized during the Classic period: the propagation of structures with fine stonework using corbeled vaults, the erection of sculptured monuments with hieroglyphs, and the construction of sumptuous tombs. Tikal and Uaxactun continued as the centers of state societies; Calakmul, Río Azul, Holmul,

TABLE 5.2 Dimensions of Palace H-Sub 5 of Uaxactun (in meters)

	Length	Width	Height	Wall Thickness	Stairs
Base	9.75	5.40	1.71	--	2.00 x 1.35
Palace	8.30	3.20	3.40	0.50	--
Room 1	6.40	1.30	2.70	0.50	--
Room 2	7.25	0.82	2.70	0.50	--
Entrance	--	1.91	1.12	0.50	--
Doorway b/w Rooms 1 and 2	--	1.27	1.48	0.45	0.30

and Caracol emerged as powerful kingdoms. During the Early Classic period, a virtual building explosion began, with a true fever of new monumental projects solicited by the growing leading class, employing diverse designs on large scales of construction. The palaces were no longer the sacred residences for exclusive use by the king; rather, their function was expanded to include the members of the royal family. With the passage of time, other nobles acquired the right to build their own palaces. The nobles wanted to remind the people that they were part of the royal lineage with divine origin and, therefore, possessed the right to occupy public positions of importance.

The palaces were built over progressively higher basal platforms, which displayed a majestic stairway in front. Better knowledge of the structural system and of the construction techniques of vaults in chamber interiors led to the building, around the year A.D. 350, of sophisticated palaces that had greater numbers of rooms and, with them, an increased capacity for greater numbers of people. The entrance doorways became wider, but the most important achievement at this time was the building of a second floor over the first. Tikal and Uaxactun were at the forefront of these architectural inventions, reflecting existing distinctions in sociopolitical development between the regional sites. However, during the second half of the Early Classic period, the aspirations of Uaxactun as a primary center were reduced by the consolidation of power by the elites of Tikal and Calakmul, which became the principal actors in the politics of the Maya lowlands (Martin and Grube 1995).

The oldest palace of the central Maya lowlands using multiple chambers has been identified in Group B at Uaxactun, underneath the palace B-2, and was dated to around A.D. 350 (Laporte 1989a). In a previous publication (Valdés and Fahsen 1995), it was demonstrated that Groups A and B became the epicenter of the ruling lineage of Uaxactun around A.D. 300, when the local ruler decided to change the seat of power for the fourth time in its history. This shift was accompanied by the construction of Str. A-5 in Group A, functioning as an acropolis; Group B was assigned more residential and administrative functions.

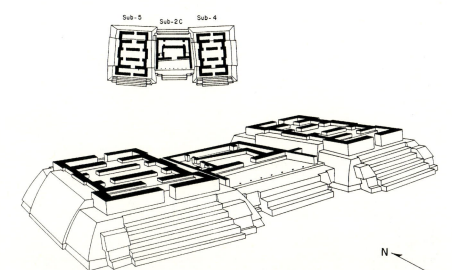

FIGURE 5.3   The royal palace of Uaxactun Sub–2C at the beginning of the Early Classic period (redrawn by F. Luin).

The palace of Group B emerged from the integration in only one block of what before were three distinct adjacent edifices. Those on the extremes had an identical form (Sub 4 and Sub 5), whereas the central one (Sub 2C) has the specific characteristics to identify it as the seat of political power and, therefore, the house of the ruler (Figure 5.3). The new palace acquired a rectangular plan with great movement of construction lines in and out, aprons on the extremes east and west, moldings everywhere, and three stairways of access in front, producing a dappled effect of light and shade typical of Maya architecture. On top of the superior terrace, the palaces Sub 4 and Sub 5 were built, each with five longitudinal chambers and two doorways (in front and rear). The central galleries enjoy greater privacy because the doors are placed off-center so that nobody could see from the exterior what was taking place in the interior. The walls were covered with a thick layer of red stucco, and the upper exterior walls were decorated with cornices and anthropomorphic masks.

In the center of this new complex, Str. Sub 2C consists of three chambers that form five rooms, which no doubt saw combined administrative and ritual functions. The plaza in front of this palace was a public space for those who witnessed the public acts. From this plaza, a wide stairway led to the first chamber of the palace. This first room has seven postholes in the floor, demonstrating the existence in antiquity of a flat roof of perishable materials or, in its absence, one of a cotton tarpaulin that was used during ceremonies only. This room must have functioned as the antechamber, or as a semipublic space reserved exclusively for elite members, before passing to the next room, where the sovereign was seated. A narrow doorway allowed entrance to the second chamber, which functioned as private space, as it probably was the place where the ruler was seated on his throne to receive in audience his nobles and foreign visitors. This is equivalent to the rooms that Peter Harrison (see Chapter 3, this volume) called "throne rooms," in which the kings received their subjects. Surrounding the throne room, the third chamber, which has a very restricted access, must have been a completely private space reserved exclusively for the ruler, who in his role as priest undertook the ancient rituals related to the sacred ceremonials of rulership, such as meditation, abstinence, and genital bloodletting.

The placement of the rooms of the palace Sub 2C is similar to the Pre-Classic structures 5C–2 of Cerros and the palace H-Sub 2 of Uaxactun, which, as previously explained, served to express "the trajectory of the sun and the trajectory of the king across the cosmos" (Robertson and Freidel 1986). This denotes that the rituals introduced during the Pre-Classic period continued to be practiced during the Early Classic and that the architecture continued to be a valuable element in accomplishing these rituals. Other features associated with ritual consisted of the dedicatory caches discovered in the palace.

With such features, this would be the first Maya palace to combine residential, administrative, and ritual functions, buttressing the hypothesis that it was the royal palace of the king of Uaxactun. The spaciousness of the rooms in the central structure made it possible for the lateral suites (Sub 4 and Sub 5) to be occupied by members of the royal family, as well as by other members of the court who helped the king in fulfilling his daily functions.

Tikal, upon observing the development reached by the Uaxactun royal court as it integrated public and ritual functions in the same building, could not be left behind, and almost at the same time the ninth successor in the dynastic line of that city, the great ruler Toh Chak Ich'ak (Great Jaguar Paw) ordered the construction of his own royal palace in the Central Acropolis (Schele and Mathews 1998). This undertaking demonstrated the great intellect and experience of the architects who years later built the second level and an internal staircase to connect the two floors (Figure 5.4). As an answer to the volume problem, three frontal doorways of access were used for the first time, displacing the traditional design of only one entrance.

This edifice (5D–46) is thought to have been built around the year A.D. 350 as the residence of the family of the governor (Harrison 1999). This is a typical example of the palaces know as *xanil nah* (Schele and Mathews 1998), as they were called in Itza Maya. The name of the sovereign who occupied this palace was identified thanks to the decipherment of the glyphs that appeared on a vessel discovered in a cache placed in a dedi-

FIGURE 5.4   The royal palace of Tikal, built by Ruler Toh Chak Ich'ak (photograph by J.A. Valdés).

catory ritual at the time of construction. The importance and symbolism of this structure was so significant that it was respected across the whole history of the city, suffering few changes and enlargements until much later in the Late Classic period, during the reign of Yax Ain II in the last part of the eighth century A.D. The reason for the interest in this palace is that it was never buried in the construction of another building as was the custom in the Maya zone. There is little doubt that this palace was considered a symbol of the grandeur of the royal dynasty strengthened by the great king, Toh Chak Ich'ak, and therefore it formed part of the identity of the city, as the building remained untouched with the passage of time even through periods of crisis.

Another palace built over a higher basal platform is also found in Uaxactun, where the Ruler A–22 ordered the construction of the enormous palace A–18 around A.D. 450, almost a century after the palace of Toh Chak Ich'ak of Tikal, who apparently belonged to the same lineage (Valdés et al. 1999). This palace (Figure 5.5) is very similar to that of Tikal, but as the newer one it was larger, spacious, and less flamboyant. It also exhibited three access doorways in front, numerous galleries, two levels, and an interior stairway that ascends to the second floor to provide access to eighteen rooms (L. Smith 1937). The importance of this edifice increases in light of the fact that here the first known Maya stone throne in the area was placed in its interior. This feature is a long bench finely stuccoed (probably painted red) with armrests on both sides. It is placed in front of the central door on the second level, where the sovereign would

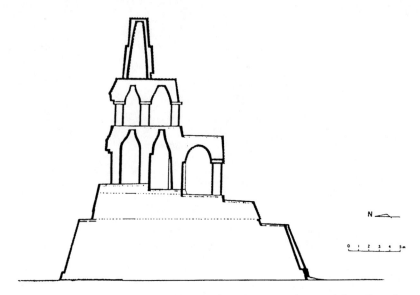

FIGURE 5.5   North-south profile of Palace A–18, residence of the ruler of Uaxactun during the last part of the Early Classic period (drawn by Raúl Anguiano).

have sat to see his subjects congregated in the plaza in front of the palace, and from where he could have participated in public acts directed to the public from this high point in the building.

The residential character of this structure was proposed by Smith (1937), who took into account the many rooms, the accommodation of burials below its floors, and the placement of dedicatory caches and offerings at the moment of its construction as well as over the following centuries.

The similarities between the royal palaces of Tikal and Uaxactun are astonishing, making it possible to conjecture that the Tikal palace also had a throne on its second level, where the king would have sat. The appearance of thrones as a new element associated with the palatial architecture was a relevant fact, as it gave comfort to the king during the long public acts and transformed the edifice into sacred space. Again, the architecture served to support the functions of rulership. It also demonstrates that residential and administrative functions were interlaced in the same structure.

The bonanza manifested by the rulers of the Early Classic period was directed toward other members of the royal family and of the court, mainly at Tikal. The construction of palaces was no longer restricted to the epicenter, but rather new elite palatial complexes appeared in other sectors of the city, as a result of the success of the local politics and economics. For the first time, nobles had the authority to erect sculptured

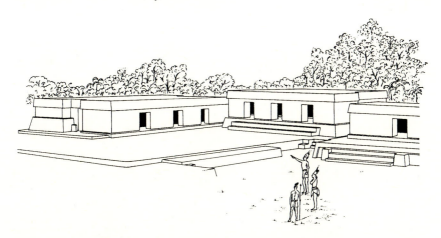

FIGURE 5.6 Buildings of the palace type at Tikal, built during the final part of the Early Classic period over low platforms (Laporte 1989).

monuments with their names inscribed, as in Group H, where a sculpture called *Man of Tikal* was discovered, with an inscription that marks the conferral of the title of *ajaw* to a local noble called K'uk' Mo and refers to events involving the ruler Yax Ain I (Valdés et al. 1994). Almost at the same time, in A.D. 416, the so-called *Ballcourt Marker of Tikal* was sculptured and placed in Group 6C–16; this monument refers to a historical event between Tikal and Uaxactun (Laporte 1989b; Schele and Freidel 1990). In Group H, the palaces are monumental, built on great basal platforms, and in Group 6C–16 they surround several patios, interconnected by passageways and stairways but on smaller platforms, all of which suggest their residential function.

All the edifices in the latter group were built between A.D. 300 and 550 during the phases Manik 2 and 3 of the Early Classic period (Laporte 1989b). These have varied forms, different numbers of chambers, variable number of access doorways, and either flat or vaulted roofs. Typological analysis of the twenty-one palaces indicates that between A.D. 300 and 378 there was a preference for buildings with broad entrances, a maximum of two rooms, and flat or vaulted roofs. For the latter part of the Early Classic period (A.D. 378–550), the situation changed, with a new architectural fashion in palaces with three frontal doorways and two or three chambers (Figure 5.6). Without a doubt, the use of three access doorways was in vogue, following the great palaces of the rulers of Tikal and Uaxactun. No stone thrones or benches were found in any of these edifices, which would relate them with administrative activities, although it has been suggested that this group was inhabited by ballplayers, as murals depicting the game decorated the structures.

The Palaces of the Late Classic Period

The political changes of the Late Classic period led to the appearance of hundreds of new cities across the Maya lowlands and, in some cases, to the development of their own independent polities as suggested by the use of particular emblem glyphs. This epoch of splendor was accomplished through ambitious urban programs of construction everywhere. From the north to the south and from the east to the west in the Maya zone, plazas were filled with palaces that have been the subject of numerous treatises and typological schemes. Abundant literature permits us to group these great edifices into regional styles, defining in some cases the political affinity between different sites. Some of these studies included those performed at Uaxactun, Tikal, and Yaxha in the central zone (Harrison 1970, 1986; Hellmuth 1978; Loten 1970; Smith 1950); Yaxchilan, Palenque, and Piedras Negras in the Usumacinta zone (Proskouriakoff 1963; Sattherthwaite 1954; Sotelo 1992); Copan in the southeastern periphery (Fash 1998; Sanders 1990); as well as those of the Yucatan Peninsula, with its buildings in the Chenes and Puuc styles (Gendrop 1983).

As a result, it can be observed that during the apogee of the Maya civilization the palaces grew in an extraordinary manner, increased their number of entrance doors to five, seven, or nine (as in the case of Tikal, where elegant edifices of as many as three floors were built), and increased their number of chambers (as shown in the Central Acropolis, with its intricate patios surrounded by structures of multiple rooms) that fulfilled varied functions, as much public as private.

Because of this, I would like to emphasize the importance of smaller palaces built on low platforms, as well as the tight connection they had with the activities of the royalty, especially in administrative events related to government matters. At the same time, we should emphasize the constant presence of interior benches from the sixth century A.D. on, in the small and great palaces of all sites, always attached to one of the walls. There is a gamut of designs and sizes for these benches, but it is believed that the majority were used for sitting and sleeping on top of comfortable mattresses of jaguar skin, as depicted on painted pottery vessels. Nevertheless, some of these benches fulfilled the role of throne and were built in the first chamber in front of the central access door to the edifice, so that the sovereign seated there could be seen by the spectators gathered in front of the palace while he controlled the assistants to the act. Many of these thrones have armrests on the sides and are very elegant in design, whereas others are rectangular benches with or without decoration.

Excavations and discoveries made by members of the Petexbatun Regional Archaeological Project were crucial in verifying that the function of the palaces built on low platforms with wide doorways and central benches was principally administrative (Demarest 1997; Inomata 1997; Palka 1997; Valdés 1997). During the excavations at Tamarindito, two small palaces were explored in the extreme north of Group B, located around a small plaza at the end of a wide causeway oriented north-south, which was used for processions arriving to greet the local authorities (Valdés 1993, 1997). The palaces 32 and 33 have a sole frontal stairway of access and three chambers, one in front and two lateral ones. The front chamber has such a wide door that it almost stretches the whole width of the room, and the interior contains a bench attached to the posterior wall.

Because of the width of the doorway, nobody could be hidden from sight from outside the palace, which makes it clear that this main space did not have domestic functions but obviously was administrative. The Tamarindito ruler must have sat on the bench in this central chamber to give audience and to attend to foreign functionaries who would arrive to reach agreements and lead discussions over government matters, such as politics and the regional economy. The palaces that had a residential function were located in a different sector of this city and were less exposed to the public view.

A very similar example, Str. M7–35, was discovered during excavations at Aguateca (Inomata 1993, 1997). During its beginnings in the Late Classic period, this palace had only one room and an ample throne in the center in front of the entrance doorway. Years later, it underwent modifications, and the dimensions of the throne room were reduced so that an additional room could be constructed on each side of the central chamber. The central space continued to hold the throne, and the lateral rooms could have served for the storage and preparation of foods and drinks that were offered to the personages who participated in the ceremonies (Figure 5.7). This edifice occupied a strategic location in the middle of the causeway that leads to the area where the sovereign and his family resided. Together with the ample open space around it, which was used for audiences and ceremonies, this structure must have fulfilled its function perfectly.

Below the throne there is a niche, and in its interior was discovered a polychrome vase with a beautiful scene of the local court, with the sovereign seated on a very elaborate throne in the company of twelve other individuals (see Inomata, Chapter 2 in Volume 1). Some of these hold their right hand over the left shoulder in a sign of submission and respect, and we can see the naturalness of the gestures and postures of the rest of the participants, including the musicians and smoking man. The beauty of the scene makes this vase one of the most exquisite artistic pieces discovered in the Petexbatun region.

Due to their characteristics, I have called this type of building "scenic palaces" or "presentation palaces," as I believe that they were built especially so that the participants in public ceremonies could observe their leaders while listening to all the conversation that took place in the interior of the chamber (Demarest 1997; Valdés 1993, 1997). The main personages would be seated on the throne, other nobles would be sitting or standing at

FIGURE 5.7 Aguateca Structure M7–35, showing the throne in the central room (photograph by J.A. Valdés).

the entrance to the palace, depending on their status, and the rest of the spectators would congregate in the plaza in front of the palace. Court scenes of this nature were painted many times in the polychrome vases of the Late Classic period, surrounding the figure of the sovereign or prince seated on the throne, conversing with other nobles of equal or lower social status, including painters or military leaders (Reends-Budet 1994).

The importance of these scenes painted on vases is that they provide real information that allows us to know architectural details that sometimes are not preserved in the field, as well as the objects utilized during the audiences, such as thrones, wide doorways, frontal steps, dividing walls, rolled curtains, offerings, vessels for liquids, and plates for solid foods. An example of this was recovered in Tamarindito (Figure 5.8), displaying the function of these edifices for the members of the royal court. This vase shows its "social value" as defined by Reents-Budet (1994), as it was used as a gift exchanged between members of the nobility. This vase forms part of the funerary offering of the ruler Chanal Balam of Tamarindito (Valdés 1997), and from its glyphic text we know that it originates in the Ik Site whose sovereign appears seated on the throne. In front of him, another noble is seated, and two other individuals are present in this event, although standing on a lower level. The individual to the left of the ruler carries a plumed bloodletter in his left hand (Schele and Grube, personal communication, 1996), used in rituals of bloodletting so that the liquid could be sprinkled on the bark or paper deposited

FIGURE 5.8 Polychrome vase from the Ik Site discovered at Tamarindito (drawn by F. Luin).

on a plate. Such a plate appears below the throne on this vase; paper within would then be burned, producing the sacred smoke needed in ritual ceremonies (Schele and Freidel 1990).

Moving to the other extreme of the Maya zone, in the far city of Copan, another edifice has been discovered with architectural features similar to those of the Tamarindito and Aguateca presentation palaces. This is Str. 10L–18 (Figure 5.9), the funerary complex of the ruler Yax Pasah, located in the southern extreme of the East Patio in the Acropolis (Fash 1998). This edifice has an ample stairway of access and a very wide doorway, upon which the image of the sovereign dancing as a victorious warrior is exalted, with an interior sculpted bench where the ruler would have been seated. Taking into account the resemblance between this structure and the Petexbatun palaces, it seems reasonable to assign to the Copan edifice an administrative function, as it is probably the location where the ruler received the members of his court and other subjects for public audiences.

Function and Significance of the Throne

As a result of the sociopolitical complexity reached during the Late Classic period, stone thrones were sculpted and covered in stucco, which was then painted in polychrome colors so they could be used by sovereigns. Although the first thrones in the Maya area have been reported for the Late Pre-Classic period at Kaminaljuyu and Abaj Takalik, their presence in the Maya lowlands began in the second half of the Early Classic period at Uaxactun. For the Late Classic period their distribution is much wider,

FIGURE 5.9   Copan Structure 10L–18 (photograph by J.A. Valdés).

and many more examples are known either through excavations of architecture or through art.

An example of the latter can be seen on the Oval Tablet in the Palenque Palace, where an elegant throne with a double jaguar head appears used by the ruler Pakal at the moment of enthronement. Nevertheless, it should be remembered that many of the thrones shown in artistic expressions such as sculpture and painted vessels must have been made of perishable materials, such as wood, because stone thrones are much less frequently found in excavations (with the exception of the beautiful carved ones from Piedras Negras and others discovered at Tikal and Dos Pilas). It should also be noted that wood palanquins and litters appear in painted scenes on polychrome vases in the Maya lowlands, as well as in the wooden lintels of Temple I of Tikal (Jones and Satterthwaite 1982; Reents-Budet 1994).

At Tikal in particular, a throne painted in red and black on white was discovered in the northern part of the Lost World Group (Figures 5.10 and 5.11), dating to the beginning of the Late Classic period, between A.D. 550 and 650, the so-called Ik phase (Laporte and Fialko 1995). To the front of the throne, the modeled stucco stands out, representing an interwoven mat, the symbol of royalty upon which the ruler would sit. From the mat falls a fringe like a short curtain, and lower down there are two niches, completely painted red in their interiors, in which vessels would be placed. The throne has a wide back that frames three sides, permitting a comfortable position for the ruler. The important discovery was that it

Palaces and Thrones in the Maya Lowlands 155

FIGURE 5.10 Drawing of the throne discovered in the Lost World Group at Tikal (redrawn by F. Luin from Laporte and Fialko 1995).

FIGURE 5.11 Detail of the throne of the Lost World Group at Tikal (photograph by J. A. Valdés).

FIGURE 5.12   Detail of the incisions on the western lateral wall of the throne from Tikal (photograph by J. A. Valdés).

was built on top of a low platform with two steps in the front, which created differences in level and social status for the individuals standing there. On its western edge, a posthole was found in the stuccoed floor. Presumably this supported a flat roof of perishable materials or a canopy of cotton cloth for protecting the ruler from the tropical sun. The throne functioned outside a structure, and in complete view of the spectators, as no wall or construction was found around it. Curiously, this throne resembles one painted on a polychrome vase discovered also in the Lost World Group, where a jaguar cub is being offered to the Tikal ruler seated on the throne.

A particular feature of this throne is the presence of incised designs on the western side of the throne, which include crosses and pyramidal platforms with frontal stairways (Figure 5.12). Of course, we do not know who made these drawings, but they could have been individuals who were trying to find the best way to pass the time during the long days of audiences. Because they are found so low on the throne, they must have been drawn by individuals sitting on the floor, although court dwarfs (who appear together with rulers on painted vases) or the small offspring of the ruler (accompanying him in these public acts) are possible candidates.

Another case of an exterior throne was discovered recently during the 1999 excavations of the palace M7–32 at Aguateca (Figures 5.13 and 5.14). This structure appears to have been one of the palaces used by the local

Palaces and Thrones in the Maya Lowlands

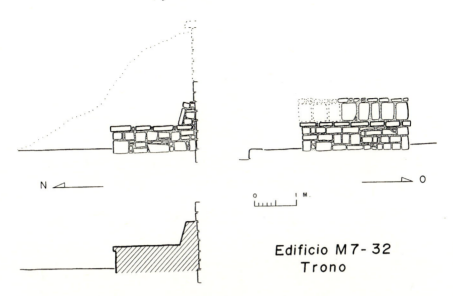

FIGURE 5.13 Drawing of the throne from Aguateca, attached to the exterior of the palace M7–32 (drawn by M. Urquizú).

FIGURE 5.14 View from the Aguateca throne during the work of restoration in 1999 (photograph by J.A. Valdés).

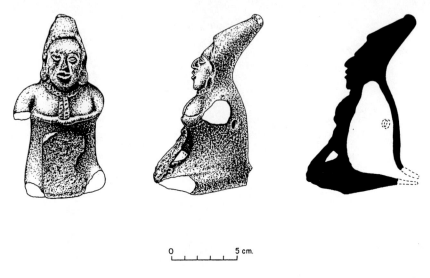

FIGURE 5.15   Female and male members of the court of Aguateca represented in the figurines and musical instruments from this site.

ruler and forms part of a complex of elite structures reserved for the royal family and court (Figure 5.15). The throne was attached to the northern wall of the main palace, and, to judge from the central location, it must have been reserved so that the ruler could use it acts less full of protocol, in which participated family members and individuals of confidence. It must have also been employed in moments of diversion, when the clowns and dancers would be entertaining or dancing.

With respect to such entertainment, it is known that the Maya enjoyed the company of magicians, comedians, musicians, and professional dancers, as well as dancing and singing masters who came together in the great urban centers to entertain and divert the court nobles. Making reference to Diego de Landa and Bernardino de Sahagún, the historian Ruz (1999) indicated that these individuals commissioned the presentation of theater pieces that were performed in Chichen Itza. The patrons admired the ability of the Maya to undertake games of illusionism "with which they deceived the people, making them believe that what was false was true, as they made it appear that houses that were not burning were burning, and made fountains with fish appear out of air. And there was nothing, just an illusion for the eyes. And they would kill themselves, slicing and cutting into pieces their bodies and other things which were apparent but not true." Furthermore, Ruz adds that in the *Relaciones Histórico-Geográficas*, the Spanish *encomendero* Juan Farfán indicated that he was present at the last celebration of the New Year in Yucatan, where he was surprised by the variety of dances that were of a thousand types.

Thousands of people attended from all the surrounding villages, to observe the dancers shining in their multicolored plumed costumes and moving to the rhythm of the music.

The same scholar indicates that the numerous clowns and musicians made their living by entertaining the nobles and refers to a song of pre-Hispanic origin from Dzitbalche, which names individuals, places, and musical instruments in the following manner:

> The sun sets in the lower slopes of the sky in the west; they sound the *tunkul*, the conch shell, and the *zacatan*, and they blow the jicara instrument.
>
> All are elected ... they have come.
>
> Afterwards, skipping, they arrive at the *popol na*, where the *Ahau Can* is ...
>
> The singing musicians, the magicians, the contortionists dancers, the jumping dancers, and the hunchbacked and the spectators have arrived.
>
> All the people have come ... to the entertainment that will take place in the middle of the plaza of our town.
>
> When the sun begins to penetrate the surface of the sky is the moment to begin fit to begin. (Ruz 1999:172)

This song makes it clear that all was not rigid in the life of the court; rather, the elite members liked to laugh and enjoy themselves, as did the townspeople, so that the royal family and the princely heir enjoyed varied spectacles that took place around the king, who would sit on his throne installed for this purpose on the exterior of the palaces or in the middle of the plazas.

This also could have taken place at Dos Pilas, where a fragmented hieroglyphic bench was discovered in the Murcielagos Group. The bench appears to refer to the ruler K'inich Kan K'awil (Wolley 1995). The interpretation of this last complex is of crucial importance, as Demarest (1997) believes that this bench was used in a presentation palace where part of the local court participated in social events related to the populace. The discovery of a standard-bearer stone is also significant, as it suggests that flags would have swung in the wind in front of the edifice; because of the low height of the walls surrounding the bench, it would have been used as an exterior throne so that the ruler would be sitting in front of the public. Once again, it is believed that a canopy of cotton cloth would have been used to shield the sovereign and his court from the great tropical heat, as was also suggested for the exterior thrones at Aguateca and Tikal.

In the Usumacinta region, the Piedras Negras Panel 3 is well-known (see Houston and Stuart, Chapter 3 in Volume 1). It depicts a courtly gathering held by Ruler 4 and a finely carved throne. The carved scene shows a very wide doorway allowing entrance to the palace, which reproduces perfectly the cases of scenic palaces or presentation palaces discussed for Tamarindito, Aguateca, and Copan, a doorway so wide that it allows observation of everything taking place inside the chamber. Thus, Piedras Negras must also be included in the list of sites that used palaces of this nature. Another very elaborate throne is the famous Throne 1 from Piedras Negras dating to A.D. 785. It was found in the interior of the palace of Ruler 7 and is now on display in the National Museum of Archaeology and Ethnology in Guatemala. The back of the throne represents the profile of Cauac, with glyphic inscriptions on the seat and supports, which mention the birth and enthronement events of the sovereign, as well as the name of the sculptors.

Because of all the previous reasons, we can conclude that palaces and thrones cannot be separated from the life of the court, as they became a complete unit during the Late Classic period. Rulers, heirs, great nobles, elite members, princesses, and queens shared these spaces and thrones, not only during formal occasions, in which they must have displayed the complexity of the administration, but also during the hours of delight that went along with times of peace. Grand and small palaces were always one of the symbols of status, and unquestionably many individuals (especially members of the court who enjoyed the prerogatives of power) invested in their construction to show with pride their power and good fortune.

Conclusion

This study has shown that the architects of the Pre-Classic period experimented with stone and stucco, reaching technological advances in the innovation of the edifices and spaces, which the architects of the Classic period employed in a more systematic manner. The creation of innovative buildings as the product of a local development was required by the growing complexity of the political ideology established by the king and his court, including among these inventions palaces with stone vaults. The success of the vaulted buildings of the Late Pre-Classic period marked the standard for the future realization of monumental constructions and helped in establishing the character (as well as prestige) of the centers closer to a complete urbanism, particularly in the sites that were continuously growing in population. With the passage of time, the activities of the nobility required more specialized architectural forms and arrangements, which marked the increasing degree of social differentiation growing between the population and particularly within the members of the court.

As a complement to the royal paraphernalia the thrones appeared, initially exclusively for the use of the sovereign, although over time other members of the court acquired the right to sit there. From the examples presented here, there is no doubt that different types of thrones and benches existed, in stone as well as wood, employed as a status symbol by the Maya rulers and other elites. With more and more frequency, thrones have been reported from the interior of edifices, although some exterior thrones are also known to exist.

Their presence in major and minor palaces must continue to be studied, although it is well–known that during the Classic period the rulers frequently visited other cities to participate in local important events, as "witnesses to the act." Through sculpted and painted art, the Maya showed for posterity the hegemony of a divine personage seated on elegant thrones in the center of these scenes. Political and economic alliances provided the impetus for these visits, which also served to validate the rights and privileges of the sovereigns and of all his royal court. With the collapse, the exuberance of the palaces and thrones associated with the splendid and comfortable life of the court had to be abandoned at the same time as the great urban centers of the Classic Maya civilization were depopulating.

However, it seems that part of this hegemonic system could have persisted in some Post-Classic sites, as on the island of Topoxte, where Structures E and G in the Main Plaza have benches with the apparent function of thrones, placed in front of the central doorway. The pottery and architectural features are clearly late (Hermes 1992). Curiously, then, elitist motifs of past epochs continued to be used. This indicated that reminiscences of the old power system, despite the changes in social organization of the Post-Classic period, lasted for several centuries afterward in the central lowlands of the Peten region.

References

Demarest, Arthur. 1997. "The Vanderbilt Petexbatun Regional Archaeological Project 1989–1994: Overview, History, and Major Results of an Multidisciplinary Study of the Classic Maya Collapse." *Ancient Mesoamerica* 8: 209–227.

Eliade, Mircea. 1991. *Tratado de historia de las religiones*. Mexico, D.F.: Biblioteca Era.

Fash, William L. 1998. "Dynastic Architectural Programs: Intention and Design in Classic Maya Buildings at Copan and Other Sites." In Stephen Houston, ed., *Function and Meaning in Classic Maya Architecture*, pp. 223–270. Washington, DC: Dumbarton Oaks Research Library and Collection.

Freidel, David, Linda Schele, and Joyce Parker. 1993. *Maya Cosmos: Three Thousand Years on the Shaman's Path*. New York: William Morrow.

Gendrop, Paul. 1983. *Los estilos Río Bec, Chenes y Puuc en la arquitectura maya*. Mexico, D.F.: Universidad Nacional Autónoma de México.

Hansen Richard. 1992. "The Archaeology of Ideology: A Study of Maya Preclassic Architectural Sculpture at Nakbe, Peten, Guatemala." Ph.D. diss., University of California–Los Angeles.

_____. 1998. "Continuity and Disjunction: The Pre-Classic Antecedents of Classic Maya Architecture." In Stephen Houston, ed., *Function and Meaning in Classic*

Maya Architecture, pp. 49–122. Washington, DC: Dumbarton Oaks Research Library and Collection.

Harrison, Peter. 1970. "The Central Acropolis, Tikal, Guatemala: A Preliminary Study of the Functions of Its Structural Components During the Late Classic Period." Ph.D. diss., University of Pennsylvania.

―――――. 1986. "Tikal: Selected Topics." In Elizabeth Benson, ed., *City States of the Maya: Art and Architecture*, pp. 45–71. Denver: Rocky Mountain Institute for Pre-Columbian Studies.

―――――. 1999. *The Lords of Tikal, Rulers of an Ancient Maya City*. New York: Thames and Hudson.

Hellmuth, Nicholas. 1978. *A General Introduction to Maya Art, Architecture, and Archaeology—Tikal-Copan Travel Guide*. St. Louis: Foundation for Latin American Anthropological Research.

Hermes, Bernard. 1992. "La secuencia cerámica de Topoxté: un informe preliminar." *Beiträge zur Allgemeinen und Vergleichenden Archäologie* 13: 221–251.

Houston, Stephen. 1998. "Finding Function and Meaning in Classic Maya Architecture." In Stephen Houston, ed., *Function and Meaning in Classic Maya Architecture*, pp. 519–538. Washington, DC: Dumbarton Oaks Research Library and Collection.

Inomata, Takeshi. 1993. "Operación 15: Estructura M7–35." In Juan Antonio Valdés, Antonia Foias, Takeshi Inomata, Héctor Escobedo, and Arthur A. Demarest, eds., *Proyecto Arqueológico Regional Petexbatún, Informe Preliminar No. 5*, pp. 35–42. Report presented to the Instituto de Antropología e Historia de Guatemala.

―――――. 1997. "The Last Days of a Fortified Classic Maya Center: Archaeological Investigations at Aguateca, Guatemala." *Ancient Mesoamerica* 8: 337–351.

Jones, Christopher, and Linton Satterthwaite. 1982. *The Monuments and Inscriptions of Tikal: The Carved Monuments. Tikal Report No. 33, Part A*. University Museum Monograph 44. Philadelphia: University of Pennsylvania.

Laporte, Juan Pedro. 1989a. "El Grupo B de Uaxactun: arquitectura y relaciones sociopolíticas durante el clásico temprano." In *Memorias del Segundo Coloquio Internacional de Mayistas*, pp. 625–646. Mexico, D.F.: Centro de Estudios Mayas.

―――――. 1989b. "Alternativas del clásico temprano en la relación Tikal-Teotihuacan: Grupo 6C–16, Tikal, Petén, Guatemala." Ph.D. diss., Universidad Nacional Autónoma de México.

Laporte, Juan Pedro, and Vilma Fialko. 1995. "Un reencuentro con Mundo Perdido, Tikal, Guatemala." *Ancient Mesoamerica* 6: 41–94.

Loten, Stanley. 1970. "The Maya Architecture of Tikal, Guatemala: A Preliminary Seriation of Vaulted Building Plans." Ph.D. diss., University of Pennsylvania.

Martin, Simon, and Nikolai Grube. 1995. "Maya Super States." *Archaeology* 48(6): 41–46.

McAnany, Patricia. 1995. *Living with the Ancestors: Kinship and Kingship in Ancient Maya Society*. Austin: University of Texas Press.

Michelet, Dominique, and Pierre Bequelin. 1995. "Elementos políticos y religiosos de un sector de la región Puuc occidental: su identificación e interpretación." In Carmen Varela, Juan Luis Bonor, and Yolanda Fernández, eds., *Religión y sociedad en el área maya*, pp. 109–134. Madrid: Sociedad Española de Estudios Mayas.

Palka, Joel. 1997. "Reconstructing Classic Maya Socioeconomic Differentiation and the Collapse at Dos Pilas, Petén, Guatemala." *Ancient Mesoamerica* 8: 209–227.

Proskouriakoff, Tatiana. 1963. *Album de Arquitectura Maya*. Mexico, D.F.: Fondo de Cultura Económica.

Reents-Budet, Dorie. 1994. *Painting the Maya Universe: Royal Ceramics of the Classic Period*. Durham: Duke University Press.

Robertson, Robin, and David Freidel. 1986. *Archaeology at Cerros Belize, Central America. Volume 1: An Interim Report*. Dallas: Southern Methodist University Press.

Ruz, Mario Humberto. 1999. "Los afanes cotidianos mayas: una historia en minísculas." *Los Mayas*, pp. 159–177. Mexico, D.F.: Conaculta-INAH.

Satterthwaite, Linton. 1954. *Piedras Negras Archaeology: Architecture*. Philadelphia: University of Pennsylvania.

Sanders, William. 1990. *Excavaciones en el área urbana de Copán*. Tegucigalpa: Secretaría de Cultura y Turismo e Instituto de Antropología e Historia.

Schele, Linda, and David Freidel. 1990. *A Forest of Kings: The Untold Story of the Ancient Maya*. New York: William Morrow.

Schele, Linda, and Peter Mathews. 1998. *The Code of Kings: The Language of Seven Sacred Maya Temples and Tombs*. New York: Scribner.

Smith, Ledyard. 1937. *Structure A-XVIII, Uaxactun*. Carnegie Institution of Washington, Publication 483. Washington, D.C.

_____. 1950. *Uaxactun, Guatemala: Excavations of 1931–1937*. Carnegie Institution of Washington, Publication 588. Washington, D.C.

Sotelo, Laura Elena. 1992. *Yaxchilan*. Tuxtla Gutiérrez Gobierno del Estado de Chiapas.

Valdés, Juan Antonio. 1989. "El Grupo H de Uaxactun: evidencias de un centro de poder durante el preclásico." In *Memorias del Segundo Coloquio Internacional de Mayistas*, pp. 603–624. México, D.F.: Centro de Estudios Mayas.

_____. 1992a. "Arquitectura maya: los palacios abovedados de la época preclásica en Uaxactun." In *Memorias del Primer Congreso Internacional de Mayistas*, pp. 344–367. Mexico, D.F.: Centro de Estudios Mayas.

_____. 1992b. "The Beginning of Preclassic Maya Art and Architecture." In Richard Townsend, ed., *The Ancient Americas Art from Sacred Landscapes*, pp. 147–157. Chicago: Art Institute of Chicago.

_____. 1992c. "El crecimiento de la civilización maya en el área central durante el preclásico tardío: una vista desde el Grupo H de Uaxactun." *U tz'ib* 1(2): 16–31 (Guatemala: Asociación Tikal).

_____. 1993. "Excavaciones en el Grupo B de Tamarindito." In Juan Antonio Valdés, Antonia Foias, Takeshi Inomata, Héctor Escobedo, and Arthur A. Demarest, eds., *Proyecto Arqueológico Regional Petexbatún, Informe Preliminar No. 5*, pp. 89–97. Report presented to the Instituto de Antropología e Historia de Guatemala.

_____. 1997. "Tamarindito: Archaeology and Regional Politics in the Petexbatun Region." *Ancient Mesoamerica* 8: 321–335.

Valdés, Juan Antonio, and Federico Fahsen. 1995. "The Reigning Dynasty of Uaxactun During the Early Classic: The Rulers and the Ruled." *Ancient Mesoamerica* 6: 197–219.

Valdés, Juan Antonio, Federico Fahsen, and Héctor Escobedo. 1994. *Obras maestras del Museo de Tikal*. Guatemala: Parque Nacional Tikal, Instituto de Antropología e Historia de Guatemala.

———. 1999. *Reyes, tumbas y palacios: la historia dinástica de Uaxactun*. Mexico, D.F.: Universidad Nacional Autónoma de México.

Webster, David, W. Fash, and E. Abrams. 1986. "Excavaciones en el Conjunto 9N–8: Patio A (Operación VIII)." In William T. Sanders, ed., *Excavaciones en el área urbana de Copán*, pp. 155–317. Tegucigalpa: Instituto Hondureño de Antropología e Historia..

Wolley, Claudia. 1995. "Investigaciones en la Estructura N5–3A del Grupo Murciélagos." In Arthur Demarest, Juan Antonio Valdés, and Héctor Escobedo, eds., *Proyecto Arqueológico Regional Petexbatún, Informe Preliminar No. 6*, pp. 281–289. Report presented to the Instituto de Antropología e Historia de Guatemala.

6

The Buenavista–Cahal Pech Royal Court: Multi–palace Court Mobility and Usage in a Petty Lowland Maya Kingdom

JOSEPH W. BALL AND JENNIFER T. TASCHEK

Symposia at recent meetings of the American Anthropological Association (Houston and Inomata 1996), the Society for American Archaeology (Christie 1998), and Dumbarton Oaks (Evans and Pillsbury 1998) have highlighted a new interest by Mayanists in better illuminating the nature, composition, and roles of the palace and court in Classic Maya civilization. Two of these have helped make clear that the term "palace" should properly be used to describe a functional type of architectural complex rather than as a label for virtually any and every chambered range building, as was the case throughout much of this century (see Andrews 1975:43–46 esp.). They also helped illuminate the range of morphological variation and size represented among Classic period Maya palaces and the highly varied depositional situations likely to be encountered among their archaeological records. In contrast, the AAA symposium focused attention on the actors who once inhabited these architectural stages, the activities they engaged in, and the significance of those activities within the broad context of Classic Maya culture and society. This volume continues an emphasis on the actors and activities associated with palaces rather than on those architectural stages. At the same time, many aspects of court life can be described only in conjunction with parallel considerations of their physical settings. We examine such an aspect in this chapter, and so although we do recognize the clear and complete distinction between "palace" and "court," we must consider both in our discussion.

Chapter Focus and Background

The archaeological records from the sites of Buenavista del Cayo and Cahal Pech are rich and potentially illuminating as to many aspects of Late Classic palace function and court life, a very few of which we previously have explored elsewhere (Ball 1993a, 1993b; Ball and Taschek 1991, 1992, 1996; Reents-Budet et al. 1994, 2000). Among the numerous possibilities that our data would allow us to address, from court composition to domestic and extradomestic court activities, we have chosen to focus on an aspect of court life that we believe has not received much attention to date: court mobility (cf. Houston 1993:125; 139–148). In using the phrase "court mobility," we mean neither the well-documented movements of royals and their accompanying parties between distinct courts seated at different centers, nor the equally well documented visits of regal personae to the courts of their subordinate liege-lords (Schele and Mathews 1991; Houston 1993); rather, we mean the wholesale transmigration of entire sets or subsets of regal actors and their activities from one royal palace to another within the same polity on some more or less recurrent basis. The concept is hardly novel. It describes a pattern common to numerous early, historical, and even modern states of many differing kinds, a pattern that is well documented virtually wherever written records exist (see esp. Geertz 1985; Kamen 1997; Steane 1999). It is, however, a pattern difficult to even recognize, much less document, when only empty palace ruins and artifactual debris remain. Nonetheless, we propose "mobility" as an attribute of at least some Classic Maya courts and, in this chapter, describe data from the western Belize Valley for one localized occurrence of the pattern.

In addressing this issue, we originally believed that we were dealing with a single pattern evidenced archaeologically in our late Terminal Classic data from Cahal Pech and Buenavista. We saw this as a possibly seasonal annual movement-pattern involving primary residence of the royal court at Cahal Pech throughout most of each year—essentially for the hot dry-season months—and their secondary residence at Buenavista during the dank, drizzly months of midwinter. Formal affairs such as state banquets or feasts requiring the presence of the regent or other court members could have been conducted at either center; however, our data indicate a more frequent or regular occurrence of these at Buenavista than at Cahal Pech despite the hypothesized lengthier period of annual residence at the latter center.[1] The distinction is between "holding court"—an activity linked to full court presence and thus residence—and conducting official court business—an activity requiring the actual presence of no more than a small, specific subset of court members. Although the local ruling elite undoubtedly did hold court at each center in conjunction with their residence there, court business could just as easily have been conducted in the absence of the full court. All that was required was the periodic—and not necessarily daily—travel of the regent or other appropriate court personnel from the palace of residence to the palace of business. Whether such travel might better be equated with periodic "business trips" or daily "commuting" we are unable to say. Elaborate formal feasting, entertaining, or ceremonial activities involving regal visitors, guests, envoys, or displays before large public gatherings could easily have been accommodated by the former pattern; however, the effective resolution of local affairs might well have required the latter. We are inclined to believe that both patterns occurred as required. Precisely such scenarios have been described for, among others, the royal courts and regents of medieval (twelfth- to sixteenth-century) England (Steane 1999), sixteenth-century and earlier Spain (Kamen 1997), eighteenth-century Russia (Massie 1981), and nineteenth-century West Africa (Mc-Caskie 1995).

It was this pattern of court mobility that we originally set out to present and document in this chapter. However, in developing our argument for the existence of a single Cahal Pech–Buenavista court (see below), we found ourselves confronting an entirely separate second instance and mode of movement. In addition to the annual seasonal pattern described above, we identified a likely long-term shift of the apparent primary dynastic seat from Cahal Pech to Buenavista (ca. A.D. 640–660) and then back again to Cahal Pech (ca. A.D. 740–760). This is reflected in what appear to be complementary alterations in the sitings of regnal burials and the use of ceremonial ball courts at the two centers during their histories.

We are uncertain as to the court's residential history during this period, especially in that such a multigeneration shift tends to suggest some major disruption in the existing dynastic or local political or regional political situations. We are unable to address this possible disruption here but do believe that continuing investigations will eventually shed some light on its nature and cause. We note that even a cursory exploration of the literature on early European and other societies, organized in ways comparable to those now generally accepted to have characterized the Classic lowland Maya, quickly reveals the extremely varied sociopolitical considerations, intrigues, and sometimes serendipitous historical circumstances that can underlie patterns of this kind (see esp. Kamen 1997:178–210; Massie 1981:7; Steane 1999:41–116). As of this writing, we can identify the period of the major transfer in dynastic ceremonial primacy back and forth between Cahal Pech and Buenavista and also believe that there is sufficient ceramic, artifactual, and architectural evidence to suggest extension of the hypothesized late Terminal Classic relationship between the two centers back into at least the fifth century A.D. The elucidation and detailed documentation of these complex diachronic situations will have to await considerably more ample presentation venues, however. What we wish to emphasize here is that the two patterns of movement were separate and distinct but resulted in complex, crosscutting depositional records that complicate one another's interpretation.

Palaces, Courts, and Court Mobility

We believe it is necessary and important to differentiate between the terms we use and to explicitly state our own usage. As employed in this chapter, "palace" refers to the "built-environment," that is, to any building, buildings, and building-complex housing or genuinely intended to house the immediate and extended members of a regnal-level family and their attendants, as well as those intended to provide a stage for the performance of socially prescribed functions, private and public rituals, and the culturally appropriate disposal and subsequent treatment of deceased court members. Conversely, by "court" we mean the royal and other regnal family members, their attendants, officers, appointees, servants, entertainers, hangers-on, and others involved in both the day-to-day maintenance and servicing of a society's ruling elite, whether hereditary or otherwise determined, and the performance of their appointed and expected organizational, administrative, adjudicative, ceremonial, ritual, and other social, political, ideological, and economic tasks within their respective culture system.

A *palace* provides a physical stage for a *court*. It is the material and thus archaeological expression of a court. It is, however, not the court or equivalent to it. A court consists of individuals together with their social identities, ranks, roles, responsibilities, activities, material associations, and other attributes. In most societies organized politically at the level of "archaic," "feudal," "galactic," "segmentary," or other early state types, the king or other equivalent *is* the court. Where the king is, the court is: The king equals the court (Fox 1977; Sanders 1981; Sanders and Webster 1988; cf. Geertz 1985:13–16). The court and its functions are associated directly with the ruler; derive from the ruler; and most properly are regarded as attributes of the ruler.

A court is ephemeral, transitory, and highly changeable as to composition and actions; a palace is concrete, stationary, and far less fluid as to physical constitution, although not actual function. Methodologically, archaeology *must* focus on the material reality that is the palace—on its physical description; architecture; iconography; spatial attributes; and on the analysis and interpretation of associated artifactual accessories. Theoretically, however, it is the living court that is of interest. It is the composition, activities, and functions of the court and its actors that anthropologists, archaeologists, art historians, and epigraphers attempt to tease from the palace and its remains.

As already observed, in many archaic as well as more complex state societies, courts are ambulant rather than stationary entities. To appreciate this, one need only consider the yearly dynamics of royal courts known from ancient China, Japan, and Southeast Asia; Pre-Colonial West Africa; Rajput and Mogul, India; historic Indonesia; Imperial Rome; Aztec and Mixtec central Mexico; Incaic Peru; czarist Russia; Renaissance Italy and medieval Europe; or the English monarchy over several centuries and numerous transformations. *Court mobility*, put simply, is a widespread, cross-culturally occurring pattern found in state societies of many kinds and grades throughout time. It is neither rare, nor unusual, nor in any way a not-to-be-expected pattern. The reality is that its nonoccurrence among the numerous courts of the Classic Maya would be far more improbable and inexplicable than its presence should be surprising. Were the pattern *not* present, in fact, we should be trying to explain why Classic Maya courts deviated in this respect from what seems to be a general cross-cultural norm.

As described historically, court mobility may result from any one or more of several factors. It may reflect the real need to demonstrate royal power and prestige or to exercise administrative functions locally throughout the length and breadth of a territorially extensive realm. Collaterally, it may reflect administrative situations demanding the personal presence of and access to "royal personae" rather than court bureaucrats (Geertz 1985). The great Khmer king, Jayavarman VII, addressed this concern by establishing a far-flung system of roadways, resthouses, and palaces throughout his domain, as at Sukhothai in Thailand (Gosling 1991:7–19). Examples of such situations abound from medieval Europe and Britain (Meade 1977; Kamen 1997; Steane 1999), including those of both Charlemagne and Charles V, whose ultimate declines many historians ascribe in part to their failures to move about their realms sufficiently widely and often to enforce what in reality was a very tenuously underwritten authority (see Bloch 1961; LeGoff 1988). Houston (1993) has suggested that similar attempts to counter poorly developed administrative infrastructures may have underlain the coexistence of the so-called twin capitals of Dos Pilas and Aguateca.[2]

Court mobility also may occur in connection with periodic activities—Rajput and Mughal pleasure palaces provide one example (Tillotson 1987:4–11; Koch 1991:103–105)—or major public occasions such as holidays, feasts, and festivals (see Steane 1999). Significant religious or other ritual occasions often engender court movements. Mobility may reflect overexploitation of the available renewable resources (fuel, food, water) of a local area within a realm and the consequent need to allow their replenishment or regeneration while still satisfying the physical needs of the court and its entourage (Steane 1999:71; 123). In a similar vein, mobility may result from intuitively recognized circumstances involving palace sanitation and court health. This was true in Britain long before Prince Albert's enlightened arrival in 1841 and had much to do with the almost frenetic and exhausting schedule of palace constructions and court movements carried out by Philip II (Kamen 1997:180–181). Finally, court mobility often results from simple considerations of physical comfort versus discomfort due to seasonal climatic or other environmental factors.

Whatever the underlying rationales, a mobile court requires the existence of more than one palace. Their formal and spatial comparability can (and generally does) vary largely on the basis of at least three factors: the specific purposes of the palace sites involved; the proportion of the full court expected to be present at each site; and the local construction history and past usage of each site. Similarly, the distances between palaces may be considerable to quite small depending on the principal reasons for court movement and the size and diversity of the realm. Other idiosyncratic factors also are likely to play roles in each particular case. This is not to suggest that there exist any simple correlations between morphology, size, separating distances, and causative factors but rather to point out that the variations potentially involved should be expected to vary at least as greatly as the factors potentially engendering court movement.

The function-related artifactual variability potentially present among palaces housing the same royal court can make the archaeological identification of multipalace court situations difficult in the extreme, and it is not unlikely that more than one such case may have been encountered in the past but not recognized. The case of Cahal Pech and Buenavista serves to illustrate one highly probable example of the mobile court pattern and to demonstrate just how uncertain the nonepigraphic behavioral data supporting such cases are even at their best.

Buenavista and Cahal Pech

The sites of Buenavista del Cayo and Cahal Pech lie just less than 5 kilometers from one another within the triangle loosely defined by the confluence of the lower Mopan and Macal Rivers at the western end of the Belize River Valley (Figure 6.1; Ball and Taschek 1991). A third, sociopolitically "major class" center, Xunantunich, also lies within this 180-square-kilometer area.[3]

Buenavista extends along the uppermost terrace of the Mopan River, slightly more than 400 meters back from its current south bank at an elevation of 343 feet (104.45 meters). Just less than 5 kilometers to its east, across a rolling bottoms and upland landscape of deep, black soils and expanses of marshland interrupted by deeply cut ravines and high limestone ridges, Cahal Pech sits atop the highest knoll of a steeply rising bluff at an elevation of 545 feet (166.03 meters). Seven hundred and fifty

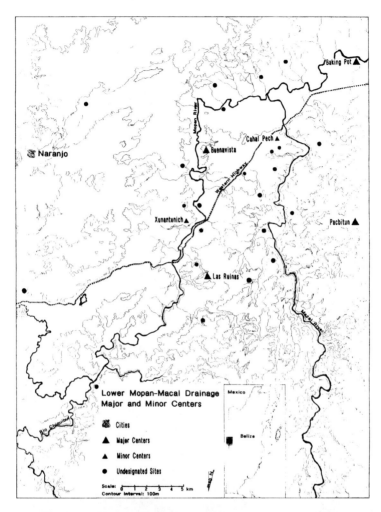

FIGURE 6.1　Map of greater lower Mopan-Macal drainage zone showing select major and minor centers.

meters to its northeast lies the deep gorge of the Macal River. Several deep ravines run down to this around the southeastern base of Cahal Pech Hill, and a permanent marsh and freshwater pond is present a short distance (130 meters) from the hill's southwestern corner.

Both Buenavista and Cahal Pech have been described well and require no extensive reintroductions here (Awe and Campbell 1989; Awe et al. 1991; Ball and Taschek 1991; Ball 1993b). Both are relatively small centers, and in this respect they are typical of sites throughout the greater Belize Valley region. Buenavista (Figure 6.2), the larger of the two, consists of roughly 12 hectares of contiguous monumental architecture spread out

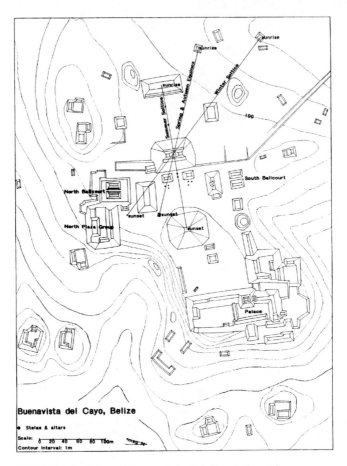

FIGURE 6.2   Map of Buenavista del Cayo site with significant referenced features identified.

over about 18 hectares of space on the highest terrace of the lower Mopan River. The Cahal Pech citadel, or core (Figure 6.3), occupies an 11-hectare area (about 27 acres) defined by the modified crest of a high limestone ridge overlooking the Macal Gorge, not at all dissimilar in size, orientation, or spatial situation from the ridge overlooking the Mopan River some 9 kilometers to the southwest that supports the Xunantunich site.

We should emphasize an important distinction between the centers of Cahal Pech and Buenavista. Whereas a palace complex *was present at* Buenavista, Cahal Pech *consisted of* an extensive palace complex and its dispersed outliers. This is an important difference. Using multiple classes of data—including site scale, internal (architectural) makeup, and plan; site placement; regional and zonal locational analyses; and extensive in situ artifact and deposit distributions and associations—we have argued in

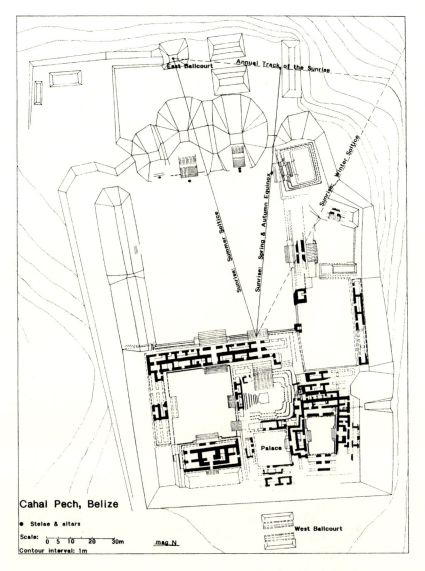

FIGURE 6.3 Map of Cahal Pech site with significant referenced features identified.

an earlier study (Ball and Taschek 1991) for the functional differentiations of Cahal Pech and Buenavista as, respectively, a *regal-residential center* (or citadel), and a multifunctional ("urban") *regal-ritual center* (see Ball and Taschek 1991:151–157 esp.; also Fox 1977:39–57).[4] Eight additional years of field and laboratory studies and their results have added details and suggested refinements to these assessments but have not substantially al-

FIGURE 6.4   Set of bowls in the Buenavista del Cayo "palace school" style.

tered them. The Cahal Pech hilltop complex *was* a high-status—or regal—residential citadel. The valley-floor, riverside Buenavista complex was a multifunctional urban center. The overall public ceremonial, economic, and multistatus residential character of this center, as indicated by its locational siting, architectural composition, internal layout, and complex artifactual record, were conjoined with a seemingly more public rather than private use of the only intermittently inhabited palace complex on its western, riverfront edge. The more public than private (albeit more occasional) use history of the Buenavista palace as compared to that at Cahal Pech is documented by qualitative differences between the depositional records from the two sites, especially by the comparative richness in presentation wares and exotica of the Buenavista palace deposits over those at Cahal Pech.

Artifacts other than ceramics, such as stone tools and implements, also indicate a functional differentiation of the Buenavista and Cahal Pech centers and their respective palace complexes. At Buenavista, a broad range of economic activities, including the production and distribution of several commodities, took place both within and without the palace confines (Ball 1993a; Ball and Taschek 1991, 1992, 1996; Kelsay 1985). At Cahal Pech, although royal residence, associated domestic and attendant support activities, regal burial, ancestral veneration, royal audience and display, and royal reception all are documented; evidence for the broad range of nonregal economic activities present at Buenavista has not been found. Restricting the current consideration to court-involved activities only, the final decorative slipping and painting of a distinctive local polychrome pottery style appears to have taken place inside or in the immediate vicinity of the south-end building complex of the Buenavista palace (Figure 6.4; Ball 1993a; Reents-Budet et al. 1994, 2000). The actual location where the unfinished green vessels themselves were produced has not been identified, but the downwind, palace-edge situation and physical configuration of the south-end platform complex would not be inappropriate, inconvenient, or otherwise unlikely as a place for such activity. No comparable findings were made at Cahal Pech, although it shared with Buenavista evidence of other domestic activities, including spinning and weaving; food preparation, food storage, and food consumption; tool maintenance; and even farming—a surprising but not unexpected regnal activity in societies organized politically at the level of complexity we believe to have existed among the Late Classic Maya of the Belize Valley (Sanders and Webster 1988; Ball and Taschek 1991; Ball 1993a, 1993b; Houston 1992, 1993, 1997; Houston and Cummins 1998; see also Fox 1977).

The Buenavista and Cahal Pech Palaces

At Buenavista, the Late Classic palace consists of a discrete complex (the West Acropolis) together with a small constellation of detached, surrounding platform structures. Five courts ringed by more than eighteen separate buildings make up the palace core. En toto, the palace complex covers about 2.5 acres (1.08 hectares), the platform-elevated core occupying nearly two (0.8 hectares) of these (see Figure 6.2).

The size of the palace at Cahal Pech to some extent is dependent on how one defines palace limits functionally and physically. Court life at Cahal Pech involved regular movement and activities throughout the entire hilltop complex, and in our judgment the entire complex constitutes a single, functionally integrated whole (see Figure 6.3). So defined, the Cahal Pech palace covers a generous 9.25 acres (3.75 hectares). A more narrow definition, limiting the actual palace only to the controlled-access, regal-residential, and administrative architecture and courtyards of the center, would yield a far more modest figure of 2.75 acres (1.1 hectares). Nonpublic support facilities would add to this an additional 0.2–.75 acres (0.08–0.3 hectares).

The Cahal Pech palace appears to have been associated closely and persistently with the *personal* activities and routines—both ritual and domestic—of private regal residence and with royal audiences and receptions. Architectural monuments and associated activities pertaining to regnal burial and ancestor veneration are situated preponderantly at and around Cahal Pech, and there is significant antiquity and continuity to their distribution extending from the Pre-Classic period into the Terminal Classic.

The Buenavista palace, in contrast, was associated with more community-oriented activities, including the formal entertainment of foreign dignitaries and possibly also of local subordinates and subjects. Several deep trash deposits rich in ceramic toasting cups, steins, and decanters; local fineware serving dishes and platters; fragments from numerous presentation vessels of both local and varied exotic origin; and abundant roasted deer, peccary, and other game scraps suggest a frequency and richness of large-scale banqueting not evident in contemporary deposits from Cahal Pech.

Buenavista and Cahal Pech: Court Social-Political Grade or Rank

Epigraphic information of any kind is exasperatingly limited for both Buenavista and Cahal Pech. However, the little that has been recovered—consisting of several appellative and rank-denotive glyphic texts on pottery and other portable objects—supports the implications of the extensive and rich contextual data from the two sites: Individuals of kingly rather than merely lordly rank were present at each from at least the late middle seventh century into the early ninth century, and the palace complexes at each thus housed true "royal" courts, albeit of territorially small realms or "petty" polities.

Space limits here prohibit detailed consideration, but we can note that the data include status-indicative contexts such as iconographically and materially regal burials and a variety of specific, distinctive artifacts and artifact assemblages ranging from composite mosaic *ajaw* belts, carved bone imitation and real stingray spines, and *spondylus* jewel cases to representations of the jester god, god K, and royal insignia–decorated personal jewelry. All data employed in this study were context-associated and were culturally significant rather than isolated or incidental. The overall collection represents a range of contexts from burials to secondary trash deposits and on-floor refuse. Lest there be any misunderstanding on this point, we emphasize that all data and deposits were *palace-associated*.

Buenavista and Cahal Pech: Court Identity

Our identification of the Buenavista and Cahal Pech palace occupants as the same individuals—members of the same petty royal court—is based on a principle of "complementary identity" as expressed in palace configuration, architectural style, and actual construction; pottery types, forms, and assemblages; artifact types and assemblages; portable art; funerary activities; and sitewide ritual architecture.[5] The identity of the two palace designs is most clearly evident in the innermost restricted-access residential quarters as identified by location, plan, and associated cultural remains. Not only are the configurations and dimensions of the courtyards and their surrounding rooms virtually identical (see Figures 6.2, 6.3, and 6.5); there is a shared use at both palaces of such details as slab-vaulted doorways to bring light into interior rooms and passages.[6] In addition, at approximately

The Buenavista–Cahal Pech Royal Court 177

FIGURE 6.5 (a) Principal interior courtyard, Buenavista del Cayo royal palace, from the northwest; Structure 31 in right background; (b) innermost residential courtyard, Cahal Pech royal palace, from the southwest; Structure 13 in background.

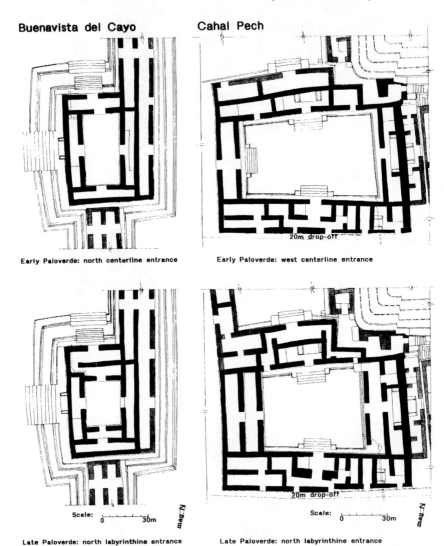

FIGURE 6.6 Comparison plans of the royal residential inner sancta at Buenavista del Cayo and Cahal Pech in the middle eighth and early ninth centuries.

the same time in the late eighth century, both inner sancta were rebuilt and made even more restricted to outside access (Figure 6.6). In each case, a *direct*, centerline portal entryway originally constructed early in the century was replaced with an *indirect*, labyrinthine passage-entry in conjunction with an expansion of the number of rooms and total amount of roofed space within the complex. Once again, a conceptually similar architectural design plainly marks the remodeling at each palace.

Environmental destruction precludes any comparison of the facade decorations originally adorning the two palaces. We can only note that brightly painted blue, green, red, orange, yellow, rose, white, and charcoal-colored carved and modeled stucco work was extensively present in both cases, and the systems of supporting armatures that once carried the decoration are identical.

Pottery vessels and assemblages can provide one potentially very powerful index of similarity, equivalence, complementarity, or differentiation for any comparable contexts. Ceramic plasticity, decorative malleability, and formal-functional specificity, when characterized minutely, precisely, and accurately through appropriate combinations of formal, typological, modal, and stylistic analysis in conjunction with chemical or physical characterization procedures, provide a complex tool for assessing these qualities. Although not foolproof, the composition of the Late Classic Cahal Pech, Buenavista, and respective palace-subset assemblages are suggestive as to the relationships of the associated user populations. In an ongoing collaborative study with Ronald L. Bishop and Dorie Budet (Reents-Budet et al. 2000), we have shown that stylistic, programmatic, and compositional as well as weaker typological and formal characteristics link the Late Classic and Terminal Classic ceramics of the Buenavista and Cahal Pech palaces far more closely to each other than to those of their respective centers and environs. This is significant, and we suggest that it strongly implies a comparably closer relationship between the occupants of the two palace complexes than between them and the extrapalace populations of their respective associated settlements. The compositional and stylistic findings are especially pertinent in that they indicate the presence at the two locations of multiple, decoratively complex, and iconographically distinctive vessels produced by the same workshops from the same clays. We do not propose that kitchen, storage, dining service, drinking, or other wares were transported regularly back and forth between the two centers—although the occasional personal favorite might well have been—but rather that the two palaces were furnished in comparable manners by the same producers and suppliers. At the same time, a formal-functional differentiation exists between the two assemblages that involves the exclusive presence or far greater occurrence at Buenavista of small toasting cups or goblets, larger quaffing vases, or "steins," very fine polychrome-decorated serving dishes, and an extensive array of fine imported exotic vessels. These were found in eight of ten palace middens sampled at Buenavista but were represented only by a small number of the locally produced large vases or steins in three of twelve such deposits at Cahal Pech. The differences suggest that the Buenavista palace assemblage included a subcomplex-like functional "supplementation," or add-on, to the basic (royal) domestic assemblage present at Cahal Pech. Thus, the two assemblages were neither equivalent nor functionally complementary yet still were very closely related.

Regnal Burials at Cahal Pech and Buenavista. Further amplifying our findings concerning the pottery assemblages characteristic of Late Classic habitational deposits at the two palaces, stylistic, programmatic, and typological ties also closely link such deposits at each site with specific interments at the other. Determination of the compositional identities of the ceramics involved in these cases is still in progress.

One of the most interesting of the contextual links identified to date involves a large, qualitatively rich, early-ninth-century refuse deposit from off the west-side rear of the Buenavista palace (Depositional Context 32–3) and a contemporary regal burial from the summit of Structure 4 at Cahal Pech (Burial CP–69–2). Excavated by Peter Schmidt in 1969, the interment's regal status is indicated by an elaborate jadeite mosaic *ajaw* belt complete with jadeite celts, a jadeite mosaic facemask, and other regalia indicative of royal status such as multiple *spondylus* valve offerings and stingray spines. The seven pottery vessels accompanying the burial all have strikingly close counterparts amid the shattered debris of the aforementioned Buenavista trash deposit (DC 32–3) and in effect represent a partial subset of that deposit's contents. In contrast, we were unable to provide a complete match for this burial subcomplex from among all the materials recovered at Cahal Pech.[7]

The shared presence at both centers of a single royal dynastic line or family—and so by inference court—from the Late Pre-Classic through the Terminal Classic periods also is suggested by an absence of any evident redundancy or contemporaneity among and the chronological complementarity of the highest-status regnal burials thus far encountered at the two sites (see Figure 6.7). Multiple late Xakal- and Madrugada-, Ahcabnal-, and Gadsden-phase burials of noble status have been recovered at Cahal Pech and its plaza-group satellites by ourselves and other excavators. None, however, were encountered at Buenavista. Interments of this elevated status dating from the Middle Classic Mills and early Late Classic Paloverde phases, in contrast, were recovered from the latter but not the former center. Finally, full Late Classic into Terminal Classic interments of noble and royal status were found at Cahal Pech, but not at Buenavista. As in other instances, these data are suggestive rather than conclusive, but the local presence of only one regal line would seem to be indicated by the distribution.

Ballcourts. The complementary distributions at Cahal Pech and Buenavista of high-status regnal burials hint at likely occasional—but not cyclic—multigenerational alternations in the apparent primacy of one

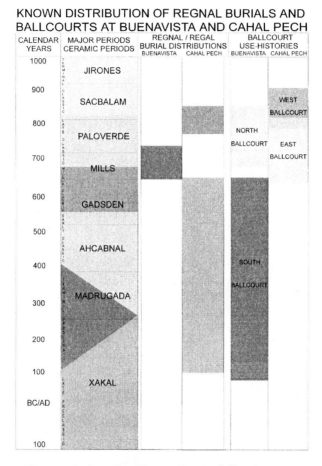

FIGURE 6.7 Late Pre-Classic–Terminal Classic ceramic-phase chronology and regal burial-ballcourt distributions for Buenavista and Cahal Pech.

center over the other. Such a pattern of switching relationships is indicated even more strongly by the chronological complementarity of the symbolically important ballcourt architecture of the two sites. Although the nature of ballcourt-related activities generally makes establishing accurate use histories for these open-air contexts difficult at best, by combining construction histories and some limited on-floor depositional data it has been possible to reconstruct at least partial outlines of these for the two centers. The combined construction and use histories suggest sequentially overlapping rather than continuously contemporaneous stagings of the ideologically and politically significant ritual ballgame at each center (Figure 6.8).

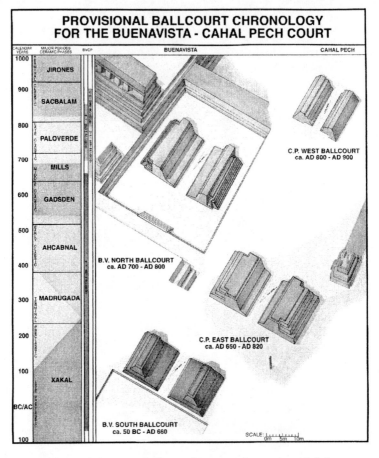

FIGURE 6.8 Schematic ballcourt histories, Buenavista del Cayo and Cahal Pech.

Buenavista del Cayo: South Ballcourt. The earliest ballcourt identified in the greater Cahal Pech–Buenavista zone is a small, open-ended, north-south complex at the southern edge of the Buenavista main plaza (see Figures 6.2 and 6.8). Built sometime during the first century B.C., the court for several centuries formed the southern edge of the central architectural plaza complex at Buenavista. After several refurbishments of the court and plaza during the Terminal Pre-Classic and Early Classic periods, the court was ritually "deactivated." In this process, its centerline cache was removed, a large number of whole pottery vessels and obsidian bloodletters were deposited on the playing-alley floor, and a sheltering thatched pole-and-daub shrine was constructed over the deposit. Finally, an 8-meter-high stuccoed masonry platform was built that closed or plugged the previously open southern side of the main plaza and blocked access to it via the deactivated ballcourt. This composite event took place sometime

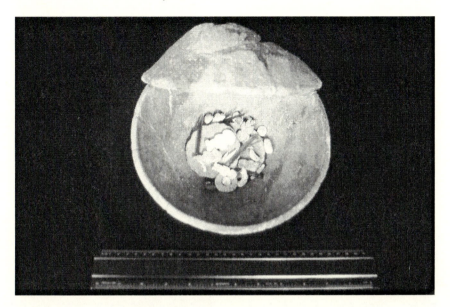

FIGURE 6.9   Center-point cache, North Ballcourt, Buenavista del Cayo.

between A.D. 640 and 660 and was contemporaneous with the construction and dedication of the large East Ballcourt at Cahal Pech.

Cahal Pech: East Ballcourt. The large East Ballcourt is the earliest such structure identified at Cahal Pech (see Figures 6.3 and 6.8). A series of construction-associated cache-deposits included the remains of two small children—arguably, at least, representing the ball-playing Hero Twins—and a set of five obsidian eccentrics. The eccentrics conformed to a caching tradition commonly associated with important lineage architecture and burials throughout the Belize Valley during the late seventh through the early ninth centuries (Otto 1995). The active lifespan of the Cahal Pech East Ballcourt has not been determined, and the task is made difficult by extensive trenching and cratering of both ranges and the playing alley by looters. Efforts to establish the use history of the court are, nonetheless, still under way.

Buenavista del Cayo: North Ballcourt. The zone's third monumental ballcourt was completed sometime between A.D. 700 and 750 at Buenavista, this time to the immediate north of that center's main plaza (see Figures 6.2 and 6.8). The new court was of an unusual sunken *I* design with an access stairway descending into it from the plaza pyramid terrace at its southern end. Other interesting features included a playing alley subflooring of tamped yellow clay and a limestone slab drain at its northwestern corner. The most interesting aspect of the court, however, was its center-point cache (Figure 6.9).

FIGURE 6.10   Center-point playing field cache pit, North Ballcourt, Buenavista del Cayo.

Placed in a marl-sealed pit at court center (Figure 6.10), the offering consisted of the two unslipped dishes (Hewlett Bank Unslipped) and their contents that originally had comprised the center-point cache of the deactivated Pre-Classic southern ballcourt.[8] The dishes and their contents—all quite typical of Late Pre-Classic and Early Classic cache materials from throughout west-central Belize—had been curated and redeposited to dedicate or ritually activate the Late Classic northern court. The jumbled contents had been supplemented by a series of fine obsidian bloodletters. Hydration analysis determined that the still pristine blades had been manufactured—and presumably used—on at least three separate occasions between about A.D. 710 and 810. We now are convinced that what at first sight would appear to be an anomalous finding indicates that the cache was disinterred, opened, added to and "renewed," reclosed, and redeposited on several occasions over the use-life of the court. Two large, red-slipped pottery urns of early-ninth-century date were found on the floor against the interior northern wall of the court. Their presence as defacto refuse indicates use of the court at least to this late. The absence of any later materials or trash suggests its abandonment not long after this time.

Cahal Pech: West Ballcourt.   A fourth, diminutive, open-ended ballcourt was built off the western edge of the Cahal Pech citadel sometime in the first half of the ninth century (see Figures 6.3 and 6.8). The court is tiny, more a final, feeble show of kingly dignity and duty than any pretense at a statement of ideological or political prowess or autonomy. Although severely damaged by treefalls and looter cratering, the small court yielded no evidence of ever having possessed a cache of any kind. The cessation of its use, unfortunately, cannot be dated.

The Significance of Regnal Rotations. The periodic alternations in the sociopolitical *primacy* and ceremonial *emphases* at Cahal Pech and Buenavista suggested by the alternating distributions of regnal burials and ballcourt architecture at each hint at changes resulting possibly from external political circumstances, possibly from ideological considerations, and possibly from the personal preferences of individuals. Steve Houston (personal communication, 1998) has suggested the possible involvement of some dynastic consideration such as a desire by royal successors to break overtly and physically with a predecessor's seat of power. Loosely analogous situations—often on far grander scales—are not uncommon in history. One such was the movement of the royal residence, the state ideological center, and the administrative capital from Thebes first to El-Amarna and then to Memphis during and following the reign of the Eighteenth Dynasty Egyptian Pharaoh Amenophis IV, better known as Akhenaten (Steindorff and Seele 1957; Redford 1984; Aldred 1988).[9]

There is one obvious and bothersome disharmony in the temporal distribution patterns of the Buenavista and Cahal Pech regnal burials and ballcourts. They are, in fact, in what appears to be almost perfect "complementary opposition" to each other. We are well aware of this and continue to seek a plausible rationale for the situation other than possible sampling error. We suspect it is in some way related to changes in the greater communal as opposed to private royal political and ideological significance of ceremonial ball-play and its physical expression, at least in the Belize Valley area, but we would welcome suggestions from others regarding this anomaly.

The Buenavista-Cahal Pech Relationship

Taken together, the Late Classic into Terminal Classic archaeological data currently available from Cahal Pech and Buenavista indicate the concurrent—albeit intermittent—use of both palaces by a population or populations of equivalent social rank and cultural role. We would further argue their actual physical identity. How far back before the eighth century this relationship pattern might have extended we cannot yet say with real certainty, although we do have indications from each site that it might have existed at least as early as the fifth century. Limited architectural data suggest that true palace complexes were present at each site by or somewhat before A.D. 700.

In addition to royal residence, some activities, such as royal audiences or tribunals and local governance, might have taken place at both centers based on the common occurrence at each of architectural facilities appropriate to such activities. We would note that the late-eighth– to early-ninth-century examples of these facilities at Cahal Pech are decidedly larger and grander than their counterparts at Buenavista, but functionally equivalent facilities were present at both centers.

Other activities—such as more personal (familial) and private royal rituals and funerary ceremonies on the one hand and more community-significant rituals and economic management on the other—appear to have occurred as the primary or exclusive functions of one center or the other. As indicated, however, there were apparent alternations in the primary functional emphasis of each center in the mid-seventh and eighth centuries that complicate this pattern.

Alternative Possibilities

There are several possible scenarios that the archaeological data do *not* support, and we should also take note of these.[10] Full and careful evaluation of all possible evidence rules against identifying Buenavista and Cahal Pech as two independent, contemporary, functionally equivalent political or ceremonial organizational centers: These were not the autonomous capitals of two separate realms.[11] In contrast to Awe and Campbell (1989), no data exist to support a successor relationship involving the decline or abandonment of one center and a coincident or successive florescence of the other. Overall occupational use and general purpose architectural construction were continuous and coeval at both sites from the Late Pre-Classic well into the Terminal Classic period.[12]

There is no evidence to indicate that the Cahal Pech and Buenavista palaces represented contemporary or generationally sequential housings of different members of the same royal family (junior siblings or offspring, multiple wives, dowagers, etc.).[13] Neither do we now see a firm basis of support for their identification as hierarchically related members of the same multicenter polity, our own earlier exploration of this possibility notwithstanding (Ball and Taschek 1991; Tourtellot 1993:227–228).[14] Finally, we see no signs of such grand-scale, back-and-forth occupations, abandonments, and reoccupations as might result from either the occurrence of cyclical, calendric "compulsive" transmigrations (Puleston 1979) or the existence of complementary social dualities (moieties) (Becker 1983).

In sum, from at least the middle eighth century on—and possibly also prior to the middle of the seventh century—Cahal Pech served as the principal royal home, stage for royal audiences and displays, and focus of private royal ritual for the lords of the western Belize Valley. During this same time, Buenavista functioned as a public center and theater for community organization, economic activity, and regal sociopolitical ceremony. Complex architectural, artifactual, ceramic, and contextual records document the systemic integrity and complementarity of the two centers and strongly support the contention that their respective palaces served but one and the same single royal court governing the same, single realm encompassing the western Belize Valley drainage of the lower Mopan and Macal Rivers.

One Court, Two Palaces—Why?

Let us turn finally to the bottom line: What might have caused a need by the Late Classic Mopan-Macal Triangle royal court for two separate palaces at Cahal Pech and Buenavista and for an apparently regular migration of the entire court back and forth between the two centers. Why might such transit have occurred?

Spatial Proximity and Its Implications

Earlier in this chapter, we reviewed several factors that historically have been responsible for court mobility. Revisiting these, it is immediately obvious that the spatial proximity of the two centers alone would seem to rule out many of them as likely motivations for migration on a scale sufficient to require the construction of two entire separate palace complexes. For example, even though the sociopolitical environment of an archaic state typically (cross-culturally) might demand the personal appearance of a regent throughout the realm to establish and maintain authority—possibly nowhere more so than at the homesites of subordinate lords—an overland move of the royal presence and display of less than 5 kilometers is hardly likely to have had any consequential effect, let alone one sufficient to justify wholesale accompaniment by the full court. Similarly, had the royal court exhausted local capacities to feed or otherwise service it at either the Buenavista or the Cahal Pech locality, a move of such distance would not have resituated it in a place more able to meet its needs.

Effective water management and waste control were good at both palaces, with conceptually similar and identically constructed courtyard drainage systems being present at each. Similarly, the local fishing, swimming, and hunting around the Buenavista and Cahal Pech palaces are unlikely to have differed greatly if at all based on present-day models and experiences.

As to periodic or regular ritual observances, including funerary obsequies and subsequent ancestral rites, royal or popular pilgrimages, retreats, or other activities that might have been aimed at polity identification and integration, we cannot completely rule these out as plausible reasons for court movements between the two centers. This is especially so given the inspectionally obvious ideological importance of the central plaza at Buenavista, the documented occurrence of royal banquets at the Buenavista palace, and the alternating importance of ceremonial ballplaying at Buenavista and Cahal Pech. However, we believe available data overwhelmingly point to Xunantunich as the Late Classic zonal focus of royal ancestral veneration in the western Belize Valley. For reasons that remain unknown, the Xunantunich site in the eighth century became the principal royal "ancestor-mountain" of the Maya lords of the Mopan-Macal Triangle. It was there, we believe, that the eighth-century lords of the Mopan-Macal Triangle entombed their dead (see Endnote 3) and performed their obsequies, and to there that the royal court or its members subsequently journeyed for the purpose of carrying out ancestral devotions and rites of intercession.[15]

More important than the straight-line distance between the two sites (4.8 kilometers; 3 miles) were the actual *topological distances* (see Abler et al. 1971:255–272 esp.) separating the two palaces—the realistic overland travel distance, courier time, and entourage time, or "real-time social distance" between them.[16] Even using these, each of the two centers lay well within the other's most conservatively defined probable economic sustaining area (estimated at 5–8 kilometers; see Ball and Taschek 1992) and responsive (or readily controllable) sociopolitical "catchment zone" (estimated at 20–30 kilometers; see Houston 1993:137–138).[17] In the end, it is most unlikely that king and court or king and courtly panoply would have migrated from Cahal Pech to Buenavista or the reverse in order to address concerns involving the maintenance of sovereign authority or to resolve problems arising from local resource depletion. Depending on the specific circumstances involved, such a move would have been either inconsequential or ineffective.

Topographic Separation and Microclimatic "Distance"

Clearly, no significant spatial or temporal distances separate the two palaces or their centers. What *does* separate them is a battery of topographic, microenvironmental, and microclimatic conditions. Temperature, airiness, wind direction, and rainfall intensity each differ significantly between these two closely neighboring locations, and the results are substantial differences in the seasonal habitability of the two palaces between the hot late winter–summer and cool fall-winter seasons. Habitability and comfort are functions of more than simplistic rainy season/dry season dichotomizations, and we have found the factors involved sufficiently complex to warrant a separate, in-depth study of their own. What we offer here are simply some initial facts and findings.

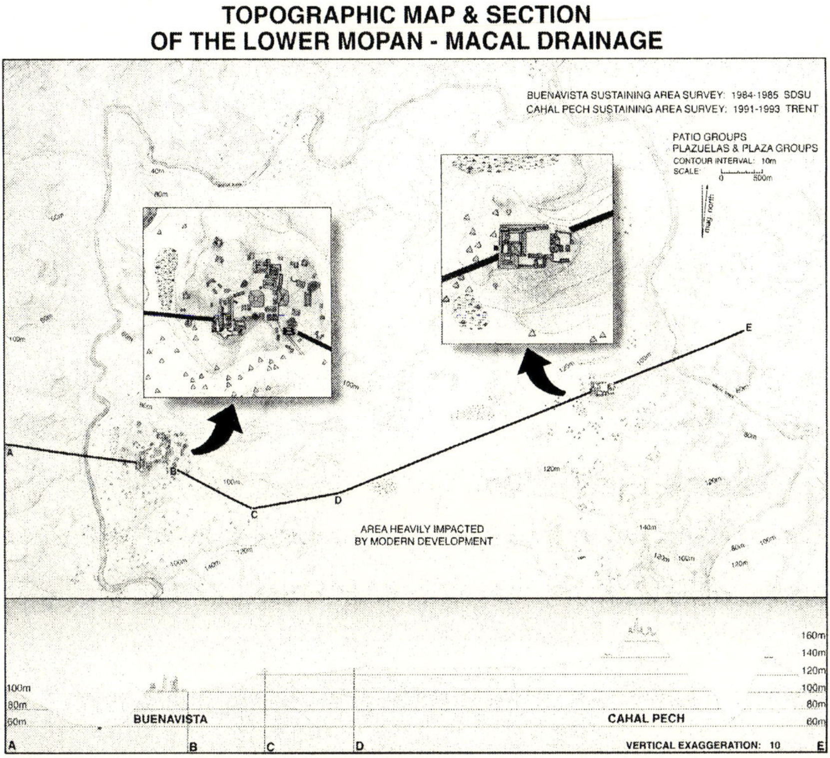

TOPOGRAPHIC MAP & SECTION
OF THE LOWER MOPAN - MACAL DRAINAGE

FIGURE 6.11   East-west topographic cross-section of the lower Mopan-Macal Triangle through Buenavista and Cahal Pech (vertical exaggeration 5:1).

First and obviously, Buenavista and Cahal Pech are characterized by sharply contrasting physical sitings—the former on a low-lying, valley-bottom river terrace, the latter along the windward edge of a lofty bluff (Figure 6.11). The Cahal Pech citadel rises up into and catches prevailing winds, thermal updrafts and other breezes, and the cooling down-valley updrafts of late afternoon (see Brown 198:26–29 esp.). The Buenavista palace lies in a virtual wind-shadow created by both its physical situation and the morphology of the enclosing monumental center. For all but the chill, drizzly, dank days of November through February, the Cahal Pech palace is refreshingly airy, balmy, and comfortable. The palace at Buenavista is closed, hot, and stuffy. For those very same few winter months, however, that Cahal Pech stands dank and cold, the Buenavista palace becomes a warm and cozy refuge.

More than 200 vertical feet (202 feet; 61.6 meters) separate the land surfaces upon which the two palaces were built. At Cahal Pech, another 25-plus feet (8 meters) of architectural mass raises the floor level of the royal residential apartments to a height of 570 feet (174 meters) above sea level. At Buenavista, the corresponding quarters also rise above the palace complex, but only some 20 feet (6 meters) to a total elevation of about 363 feet (110.6 meters).

The overall effect of 200-plus feet of elevation combined with other microenvironmental variables is a real diurnal temperature difference between the two palaces of 6–8 degrees Fahrenheit. This is more than enough to be noticeable and easily means the difference between discomfort and comfort during the hot months of March into September as well as the wet and chilly months of November into February. We speak to this from anecdotal local information, from official meteorological records, and from nearly fifteen years of direct personal experience and supporting journal data. A GIS-based study still in progress also suggests that significant "comfort-level" differences in rainfall and wind patterns and shadow/shade effects are present between the two centers. The bottom line is that the Cahal Pech palace appears to have functioned as the primary residence for members of the Mopan-Macal Triangle royal court throughout most of the year, whereas Buenavista—principal community ceremonial, economic, and organizational center for the realm—provided only what amounted to a "winter palace." It merits noting that Buenavista incorporates architectural platforms, marker-monuments, and formally defined sight lines for both the summer and winter solstices as well as for the vernal and autumnal equinoxes (see Figure 6.2). Cahal Pech includes similar facilities only for the summer solstice and equinoctial events (see Figure 6.3). In fact, the center is laid out so as to preclude the direct on-site marking of the winter solstice. If we reject the premise that the event itself was not important, it suggests the possibility that the ability to mark and celebrate its occurrence was not important at Cahal Pech—possibly, we would argue, because the court was not in residence at that time.[18]

As to the proximity of the two palaces, it ought be remembered that among other pedestrian peoples alternative palace sites are often similarly near. The "country palace" (Cahal Pech?) of the powerful mid–nineteenth century Asante king, Kwaku-Dua-Panin, lay only some 3.5 miles outside the capital city of Kumase (Buenavista?) at Eburaso (McCaskie 1995:373). The country palace of his predecessor, Osei-Yaw-Akoto, was located about 5 miles from the capital, and it is here that this *asantehene* ("king" of the Ashante) is recorded to have conducted both public affairs and private rituals of a nature generally reserved to the official state center at Kumase (McCaskie 1995).

Even the archetypal examples of seasonal courts—the Summer and Winter Palaces of Czar Peter the Great—also actually lay only a little over a mile from each other on opposite banks of the River Neva (Massie 1981:605). Yet a third palace situated across the river from the residential Winter Palace was used by Peter for formal banquets and other affairs of

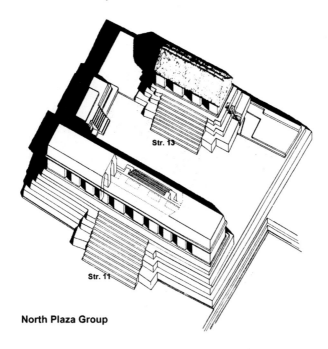

FIGURE 6.12 Axonometric reconstruction of the North Plaza Group at Buenavista seen from the southeast.

state (Massie 1981:603–604). This czar moved regularly among these three locales, accompanied by whatever portion and magnitude of the full royal court that was required.

The Mopan-Macal Triangle court resided at Cahal Pech throughout most of the year, and most court functions probably took place there. Sovereigns or their representatives likely traveled back and forth regularly between Cahal Pech and Buenavista to conduct public zonal and community affairs, but such business required no more than the availability of an appropriate administrative audience hall or tribunal and the occasional provision of suitable but limited accommodations. Such facilities have been identified at Buenavista.

The North Plaza Group (see Figures 6.2 and 6.12) is fronted by an architecturally splendid—and almost grotesquely out of place—formal *audiencia* (Structure 11).[19] In service throughout the eighth century, the complex appears to have fulfilled at Buenavista whatever societal functions were associated with Late Classic *audiencia*-type buildings. Physically isolated from the palatial West Acropolis, its built-in residential facilities (Structure 13) were minimal but comfortable. Associated off-platform refuse evidences regular if not continuous high-status elite (noble or royal) habitational use from the late fifth century through the eighth century.

We are not able to determine from the recovered archaeological evidence whether the local sovereign and retinue, royal representatives, and other court officials traveled to and fro daily between the palace of residence and the palace of court affairs (when these did differ)—as, for example, did Philip II of Spain (Kamen 1997), Asante kings (McCaskie 1995), and many other regents—or only made appearances periodically as required—as did most medieval English monarchs, among others (Steane 1999). We are inclined to believe that the royal transit occurred on a periodic rather than daily basis, but we admit that this represents a logical assumption rather than a substantiated inference. What we believe can be certain, however, is that such royal peregrinations were carried out far more as elaborate processional displays than as mundane commutes or trips. The designed role and importance of such royal processionals as instruments of societal integration and subjugation in archaic states on a worldwide basis has been documented over and over again (e.g., Geertz 1985 [Elizabethan England; Indonesia; North Africa]; Freeman and Warner 1990:65–66 [Angkor]; Jessup 1990:193–209 [Indonesia]). With respect to the Belize Valley, we have no doubt that the zonal regent's progress from center to center was a political act of precisely this kind. How often it took place, however, we currently are unable say.

Conclusion

In the eighth and early ninth centuries A.D., contemporary royal palace complexes were present at the western Belize Valley centers of Cahal Pech, Buenavista del Cayo, and Xunantunich.[20] We have tried to show in this chapter that at least the Cahal Pech and Buenavista palaces served concurrently to house the selfsame members of but a single royal court.[21] Why two palaces for one court? Like other royals across space and time, from Pre-Colonial Africa to medieval Europe and czarist Russia, the Maya sovereigns of the Mopan-Macal Triangle moved members of the royal court, court functions, or the entire court itself from place to place as needed or desired and built additional palace facilities as thereby required. In the case of the palaces at Cahal Pech and Buenavista and the recurrent Late Classic court movements between them, we see at work no matters of state; no momentous historical event; no grand cosmological or ideological design; no in any otherwise culturally or calendrically "compelled" actions. What we do see are simply the archaeological reflections of mundane arrangements involving seasonal palace comfort and habitability and the personal preferences of individuals, perhaps tempered to some extent by lineal ritual obligations.

Zonal administrative activities, economic organization, ceremonial community integration, and broader regional political responsibilities might have required a periodic royal or noble presence at Buenavista, as suggested by the siting there of royal banqueting facilities and ballcourts, but these were not sufficient to demand the resident presence at that center of the entire royal court or the construction there of a full-service palace complex suitable to house it. Considerations of personal comfort and household privacy together with family traditions and resulting ritual obligations exerted a far more powerful pull from atop Cahal Pech Hill. In the end, we contend, it was these same considerations rather than administrative needs or concerns that brought about the construction and contemporaneous use of separate palaces at Cahal Pech and Buenavista to serve the needs of but one royal court.

And what do *we* learn from this? On a particularist level, we can add one more simple fact to our overall understanding of the life and workings of Classic Maya courts: At least some of them maintained, made use of, and were associated with multiple palace sites; at least some of them engaged in a dynamic palace-to-palace mobility. On a more general level, the lesson of this finding is also quite simple: In the ambulant quality of their royal courts, as suggested by the western Belize Valley data, the ancient Maya have revealed themselves once more to have been little different from and much akin to many other peoples—a creatively extraordinary but in the end very accessible, comprehensible, and human expression of prescientific humanity.

References

Aldred, Cyril. 1988. *Akhenaten: King of Egypt*. London: Thames and Hudson.

Abler, Ronald, John S. Adams, and Peter Gould. 1971. *Spatial Organization: The Geographer's View of the World*. Englewood Cliffs, NJ: Prentice-Hall.

Andrews, George F. 1975. *Maya Cities: Placemaking and Urbanization*. Norman: University of Oklahoma Press.

Ashmore, Wendy, and Richard M. Leventhal. 1993. "Xunantunich Reconsidered." Paper presented at the Belize Conference, University of North Florida, Jacksonville.

Awe, Jaime J., and Mark D. Campbell. 1989 *Cahal Pech, Cayo, Belize: A Preliminary Guide to the Ancient Ruins*. Benque Viejo: Belize Tourism Industry Association.

Awe, Jaime J., Mark D. Campbell, and Jim Conlon. 1991. "Preliminary Analysis of the Spatial Configuration of the Site Core at Cahal Pech, Belize, and its Implications for Lowland Maya Social Organization." *Mexicon* 13(2): 25–30.

Ball, Joseph W. 1993a. "Pottery, Potters, Palaces, and Polities: Some Socioeconomic and Political Implications of Late Classic Maya Ceramic Industries." In Jeremy A. Sabloff and John S. Henderson, eds., *Lowland Maya Civilization in the Eighth Century A.D.*, pp. 243–272. Washington, DC: Dumbarton Oaks Research Library and Collection.

_____. 1993b. *Cahal Pech, the Ancient Maya, and Modern Belize: The Story of an Archaeological Park*. San Diego: San Diego State University Press.

Ball, Joseph W., and Jennifer T. Taschek. 1991. "Late Classic Lowland Maya Political Organization and Central-Place Analysis: New Insights from the Upper Belize Valley." *Ancient Mesoamerica* 2: 149–165.

_____. 1992. "Economics and Economies in the Late Classic Maya Lowlands: A Trial Examination of Some Apparent Patterns and Implications." Paper presented at the Wenner-Gren Foundation symposium The Segmentary State and the Classic Lowland Maya: A "New" Model for Ancient Political Organization. Cleveland State University.

_____. 1996. "Beyond Residence, Ceremony, and Burial: Artists, Craftsmen, Specialized Production, and the Late Classic Maya Court." Paper presented at ninety-fifth annual meeting of the American Anthropological Association, San Francisco.

Becker, Marshall J. 1983. "Kings and Classicism: Political Change in the Maya Lowlands during the Classic Period." In Arthur G. Miller, ed., *Highland-Lowland Interaction in Mesoamerica: Interdisciplinary Approaches*, pp.159–200. Washington, DC: Dumbarton Oaks Research Library and Collection.

Bloch, Marc. 1961. *Feudal Society*. Chicago: University of Chicago Press.

Christie, Jessica J. (Organizer). 1998. *Maya Palaces and Elite Residences*. Symposium at the sixty-third annual meeting of the Society for American Archaeology, Seattle.

Braswell, Jennifer B. 1998. "Archaeological Investigations at Group D, Xunantunich, Belize." Ph.D. diss., Tulane University.

Brown, G.Z. 1985. *Sun, Wind, and Light: Architectural Design Strategies*. New York: John Wiley and Sons.

Evans, Susan T., and Joanne Pillsbury (Organizers). 1998. *Ancient Palaces of the New World: Form, Function, and Meaning*. 1998 Pre-Columbian Symposium, Dumbarton Oaks Research Library and Collection, Washington, DC.

Fox, Richard G. 1977. *Urban Anthropology: Cities in their Cultural Settings*. Englewood Cliffs, NJ: Prentice-Hall.

Freeman, Michael, and Roger Warner. 1990. *Angkor: The Hidden Glories*. Boston: Houghton Mifflin.

Geertz, Clifford. 1985. "Centers, Kings, and Charisma: Reflections on the Symbolics of Power." In Sean Wilente, ed., *Rites of Power: Symbolism, Ritual, and Politics since the Middle Ages*, pp.13–38. Philadelphia: University of Pennsylvania Press.

Gosling, Betty. 1991. *Sukhothai: Its History, Culture, and Art*. New York: Oxford University Press.

Houston, Stephen D. 1992. "Weak States and Segmentary Structure: The Internal Organization of Classic Maya Polities." Paper presented at the Wenner Gren Foundation Symposium The Segmentary State and the Classic Lowland Maya: A 'New' Model for Ancient Political Organization, Cleveland State University.

_____. 1993. *Hieroglyphs and History at Dos Pilas: Dynastic Politics of the Classic Maya*. Austin: University of Texas Press.

_____. 1997. "Estados Débiles y Estructura Segmentaria: la Organización Interna de las Entidades Políticas Mayas." *Apuntes Arqueológicos* 5(1): 67–92 (Guatemala: Escuela de Historia, Universidad de San Carlos).

Houston, Stephen D., and Tom Cummins. 1998. "Body, Presence, and Space in Andean and Mesoamerican Rulership." Paper presented at the Dumbarton Oaks Symposium, Ancient Palaces of the New World: Form, Function, and Meaning. Washington, DC.

Houston, Stephen D., and Takeshi Inomata (Organizers). 1996. *Royal Courts of the Classic Maya: An Anthropological Perspective*. Symposium at the ninety-fifth annual meeting of the American Anthropological Association, San Francisco.

Jessup, Helen I. 1990. *Court Arts of Indonesia*. New York: Asia Society Galleries and H.N. Abrams.

Kamen, Henry. 1997. *Philip of Spain*. New Haven and London: Yale University Press.

Kelsay, Richalene G. 1985. "A Late Classic Lithic Finishing Station at Buenavista del Cayo, Belize." Paper presented at the fiftieth annual meeting of the Society for American Archaeology, Denver.

Koch, Ebba. 1991. *Mughal Architecture*. Munich: Prestel-Verlag.

LeGoff, Jacques. 1988. *Medieval Civilization, 400–1500*. Oxford: Blackwell.

Leventhal, Richard M., and Wendy Ashmore. 1995. "Xunantunich in a Belize Valley Context." Unpublished paper in authors' possession.

Leventhal, Richard M., W. Ashmore, L. LeCount, V. Hetrick, and T. Jamison. 1992. "Xunantunich Archaeological Project: 1992 Research." Paper presented at the ninety-first annual meeting of the American Anthropological Association, San Francisco.

Massie, Robert K. 1981. *Peter the Great: His Life and World*. New York: Ballantine Books.

McCaskie, T. C. 1995. *State and Society in Pre-Colonial Asante*. Cambridge: Cambridge University Press.

Meade, Marion. 1977. *Eleanor of Aquitaine: A Biography*. London: Penguin Books.

Puleston, Dennis E. 1979. "An Epistemological Pathology and the Collapse, or Why the Maya Kept the Short Count." In Norman Hammond and Gordon R. Willey, eds., *Maya Archaeology and Ethnohistory*, pp. 63–71. Austin: University of Texas Press.

Otto, Barbara E. 1995. "The Eccentrics of Buenavista: Typology, Terminology, and Meaning." Master's thesis, San Diego State University.

Redford, Donald B. 1984. *Akhenaten: The Heretic King*. Princeton: Princeton University Press.

Reents-Budet, Dorie, R. L. Bishop, B. MacLeod, V. Fields, and J.W. Ball. 1994. *Painting the Maya Universe: Royal Ceramics of the Classic Period*. Durham: Duke University Press.

Reents-Budet, Dorie, R.L. Bishop, J.T. Taschek, and J.W. Ball. 2000. "Out of the Palace Dumps: Ceramic Production and Use at Buenavista del Cayo, Belize." *Ancient Mesoamerica* 11:99–121.

Robin, Cynthia, and Jason Yaeger. 1996. "Ancient Maya Royalty and Expressions of Power at Xunantunich." *ECO-Journal of Environmental Information* 1(3): 32–36. Belize City: Environmental Conservation Organization.

Sanders, William T. 1981. "Classic Maya Settlement Patterns and Ethnographic Analogy." In Wendy Ashmore, ed., *Lowland Maya Settlement Patterns*, pp. 351–369. Albuquerque: University of New Mexico Press.

Sanders, William T., and David L. Webster. 1988. "The Mesoamerican Urban Tradition." *American Anthropologist* 90: 521–546.

Schele, Linda, and Peter Mathews. 1991. "Royal Visits and Other Intersite Relationships among the Classic Maya." In T. Patrick Culbert, ed., *Classic Maya Political History: Hieroglyphic and Archaeological Evidence*, pp. 226–252. Cambridge: Cambridge University Press.

Steane, John. 1999. *The Archaeology of the Medieval English Monarchy*. London: Routledge.

Steindorff, George, and Seele, K.C. 1957. *When Egypt Ruled the East*. Chicago: University of Chicago Press.

Taschek, Jennifer T., and Joseph W. Ball. 1987. "Regal-Ritual Residences and Administrative Hubs: Differential Structure and Function among the Major Centers of the Upper Belize Valley." Paper presented at the fifty-second annual meeting of the Society for American Archeology, Toronto.

Tillotson, G.H.R. 1987. *The Rajput Palaces*. New Haven: Yale University Press.

Tourtellot, Gair. 1993. "A View of Ancient Maya Settlements in the Eighth Century." In Jeremy A. Sabloff and John S. Henderson, eds., *Lowland Maya Civilization in the Eighth Century A.D.*, pp. 219–241. Washington, DC: Dumbarton Oaks Research Library and Collection.

Yaeger, Jason R. 1997. "The 1997 Excavations of Plaza A-III and Miscellaneous Excavation and Architectural Clearing in Group A." In Richard M. Leventhal, ed., *Xunantunich Archaeological Project—1997 Field Season*, pp. 24–55. Unpublished annual field reports, University of California–Los Angeles.

Yaeger, Jason R., and Wendy A. Ashmore. 1993. "Xunantunich at the End of the Classic: Dynamics of Settlement in a Time of Crisis." Paper presented at the fifty-eighth annual meeting of the Society for American Archaeology, St. Louis.

Notes

1. These data include the number, ceramic-content quality and compositional richness, and artifactual functional diversity of comparably sized palace trash deposits encountered at the two sites. Summary discussions of these attributes are presented where appropriate below.

2. Houston argues that the existence at each of these two centers of equivalent palace facilities concurrently utilized by members of the same royal family is a reflection of efforts by those regents to use their personal presence to reinforce their authority to weakly integrated subject populations. He posits a similar rationale for the periodic visits of royals from Piedras Negras and Yaxchilan to the courts of subordinate *sajal* within their respective realms.

3. Although we chose not to examine the possible sociocultural and historical relationships of Cahal Pech and Buenavista to Xunantunich in this chapter, the authors are convinced that the latter was an integral part of the same central place system to which the two former centers belonged. We believe that Xunantunich served a very special *and specialized* role in the system during much of the middle through late eighth century—that of regnal or noble necropolis and royal ancestor shrine. If we are correct, it is highly likely that the center continued to enjoy importance as a focus of "elite" ancestral veneration well into the ninth century.

We see Structure A-6 (El Castillo) as a royal ancestor-mountain, but, unlike others, we believe it to have been the ancestral focus for the entire western or upper Belize Valley rather than for the single (Xunantunich) center and its immediate sustaining area alone. We believe Structures A-2, A-3, A-4, A-7, A-8, and A-9 served as noble funerary monuments over the eighth century, and although the 1990s UCLA Xunantunich Archaeological Project failed to investigate this possibility, sufficient data do exist from work by earlier researchers to support its viability (e.g., Gann 1925). The comparatively simple palace compound at Xunantunich (Plaza A-III) likely served to house local royalty only periodically in conjunction with regnal funerary rites or on occasions of ancestral devotional observances. The impressive, Cahal Pech–like, ninth-century *audiencia* (Structure A–13) suggests a decided if brief role for the center as a principal stage for regal display and public administrative activities during the early ninth century, a time of troubles in the Belize Valley as elsewhere across the southern lowlands and, as such, a time during which a highly defensible ridgetop retreat might well have served local rulers as the administrative hub of choice.

Crucial to evaluating our hypothesis is a single, precise, and currently unavailable comparative parallel construction and use-history chronology for the late Terminal Classic *audiencias* at Xunantunich (A–13), Cahal Pech (Structure 1), and Buenavista (Structures 11 and 36). To the extent possible based on available data, such a determination is now in progress.

The authors must here also remark that numerous recent suggestions (Leventhal et al. 1992; Ashmore and Leventhal 1993; Yaeger and Ashmore 1993; Leventhal and Ashmore 1995; Robin and Yaeger 1996; Braswell 1998) to the effect that Buenavista failed as a center, was largely abandoned, and was replaced by Xunantunich sometime around A.D. 750 *or earlier* are not only premature in the extreme but also controverted clearly and obviously by even our limited published data (Ball and Taschek 1991; Ball 1993a; 1993b).

4. In this study we also evaluated the functional role of Xunantunich based on the data available in 1990. Extensive subsequent work by the Xunantunich Archaeological Project (1991–1997) has provided much new data concerning the nature of Xunantunich, data far too extensive to consider here. Readers are directed to a recent article by Robin and Yaeger (1996) for a good, up-to-date summary discussion of their import.

5. We have struggled to find a succinct but accurate way of describing this concept without complete satisfaction. Briefly, the Late into Terminal Classic archaeological records of the two palaces as expressed in the stated material classes are virtually identical and represent a single, shared material cultural complex with two exceptions. First, certain specific activities—regnal burial and ritual ball-playing (see following section)—occurred in a chronologically complementary manner at one center or the other from the Late Pre-Classic onward. Second, some specialized activities—ostentatious banqueting and the decorative painting of the local palace-school polychrome pottery (see Ball 1993a)—appear to have occurred only at Buenavista. We regard the latter activities as supplemental to the general body of court domestic and administrative routines, the full range of which are represented in the late Terminal Classic records of both palaces.

6. The two palaces also share a well-defined masonry technology that is distinct from that of the Late Classic Peten veneer facing tradition. This local masonry construction mode—which is also shared by the Xunantunich palace (Plaza A-III)—employs regularly coursed facing masonry that deteriorates (breaks up) into discontinuous and disorganized courses of small limestone chunks immediately adjacent to vaulted doorways. The tooth to anchor surface plaster is provided by continuous chinking with flat spalls in both vertical and horizontal joints.

7. One red-slipped (Tinaja group) tripod dish; a reddish brown on cream linear crosshatch design bowl; and two red on cream to buff "petal" or "feather" motif

bowls are typical of dining servicewares common at both sites as well as elsewhere throughout the valley. However, a red and black on cream pyriform pedestal vase bearing a seated personage engaged in penal bloodletting matches several vessels from Buenavista palace deposits but none from Cahal Pech. Finally, two probable imports from the central Peten—a high-gloss, fluted blackware vase and a Zacatel cream-polychrome "checkerboard" design dish—each have multiple exact matches at Buenavista and also are known from Uaxactun and Tikal. Neither, however, has any counterparts or similarities among the massive corpus of Late and Terminal Classic ceramics recovered to date from Cahal Pech.

8. We recovered the north ballcourt centerpoint cache in 1984. It consisted of two broken and eroded Hewlett Bank dishes set lip to lip and their jumbled contents. We easily recognized these contents to be of generic Late Pre-Classic/"Proto-Classic"/Early Classic origin-date and were troubled by the otherwise documented Late Classic construction age of the ballcourt. The three hydration dates obtained only further confused the situation. In 1988 we excavated the southern ballcourt, including its emptied and refilled centerpoint cache pit. The matrix soil, artifactual inclusions, and other associated debris from this pit all passed into our laboratory storage facility until early 1992, when sufficient lab staff to carry out their processing and recording finally were available. During the processing, our lab supervisor, JoAnne Gilmer, recognized two nonfitting sherds of Hewlett Bank Unslipped and whimsically "tried" each against the broken vessels recovered from the northern court in 1984. Each fit neatly to a broken edge of one of the dishes, although neither could be joined to the other. We can conceive of little stronger evidence to support our interpretation of the northern court cache's history.

9. Peter the Great's eighteenth-century shift of the imperial Romanov residence and the Russian administrative capital from Moscow to St. Petersburg is another well-known case of such movement, as is Philip II's sixteenth-century transfer of the primary Hapsburg dynastic residence, principal regal ceremonial center, and state administrative seat from Valladolid to Toledo and then to Madrid. It merits noting that entirely different reasons ranging from ideological considerations and issues of administrative centralization to mundane matters of accessibility and pure physical comfort underlay each of the three cited cases (see especially Massie 1981:52, 355, 602–612; Kamen 1997:179–188). Such movements, in other words, are not easily ascribable to any single specific factor or cause.

10. Limitations of space again here require an abbreviated presentation of these alternatives and our reasons for their rejection. We will address these more fully in future treatments of the Buenavista–Cahal Pech–Xunantunich central place system.

11. We base this on the combined significance of the proximity of the two centers to each other; their effectively complete occupational contemporaneity; the major differences in their overall scales, site designs, architectural makeups, and functional roles as indicated by artifact distributions; and the application of central place analysis to the two centers within their larger geographic and settlement contexts (see Ball and Taschek 1991 for full exposition of this evaluation). As we point out again in the next section, the two centers lay well within each other's most likely economic and sociopolitical "catchment zones," or spheres of

control, estimated respectively at 5–8 kilometers (Ball and Taschek 1992) and 20–30 kilometers (Houston 1993). Note that we are here considering the Buenavista and Cahal Pech *centers—not* the palace complexes.

12. Neither center appears ever to have been abandoned completely from the late Middle Pre-Classic well into the Terminal Classic. Nonregal supporting populations always were present within and surrounding the Buenavista center and throughout the countryside immediately around Cahal Pech. Furthermore, trash deposits associated with each of the late Terminal Classic palaces suggest that at no time was either completely empty of some inhabitants, possibly resident service or maintenance personnel.

13. As already indicated, the composite archaeological records from each palace—including architecture, pottery, and artifacts—document the contemporary presence at each of a corporate group of the same rank and social identity. In other words, the Late Classic Cahal Pech and Buenavista palaces were utilized either by the same royal body or by two absolutely equal and contemporary groups of royalty.

14. There is a subtlety here in that Cahal Pech was a "palace center," whereas a palace was present as one constituent of the center at Buenavista. We recognized this in our earlier analysis (Ball and Taschek 1991) but failed to fully grasp its significance. In that study, we characterized the Cahal Pech, Buenavista, and Xunantunich *centers* as functionally *complementary*. What we failed to recognize is that even though they might have been complementary *as centers*, they were *redundant as palace sites*. This is a subtle but important distinction.

15. We would point out that the comparatively "basic" and spare nature of the palace complex at Xunantunich gains considerable understandability in this light. Given the well-established longevity and tenacity of tradition among the Maya, we must also note here that no ethnographic or ethnohistoric traditions exist today that suggest any special importance for the Buenavista locality that might have elevated it above or countered the obvious commanding visual prominence and presence throughout the upper Belize Valley of Structure A–6—the Sacred Mountain—at Xunantunich.

16. With help from some local residents, we determined the most likely real-world (direct but realistic) travel parameters for these to be: (1) real travel distance: 4.6 miles or 7.4 kilometers; (2) slow-walk/strolling-time: 1:10–1:30 hours; (3) courier/running time: 20–25 minutes; and (4) entourage/procession time: 2:30–3:30 hours (or considerably more depending upon expected "stops" and their associated rites/drinking/meal consumption as reflected in contemporary Maya processional observances; see Geertz 1985:22–23; Steane 1999:71–72).

17. We should note, however, that the two centers are associated with two separate drainage hinterlands and that the upriver resources potentially available to Cahal Pech would have differed from those accessible to Buenavista from its valley-bottom environs.

18. An interesting aspect of the Cahal Pech East Ballcourt involves the precise placements of the dual equinoctial and summer solstice markers at its respective southern and northern ends. These were such that at the vernal equinox the sun rose immediately off the southern end of the ballcourt and each day thereafter rose slightly to the north directly over and traversing the length of the court until reaching its northern end at the summer solstice. Thenceforth, as viewed from the

ceremonial observation station in the portal at the east foot of Structure 13, the rising sun retraced its path southward until finally passing over the south-end marker at the autumnal equinox. Over the following six months, the sun at first rose ever farther southward—away from the court and off the site—until its eventual reversal at the winter solstice and ultimate return at the vernal equinox.

19. Since we introduced this term in the mid-1980s (Taschek and Ball 1987), it has come to be used widely to describe a building-type consisting of two back-to-back ranges of individually accessed rooms flanking a central portal connecting one seemingly more "public" plaza or courtyard with a more "private" or restricted-access counterpart, the latter typically associated physically with high-status occupancy and other activities. Functionally, the *audiencia* was both a screen and a controlled access passageway between more public and more private zones of high-status social activity. Although now commonly used in this manner, the term has never been defined formally. To that end, an *audiencia* was a multiroom range structure that separated more public civic-religious courtyard space from more private elite status space and functioned both as a screen and a controlled-access passageway between the two. A variety of activities as yet poorly understood were associated with these buildings. What we can say is that these activities involved a controlled and culturally defined interfacing of high-status members of society and others, and that matters of local administration and adjudication as well as of "foreign" affairs appear likely to have been conducted within them based on associated artifactual data. Further, based on the same artifactual data, the actors involved and activities engaged in appear to have differed considerably and fundamentally in each of the two courtyard areas separated by *audiencia*-type buildings in all those cases systematically investigated (Cahal Pech; Buenavista; Las Ruinas; Xunantunich). We propose that these buildings served as architectural screens, interfaces, and portals between the restricted private worlds and approachable public worlds of local elites and their constituencies, including both local subordinates and extralocal peers and superiors.

20. Architectural testing has revealed that the Cahal Pech and Buenavista palaces each grew gradually by accretion over the late seventh through early ninth centuries and that each had been built over and incorporated portions of early-seventh- and late-sixth-century palatial predecessors. In contrast, the construction of a palace at Xunantunich appears to have been conceived and undertaken as a single event no earlier than sometime during the eighth century (Yaeger 1997).

21. As previously indicated, although we have chosen not to discuss the palace at Xunantunich further at this time, we believe that it, too, belonged to the Lower Mopan–Macal royal court central place system but that it owed its existence to reasons functionally very different from those that produced the redundant duo at Buenavista and Cahal Pech (see Endnotes 3 and 4). We should also note that we do not exclude the possible existence of other, as yet unidentified members of this palace circuit situated farther afield—as, for example, at the regal-ritual city of Naranjo.

7

Life at Court:
The View from Bonampak*

MARY MILLER

When we think about what life at court was like for the Maya, our minds usually generate pictures based on the Bonampak murals, for, indeed, more than any other work from the pre-Hispanic past, those murals do seem to offer us an illustration of Maya life. In fact, the murals of Bonampak are known almost completely as illustrations for one thing or another.

What makes us think that the Bonampak murals provide a view of palace life? Clearly some portions of the painting—say, the great battle painting—take place away from standing architecture. But all other scenes transpire in association with architecture, animating what might otherwise be understood only archaeologically as unarticulated platforms or steps, and thus providing a way to read—and even historicize—Maya architecture. Additionally, the paintings depict two thrones in use. The single most important piece of Maya furniture—the throne—also explicitly refers to the Maya palace, its exclusive place of use. Even more specifically, two known thrones with inverted trapezoidal legs, like those of the paintings, had particular palace contexts: first, the throne of the Oval Palace Tablet, House E, the Palenque palace; and second, Piedras Negras Throne 1, which had been set into the wall of J-6, within the Piedras Negras West Acropolis palace complex. Such placements confirm that the Bonampak paintings are referring in some scenes to activities at the heart of palace complexes.

---

*Students in my seminar on Mesoamerican painting in fall 1997 contributed to analysis of the Bonampak paintings, especially Rachel Cane, Scott Brown, and Amy Kurtz. Work by Karl Taube and Stephen Houston, members of the Bonampak Documentation Project, has stimulated new thinking about Bonampak. Regan Huff and Lisa Senchyshyn have prepared new images used in this study.

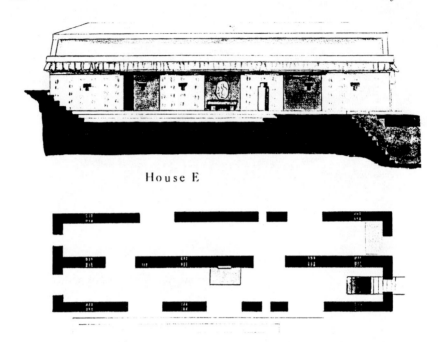

FIGURE 7.1 Palenque Palace (redrawn by Gillett Griffin; used by permission).

Ironically, the architecture at Bonampak itself offers few clues to its meaning, although in general the Maya architecture of Chiapas is more richly explicit in its iconographic coding than Maya architecture elsewhere. For comparison, the Palenque palace merits consideration, for the palace there seems not only to be the architecture of courtly life but also to represent that architecture in action. In other words, whereas architecture elsewhere is often silent about function, and whereas the Bonampak murals may depict functioning architecture, the Palenque palace provides architecture wherein meaning and function is pronounced by its facades and furnishings (Figure 7.1).

At the heart of the Palenque palace lies the iconography of rulership, embedded in House E, with the throne installed at the Oval Palace Tablet. Later, a more public throne would be installed in House AD, in front of the Palace Tablet. These two throne rooms both celebrate installation in office and attendant rituals. In House E, the iconography of accession is also emphasized by the use of the Bicephalic Monster over the doorway that links it to the northeastern court of the palace, the transitional location between the house of accession, and the courtyard of war and sacrifice. House E signaled a humble origin of Maya rulership in its exterior form, perhaps ever more important as grander and larger colonnades grew up around it, in which the building replicated aspects of a thatch structure, particularly in the finish of the mansard roof (Robertson 1985:8–9). Additionally, like many a perishable structure of the Maya, its exterior was painted white (and then adorned with painted flowers) throughout its history, unlike the rest of the palace, which came to be painted red. In other words, the pattern that Stone (1989) has demonstrated, in which Maya lords sought to identify themselves as humble agriculturalists during rituals of accession, may also hold true for the structures of accession, in which they may have sought to call upon the iconography of peasant agriculture. Whereas the Maya called upon this simple agricultural past during accession ceremonies, the Aztecs invoked a past when they were nomadic hunters and gatherers, or Chichimecs. Put simply, Mesoamerican peoples invoked the past in order to affirm authority. What is preserved in stone at Palenque may in fact be a clue that the architecture of accession may frequently have been a perishable structure, and the thatched features on the upper margins of some accession stelae may be further indication of this practice, as seen on Copan Stela J or Mayapan Stela 1.

Maize iconography also forms a theme of House E and its surrounding courtyard at Palenque, underscoring Stone's association of maize rituals and accession. At the top of a stairway from the subterranean passages into the tower court, the Maize God flourishes; within House E, a throne was once placed within the maws of the Underworld, an iconographic conceit also featured on Pakal's sarcophagus lid, and from these underworld maws the Maize God was reborn (Robertson 1985:figs. 67; 118). Presumably House E, then, featured maize ceremonies. Because rulers are often depicted as the youthful, growing maize in ear, the emphasis probably falls on green corn ceremonies (Taube 1985). We should probably also keep in mind the sort of ceremonial gardens kept within palace precincts by both Aztec and Inka rulers as well as symbolic cultivation. The common depiction of tamales and tamale presentation on Maya ceramics (see Reents-Budet, Chapter 7 in Volume 1), usually in throne rooms, may well have been a part of maize rituals and associated with accession and its renewal over the years on, say, anniversaries of the first event.

House B bears the iconography of the mat on its upper facade, indicating that it was a *popol na*, or mat house, in other words a communal lords' house, probably related to similar concepts across the native Americas (cf. Miller 1998; Stomper n.d.). House B was originally one large open room before later partitions were thrown up and was equally accessible to both House E and the northeastern court; presumably the attending lords needed to participate in both the court of rulership out its backdoor and the court of tribute and sacrifice to which it faced. The access to House E was particularly indirect, so that lords attending from House B might slip in and out without great attention.

The iconography of the northeastern courtyard treats warfare and its principal results: tribute and sacrifice. Nine gross captives carved of distinctive rock visually grovel along the sloping eastern wall; texts on loincloths note that captives were "dressed," probably for sacrifice. Directly across the courtyard, nobles from Pomona reveal their fealty to Palenque, and they flank steps that relate the early-seventh-century assault on Palenque and the attendant destruction of their ritual images, from which the site clearly recovered. The physical evidence for tribute can be seen in the distinctive types of limestone, which were probably imported from the surrounding region. It is worth remembering that when the Aztecs imposed their most crippling tax burdens they insisted that subject cities bring stone.

No such elaborate palace spaces exist at Bonampak. In fact, the courtyards that signal palace architecture at Palenque and Piedras Negras are altogether absent from the site. Nevertheless, the Bonampak building that houses the murals (Structure 1) might be encompassed by a very general description of palace architecture, with its three-chamber design (Figure 7.2). However, the entire configuration of Structure 1 at Bonampak is unusual, especially in the way it makes the observer walk outside of the building in order to gain access to the next room. This design would suggest that the building was planned to create space for murals, and thus the designer maximized wall space. Additionally, the built-in wrap-around benches were apparently planned from the first, in what was a unique local adaptation. The benches helped protect the paintings from casual wear and tear (Figure 7.3). They, too, were painted, and in Room 1 they were painted with the stepfret patterning that most commonly occurs on Maya underwear—thus also making the building akin to something worn, adorned from the inside out, in concentric circles (Figure 7.4). Mesoamericanists have long noted analogies between headdresses and roofcombs; the relationship between articles of attire and architectural features may be able to be expanded.

The exterior was painted in broad vertical bands of red and salmon on cream, with a running glyph band at the cornice level that once included about 130 glyphs (Figure 7.5). In other words, candy-cane stripes descended from the glyph band, giving the appearance of a striped building. Such striping was part of the iconography of warfare in Mesoamerica. Skin "striped" with an obsidian blade electrified the body with all-over pain, so that the warrior was less likely to give in to sleep, and his hunger was dulled. Even before entering the fray, the Maya warrior was pumped up with adrenaline, ready to fight for hours. Structure 1, then, when its facade could be seen, revealed the iconography of striped human flesh, aggressively announcing that it is a warrior building.

Although we see Bonampak Structure 1 today as defined by its stone architecture, the building was probably very different in its appearance to

Life at Court: The View from Bonampak 205

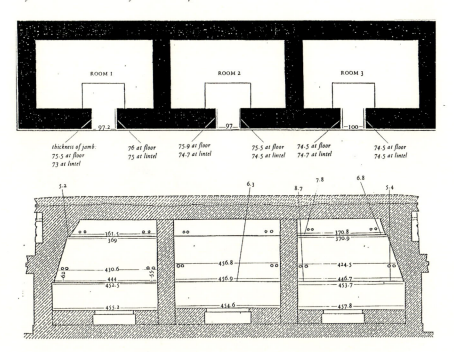

FIGURE 7.2 Bonampak Structure 1, plan and section (drawing by Regan Huff; courtesy Bonampak Documentation Project).

FIGURE 7.3 Bonampak murals, Room 1, view of bench and lintel (copy by Antonio Tejeda after Ruppert, Thompson, and Proskouriakoff 1955).

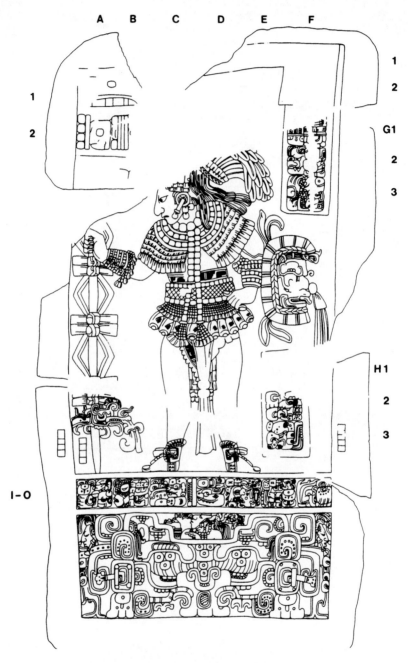

FIGURE 7.4   Detail of Stela 1, Bonampak (rawing by Peter Mathews; used by permission).

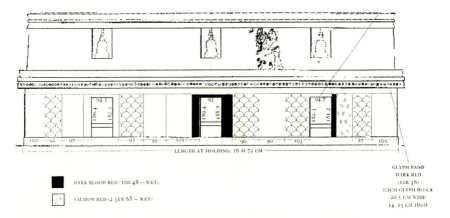

FIGURE 7.5 Bonampak Structure 1, elevation (drawing by Regan Huff; courtesy Bonampak Documentation Project).

the Maya. Flimsy curtain holders line the inside door frame, allowing cloths to be stretched across the doorways. Additionally, some cornice fragments on the ground may have "curtain" holes. What was suspended from the front of the building was probably much like an awning. "Curtains" often seem to be inside palaces, but there is usually no means for the attachment of heavy sheets of cotton *inside* the palace. Cotton awnings would have expanded the functional and protected palace area, turning what seem today to be hot and public stoops into private and shady extensions of the palace. The scenes, then, of palace life on Maya vessels, commonly articulated by steps, thrones, pillars, doorjambs, and curtains, generally refer to the continuous palace, from its dark, airless interiors to the brighter and more spacious tentlike spaces of the stoop.

On the surface, then, the courtly life of the late eighth century presented in the Bonampak murals is a picture of the well-fed and even the complacent. But we might imagine the cultural backdrop against which the visual narrative is set: Simply put, population and its attendant demands outstripped the environment, which could no longer provide enough food, fuel, and material for shelter. Without adequate supplies of maize and beans, without wood to cook—and, more important, without the ability to reduce limestone to the quicklime necessary to effect the nixtamalization of maize (without which maize has little nutritive value)—the Maya may have been driven to pursue any route to get them. Warfare wracked many sites; kings fell captive or hostage. Cities were burned. But a city burned was a city that might not have been able to be rebuilt, for where would the thatch or timbers come from? Not from a rainforest reduced to patchy scrub bordering tare-choked fields. An environment destroyed must have led to utter degradation, first of the physical world of the Maya and, ultimately, even the spiritual. It is in this cultural dissonance between courtly elegance and the horror of the battlefield that we find some of the most moving and disturbing images of the ancient Maya at Bonampak.

A reality constructed visually is *a* reality, but it is not the same reality that a historian would relate or an archaeologist would find on the ground. These realities may all be in conflict, or seemingly so: We find the seamless carving of Parthenon frieze figures to be an expression of the highest ideals of fifth-century B.C. Greece, but in fact we could juxtapose these remarkable works against a story of death, disease, and political malfeasance in Athens. Remarkable works of art are often *more* than the expression of their time, which is why they are an altogether different kind of artifact from most of the detritus of the archaeological past. Works of art are imbued with ideology and meaning by their makers. Works of art were constructed by their makers; what archaeologists can construct can never have the intent or viewpoint of an ancient work of art. In this we should recognize that the murals of Bonampak are far more than illustration and that their construction may *tell* as much about the Bonampak court as *illustrate* it; they project a noble ideal rather than passively record their lives.

The paintings of Bonampak appropriate the key architectural settings of any Maya site and represent them all: palace, pyramid, presentation steps for captives—there is even the suggestion of a ballcourt in the presence of two individuals attired for ball-playing in Room 1. What is represented at Bonampak is nothing less than the complete architectural configuration of, say, the entire ritual precinct of a Palenque. This artistic conception of Maya space and ritual is conflated, letting us see that the lords of Bonampak "own" it all, a sort of Potemkin village in which the fiction is more compelling than the fact, particularly when presented with such conviction. In Room 1, the hieroglyphic text notes King Chan Muwan as the owner of the building: In owning the building, he may own the unfolding narrative as well. By extension, he pretends to dominate an architectural and ritual realm.

The explicit furniture of the palace chamber of the Usumacinta, the wedge-legged throne, defines the palace life of the Bonampak murals. Interestingly enough, Karl Ruppert reported such a throne (he called it a "square altar") across the plaza from Structure 1, adjacent to Structure 16, although its current location is unknown (Alejandro Tovalin, personal communication, 1999). With a plain top surface measuring 1.05 meters by 1.6 meters, such a throne would have been large enough for two or three individuals to sit on—exactly what is depicted in Rooms 1 and 3. Was it once within Structure 2, adjacent to Structure 1, and thus within a building that might have accommodated palace function? We cannot know, but the very representation two times of this significant piece of furniture would seem to underscore its role in courtly rituals.

Life at Court: The View from Bonampak 209

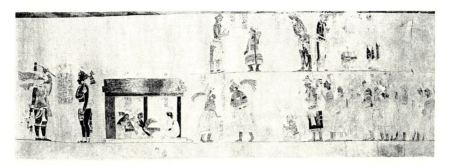

FIGURE 7.6 Uaxactun painting (copy by Antonio Tejeda after Smith 1950).

Of course, such a plain throne pales beside the grand ones excavated at neighboring Piedras Negras, Yaxchilan, and Palenque, or even the painted versions in Bonampak Rooms 1 and 3. But a parallel may also be seen in costume: Archaeologically excavated adornments are usually found to be much smaller than the way the Maya depicted them. In their representations, the Maya frequently enhanced their representations and even diminished those of their enemies. Without grand architecture, without highly elaborated furniture, the lords of Bonampak may have willingly settled for the elaborated representation of ritual and for the acquisition of its trappings, ranging from furniture to costume. In short, the Maya felt free to paint a world far grander than the one they actually inhabited.

In their remarkable ability to describe a world of ritual and its settings that goes far beyond the constraints of the building itself, the Bonampak murals may also be part of a painting and manuscript tradition that is nearly unknown to modern observers. At Uaxactun, fragmentary paintings from the late fifth century feature many conventions that are otherwise known only in the Bonampak paintings. The figural program features members of the court at about one-quarter life-size, and they reenact the rituals that would have taken place within the palace (Figure 7.6). A visiting warrior in Teotihuacan dress receives a cordial welcome; women gather on the stoop of a palace, its roof decorated with woven mat signs. Like the Bonampak murals, the Uaxactun murals include numerous musicians. These musicians demonstrate the great skill of the painters, for the figures overlap one another, and a single musician turns to the man behind him, in part of a formula for the representation of musical retinues that would be repeated 300 years later, at Bonampak.

Underneath the Uaxactun paintings was a running 260-day count, the ritual calendar of divination characteristic of many Mesoamerican books known from the time of the Spanish Conquest, a thousand years later. Events are punctuated along the linear day count, perhaps to be correlated with the elaborate figural scene above. Framed by a broad red outline, as are Maya books, the Uaxactun painting gives us the sense of what a Maya book of the period would have looked like as well as a preview of the later paintings at Bonampak.

If Uaxactun and Bonampak can be linked across 300 years, then they are clearly only traces of a much broader tradition, but perhaps traces of the tradition of the book rather than of the mural. What also links Uaxactun and Bonampak across 300 years is the standardization of ritual. The Uaxactun painting is only a fragment, but its subjects are encompassed by those of Bonampak. Nevertheless, the Bonampak murals are a far more powerful artistic achievement in many respects. For one thing, they both reveal emotion—rare in Pre-Columbian art—and command it from the viewer. Second, individual master painters of a remarkable team effort also stand out, giving particular character to a single wall, for instance. Furthermore, few other ancient Mesoamerican works are so experiential for the viewer, and this might well have been as true in antiquity as it is today. Finally, in sandwiching the room celebrating battle between rooms celebrating additional dynastic events, the paintings also provide a united, harmonious narration of a world that seems simultaneously fractured by war and sacrifice—a window on the dissonance that the Maya themselves could not recognize.

Room 1 features an Initial Series text that indicates this room's likely primacy in the reading order. Above the text, lords in white mantles—some of whom are explicitly titled *ajaw*—approach a royal family assembled on a throne, including a small child who is held up to the lords by a servant. A bundle to the right of the throne bears a few glyphs that identify the contents as five 8,000-bean counts of cacao, in what would have been a substantial tribute or tax payment in a world where the cacao bean was one of the few standard means of exchange. The lords, then, are presumably paying their taxes and cementing their loyalty to the royal family at the same time (Figure 7.7). The text below notes an installation in office, possibly of a child described as a kinsman of the Yaxchilan royal family, and also notes the dedication of the building in A.D. 791. This is the only reference to installation in office, usually one of the principal subjects of palace iconography. Visually, the emphasis is given to tribute, not a subject of the monumental text. Such seeming inconsistencies may serve to open up the questions that can be asked about the meaning of verbal statements.

Throughout the program, only a viewer seated on the built-in bench could have studied the northern wall over the doorway. In Room 1, this northern wall shows three principal lords preparing for celebration and dance (Figure 7.8). A servant to the right of the lord at center daubs his master with red paint; a servant strains to secure a feather backrack in the frame of the lord at left. Recent infrared photography unmasks the long-

FIGURE 7.7 Bonampak murals, Room 1, upper southern wall (digital enhancements by Doug Stern to photographs of Enrico Ferrorelli, copyright National Geographic Society; used by permission.

invisible skill of the painter, who applied a lively final black outline over the blocked-out colors (Figure 7.9). Body contours and the rendering of torsion reveal a deep understanding of human form and the foreshortened, rounded way in which the eye *sees* rather than *knows*. Not only is the rendering of hands especially meticulous; the detail of the line also indicates close kinship to the sculptural tradition of Yaxchilan rather than to the small-scale paintings of Maya vases.

Dressing is a ritual with a number of implications. Backracks and headdresses were bulky and valuable, composed almost entirely of luxury materials. Jade collars and cuffs, jaguar pelts, and fine cottons all required some means of storage. What did the Maya use as closets and bureaus? Wooden and wicker chests probably held most ritual attire; Maya lords may have then hoisted such boxes up to the rafters, the way that *cofradía* (ritual brotherhoods) costumes and idols are kept in highland Guatemala today. A building with stone vaulting would have been an ideal place for such storage, because it would also have protected valuables from fire, should a roof be set afire. The hoisting up and down of

FIGURE 7.8 Bonampak murals, Room 1, north wall (copy by Felipe Dávalos; courtesy Florida State Museum).

FIGURE 7.9 Infrared detail of dressing scene, Room 1, northern wall (courtesy Bonampak Documentation Project).

ceremonial attire may well have been ritualized. The depiction in Room 1 could refer to the space inside Room 1 where ceremonial attire may have been stored and where dressing would then transpire.

The dressing ritual also includes the painting of the body. The strangely drawn hand of the attendant to the right of the principal dancer may be an attempt to show a hand that is dripping with pigment. Here, responsibility for bringing pigments to the court may rest in the hands of the *ah naabs* (court attendants with responsibility for painting) who do the painting; other *ah naabs* may have the job of bringing in the merchant packs that sit on the palace steps.

The principal lords of the dressing-scene on the northern wall are represented a second time, dancing, on the badly destroyed wall one sees upon stepping into the room. The sequence is clear: Dressing precedes performance. But in making such sequences specific, the Maya painters emphasize the narrative that threads its way through the rooms. Protagonists reappear from scene to scene, providing a sense that the story moves both backward and forward in time. In this regard, the paintings are more visually narrative than any other Pre-Columbian work of art. If we were to describe this in linguistic terms, we might say that the paintings are like a series of verbal events—and in this, they differ from the more typically nominative representations of Maya stelae—or of almost all other Pre-Columbian works of art. The paintings of Bonampak may be the only monumental works of Maya art that surpass visually the narrative complexity of Maya writing.

The ritual of dancing is known primarily from Yaxchilan. It may have taken place on the Bonampak plaza, or in one of the smaller buildings flanking it, so that the other participants could take their places. In the sixteenth century, Fray Diego de Landa described the small radial platforms at Chichen Itza as the loci for performances. In most Yaxchilan instances, a principal lord—usually one of the Jaguar kings of Yaxchilan—dances with a liege-lord, generally in what would seem to be acts of détente, conciliation, and perhaps harmony. At Yaxchilan, ruling kings commonly dance with subordinates from the hinterland on lintels; at Piedras Negras, according to the text recorded on Wall Panel 3, a Yaxchilan king dances with the Piedras Negras ruler, presumably as equals. At Bonampak, according to the texts, none of the three dancers is Chan Muwan; one may well have been a member of the Yaxchilan ruling family. This dancing may well establish harmony among a coalition of Bonampak, Lacanha, and Yaxchilan lords, but it may well also identify Yaxchilan as the superior power.

On the lowest register of Room 1, Maya musicians and regional governors flank the dancers at center. Here the Maya artist attempts to represent aspects of movement and sound otherwise unknown in Maya art.

FIGURE 7.10   Infrared detail of drummer, Room 1 (courtesy Bonampak Documentation Project).

The maracas players move as if in stop motion, their arms changing frame by frame; the drummer's hands were painted palm up, the fluttering motion evident (Figure 7.10). In this, the painted wall attempts to represent sound itself. What's remarkable is that the Maya artist knows here what the eye and brain will *believe*, a step even beyond the problem of what one knows and what one sees. Such sophisticated phenomena are completely unexpected—but the Maya artist represents aspects of motion that would not be captured by Western artists until the late nineteenth century.

In addition to the ritual of dance, the long four-wall scene of the lowest register of Room 1 provides insight into other noble activities. The most obvious of these is musical performance, an activity rarely given its ritual due in modern times, if only because of the omnipresence of recorded music. The Bonampak musicians enter in clockwise fashion, counter to the usual processional direction. Musical performance itself is highly ritualized and conventionalized. In Maya musical bands, the maracas lead off, followed by turtle shells and drums, with trumpets bringing up the rear. However, what the artist has tried to represent here in Room 1 as well as in Room 3, where musicians also appear, is that they are moving in a circle and moving around the stationary *huehuetl*, as the Aztecs called this drum. The usual representation of musical performance is on the surface of cylinder vessels, which lend themselves to the subject so neatly that observers do not notice that the performance is in a circle. Needless to say, this courtly ritual does not transpire inside the palace but on the adjacent plaza or possibly a courtyard.

In addition to the ritual performance of instrumental music, several members of the procession presumably sing, and some explicitly bear the title of singer. Singing, too, had ritualized qualities, and from what we know of sixteenth-century accounts singing and instrumental performance were almost always united.

Long the most revered figures in the paintings, a group of performers is wedged into the northeastern corner of Room 1 (Figure 7.11). Two wear the hoods also seen on the ballplayers of Yaxchilan Hieroglyphic Stairs 2, as well as abbreviated ballgame yokes (Figure 7.12). One holds an ear of tender green maize in his hand; a Maize God impersonator sits at their feet. The Maize God, of course, is resurrected from an underworld ballcourt by the Hero Twins in the central Maya religious narrative, and it may be just this drama that is about to transpire here at Bonampak, with the Hero Twins in a disguise very similar to the one they wear on the Princeton vase (Coe 1973:42). A new king is often likened to maize and may wear maize in his headdress (Stone 1989); here, the significance is probably the exaltation of the royal family, perhaps in the person of the small child.

Parasols also serve ritual functions. Made of precious feathers, they were probably stored in vaults when not in use. At Bonampak the parasols have been taken out by their bearers and put in use; they function in the painting on several levels. First of all, and most strikingly, they work as paired colophons to the Initial Series text, carefully reversing colors and view from eastern wall to western wall, in a way visually underscored by the visibility of the bearers on the west and their invisibility (one can see their feet) on the east. But the manipulation and demonstration of these parasols is very likely highly ritualized, as is their representation. They are borne into battle in Room 2; capturing, breaking, and displaying them was probably a war ritual; the round banner stones with pierced centers, into which such trophies would be set, survive today at Bonampak, directly in front of Structure 1.

One last ritual of Room 1: Some of the *sajals* (regional governors) who stand around in Room 1 are smoking very small cigars, or what almost appear to be cigarettes (Rosas 1991:46). *Cigar* is a Maya word (Miller and Taube 1992:169); the only modern packaged commodity sold in vigesimal packets today is the cigarette. The K'iche merchants who purveyed tobacco across Mesoamerica probably sold cigars—or possibly these very slender *tiparillos*—in bundles of twenty.

The very sensibility of Room 2 differs from Room 1: A single battle scene encompasses all three walls surrounding the viewer upon entrance into the space, seemingly drawing any viewer into the fray. Dozens of combatants charge into battle from the eastern wall, banners and

FIGURE 7.11 Bonampak murals, Room 1, northeastern corner (copy by Felipe Dávalos; courtesy Florida State Museum).

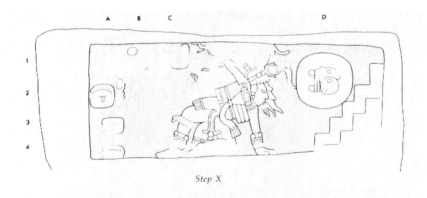

FIGURE 7.12 Yaxchilan Hieroglyphic Stairs 2, Step X (drawing by Ian Graham, CMHI 3:163; copyright 1982 by the President and Fellows of Harvard College).

weapons held high, converging under a large elbow of text on the southern wall, where jaguar-attired warriors, including Chan Muwan, strike the enemy with such energy that one body almost seems to fly right out of the picture plane. The text itself offers only an enigmatic date, perhaps to be located a few years before the Initial Series text. In the upper western vault, defenders try to protect a wooden box, perhaps the same one that then appears under the throne in Room 3. Damage along the joint of the wall and bench may conceal concentrated captive-taking and dismemberment. Unusual dark pigments used in the background indicate that the violence takes place in the dark.

Time is shown in sequence, with preliminaries followed by the climax of conflict, and ending with the mopping up of the defeated. Some individuals are rendered more than once, providing evidence of the Maya ability to create a narrative into which a sequence was embedded—or what is called "simultaneous narrative" in European art, typically understood to be one of the breakthroughs of fifteenth-century painters in Italy.

On the northern wall Chan Muwan, accompanied by warriors and female dynasts, including his Yaxchilan wife, receives presented captives on a staircase (Figure 7.13). Maya constellations oversee the sacrifice, including the Turtle at right (Orion) and the Peccaries, probably indicating that the sacrifice begins at dawn. Whereas war takes place away from the ceremonial precinct, the display and sacrifice brings the most important rituals of war's aftermath into the palace.

As we read across the wall, we see the captives at right, essentially stripped but with ropes (texts elsewhere call a presentation of captives an "adornment," a wonderful piece of wartime disinformation from the eighth century, since they are in fact stripped) and loincloths, proud, angry. Reading across in a zig-zag to far left, we see the figure partly truncated by the huge cross-tie holes of the vault, who either pulls the fingernails or trims off the ends of captives' digits (in Belize, archaeologists at Caracol have now found many offerings of what they call "fingerbowls"—small ceramic vessels that contain the bones of fingers [Chase and Chase 1998:309]), making such arterial cuts that blood spurts and arcs from captives' hands. Elegantly drawn, with sweeping, continuous lines defining body outline, eyes, hands, and hair, these captives are among the most beautiful figures in all of Maya art. Most also seem to have lost their teeth, and one howls in agony. A single captive presented on the upper tier appeals to Chan Muwan, who stares over his head. At his feet, a dead captive sprawls, cuts visible across his body; his foot leads to a decapitated head, gray brains dribbling from the open cranium.

No figure in Maya art is painted with greater understanding of the human anatomy or with more attention to the inherent sensuality of naked flesh than this dead captive of Room 2. For any individual seated on the

FIGURE 7.13 Bonampak murals, Room 2, northern wall (copy by Antonio Tejeda; after Ruppert, Thompson, and Proskouriakoff 1955).

bench, the captive's body is in the center of what one can see. The eroticized body of the dead captive of Room 2, sprawled on the diagonal, dominates the scene altogether and undermines the representation of victory.

Why bring this scene into Structure 1? This single scene, more than any other, is powerfully interactive, since the victorious warriors of the lowest level stand visually poised to crush any visitor who crosses the threshold. But who would be the victim? The only possible answer is the next captive to walk through the door, the one who would take the place of the fellow now dead, but whose eroticized body still has sexual power. The purpose we can only imagine, but we should not exclude rape, particularly given the frequent dorsal view of captives, whose humiliation would be complete before being given the release of death. The central chamber of Structure 1, then, might well be a chamber of the ultimate authority—military, political, and even sexual.

What did the Maya see when they saw this wall? Surely they saw some or all the above, and surely they recognized above all the power of their

FIGURE 7.14 Bonampak murals, Room 3, eastern, southern, and western walls (copy by Antonio Tejeda; after Ruppert, Thompson, and Proskouriakoff 1955).

king. They may also have seen in the very painting itself a sort of conspicuous consumption that emphasized the wealth and power of those who had commissioned it, for as Diana Magaloni has demonstrated (1998:70), the dominant blue pigment featured is azurite, a valuable mineral. When observers looked at these walls of azurite, they saw preciousness itself, much as a European might have been awed at the site of a wall of gold. But what the warlord at left holds out to Chan Muwan is a jade bead, and in his hand is a bundle of quetzal feathers. These two blue-green materials—jade and quetzal feathers—symbolize preciousness and transience itself, and at the time of the Spanish Conquest they were linked in metaphorical speech by Aztec poets to represent all things of value. Victory at Bonampak may have meant, indeed, that one rounded up the maize crop and hauled off the skilled workers, including artists, and took important captives for sacrifice. But what most pleased the king in this painting was loot—the jade and feathers that he stripped from his foes.

In Room 3, the lords of Bonampak don great "dancer's wings" for a final orgy of autosacrifice and captive dismemberment, all arrayed against a large pyramid (Figure 7.14). Whirling lords have pierced their penises, and blood collects on the white, diaperlike cloth at the groin while captives—perhaps with skin painted to resemble jaguars—led in from the side are slaughtered at the center of the southern wall.

Microtexts—the size of many a pot inscription—are painted in several locations, but an especially fine example located at the center of the

FIGURE 7.15 Bonampak murals, Room 3, upper eastern wall (digital enhancements by Doug Stern to photographs of Enrico Ferrorelli, copyright National Geographic Society; used by permission).

southern wall, where it would easily be spotted, names Itzam Balam, the coeval king of Yaxchilan, in association with a scene of tiny-scale dancers, again, at the scale of figures on ceramics. What's unusual about the positioning of this central microtext is that it appears to be on a banner that has been unfurled between two lords in wings. If this were indeed a large unfurled cloth, then this would be a unique representation in Maya art of the sort of painting on cloth known as a *lienzo* in central Mexico at the time of the Spanish invasion. Of course, the very presence of large cloth paintings would have provided a means for the transmission of courtly art and ritual about which modern scholars have been completely unaware.

In the upper vault scenes, Maya artists have rendered other intimate views of palace life. A band of deformed musicians performs on the western vault. The ladies of the court gather in the throne room depicted in the upper eastern vault, first to pierce their tongues and then to run ropes through them, and also to instruct a little child—presumably the same one featured in Room 1—who holds out a hand for piercing (Figure 7.15). This central ritual conducted by women is also known from monuments at Yaxchilan; there the subject is usually portrayed on lintels or monuments confined to specific architectural spaces that run along the main plaza. At Bonampak, strikingly, five women cluster on or near the throne, in what is the single most important female gathering known from the Maya past. We see in this the ability of women to occupy powerful spaces while separated from men, and these may very well be the sorts of spaces commissioned by women at Yaxchilan in palace structures that hug the plaza, especially Structures 21 and 23. Rendered only in the first and final scenes of the program, the little child may have the ostensible motivation for the entire sequence of events.

Only a handful of these rituals could ever have transpired inside Structure 1, or even in a Structure 1 expanded by awnings that swept onto the patio in front of the building. The paintings capture the sweep of processional space, towering pyramids, and private quarters that feature elaborate furniture. They show not only the rituals of warfare conventionally celebrated in Maya art—the sacrifice that took place within ceremonial precincts—but also the mayhem of warfare, a subject not attempted in any other surviving southern lowland Maya work. They unite the palatial world of God L (although he is not pictured, his is the world of trade and tribute) with the agricultural world of the Maize God—two Maya gods often juxtaposed as opposites or enemies; and then they frame their relationship within the context of religious and political war, as occurs at Cacaxtla.

By the year A.D. 800, no Maya ruling family had the resources to transform a town into a Palenque or a Piedras Negras in terms of the built environment. But they could dance the dances, perform the dramas, and carry out the sacrifices that the architecture of one of those grand cities made permanent. At Bonampak, a bare minimum of the architecture depicted in the paintings is present: A pyramid, massive steps, and probably a throne room all overlook the plaza and attendant platforms. In the murals of Bonampak, we see the story writ large for which the Bonampak lords wished to be remembered, without having built but a fraction of the city over which they saw themselves as masters. In this regard, how prescient these Bonampak lords were, for they created the first virtual Maya city—the Bonampak murals being their holograph.

References

Chase, Diane Z., and Arlen F. Chase. 1998. "The Architectural Context of Caches, Burials, and Other Ritual Activities for the Classic Period Maya (as Reflected at Caracol, Belize)." In Stephen D. Houston, ed., *Function and Meaning in Classic Maya Architecture*, pp. 299–332. Washington, DC: Dumbarton Oaks Research Library and Collection.

Coe, Michael D. 1973. *The Maya Scribe and His World*. New York: Grolier Club.

De la Fuente, Beatriz, ed. 1999. *La pintura mural prehispánica en México, II, Area Maya, Bonampak*. 2 vols. Mexico, D.F.: Universidad Nacional Autónoma de México.

Magaloni, Diana. 1999. "El arte en el hacer: técnica pictórica y color en las pinturas de Bonampak." In Beatriz de la Fuente and Leticia Staines Cicero, eds., *La pintura mural prehispánica en México, II, Area Maya, Bonampak, Tomo II, Estudios*, pp. 49–80. Mexico D.F.: Universidad Nacional Autónoma de México.

Miller, Mary. 1998. "A Design for Meaning in Maya Architecture." In Stephen D. Houston, ed., *Function and Meaning in Classic Maya Architecture*, pp. 187–222. Washington, DC: Dumbarton Oaks Research Library and Collection.

Miller, Mary, and Karl Taube. 1992. *The Gods and Symbols of Ancient Mexico and the Maya: An Illustrated Dictionary of Mesoamerican Religion*. London: Thames and Hudson.

Robertson, Merle Greene. 1985. *The Sculpture of Palenque, Volume II: The Early Buildings of the Palace and the Wall Paintings*. Princeton: Princeton University Press.

Rosas, Mauricio. 1991. "Epigrafía e iconografía." In *Bonampak*, pp. 41–54. Mexico, D.F.: Citibank.

Ruppert, Karl, J. Eric S. Thompson, and Tatiana Proskouriakoff. 1955. *Bonampak, Chiapas, Mexico*. Washington, DC: Carnegie Institution of Washington.

Smith, A. Ledyard. 1950. *Uaxactun, Guatemala: Excavations of 1931–1937*. Washington, DC: Carnegie Institution of Washington.

Stomper, Jeffrey. 1996. "The Popol Na: A Model for Ancient Maya Community Structure at Copán, Honduras." Ph.D. diss., Yale University.

Stone, Andrea. 1989. "Disconnection, Foreign Insignia, and Political Expansion: Teotihuacan and the Warrior Stelae of Piedras Negras." In Janet Berlo and Richard Diehl, eds., *Mesoamerica After the Decline of Teotihuacan*, pp. 153–172. Washington, DC: Dumbarton Oaks Research Library and Collection.

Taube, Karl. 1985. "The Classic Maya Maize God: A Reappraisal." In Virginia M. Fields, ed., *Fifth Palenque Round Table, 1983*, pp. 171–181. San Francisco: Pre-Columbian Art Research Institute.

8

Triadic Temples, Central Plazas, and Dynastic Palaces: A Diachronic Analysis of the Royal Court Complex, Calakmul, Campeche, Mexico

WILLIAM J. FOLAN, JOEL D. GUNN, AND MARÍA DEL
ROSARIO DOMÍNGUEZ CARRASCO*

The principal objective of this chapter is to offer a diachronic sociopolitical and economic model of Calakmul, Campeche, Mexico. Calakmul is a regional capital situated in the geographical heartland of the lowland Maya area. Our perspective is from its temples, central plaza, and palaces situated on the artificially leveled dome on which the city center is built. We mapped the site during eighty-seven months of fieldwork between 1982 and 1994 (Folan et al. 1995b; May Hau et al. 1990; Pincemin et al. 1998) (Figure 8.1). Our model includes exposition of a royal court complex. We believe the tripartite nature of Maya culture in Calakmul (Folan 1994; Folan in Sharer 1994) is aptly expressed by its place-name—*ox-té-tun* (three-stone place)—and by the conceptually parallel building complex crowning Structure II from the Pre-Classic period (Braswell et al; 1999). The complex symbolism continued into the Early Classic period.

---

*This chapter was read by Don Dumond, Stephen Houston, Takeshi Inomata, and Joyce Marcus, with David Bolles contributing toward our better understanding of Maya terminology. We are also grateful for the equally astute observations made by two anonymous readers. Although their comments have been very helpful, all errors or omissions are the exclusive property of the authors. We wish to acknowledge the support of the Universidad Autónoma de Campeche, the State of Campeche, la Secretaría de Educación Pública/Instituto Nacional de Antropología e Historia, the Secretaría de Desarrollo Urbano y Ecología, the National Geographic Society, CONACYT, and the Center for Maya Research during various facets of the Calakmul Project.

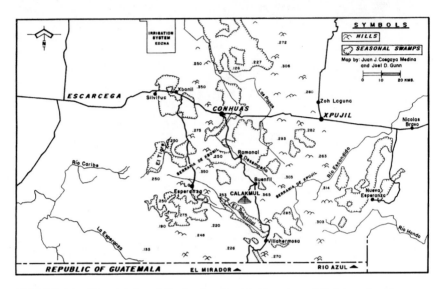

FIGURE 8.1 The Calakmul Basin showing the location of Calakmul and related sites, settlements, bajos, hills, arroyos, and rivers (INEGI with additions by Joel D. Gunn; drawn by Juan José Cosgaya M.).

This is attested to by the dynastic-period, three-part roof combs imposed on Early Classic Structure III and its associated architecture and royal tomb. The sum of the structures is analogous to the sociopolitical organization evolved around the Cross Group in Palenque as described by Berlin (1963).

We assume (see also Houston and Stuart, Chapter 3 in Volume 1), that royal courts represent the vortices of Maya society. The court was composed of the king, queen, the royal household, highest-status elites, and their families. The members and relative importance of royal courts were as cyclical as that of Maya regional states (Marcus 1998:Figure 3.1). Numbered within the royal court are members of their retinue, including artisans. We note that not only the presence of the highest ranking members of society can be defined through ceramics and artifacts, but court artisans in particular can be located in temples and palaces by tracking the material stages of manufacture, uses, and refabrication of their tools. These tools, associated ceramics, and a model of Maya class structure provide a guide to the activities being carried out by the royal court in its architectural environs. This integrated model is also based on the archaeological and ethnographic literature of Mesoamerica, including architecture (Ruppert and Denison 1943), settlement patterns (Ashmore 1981), and cultural materials recorded at Calakmul (Domínguez et al. 1996, 1997, 1998a; Gunn 1997). As supporting adjuncts to the Classic period reconstruction, we employ the sixteenth-century ruling authority and settlement pattern of Chicxulub, Yucatan (Restall, Chapter 11 in this volume), and the nineteenth-century Noh Cah Santa Cruz Maya (Dumond 1997), which also exercised a triadic form of government up to 1901. The underlying continuity through these millennial-scale transformations of lowland architecture is the enduring cosmology of Maya culture itself.

It is our intention to demonstrate how the sociopolitical and economic organization of the Maya court at Calakmul reflects the flow of cultural materials through the complex. We will provide a description of elite structures and a discussion of relative artifact distributions within these structures. We will demonstrate the degree of publicness and accessibility to public structures by people living within, near, and outside the royal community (Tourtellot et al. 1992) through the distribution of figurines from Calakmul analyzed by Ruíz Guzmán et al. (1998). Interpretive models from lowland Maya ethnology and history will follow. Finally, an architectural time line will be used to integrate artifact analyses and ethnohistoric analogy with Calakmul's massive elite acropolis. In our discussion of the ruling court at Noh Cah Santa Cruz, we will make use of the remarkable continuity of Maya culture from ancient to modern times to draw an analogy of the structure of ancient royal courts.

Researchers have focused great attention on Mesoamerican "courts" and "plazas," which include the people living and working within the associated structures and their activities, as well as the buildings and open spaces forming them. The predecessors of Classic-period royal courts and plazas have been recorded by many investigators from the Middle Pre-Classic onward (Lowe 1989). Much of this work implies a broad range of ritual and domestic activities within royal precincts. As an example, excavations by William J. Folan in Dzibilchaltun, Yucatan, in 1960, 1961, and 1962 investigated Temple Structure 38 and Residential Buildings 384, 385, and 386, built on a raised platform and distributed around a patio (Andrews and Andrews 1980; Folan 1961, 1969). A deer-head pectoral associated with the principal burial in Structure 384 supported the idea that this group was inhabited by a Ceh Pech ruling household. They carried out sacred and secular activities interpreted as contributing to a Late Classic and Terminal Classic period royal court complex centered around Dzibilchaltun's main plaza. Activities included culinary, dormitory, mortuary, and religious functions. Comparable activities were described by Bishop Diego de Landa (Tozzer 1941) for sixteenth-century Maya residing in similar buildings. The controlled excavations in Dzibilchaltun during 1961–1962 motivated the search for different activities during investigation of other sites within and without Mesoamerica, including those at Calakmul twenty years later.

Some researchers question whether the ancient Maya inhabited religious buildings in a domestic sense, supposing rather that they limited their use to sacred and selected secular activities. Chase and Chase (per-

Table 8.1 Chronological Sequence of Calakmul, Campeche, Mexico

Christian Calendar G.M.T.	Principal Period	Calakmul	Uaxactun	Tikal	El Mirador	Nakbe	Becan
1550	Proto Historic	Cehache					?
1450							
1350	Late Postclassic						Lobo
1250							
1150	Early Postclassic	Halibe		Caban	Post Lacna		Xcocom
1050							
950	Terminal Classic		Tepeu 3	Eznab			
850							
750	Late Classic	Ku	Tepeu 2	Imix	Lacna	Uuc	Chintok
650			Tepeu 1	Ik			Bejuco
550							Sabucan
450	Early Classic	Kaynikte	Tzakol	Manik	Acropolis	UAC	Chacsik
350							
250							
150	Proto Classic	Takan	Chicanel	Cimi	Paixbancito	Ho	Pakluum
50					Cascabel	Kan	
50				Cauac			
150	Late Preclassic						
250				Chuen		Transition Ox Kan	
350		Zihnal	Mamom	Tzec			Acachen
450							
550	Middle Preclassic				Monos		
650		?			?	Ox ?	
750				Eb			
850							

sonal communication, 1998, and Chapter 4 in this volume) identified secular activities at Caracol on the facade of the impressive Caana temple, where several rooms were inhabited by people who ate, slept, and made use of storage space. Contrary to Calakmul, it seems that they did not prepare meals within those areas. Some other buildings like the Caana temple may also have been inhabited.

Most researchers are easily convinced that palaces, in contrast to temple structures, were used to house elite families and their retainers. The occupying royalty would have shared most of the same needs as others, whether in power or not, sacred or secular in disposition, of a high or a lower class. These include cooking, eating, receiving guests, sleeping, and washing, in addition to sacred activities in vaulted areas and their associated platforms and stairways.

Our analysis of the contents of sacred and secular structures in Calakmul during the final days of occupation suggests that a full range of life activities was carried out in temples as well as palaces. For example, in addition to cooking and serving wares (Table 8.1), more than fifty *metate* fragments and 250 complete and/or incomplete *manos* were located on top of Structure II. These artifacts unquestionably indicate food preparation and consumption. Through the distribution of other functionally identifiable artifacts, we also find that the wide terraced zones forming the facade of Structure II at Calakmul were used for a range of activities.

Although many archaeological sites are no longer visited by the contemporary Maya, some ancient sites such as Coba in Quintana Roo, Mexico, continue their sacred function up to the present day (Folan et al. 1983). Chichen Itza is another example (Folan, personal observation). Other historic courts, plazas, and associated architecture continued to function as a court in places like the city of Campeche during the Colonial period. A court and its plaza was also present up to the first year of the twentieth century at Noh Cah Santa Cruz in Quintana Roo as one of the major towns inhabited by the Maya.

Cultural Setting

Calakmul represents one of the largest, most prominent regional centers in the Maya area (Folan et al. 1995b). A detailed map of Calakmul's 30-square-kilometer topography and its structures (May Hau et al. 1990; see Figure 8.2) has revealed 6,250 architectural foci. Together they form a concentric urban plan (Folan 1985; Folan et al. 1995b). Demographic analysis by Fletcher et al. (1987), Fletcher and Gann (1994), Folan (1988), and Folan et al. (1997) has shown that during the Late Classic–period Calakmul had 37 percent more inhabitants than Tikal living within its 22.5-square-kilometer core. In the 1970s, Flannery (1972) and Marcus (1973, 1976) used central-place theory to delimit the "inner core" of the Calakmul state. Using emblem glyphs, Marcus (e.g. 1976, 1988, 1992, 1993, 1995, 1998; Folan et al. 1995a) drew attention to the four hierarchical tiers that comprised each of the Maya regional states. She noted that the Calakmul state (its inner core of contiguous dependencies plus its far-flung dependencies) covered at least 10,000 square kilometers. Our own study builds on this earlier work and expands the territory encompassed by the Calakmul state to more than 13,000 square kilometers. Our work includes the distribution of ceramics around Oxpemul and nearby settlements, including the distribution of twentieth-century chicle centers and camps identified by Avila Chi and Folan (1990; Folan 1992, 1998b). Our model suggests that Calakmul's regional state of more than 13,000 square kilometers (Folan 1998b) is somewhat more extensive than the 7,225 square kilometers suggested by Hauck's (1975) analysis on communication networks. The Avila Chi/Folan study investigates the location of approximately 600 chicle camps established in and around ancient Maya cities. Data were recorded on site size, aguadas, and number of stelae as-

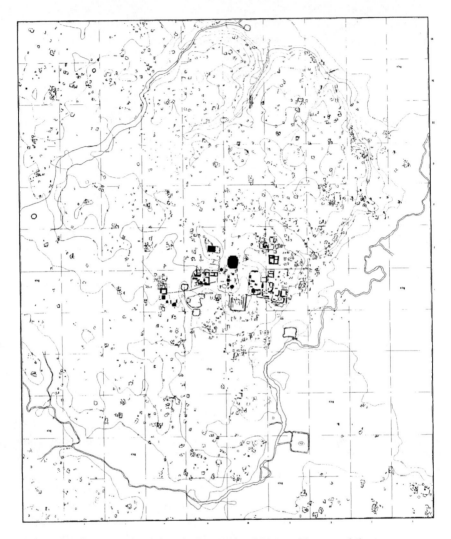

FIGURE 8.2 Map of Calakmul, Campeche, México, 30 square kilometers (Jacinto May Hau, Rogerio Couoh Muñoz, Raymundo González Heredia, William J. Folan (1990), Centro de Investigaciones Históricas y Sociales, Universidad Autónoma de Campeche).

sociated with these camps within the territories of eleven *centrales chicleros*. These were located in the Peten area of Campeche in the southern half of the 1.5 million acre Calakmul Biosphere Reserve (Folan et al. 1992) and neighboring Guatemala. R.E.W. Adams (1986) believes that Calakmul's regional state may have extended to 30,000 square kilometers, approximating the territory of the modern municipality of Champoton, Campeche, as of a few years ago.

The degree of success with which state activities were carried out appears to have been influenced by environmental circumstances (Folan et al. 1983). Calakmul was abandoned around A.D. 900 following a severe, extended drought (Gunn and Folan 1996, Gunn et al.1994, 1995). A study by Gunn et al. (1994) on the discharge of the Candelaria River shows the drought's maximum severity occurred around A.D. 850. This is some forty years before the last monuments in Calakmul, and those in at least two of its tributary cities were dedicated in A.D. 889 (Braswell et al. 1999; Marcus 1989). This drought was later verified by Hodell et al. (1995) through lake bottom coring of Laguna Chichancanab, Quintana Roo. The results of studies by Fialko et al. (1998) between Yaxha, Nakum, and Tikal support the Gunn et al. (1994, 1995) proposal that during times of ideal climate, with an equitable mix of wet and dry seasons, upland *milpas* abundantly supplemented the produce of lowland horticulture. During periods of long dry seasons the edges of *bajos* and island communities in raised areas within the bajos supplied adequate but not abundant subsistence to maintain continuity (see also Folan and Gallegos 1996, 1998). During periods of prolonged drought people moved out to rivers and lagoons. In the Petexbatun region, however, quick abandonment was due to military aggression, according to Demarest and Escobedo (1998; see also Ponciano et al. 1998).

The Calakmul Acropolis and Its Architectural Components

The architectural structure of the Calakmul acropolis precinct has been generally triadic in design since before Christ. It parallels Heinrich Berlin's (1963:91) concept of a triadic architectural complex at Palenque. The triad in Palenque comprises the larger and higher Temple of the Cross, flanked by the lower and smaller temples of the Foliated Cross and the Sun. Roof combs top these three temples. Although each was associated with historic individuals and a different god, he notes that "the visual impression already anticipates the formula: three in one" (see Sharer [1994:284–289] for a more complete description of this group). According to Proskuriakoff (1963), the triadic character of Maya culture is one of its earliest principles. She illustrates this when referring to group A–5 in Uaxactun dating to A.D. 340 during the Early Classic. George Andrews (1975) later refers to this architectural design as being generic Maya in character.

The Pre-Classic

During the Pre-Classic the main plaza in Calakmul functioned as a public area surrounded by four major structures. Structure II supported three thatched temples initiating a pattern of triadic architecture. We maintain that the three earliest structures on top of Structure II were occupied in one form or another since c. 300 B.C. during Late Pre-Classic times, including

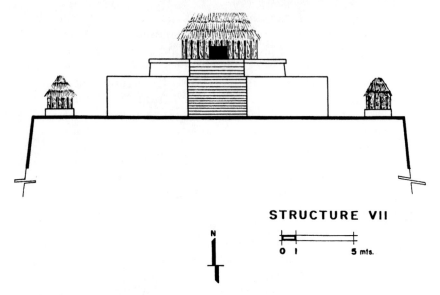

FIGURE 8.3 The upper southern facade of the triadic Temple VII suggesting its first known construction period during the Pre-Classic period (reconstruction drawing by María del Rosario Domínguez Carrasco and Aida Amine Casanova Rosado).

Building II-F. This is attested to by the Late Pre-Classic serving and cooking vessels found at floor level. Structure VII was also topped by three thatched temples (Figure 8.3). In the case of Structure II and Structure VII, the central temples were higher than the other two, as in Palenque. Structure V was a small thatched building fronting Structure II, and Structure IV was formed by three thatched buildings joined by low platforms.

Structure IV represents a different design, although it is also tripartite in character. It, like Structure V, was investigated by means of looters' trenches and tunnels (Alvarez Aguilar et al. 1995). The three principal components of Structure IV were each aligned with the other, forming an E-Group, an architectural form extant since Pre-Classic times. The structures of the group appear to form a large sundial recording the equinoxes and solstices. Ruppert and Denison (1943) first noted this E-Group configuration at Uaxactun. The sundial concept was later tested by Morales López (Folan et al. 1995b:Figure 4) at Calakmul. Temple Structure V (Pincemin 1988) faces Structure II. This and several other structures were excavated and reconstructed by INAH (Carrasco and Boucher 1994; Nieves et al. 1995).

To summarize, the plaza and its flanking structures are thought to have served as a platform for sacred, occupational, productive, distributional, and administrative roles of the Pre-Classic royal court. Other activities included astronomy and calendrics associated with the beginnings of standard lowland Maya practice in Calakmul. This design reflected an underlying triadic design presaged in other lowland cities to the south.

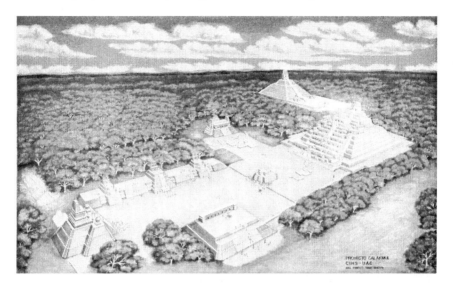

FIGURE 8.4 Reconstruction rendition of the main plaza of Calakmul during the Terminal Classic period with Structure I in the upper-right background and Structure II to the right; Structure III is to the immediate left (or northeast) of Structure II (painting by Ernesto Tamay Segovia; photo by Eldon Leiter).

The Classic

One of the principal purposes of our research on Calakmul is to define the sources, production, and use of the archaeological materials associated with its now two-level plaza sloping toward the north, including Structures I, II, III, and VII, as well as the contexts in which those artifacts were discarded during the Classic period (Figure 8.4).

Structure I was a pyramid more than 50 meters high during the Classic period. It currently has a collapsed temple on its summit (Zapata and Florey Folan 1989–1990). The base is larger than Temple IV at Tikal and, according to Carramiñana (personal communication, 1997), may have been used for astronomical purposes given its alignment, which contrasts with nearby buildings.

Structure II is currently a 55-meter-high zoned pyramid with a 140-meter-square base. Three impressive stairways scale the northern facade facing the plaza. The terraced zones on the low sides of the pyramid are between 3 and 6 meters wide in four directions. The upper reaches of the pyramid contain two building complexes raised on a 30-meter-high upper platform.

The first complex is toward the back of the platform. Here resides the Pre-Classic building triad. It centers on the 25-meter-high Building II-A temple, remodeled during the Classic. Two raised thatched-roofed structures are located below on either side. The structure to the east is Building II-C and to the west is Building II-F.

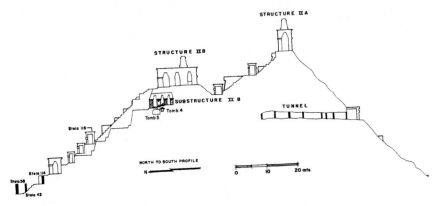

FIGURE 8.5 Section drawing of Structure II acropolis showing the locations of Stelae 114, 115, 116, various buildings, and the room at the rear (south) of Building II-A. Note location of the tunnel to the south where the Late Pre-Classic nature of Structure II was determined (architectural reconstruction by Abel Morales L. and Ernesto Tamay S.; redrawn by Aida Amine Casanova R. and Fabian Pérez J.). Also present is Building II-B-sub showing its associated tombs and their location below building II-B (redrawn from Carrasco et al. 1999:Figure 5).

The second complex lower down at the front of Structure II's upper platform includes palace Building II-B sub and Building II-B (Figure 8.5). During the Early Classic, Structure II-B-sub was added to the platform. It is reported that Jaguar Paw, who was not killed in Tikal (cf. Marcus and Folan 1994), was buried in this building during the Late Classic (Carrasco et al. 1999). Building II-B was built during the Late Classic and remodeled during the Terminal Classic (Folan et al. 1995b). It is a three-range, vaulted structure with three entrances. Restructuring during the Terminal Classic included dividing its interior into three separate units forming nine rooms. These incorporated a steambath and two benches. Building II-B fronts Buildings II-A, II-C, and II-F. The smaller Late Classic vaulted Palace Buildings II-G and II-H are located to the east and west of Structure II-B, forming a three-building alignment.

In addition to marking the southern limits of the main plaza, the Structure II acropolis is one of the largest buildings in the Maya area and one of the principal centers of ruling authority since the Pre-Classic. As such it conforms to the *ox-té-tun* place-name—three-stone place. It housed the principal offices of the Calakmul government. Through the whole of its construction and restructuring, the Pre-Classic triadic design was faithfully maintained until converted into a quadrangular unit during the Classic with the addition of the II-B complexes.

As our study focuses on the Terminal Classic, the design of modifications to Structure II are important to our understanding of Terminal Classic social outlook. Structure II was undergoing additional renovation prior to its abandonment. Restructuring included the addition of rooms to its facade, the raising and partial replacement of its lower central stair-

Triadic Temples, Central Plazas, and Dynastic Palaces in Campeche

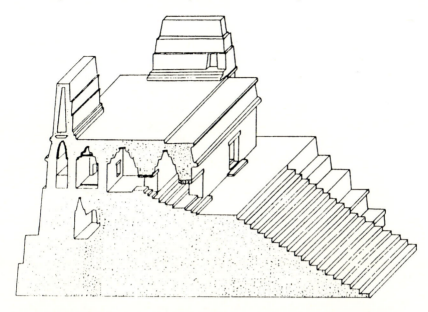

FIGURE 8.6 Artist's rendition of a section drawing of Structure III during the Terminal Classic showing the location of Early Classic Tomb 1 (drawing by Sophia Pincemin 1994).

way leading to Building II-B, the upper stairway leading to Building II-A, and the floor area within the same building. Other renovations include earthen, plastered-over additions to the sides and rear of Building II-B. We will later explore the implications of this redesign.

Equally important to understanding the social design of Calakmul are the multiple stelae associated with Structure II and other buildings. Their texts describe dynastic events covering more than 400 years from A.D. 431 to A.D. 889. Stelae were recorded by our project (Marcus 1985, Pincemin et al. 1998), the Carnegie Institution of Washington (Ruppert and Denison 1943), and Lundell (1933), who discovered Calakmul in 1931.

The Lundell Palace (Structure III) on the eastern side of the plaza represents both continuity with the Pre-Classic triadic design and a Classic-period departure toward dynastic power. It is a twelve-room building with triadic roof combs (Alvarez A. and Armijo T. 1989–1990) (Figure 8.6). Structure III again follows the triadic tradition established on the summit of earlier Structure II. Its two-level roof and triadic components represent a replica of the ruling court structures on top of Structure II during the Pre-Classic. The central rear room is higher than the two other narrow rooms at the northern and southern limits of the building. The hollow roof comb to the south was provided with an entryway. Structure III has a stucco-masked facade and three entrances. Its principal staircase is to the west with a narrow staircase to the south that may have allowed access to lower-status members of the household.

Based on several criteria, Structure III is defined as a palace. It resembles palaces on a worldwide basis (Flannery 1998); it is proximate to Structure II, combined with its compliment of elite ceramic and artifact associations (Haviland and Moholy-Nagy 1994). It is presumed that the royal household and some close collaborators lived in Structure III, with its three roof combs continuing the *ox-té-tun* symbolism discussed above during much of the Classic period. It, too, was restructured during the Terminal Classic through the addition of entryways and stairways. Several of its rooms remain vaulted today.

During the Classic, Structure IV-a, -b, and -c, as the now enlarged Pre-Classic Type E complex, still formed the eastern limits of the plaza. Structure VI is the western element of this group. It was crowned by a building of perishable material. Structure VI may be an unfinished, truncated building.

On the north of the plaza, Structure VII is a triadic, 26-meter-high, three-range, single-entrance, Late Classic building with a now vaulted temple. It was remodeled during the Late Classic, including a patolli track on the floor of its front room. It is flanked by two small thatched-roofed adoratories located below on its eastern and western sides (Domínguez 1992; Domínguez and Gallegos 1989–1990). Structure VII is a smaller, mirror image of the larger, complementary Structure II. It is therefore assumed to have participated as an extension element of the triadic character of the complex nature of Maya society.

Immediately behind Structure VII is a wall (6 meters high by 1.8 meters thick) associated with what is believed to have been a raised area, perhaps used as a market or garrison. This was suggested by Tourtellot et al. (1988) for a similar feature in Sayil. This 1-kilometer-long wall to the north of the 1.75-square-kilometer central platform was, like Structure VI, apparently not completed by the ancient Maya. The plaza also features a nearby quarry and water-catchment facilities (Domínguez and Folan 1996; Gallegos 1985, 1994).

Most of the structures of the central plaza, including the palace Structure III, in and around the plaza would be classified as public buildings based on Flannery's (1976, 1998), Marcus and Flannery's (1996), and Sanders's (1974) definition (i.e., they required corvée labor to construct them). They are thought by us to provide a stage for the sacred and secular activities of the society with a degree of functional overlap. They are also thought to reflect the concepts and mores of Maya elite society and its royal court.

Ceramics, Tools of the Trade, Products, and the Remains of Those Who Made and Used Them

During our excavations in Calakmul, a special effort was made to record all culturally modified material encountered by horizontal and vertical stratigraphic proveniences within rooms, on platforms and stairways, and on other architectural features (Domínguez et al. 1996, 1997, 1998b; and Gunn 1997). During excavation, material above floors was separated from that on floors. These data were used to determine activities within the single-roomed temple located on top of Structure I, the eighty-six rooms of Structure II (some of which had low platforms to the left of their entryway and internal niches), the twelve rooms of palace Structure III, and the three-range temple and flanking *adoratorios* (shrines) of Structure VII.

As will be demonstrated by patterned artifact distributions, we have every reason to believe that the artifacts from floor levels were not left by squatters, occasional visitors, or pilgrims. On the contrary, they represent the remains of a functioning society during the Terminal Classic at the very latest. Among the many sources of evidence supporting this contention is the fact that stelae continued to be erected in Calakmul throughout the Terminal Classic period up to the end of the ninth century (Braswell et al. 1999; Marcus 1985). The artifacts do not include Post-Classic materials, except for one miniature censer and a few censer fragments not associated with floors but with fallen debris. A pottery pestle related to Chichen Itza and a copper ring were excavated on the surface of Building II-F.

In general terms, as archaeologists we feel obliged to infer our perception of Calakmul from an evenhanded analysis of all categories of material culture registered during excavations. We have analyzed this material utilizing modified versions of statistical techniques applied to Late Pleistocene tool kits in Europe by Binford and Binford (1966). In the case of Calakmul, these materials include architecture, ceramics, lithics, figurines, bone, shell, and hieroglyphic texts. It is from the synthesis of these materials that emerges the understanding of Calakmul culture in particular and past cultures in general. Detailed analysis of stone and ceramic artifacts informs us when and where various functions were being performed. We also draw upon analogies from ethnohistoric and ethnographic information and paleoclimatology to inform our conclusions.

A general lack of archaeological data characterizes the literature regarding the uses and functions of buildings. In some cases,-for example, in Andrews V's (1992) careful excavations in Copan—no artifacts were found in some rooms. In excavations other than Copan, artifact collections have not been adequately recorded. Our detailed artifact record of the lower facade of Temple Structure II discovered artifact assemblages that Haviland and Moholy-Nagy (1994) have classified as those of a household in Tikal. The artifacts from the top of Structure II, however, include a greater number and diversity of rare specimens such as imported chert and polychrome ceramics. These are associated with the palaces of Tikal (Haviland and Moholy-Nagy 1994). In contrast to Structure II, the

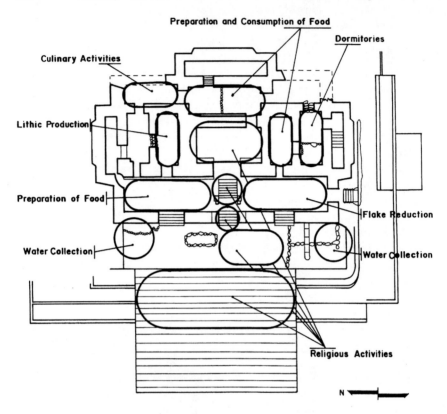

FIGURE 8.7 Structure III activity areas (Domínguez, Gunn, and Folan 1997:Figure 7 [revised rendition]).

palace Structure III inventory suggests few production activities of any type (Figure 8.7). The artifacts from Structure III indicate a palace as opposed to a household according to Haviland and Moholy-Nagy's (1994) definition for Tikal. Structure III also includes an architectural effort to guard the privacy of the occupants. An elevated platform and restricted inner access would have served to protect them from intruders.

The artifacts registered at Calakmul represent ceramics and special deposits of domestic refuse, including lithics defined by Hattula Moholy-Nagy (1997:297) as "discarded durable material, distinct from biodegradable waste or garbage." According to her, "debitage is a special kind of refuse generated by the production of artifacts by reductive processes." Moholy-Nagy believes that the majority of pre-Hispanic lithic artifacts from Tikal were produced and utilized by highly skilled, independent, part-time specialists involved in household industries, in contrast to expedient production by nonspecialists for personal or household use. We find a similar distribution of activities in the case of Structure II of Calak-

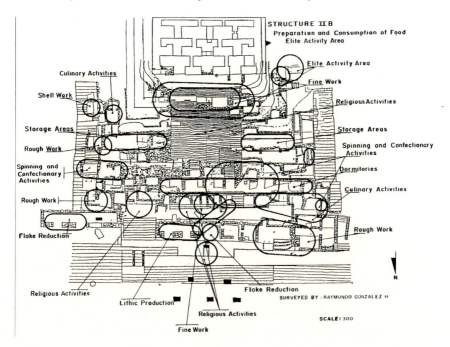

FIGURE 8.8 The lower facade of Structure II showing the location of activity areas based on the analyses of ceramics and lithics registered during excavation (Domínguez C. et al. 1997; drawing by Raymundo González H. and Juan José Cosgaya M.).

mul from its summit and the lower zones of its principal facade. The unexcavated zones from its other three sides seem also to have been used for habitation and, perhaps, production purposes. More than 15,000 lithic artifacts were recorded in Calakmul. They are of various types produced from local and imported materials. The totality of the artifacts registered include *manos* and *metates*, points, chert bifaces, obsidian cores, and prismatic blades. The lithics are complemented by many additional artifact types, including bark beaters, spindle whorls, centrally perforated sherds, bone awls and needles, manta ray spines, deer-antler mallets, stone beads, jade and pyrite plaques, and other artifacts of bone and shell, including *Spondylus*. The disposition of some floor-related artifacts indicates careful placement. Some *metates* were found turned upside-down, and obsidian cores and some points were found carefully tucked into wall niches (Florey Folan and Folan 1994). Combinations of tools forming kits associated with food, chipped stone, wood, and cloth-related functions were located in the rooms excavated on the facade of Structure II (Figure 8.8).

Other activities were carried out in areas that may not have been roofed but could have been protected by *ramadas* (perishable shelters)

Reents-Budet, Chapter 7 in Volume 1). Some of these areas seem to have been used to store consumables in large jars, as in the case of the upper facade of Structure II (Domínguez et al. 1997). The Structure III palace contained a considerable amount of Terminal Classic ceramics as well as more obsidian from highland Mexico than from Guatemalan sources. This suggests a link between Calakmul's secular elite and highland Mexico during the Terminal Classic (Braswell et al. 1997). Associated with Structures II and III were more than 100 fragments and/or complete trough-type limestone and small-tripod green stone in addition to slab-type *metates*. Numerous bone, shell, and other associated artifacts were excavated, including quantities of spindle whorls for producing yarn. Bone needles are also represented. These items were probably used to produce woven cloaks of great value as exchange and tributary items (Peniche Rivero 1990). These mantas often appear in what are believed to be royal court scenes painted on polychrome vases and murals (Coe 1973).

Some twelve tons of ceramics were excavated. These were analyzed and published by Domínguez (1994; see Table 8.1). Ceramic sherds recorded on Structure II can be classified as follows: 40 percent from the Late Classic and 60 percent from the Terminal Classic with more ollas than plates represented. This cultural material was left by the inhabitants of Calakmul living within these structures mainly during the Terminal Classic (Domínguez et al. 1996).

Large quantities of monochrome, bichrome, and polychrome ceramics were recorded from excavated architecture in Structure II (2,930 square meters) and Palace Structure III (975 square meters). But of the total amount of ceramic material identified in Calakmul, there exists a lower percentage of polychrome sherds on Temple Structure II than Palace Structure III. Plates and bowls predominated in the latter. These wares and artifacts do not represent postdynastic collapse deposits. They represent the use of the buildings during the Terminal Classic. Most of the ceramic types identified by Domínguez (1992) pertain to the Terminal Classic, as do the greater amount of the ceramics excavated by us elsewhere in Calakmul. In some cases these artifacts border on the last dynastic date in Calakmul of A.D. 889 (Marcus 1985). The greatest percentage of the 9,297 large sherds on or near the floor from the lower facade of Structure II are from the Terminal Classic, including up to 100 partially reconstructible examples of basins, bowls, jars, and plates. There still remain 3,000 sherds to be identified.

We have been able to distinguish between the Late Classic and Terminal Classic ceramics of Calakmul associated with the lower facade of Structure II principally on the basis of slipped monochromes. The chronology of types without slip, such as Encanto Striated and Cambio, were established based on their association with slipped types definitely identifiable as pertaining to the Terminal Classic.

Ceramic types notwithstanding, the greater percentage of the figurines from Calakmul date to the Late Classic. It is possible, however, that the Calakmuleños continued to produce mold-made figurines into the Terminal Classic using Classic molds. The excavation records of the figurines' place of discovery, as well as those of the ceramics and lithics, provide convincing distribution patterns indicative of a eufunctional society.

The lithic artifacts from the upper zones of the Structure II lower building facade, those from the lower stratigraphic levels of the principal staircase, and those found on the floor of rooms or other surfaces are considered by us to be in their primary sociological context or discards in the general area of their final usage. Because of their relatively small quantities, we also believe that the presence of these lithics are the product of use rather than workshop production, with one exceptional case at the base of the Structure II, where several kilograms of flakes were recorded. By way of comparison, Clark (1991:262) recorded more than 23 kilograms of workshop debris on the floor of an abandoned Lacandon knapper's house and 2 kilograms of the same type of material recovered from a similar dwelling. Our small quantities of lithics—seldom more than a few pieces—indicate to us that the flakes recovered on floors represent a minimal amount of chipping debris associated with use and resharpening, not fabrication. The collection of debris as a whole recorded by us in Calakmul represents a record of past use activity in houses, rooms, or open spaces, whether they represent complete or broken artifacts or flakes. We also found this to be the case in sites such as Dzibilchaltun (Folan 1969), Huamango (Florey Folan and Folan 1981), and Cerrito de la Campana (Folan et al. 1987) in the state of Mexico. In the aforementioned sites, large quantities of cultural materials were found both on and above the floor of some rooms, especially those used for culinary practices, with less cultural materials being recorded in rooms classified ethnohistorically as dormitory areas (cf. Barba and Manzanilla 1986; Inomata and Stiver 1998).

Several regal burials of ancestors of considerable importance to the royal court (Fitzsimmons 1998; McAnany 1998; Pincemin 1994) were recorded in Calakmul Structures II-H, III, and VII (Figure 8.12). This importance is emphasized by the duct connecting Tomb 1 of palace Structure III with the exterior of the building (Pincemin 1988). The tombs included jadeite mosaic masks, often depicted in royal court scenes, as are the hieroglyphic-incised jadeite plaques and polychrome and codex-style ceramics excavated in Calakmul (Coyoc 1989; Folan et al. 1995b; Folan and Morales 1996; Pincemin 1988; Tiesler et al. 1998). Not only do the masks, plaques, and ceramics reflect the royal court life of high-status individuals but also the remains of jaguar-skin cloaks (claws and teeth), headdresses (beads), mosaic encrusted-pyrite ear ornaments, beaded-shell capes (shells), and obsidian and manta ray–spine bloodletters. Jadeite fragments were found in lapidary areas in Buildings II-A and II-H and on Structure VII. At times the concentrations of discard production debris noted above tombs may parallel the discard of obsidian in association with tombs of Tikal (Moholy-Nagy 1997). Also recovered were fragments of *petates* (woven mats) and other bedding as well as resin and seeds. A codex-style vessel from a tomb in Structure II-H (Folan and Morales 1996) was produced in Nakbe, according to Reents-Budet and Bishop (1997). The imported ceramic piece is an exception rather than the rule, even though Calakmul and Nakbe may be connected by a *sacbe* (Folan et al. 1995a). Reents-Budet and Bishop (1997) have determined by neutron activation that virtually all tested vessels were produced in Calakmul and not elsewhere. This is generally the case with many other sites in the area.

What surprises us is that with the exception of durable materials such as jade, obsidian, and other rare lithic materials (granite, jasper, chalcedony, tuff, welded tuff), as well as some saltwater shells, it would seem that few durable goods were exchanged between Calakmul and centers outside the limestone platform of the Yucatan Peninsula. Given the immense size of the city, it seems likely that less archaeologically visible materials such as cacao, cloth, salt, and other perishables were traded. They are depicted on polychrome vessels and reported in the ethnohistoric record (Folan 1979; Piña Chan 1978). Voorhies (1982, 1996) analyzed the likely character of trade between highland and lowland habitats and points out that most potential trade goods from the lowlands would be of perishable nature. The Calakmul assemblage appears to support this contention. Because of proximity, Calakmul bears an apparent relationship with the Rio Bec region to the north and east, but there exists only a few architectural similarities within the city.

Some thirty-six deposits of secondary human skeletal material consisting of fragments analyzed by Vera Tiesler et al. (1998) were located in the rubble covering the lower facade of Structure II (Figure 8.9). Some of these may have been Post-Classic in time if they were not included within the sacred inventory of their associated buildings. Many were associated with obsidian blade and shell fragments as well as animal bones. They included a partially articulated human skeleton within the ash layer fronting the Cycle 8 Stela 114 dating to A.D. 431 (Pincemin et al. 1998).

Structure I activities denote the serving of foodstuffs and water storage recorded around a collapsed, narrow room on its summit; production activities were virtually nonexistent.

On top of the Structure II pyramid, behind the base of Building II-A, artifacts from the floor area of a room represent a variety of activities

Triadic Temples, Central Plazas, and Dynastic Palaces in Campeche 241

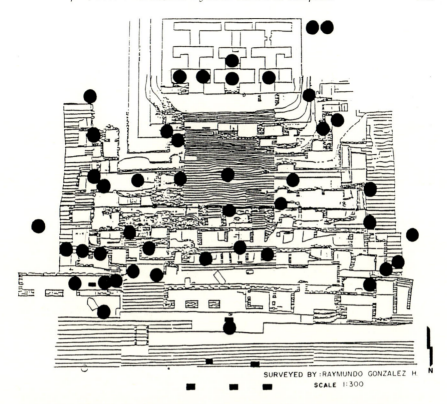

FIGURE 8.9 Lower facade of Structure II showing the location of skeletal material mainly located among collapsed masonry (Tiesler et al. 1997; location of skeletal material by Abel Morales Lopez; drawing by Raymundo González H.).

common to Structure II but no evidence of extensive lithic or other types of production (see Figure 8.5). A consortium of artifacts and features include a hearth, one complete *mano* and *metate*, a ceremonial serving vessel, and large quantities of cooking-vessel sherds. Other items recovered were two obsidian cores, four obsidian blades, an obsidian point fragment, five chert points, two biface scrapers, two stone spindle whorls, a chert flake, a perforated disk, a perforated Oliva shell, a fragment of mother-of-pearl, a miniature ceramic vase, and one unidentified shell (Morales 1994).

The sometimes burned floors of several rooms associated with the lower facade of Structure II contained deposits of ceramics as well as lithics and ash, leading to the conclusion that the inhabitants were living, preparing food, sleeping, and carrying out shell, bone, and textile production activities. Only Room 60–61 near the base of the Structure II staircase contained enough flakes to suggest production activity ap-

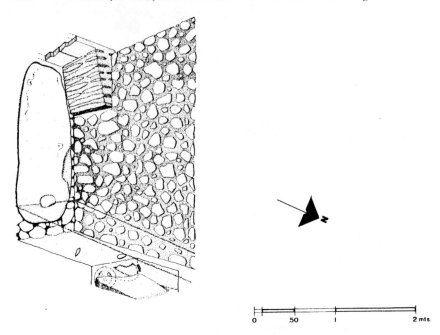

FIGURE 8.10 Cycle 8, Stela 114 at Calakmul located in a partially vaulted niche. A round miniature altar supported by a layer of ash was found at its fire-blackened base (Pincemin et al. 1998; original drawing by Juan José Cosgaya M.).

proaching that reported by Clark (1991) for the Lacandon. Approximately 7,000 flakes were found on the floor weighing 24 kilograms. The dimensions of this deposit are 1.8 meters long, 1.4 meters wide, and 10–15 centimeters high. This is analogous to the pile of workshop debris (approximately 0.5 meters in diameter and 10–15 centimeters thick) abandoned in K'in Paniagua's house in Naja, Chiapas, as determined by Clark (1991:254). The 7,000 flakes represents 46 percent of all lithics recovered by our project in Calakmul. This room is on the first zone above and behind the Cycle 8 stela located in a vaulted shrine (Figure 8.10). Two intrusive vessels containing the remains of snakes, paralleling the emblem glyph for Calakmul (Pincemin et al. 1998)—and thus associated with the royal court—were located below the broken floor fronting the stelae.

Other areas of Structure II show alternate functional foci with combinations of tools representing kits (Figure 8.11; see Gunn et al. 1999). The most recognizable tool kit is a snapped bifacial point and an obsidian blade. Others are identifiable by numerical analysis. A factor analysis of room inventories, and subsequent cross-tabulation evaluation of relationships, support the following suite of eight tool kits from the Structure II acropolis precinct at Calakmul.

Triadic Temples, Central Plazas, and Dynastic Palaces in Campeche

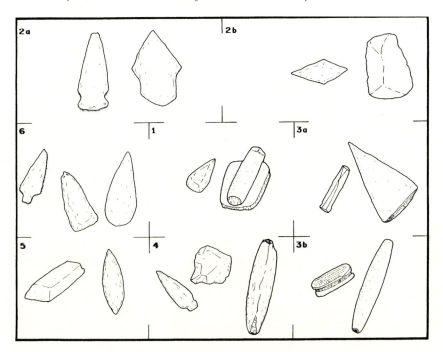

FIGURE 8.11 Tool kits from the rooms in Structures II and III. The combinations of tools were extracted by factor analysis from the presence or absence of tool types in rooms (Gunn et al. 1999). See text for discussion of tool-kit functions. Tool-kit probabilities, that is, the probability that they occurred by chance, were calculated by Fischer's Exact Probability method (1 p=.005, 2a p=.006, 2b p .001, 3a not calculated, 3b p=.005, 4 p=.004, 5 p=.06, 6 p=.001).

1: 1. *Manos* and *metates*. Factor 1 represents a number of types of apparent mixed functions (point tips, utilized flakes, *metates*, mortars, preforms, celts, tortoise shell scrapers, chunks, and picks). Although some of this functional ambiguity is attributable to number sizes in the data matrix, some of it seems to represent a complex group of tools. Some of the tools are associated with food preparation such as *manos* and *metates*. Others probably represent tools that have a wide range of uses and therefore tend to occur systematically with other tools among the rooms.

2: 2(a). Notch-broad stems. The positive aspect of the second factor points to an alliance between notch stem points, probably used for cutting, and broad stem points. The broad stems appear to be a multipurpose tool with needle-sharp tips and heavily resharpened beveled blade edges. The combined features of the two types suggests a cutting and punching activity, perhaps the sewing of hides or bark. 2(b). Scraper-point. The negative aspect of the second factor contains scrapers and pointed stem points. Cores are also present. This would seem to suggest the locations of weapons manufacture, probably that of *atlatls*, judging by the size and morphology of pointed stemmed points. The scrapers could have been used for preparing shafts.

3: 3(a). Obsidian. Obsidian appears in lone opposition to the other types in the third factor. The complimentarity of the distribution implies use in nonrelated functions. For example, if obsidian was used for cutting hair, the isolation of obsidian would mean that hair-cutting was not performed in the same premises as atlatl manufacture. 3(b). Bark beaters–*mano*. *Manos* and bark beaters appear as a combination of tools occurring in the same space, but perhaps, or perhaps not, as a tool-kit association. The bark beaters must have been used in bark cloth preparation, whereas *manos* imply the grinding of corn or other seeds. However, the so-called *manos* are highly varied in morphology and often show evidence of end damage resulting from use as hammers. They could have been used as part of a paper-production kit as well.

4: 4. Chisels-denticulates-straight stems. The straight stem points appear to amalgamate with the lanceolate in this context. Also present are robust denticulate scrapers and chisels. The combination suggests some sort of incising tool kit. It could have been used for quarrying, working wood, or perhaps engraving stelae.

5: 5. Bipoint-polisher. The bipoints and polishers together suggest some sort of very special craft. The snapped points found widely distributed through the site, and associated with obsidian blades in a near one-on-one relationship, could be manufactured by dividing bipointed bifaces in two. It is also possible that the two tools are associated because of some sort of incidental convergence of their spatial distributions. Although the sample sizes are small, small stems are found in a complementary distribution to this tool kit.

6: 6. Adzes–small stems. Small stem points and adzes suggest a woodworking kit of some specialized form. Axes are also present in this association.

Ethnohistory, Ethnology, and Calakmul

The Terminal Classic period in Calakmul was probably initiated by some sort of social trauma, perhaps an early phase of the ninth-century drought (Gunn and Folan 1996; Gunn et al. 1995; see Chichancanab core, in Hodell et al. 1995). Judging from the stratigraphy of ceramics recovered from El Laberinto Bajo (Domínguez and Folan 1996), the break between the Late Classic and Terminal Classic occurred about A.D. 800, with the Terminal Classic ending around A.D. 900. Ethnohistorical reports may provide insights into the character of such a disruption. According to Landa's (Tozzer 1941:146–147) sixteenth-century account, droughts in the Yucatan Peninsula brought famine. This in turn encouraged thievery. Thievery produced slaves and the selling of those who stole, from which stemmed discords and war among themselves and other towns. We believe that these same conditions could well have marked the late Terminal Classic transition of Calakmul. This may also have been the case elsewhere during the Terminal Classic.

Ethnographic evidence may help understand the figurines excavated by us in Calakmul. Left figurines mark visitations to sacred precincts. The ceramic assemblage from Calakmul included more than 700 fragments of figurines and musical instruments analyzed by Ruíz Guzmán (1998). Twenty-five percent of these unreconstructible figurine fragments were found on floors almost entirely associated with Structure II. Ruíz has identified some sixty figurines and musical instruments as representing nine deities from the Maya pantheon. Individuals from the city, and perhaps the regional state, left figurines and musical instruments in rooms and on stairways. Public feasting and other rituals associated with the ballgame can be attested by nineteen ballplayer figurines located across the front of the Structure II acropolis. These may be similar to those alluded to by Fox (1995) in Cotaguana, Honduras. Most figurines date principally to the Late Classic in 89 percent of the cases. They were made in Calakmul based on chemical analysis by Bishop et al. (1998). The seeming discrepancy between the dating of the great majority of the figurines and ceramics is, as noted, probably due to reutilizing Classic molds during the Terminal Classic. In reality, an unknown quantity of these stylistically Late Classic figurines were produced with Terminal Classic clays. This could be taken as a statement in clay regarding the moribund character of Terminal Classic society compared to the more dynamic Late Classic social milieu.

The placement of figurines on the front of Structure II seems analogous to Lacandon censers found associated with pre-Hispanic structures in and around Bonampak, Chiapas, by Rosas Kuri (personal communication, 1999). Similar activities can be observed among the contemporary highland Maya of Chiapas who place censers and offerings on the steps of local churches (they now remove them following worship due to the urban setting of the practice). Even more impressive, in Calkini, Campeche, small anthropomorphic and zoomorphic effigy whistles, ocarinas, and flutes produced in Tepakan, Campeche, are given to children to blow during Chac Chac and Catholic Semana Santa ceremonies to petition for rain. After their use, they are left in the church. If they are broken, they are replaced by religious authorities. Similar ceremonies transpire on the Day of the Dead in Calkini, Campeche, and Ticul, Yucatan (Asunción Pech Cocom and Alejandro Kim de Bolles, personal communication, 1998). The whistles and other instruments in Calkini are abandoned after breakage and new ones acquired. In Ticul they are discarded.

Tourtellot et al. (1992) once posed a query as to the public nature of buildings such as Structure II. From analysis of Calakmul architecture, it can be said that Structure II represents a more public function than the Structure III palace (Alvarez and Armijo 1989–1990). There, access to the inner rooms was limited to assure the privacy of the royal court. Similarly guarded facilities are suggested by Haviland and Moholy-Nagy (1994) for the palaces of Tikal. The distribution pattern of ancient figurines and musical instruments in Calakmul appears to support this inference. They define more limited access to palace Structure III than temple Structure II. Figurine fragments occurred in large numbers in many of the roofed over areas of the Structure II acropolis as well as on their stairways (Ruíz G. 1998) (Figure 8.12). This is the case up to and including its least-accessible recesses behind Building II-A.

Figurines occurred only sporadically inside the Structure III palace (Figure 8.13). The exceptional space is the once-vaulted central room with interconnected niches where a large concentration of figurines may indicate the presence of an *oratorio* (chapel). This could be associated with the Early Classic tomb of the ruler identified by Joyce Marcus as Long-Lipped Jawbone (Folan et al. 1995b; Marcus 1985). Inferred from the presence of stelae bases, two up-till-now-unlocated stelae were removed from the back of this room during pre-Hispanic times (Alvarez and Armijo 1989–1990).

Noh Cah Santa Cruz and Calakmul Social Structure

Perhaps due to a pervasive concept of the so-called Maya collapse, the Maya are generally regarded by some as being dead and gone. Few are aware that the eastern half of the Yucatan Peninsula was an independent Maya state (Folan 1998a) as late as the first year of the twentieth century, or that the Mexican state of Quintana Roo was a Mexican territory as late as 1974. Books by scholars of Maya history (Bricker 1981; Lapointe 1983; Reed 1964), most recently Dumond (1997), have brought to light a fully developed recent Maya polity that waged a successful war for independence from Mexico for fifty-eight years. This polity, set in the matrix of the eastern Yucatan Peninsula, is referenced in Colonial-period maps as "The Wild Territories." It appears to have been seldom penetrated by Colonial culture, except by occasional expeditions. As such, Quintana Roo represents cultural continuity with the ancient Maya. The half-century of home rule by the Maya of the region can probably best be regarded as a revitalization movement (Bricker 1981:5, 87; Wallace 1970)

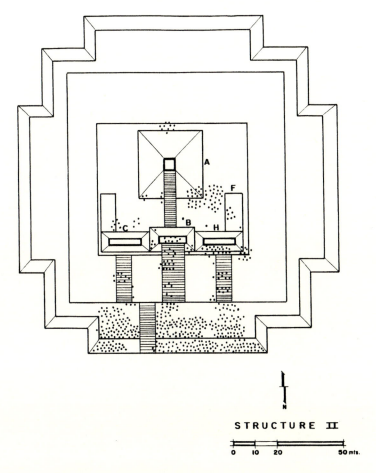

FIGURE 8.12 Structure II, Calakmul, Campeche. Quantitative distribution of figurines, effigy whistles, ocarinas, and flutes.

with its roots in Classic Maya principles of social cosmology. This concept, rather than the term "caste war," applied by contemporaries to disparage the character of this once nearly forgotten episode of Maya history, would be preferable.

The form, use, and economic patterns of the Maya of Quintana Roo during the mid-to-late nineteenth century are reminiscent of those at Calakmul displayed in Structures II and III. In effect, a ruling court existed at Noh Cah Santa Cruz around 1864 (Dumond 1997). Rents and other obligations were paid to, and orders to attack indigenous and nonindigenous communities emanated from, the Talking Cross housed within the Balam Na, a European-style temple built for the Maya by captive masons in Noh Cah Santa Cruz.

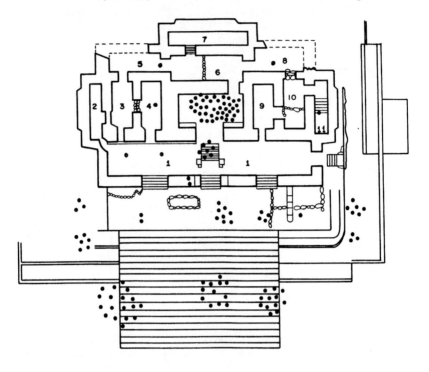

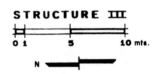

FIGURE 8.13 Structure III, Calakmul, Campeche. Quantitative distribution of figurines, effigy whistles, ocarinas, and flutes.

The temple was also the depository of the wealth brought back by the Maya after their war campaigns. War loot, monopolies associated with alcohol, and tribute fueled the economy. Located behind the Balam Na were artisans and jewelers (Dumond 1997) (Figure 8.14). These skilled individuals may have also contributed to the economic well-being of the Santa Cruz Maya.

We suggest that the relatively isolated inhabitants of Quintana Roo retained some of the elements of the pre-Hispanic Maya through a direct lineage of belief and practice, however modified, by intervening years of contact with Spanish colonialists. The historic Maya of Noh Cah Santa Cruz and their temple-oriented economy, architecture, and nineteenth-century ruling court is similarly structured to principal pre-Hispanic cen-

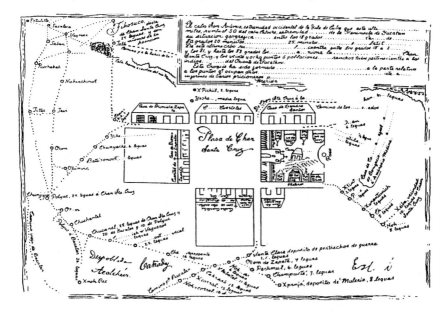

FIGURE 8.14   Noh Cah Santa Cruz and vicinity circa 1860 (drawn from a photograph, courtesy of Alfredo Barrera Vasquez, Dumond 1997:Figure l; reprinted from the *Machete and the Cross: Campesino Rebellion in Yucatan* by Don E. Dumond by permission of the University of Nebraska Press © 1997).

ters such as Calakmul with its king, his royal court, and palace. The Noh Cah Santa Cruz plaza thus underscores the tenacity of their cultural memory despite some 300 years of European contact reflected in the distribution of their principal structures, associated offices, and functions.

The court in Noh Cah Santa Cruz included the Talking Cross and the *tatich*, or patron (chief priest) of the Cross. The Balam Na temple rims the eastern side of the large plaza. The *tatich* lived with his family on each side of this temple housing the Cross. The patio of the *artesanos* (artisans) and *plateros* (silversmiths) was located behind the temple. Like in sixteenth-century Chicxulub, a governor resided to the north of the Balam Na temple. The most important military commander resided to the south. The *tatich*, governor, and principal military commander were accompanied by their families and closest attendants. These individuals, living on either side of the Balam Na temple (where a priest also lived in the church praying and singing all day [Dumond 1997:307]), formed in this manner a basic triadic complex related to the religious, civic, and military aspects of the society.

The settlement pattern of the plaza at Chicxulub and Noh Cah Santa Cruz buildings and their associated functions are similar to the summits of Structure II and Structure VII of Calakmul during the Late Pre-Classic and onward with the centrally located Balam Na also being the largest and highest building. If we assume a similar social structure, the *tatich* lived in the equivalent of the Early and Late Classic Palace II-B-sub and II-B in Calakmul that straddled much of the width of the temple Structure II upper platform. Palace Building II-B was perhaps inhabited by members of the royal court at that time, including the sovereign's speaker. This further suggests that the control of artisans on the Structure II zones during the Terminal Classic in Calakmul was exercised through a similar mechanism to that of the Talking Cross through the *tatich* over sacred and secular matters including the artisans and jewelers.

Another pattern that emerges from the study of the Noh Cah Santa Cruz Maya (Dumond 1997) is that the royal court could also have changed its location from place to place throughout the regional state. Ball reports a shifting residence by Maya authorities in Belize during Classic times.

At one time, the *tatich* also held the position of governor and the most important military commander, thus demonstrating a considerable overlap of privileges and responsibilities. The Talking Cross, through the *tatich*, thus controlled the sacred, civil, and military aspects of society, including the acquisition, production, and distribution of scarce resources associated in part with the workshops located behind the Balam Na temple. After 1864, the pattern of selection of leaders changed. The principal military commanders were often different individuals who at times held more than one office but not all three at the same time, as could have been the case up to 1864. Although the governor—elected by his most important military commanders—the military commander himself, and the *tatich* ideally worked out their power structure among themselves on a mutually beneficial basis, it was the *tatich* who was the most powerful during the twentieth century after the cessation of military operations. According to Dumond (1997), however, there were disagreements, at times leading to the demise of at least one of the parties concerned. Although the *tatich* in 1864 was a former military commander before assuming his other roles, it is not yet understood how the *tatich* was selected in Noh Cah Santa Cruz after that year. It may have been an ascribed status, like some of the other two leaders, or perhaps earned in some cases. Dumond (personal communication, 1998) believes, however, that the *tatich* somehow moved up through the priesthood. Whatever the situation, there is some evidence suggesting the importance of lineal or collateral relationships in all three forms of government through which Noh Cah Santa Cruz transitioned. Similar transitions may have been experienced by the Classic Maya royal families as reported during the rule of the Three Brothers in Chichen Itza (Tozzer 1941). That rule began to disintegrate when one of the brothers left.

It is of interest that during the half-century interlude that the Noh Cah Santa Cruz Maya maintained a recognizable hegemony, they maintained the fluid governmental structure of a heterarchy (Brumfield 1995; Ehrenreich et al.1995), for the most part, but also may have adopted a hyperhierarchized (Flannery 1972) form of government for part of their tenure. It could be that the triadic structure emblemized in the architecture of Palenque, Calakmul, Noh Cah Santa Cruz, and other Maya cities contained the seeds of a flexible heterarchical government principle that facilitated adjustments to an unpredictable and fluid social and physical environment.

A Pre-Columbian Architectural Complex, Its Occupants, and Their Activities

If we permit ourselves to go back in time, a comparison can be made between the Terminal Classic Calakmul royal court with its Divine King, and the Noh Cah Santa Cruz society (Folan 1998a). Both represent temple-oriented economies, with temple Structure II and the Balam Na Temple dominating the landscape in both cases. At Calakmul the political, military, and religious functions were supervised by the sovereign, his family, and his advisers associated through time with triadic architecture on Structure II. We have no immediately apparent ethnohistoric guidelines to interpret the activities of triadic Structure VII except for what we have learned from the Noh Cah Santa Cruz Maya. The Building II-B palace also exhibits evidence of habitation, including culinary activities associated with hearths and *metates* (Folan et al. 1989) (Figure 8.15) and a larger percentage of monochrome pottery than recorded among the comparatively lower-status residents of the lower facade of Structure II. Also in contrast to the lower zones of Structure II is the lack of lithic production evidence in Building II-B, with no primary production flakes but only secondary and tertiary consumption flakes being recorded. Indications of bead, bone, and shell production, also evident on the facade below, are absent on top of Structure II.

In general terms, the inhabitants and activities of the lower zones of Structure II and the Building II-B palace were of a lesser status than the inhabitants and activities of the Structure III palace based on artifact associations. The activities appear to pertain to both genders as interpreted from iconography (cf. Coe 1973). The Structure II and Building II-B artifacts included sixteen spindle whorls for production of yarn found mainly on staircases and the front platform.

In the Building II-A temple, male ceremonial activities predominated, signaled by vessels such as dishes and plates, with the majority of the associated bowls being polychrome. This suggests a division of labor based on gender and status as depicted in Maya iconography, ethnohistory, and ethnography. In the case of the chipped stone, the majority of flakes from temple II-A were tertiary flakes. The totality of the artifacts (including

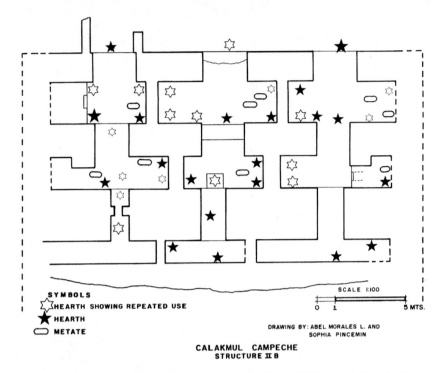

FIGURE 8.15 Building II-B palace at Calakmul (Folan, Folan, and Cauich Mex 1990; drawing by Abel Morales L. and Sophia Pincemin D.).

finished miniature shell objects or others of jade and pyrite) indicate personages of higher status than those of Building II-B. This is also the case with the activities that dominated the summit of the Structure I temple. The activities of Structure VII temple are similar to those of the Building II-A temple, including sacred and secular tasks related to habitation and some lithic modification, including the working of jade. Do production activities on the summit of Structures II and VII mark a different overall function of these buildings? When we excavate the lower part of Structure VII, we may learn the answer.

The distribution of ceramics and lithics on triadic Structure II demonstrates a flow from primary manufacture and reduction at the bottom to final expenditure and use at the top of the pyramid. In the same manner that the early stages of lithic reduction was most prevalent farther out from major centers, whereas those closer to those centers were relatively more associated with later stages of lithic reduction (Fedick 1991; Moholy Nagy 1997), the earliest stages of lithic production associated with Structure II took place near its base, with later stages of lithic modification taking place up the front and on top of the structure. The pyramid, its occu-

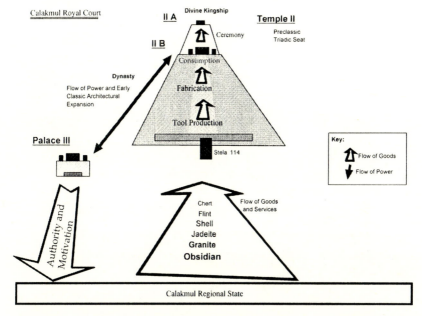

FIGURE 8.16 The Pre-Classic acropolis organized around pyramid Structure II crowned with a triadic architectural symbol. These structures reflected the royal court. The increased population and administrative responsibilities of the Early Classic dynastic period, not to mention increased ceremonial demands, precipitated construction of Palace Structure III down pyramid to the left.

pants, and its artifacts have thus provided an architectural metaphor of a hierarchical society. As one proceeds up the pyramid, nobler status increases. In reverse perspective, authority, inspiration, and motivation flow down the pyramid, providing order and tradition for Calakmul's vast populations (Figure 8.16).

Conclusion

We conclude that the principal plaza, temples, and palaces of Calakmul as a conceptual whole represent a royal court including sacred, secular, and military elements based on a triadic social cosmology. At a minimum, it was symbolically centered on the summit of Structure II since Pre-Classic times, a place where closely related religious, political, and military aspects of Calakmul society were located with overlapping but distinct functions. These authorities also resided on the summit at some time during the Pre-Classic and Classic periods. The manufacture, use, reworking, and distribution of tools, and the activity areas essential for production of clothing and jewelry as well as food preparation and shelter, took place on and about the base and zones of Structure II during the

Terminal Classic. Based on the Calakmul findings, the debitage associated with the basal zone of Structure II is clearly related to Hayden and Cannon's (1983) third consideration: the economy of effort that suggests that it would have been more efficient to establish temporary or even permanent production areas where the largest deposits of lithic debitage were located. This is especially the case on the lower facade of buildings like Structure II. This strongly supports our argument that these lithics represent the debitage from at least temporary, if not permanent, production areas. This contrasts with Palace Building II-B and Palace Structure III, which, like temple Structure I and Building II-A, were consumers rather than producers of goods. In essence, the rooms located on the zones rimming Structure II represent the production class and the buildings on top the consumption class. This recalls Moholy-Nagy's speculation (1997:310) regarding the Gran Plaza (Group 5D–2) at Tikal. She suggests that the material excavated from the Gran Plaza might be secondary in nature, yet she also leaves open the possibility that the chert and obsidian waste found with tomb burials may have been generated in the Gran Plaza instead of being brought in from workshops in the surrounding area.

We believe that Palace Structure III, with its three roof combs and *ox-té-tun* symbolism, including the raised rear room of the building imitating the earlier Pre-Classic triadic Structure II, was built as one of the first vaulted manifestations of Classic-period dynastic Calakmul. It gives the impression that the triadic concept at Pre-Classic Structure II was transposed to the top of the dynastically related palace Structure III below. Its ground-level location in comparison to the 55-meter-high Structure II (or, if you wish, from the mountain to the plain) seems to suggest a period of less armed conflict in comparison to, for example, later, fortified Terminal Classic sites (Demarest and Escobedo 1998; Inomata and Stiver 1998; Webster 1979). In this way Structure III became the residence of the royal household, including an individual whose name may be depicted on the front of Stelae 114 (Pincemin et al. 1998). He can be considered the founder of a lineage household (Folan 1990; see also McAnany 1995; Ringle and Bey, Chapter 9 in this volume), who was buried beneath Room 6 of Structure III around A.D. 350. The three plaques accompanying his burial may also represent the triadic nature of ancient Maya society related to Calakmul's *ox-té-tun* title.

It was around A.D. 350 that important modifications were made to the triadic structures in Temple Structure II, including the addition of masks to its facade. Although the inner recesses of Palace Structure III were accessible only through a single entryway during the Early Classic, it may be surmised that the interior residence of the sovereign was symbolically divided into three components, all located below one of the triadic roof combs. The divine component (*ajaw*) was still in the middle, the political component (*halach uinic*) to the north, and the military component (*yax batab*) to the south, to use the apparently parallel terminology of Chicxulub as well as the Noh Cah Santa Cruz Maya as late as the beginning of the twentieth century (Dumond 1997). The triadic design also reflects Berlin's concept of "three-in-one," which he devised for the Palenque triad. These components were accessible in Structure III through an entryway in the middle of Room I that served a combined reception-culinary function. The room below the roof comb to the south was a throne room with a raised, hollow dais reached by stairs suitable for special sound effects. These might include disembodied voices similar to the oracle of Cozumel (Tozzer 1941), as suggested by Braswell (personal communication, 1998), and of the Talking Cross at Noh Cah Santa Cruz. In fact, the entrance to the southern roof comb on top of Structure III may have facilitated the entry of an assistant to an area within the base of the roof comb. Once there, he could create sounds similar, perhaps, to those made in the church at Calkini, when sounds imitating thunder were produced on the roof by dragging large chains back and forth along the vault. It is also possible that sunlight could have been flashed within this and other rooms of Structure III, as was also done in Calkini to represent lightning (Asunción Pech Cocom, personal communication, 1998).

Sometime during the Late Classic period or later, the central room vault of Structure III collapsed, and four new entryways were opened into the inner recesses of the building from the reception area, essentially dividing it into three or more independent areas provided with a hearth and *metate*; eighty-nine whole or incomplete *manos* were associated with the building. Also present were various and sundry ceramics and artifacts also associated with Late Classic palaces in places such as Tikal (Haviland and Moholy-Nagy 1994). The main reception room continued its culinary and other social functions as described by Folan (1969; for Dzibilchaltun) and Landa (Tozzer 1941; for the northern Yucatan Peninsula in general). The secondary steps and platform associated with the building continued to represent spaces important for both sacred and secular activities associated with figurines in one case (Ruíz G. 1998) and spindle whorls in the other (Domínguez et al. 1998c). Some lithics according to Armijo (personal communication, 1985) were modified on the roof of Structure III.

It is thought that Building II-B sub and the Late Classic Building II-B were added to the front of the triadic Structure II as three-range palaces for the use of the royal court. The latter resembles the facade of Palace Structure III, thereby converting the upper part of Structure II into a Classic-period quadrangular palace/temple complex, as in the case of the once-triadic Structure A–5 in Uaxactun. Structure A–5's three original, Early Classic roof combs were still visible following the addition of the palace during the Late Classic (Proskouriakoff 1963). Later on, close to the end of the late Terminal Classic, new influences begin to arrive in Calakmul, principally from the north, as demonstrated by ceramics (Domínguez 1994). It was at this time that Building II-B was divided into three separate areas apparently following the *ox-té-tun* nature of Maya society. At least two tombs were sacked around A.D. 800, perhaps signaling a dynastic change. A new floor was laid. Its rear room and steambath were filled with stone to prevent the collapse of the rear vault. A burial was made in the central area, supplied with a large, poorly formed altar abutting the rear wall of the building. Spheres of ash fronted it, and a yellow jasper knife fragment offering was left on top of it. These seemingly new arrivals are associated with new ceramic types and the modifications to Building II-B. They would also have been responsible for adding more than sixty rooms to the facade of Structure II, associated with full-time specialists engaged in activities similar to processes that had transpired in Noh Cah Santa Cruz in the 1860s. In this fashion, Structure II was converted from an *ox-té-tun* sacred/secular concept to one that also included production activities. The artifacts recovered from Building II-F differ significantly from those recovered in association with Temple Structure II-A, with its polychrome pottery and exotic materials such as jade. To our knowledge, no one resided in Structure II or Structure III during the Post-Classic period, although evidence does exist of later visitors in the form of the three censers and censer fragments found among fallen masonry and on a raised platform in the nearby Laberinto Bajo.

The triadic Structure VII marking the northern limits of the plaza experienced a history similar to Structures II and III. It had a vaulted temple added to it, as well as a royal burial sometime around A.D. 780. Domínguez and Gallegos (1989–1990) recorded, in addition to religious activities, areas dedicated to lapidary, lithic production, and culinary activities associated with its female and male inhabitants. This suggests that although not as extensively excavated as Structure II, Structure VII (like Structure II) could claim both limited production and consumption components as part of its economic structure. Production areas on the summit signal a fundamentally different overall use configuration for the building, however.

In sum, the principal symbolic location of the royal court in Calakmul, including the residence of the sovereign (*ajaw*), the governor (*halach uinic*), and principal military commander (*yax batab*), was located on top of Structure II up to the fourth century. At that time Palace Structure III was built with its three roof combs as a dynastic ruler's royal household. This would have made it more accessible to a general populous. Structures II-B and II-B-sub may represent the Divine King's principal speaker's (*ajaw can*) residence during the Early and Late Classic periods. It is also possible that Room 1 of Palace Structure III also may have been associated with the *ajaw can* as the sovereign's speaker. This personage parallels that of the *tatich* in Noh Cah Santa Cruz, who was the speaker for the equally divine Talking Cross.

It is suggested that other triadic Pre-Classic structures in places such as El Mirador (Hansen 1990), as well as Tikal (Andrews 1975), Uaxactun (Proskuriokoff 1963), and possibly Caracol (A. Chase and D. Chase, personal communication, 1998) were the official locations of a religious, civil, and military power as described by us for Calakmul. Much later this is the case for Chicxulub and for Noh Cah Santa Cruz, where the Talking Cross was equivalent to a Divine King. This is perhaps analogous to the Cross-like world tree in Palenque that supports a double-headed serpent bar considered to be "one of the primary symbols of kingship" (see Sharer 1994:287; see Restall, Chapter 11 in this volume). In the case of Calakmul, and perhaps elsewhere, these functions were also established at plaza level during the early dynastic years of lowland Maya society in the form of a royal family inhabiting triadic Palace Structure III. This appears to be a response to a new dynastic order that still recognized the importance of the triadic nature of the Maya as manifested and maintained on top of Structures II, including the addition of Palace Building II-B and II-B-sub. Structure VII located at the northern end of the plaza up to final abandonment was also part of this process, evidenced by the continuation of its triadic nature.

It was not until our excavations at Calakmul that we discovered in finer detail what some of us had suspected in the late 1950s motivated by the teachings of Taylor (1948) and supported by Román Piña Chan. Although investigators have always thought that some of the cultural materials found on the floors, platforms, and stairways of excavated structures in Mesoamerica constitutes only discard in the truest sense of the term, it was also thought by others to reflect a past reality identified at Calakmul for the Terminal Classic period at a minimum. We believe that even though some disposal functions in these rooms were suspended during the Terminal Classic, the essential economic and religious patterns of the society were carried forward. In a broad sense, then, we see a pale but royal shadow of Calakmul's Late Classic court grandeur. We are peering through a 1,000-year lens focused on a Pre-Classic–period cultural reality that includes a triadically organized *ox-té-tun* society.

References

Adams, Richard E.W. 1986. "Río Azul." *National Geographic* 169(4): 420–451.

Alvarez Aguilar, Luis Fernando, and Ricardo Armijo Torres. 1989–1990. "Excavación y consolidación de la Estructura III de Calakmul, Campeche." *Centro de Investigaciones Históricas y Sociales, Información* 14: 42–55. Campeche: Universidad Autónoma de Campeche.

Alvarez Aguilar, Luis Fernando, A. Casanova Rosado, Ma. del Rosario Domínguez Carrasco, W. J. Folan, A. Morales López, and A. Zapata Castorena.

1995. "Calakmul, Campeche: un acercamiento a la reconstrucción arquitectónica de la Gran Plaza y aus alrededores." *Belizean Archaeology*. In press.

Andrews, George F. 1975. *Maya Cities: Place Making and Urbanism*. Norman: University of Oklahoma.

Andrews, E. Wyllys V. 1992. "Continuity and Change in a Royal Maya Residential Complex at Copan." *Ancient Mesoamerica* 3: 63–88.

Andrews, E. Wyllys IV, and E. Wyllys Andrews V. 1980. "Excavations at Dzibilchaltun, Yucatan, Mexico." *Middle American Research Institute Publication No. 48*. New Orleans: Tulane University.

Ashmore, Wendy. 1981. *Lowland Maya Settlement Patterns*. Albuquerque: University of New Mexico Press.

Avila Chi, Rubentino, and William J. Folan. 1990. "Aguadas, campamentos chicleros, ruinas y estelas de la reserva de la Biósfera Calakmul y alrededores." Manuscript in possession of the authors.

Barba, Luis, and Linda Manzanilla N. 1986. "Estudios de áreas de actividad: Coba, Quintana Roo." In Linda Manzanilla N., ed., *Análisis de dos unidades habitacionales mayas del horizonte clásico*, pp. 69–115. México, D.F.:Universidad Nacional Autónoma de México.

Berlin, Heinrich. 1963. "The Palenque Triad." *Journal de la Société de Americanistes* 52: 91–99.

Binford, Lewis R., and Sally R. Binford. 1966. "A Preliminary Analysis of Functional Variability in the Mousterian of Levallois Facies." *American Anthropologist* 68: 238–295.

Bishop, Ronald L., Roberto Ruíz Guzman, and William J. Folan. 1998. "Figurines and Musical Instruments of Calakmul, Campeche, Mexico: Their Chemical Classification". *Los Investigadores de la Cultura Maya* 7. Campeche: Universidad Autónoma de Campeche.

Braswell, Geoffrey, Joel D. Gunn, María del Rosario Domínguez C., William J. Folan, and Michael D. Glascock. 1997. "Late and Terminal Classic Obsidian Procurement and Lithic Production at Calakmul, Campeche, México." Paper presented at the sixty-third annual meeting of the Society for American Archaeology, Seattle.

Braswell, Geoffrey E., Joel D. Gunn, María del Rosario Domínguez Carrasco, William J. Folan, Laraine A. Fletcher, Abel Morales Lopez, and Michael D. Glascock. 1999. "Defining the Terminal Classic at Calakmul, Campeche." In Don S. Rice, Prudence M. Rice, and Arthur A. Demarest, eds., *The Terminal Classic in the Maya Lowlands: Collapse, Tradition, and Transformation*.

Bricker, Victoria Reifler. 1981. *The Indian Christ, the Indian King*. Austin: University of Texas Press.

Brumfield, Elizabeth M. 1995. "Heterarchy and the Analysis of Complex Societies: Comment." In Robert M. Ehrenreich, Carole L. Crumley, and Janet E. Levy, ed., *Heterarchy and the Analysis of Complex Societies*, pp. 125–131. Archaeological papers of the American Anthropological Association No. 6. Washington DC.

Carrasco Vargas, Ramón, and Sylviane Boucher. 1994. "Calakmul: espacios sagrados y objetos de poder." *Arqueología Mexicana* 2(10): 32–38.

Carrasco Vargas, Ramón, Sylviane Boucher, Paula Alvarez González, Vera Tiesler Blos, Valeria García Vierna, Renata García Moreno, and Javier Vázquez

Negrete. 1999. "New Evidence on Jaguar Paw, a Ruler from Calakmul." *Latin American Antiquity* 10: 47–58.

Clark, John E. 1991. "Modern Lacandon Lithic Technology and Blade Workshops." In Thomas R. Hester and Harry J. Shafer, eds., *Maya Stone Tools*, pp. 251–265. Monographs in World Archaeology No. 1. Madison, WI: Prehistory Press.

Coe, Michael D. 1973. *The Maya Scribe and His World*. New York: Grolier Club.

Coyoc Ramírez, Mario. 1989. "Entierros explorados en la zona arqueologica de Calakmul, Campeche." *Centro de Investigaciones Históricas y Sociales, Información* 14: 85–105. Campeche:Universidad Autónoma de Campeche.

Demarest, Arthur A,. and Héctor L. Escobedo. 1998. "Acontecimientos, procesos y movimientos de poblaciones en el clásico terminal y el colapso maya." In Juan Pedro Laporte and Héctor L. Escobedo, eds., *XI Simposio de Investigaciones Arqueológicas en Guatemala*, pp. 699–712. Guatemala: Ministerio de Cultura y Deportes, Instituto de Antropología e Historia, Asociación Tikal.

Domínguez Carrasco, Ma. del Rosario. 1992. "El recinto superior del Edificio VII de Calakmul, Campeche: Una interpretación diacronica de su desarrollo desde el punto de vista de la arquitectura y el material cerámico." Licenciatura thesis. Escuela Nacional de Antropología e Historia, INAH, México.

———. 1994. *Calakmul, Campeche: un análisis de la cerámica*. Colección Arqueología 4. Campeche: Centro de Investigaciones Históricas y Sociales, Universidad Autónoma de Campeche.

Domínguez Carrasco, Ma. del Rosario, and Miriam Judith Gallegos Gómora. 1989–1990. "Informe de trabajo del Proyecto Calakmul, 1984, Estructura VII." *Centro de Investigaciones Históricas y Sociales, Información* 14: 56–84. Campeche:Universidad Autónoma de Campeche.

Domínguez Carrasco, Ma. del Rosario, Joel D. Gunn, and William J. Folan. 1996. "Calakmul, Campeche: sus áreas de actividades ceremoniales, cívicas y domésticas derivadas de sus materiales líticos y cerámicos." In *Los Investigadores de la Cultura Maya* 4: 80–106. Universidad Autónoma de Campeche, México.

———. 1997. "Interpretaciones de actividades líticas en la Estructure II de Calakmul y su relación con los Edificios III y VII de la Plaza Central." In Juan Pedro Laporte and Héctor L. Escobedo, eds., *X Simposio de Investigaciones Arqueológicas en Guatemala*, pp. 615–632. Guatemala: Ministerio de Cultura y Deportes, Instituto de Antropología e Historia, Asociación Tikal.

———. 1998a. "Calakmul, Campeche: sus áreas de actividades ceremoniales, cívicas y domésticas observadas de un análisis de su artefactos de piedra." In *Los Investigadores de la Cultura Maya* 2(5): 526–540. Campeche: Universidad Autónoma de Campeche.

———. 1998b. "La cerámica y lítica de Calakmul, Campeche, México: Un análisis contextual de las Estructuras I, II, III y VII." In Juan Pedro Laporte and Héctor L. Escobedo, eds., *XI Simposio de Investigaciones Arqueológicas en Guatemala*, pp. 605–622. Guatemala: Ministerio de Cultura y Deportes, Instituto de Antropología e Historia, Asociación Tikal.

Domínguez Carrasco, Ma. del Rosario, William J. Folan, Abel Morales López, and Roberto Ruíz Guzmán. 1998c. "Hilado, confección y lapidación: los quehaceres cotidianos de los artesanos de Calakmul, Campeche, México." Paper presented at the XII Simposio de Investigaciones Arqueológicas en Guatemala, Guatemala.

Domínguez Carrasco, María del Rosario, and William J. Folan. 1996. "Calakmul, México: Aguadas, bajos, precipitación y asentamiento en el Petén campechano." In Juan Pedro Laport and Héctor L. Escobedo, eds., *IX Simposio de Investigaciones Arqueológicas en Guatemala*, pp. 171–193. Guatemala: Ministerio de Cultura y Deportes, Instituto de Antropología e Historia, Asociación Tikal.

Dumond, Don E. 1997. *The Machete and the Cross: Campesino Rebelión in Yucatan*. Lincoln: University of Nebraska Press.

Ehrenreich, Robert M., Carole L. Crumley, and Janet E. Levy, eds. 1995. *Heterarchy and the Analysis of Complex Societies*. Archaeological Papers of the American Anthropological Association No. 6. Washington DC.

Fedick, Scott L. 1991. "Chert Tool Production and Consumption Among Classic Period Maya Households." In Thomas R. Hester and Harry J. Shafer, eds., *Maya Stone Tools*, pp. 103–118. Monographs in World Archaeology No. 1. Madison, WI: Prehistory Press.

Fialko, Vilma, William J. Folan, Joel D. Gunn, and Ma. del Rosario Domínguez Carrasco. 1998. "Land Use in the Peten Region of Guatemala and Mexico." Paper presented at the sixty-third annual meeting of the Society of American Archaeology, Seattle.

Fitzsimmons, James L. 1998. "Classic Maya Mortuary Anniversaries at Piedras Negras, Guatemala." *Ancient Mesoamerica*: 271–278.

Flannery, Kent V. 1972. "The Cultural Evolution of Civilizations." *Annual Review of Ecology and Systematics* 3: 399–426.

_____., ed. 1976. *The Early Mesoamerican Village*. New York: Academic Press.

_____. 1998. "The Ground Plans of Archaic States." In Gary M. Feinman and Joyce Marcus, eds., *Archaic States*, pp. 15–57. Santa Fe: School of American Research Press.

Fletcher, Laraine A., and James Gann. 1994. "Análisis gráfico de patrones de asentamiento: el caso Calakmul." In William J. Folan, ed., *Campeche maya colonial*, pp. 85–121. Colección Arqueología 3. Campeche: Universidad Autónoma de Campeche.

Fletcher, Laraine A., Jacinto May Hau, Lynda M. Florey Folan, and William J. Folan. 1987. *Un análisis estadístico preliminar del patrón de asentamiento de Calakmul*. Campeche: Centro de Investigaciones Históricas y Sociales, Universidad Autónoma de Campeche.

Florey Folan, Lynda M., and William J. Folan. 1981. "Arqueología: el palacio." In Román Piña Chan, ed., *Investigaciones sobre Huamango y región vecina*, pp. 249–258. México, D.F.: Secretaría de Turismo de Estado de México.

_____. 1994. "Proyecto Calakmul: Informe de Trabajo. Estructura II." Report on file, Consejo de Arqueología, INAH, México, D.F.

Folan, William J. 1961. "Excavation and Restoration of Structure 38." In E. Wyllys Andrews IV, ed., *Preliminary Report on the 1959–60 Field Seasons, National Geographic Society-Tulane University Dzibilchaltun Program*, pp. 11–13. Middle American Research Institute, Miscellaneous Series 11. New Orleans: Tulane University.

_____. 1969. "Dzibilchaltun, Yucatan, México, Structures 384, 385 and 386: A Preliminary Interpretation." *American Antiquity* 34: 434–461.

———. 1979. "La organización sociopolitico de los habitantes de la Península de Yucatán a través del tiempo." *Boletín de la Escuela de Ciencias Antropológicas de la Universidad de Yucatán* 6(34): 34–45.

———. 1985. "Calakmul, Campeche: un centro urbano, estado y región, en relación al concepto del resto de la Gran Mesoamérica." *Centro de Investigaciones Históricas y Sociales, Información* 9: 161–185. Campeche: Universidad Autónoma de Campeche.

———. 1988. "Calakmul, Campeche: El nacimiento de la tradición clásica de la Gran Mesoamerica." *Centro de Investigaciones Historicas y Sociales, Información*, 13: 122–190. Campeche: Universidad Autónoma de Campeche.

———. 1990. "Calakmul y su estado regional durante el clásico." In Amalia Cardós de Méndez, ed., *Nuevos hallazgos, nuevas ideas*, pp. 505–520. México, D.F.: Museo Nacional de Antropología, INAH.

———. 1992. "Calakmul, Campeche: A Centralized Urban Administrative Center in the Northern Petén." *World Archeology* 24(1): 58–168.

———. 1994. "Calakmul, Campeche, México: una megalópolis maya en el Petén del norte." In William J. Folan, ed., *Campeche maya colonial*, pp.55–83. Colección Arqueología 3. Campeche: Universidad Autónoma de Campeche.

———. 1998a. "Review. The Machete and the Cross: Campesino Rebellion in Yucatan by Don E. Dumond." *Revista Mexicana del Caribe* 5: 257–261.

———. 1998b. "La Península de Yucatán in vísperas de la conquista: un modelo diacrónico de desarrollo y decaimiento." *Gaceta Universitaria*, 8(41/42): 25–38.

Folan, William J., Joel Gunn, Jack Eaton, and Robert Patch. 1983. "Paleoclimatological Patterning in Southern Mesoamerica." *Journal of Field Archaeology* 10: 453–468.

Folan, William J., Lynda Florey Folan, and Antonio Ruíz Pérez. 1987. *Cerrito de la Campana: una avanzada en la ruta teotihuacana al noreste de la Gran Mesoamérica*. Campeche: Universidad Autonóma del Sudeste.

Folan, William J., Betty Faust, Wolfgang Lutz, and Joel D. Gunn. 1997. "Social and Environmental Factors in the Classic Maya Rise and Collapse." Paper presented at the Latin American Regional Meeting on Population and Environmental Research, American Association for the Advancement of Science and the IIASA, Mérida, Yucatán, April 22–25.

Folan, William J., Lynda Florey Folan, and Juan Pablo Cauich Mex. 1989. "Estructura IIB, Calakmul, Campeche: su excavación y consolidación durante la temporada 1988–1989 y el análisis preliminar de sus actividades asociadas." *Centro de Investigaciones Históricas y Sociales, Información* 16. Campeche: Universidad Autónoma de Campeche.

Folan, William J., José Manuel García Ortega, and Ma. Consuelo Sánchez González. 1992. *Programa de manejo, reserva de la Biosfera, Calakmul: Primer Borrador*. 4 vols. Campeche: Centro de Investigaciones Históricas y Sociales, Universidad Autónoma de Campeche, Secretaría de Desarrollo Social, Campeche.

Folan, William J., Joyce Marcus, and W. Frank Miller. 1995a. "Verification of a Maya Settlement Model Through Remote Sensing." *Cambridge Archaeological Journal* 5: 277–283.

Folan, William J., Joyce Marcus, Sophia Pincemin, María del Rosario Domínguez Carrasco, Laraine Fletcher, and Abel Morales López. 1995b. "Calakmul, Campeche: New Data from an Ancient Maya Capital in Campeche, Mexico." *Latin American Antiquity* 6: 310–334.

Folan, William, J., and Abel Morales López. 1996. "Calakmul, Campeche, México. La Estructura II-H, sus entierros y otros funciones ceremoniales y habitacionales." *Revista Española de Antropología Americana* 26: 9–28. Madrid: Facultad de Geología e Historia, Universidad Complutense.

Folan, William J., and Silverio Gallegos Osuna. 1996. "El uso del suelo del sitio arqueológico de Calakmul, Campeche." *Yum Kax* 2(3): 7–8.

_____. 1998. "Uso del suelo en el Estado de Campeche, México y alrededores." *Los Investigadores de la Cultura Maya* 2: 459–478. Campeche: Universidad Autónoma de Campeche.

Fox, John Gérard. 1995. "Los campos de pelota y poder social en Mesoamérica sureste." *Investigadores de la Cultura Maya* 1: 95–110. Campeche: Universidad Autónoma de Campeche.

Gallegos, Judith. 1985. "Calakmul, Campeche: una cantera." Report on file, Consejo de Arqueología, INAH, México, D.F.

_____. 1994. "Explotación de piedra caliza en el Petén campechano." *Mayab* 9: 8–17.

Gunn, Joel D. 1997. "Room and Artifact Lithic Analysis from Temple and Palace Contexts at Calakmul." Paper presented at the sixty-second annual meeting of the Society of American Archaeology, Nashville.

Gunn, Joel D., William J. Folan, and Hubert R. Robichaux. 1994. "Un análisis informativo sobre la descarga del sistema del Río Candelaria en Campeche, México: reflexiones acerca de las paleoclimas que afectaron a los antiguos sistemas mayas en los sitios de Calakmul y El Mirador." In William J. Folan, ed., *Campeche maya colonial*, pp. 174–197. Colección Arqueología 3. Campeche: Universidad Autonóma de Campeche.

_____. 1995. "A Landscape Analysis of the Candelaria Watershed in Mexico: Insights into Paleoclimates Affecting Upland Horticulture in the Southern Yucatan Peninsula Semi-karst." *Geoarchaeology* 10(1): 3–42.

Gunn, Joel D., and William J. Folan. 1996. "Tres ríos: Una superfície de impacto climatico global interregional para las tierras bajas de los mayas del suroeste." *Los Investigadores de la Cultural Maya* 4: 57–79. Campeche: Universidad Autonóma de Campeche.

Gunn, Joel D., María del Rosario Domínguez Carrasco, and William J. Folan. 1999. "Lithic Technology Among the Maya Elite at Calakmul, Campeche during the Terminal Classic." In preparation.

Hansen, Richard D. 1990. *Excavations in the Tigre Complex El Mirador, Peten, Guatemala*. Papers of the New World Archaeological Foundation No. 62. Provo: Brigham Young University.

Hauck, F. R. 1975. "Pre-Conquest Maya Overland Routes in the Yucatan Peninsula and Their Economic Significance." Ph.D. diss., University of Utah.

Haviland, William A., and Hattula Moholy-Nagy. 1994. "Distinguishing the High and Mighty from the Hoy Polloi at Tikal, Guatemala." In Diane Z. Chase and Arlen F. Chase, eds., *Mesoamerican Elites: An Archaeological Assessment*, pp. 51–60. Norman: University of Oklahoma Press.

Hayden, Brian, and Aubrey Cannon. 1983. "Where the Garbage Goes." *Journal of Anthropological Archaeology* 2: 117–163.

Hodell, David A., Jason H. Curtis, and Mark Brenner. 1995. "Possible Role of Climate in the Collapse of Classic Maya Civilization." *Nature* 375: 391-394.

Inomata, Takeshi, and Laura Stiver. 1998. "Floor Assemblages from Burned Structures at Aguateca, Guatemala: A Study of Classic Maya Households." *Journal of Field Archaeology* 25: 431-452.

Lapointe, Marie. 1983. *Los Maya rebeldes de Yucatan*. Zamora, Michoacan: El Colegio de México.

Lowe, Gareth. 1989. "Algunas aclaraciones sobre la presencia olmeca y maya en el preclásico de Chiapas." In Martha Carmona Macías, ed., *Preclásico o Formativo: Avances y Perspectivas*, pp. 363-384. México, D.F.: Museo Nacional de Antropología e Historia, INAH.

Lundell, Cyrus Longworth. 1933. "Archaeological Discoveries in the Maya Area." Proceedings of the American Philosophical Society, vol. 72, no. 3, pp. 147-179.

Marcus, Joyce. 1973. "Territorial Organization of the Lowland Classic Maya." *Science* 180: 911-916.

_____. 1976. *Emblem and State in the Classic Maya Lowlands: An Epigraphic Approach to Territorial Organization*. Washington, DC: Dumbarton Oaks Research Library and Collection.

_____. 1985. *The Inscriptions of Calakmul: Royal Marriage at a Maya City in Campeche, Mexico*. Museum of Anthropology, Technical Report No. 21. Ann Arbor: University of Michigan.

_____. 1988. "The Calakmul State and Its Expansionist Policies." Manuscript on file at the University of Michigan.

_____. 1989. "Epigrafía de Calakmul, Campeche." Paper presented at the Primer Congreso Internacional de Mayistas, Homenaje a Alberto Ruz Lhuillier. Centro de Estudios Mayas, UNAM, San Cristobal de las Casas.

_____. 1992. "Dynamic Cycles of Mesoamerican States." *National Geographic Research and Exploration* 8(4): 392-411.

_____. 1993. "Ancient Maya Political Organization." In Jeremy A. Sabloff and John S. Henderson, eds., *Lowlands Maya Civilization in the Eighth Century A.D.*, pp. 111-183. Washington, DC: Dumbarton Oaks Research Library and Collection.

_____. 1995. "Where Is Lowland Maya Archaeology Headed?" *Journal of Archaeological Research* 3(1): 3-53.

_____. 1998. "The Peaks and Valleys of Ancient States: An Extension of the Dynastic Model." In Gary M. Feinman and Joyce Marcus, eds., *Archaic States*, pp. 59-94. Santa Fe: School of American Research Press.

Marcus, Joyce, and William J. Folan. 1994. "Una estela más del siglo V y nueva información sobre Pata de Jaguar, gobernante de Calakmul, Campeche en el siglo VII." *Gaceta Universitaria* 4(15-16): 21-26. Campeche: Universidad Autónoma de Campeche.

Marcus, Joyce, and Kent V. Flannery. 1996. *Zapotec Civilization*. London: Thames and Hudson.

May Hau, Jacinto, Rogerio Cohouh Muñoz, Raymundo González Heredia, and William J. Folan. 1990. *El mapa de Calakmul*. Campeche: Centro de Investigaciones Históricas y Sociales, Universidad Autonóma de Campeche.

McAnany, Patricia A. 1995. *Living with the Ancestors: Kinship and Kingship in Ancient Maya Society*. Austin: University of Texas Press.

———. 1998. Ancestors and the Classic Maya Built Environment. In Stephen D. Houston, ed., *Function and Meaning in Classic Maya Architecture*, pp. 271–298. Washington, DC: Dumbarton Oaks Research Library and Collection.

Moholy-Nagy, Hattula. 1997. "Middens, Construction Fill, and Offerings: Evidence for the Organization of Classic Period Craft Production at Tikal, Guatemala." *Journal of Field Archaeology* 24: 293–311.

Morales, López, Abel. 1994. "Informe preliminar del Proyecto Calakmul en Campeche: Temporada de campo noviembre y diciembre de 1993 y de febrero a marzo de 1994." Report on file, Consejo de Arqueología, INAH, México, D.F.

Nieves, Lucía M., Lourdes Esparza, and Paco Nieto. 1995. "Trabajos arqueológicos en la plaza central de Calakmul, Campeche, México." In Carmen Varela Torrecilla, Juan Luis Bonor Villarejo, and Yolanda Fernández Marquínez, eds., *Religión y sociedad en el área maya*, pp. 93–108. Madrid: Sociedad Española de Estudios Mayas.

Peniche Rivero, Piedad. 1990. *Sacerdotes y comerciantes: El poder de los mayas e itzaes de Yucatán en los siglos VII a XVI*. México, D.F.: Fondo de Cultura Economica.

Pincemin Deliberos, Sophia. 1988. "Informe de la temporada noviembre-diciembre de 1988 en Calakmul, Campeche, Estructura V." Report on file, Consejo de Arqueología, INAH, México, D.F.

———. 1994. *Entierro en el palacio: la tumba de la Estructura III de Calakmul, Campeche*. Colección Arqueolgía No. 5. Campeche: Universidad Autonóma de Campeche.

Pincemin Deliberos, Sophia, Joyce Marcus, Lynda M. Florey Folan, Ma. del Rosario Domínguez Carrasco, and Abel Morales López. 1998. "Extending the Calakmul Dynasty Back in Time: The Discovery of a the Fifth Century Stela from a Maya Capitol in Campeche, México." *Latin American Antiquity* 9: 310–327.

Piña Chan, Román. 1978. "Commerce in the Yucatan Peninsula: The Conquest and Colonial Period." In Thomas A. Lee Jr. and Carlos Navarrete, eds., *Mesoamerican Communication Routes and Cultural Contacts*, pp. 37–48. Papers of the New World Archaeological Foundation No. 40. Provo: Brigham Young University.

Ponciano, Erick, Takeshi Inomata, Daniela Triaden, Estela Pinto, and Shannon Coyston. 1998. "~Aguateca, evidencias de un abandono repetino en el clásico tardío." In Juan Pedro Laporte and Héctor L. Escobedo, eds., *XI Simposio de Investigaciones Arqueológicas en Guatemala*, pp. 685–697. Guatemala: Ministerio de Cultura y Deportes, Instituto de Antropología e Historia, Asociación Tikal.

Proskuriokoff, Tatiana. 1963. *An Album of Maya Architecture*. Norman: University of Oklahoma Press.

Reed, Nelson. 1964. *The Caste War of Yucatan*. Stanford: Stanford University Press.

Reents-Budet, Dorie, and Ronald Bishop. 1997. "La cerámica policromada de Calakmul, Campeche." Paper presented at the VII Encuentro Los Investigadores de la Cultura Maya. Universidad Autónoma de Campeche, Campeche.

Ruíz Guzmán, Roberto. 1998. "Las figurillas e instrumentos musicales de Calakmul, Campeche. Descripción, análisis e interpretación: una tentativa tipológica." Licenciatura Thesis, ENAH, SEP.

Ruíz Guzmán, Roberto, Ronald Bishop, Ma. del Rosario Domínguez Carrasco, and William J. Folan. 1998. "Figurines and Musical Instruments of Calakmul,

Campeche, Mexico: Its Sociocultural and Chemical Classification." Paper presented at the IV Congreso Internacional de Mayistas, Antigua, Guatamala.

Ruppert, Karl, and J. H. Denison Jr. 1943. *Archaeological Reconnaissance in Campeche, Quintana Roo and El Peten.* Carnegie Institution of Washington Publication, No. 543. Washington DC.

Sanders, William T. 1974. "Chiefdom to State: Political Evolution at Kaminaljuyu, Guatemala." In Charlotte B. Moore ed., *Reconstructing Complex Societies: An Archaeological Colloquium,* pp. 97–116. Supplement to the Bulletin of the American Schools of Oriental Research 20. Cambridge, MA.

Sharer, Robert J. 1994. *The Ancient Maya.* Stanford: Stanford University Press.

Taylor, Walter W. 1948. *A Study of Archaeology.* Memoirs of the American Anthropological Association No. 69. Kenosha, Wisconsin.

Tiesler, Vera, Mario Coyoc, Ma. del Rosario Domínguez Carrasco, William J. Folan, and Abel Morales López. 1998. "Los restos humanos de contextos funerarios y extrafunerarios de Calakmul, Campeche." Paper presented at the XII Simposio de Investigaciones Arqueológicas en Guatemala. Guatemala: Ministerio de Cultura y Deportes, Instituto de Antropología e Historia, Asociación Tikal.

Tourtellot, Gair, Jeremy A. Sabloff, and M. Smyth. 1988. "Mapping Community Patterns at Sayil, Yucatan, Mexico: The 1985 Season." *New World Archaeology* 8(2–3): 1–24.

Tourtellot, Gair, Jeremy A. Sabloff, and Kelli Carmen. 1992. "An Archaeological Assessment of Maya Elite Behavior in the Terminal Classic Period." In Diane Z. Chase and Arlen F. Chase, eds., *Mesoamerica Elites: An Archaeological Assessment,* pp. 80–99. Norman: University of Oklahoma Press.

Tozzer, Alfred M. 1941. *Landa's Relacion de las Cosas de Yucatan.* Papers of the Peabody Museum of American Archaeology and Ethnology, vol. 18. Cambridge: Harvard University.

Voorhies, Barbara. 1982. "An Ecological Model of the Early Maya of the Central Lowlands." In Kent V. Flannery, ed., *Maya Subsistence,* pp. 65–95. New York: Academic Press.

Voorhies, Barbara. 1996. "The Transformation from Foraging to Farming in Lowland Mesoamerica." In Scott L. Fedick, ed., *The Managed Mosaic: Ancient Maya Agriculture and Resource Use,* pp. 17–29. Salt Lake City: University of Utah Press.

Wallace, Anthony F.C. with Sheila C. Steen. 1970. *The Death and Rebirth of the Seneca.* 1st ed. New York: Knopf.

Webster, David. 1979. *Cuca, Chacchob, Dzonot Ake: Three Walled Sites of the Northern Maya Lowlands.* Occasional Papers in Anthropology 11. University Park: Pennsylvania State University.

Zapata Castorena, Alica, and Lynda Florey Folan. 1989–1990. "Investigaciones arqueológicas en la Estructura I de Calakmul, Campeche." *Centro de Investigaciones Históricas y Sociales, Información* 14: 27–41. Campeche: Universidad Autónoma de Campeche.

9

Post-Classic and Terminal Classic Courts of the Northern Maya Lowlands

WILLIAM M. RINGLE AND GEORGE J. BEY III

In examining court life among the northern Maya, it is perhaps appropriate to begin with a brief discussion of the criteria deemed most relevant to northern Yucatan. Inasmuch as "court" is not a native term, the topic implicitly invokes reference to the European court or its extension to other societies. In our view, two factors qualify an institution for inclusion under this rubric. First, as the primary articulation between a paramount and a dependent nobility, a court presupposes a monarchy of some sort and is distinguishable from a council. The court requires the presence of a ruler, although he need not be uppermost in the political hierarchy and may in fact be an attendant at a higher-level court. Courts are usually charged with a specific set of responsibilities; others may be reserved for the ruler or nobility alone. Second, the court cannot be defined strictly as an administrative organ, for performance and display are key elements of court life, often in patterns so orchestrated as to be almost ritualized. Because of the centrality of actors and audience to court life, the court should not be equated with the palace, access to which may be restricted to the ruler's household, or to the ruler's executive actions, since those may be decided upon in isolation or in the presence of a particular subset of subordinates.

Inasmuch as the primary actions of the court usually involve exchanges of wealth and power—the formulation of policy, the dispensation of justice, the conduct of diplomacy, the awarding of benefits, the reception of tribute and fealty—the court represents the nexus of many competing interests and so invites analysis from a variety of perspectives. The court was, for instance, a way for the ruler to maintain a close cohort of supporters or, conversely, to prevent potential rivals from making mischief from their own seats of power. For the nobility, the court provided a variety of avenues for economic and social advancement, from service to the paramount as counselor or captain, to proximity to the leader's largesse, to access to potential alliances both political and romantic.

Although courtly festivities and dance were complementary to the more serious tasks of governance, the stakes were hardly frivolous. The elements of pomp and conviviality were a central medium of communication, allowing courtiers to monitor the often rapid changes in status and favor. Displays of wealth and wit were often a means of self-promotion and personal advancement. History is replete with stories of fortunes made less on the basis of political or military acumen than by charm and personal friendship. But as Elias (1983) has shown, the extravagant expenditures required of court life were, from the royal point of view, a potent means of controlling the growth of noble fortunes. At Versailles, for instance, the combination of such expenditures with declining rents and a ban on engagement in commerce periodically bankrupted a large fraction of the aristocracy. It is intriguing to speculate whether the increasing lavishness of Late Classic Maya subelite life may reflect a similar dynamic.

Although "court" also has architectural connotations, it is clear that this architectural space by no means confines the social court, as any number of accounts of the peripatetic life of courtiers and kings attest (see Ball and Taschek, Chapter 6 in this volume). Neither are the court and the palace coextensive, since large sections of palaces were frequently reserved for royal domestic quarters, and palace attendants did not always perform similar functions for the court as a whole. Yet the court was often, in some sense, an attempt to encompass a semi-independent nobility within an overarching royal household. Nobles might be required to live a portion of the year in palace apartments, as was the case at Versailles and St. Petersburg, or they might build second homes to be nearer the court during its season. On occasion, the entire court might also be lodged within the country manors of noble courtiers, reversing this pattern of household hospitality.

Obviously a court in some sense is present in any society in which a leader convenes with lesser nobility. But in examining the case of the northern Maya, we may question the extent to which palace and court were coextensive, and whether courts were permanent institutions requiring dedicated facilities. As for the performative aspect, certainly Maya elite life was not lacking in pomp, but can the occasions for public display be related to court behavior? And if we grant that there were courts, at how many levels in the political hierarchy did they exist, and whom did courtiers represent at court? This discussion therefore focuses on three aspects of court life: the ethnohistorical evidence for northern Maya court organization, evidence for the types of social units represented at court, and the identification of possible archaeological correlates of courts during the Late Classic and Post-Classic periods.

The Protohistoric Maya Court

We begin, therefore, with the political organization of the late pre-Hispanic Yucatecan Maya. For the past half-century, our understanding of the political structure of the northern Maya has been based largely upon the classic studies of Ralph L. Roys (1943, 1957; Scholes and Roys 1948; Roys et al. 1959), who mined the great majority of native and Colonial ethnohistorical documents available for the area. Further studies by Farriss (e.g., 1984) amplified but did not appreciably alter Roys's account. During the past decade, the major contributions have been related studies by Quezada (1993) and Okoshi H. (1992), both of which contest some of Roys's interpretations of native terminology. Restall (1997) extends this critique by emphasizing the central organizational importance of the *cah* (town) and *ch'ibal* (patriline) while also casting doubt on the utility of certain other native political units. Also relevant is Grant Jones's recent exhaustive study of the kingdoms around Lake Peten Itza (Jones 1998). These polities claimed descent from fugitive elites from both Chichen Itza and Mayapan, most of whom probably arrived following the collapse of Mayapan around A.D. 1451.

The major primary sources include several sixteenth-century native documents that provide information on the history, lands, and lineages of important families. These include the *Chronicle of Calkini*, from the Ah Canul territory of the western peninsula (Barrera V. 1957; Okoshi H. 1992; Roys 1929),[1] the *Chronicle of Chacxulubchen* (a.k.a. the *Chronicle of Chicxulub* or *Nakuk Pech*), a document from the Cehpech province (Brinton 1882, Martínez H. 1926), the Yaxkukul land survey documents (Barrera V. 1984; Martínez H. 1926), also from the Cehpech province, the Mani land treaty from the province of the same name (Roys 1943:175–194; Stephens 1963[1843]), the Xiu family papers, also from the Mani province, and several other unpublished documents from towns such as Tekanto (transcribed by V. Bricker).[2] In addition, some relevant information can be gleaned from the *Chilam Balams of Tizimin* (Edmonson 1982) and *Chumayel* (Edmonson 1986; Roys 1933). Although in Chontal and from Tabasco, the Paxbolon papers (Scholes and Roys 1948; Smailus 1975) offer a glimpse of the social organization of a neighboring Maya group during the same period. The important Spanish sources include, of course, Landa (Tozzer 1941), López de Cogolludo (1957), Ciudad Real (1976), and the *Relaciones de Yucatán* (de la Garza et al. 1983).

To briefly review Roys's interpretation of Late Post-Classic political structure, the highest organizational level was translated as *provincia* in early sources, referring to the eighteen or so regions familiar from late prehistoric maps of northern Yucatan. There apparently was no native term for these units, although they are sometimes referred to erroneously as *cuchcabalob*. Roys envisioned a broad spectrum of political centralization among these provinces, from those under the centralized control of a *halach uinic* to *provincias* with no primate centers, sometimes even composed of mutually antagonistic communities. In Roys's view, the *provincia* was ultimately a territorial entity, whatever its degree of political coherence.

Roys (1943:11) noted that the *cuchcabal* more properly refers to the jurisdiction subject to a particular town or city.[3] Okoshi H. (1992) and Quezada (1993) have developed this into a critique of the Roys's interpretation of the *provincia*. They observe that a given *cuchcabal* is always associated with a toponym, so that in their view the administration of several subject towns by a primate center is the essence of the *cuchcabal*.[4] Their list is thus somewhat different from Roys. For instance, Roys's Cupul province, which he viewed as being composed of several independent and frequently antagonistic *cacicazgos*, is viewed by them as composed of several *cuchcabalob*: Saci, Chichen Itza, Popola, Ek Balam, and Tizimin. *Halach uinicob* were invariably in charge of *cuchcabalob*, although not all *provincias* had *halach uinicob*. But all *cuchcabalob*, in their view, were subject to a single town and ruler. Due to the vagaries of their histories, however, *cuchcabalob* were not necessarily territorially contiguous.

Within the *cuchcabal* were various subdivisions, where again there is some disagreement among authorities. All agree that the fundamental second-level jurisdictional unit was the *batabil*, whose functionary was designated the *batab*. Although commonly viewed as having jurisdiction over a single town, *batabob* such as Nakuk Pech might rule over small nearby hamlets (*cacab*) as well. Occasionally *batabob* were politically independent, although others, such as Nakuk Pech, owed allegiance to higher-ranking *batabs* (discussed below).

The smallest unit was the *cuchteel*. Roys (1943:7), following the Colonial dictionaries, viewed this as a ward, or *barrio*, of a town led by an *ah cuchcab*. Quezada (1993:39, note 60) notes that *cuchteel* has a number of associated meanings: a subject or vassal, a household (perhaps led by an *ah cuch nal*), a parishioner, as well as a territorial division of a town. *Cuchteelob*, he argues, were also identified with a toponym, and he suggests members of the *cuchteel* had common access to designated land parcels. The *ah cuchcab* had the duties of representing the *cuchteel* that elected him. He also collected tribute, arranged for the mobilization of labor and perhaps military service from the group, as well as congregating ward members for festivities (de la Garza et al. 1983:1:123). Thus, the *cuchteel* was also a taxation unit (Quezada 1993:41–42). However, there is no evidence that the *ah cuchcab* was a lineage head, consistent with the apparent lack of residential segregation by patronym in early census data (Roys et al. 1959).[5]

A final term of relevance is the *tzucub*, unfortunately infrequent in Colonial texts. For Quezada (1993:15–16, 45–50), the *tzucub* was essentially an extended noble lineage, providing mutual support for the *batabob* and *halach uinicob* sharing a common patronym. In his view the *tzucub* crosscut provincial boundaries, for although patronyms were often dispersed among several different *provincias*, members of the same patronym apparently recognized obligations of hospitality (e.g., Roys 1957; Tozzer 1941:99).[6] Okoshi, however, insists that the term referred primarily to a territorial division of the *cuchcabal*, in this case referring to individual towns subject to a paramount. Thus, for him the *tzucub* did *not* crosscut provincial boundaries and had no necessary relation to kinship. This has the backing of the dictionaries, for *tzuc* among other things is a (numerical) classifier of towns; other terms are used for *linaje* (see discussion below).[7]

A similar term, *tzucub te*, occurs in the *Chilam Balam of Tizimin* (Edmonson 1982) associated with toponyms rather than patronyms.

u yax ilcob/u lumil/Yucatan/tzucub te
they first saw the land of Yucatan, *tzucub te*
(ll. 173–176)

uai ti tzucub te/Mayapan
here in the *tzucub te*/(of) Mayapan
(ll. 2093–3094)

tu yax cheil/tu tzuc teil cab
at the ceiba/at the *tzuc(ub)te* of the town
(ll. 2909–2910)

Chac Temal/tu lumil tzucub te/Tah Uaymil
Chetumal/in the *tzucub te* land/Uaymil
(ll. 2971–2972)

uai tu chumuc tzucub te/May cu/Mayapan
here in the middle of the *tzucub te*/cycle seat/Mayapan
(ll. 5259–5261)

Although we disagree with Edmonson's interpretation,[8] *tzucub te* does seem to reference a capital or polity (since it is also applied to Yucatan as a whole), perhaps metaphorically as a world tree.[9] None of the passages supports Quezada's hypothesis. We dwell on this because below we present a more detailed critique of the evidence for extended patrilineages or patriclans in Yucatan.

Within the provincial government, each *batab* had under him several officials, the titles of which varied from province to province. The *ah kulelob* and the *ah cuchcabob* formed a council representing each of the *cuchteelob*. According to Roys (1943:63), the *ah cuchcab* was the elected representative of the *cuchteel*, the *ah cuchcabob* forming an influential council able to exert considerable sway over the *batab*.[10] In the Calkini document, the tier below the *batab* was referred to as *ah canob*, "the speakers," recalling similar titles elsewhere in Mesoamerica, such as *tlatoani*, that emphasize the importance of oratory.[11] Consistently there are three of these, although the first is consistently referred to as *u kul(el)* while the second and third have ordinal designations.[12] Since the latter two are frequently "named" Ah Kul as well, it underscores the complexities of official titles and the dangers of assigning rank strictly on their basis. Perhaps the most egregious example of this comes from the *Chronicle of Chacxulub Chen*, where Nakuk Pech, leader of a very minor Pech town, refers to himself as a *halach uinic*, a title virtually all authorities believe was reserved for the provincial paramount. In another section he refers to himself as the *yax batab* ("first *batab*"), although, as is discussed below, he was clearly of the third tier within the province, if that.

Another office of much recent archaeological interest was the *holpop*. As is well known, the *holpop* had responsibilities for certain festivities held in the *popol na*, or council house, but also had political jurisdiction over certain towns as well, at least occasionally at a level equivalent to *batab* (Quezada 1993:43, citing the *Relaciones* of Hocaba and Sotuta [de la Garza et al. 1983:134, 146]). Quezada (1993:43) advances the interesting suggestion that it may be characteristic only of certain regions of Yucatan, specifically the *cuchcabalob* of Hocaba, Sotuta, and Calotmul. This is based upon occurrences of the terms in the *Relaciones*, but *holpopob* are also mentioned in the *Chronicles of Chacxulub* and *Calkini*, the *Chilam Balam of Chumayel*, and once in the *Tizimin*. The office was therefore once fairly widespread. One explanation for its rarity in texts might be that it was a title entrusted to officials usually marked by other titles, such as *batab* or *ah kulel*. Another is that certain of the Spanish reforms specifically targeted the activities of *holpops*, such as dance festivities and lineage activities, and so that office may have rapidly disappeared.

Types of Courts

At the time of the Spanish Conquest, courts were held at several levels. At the highest level was the court of the regional or provincial capital and, at the lowest, those around the leaders of individual townships, the *batabob*. Occasionally there seems to have been a middle ground as well, for certain towns within a province might cluster together and be internally ranked. In the *Chronicle of Chacxulub*, for instance, the narrator, Nakuk Pech, was the "guardian" and *batab* of Chacxulubchen, itself composed of two districts. Nakuk Pech was placed in office by Ah Naum Pech of Motul, the provincial capital, but was the son of Ah Kom (Martin) Pech of Xul Kum Chel (Figure 9.1). Most of the activities that Nakuk Pech records, such as various tribute-paying episodes and battles fought as allies of the Spanish, were in the company of his father and uncles, espe-

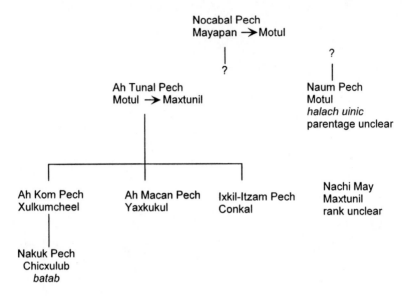

FIGURE 9.1   Genealogy of the Pech family in the *Crónica de Chacxulubchen*.

cially Ah Macan Pech, his paternal uncle and *batab* of Yaxkukul. Significantly, he never mentions attendance at the Motul court. Nakuk Pech clearly places himself in a subservient position to all three of the above individuals by referring to them as *in yum* ("my lord"), the only Maya so referenced in the document.[13]

Yet despite what would seem to be a rather humble noble rank, Nakuk Pech briefly mentions a full complement of his own officers, including two *ah kulelob*, two *holpopob*, and two *ah kinob*, as well as several *nacomob/holcanob*. None possessed the Pech patronym. (Here the *holpop* would seem to have displaced the *ah can* of the Calkini chronicle, although the *holpopob* are consistently mentioned after the *ah kulelob* in the Chacxulub document.) Thus, even this third-tier site would seem to have had a rather complex court, to which presumably were added *ah cuchcabob* as representatives of the people.

Similarly, in his recent study of the Calkini document, Okoshi (1992:190) notes the *batab* of Calkini, the principle Canul town, was the immediate head of three subject towns (Mopila, Nunkini, and Tepekan), which Okoshi believes formed a *cuchcabal*. This leader was also recognized as the lord of the province of Ah Canul by the other *batabob*, although he was never accorded the title of *halach uinic*. Thus, here a single individual was the center of both a local and provincial court. Like the Ceh Pech courts, lower officials often did not share the patronym of the ruling lines. Documents indicate a similar organization for the Xiu province (see note 3).

Mul Tepal

Mul tepal has gained a measure of popularity in recent years as a model for some of the more important northern Maya polities and courts. Several commentators have suggested that the governance of cities such as Chichen Itza, Xcalumkin, and Mayapan could be characterized as "joint rule," based upon a literal interpretation of the term (e.g., Grube 1994; Marcus 1993; Schele and Freidel 1990). This form of government is said to have occurred at Mayapan, and because of Landa's story of the three brothers ruling Chichen (repeated in no native source), it has been suggested there as well. It is well to remember, however, that Maya mentions of *mul tepal* are to be found only in the books of *Chilam Balam*, once in the *Chumayel* and twice in the *Tizimin*, both texts dating to the late eighteenth–early nineteenth centuries. It does not occur in sixteenth-century documents, native or Spanish.

Although some sixteenth-century accounts do indicate Mayapan was a confederacy of sorts, the interpretive problems presented in the documentation amassed by Roys (1962) should not be oversimplified. Few of the early writers were impartial observers: Gaspar Xiu was a descendent of that ruling house, and Nachi Cocom, who gave Landa much information, was from the opposition. Thus, the former tends to concentrate on the last period of Mayapan after the success of the Xiu rebellion, emphasizing the treachery and Mexican derivation of the Cocoms. Landa and Herrera present fuller and more sympathetic information on the Cocom role at Mayapan and its relation to Chichen. It is also interesting that every reference to Mayapan in the *Relaciones de Yucatán* comes from the Colonial province of Merida; not a single mention can be found in the twenty-five reports from the Valladolid *provincia* (de la Garza et al. 1983). This may suggest the hegemony of Mayapan was considerably attenuated in eastern Yucatan.

Several sources agree that even though families within Mayapan each had authority over particular subject towns, ultimate authority was in fact vested in a single lord from one of two paramount factions, the Cocoms and Xius (the Chel family was a distant third). López de Cogolludo, for instance, states:

> This land of Yucatan, which the natives call Maya, was governed for a long time by a Supreme Lord, and the last descendent of these was Tutul Xiu, he who was the lord of Mani and its hinterlands. . . . It thus seems to have had a monarchy, which according to the truest sentiment of authors is the best for the preservation of kingdoms. This king had for his capital a populous city called Mayapan (from which must have derived the naming of this land as Maya) that by wars, and by discord between him and his vassals, being the only justice the degree of power of each one (unhappy times, in which there

was no supreme lord equal in power and justice), terminated this government. (López de Cogolludo 1957[1688]:179)[14]

Ciudad Real, writing a century earlier, provides a somewhat fuller picture:

> In this region ... a very populous city was founded, called Mayapan, in which (as if it was a court) resided all the chiefs and lords of the Maya province, and there they supported them with their tribute. Among these were two leaders, whom the others recognized as superiors and acknowledged vassalage and for whom they had the greatest respect. One they called Cocom and the other Xiu, and the elderly Indians said that the Xiu, supported by other lords, killed the Cocom, who was more senior and renowned than he. (Ciudad Real 1976[c.1589]:II:367–368)[15]

Gaspar Xiu, in parallel passages in several of the *Relaciones* (*Citilum, Kizil, Tekanto, Dzan*), affirms that one of the Tutul Xiu lords was the absolute ruler of Mayapan, ruling more by craft than force (de la Garza et al. 1983:181–183, 198–200, 215–217). Similar views are voiced in several other reports. The *Relaciones de Cansahcab* and *Izamal* (de la Garza et al. 1983:I:94, 305) indicate that one of the rulers of Mayapan, possibly the last, was named Ah Xupan (Xiu),[16] and furthermore that the leader and founder of the Ahkinchel province was formerly his *criado* (servant or vassal). Since the Chels are stated in other sources to be the third major family at Mayapan, the fact that they were subservient to Ah Xupan further confirms the inequalities of the major families.

Other *Relaciones* affirm the presence of a paramount, but maintain that initially the Cocom family was dominant. Thus Herrera: "The lords of Yucatan, believing that they could not be preserved unless one man governed, determined to give the ruling power to the Cocom family, who were so rich that they possessed twenty-two good pueblos" (quoted in Roys 1962:61). Much the same thing is said by Landa, who states the reign of the Cocom immediately followed the foundation of Mayapan by Kukulcan (Roys 1962:57; Tozzer 1941). The *Relación de Mama* (de la Garza et al. 1983:I:110), from Xiu territory, clarifies this by stating: "They were subjects of a lord called Tutul Xiu, a Mexican name, who they said was a foreigner coming from the west, and on coming to this province was acclaimed as king by common consent of his nobles, by virtue of his valor. Before he came they were subjects to Cocom, who was the native lord of a great part of these lands."[17]

There thus seems to be fairly abundant information indicating that Mayapan was a monarchy dominated by two families, possibly sequentially. In our view, *mul tepal* refers not to joint rule but to a type of court composed of powerful "vassals" who, although acknowledging subservience to a paramount, nevertheless retained considerable holdings and rights.[18] Historically some of these polities may have been more extensive, such as Uxmal, Chichen Itza, and Mayapan but deviated chiefly in scale and splendor from the regional courts of *batabs, ah kulelob,* and *ah cuchcabob*. In these regional courts the courtiers were lords in their own right, of course, so that differences in dwellings and civic architecture were not as extreme as in lower-level polities.

Grube (1994) has argued for Classic-period *mul tepal* on epigraphic grounds, noting the apparent absence of a paramount at some sites and the frequent mention of various *itahs*, or "companions/friends," in lintel dedication texts and in rituals. There is nothing particularly surprising about this, however, since such "companions" or "captains" are mentioned in many of the ethnohistorical documents where it is clear they were subservient to the paramount lord.[19] Typically they were the warlords, *holpops, batabs,* or other close associates of the leader. Their appearance on lintel dedications is also unsurprising, since buildings such as the Monjas, the Temple of the Three Lintels, and the Temple of the Four Lintels were civic structures of some sort (Lincoln 1990:608; Ringle 1990) which probably had rooms for each of the major noble segments.

Court Architecture

Despite the several mentions of the activities of "courtiers," there is almost no mention of the architectural spaces within which these events took place. About the only passages actually refering to buildings occur in the *Chronicle of Calkini*. There we read: *"heklayobi tix xoti u patanob (tu) tancabal Napot Canche uay Calkinie ("The tribute of these people was assessed in the tancabal of Napot Canche here in Calkinie")."* A similar passage reads:

> *lay tun Naapot Canche ti kamiob ti patan ca ti*
> then Naapot Canche received them with tribute when
> *uliob tu tancabale ti tacan u batabob tumen lay Nachanchee Canule*
> they arrived in the *tancabal* where his *batabob* had gathered for Nachanche Canul (Calkini f. 16)

Both passages establish the *tancabal*, literally "in the middle of the town/region," as the locus of tribute presentation and noble congregation but, unfortunately, do not clarify whether this was an indoor or outdoor area. Roys (1929) translates *tancabal* as a "reception hall," but Barrera Vásquez prefers a translation as *cortile* (yard or patio). *U tancabil yotoch ku* is the patio of a church in the Cordemex dictionary (Barrera V. 1980:773).

Another passage concerning the presentation of tribute suggests the latter sense, also linking this activity specifically with the *popol na* (council house):

bitun u cah u chic	there occurred
u banal u cuchteel tu tancabal	the assembling of the subjects in the patio
tu chi yotoch	at the doors
tu popolnaob	of the council houses
ca hop u mulcanob	then began the public consultation
ti ca tal u paabaob	then came their breaking up
ca likiob ca talob	and they departed and came to ... (Calkini f. 14)

Tancab is also glossed as *corte* in the dictionaries with much the same ambiguity between the social and architectural aspects of the court as in English. Thus, *u tancabal ahau* is the "court, place where the king is" and the "royal palace," and *u tancabal yum cab* the "court of the king" (Barrera V. et al. 1980:773).

These passages suggest that archaeological attention might profitably be redirected to plazas and patios, rather than buildings, as the loci of court life. This is perhaps not altogether surprising given the limited ability of the Maya to enclose interior spaces sufficiently roomy for large gatherings (Kurjack 1994—the colonnaded halls of Chichen may be an exception.) Emphasis on open spaces as the loci of significant acts of display and performance may modify our perception of architectural space. Building facades, for instance, may be less an advertisement of what is within than a backdrop or stage set for the events taking place before them (see also Reents-Budet, Chapter 7 in Volume 1).

Mayapan still provides virtually the only example of a Post-Classic site in northern Yucatan described in sufficient detail for comparison. There Tatiana Proskouriakoff (1962:90) identified the colonnaded halls as akin to men's houses but noted that since "the number of such independently located halls is close to what Roys [1957] has estimated as the number of provinces under the hegemony of Mayapan, ... it is possible that each of these halls served the nobility of a specific province." Given the overwhelming dominance of censers in the pottery assemblages of these structures, collonaded halls are unlikely to have been residences and instead were almost certainly *popol nas*. Usually a "raised shrine" (Smith's [1971:108] "ceremonial shrine") faced the midline of the colonnade in ceremonial groups. Defined as a small, one-room structure standing on an independent platform, these usually had a single bench against the rear wall, although some had no furniture. Unlike shrines within the halls, provisions for statues in raised shrines were infrequent. We would suggest these may have been places from which leaders either addressed the members of their *cuchcabal/cuchteel* or received tribute. Another possible locus for these actions is the somewhat larger and more elevated "oratory" which also

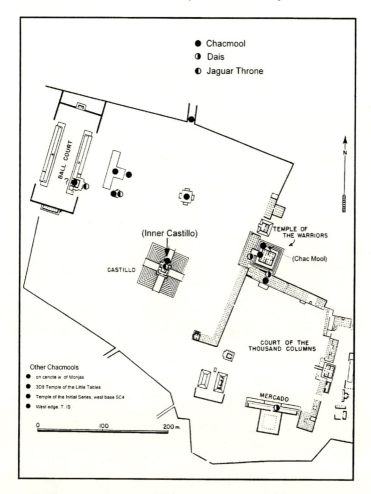

FIGURE 9.2   Location of chacmools, sculpted benches, and jaguar thrones at Chichen Itza (map from Ruppert 1943:Figure 1).

usually faced the colonnaded hall somewhat behind the raised shrine (Proskouriakoff 1962:90–91; Smith's [1971:107] "Type B" oratory). It too had a raised bench on the interior but did not have any statuary. Only two were excavated within the site core (Q–82, Q–153). Ceramic evidence from the former was similar to that of the raised shrines in having a higher percentage of ceremonial types, although the latter had a substantially higher fraction of utilitarian sherds (Smith 1971:107, Table 14). Perhaps this was because of tribute exchange or the presentation of prepared foodstuffs.

Some suggestion that the ethnohistoric use of plazas as court settings was true for much earlier times comes from the placement of thrones at Terminal Classic sites such as Uxmal and Chichen Itza (Figure 9.2). At Chichen, a jaguar throne is set in the doorway of the Lower Temple of the

Jaguars and faces out onto the Gran Nivelación, particularly the area before the *tzompantli*. The reliefs on the walls behind are familiar as an extensive record of tribute presentation and fealty by processions of warriors. At the center of these prestation scenes in the uppermost register is an individual seated on precisely such a throne with a "sun disk" backdrop. In addition to the well-known jaguar throne from within the Castillo substructure, LePlongeon discovered a "sculpture of a reclining jaguar" buried atop the Platform of the Eagles (Miller 1985:7), a relatively low, flat-topped radial structure in the main plaza. A final jaguar throne was discovered at the foot of the stairway fronting Las Monjas (Bolles 1977: 230). It too may have overlooked a large open area.

At Uxmal two jaguar thrones have been found (see Kowalski 1987:229–236 for a general discussion of jaguar thrones). Stephens (1963) partially unearthed a bicephalic jaguar throne from within what has since been shown to be a low radial platform (or *adoratorio*) located along the midline of the terrace of the House of the Governors (Ruz 1953). A similar, although poorly preserved, platform was centrally located within the Monjas complex (Ruz 1953:2). Fragments of a destroyed jaguar throne were also found within its rubble, although it is unclear when and by whom (see Kowalski 1994:112, Figure 31). Schele and Mathews (1998:285–286) suggest columnar stone monuments, called *picotes* and possibly representing the axis mundi, formed a third component of these throne-platform-column complexes.

As with the Chichen jaguar thrones, both Uxmal thrones were placed for maximum visibility within important plaza areas. Generalizing to other northern Maya sites, it may be that such centrally located *adoratorios* often functioned as supports for outdoor thrones or benches used for activities such as tribute presentation, rather than as shrines.[20] Since many documentary sources state the actual amount of tribute demanded was negligible, the true purpose was probably to publicly manifest relations of dominance and subservience.

Interestingly, another type of sculpture seems to follow this pattern—the *chacmool*. Miller (1985) has convincingly demonstrated their iconographic role as captives, but what interests us here is their location at Chichen Itza (Figure 9.2). Only certain examples remain in situ, but virtually all in the northern part of Chichen are associated with places of high visibility. The inner Castillo shows their association with jaguar thrones; another was apparently found buried deep below the Temple of the Eagles below another jaguar throne. Only the jaguar throne of the Lower Temple of the Jaguars lacks one, but an unprovenienced *chacmool* does come from the ballcourt.[21] Other *chacmools* are associated with serpent column temples, the *tzompantli*, and the Temple of Venus bordering on, or centered within, the plaza and the Court of the Thousand Columns.

Thus, rather than being the by-product of building placement, the plaza instead may be seen as a socially and ritually charged field *about*

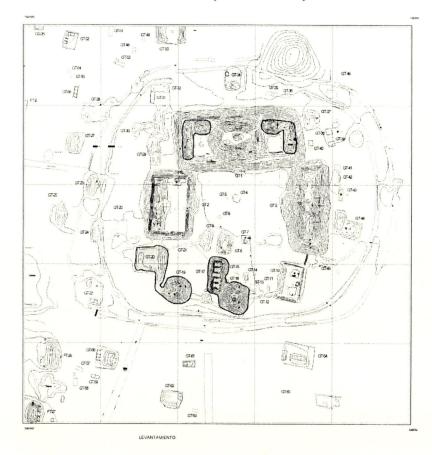

FIGURE 9.3 Plan of the central precinct of Ek Balam; temple assemblages are shaded.

which buildings were built. In other words, such spaces are owed primacy in understanding site layouts. Such a view is implicit in the suggestion that the number of plazas present at a site might be a measure of its political rank (Turner, Turner, and Adams 1981). We must, however, be sensitive to the nature of these open spaces, for public access varied enormously. Clearly the Monjas quadrangle had a much more restricted audience than the open-air platform of the Governor's Palace. A similar contrast between the public and private roles of courts and plazas might be drawn between the plaza around the Castillo versus the enclosed Court of the Thousand Columns at Chichen.

At present, several regional styles of plaza formation can be identified. In our own work at Ek Balam and its environs, we have pointed out the widespread distribution of temple assemblages (Figure 9.3). In the temple assemblage, two sides of a plaza are delimited by a pyramidal mound and a "long house," and the center is often occupied by an *adora-*

torio. The long house we have interpreted as a *popol na* (council house, literally "mat house"). At many sites, temple assemblages are associated with either *sacbeob* (causeways) or ballcourts or both (Bey and Ringle 1989; Ringle 1990; Ringle and Bey 1992). Temple assemblages range from single examples at the centers of modest hinterland sites to enormous examples such as the Str. 44 complex of Dzibilchaltun and perhaps the Governor's Palace and Great (South) Pyramid of Uxmal. A distinctive regional subvariant is the serpent temple assemblage of Chichen Itza. As we have shown (Ringle and Bey 1992), this assemblage also usually includes a ballcourt, *sacbe*, and gallery-patio structure. This evolved into similar complexes at Mayapan during the Late Post-Classic, as Proskouriakoff (1962) first noted, although they lack the associated ballcourts, *sacbes*, and gallery-patio structures. Three of these help form the southern section of the site core of Mayapan (discussed below).

Ek Balam is distinctive in having several temple assemblages within the urban limits, including multiple examples around the main plaza. These are associated with *sacbeob* connecting them to outlying groups of elite buildings. Our interpretation is that these causeways link not a royal palace to outlying noble compounds, or two groups related by kinship, as Kurjack (1979, 1994) has suggested, but rather "court" houses with the outlying temples and residences belonging to the same elite "family" (Bey and Ringle 1989; Ringle and Bey 1992). This view is predicated upon a segmentary view of northern Maya political and social organization, such that the major buildings along a single *sacbe* would all belong to the same segment, whether within the walls of the center or not.[22] This is much the same view that Okoshi independently arrived at from his studies of the Calkini text:

> Thus, in the Canul province, the leader of the hamlets sent their delegates, *ah cuchcabob*, before the ruler of their community to represent their interests. These delegates lived in the principle town, in the ward designated for each of the hamlets. (I refer to a subdivision of the principle settlement, whose number corresponded to the number of places.) It is to be noted that in each one of these wards, there was not only the house of the delegate of a hamlet but also the residence of the leader of that place for use whenever it was necessary to come before the governor of the community. Thus, I consider that a barrio or a district included both the hamlet and the ward to which it corresponded in the principle settlement. (Okoshi 1992:251)[23]

In contrast to the popularity of temple assemblages across the northern plains, Dunning (1992:107–113) has identified two widespread site core plans in the Puuc zone of western Yucatan. Although formally distinct from the temple assemblage, we believe they ultimately reflect segmentary organization as well (Figure 9.4). The first consists of a "palace," a large, multiroomed, often multitiered building with evidence for residential function, connected via a *sacbe* to a quadrangle or a quadrangle-and-

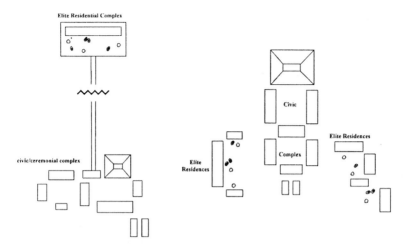

FIGURE 9.4 Dunning's Puuc site core architectural patterns (after Dunning 1992:Figures 5–19, 5–20).

pyramid complex. Usually the palace is placed to the north and the quadrangle to the south, as at Sayil and Labna. Frequently, the quadrangles possess little evidence for residential activity: Both the Mirador and Double Plaza complexes of Sayil lack *chultuns*, for instance (Dunning 1992:109, 111; Tourtellot et al. 1988:18–19).[24] The second pattern, at sites such as Nohpat and Yakalxiu, is characterized by large temple mounds fronted by a series of courts. Sometimes the courts nearest the pyramid may be raised, forming terraces, and there may be several such courts forming a descending series.

When examined in this light, the internal organization of Uxmal becomes somewhat more intelligible (Figure 9.5). The walled area of Uxmal (Graham 1992) consists largely of four or five of Dunning's second class of site core complexes (the Grupo Norte, the Adivino-Pajaros complex, the Cementerio, and the Templo Sur-Palomar, with the Temple de la Vieja being a possible fifth). All are approximately oriented toward the center of the walled zone. Two of the major remaining structures—the Palace of the Governors and the Great Pyramid—are usually considered independently, but the site plan suggests they may instead have formed an immense temple assemblage.[25]

We identify the Monjas quadrangle as the primary meeting place for the Uxmal court; by extension, certain quadrangles probably played a similar function at other sites (e.g., Tiho).[26] This is supported by the general lack of domestic features in such quadrangles, their placement relative to other "civic" structures, such as pyramids and *sacbeob*, and, perhaps most important, by formally defined entries. The "court" quadrangle seems identifiable at several Puuc sites by the presence of an arched entry, either as a freestanding structure (e.g., Sayil, Kabah[27]), as an

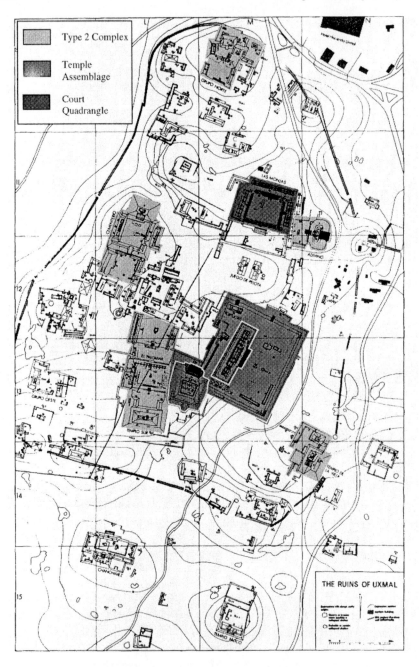

FIGURE 9.5   Uxmal: Plan of the structures within the enclosure wall (Graham 1992).

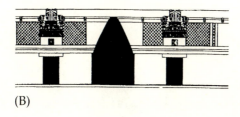

FIGURE 9.6 Two Puuc arched entryways. (a) El Arco, Labna (Pollock 1980:Figure 79); (b) central section of the central south facade, Las Monjas, Uxmal (Schele and Mathews 1998:Figure 7.11).

individual building (the Arco of Labna), or incorporated into the quadrangle, as with the western building of Las Monjas (Figure 9.6). The presence of the jaguar throne at the center of the Monjas quadrangle and the iconography of its buildings also reinforce this interpretation. Jeff Kowalski (1990:29), for instance, found fragments of "several human figures (captives, torchbearers, and musicians)," undoubtedly from the facade of the north building and all suggestive of the sorts of court activities mentioned by Landa (Tozzer 1941:27). At Labna and Sayil, the architectural associations of the quadrangles appear to be shared by two contiguous quadrangles (Gallareta N. et al. 1992; Pollock 1980:Figure 3; Tourtellot et al. 1988). The Labna Arco opens onto the court formed by Strs. 7–1, as does the *sacbe* from the Palace. Adjacent to this is another more formal court defined by Strs. 4–7 and the Mirador pyramid. The equivalent of the *adoratorio* here is a centrally located circular platform. Although no throne survives, a monumental phallus (Sculpture M1) was found just south of this plaza (Pollock 1980:51).

Quadrangles may thus be markers of a certain level of political importance. Those of Labna and Sayil probably functioned as the court spaces of small polities. Labna seems to have been under the control of a single important group based in the palace, the latter being connected by a *sacbe* to the quadrangle. Sayil was slightly more complex, since it had two such palace-quadrangle groups, each placed end-to-end along its *sacbe* and perhaps reflective of the presence of two important families. In Post-Classic terms, these may have been equivalent to the major *batabilob*, some of which were probably politically independent. At Uxmal, however, the site layout, the absence of a typical palace structure, and the scale of construction would suggest that the Monjas was not the local court of a very large *batabil* but rather of a more complex order—the Terminal Classic equivalent of the *cuchcabal*. Others have suggested that Uxmal was a regional capital on general grounds of size, architectural elaboration, and its intersite *sacbe* connections. We argue that an even more potent indicator is the four or five Type 2 complexes within its enclosure wall, one of which normally forms the core of lesser sites. These were probably the compounds of important segments who were either based in Uxmal or had their chief seat in other towns within the *cuchcabal*, the equivalent perhaps of the *batabob*.

The layout of Late Post-Classic Mayapan bears certain similarities to those of Uxmal and Chichen Itza for two reasons. First, all three may have derived their importance, at least in part, from being major shrine centers of the cult of Quetzalcoatl (Ringle et al. 1998). Second, Mayapan is simply a variant of the type of segmentary organization seen previously at Ek Balam, Chichen, and Uxmal and seems to demonstrate many of the organizational features mentioned in the ethnohistorical literature. Apart from "segmentary" architectural groups, there is often very little in the way of specialized structures at the center of many of these sites. This was first demonstrated by Proskouriakoff's (1962) penetrating analysis of the site center of Mayapan, in which she identified two basic complexes, the Basic Ceremonial Group (BCG) and the Temple Assemblage (TA). The BCG is marked by a colonnaded hall, a shrine, and usually an oratory. The latter two usually face the midline of the colonnade when there are no other constraints. In the TA, a temple is at right angles to the hall, and the shrine is rotated to face it. The eleven such groups in the site core match up well with Landa's (Tozzer 1941:40) statement that there were "twelve priests" at Mayapan; the twelfth group may have been the outlying Itzmal Ch'en complex.

A variant of the TA, the Serpent Temple Group (STG), is decorated with serpent sculpture, especially on its columns and balustrades. We would refine Proskouriakoff's typology by suggesting that the primary division was between STGs and BCGs, with the remaining temple assemblages probably being variants of the BCG or special-purpose structures.[28] As can be seen in Figure 9.7, all three STGs are south of the main plaza and all the BCGs are to their north, save for the aberrant Q–64 hall. Surrounding the main plaza are the radial pyramid Q–162, the major round structure Q–151, and six colonnaded halls. The latter in some cases appear to have had associated shrines and, in the case of Q–81, perhaps an oratory as well.

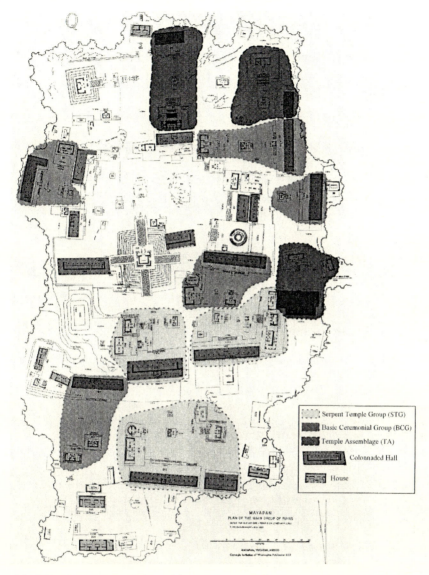

FIGURE 9.7   Mayapan: Plan of the main group of ruins (Proskouriakoff 1962).

The core of Mayapan thus comprises several smaller plazas formed by either BCGs or STGs, with colonnaded halls delimiting the main plaza. Placement of the colonnaded halls and limitations of access may indicate that each inner hall belonged to one of the complete groups surrounding it. Since there are fewer of the inner halls than surrounding groups, some apparently were not represented. If true, we can again see the "infield-outfield" pattern of civic (and court) organization (although we must remember that the site core was also the result of two centuries of accretionary growth). Actually this was doubly so, for each complex would also be representative of a distant *batabil* or *cuchcabal* forming part of the confederacy.[29]

Landa noted that nobles had their "houses" located within the inner wall of Mayapan, and Gaspar Antonio Chi makes the famous comment that "lords and nobles in the land remember the sites of their former homes" (Tozzer 1941:230). Some authors have taken Landa at his word and have assumed that these halls were noble residences. Excavations of three colonnaded halls by the Carnegie Project (Shook 1954; Shook and Irving 1955) effectively dispelled the notion that they were residential buildings, however. Deposits from within the main halls were overwhelmingly dominated by censer fragments, although domestic pottery was sometimes associated with an anteroom at one end (Smith 1971:109, Table 18). Of course houses need not indicate residences and may have referred to noble structures with other functions. We would agree with Roys that each hall represented a major family, although whether each corresponded to a major *cuchcabal*, or whether major families such as the Cocoms or Xius might be represented by multiple halls (corresponding to the important "descent lines" within them), remains unclear.

It is tempting to hypothesize some sort of ethnic differentiation between the BCG and STG, although excavations of these groups were unfortunately insufficiently broad for categorical statements. The obvious derivation of the serpent temple from similar structures at Terminal Classic Chichen Itza (and nowhere else to our knowledge), suggests they may have belonged to eastern *cuchcabalob*. The group containing Hall Q-212 is also the only STG with a round temple and, hence, may have belonged to the dominant Cocom faction. In contrast, excavation of the colonnaded Hall Q-151 (Shook and Irving 1955) demonstrated it had a series of Puuc-style masks across the base of the front colonnade. These "Chac" masks are strikingly similar to those decorating the tops of several huts on the facade of the southern building of the Nunnery and elsewhere. In view of the size and location of the Q-151 group, it is tempting to see it as having belonged to the Xiu faction. By extension, the remaining BCGs may also be attributable to other western *cuchcabalob*.

Another architectural feature that may be related to the hierarchical position of a given center is the presence or absence of enclosure walls. Although walls may well have had a defensive function, either real or symbolic (cf. Bey and Ringle 1989), they also delimited the civic centers of the most important polities and so were marks of rank.[30] Just as the quadrangles of the Puuc zone defined private spaces, so too enclosure walls limited access to main plazas. This is most evident at Ek Balam (Figure 9.3), where two circular enclosure walls defined the monumental core of the site center and limited entrance to it by means of four gates. Access was further limited to the main plaza by a series of low rectangular platforms connecting the major buildings and creating what was in effect a private space similar to the enclosed quadrangles of the Puuc zone.

Were the Maya Examples of House Societies?

Related to the forgoing discussion of the "segmental" architectural components of site centers is the identity of the social unit or office utilizing these complexes. In the Introduction to Volume 1 of this series, Inomata and Houston pose the interesting question of whether the Maya can be considered a "house society" and thus, given the arguments above, whether the structures about court plazas might better be considered as "great houses" rather than "lineage houses." Given the notorious difficulty of digging up kinship, Lévi-Strauss's notion of the house society is initially attractive in providing an alternative to lineage theory with potentially recoverable material correlates. Furthermore, the complex societies included under this rubric seem at first glance to offer many parallels with those of ancient Mesoamerica, especially those from Southeast Asia. But since most authorities emphasize lineages as a basic organizational feature of Maya society, some discussion of the evidence for such units is first necessary.

Maya Lineages

Carsten and Hugh-Jones (1995:18–20) note that whereas Lévi-Strauss chose to accommodate lineage theory to his theory of house societies, the latter position may also provide further ammunition for the radical critique of classical lineage theory (e.g., Kuper 1982, 1988). It is perhaps true that we sometimes forget that lineage theory is a relatively recent construct in anthropological thought and overlook the wide variety of ways the term has been used.

In most (Maya) archaeological usage, "lineage" has what might be called a strong sense of an enduring, branching corporate descent group possessing rights and obligations, as well as being recognized as such by its members. Indeed, some would assign all those with a given patronym to a single patrilineage. Quezada's (1993:44–50) interpretation of *tzucub* mentioned above also falls within this interpretation of the word, although he would limit it to nobility. Proponents often cite Landa's well-known statement that "the Indians say that those bearing the same name are all of one family" and that a stranger, on arriving at a new place, "makes use of his name, and if there are any of the same name there, they receive him at once and treat him with the greatest kindness" (Tozzer 1941:99). Landa further indicates that inheritance was usually patrilineal and that patronyms were exogamous, also confirmed by census data (Jones and Ringle 1990; Roys et al. 1959). This is basically what led Roys

(1957:35) to conclude that patrilineages included both nobles and commoners.[31]

At the other extreme, we have what Goody (1983:222–239, 1990) refers to as *lignage*, noting that "one of the major problems has been that comparative analysis has begun, almost inevitably, by taking a term from medieval Anglo-French law, lineage/*lignage*, and then developing the concept as a term of art for very different social contexts." He continues:

> *Lignages* were not formally constituted corporations in the same way [as Chinese lineages], but groups of kin linked together by claims to status and estate in aristocratic and mercantile families. These groups existed within a society that was largely cognatic (bilateral) in its kinship organization and had long abandoned, if it had ever possessed, unilineal lineages of any other kind; and the *lignages* consisted of "descent lines" rather than the much more extensive kind of group found in China, or in a different form in Africa. (1990:77)

Goody (1983:224) further points out that patterns of inheritance or political succession are not always trustworthy guides to descent. Property and office are by their nature of limited availability and so may require different rules of transmission, whereas rules of descent are applicable to all.

To turn Goody's point on its head, we contend that part of the confusion with regard to the Maya is linguistic, and that it is the sense of *lignage* as "genealogy" or "pedigree" that better characterizes the relationships of Maya nobility. Several proponents of the strong sense of lineage, including Roys, have drawn support from definitions of certain native terms as *linaje* in sixteenth-century Spanish dictionaries. For instance, the term *ch'ibal* (sometimes incorrectly spelled *chibal* in documents) is defined in the Motul dictionary as "casta, linaje, genealogía por línea recta; de aquí sale."[32] Other dictionaries indicate this refers to descent through the male line, although not all sources agree. But during the sixteenth century, *linaje* would have been cognate to *lignage*, referring to the relative ranking of individual families or descent lines.

It is possible *linaje* was being used as the closest Spanish equivalent to a novel kin term, but if patrilineages were important, there is remarkably little mention of them in native texts. Outside of the chronicles of Calkini and Chicxulub, there is but a single mention of *ch'ibal* in other sixteenth-century documents (and none of *dzacab*, the putative term for the matriline). In the two chronicles, there is often enough ambiguity that either sense might be attributed to the term. Several instances, however, appear to be inconsistent with the strong sense of lineage. In the Chicxulub chronicle, the term *yax ch'ibal* ("first or most important lineage/*lignage*") is used several times, each time with reference to a specific town (rather than the entire *provincia*), and to a specific individual, rather than the common patronym.[33] Since two of the individuals mentioned, Ah Kom Pech and Ah Macan Pech, were brothers and thus would have belonged to the same patrilineage, it is difficult to understand why they are designated as representatives of the *yax ch'ibal*s of their respective communities unless *ch'ibal* had a much more restricted meaning. As Roys (1943:35–36) notes: "The Pech family was so numerous that this could hardly have been much of a distinction [i.e., if a lineage in the strong sense was being referred to]; and I suspect that it refers rather to their own high rank among members of this name." Since the individuals mentioned were all community leaders, an interpretation of the "first or ruling family of X" seems preferable.

In the Calkini Chronicle, another passage reads "*u kul ti ah kul canche—na moo u naal lay u ch'ibal na may canche yetel batab che lay u ch'ibal ti cimi te manie yetel ah balam dzul manan ch'ibal heuac teob ti sati te chakane*" (his deputy was [Ah] Kul Canche, whose *naal* was Na Moo and whose *ch'ibal* was Na May Canche. The *ch'ibal* of Batab Che died there at Mani and Ah Balam Dzul did not have a *ch'ibal* because he lost it at Chakan; *Crónica de Calkini*, f. 14, ll.16–20). Instead of referring to a patronym, here *ch'ibal* makes reference to a prestigious individual, Na May Canche, who was one of the founders of the province and a direct paternal ancestor of the narrator.[34] Again, *ch'ibal* as *lignage*/descent line seems closer to the sense of the passage. Furthermore, *ch'ibal* as lineage in the strong sense is incompatible with the second clause: clearly the Che patronym was not extinguished at Mani, but a particular descent line may well have. The final clause is echoed in another passage reading "*naa hau ku—manan u ch'ibal*" (Na Hau Ku, he did not have a *ch'ibal*; *Crónica de Calkini*, f. 18, l. 9). Obviously, these statements are an impossibility if *ch'ibal* referred to an extended patrilineage, but Ah Balam Dzul and Na Hau Ku may well have lost their immediate paternal relatives.

Thus, instead of enduring corporate kin groups, we have independent, ego-focused descent lines. The *ch'ibal* of the *Chicxulub Chronicle* includes individuals who are direct descendants of a recent paternal ancestor, but it apparently did not extend to the highest-ranking Pech—Naum Pech—who was from a corollary line. The final two citations given above would further suggest that the sense of *ch'ibal* is that of a noble family, although we must acknowledge the elite bias of our sources.

A more limited interpretation of Maya lineages is perhaps more in line with expectations, given the restricted possibilities of unilineal descent groups as a basis for complex societies. As has often been noted, unilineal descent groups are exclusive, patrilineal descent groups in particular tending to factionalism and conflict. Greater stability demands crosscutting ties, such as matrilocal residence, or a greater emphasis on bilateral or ambilineal descent. As Roys pointed out some time ago, unilineal descent has only a limited ability to explain the general distribution of patronyms across *provincias* and the lack of residential segregation by patronym in early census data (Roys et al. 1959:199) . Further afield, Hill and Monaghan (1989) have argued that the Quiche term *chinamit* and the Pokomam term *molab*, usually defined as "lineage," were in fact residential divisions with only a nominal basis in kinship.[35] And despite Landa's mention of ritual hospitality among bearers of the same patronym, there must have been many instances where members of the same name wound up on opposite sides of political and military disputes.[36]

Bilateral or ambilateral (Barnes 1962) descent would also better agree with parentage expressions in hieroglyphic texts, with bilateral names in documents such as the *Crónica de Calkini*, and with patterns of residence. A bilateral pattern of descent (or affiliation), perhaps with a patrilineal emphasis, is not incompatible with an emphasis on ancestors, or with patrilineal succession to office, and would provide the needed flexibility for the complex political and residential landscape of northern Yucatan. But the question then arises: What precisely was the basis for what seem to be clear segmentary site layout patterns if ego-focused bilateral kinship was the norm?

House Societies

Lévi-Strauss (1982, 1987) proposed the "house society" as an alternative to (or perhaps an evolution from) unilineal descent groups as the organizational basis for certain societies. In a house society, kinship patterns, although present, appear insufficient to explain social organization or the transmission of rights and goods. In Lévi-Strauss's view, such societies are usually complex and their kinship cognatic. In the second section of *The Way of the Masks*, he defines the social house as "a corporate body holding an estate made up of both material and immaterial wealth, which perpetuates itself through the transmission of its name, its goods, and its title down a real or imaginary line, considered legitimate as long as this continuity can express itself in the language of kinship or of affinity and, most often, of both" (1982:174) adding elsewhere that "'houses'— called by this name in their language—and taken by anthropologists as mere buildings, are the actual bearers of rights and duties" (Lévi-Strauss 1987:151). Although descent is often the language expressing membership in the house, the net effect is often subversive of such structures, since members may also be recruited by alliance (marriage, adoption, fictitious descent). "[The] descent line . . . is recognized as legitimate as long as the continuity can be expressed in the language of descent or alliance or, most often, of both together" (Lévi-Strauss 1987:152). Medieval noble houses fall within this category, according to Lévi-Strauss, and Southeast Asian specialists have also been quick to apply the concept to the complex cognatic societies of that region.

In the case of Medieval houses, Goody (1983:228–230) notes that one argument for the emergence of the European noble house was a strong desire to maintain estates impartible, such that patrilineal inheritance and primogeniture were emphasized in a society that was largely bilateral overall. Similar processes may well have been operating in the patterns of succession at Classic-period sites. Although these tend to follow patrilines (Hopkins 1988), most Late Classic parentage expressions emphasize both parents. (In some cases, such as K'ak' Tiliw Chan Chaak of Naranjo, the father is recognized hardly at all.) And despite similar patterns of succession in early Colonial times, Roys (1929, 1940) noted the presence of the *naal* matronym in the *Crónica de Calkini*. We also have examples where patrilines were interrupted, apparently without significant political upheaval. Rather than the traumatic experience Schele and Freidel (1990:221–222) paint, the interruption of normal patrilineal succession instead seems to have been downplayed at Tikal and Palenque. At Palenque, rulers previous to the current patriline were proudly cited on the Temple of the Cross and elsewhere. In the case of Palenque's two queens, Yohl Ik'nal and Sac K'uk', although strict patrilineal inheritance of office may have been violated, mechanisms of affiliation may instead have preserved the royal dynasty and house, especially since their husbands did not rule.

Linguistic Evidence

Some evidence of "house" as a native political and civic classification may be found in the Colonial dictionaries. Roots generally meaning "house" (Yucatec *otoch* or *na*) were used to refer to residential groups, including towns, at the same time that roots meaning "town" (such as *cah* or *cab*) seem to make reference to houses. We read, for instance, that *otoch cahil* means "dependent settlement (*colonia*)" and that *otoch cab*, in addition to meaning an inn, can also mean "someone's land or homeland, a house belonging to someone" (Barrera V. et al. 1980:608). A term for *barrio* is *chi'nail* (Barrera V. et al. 1980:101). This is a derivative of *chi-na*, literally "mouth of the house," but more properly a synonym for *chi otoch*, "door [of a house]." We return to these meanings below.

Otoch and *na* more commonly refer to the house and household, and it was on this basis, rather than on kin reckoning, that civic entitlement was allotted. Thus, *ah otochnal* means "native or citizen of some town or province, inhabitant or citizen of a town, lord of the house" (Barrera V. et al. 1980:608). The family too is often conceptualized in terms of *u ba'al yotoch*, literally "the contents of the house." *U ba'alen yotoch David* means "I am of the house and family of David" (Barrera V. et al. 1980:31), and *ba'al nail* is glossed as "domestic, familial, member of the house and family who is in the charge of the head of the household" (Barrera V. et al. 1980:36).[37]

Reciprocally, although *cah* was the morpheme commonly used to refer to a town, it too sometimes had a house or household referent, at least metaphorically. In addition to the definitions associated with *pueblo, cahan* is "a married man who lives in his own house and not with his father or father-in-law" (Barrera V. et al. 1980:281). In other words, it was a synonym for *ah otochnal*. *Cahen cah* means to "establish dwellings, to live in separated rooms, to lodge or put in houses."[38] *Cahcunah* means "to put a son or son-in-law in a house to live independently" (Barrera V. et al. 1980:281). *Cahsah* means much the same thing, the *s* serving as a causative suffix. Note also the bilateral nature of such an action.

Glyphic Texts

If northern Maya nobles of the Late Classic period defined themselves in terms of houses, it may be expected that some evidence would be present in hieroglyphic texts, especially those of Chichen Itza. Work first by Kelley (1982), and then greatly amplified by Krochock (1988, 1991), demonstrated that most of the events recorded at Chichen involved the "dedications" of structures, particularly stone lintels. As noted by Krochock (1988:100) and further discussed by Ringle (1990) and Grube (1994), several structures (e.g., Las Monjas, Temple of the Four Lintels, Temple of the Three Lintels, etc.) had lintels each dedicated by a distinct individual. (Conversely, the lone lintel of the Temple of the Initial Series was apparently dedicated by more than one person.) Furthermore, dedicators often mention two or three associated figures, sometimes connected to them by the *itah* (companion) glyph. Ringle (1990) attempted to explain this pattern by suggesting these buildings were communal structures of some sort, probably *popol nas*, and that the dedicators were second-tier officials, probably *holpops*. Grube (1994:329) endorsed a public function for the Monjas but suggested that the Four Lintels was a residence, despite the fact that exactly the same pattern of joint "ownership" can be observed in both structures. It is highly unlikely that the families of Chichen's richest and most powerful lived cheek-by-jowl in a two-room building like the Temple of the Four Lintels, far from the central city.

More than thirty "house" glyphs occur at Chichen Itza, including twelve from the Four Lintels and five from Las Monjas. Most form part of a dedication phrase, either directly following the verb (e.g., Figure 9.8c) or following the object being dedicated, such as *pacab* (lintel) (Figure 9.8a, b). Invariably a personal name follows, although house glyphs can occur without a name in nondedication phrases. The main interpretive difficulty arises from the compound T59.679:24 that usually precedes the house glyph. Krochock (1988:101–102) forwarded the plausible reading of *tial*, which can mean "owner" or "for, with the end of," endorsed by Schele and Freidel's (1990:359) reading of "it was owned by." Both forms

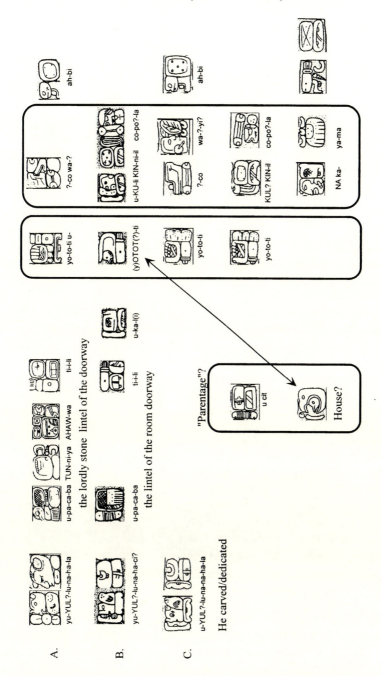

FIGURE 9.8 House "dedication" texts from Chichen Itza. (a) Monjas Lintel 4: D5-E4 (Bolles 1977:271[drawing by I. Graham]); (b) Four Lintels 2:B3-B7 (Krochock 1989); (c) Three Lintels B2-I2 (Krochock 1989).

of *tial* are invariably possessed in native documents, however. Furthermore, there is no indication that /a/ is represented by these glyphs.

A more likely reading is a derived form of *ti*, "mouth," plus an adjectival suffix, probably -*il*. In the passage above from the *Chronicle of Calkini*, *chi otoch* is used to indicate the door of the *popol na*; here the lintel is being described as a "door lintel of the house."[39] In the Chichen texts *ti yotot* is not possessed because it is an adjectival phrase modifying the possessed lintel glyph, just as the stone glyph is unpossessed when it directly follows the lintel glyph (Figure 9.8a). One remaining difficulty is that parallel passages from the Four Lintels have T1:669:24 intervening between the *tiil* and *yotot* (Figure 9.8b). Here Grube's (1994:322) reading of T1.669.24 as *u k'al*, meaning perhaps "room," would suggest that a literal translation of these passages would be "was dedicated/carved, his lintel of the mouth of the room of the house, [name]," or "[name] dedicated/carved the lintel of the room doorway."

Unfortunately, this renders most of these passages uninformative with regard to the existence of noble houses, since the house glyph in this interpretation would refer only to the specific structure being dedicated by various individuals, rather than by the houses of those individuals. Parentage expressions might be thought to be another source of information, but these are rare in the north and the terms frequently undeciphered. However, a tentative example comes from the House of the Three Lintels (Figure 9.8c). There a house indicating the "dedication" of the house by "Jawbone" is followed by passages mentioning a man and a woman. Possibly this is a parentage expression, since the glyph preceding the woman is a known "child of mother" glyph. The glyph preceding the male name is *u-ci-ti*. *Cit* is cited in the Cordemex as a reverential term for father or for the paternal uncle.[40] This is followed by a *yotot* glyph and then the name of Kinil Co-?-la. If our identification of the father glyph is correct, this would indicate that Jawbone is a son of the house of his father. Also notable is the similarity of the house glyph variant from the Temple of the Four Lintels (Figure 9.8b) to the "child of mother" glyph in this parentage statement. Since the latter is preceded by a /y/, it too may read "house," indicating Jawbone is of the house of Lady Kayam.

Archaeological Evidence

The iconography of certain quadrangles suggests that the components of the court were conceptualized as houses. At Uxmal, stone images of thatched huts were placed above the doorways of three of the four Monjas quadrangle structures (all except the east building). Two similar huts adorn the facades above the flanking doorways of Labna's Arco; indeed, the parallel is striking (Figure 9.6). Traces of modeled stucco indicate stucco figures were once placed within their doorways (Pollock 1980:43).

Although the Uxmal huts are today empty, perhaps one having held similar sculptures, their roofs are surmounted by mosaic masks. It is interesting that in both cases stone huts occur not on palaces or residences but on the facades of complexes we have identified as court areas. A possible interpretation is that such houses represent political segments of the polity, either wards, noble houses, or entire towns. The placement of figures within the doorways suggests that descent lines may have perceived themselves as houses (see the linguistic evidence presented above).

In northern Yucatan, one striking pattern emerging during the Late Classic period at many larger sites, and, perhaps related to the emergence or expansion of noble "houses," is the appearance and elaboration of palace structures. In the Puuc area such structures are extensive and often multileveled, as at Sayil and Labna,[41] but examples can be found throughout the northern plains. At Ek Balam, Structure GT-3 is the second largest building and forms the eastern side of the main plaza. Although badly collapsed, it clearly consisted of several tiers of vaulted rooms. But during the Florescent period, several buildings were enlarged by the addition of tiers of rooms to form similar minipalaces. Our excavation of the outlying FT-27 is a good example of an existing Early-Middle Classic stepped pyramid later amplified by the addition of a series of rooms across its western facade. A similar line of rooms was added to the base of GT-1, the main acropolis, and restoration of Str. GT-16 by Leticia Vargas has shown a pattern similar to that of FT-27. Substantial deposits of domestic pottery, *manos*, and *metates* suggest at least some of the rooms functioned as residences, although whether permanently or not is uncertain.

Clearly beyond the scale of a single extended family, and probably even a "descent line," such structures are perhaps identifiable as noble houses incorporating a mixture of kin, subjects, retainers, and servants. From a symbolic point of view, the housing of all these people in a single large "palace" complex, if only temporarily, suggests the house was a powerful metaphor for describing the polity. (It remains to be demonstrated the extent to which these buildings were in fact residences.) Palace elaboration may reflect the consolidation of power by certain descent lines during the Late Classic period, perhaps through continued appropriation of land and especially labor in the form of community holdings. Such large palace structures may then have been necessary to periodically accommodate officials of subject communities, who may have had no necessary kinship relation to their overlord. Alternatively, Kurjack (1994:313) has suggested palaces may have housed kin groups whose males comprised an effective military unit; by extension, their growth was a function of escalating conflicts during the late Terminal Classic period. Perhaps the house, rather than kin ties, formed a more flexible basis for incorporating additional warriors.

It is worth noting, however, that most military iconography comes not from palace structures but from those we have identified as court buildings. This may reflect a similar dynamic in which the elaboration of court facilities reflects the widening of military alliances among noble families and their retainers. This is perhaps clearest at Chichen, where warrior columns, sculptured benches with warrior processions, and *chacmools* all contribute to the colonnade surrounding the Court of the Thousand Columns. Sculptures of captives and warrior figures also decorate the facade of the Monjas quadrangle of Uxmal (Kowalski 1994). At Ek Balam, several sculptures of warriors and captives were found in and around the main plaza, confirming a remark in the *Relación de Ek Balam*: "It [Str. GT–1] has many figures of stone that appear to be armed men" (de la Garza et al. 1983:II:138). Leticia Vargas's recent excavation of the lower tier of Str. GT–1 of Ek Balam will provide further supporting evidence when published and may suggest that the lowest tier of rooms fronting the plaza functioned similarly to those about quadrangle plazas.

Discussion

Archaeologists have often been reluctant to apply ethnohistorically derived models to the Classic period because of the combined transformations of the Spanish Conquest, the collapse of Mayapan, and the still earlier abandonments of the Terminal Classic period. Although not wishing to minimize these changes, we argue that northern Maya political structure can be understood within a single transformational framework with significant historical continuities. One such continuity was the court, whose archaeological vestiges indicate that it literally formed the center of northern Maya political life. One component of the court, the Temple Assemblage, is clearly visible in Classic-period sites and may well extend back to the Late Formative. These remains are consistent with a feudal-like monarchy held together by a network of alliances and tribute obligations among the major noble segments. The size and organizational details of such courts evolved over the centuries, as perhaps did the nature of the monarchy (cf. Lincoln's [1990] argument for dual rulership at Chichen), but not to the extent of historical discontinuity.

We reiterate that Post-Classic Maya courts occurred throughout the hierarchy of a given *provincia*, as was probably also true during the Late Classic. Those at the highest level might be not only larger and more sumptuous but also qualitatively different from lower courts. It was not just that higher courts had greater power and authority; court attendance at the highest level might have been for quite different reasons than at courts of lesser importance. Courts at the local and district levels were probably the bailiwick of a single ruling family and included councilmen (*ah cuchcabob*) from the community. At regional centers, there seems not to have been a parallel council representative of the *cuchteelob* at the polity level. Instead, the components of the court were the leaders of subject towns, or *cuchcabalob*, and their agents (e.g., Landa's *caluacs*).

From an architectural perspective, then, the court would seem to have met within certain of the formally defined plazas enclosed by multiroom structures. In late Terminal Classic western Yucatan, such quadrangles are typically separated from palace structures. Since the latter are usually identified as the residences of the highest nobility, this would suggest some separation between the social spheres of the paramount's household and the court. The absence of burials and the paucity of domestic facilities also suggest that quadrangle rooms were only occasionally fully utilized by court officials. In contemporary eastern Yucatan, in contrast, the pattern is variable. The Court of the Thousand Columns at Chichen is perhaps the closest homologue, but at Ek Balam there was apparently no equivalent to the independent quadrangle. Rather, the impression is that buildings of several different functions—*popol nas*, multitiered "palaces," temples—were all clustered about a single main plaza that nevertheless was probably the primary locus of court activity. At Post-Classic Mayapan, houses seem to have been excluded altogether from the site core, except for a few scattered examples. Instead, multiple BCGs and STGs predominate. But common to all these examples is an "infield-outfield" organization, in which residences at court were linked either to noble complexes outside the site cores via *sacbeob* or to ruling households in subject communities.

We emphasize that large plazas or patios varied significantly in access, which presumably reflects function and the degree to which activities were confined to the court alone. Large open areas such as the Gran Nivelación of Chichen Itza, the Mirador "flats" of Sayil, and perhaps the House of the Governors platform seem designed for more public spectacles. Others were much more confined, such as the Monjas of Uxmal, the Court of a Thousand Columns at Chichen, and the main plaza of Ek Balam, thus reflecting a more restricted audience.

Finally, there is the question of whether courtiers represented lineages or some other social unit. Clearly, descent was a central preoccupation of Maya nobility, but the data presented above suggest they were not members of lineages as classically defined. Still, evidence for emically recognized noble houses is suggestive, but hardly conclusive. Our uncertainty is in part the result of certain ambiguities in the concept itself. To the question "Why is a house not a lineage?," Carsten and Hugh-Jones (1995:20) would respond "Why is a lineage not a house?" Yet this does not seem to get us much farther along a murky path. For instance, what precisely is the distinction between household organization and the "house"? Since the former is virtually a universal aspect of human society, if we simply equate the two, the concept of the house society loses much of its discriminatory power. Do we distinguish Houses versus houses, as Sellato has suggested (quoted in Waterson 1995:52–53), and, if so, are there independent means whereby we might distinguish the social House archaeologically? And given the "subversive" use of kin terminology in the house society, can we distinguish between a society truly organized on lineage principles from one based upon the house, especially given the limitations of the archaeological and epigraphic records? Finally, discussions of house societies have concentrated on considerations of descent, alliance, and ritual. Although it would not seem too difficult to meld these with more general models, such as the segmentary or tributary state, the economic factors particular to the formation of house societies have yet to be elaborated.

Nevertheless, in looking at Maya political organization and site planning, there does appear to be a strong tendency to promote low-level, house- or household-based institutions and architecture to levels increasingly higher in the hierarchy. Despite increasing differences of wealth, status, and power in the larger centers, public architecture continued to be presented in terms that were often only highly elaborated versions of humbler antecedents. The quadrangle of the court is an example whose ultimate referent is the domestic patio group, much as the court of the *batab*, his deputies, and the *ah cuchcabob* mirrored the authority of the *ah otochnal* over the extended household.

Consideration of the Maya as a house society and the court as the locus of interaction between such houses may provide a complement to the many discussions of Maya site layouts as cosmological templates. Instead of interpreting the importance of structures solely as symbols within rigid cosmographic or ritual schemata, the house society may suggest a complementary social and political dynamic affecting both the nature of the house itself and the type of settlement associated with it. As "moral actors," in Lévi-Strauss's words, houses may also be ascribed a certain intentionality in terms of ambition and positioning relative to other houses.

We acknowledge that our hypotheses are tentative and based on the architectural patterns of relatively few examples. Hopefully, with the publication of the mass of excavations carried out in northern Yucatan in recent years, a better understanding the growth of civic centers and individual structures will emerge. The targeting of plaza areas in future projects would seem to be particularly worthwhile, and perhaps with luck we may eventually know with certainty the actors on these most important of stages.

References

Barnes, J.A. 1962. "African Models in the New Guinea Highlands." *Man* 62(2): 5–9.
Barrera Vásquez, Alfredo, ed. 1957. *Códice de Calkiní*. Campeche: Talleres Gráficos del Estado.

———. 1984. *Documento n.1 del deslinde de tierras en Yaxkukul, Yuc.* Colección Científica, Lingüística 125. México, D.F.: Instituto Nacional de Antropología e Historia, Centro Regional del Sureste.

Barrera Vásquez, Alfredo, et al. 1980. *Diccionario Maya Cordemex.* Mérida, México: Ediciones Cordemex.

Bey, George J., and William M. Ringle. 1989. "The Myth of the Center." Paper presented at the fifty-fourth annual meeting of the Society for American Archaeology, Atlanta.

Bolles, John S. 1977. *Las Monjas.* Norman: University of Oklahoma.

Bricker, Victoria R. 1990a. *A Morpheme Concordance to the Book of Chilam Balam of Tizimin.* Middle American Research Institute, Publication No. 58. New Orleans: Tulane University.

———. 1990b. *A Morpheme Concordance to the Book of Chilam Balam of Chumayel.* Middle American Research Institute, Publication No. 59. New Orleans: Tulane University.

Brinton, Daniel G., ed. and trans. 1882. "The Chronicle of Chac-Xulub-Chen." In *The Maya Chronicles.* Philadelphia: Brinton's Library of Aboriginal American Literature, No. 1.

Carsten, Janet, and Stephen Hugh-Jones. 1995. "Introduction." In Janet Carsten and Stephen Hugh-Jones, eds., *About the House: Lévi-Strauss and Beyond.*, pp. 1–47. Cambridge: Cambridge University Press.

Ciudad Real, Antonio de. 1976. *Tratado curioso y docto de las grandezas de la Nueva España.* Serie de Historiadores y Cronistas de Indias, 6. México, D.F.: Universidad Nacional Autónoma de México.

de la Garza, Mercedes, et al., eds. 1983. *Relaciones histórico-geográficas de la gobernación de Yucatán: Mérida, Valladolid y Tabasco.* 2 vols. México, D.F.: Instituto de Investigaciones Filológicas, Centro de Estudios Mayas, Universidad Nacional Autónoma de México.

Dunning, Nicholas P. 1992. *Lords of the Hills: Ancient Maya Settlement in the Puuc Region, Yucatán, Mexico.* Madison, WI: Prehistory Press.

Edmonson, Munro S. 1982. *The Ancient Future of the Itza: The Book of Chilam Balam of Tizimin.* Austin: University of Texas Press.

———. 1986. *Heaven Born Merida and Its Destiny: The Book of Chilam Balam of Chumayel.* Austin: University of Texas Press.

Elias, Norbert. 1983. *The Court Society.* New York: Pantheon Books.

Farriss, Nancy M. 1984. *Maya Society Under Colonial Rule: The Colonial Enterprise of Survival.* Princeton: Princeton University Press.

Gallareta Negrón, Tomás, José Huchim Herrera, Carlos Peraza Lope, Carlos Perez Alvarez, and Lourdes Toscano Hernández. 1992. "Planteamientos y resumen de los trabajos de campo del Proyecto Arqueológico Labná, temporada 1991." Report on file, Centro INAH Yucatán, Mérida.

Gallareta Negrón, Tomás, Lourdes Toscano Hernández, Carlos Pérez Alvarez, Carlos Peraza Lope, et al. 1993. "Restauración e investigaciones arqueológicas en Labná: la temporada de campo de 1992." Report on file, Centro INAH Yucatán, Mérida.

Goody, Jack. 1983. *The Development of the Family and Marriage in Europe.* Cambridge: Cambridge University Press.

_____. 1990. *The Oriental, the Ancient, and the Primitive: Systems of Marriage and the Family in the Pre-industrial Societies of Eurasia*. Cambridge: Cambridge University Press.

Graham, Ian. 1992. *Corpus of Maya Hieroglyphic Inscriptions, Volume 4, Part 1: Uxmal*. Peabody Museum of Archaeology and Ethnology. Cambridge: Harvard University.

Grube, Nikolai. 1994. "Hieroglyphic Sources for the History of Northwest Yucatan." In Hanns J. Prem, ed., *Hidden among the Hill.*, pp. 316–358. *Acta Mesoamericana* 7. Möckmühl: Verlag Von Flemming.

Grube, Nikolai, and Linda Schele. 1991. "*Tzuk* in the Classic Maya Inscriptions." *Texas Notes on Precolumbian Art, Writing, and Culture* No. 14.

Hill, Robert M. II, and John Monaghan. 1987. *Continuities in Highland Maya Social Organization: Ethnohistory in Sacapulas, Guatemala*. Philadelphia: University of Pennsylvania Press.

Hopkins, Nicholas A. 1988. "Classic Maya Kinship Systems: Epigraphic and Ethnographic Evidence for Patrilineality." *Estudios de Cultura Maya* 17: 87–121.

Houston, Stephen, and David Stuart. 1996. "Of Gods, Glyphs, and Kings: Divinity and Rulership Among the Classic Maya." *Antiquity* 70: 289–312.

Jones, Grant D. 1998. *The Conquest of the Last Maya Kingdom*. Stanford: Stanford University Press.

Jones, Grant D., and William M. Ringle. 1990. "Population and Society in a Sixteenth-Century Maya Town." Paper presented at the eighty-ninth annual meeting of the American Anthropological Association, New Orleans.

Kelley, David H. 1982. "Notes on Puuc Inscriptions and History." *The Puuc: New Perspectives [Supplement]*, pp. 1–18. Pella, Iowa: Central College.

Kowalski, Jeff K. 1987. *The House of the Governor*. Norman: University of Oklahoma Press.

_____. 1990. "A Preliminary Report on the 1988 Field Season at the Nunnery Quadrangle, Uxmal, Yucatan, Mexico." *Mexicon* 12(2): 27–33.

_____. 1994. "The Puuc as Seen from Uxmal." In Hanns J. Prem, ed., *Hidden among the Hills*, pp. 93–120. *Acta Mesoamericana* 7. Möckmühl: Verlag Von Flemming.

Krochock, Ruth J. 1988. "The Hieroglyphic Inscriptions and Iconography of Temple of the Four Lintels and Related Monuments, Chichen Itza, Yucatan, Mexico." Master's thesis, University of Texas at Austin.

_____. 1989. *Hieroglyphic Inscriptions at Chichén Itzá, Yucatán, México: The Temples of the Initial Series, the One Lintel, the Three Lintels, and the Four Lintels*. Research Reports on Ancient Maya Writing, No. 23. Washington, DC: Center for Maya Research.

_____. 1991. "Dedication Ceremonies at Chichén Itzá: The Glyphic Evidence." In Virginia M. Fields, ed., *Sixth Palenque Round Table, 1986.*, pp. 43–50. Norman: University of Oklahoma.

Kuper, Adam. 1982. "Lineage Theory: A Critical Retrospect." *Annual Review of Anthropology* 11: 71–95.

_____. 1988. *The Invention of Primitive Society*. London: Routledge.

Kurjack, Edward B. 1979. "*Sacbeob*: parentesco y desarrollo de estado maya." In *Los procesos de cambio en Mesoamerica y áreas circunvecinas*, pp. 217–30. Sociedad Mexicana de Antropología, XV Mesa Redonda, Universidad de Guanajuato.

_____. 1994. "Political Geography of the Yucatecan Hill Country." In Hanns J. Prem, ed., *Hidden among the Hills*, pp. 308–15. *Acta Mesoamericana* 7. Möckmühl: Verlag Von Flemming.

Lévi-Strauss, Claude. 1982. *The Way of the Masks*. Vancouver: Douglas and McIntyre.

_____. 1987. "The Concept of 'House.'" In *Anthropology and Myth: Lectures, 1951–1982*. London: Basil Blackwell.

Lincoln, Charles E. 1990. "Ethnicity and Social Organization at Chichen Itza, Yucatan, Mexico." Ph.D. diss., Harvard University.

López de Cogolludo, Fray Diego. 1957. *Historia de Yucatán*. edited by J. Ignacio Rubio Mañe. Colección de Grandes Crónicas Mexicanas 3. México: Editorial Academia Literaria.

Marcus, Joyce. 1993. "Ancient Maya Political Organization." In Jeremy A. Sabloff and John S. Henderson, eds., *Late Lowland Maya Civilization in the Eighth Century A.D.*, pp. 111–184. Washington, DC: Dumbarton Oaks Research Library and Collection.

Martínez Hernández, Juan, ed. 1926. *Crónica de Yaxkukul*. Mérida: Talleres de la Compañía Tipográfica Yucateca.

_____. 1929. *Diccionario de Motul maya-español, atribuído a Fray Antonio de Ciudad Real y Arte de lengua maya por Fray Juan Coronel*. Mérida: Talleres de la Compañía Tipográfica Yucateca.

Miller, Mary E. 1985. "A Re-examination of the Mesoamerican Chacmool." *Art Bulletin* 67: 7–17.

Okoshi Harada, Tsubasa. 1992. "Los Canules: Análisis etnohistorico del Códice de Calkini." Ph.D. diss., Universidad Autónoma de México.

Pollock, H.E.D. 1980. *The Puuc*. Memoirs of the Peabody Museum of Archaeology and Ethnohistory, vol. 19. Cambridge: Harvard University.

Proskouriakoff, Tatiana. 1962. "Civic and Religious Structures of Mayapan." In *Mayapan, Yucatan, Mexico*. Carnegie Institution of Washington, Publication 619. Washington, DC.

Quezada, Sergio. 1993. *Pueblos y caciques yucatecos, 1550–1580*. México, D.F.: El Colegio de México.

Restall, Matthew. 1997. *The Maya World: Yucatec Culture and Society, 1550–1850*. Stanford: Stanford University Press.

_____. 1998. *Maya Conquistador*. Boston: Beacon Press.

Ringle, William M. 1990. "Who Was Who in Ninth-Century Chichen Itza." *Ancient Mesoamerica* 1: 233–243.

Ringle, William M., and George J. Bey. 1992. "The Center and Segmentary State Dynamics." Paper presented at the Wenner-Gren Conference on the Segmentary State and the Classic Maya Lowlands.

Ringle, William M., Tomás Gallareta Negrón, and George J. Bey III. 1998. "The Return of Quetzalcoatl: Evidence for the Spread of a World Religion During the Epiclassic Period." *Ancient Mesoamerica* 9: 183–232.

Roys, Ralph L., ed. 1929. "Crónica de Calkini." Unpublished manuscript in the Latin American Library, Tulane University.

_____. 1933. *Book of Chilam Balam of Chumayel*. Carnegie Institution of Washington, Publication 438. Washington, DC.

———. 1940. *Personal Names of the Maya of Yucatan*. Contributions to American Anthropology and History, No. 31. Carnegie Institution of Washington, Publication 523. Washington, DC.

———. 1943. *The Indian Background of Colonial Yucatan*. Carnegie Institution of Washington, Publication 548. Washington, DC.

———. 1957. *The Political Geography of the Yucatan Maya*. Carnegie Institution of Washington, Publication 613. Washington, DC.

———. 1962. "Literary Sources for the History of Mayapan." In *Mayapan, Yucatan, Mexico*. Carnegie Institution of Washington, Publication 619. Washington, DC.

———. 1965. "Lowland Maya Native Society at Spanish Contact." In Gordon R. Willey, ed., *Handbook of Middle American Indians, Volume 3: Archaeology of Southern Mesoamerica, part 2*, pp. 659–678. Austin: University of Texas Press.

Roys, Ralph L., France V. Scholes, and Eleanor B. Adams. 1959. "Census and Inspection of the Town of Pencuyut, Yucatán, in 1583 by Diego García de Palacio, *oidor* of the Audiencia of Guatemala." *Ethnohistory* 6: 195–225.

Ruppert, Karl. 1943. *The Mercado, Chichen Itza, Yucatan*. Contributions to American Anthropology and History, No. 43. Carnegie Institution of Washington, Publication 546. Washington, DC.

Ruz Lhuillier, Alberto. 1953. *Uxmal: temporada de trabajos 1951–1952*. Unpublished report on file Centro de Yucatán, INAH.

Schele, Linda, and David Freidel. 1990. *A Forest of Kings: The Untold Story of the Ancient Maya*. New York: William Morrow.

Schele, Linda, and Peter Mathews. 1998. *The Code of Kings*. New York: Scribner.

Scholes, France V., and Ralph L. Roys. 1948. *The Maya Chontal Indians of Acalan-Tixchel: A Contribution to the History and Ethnography of the Yucatan Peninsula*. Carnegie Institution of Washington, Publication 560. Washington, DC.

Shook, Edwin M. 1954. "Three Temples and Their Associated Structures at Mayapan." Current Reports, No. 14. Washington, DC: Carnegie Institution of Washington.

Shook, Edwin M., and William N. Irving. 1955. "Colonnaded Buildings at Mayapan." Current Reports, No. 22. Washington, DC: Carnegie Institution of Washington.

Smailus, Orwin. 1975. *El Maya-Chontal de Acalan*. Centro de Estudios Mayas, Cuaderno 9. México, D.F.: Universidad Autónoma de México.

Smith, Robert E. 1971. *The Pottery of Mayapan*. Papers of the Peabody Museum of Archaeology and Ethnology, vol. 66. Cambridge: Harvard University.

Smyth, Michael P., José Ligorred P., David Ortegón Z., and Pat Farrell. 1998. "An Early Classic Center in the Puuc Region: New Data from Chac II, Yucatan, Mexico." *Ancient Mesoamerica* 9: 233–258.

Stephens, John L. 1963. *Incidents of Travel in Yucatan*. New York: Dover Press.

Tourtellot, Gair, Jeremy A. Sabloff, *et al.* 1988. "Mapping Community Patterns at Sayil, Yucatan, Mexico: The 1985 Season." *Journal of New World Archaeology* 7(2/3): 1–24.

Tozzer, Alfred M. 1941. *Landa's Relación de las Cosas de Yucatan*. Papers of the Peabody Museum of American Archaeology and Ethnology, vol. 18. Cambridge: Harvard University.

Turner, Ellen Sue, Norman I. Turner, and R.E.W. Adams. 1981. "Volumetric Assessment, Rank Ordering, and Maya Civic Centers." In Wendy Ashmore, ed.,

Lowland Maya Settlement Patterns, pp. 71–88. Albuquerque: University of New Mexico Press.

Waterson, Roxana. 1995. "Houses and Hierarchies in Island Southeast Asia." In Janet Carsten and Stephen Hugh-Jones, eds., *About the House: Lévi-Strauss and Beyond*, pp. 47–68. Cambridge: Cambridge University Press.

Notes

1. A recent volume by Restall (1998) translates the Calkini, Chacxulubchen, and Paxbolon documents (among others) and provides a valuable overview of each document.

2. Unless otherwise indicated, "Maya" indicates Yucatec Maya. Because the documents discussed date to the Colonial period, traditional orthography has been retained. The principal correspondences are Colonial c, k, pp, dz, and uV/Vu to k, k', p', ts', and wV/Vw in the Cordemex dictionary (Barrera V. et al. 1980). Distributional arguments are based upon concordances to the texts transcribed by Victoria Bricker (all texts except Paxbolon, Yaxkukul, Calkini) and myself. In addition, we have relied on published concordances to the *Chilam Balams of Tizimin* and *Chumayel* (Bricker 1990a, 1990b).

3. There is some variance in native usage. For instance, the Mani land treaty reads *halach uinic don francisco de montejo xiu/gouernador uay ti cah/yetel tu cuchcabal tutul xiu*, indicating Francisco Xiu was *halach uinic* of the Tutul Xiu province (*cuchcabal*) and governor of the town of Mani. Yet a few lines later, we have *yetel u cuchcabalobe/ah petuob/ah calotmulobe/yetel ah hunactiob*, which Roys (1957:185) translates as "the districts (*cuchcabalob*) of the people of Peto, Calotmul, Hunacti," noting that "Hunacti was one district, and the lands of Peto, Tzuccacab and Calotmul constituted another; but both were associated with Mani." Thus, the jurisdiction of the *cuchcabal* could encompass either the entire province or major subdivisions within it. This perhaps is the best way to interpret another entry between these two: *yetel tun u chayanob/gouernadoresob yanob/ tu cuchcabal mani* ("and the rest of the governors of the *cuchcabal* of Mani"). Although Mani could be another name for the Tutul Xiu *provincia*, it more likely refers to the jurisdiction over towns immediately subject to Mani.

4. They also disagree somewhat on the nature of the *cuchcabal*, based upon their respective definitions of *cuch*. Okoshi suggests it refers to a particular office or jurisdiction (a set of duties), whereas Quezada (1993:21) maintains it refers instead to a place, a political seat.

5. The Cordemex citation of the *ah cuchcab* as a lineage head is a translation of a conjecture by Roys; no primary source suggests it was a kin term.

6. Quezada's (1993:46, n. 89) main evidence is a definition in the Motul dictionary (Martínez Hernández 1929) pairing the term with several "lineages," such as *u tzucob Ah Canulob*. This is the only such passage in sixteenth- and seventeenth-century texts, and it is open to other translations, such as references to *provincias* rather than patrilineages.

7. A passage in an unpublished document from the Tutul Xiu town of Sabacche supports Okoshi: *Tu cahal Mani tu lahun ca kal u kinil uy uil mayo ychil yabil de mil quinientos noventa y seis anyos/ Tu hoksah u baob Gaspar Keb yetel Geronimo Keb Francisco Keb José Keb ah otochnalob ychil u tzucul u cahal San Antonio Ah Sabacche uay ti*

cah Mani/ Cat chicanpahiob yetel yunil u petisionob tintan cen alcalde Francisco Nauat ordinario ti cah tumen noh ahau ah tepale ("In the town of Mani on the thirtieth of the month of May in the year 1596/Gaspar Keb presented himself, as did Geronimo Keb, Francisco Keb, [and] José Keb, householders in the division [/,of?] the town of San Antonio Sabacche. Here in the town of Mani where they appeared with the letter, the petitions, before me, I who am alcalde Francisco Nauat *ordinario* to the town by order of? the great lord, the ruler"). *Tzucul* could here be a parallel couplet with *u cahal* (town) and thus be a synonym or be a part of Sabacche, but there is no hint it functioned as a kin unit. A passage from the Ch'ontal Paxbolon papers also mentions the term *tzucul: u chun u cahibal ta tecel ta ca(ha)lob tamactun u kaba ta ui ba than acalan u kaba ta mexi than u petel mactun uinicob cheba checel u tuzucul cah dzibil u hidzibal tu patay* ("Beginning at the start, when they were in their towns, in Tamactun, as it is called in the language here, Acalan as it is called in the Mexican language, all the Mactun people dispersed[?] in their towns as is written. The end [of the list] is written on the reverse"; Smailus 1975:46). Although Smailus glosses *tzucul* as *barrio*, the designated list specifically mentions towns.

8. Edmonson's (1982:note to 1.25) gloss states, "*Tzucub Te* 'grove of trees,' a sacred grove, the most famous of which was always at the cycle seat, in this case Chichen Itza." The Cordemex dictionary indicates *tzucub te* is a synonym of *tzucul*.

9. Cf. Grube and Schele (1991) for possible Classic-period hieroglyphic correlates.

10. Quezada (1993:42–44) maintains the reverse—that the *ah cuchcab* was the appointee of the *batab* while the *ah kulel* was elected by members of the *cuchteelob*. This is suspect because in both the Calkini and Chacxulub chronicles it is the *ah kulelob* who consistently accompany their migrating leaders to new towns, whereas the *ah cuchcabob* are mentioned hardly at all.

11. Houston and Stuart (1996:295, note 3) have recently suggested that *ajaw* may derive from the proto-Cholan root **aw*, "to shout."

12. *Ah kul Calam u kul; Ah Kul Cob u canac yah canob, Ah Kul Chim u yoxnac yah canob* (MS. p. 11). Ah Kul Calam was his *kul*, Ah Kul Cob his second speaker, Ah Kul Chim his third speaker.

13. One passage may suggest that Ah Macan Pech was the overlord of the western Cehpech district (ll. 499–501, MS. p. 35). Those concerning Ah Kom Pech may have been more marks of filial respect by Nakuk Pech.

14. "Esta tierra de Yucathan, a quien los naturales de ella llaman Maya, fue gouernada muchos tiempos por vn Señor Supremo, y el ultimo descendiente de ellos fue Tutul Xiu, el que era Señor de Mani, y sus comarcas . . . Asi parece aver tenido gouierno Monarquico, que segun el mas valido sentir de los Escritores, es el mejor para la conseruacion de los Reynos. Tenia este Rey por cabecera de su Monarquia vna Ciudad muy populosa, llamada Mayapan (de quien debia de deribarse llamar a esta tierra Maya) que por guerras, y discordias entre el, y sus vassallos, siendo solo justicia el mayor poder de cada uno (infelizes tiempos, en que no tiene el Señor supremo igual el poder con la justicia) acabo este gouierno" (López de Cogolludo 1957 [1688]:178–179).

15. "En aquella guardianía . . . estovo fundada una ciudad muy populosa, llamada Mayapán, en la cual (como si fuera corte) residían todos los caciques y

señores de la provincia de Maya, y allí les acudían con sus tributos. Entre éstos había dos principales, a quien[es] los demás reconocían superioridad y vasallaje y tenían grandísimo respeto; el uno se llamaba Cocom y el otro Xiu, y dicen los indios viejos que el Xiu, ayudándose de otros principales, mató al Cocom, que era más señor y más principal que él" (Ciudad Real 1976 [ca. 1589]:II:367–368).

16. There is also mention of another Mayapan king, Cotecpan, in the *Relación de Muxuppip* (de la Garza et al. 1983:I:376): "Y el rey que los gobernaba se llamaba y tenía por nombre Cotecpan, que quiere decir en nuestro romance hombre sobre todos" ("And the king who governed them was called and had the name of Cotecpan, which is to say in our language 'lord over all'"). As Roys (1962:55) notes, this is partially a Nahua name, *tecpan* meaning "palace." Muxuppip was a Ceh Pech town, but we know nothing further about this individual.

17. "Eran sujetos a un señor que llaman Tutulxiu, nombre mexicano, el cual dicen era extranjero venido de hacia poniente, y venido a esta provincia lo alzaron los principales de ella con común consentamiento por Rey, visto las partes que tenía de valor; y antes que viniese eran sujetos al Cocom, el cual era señor natural de much parte de estas provincias."

18. In arguing against *mul tepal* among the Peten Itzas, Jones (1998:105) states "such 'shared rule' was tempered by a strong principle of lineage domination by a single group of closely related males, two of whom 'ruled' as a dual persona."

19. E.g., the Paxbolon papers (Smailus 1975:26, 46–47), the *Relación de Ek Balam*, etc. Whether the frequent reference to four companions is a trope or corresponds to an actual number of companions remains unclear, though ethnohistorical documents such as the *Crónica de Calkini* indicate a fixed number of incumbents for certain offices. It should also be noted that the interpretation of this glyph is strongly contested by Houston, Stuart, and others, who argue that it is a verb of some sort (Houston, personal communication, 1998).

20. See the discussion of representations of outdoor thrones by Reents-Budet (Chapter 7 in Volume 1 of this series).

21. Given their association with serpent columns, a more likely place for the *chacmool* may have been the Upper Temple of the Jaguars.

22. The *Relación of Ek Balam* states that Ek Balam was founded by a king and his four "captains," each of whom was responsible for a building bordering the main plaza. Our excavations have determined these in fact date to widely differing time periods, though the *sacbe* system may well have been built in a relatively short period of time during the Florescent period. Many of the buildings also underwent extensive modifications at this time.

23. "Ahora bien, en la provincia de los Canules, los dirigentes de las aldeas enviaban sus delgados, *ah cuch cabob*, ante el gobernante de su pueblo para que el representaban sus intereses: éstos vivían en el asentamiento principal, en un sector que estaba designado para cada una de las aldeas. Con esto me refiero a la subdivisíon del asentamiento principal, cuyo numero concordaba con el de las parajes. Es de señalarse asimismo que en cada uno de dichos sectores, había no solamente la casa del delgado de un aldea sino también la residencia del dirigente de ésta para la utilizara siempre y cuando necesitare acudir ante el gobernante de su pueblo. Asi pues, considero que un barrio o una parcialidad abarcaba una aldea y el sector que el le correspondia en el asentamiento central" (Okoshi 1992:251–252).

24. We also found few water storage facilities and no permanent sources within the enclosure walls of Ek Balam. The five or so small *chultuns* could hardly have served the needs of all these buildings if they were fully occupied year-round.

25. This interpretation is admittedly tentative and requires further evidence. One problem in identifying the Governor's Palace as a long house/*popol na* is that it consists of a series of rooms rather than long corridors, and these open onto the terrace rather than onto the plaza facing the Great Pyramid. Another question is why both a central temple assemblage and quadrangle are present if both were elsewhere involved with court activities. Possibly this reflects a spatial segregation of court functions not present in eastern Yucatan, with the Governor's Palace being involved more with the performance of public rituals and ceremonies.

26. The quadrangle at Chac II (Smyth et al. 1998) would seem to have grown out of an earlier temple assemblage complex.

27. Located near to 1B2, the largest pyramid, which has a forecourt to its south. Just south of this is a poorly reported quadrangle (Pollock 1980:Figure 281).

28. Two of the three TA colonnaded halls are extremely small (Q–64, Q–97a); the other (Q–142) has an aberrant floor plan.

29. See Jones (1998:64, 71–74, 82–104) for extended treatment of the Itza version of this type of arrangement.

30. Earlier (Bey and Ringle 1989) we pointed to a possible correspondence between the roughly circular layout of northern wall systems and the circular maps of native provinces done by early Colonial Maya. Okoshi (1992) has also suggested that *peten*, "province," derives from the root *pet*, "round."

31. Roys's views changed somewhat over time. At first he maintained that "Yucatecan society was also divided vertically into lineage groups. Many of these included nobles and commoners alike, a circumstance which must have contributed greatly to social solidarity. . . . The lineages had its own patron deity, sometimes a deified ancestor, and such matters were discussed in their hieroglyphic books." (Roys 1943). In later years he was more cautious: "These groups are called lineages in the present study, although a good many of them contained too many members and were too widely dispersed to be considered lineages in the anthropological meaning of the term" (Roys 1957:4). Similar sentiments were presented in his synthetic article for the *Handbook of Middle American Indians* (Roys 1965).

More recently, Farriss has also noted the poverty of the evidence: "However, we lack evidence for any functionally significant kinship organization beyond the extended family. . . . If phratries, moieties, clans, or any equivalent to the Aztec *calpulli* or the Andean *ayllu* existed, the evidence has yet to surface. In its absence we must conclude tentatively that beyond the level of the extended family (which retained its vitality because of its relatively small size and its strong links with the unchanging mode of food production) social grouping had shifted from lineage to locality; to the territorially based community of village or town and the wards or precincts into which they were divided" (1984:137).

Restall (1997:Chapters 4, 7) provides further discussion of the Colonial *ch'ibal*, which he argues was restricted to a town (*cah*).

32. *Ch'ibal* is not restricted to kinship alone but can also indicate membership in or inheritance of a particular profession or office: *ch'ibal a tal, a talel ti' almehenil, tah miatsil, tah okolil* ("You come from the *ch'ibal*, you come from nobility, wise

men, thieves, etc."; Barrera V. et al. 1980:133–134). This is how it is used in the Chilam Balam of Chumayel. *Ch'ibal* is not used with patronyms in either the Tizimin or Chumayel (Bricker 1990a, 1990b).

33. *Lai tun ulicob tu cahalob y+ uy ah kulelob y+ u holpopob. /Bay tu cahal yaxkukul bay tu cahal xulkum cheel bai tu cahal maxtunil yax ch'ibal macan pech yax ch'ibal tah kom pech xulkum cheel yetulcob ix yah kinob yax ch'ibal macan pech yax ch'ibal tah kom pech xulkum cheel yetulcob ix u cuchulob tu pachob ca uliob uai ti cahtale* (Chicxulub, ll. 177–178; "Then they came to the towns with their *ah kulels* and their *holpops*. Here to the town of Yaxkukul, here to the town of Xulkum Chel, here to the town of Maxtunil, [of] the first *ch'ibal* Macan Pech, [of] the first *ch'ibal* Ah Kom Pech [of] Xulkum Chel and together [with them] came the priests of the first *ch'ibal* [of] Macan Pech, the first *ch'ibal* of Ah Kom Pech [of] Xulkum Chel and their subjects came behind them here to this town").*Tumen in yum tah kom pech u mehen tah tunal pech yax chibal maxtunile/mektantic cah lae/cat uli dzulob uai/tu lumil ca cabob lae* (Chicxulub, ll. 184–186); "Because my lord Ah Kom Pech sent Ah Tunal Pech of the first *ch'ibal* of Maxtunil, to govern that town"). *Ca binon y+ in yum ah macan pech yax chibal yax kukul y+ yxkil ydzam pech yax chibal cumkal* (Chicxulub, ll. 209; "Then we came with my lord Ah Macan Pech, of the first *ch'ibal* of Yaxkukul and Ixkil Idzam Pech, of the first *ch'ibal* of Conkal").

34. Indicating furthermore that *ch'ibal* is not reducible to "patronym" but refers to a specific descent line.

35. The Yucatec cognate is *molay*, "junta, congregación, colegio y ayuntamiento," ("meeting, congregation, academy, township or council"). *Mol tepal* is probably the more correct form of *mul tepal* (Barrera Vasquez et al. 1984:528). It, too, has no specific kinship associations.

36. Ethnohistorically, the scarcity of marriages between individuals of the same patronym may be explicable by other factors, including the large number of patronyms in relatively small villages. Individuals with a common patronym were likely members of a few closely related families, marriage among whom was discouraged on grounds of closeness.

37. The other two words given for family in the Cordemex are *cuchcabal* and *mekelte*. Both are common in discussions of government: the former has been discussed above, and *mekelte* refers to the act of governing. There does not appear to be an equivalent word for family without these associations of rulership.

38. "Establecer moradas, vivir en allas con separación, arrancharse en casas."

39. David Stuart and Stephen Houston (personal communications, 1998) had also come to this conclusion. Here *ti* lacks a possessive pronoun but has suffixes because "door" is functioning as an adjective modifying "lintel." Note that here *tiil otot* is expressly indicated phonetically, rather than *chi otoch*, indicative of a spelling closer to Cholan forms in the Chichen texts. Whether this reflects the spoken language of Chichen, the nature of the hieroglyphic language, or whether historical reconstructions of Classic-period phonology are in error, is unclear.

40. *Cit* also occurs in several northern glyphic texts in nominal phrases. These we would interpret as a title or honorific, examples of which can be found in the *Chilam Balam* books.

41. Toscano (in Gallareta et al. 1993) has shown that the Labna palace grew from a temple assemblage–like complex.

10

Post-Classic Maya Courts of the Guatemalan Highlands: Archaeological and Ethnohistorical Approaches

GEOFFREY E. BRASWELL*

When don Pedro de Alvarado entered the highlands of Guatemala in early A.D. 1524, he was searching for a territory that his Tlaxcallan allies called Quahtemallan. The existence of powerful kingdoms[1] in the Guatemalan highlands was known to the Spaniards because a delegation from that region had sought out Hernán Cortés in northern Mexico three years earlier. In less than four months, by skillfully manipulating the extant enmity between indigenous peoples, Alvarado and the Kaqchikel,[2] his temporary allies, were able to defeat the K'iche', Tz'utujil, and Pipil. The first of many revolts led by the Kaqchikel began in August A.D. 1524, but it was quickly suppressed. By late A.D. 1525, three more powerful groups—the Chajoma' (known to the Kaqchikel as the Akajal and also called the Sacatepequez), the Poqomam, and the Mam—all submitted to Spanish domination.

The historical chronicles, *relaciones*, and early Colonial histories that describe the conquest of Guatemala and the events that followed are one of the richest sources of data we have on Maya society at the time of conquest. Historical details are complemented by ethnographic information provided by dictionaries or gleaned from early legal documents and

---

*I thank Robert M. Hill for sharing his thoughts; his work has deeply influenced my own thinking on K'iche'an social structure. Judith Maxwell, as always, guided my limited forays into Kaqchikel and Nahua linguistics. I thank her and Xta Ixim Nikte' for help in translating some particularly difficult titles. I also thank Joyce Marcus, Andrew Shryock, Dennis Tedlock, Stephen Houston, and Takeshi Inomata for their sound comments and suggestions on an earlier draft of this chapter. A special debt is owed to Susan Gillespie and Rosemary Joyce, who shared critical, in-press manuscripts with me.

Colonial records. Indigenous sources, such as the *Popol Wuj* and the *Annals of the Cakchiquels* (or the *Memorial de Tecpán Atitlán*), afford glimpses of how Maya people remembered and chose to recount their own history. With the notable exception of *relaciones geográficas*, which are quite rare for Guatemala, the diversity and depth of ethnohistorical sources are without parallel in other parts of the Maya region.

Compared to the Maya lowlands, the Maya highlands have seen relatively little archaeological investigation. Unstable political conditions have contributed as much to this neglect as the lack of Classic-period monumental stone architecture and carved monuments with hieroglyphic texts. Nonetheless, the great preponderance of work has focused on Post-Classic sites, especially those that can be linked to ethnohistorical sources. In this respect, too, the highlands of Guatemala are unique in the Maya region.

This chapter summarizes the archaeological and ethnohistorical data that have been brought to bear on questions related to the function and structure of the Late Post-Classic royal courts of the highland Maya. I begin with a brief description, drawn from ethnohistorical sources, of the players that filled the stage of highland Maya courts. Next, I turn to archaeological data on the Post-Classic period. In reviewing this body of work, I focus on interpretations of Maya royal courts as places of interaction rather than as physical spaces. Then I concentrate on two areas of current ethnohistorical research of relevance to Maya courts: social structure and the organization of Late Post-Classic political systems. Although I describe most archaeological projects conducted at Post-Classic sites in the Guatemalan highlands since 1970, my review of ethnohistorical studies is limited in scope because of the quantity of work on the subject.

Dramatis Personae

What kind of people made up Post-Classic highland courts? First, the central precincts of capitals such as Iximche' and Q'umarkaj were homes to individuals from at least three strata of society: slaves (*muna'* in Kaqchikel), vassals (*alk'ajola'*, "sons") and the ruling elite (*ajawa'*, "lords"). People could become slaves in several ways—being captured in war (Coto 1983:206), as a result of committing robbery, because they or a member of their family profaned a temple or priest (Fuentes y Guzmán 1932–1933:6:12–13), or because they married a slave, were born to slave parents, or were sold into slavery by relatives (Las Casas 1909:616–618). Various words for "slave," such as *mun* (which also can mean "laziness," "sloth," or "gluttony"), *alab'itz* ("of bad descent"), and *tz'i'* ("dog") are suggestive of how people became slaves and how slaves were viewed. We are told specifically in Thomás de Coto's (1983:206) dictionary that "in ancient times 'dog' meant a slave captured in war." We can assume that slaves belonging to the *ajawa'* conducted many of the quotidian chores of the aristocratic court: preparing food, running errands, washing and mending clothes, and even serving as sources of sexual diversion (Carmack 1981:151). Excavations in palace structures at Q'umarkaj have revealed hearths and water tanks where slaves would have worked, and Robert Carmack (1981:Figure 9.11) has identified what he believes to be slaves' quarters within the Kaweq palace complex.

Some vassals lived inside the central precinct of highland capitals and served as warriors, although this occupation was not limited to *alk'ajola'*. As in other Mesoamerican societies, military service was one of the primary ways to achieve social mobility. There are indications that soldiers lived within palace compounds and enjoyed high-earned status (Carmack 1981:294). It may be that young soldiers, of both vassal and noble birth, slept in mens' houses attached to the Kaweq palace.

There also is strong evidence that vassals visited courts for economic reasons. The *Annals of the Cakchiquels*, for example, relates an incident where a Kaqchikel woman named Nimapam Ixkakaw ("Big-belly Lady-Cacao") traveled to Q'umarkaj to sell tortillas. There she was accosted by a resident soldier in the royal guard, an incident that provided the pretext for a revolt among the K'iche' (Arana X. and Díaz X. 1573–1605:41). This kind of saleswoman was called *ajk'ay* or *k'ayil* ("of the market" or "vendor"). Other traveling merchants, some of whom achieved very high status, were called *b'eyom* or *ajb'eyom* ("travelers" or "of the road people"). These itinerant merchants often sold valuable items traded over long distances rather than food or locally produced goods of daily necessity.

Vassals could achieve significant status as musicians. These included *q'ojomanela'* ("drummers" or "instrument players"), *bixanela'* ("singers"), and *xulanela'* ("flautists"). We also know that specialized artisans were attached to the royal court. In general, these were called *ajtoltekat* (literally "of the Toltecs" but figuratively "artisan"). Some may have been vassals of very high earned status; others undoubtedly were *ajawa'*. The *Annals of the Cakchiquels* relates an incident in which an attacking K'iche' army was annihilated by the Kaqchikel. In addition to killing two important K'iche' lords, the *Q'alel Achij* and the *Ajpop Achi'*, four important artisans were executed (Arana X. and Díaz X. 1573–1605:46). The fact that these individuals accompanied an army suggests that their occupations did not exclude them from military service. These artisans were the *ajxit* ("jeweler" or "gem-worker"), *ajpwaq* ("precious metalsmith"), *ajtz'ib'* ("scribe" or "painter"), and *ajk'ot* ("sculptor"). Archaeological evidence for metallurgy has been found in the form of twenty-six mold fragments recovered from Mound 8 of the Reguardo plaza group, located 750 meters southeast of the epicenter of Q'umarkaj (Weeks 1977). Thus, we can associate metalworking directly with the royal court of the K'iche'.

The role of the *ajtz'ib'* is particularly enigmatic. There are no surviving Mayan hieroglyphic texts from the Guatemalan highlands that postdate the Terminal Pre-Classic period.³ De Palacio (cited by Carmack 1973:127) and several other Colonial authors noted that the highland Maya had "books," but it is not clear if they were written or pictorial manuscripts. Bartolomé de las Casas (1957:346) wrote that highland Maya books contained "figures and characters by which they could signify everything that they desired." Francisco Antonio de Fuentes y Guzmán (1932–1933:7:108, 112) saw two manuscripts and included a copy of one in his writings. Based on this source, Carmack (1973:13, 127 Footnote 39) suggests that highland Maya manuscripts were similar to Mixteca-Puebla texts. The root *tz'ib'* in K'iche'an languages can be used to mean either "word" or "paint" (Coto 1983:207, 420). We may conclude, therefore, that these texts were not complete representations of spoken language but served as pictorial mnemonic aids for recalling oral narratives. It also may be that the parietal art of the Late Post-Classic, stylistically related to Mixteca-Puebla murals in highland Mexico, was produced by the *ajtz'ib'a'*.

The *ajawa'*, or noble class, contained many named status positions that Carmack (1981:158–159) equates with minimal and principal lineages. Among the Kaqchikel, one of these roles was *lolmay* ("ambassador"). Such emissaries were free to travel long distances. In his fourth letter to the Crown, written in A.D. 1520, Cortés (1961:218–219) mentions that a delegation from Guatemala met with him near Panuco. These Kaqchikel ambassadors sought an alliance with the Spaniards against the K'iche'.

A long list of *ajawa'* status positions is presented in the *Historia Quiché de don Juan de Torres* (Recinos 1957:48–56). Among the titles and names of the Tamub (a factional group of the K'iche') included in this document are: *Maku[p]il Tuch* ("Bracelet Keeper"), *Saqrij Tum* ("Honorable Palm"), *Saqrij Kamachal* ("Honorable Enchanter"), *Popol Winaq Istayol* ("Councilman White Salt [or Heart]"), *Tzuqtzumay* ("Feeder-gourd"), *Su'y* ("Polisher"), *Popol Winaq Xok* ("Councilman Digging Stick"), *Tz'oqoqob Kik'* ("Extractor of Blood"), *Tuj* ("[Lord] Sweatbath"), *Ub'aq'wach Meba Uqalachij* ("Eye of the Orphan of the ... Men"), *Tz'aqi' Istayol* ("Walls Salt"), *Yakola' Awan* ("Farmer [of the] Mature-Milpa"), *Yakola' Ajbaq* ("Farmer of the Bone"), *Aj Tojil* ("[Lord] of Tohil"), *Yakola' Ixtux* ("Farmer [of the] Female"), *Popol Winaq Tz'ab'* ("Councilman Elect"), *Popol Winaq Pikaxul* ("Flute-Playing Councilman"), and *Nim Chokoj* ("Great Giver-of-Banquets"). Many more *ajawa* titles that do not appear in this list were used by the K'iche' and Kaqchikel. It is particularly important that many K'iche'an titles reflect participation in councils. Kaqchikel and K'iche' courts were places where many men, representing their own great houses as well as larger factional groups, met to make political decisions. The presence of numerous *nimja* (literally "great houses") at highland capitals and secondary centers supports this conclusion.

Comparatively little is known about the structure of K'iche'an religious hierarchies. Presumably this is because Spanish interest in the matter was focused on dismantling the system (Hill and Monaghan 1987:34). Coto (1983), for example, does not include an entry for *sacerdote* or *cura* in his otherwise illuminating dictionary, but does gives four cognates for *brujo*: *ajitz* ("of evil"), *ajq'ij* ("of the day"), *jalom* ("false one"), and *nawal* ("spirit"). Robert Hill (1984:305,308) has noted that one of the meanings of *molab*, the Poqomam equivalent of the *chinamit*, is "church" or "congregation" (Zúñiga 1608:272). It may be that each of these bodies maintained temples and shrines in its area and supported local priests. Given that failure to respect a priest was a serious crime, we may infer that they held high status. The most powerful priests in residence at the capitals of the K'iche' and Kaqchikel were members of the *ajawa'* class. Carmack (1981:Table 6.3) argues that titles such as *Aj Tojil*, *Aj Q'ukumatz*, and *Aj Awilix* were inherited priestly roles. We also may assume that the Tamub *Tz'oqoqob Kik'* ("Extractor of Blood") performed sacrificial rituals. Although many prognostications were undertaken by *ajq'ija'*, prophets were known as a *saqiwachinela'* ("white-faced ones") (Coto 1983:441). The latter commanded high status, but it is doubtful that they were drawn from any particular class of society.

The highest lords of the *ajawa'* class are known to us as kings, although there is little reason to think of them as absolute monarchs. At the Kaqchikel capital of Iximche', two nobles, the *Ajpop Sotz'il* and the *Ajpop Xajil*, shared power. It is likely, however, that the head of the Tuquche' *amaq'* (a large faction within the Kaqchikel polity) may have held an equal position before that faction was expelled from Iximche'. According to las Casas (1909:615–616), the K'iche' were ruled by four lords, including a "king" (*Ajpop*), a "king-elect" (*Ajpop K'amja*, literally "[Lord-]of-the mat Receiving-house"), and two important war captains. Las Casas asserted that the *Ajpop* was succeeded by the *Ajpop K'amja* and that both captains shifted upward in status position. Because these usually were brothers, sons, or other relations of the *Ajpop*, rulership was fixed within the family but did not follow strict rules of primogeniture. In other words, kingly status could pass to different members of the same line or even to more distant affines. Rulership, then, was both inherited and earned, as among the Aztecs. Las Casas noted that whereas the *Ajpop* sat beneath four decorative canopies, the other high lords sat below three, two, and one canopy, further illustrating the hierarchical nature of quadripartite rulership. The *Ajpop* also was distinguished from other *ajawa'* as the only one who wore a particular nosepiece, a tradition that may have been adopted from the Mexican highlands.

In contrast, Pedro de Betanzos (in Carrasco 1967:252–257) claimed that rulership at Q'umarkaj was shared equally between four lords and that their political authority did not extend beyond the city. Carmack

(1981:169–171) argues that Betanzos has confused leadership roles in the four "principal lineages" residing in the town with the political statesmen called the *Ajpop, Ajpop K'amja, Q'alel* ("Judge" or "Courtier"), and *Ajtz'ij Winaq* ("Person of Words"). The point of confusion is that the same individuals often occupied high offices within their own great house and within the K'iche' polity.

Because of the paucity of relevant native sources, we know far less about Tz'utujil rulers. Although the Tz'utujil court contained a complex cast of titled aristocrats, rulership was shared by two individuals: the *Ajpop* and *Ajpop Q'alel*. The qualified title of the second leader suggests that the division of status was not equal; the *Ajpop Q'alel* played lesser king to the *Ajpop*. But we do not know which of the corulers of the various K'iche'an polities held more political power, or even if the division of secular power was institutionalized rather than determined by the ability of the individuals who held office.

It often is assumed that divided rulership is a result of power-sharing alliances between different factions. Carmack (1981), for instance, interprets the complex political structure of the K'iche' as a hierarchically organized division of power among four "principal lineages" he sees as living at Q'umarkaj. Alternatively, it may be that the distinction between power and divine authority was the basis for divided rulership. Kingship often involves two contradictory pressures: the preservation of power and the maintenance of sacred authority. A fully sacred ruler cannot directly exercise force because he is distanced from the populace. Power-sharing can result from the growth of sacred authority at the expense of profane prerogative, that is, if a king adopts a divine role, it becomes more difficult for him to wield earthly power. "Divine kingship" is an oxymoron, and I believe that the opposed centripetal and centrifugal tendencies of sacred rulership were an important source of instability in Maya political systems.

Although we can conclude that K'iche'an society was ruled by an upper stratum of nobles, succession was based not simply on hereditary rank but also on ability, and status was determined not only by seniority and authority but also by military prowess and power. As in Polynesia, K'iche'an status systems were "based on complex patterns representing opposing concepts of ascription and of achievement, of sacred and secular, of formal and pragmatic" (Goldman 1970:7). Rigid models focused on lineage and descent seem too idealized to account for this dynamic between power and position.

Archaeological Research

Until the 1970s, with a few notable exceptions, archaeologists working at Post-Classic sites in the Guatemalan highlands tended to stress the identification of sites mentioned in ethnohistorical documents. These scholars also were interested in understanding the timing of "Mexican" influence at Post-Classic sites, particularly in discovering whether the source of that influence was the Early Post-Classic Toltecs or the Late Post-Classic Aztecs (e.g., Lothrop 1936; Thompson 1943:122–132). In addition, highland archaeological data were used to evaluate various correlations proposed for lowland Maya calendars (Wauchope 1947, 1948). More recently, trained archaeologists have left the interpretation of Post-Classic sites to ethnohistorians who are less absorbed by chronological issues. Although this has led to more interesting questions being asked of archaeological data, they often are answered without a clear understanding of culture history.

Many of the largest Post-Classic sites of the Guatemalan highlands have seen considerable archaeological investigation. Important centers have been subject to mapping and intensive excavations, such as the Tz'utujil capital of Chwitinamit-Atitlan (Lothrop 1933); the Mam settlement of Saq Ulew (Woodbury and Trik 1953); the Chajoma' capital of Saqik'ajol Nimakaqapek (Lehmann 1968); the Kaqchikel capital of Iximche' (Guillemín 1959, 1964, 1965, 1967, 1968, 1969, 1977; Guillemín and Anders 1965); the K'iche' capital of Q'umarkaj (de Szecsy 1979; Wallace 1977; Weeks 1977, 1997; Wauchope 1949, 1970) as well as other sites in the Santa Cruz del Quiché region (Fox 1975, 1977; Weeks 1976, 1980, 1983a, 1983b, 1983c); and a series of K'iche' and Achi' towns and fortresses in the Río Chixoy drainage (Breton 1993; Fauvet-Berthelot 1986; Ichon 1979, 1992; Ichon and Grignon C. 1981, 1983; Ichon and Hatch 1982; Ichon et al. 1980, 1996).

Several smaller archaeological projects have looked at Post-Classic highland Maya sites in recent years. *Ri Rusamäj Jilotepeke*, a survey and excavation project conducted in the *municipio* of San Martín Jilotepeque, located and sampled eighty-two sites with Post-Classic components (Braswell 1996, 1998). As part of this project, test excavations were conducted at O'ch'al Kab'owil Siwan, first the seat of the Kaqchikel Xpantzay and later a short-lived capital of the Chajoma' (Braswell 1993, 1996). In 1991, Hill (1996) conducted a brief reconnaissance of the western Chajoma' region and located and mapped several Classic and Post-Classic sites. In 1993, members of the continuing *Proyecto Arqueológico del Área Kaqchikel* conducted exploratory excavations at the Late Post-Classic Kaqchikel site Chitaqtz'aq in the municipio of Sumpango. Ceramics and obsidian artifacts from the site have been studied (Robinson 1997, 1998).

Unfortunately, with the exception of the Saq Ulew and the Río Chixoy reports, most archaeological publications about highland Post-Classic sites are preliminary or incomplete. Lehmann (1968) published a brief guide to the ruins of Saqik'ajol Nimakaqapek and erroneously concluded that it was the Poqomam capital Mixco Viejo (Carmack 1979). The site still is widely known by this name (e.g., Sharer 1994:427). Lehmann died before completing an excavation report, and most of what we know about the archaeology of the Chajoma' capital is derived from well-documented but small-scale household excavations and analyses of funeral deposits (Fauvet-Berthelot 1986; Fauvet-Berthelot et al. 1996; Ichon and Grignon C. 1984). A brief ceramic report describing materials excavated by Lehmann was prepared by Navarrete (1962), who did not have access to detailed site plans or excavation notes.

Like Lehmann, Jorge Guillemín published only brief and tantalizing descriptions of his extensive excavations at Iximche', the capital of the Kaqchikel polity, but he did not prepare an adequate map of the site. Guillemín's principal contribution was the uncovering and consolidation of two large architectural clusters separated by a low wall. Each includes two temples, a ceremonial plaza with altars, a ballcourt, and a palace complex. A third, more modest group containing smaller palace and temple structures witnessed limited excavations, and a fourth similar cluster was tentatively identified. Guillemín (1977) argued that the larger two of these complexes should be assigned to the *Ajpop Xajil* and *Ajpop Sotz'il*, whereas the smaller two belonged to the *Ajuchan* and the *Q'alel Achi'* (two lesser rulers). In other words, the repetitive architectural pattern of Iximche' reflects what Guillemín interpreted to be a quadripartite division of rulership among four lords. Although quadripartite rulership was once a part of the Xajil *amaq'* (a major faction of the Kaqchikel), the Kaqchikel polity seems to have been ruled by only two kings (Arana X. and Díaz X. 1573–1605:36 and 44). Thus, if Iximche' really does consist of four repetitive groups, it must do so for another reason.

Guillemín's ceramics from Palace Complex I and II have been analyzed (Nance 1998). Whittington and Reed (1998) have included a sample of skeletal materials from Iximche' in a recent study of paleodiet. For the most part, however, materials excavated from the site remain unstudied because we lack information on context. Guillemín (1967) was of the opinion that artifact analyses, particularly ceramic studies, were of little importance for understanding a protohistorical site. For this reason, much of his material from Iximche' is provenienced only by major architectural group or year of excavation (C. Roger Nance, personal communication, 1992).

Results of the State University of New York at Albany's Quiché Project, including brief summaries of exploratory excavations conducted in what is thought to be the Kaweq palace of Q'umarkaj (Carmack 1981; Wallace 1977) and more extensive descriptions of work at Chisalin (Weeks 1983b), have been published. Kenneth Brown, however, has not published the results of his three seasons of extensive excavations in the center of Q'umarkaj (Weeks 1997). Thus, a detailed map of the site (Wallace 1977:Figure 4) and illustrations of two mural fragments (Carmack 1981:Figures

9.12 and 9.13) are the most tangible advances in Q'umarkaj archaeology since the days of Wauchope (1949, 1970). We still lack an adequate understanding of the ceramic chronology and construction sequence of the central precinct and royal court of the K'iche' capital. Excavation and artifact analyses have contributed little to our understanding of the function of the buildings and the activities conducted in the K'iche' royal court.

Nonetheless, ethnohistorians working at Q'umarkaj have formulated many conclusions about the architecture and history of the site. Individual buildings have been identified by interpreting ethnohistorical accounts (Carmack 1981:264–272). The Temple of Tojil, described clearly in an account by fray Francisco Ximénez (1929–1931:1:74–75), is the most securely identified structure at the site. The spatial arrangement of buildings, understood from surface architectural features and limited excavations, also has been an important focus of speculation. Wallace (1977) identifies what he interprets as "ritual-council-palace" complexes. Apparent divisions between these complexes, inferred from the site map, are thought to be boundaries between "moiety wards" (Carmack and Wallace 1977; Wallace 1977) and even "lineage precincts" (Carmack 1981; Fox 1994).[4] The subjective nature of these assignments is demonstrated by the fact that project members do not agree on the location of such divisions or which lineage should be assigned to which architectural group (Carmack 1981:222–228; Wallace 1977). The association of these arbitrary divisions with particular kinship groups seems entirely conjectural. More to the point, the correlation of structures in the K'iche' royal court with particular segments of society is not derived from archaeological evidence.

John Fox, although principally an ethnohistorian, uses architectural patterns to draw conclusions about the political and ideological geography of K'iche'an society. First, he describes certain architectural complexes that he calls K'iche' "conquest-administrative enclaves" and Kaqchikel "garrison plazas" (Fox 1977:95). The presence of "garrison plaza" groups at Saqik'ajol Nimakaqapek and at Chinautla Viejo, for example, is interpreted as indicating conquest of those Chajoma' and Poqomam capitals by the Kaqchikel (Fox 1981). But because the complex that Fox associates with the K'iche' is found not only at K'iche' but also at Mam and Kaqchikel sites, and because his characteristic Kaqchikel pattern is found at Kaqchikel, K'iche', Poqomam, and Chajoma' centers, we might conclude that these two architectural configurations do not correlate well with particular ethnic groups and their political expansion.

Fox (1994) recently has used structure, lineage precinct, and moiety-ward identifications to interpret the architectural patterning of Q'umarkaj as a large, counterclockwise-rotating K'iche'an cosmogram. Astronomical alignments—particularly with conjunctions of Venus and solstitial sunsets—are seen as supporting evidence for this interpretation, as well as indicating broad structural symmetries of domination versus subordination, day versus night, and the rainy fertile summer versus the dry death of winter. Fox (1994:167–170) sees this cosmogram—centered at Q'umarkaj—replicated over the entire central highlands. To him, the actions of individuals and political factions were determined by a calendar-derived "ideological calculus" patterned in the human occupation of the landscape (Fox 1994:158). My experience as an archaeologist suggests that it is not easy to determine precise alignments from unexcavated buildings that have been thoroughly stripped of facing stones. Moreover, I hesitate to accept that the entire history of the Post-Classic highlands, including factional conflicts led by thinking individuals, was subject to a cosmological predestination encrypted in settlement patterns.

Many archaeologists and ethnohistorians agree that certain long range structures characteristic of Post-Classic highland sites served as "council houses" (e.g., Arnauld 1997; Carmack 1981; Wallace 1977). Carmack (1981:159–160, 289) calls all such range structures *nimja* ("great house"), and suggests that they were used for the lectures, bride-price giving, and feasting associated with marriages. They also were the meeting places of councils, the locations of the court of lineage chiefs, and the places where rulers sat in judgment. In some cases, he concludes, *nimja* were used by more than one lineage. In short, *nimja* were the *salones de usos múltiples* of the Post-Classic highland Maya. Alternatively, as Hill (1996) suggests, we should equate long structures not with clans or lineages but with individual *chinamit*, the fundamental unit of Post-Classic highland land tenure.

Reports detailing excavations of these range structures are few, but urn burials have been found in council houses at Q'umarkaj (Carmack 1981:287), Saqik'ajol Nimakaqapek (Fauvet-Berthelot et al. 1996), and Kawinal (Ichon et al. 1980:203), and also are known from O'ch'al Kab'owil Siwan (Braswell 1996:334). We can conclude, therefore, that this burial pattern was practiced not only by the K'iche' but also by the Chajoma' and Kaqchikel. Carmack (1981:288) points out that this is consistent with López Medel's claim that just rulers were buried beneath the place where they sat in judgment.

Arnauld (1997) has added an interesting twist to the interpretation of these common features of Post-Classic courts. She notes that in the eastern portion of the central highlands there is a distinction between *nimja* (with stairs on only one facade of the supporting platform) and true council houses (with stairs on all four facades). The latter, she argues, are derived from the *popol na* ("mat house") of the northern lowlands (Arnauld 1997:122–123). She goes on to define an archaeological complex characteristic of the Verapaz that consists of a central temple-pyramid (often with stairs on all four sides), council houses oriented to the central temple-pyramid, and *nimja* oriented with the topographic relief of the landscape. These "Verapaz plazas" are common at Achi', Chajoma', and Poqomam sites. Arnauld defines a second architectonic configuration, called the "radial pyramid-temple complex," that consists of combined *nimja*–council houses and laterally positioned temple-pyramids. This second complex is characteristic of the western portion of the central highlands and commonly is associated with the K'iche' and Kaqchikel. Both the eastern and western patterns, she argues, are derived from the basic plan of Chichen Itza and Mayapan (Arnauld 1997:123–124).

Ethnohistorical Approaches to Social and Political Structure

Ethnohistorians long have relied on three basic sources of data for their interpretations of Post-Classic highland Maya courts. These are postconquest native accounts, early Colonial dictionaries, and a variety of Spanish documents including histories, *relaciones*, and legal documents (see Carmack [1973] for a discussion of most of these important sources). The *Popol Wuj*, the *Annals of the Cakchiquels*, and the *Rabinal Achi'* are the best-known and longest of the indigenous narratives, but legal documents and petitions written in both Spanish and Mayan languages have been particularly useful for understanding political geography. It is notable that the vast majority of indigenous Colonial documents were written by either the K'iche' or Kaqchikel. There is only one extant early document in Tz'utujil (the *Título San Bartolomé*), and two others survive in Spanish (the *Relación de los Caciques y Principales del Pueblo Atitlán* and the *Testamento Ajpopolajay*). I know of only three early Colonial documents written from the perspective of the Q'eq'chi' (the *Título Cacoj*, the *Título Chamelco*, and the *Testamento Magdalena Hernández*), only one of which is in that language. A single document is written in Poqomchi (the *Título Chama*), and only one very brief Spanish manuscript (the *Título Mam*) provides a Mam perspective on pre-Conquest and early Colonial events.

Colonial dictionaries always have been used as tools for understanding native Maya documents, but some researchers (Miles 1957; Feldman 1985; Hill 1984; Hill and Monaghan 1987) also use them extensively as sources of ethnohistorical data. Unfortunately, many of the earliest and most important dictionaries have yet to be published (e.g., Vico ca. 1550; Morán 1720; Zúñiga 1608). Colonial dictionaries are particularly important for clarifying issues of social and political structure, as well as occupational specialty. For example, although the morpheme *mun* survives today in Kaqchikel words like *munil* ("sloth" or "laziness") and *muninïk* ("to crave" or "to covet"), in the Tz'tujil *muninem* ("to be gluttonous"), and in the K'iche' *munixik* ("to desire to eat" or "to covet a role"), it has lost its original meaning of "slave" or "disobedient one" in many highland Mayan languages.

The Chinamit *and Other Units of Social Integration*

The basic unit of group organization among the Kaqchikel and K'iche' was the *chinamit*, called the *molab* in Poqomam. Debates concerning the nature of the *chinamit* have focused on whether it was essentially a descent group or a territorial unit. Carmack (1977:12–13; 1981:164–165) has argued that the *chinamit* was a feudal estate headed by a hereditary chief of a dominant lineage. Others have directly equated *chinamita'* with patrilineal lineages (e.g., Carrasco 1964:324). This second identification, however, is unlikely for two reasons. First, *chinamita'* could be large groups containing thousands of members. It is difficult to see how a structure as fragile and prone to conflict as the patrilineal descent group could have grown to this size. Second, the *chinamit* was fundamentally endogamous. Hence, common descent probably did not serve as an organizing principle (Hill 1984).

Hill (1984, 1996; Hill and Monaghan 1987) views the *chinamit* as a territorial unit with many similarities to the Aztec *calpulli* and modern closed corporate communities. He does not consider kinship to be a critical factor in determining group membership. We must recognize, however, that leadership roles in some *chinamita'* became fixed within certain families and particular lines for several generations. A suitable analogy may be found in Victor Goldkind's (1965, 1966) reanalysis of Chan Kom. Although political control over contemporary *ejido* lands theoretically cannot be established in one line, it often becomes so because of the ambitions of a particular man or family. I suggest, then, that the heads of *chinamita'* might have been "*caciques*" in Goldkind's sense. They tried and often were successful at maintaining a politically powerful role in their descent line for more than one generation. Thus, concurring with Hill, I am not convinced that the lineage was a particularly consequential structure. But I do see both the line and a larger, *metaphoric* sense of kinship as two foundations of K'iche'an society.

A fourth possibility is raised by a new and exciting body of work that argues that Formative and Classic peoples of southern Mesoamerica were organized as "house societies" (e.g., Gillespie 1995; Gillespie and Joyce 1997, 2000; Joyce 1996, 1999a). Most recently, this model has been applied to the Late Post-Classic Maya of the northern lowlands (Joyce 1999b; Ringle and Bey, Chapter 9 in this volume). It may be that the *chinamit* of the Late Post-Classic highlands was a kind of fictional kin group that included many families loosely bound by the "the language of kinship or of affinity and, most often, of both" (Lévi-Strauss 1983:174). These corporate bodies, called "houses" (Lévi-Strauss 1983, 1987), potentially could include the thousands of individuals who made up the *chinamita'*. The use of "*nimja*" to describe the range structures associated with the *chinamita'* may reflect the conflation of the name for a social unit with the structure where that group conducted its business. There even was an important K'iche' group known as the *nijaib* ("people of the great houses"). Therefore the *chinamit*, although fundamentally a corporate group based on land tenure, may have used the metaphor of kinship to build group solidarity. This is consistent with Hill's (1984:307) supposition that lesser members of a *chinamit* may have adopted the family name of the *cacique* as an acknowledgment of his authority and control over an area. As I will outline below, there are other aspects of the house society model that are consistent with K'iche'an society.

Most members of a *chinamit* practiced endogamous marriage, but more powerful individuals married into prominent families in other *chinamita'*. According to Hill (1996:63), alliances between *chinamita'*—called *amaq'i'*—were formed and strengthened by such marriages. In this model, leadership roles in K'iche'an society were divided among *amaq'i'*. For this reason, after the Tuquche' *amaq'* was eliminated from the Kaqchikel polity, rulership was divided between the *Ajpop Sotz'il* and the *Ajpop Xajil*, the leading aristocrats of the remaining two Kaqchikel *amaq'i'*. John W. Fox and Garrett Cook (1996:811–812) see *amaq'i'* as community segments tied together by kinship. In their model, major lineages, including those that ruled at Q'umarkaj, contained more than one *amaq'i'*. Thus, Hill views the *amaq'* as the largest unit of organization within each K'iche'an polity, whereas Fox and Cook (1996) and Carmack (1981:Table 6.2) see major lineages and moieties as still larger units. But there is no ethnographic evidence supporting the contention that the highland Maya ever were organized in moieties.

Above the *chinamit* level, models of highland social organization proposed by Carmack (1981), Fox and Cook (1996), and Hill (1984, 1996; Hill and Monaghan 1987) all suffer from the overidealization of a rather chaotic reality. It is difficult to see how the carefully nested hierarchies of these models are expressed in Colonial documents. *Chinamita'*, *amaq'i'*, and the great houses described in the *Popol Wuj* may be more synonymous than most ethnohistorians have supposed. Alternatively, *amaq'i'* may have been large factional units that cross-cut descent and territorial units. An important question for which there is no clear answer is: Could members of the same *chinamit* belong to different *amaq'i'*?

The word "*Amaq'*" has ethnic connotations and often is translated as "tribe." Many K'iche'an nobles claimed to be recently arrived conquerors. In some cases, *amaq'* was used to describe commoners living outside of K'iche'an capitals. Perhaps, then, it refers to the descendants of people who already were living in a particular territory when the K'iche'an elite arrived. Larger units of social identity, therefore, may have had an ethnic component. Coto (1983:LXXXV) defines *amaq'* as "stranger" or "place." The first can have ethnic implications, and the second suggests something akin to a territorial unit. In particular, the morpheme can be combined to form a verb meaning "to settle as a neighbor," which has both the sense of place and otherness. The root often is used to describe something lasting or permanent and, in Colonial times, could be combined to form *amaq'ib'äl*, meaning "old or former household." This last definition is particularly intriguing. If we suppose that the sense of antiquity implied in *amaq'ib'äl* refers to a Pre-Columbian past, it may be that the *amaq'* was a kind of social house that ceased to exist after the Conquest. Thus, the hierarchical and qualitative distinctions between *amaq'*, *chinamit*, and *nimja* are not particularly clear. According to Dennis Tedlock (personal communication, 1998), there is "no good evidence that *chinamit* labels a category that is not subsumed under *nimja/amaq'* terminology."

Political Organization

The nature of K'iche'an political organization also has been a focus of ethnohistorical research. An important contribution to Maya studies is the proposal that the K'iche'an political system was a segmentary state. The first explicit use of Aiden Southall's (1956, 1988) model to describe Post-Classic highland polities is attributable to Fox (1987), but it is apparent from earlier writings that other scholars considered K'iche'an society to be organized in segmentary lineages (e.g., Carmack 1981; Fox 1981; Wallace 1977).

Although K'iche'an society was in no way monolithic, it is not clear that segmentation always followed lineage boundaries (e.g., Braswell 1996; Hill 1984; Hill and Monaghan 1987). But segmentary states need not be partitioned according to kinship principles (Southall 1988:71). In the K'iche'an case, it might be productive to consider segmentation along factional boundaries. I am thinking specifically of Elizabeth Brumfiel's (1994:4) definition of factions as "structurally and functionally similar groups which, by virtue of their similarity, compete for resources and positions of power or prestige." The conflict between the Tuquche' and the other *amaq'i'* of the Kaqchikel, which resulted in the expulsion and the *kamib'äl* ("death") of the Tuquche'(Arana X. and Díaz X. 1573–1605:49–50), can be interpreted as a factional conflict.

It is not universally accepted that the various K'iche'an kingdoms formed a segmentary state. Brown (1983, 1985; Fox et al. 1992:Note 1) agrees that the K'iche' polity was segmented along lineage lines but regards it as an advanced chiefdom. Marcus (1993), citing Southall (1991:91), notes that segmentary states are not state-level societies. Instead, she points out that the segmentary state is an intermediate category between acephalous societies and unitary states. The Alur, then, were a ranked society, but not any kind of state.

From a different perspective, it is unclear if Southall's (1988:52) recent definition of the segmentary state as "one in which the spheres of ritual suzerainty and political sovereignty do not coincide" fits the K'iche'an case. We simply do not know enough about the ritual role of the K'iche' and Kaqchikel kings to say that this definition is satisfied. If las Casas (1909:615–616) was correct in his assertion that the rulers of the Kaqchikel, Achi', and Tz'utujil had to be confirmed in office by the *Ajpop* of Q'umarkaj, then perhaps the definition would hold. Las Casas's informants were K'iche', so it is natural that their perspective emphasized the importance of their own ruler. The issue is further complicated by tribute; what is viewed as required tribute by the receiver may be considered a gift by the provider. There is no doubt that items were exchanged between the rulers of the Kaqchikel, K'iche', and Tz'utujil. But gift-giving between rulers may have solidified their ritual and political status in several apparently contradictory ways. The acts of both giving and receiving can be manipulated to reinforce status.

The prime sanction held by K'iche'an kings was "control over the means of destruction" (Goody 1971). The numerous rebellions by K'iche' and Kaqchikel factions reported in documents like the *Annals of the Cakchiquels* attest that this sanction was both frequently needed and regularly employed. The necessary exertion of destructive power is not particularly consistent with ritual suzerainty. Instead, K'iche'an kings seem more like the heads of large factions defined, in part, by ethnic criteria. Their rulership was based more on military prowess and threat than on any ritual authority. The setting of a highland capital often was chosen because of its strategic value as a defensive location or as a place from which raids could be launched, not because of its central position in the political landscape. For this reason, I consider sites like Q'umarkaj and Iximche' more as military and logistical strongholds than as true political or economic central places. The abandonment of O'ch'al Kab'owil Siwan by the Chajoma' sovereign Amolaq' Lajuj No'j and subsequent founding of Saqik'ajol Nimakaqapek are consistent with this interpretation of K'iche'an capitals (Braswell 1996:330). In this case, the Chajoma' royal court was moved to be closer to four smaller communities that had staged an unsuccessful rebellion.

Were Post-Classic K'iche'an polities organized as one or more states? To a great degree, the answer depends on how one chooses to define the state. According to a recent operational definition, archaic states are characterized by:

(1) a change in the settlement hierarchy from three to four levels; (2) a change in the decision-making hierarchy from two to three (or more levels); (3) a fundamental change in the ideology of stratification and descent, such that rulers were conceded a sacred supernatural origin (establishing their divine right to rule) while commoners were seen as having a separate descent of nondivine origin; (4) the emergence of two endogamous strata, the result of severing the

bonds of kinship that had once linked the leaders to followers in a branching continuum of relationships; (5) the evolution of the palace as the ruler's official residence; (6) the change from a single centralized leader (e.g., a chief) to a government that employed legal force while denying its citizens the use of personal, individual force; and (7) the establishment of governmental laws and the ability to enforce them. (Marcus and Feinman 1998:16–17)

Current archaeological research sheds some light on the first of these seven criteria. Settlement surveys in the eastern (Hill 1996) and western (Braswell 1996, 1998) portions of the Chajoma' kingdom reveal a simple settlement hierarchy consisting of three levels. The smallest sites are simple sherd and lithic scatters, most of which represent isolated households. Intermediate-sized sites contain isolated structures or small groups, usually consisting of earthen or *laja*-faced earthen platforms. Only four multigroup sites are known: O'ch'al Kab'owil Siwan (Braswell 1996:Figures B.7-B.15), Saqik'ajol Nimakaqapek, Las Vegas, and El Horno. The first two were sequential capitals of the Chajoma'. The last two, which are much smaller and best considered as second-tier sites, have yet to be subject to archaeological scrutiny (Hill 1996:70–73). Survey within the territory dominated by the Kaqchikel polity also has revealed just three levels of settlement: Iximche', second-tier sites such as Chitaqtz'aq, and artifact scatters (Robinson 1990, 1997, 1998).[5] The K'iche' capital of Q'umarkaj is neither significantly larger nor more elaborate than Iximche' or Saqik'ajol Nimakaqapek. Thus, there is no reason to posit that the settlement hierarchy of the entire K'iche'an world consisted of more than three levels.

The number of levels in K'iche'an decision-making hierarchies is less clear, reflecting as much about the idealized and unrealistic formulation of the concept as about the organization of Maya administration. Ethnohistorical sources do not describe individuals or councils that made metadecisions. Rather than formulating procedures and policies about administration, K'iche'an elites participated directly in decision making. Particular issues of sufficient moment were passed upward within the political system. If the identification of *nimja* as the seats of *chinamita'* is correct, we can conclude that some administrative activities were conducted at these structures by individual leaders. More important decisions may have been made by *chinamit* councils that also met in these structures. The repetitive titles held by the lords of groups like the Xajil, Sotz'il, and Tuquche' suggest that each contained both individuals and councils that made decisions. At the top of the hierarchy were individuals and councils representing each of these larger alliances, as well as the king and his council of advisers. It is conceivable, therefore, that a particular administrative decision might pass through as many as six or seven levels within a decision-making hierarchy.

The degree to which the *ajawa'*, particularly rulers, were distinguished from commoners is somewhat ambiguous. Society contained three essentially endogamous strata *(ajawa', alk'ajola',* and *muna')*. But creation and migration myths do not imply distinct supernatural origins for the ancestors of rulers. The *Popol Wuj* gives primacy to the creation of the founders of the four great clans of the K'iche', but there is no qualitative difference in how they and other mortals were created: All mankind was made of water and white and yellow maize. Furthermore, the creator gods were unhappy with the divine powers of the founders and so weakened them. This accentuates the difference between the members of the four great clans and their divine creators, and serves to identify the founders as human. The corresponding portion of the *Annals of the Cakchiquels* relates a slightly different story but also fails to stress a separate and divine creation of the kingly line. K'iche'an society, then, was based on both kinship and class. This is consistent with the house society model, formulated to describe societies that appear to be transitional between kinship- and class-based.

There is no doubt that K'iche'an rulers lived in palaces. Webster (1997; Chapter 5 in Volume 1) has proposed that Classic-period centers were little more than large palaces or the location of royal courts. In fact, Post-Classic centers such as Q'umarkaj, Saqikajol Nimakaqapek, Saq Ulew, and Iximche' fit his model much better than do highly urbanized Classic cities like Calakmul (Braswell et al. 2001). The stages upon which the royal courts of the Post-Classic highland Maya performed are profitably seen as the entirety of these sites, and not as small portions of more complex and metropolitan wholes. In other words, Post-Classic highland capitals were elaborate great houses or conglomerations of several great houses.

Behavior was codified in K'iche'an society in ways that can be construed as lawlike, also consistent with the house society model. For example, punishments for crimes like theft and the disrespect of priests were firmly established, and the government was obliged and empowered to enforce standards of behavior. Yet it is less certain that the exertion of force was monopolized by a central government. Coercive power seems to have been the license of whoever could control and maintain it. Conflict and violence, which in at least one case resulted in the overthrow of a K'iche' king, was justified by victorious factions in their official histories.

K'iche'an political systems, therefore, fulfill some of the defining criteria of the archaic state but fail to meet others. The dichotomy of "chiefdom" and "state" is not a productive way to conceive of their organization and function. Instead, the house society model, particularly its emphasis on both class and kinship as organizing principles, seems a more fruitful approach to understanding K'iche'an political systems.

Marcus (1993, 1998) describes one way that such "semistates" can form. In her Dynamic Model, autonomous polities with some of the attributes of archaic states (particularly the notion of kingship) emerge while former provinces of a decaying state gain their independence. Such *cacicazgos* or *señoriales* control much smaller territories than their parent state and resemble principalities. This process may explain the proliferation of small Maya kingdoms in the Late Classic period but cannot describe the emergence of K'iche'an polities during the Late Post-Classic. The central Maya highlands were never organized as a large Classic or Early Post-Classic state, so the K'iche', Kaqchikel, Chajoma', and other Late Post-Classic kingdoms cannot be viewed as products of political disintegration.

Two alternative models for the formation of semistates might apply to K'iche'an kingdoms. The first is that they are the product of autochthonous development. Cultural evolutionists may wish to interpret K'iche'an kingdoms as "maximal chiefdoms" on the way to becoming archaic states. But ethnohistorical data do not support this position. The century before the arrival of Pedro de Alvarado was not a time of consolidation but of fission and the budding-off of new polities—a process more consistent with ranked societies than with potential states. A second possibility is that K'iche'an polities acquired some of the trappings of statehood through emulation (Braswell 2001). This is much more likely, especially since many of the *ajawa'* titles are borrowed from Nahua.[6] As has been documented (e.g., Navarrete 1996), the last century before the Spanish Conquest saw not only the emergence of K'iche'an kingdoms, but also the introduction of many aspects of highland Mexican culture.

Conclusions

Archaeological data—for the most part derived from architectural maps and not from subsurface explorations—have been used in three distinct ways to understand Post-Classic Maya courts. First, the function of individual buildings has been posited from their basic form. Range structures are lineage houses or buildings where landholding groups resolved their affairs; they were places of judgment and marriage rituals; they were council houses and sepulchers for the burned remains of leaders. They also may have been part-time or permanent residences, especially if a title or office became fixed in a particular family. Temples, in contrast, are tall and often have square bases. Altars are low and associated with temples and open plazas. Palaces are low compounds with many rooms. In short, archaeologists of the Maya highlands have used the same simple criteria for determining building function as many of their counterparts in the lowlands. Unfortunately, these assumptions hardly ever are subject to testing (cf. Nance 1998). Detailed site maps, carefully checked through excavation, are uncommon in the highlands. Clear accounts of the artifacts recovered from primary contexts in Post-Classic buildings are even rarer.

Second, the frequent and repetitive nature of some architectonic complexes—such as Wallace's (1977) "ritual-council-palace" group, Guillemín's (1977) "palace-temples-altars" group, Fox's (1977) "garrison plaza" and "conquest-administrative enclaves," and Arnauld's (1997) "Verapaz plaza" and "radial pyramid-temple" complexes—are seen as keys to political and social organization. The presence of multiple examples of these complexes at a single site frequently is assumed to replicate the decentralized or segmented nature of Post-Classic rule. At Iximche', for example, the replication of architectural form is seen as indicating quadripartite rule (Guillemín 1977). At Q'umarkaj, a perceived four-part division in site plan is interpreted as indicating the presence of the four great lineage groups of the K'iche' (Carmack 1981). The appearance of particular arrangements at various sites is seen by Fox (1977) as indicating the imposition of Kaqchikel or K'iche' dominance. Arnauld (1997) suggests that two distinct architectural complexes tend to be associated with different ethnic groups, but both are derived from antecedents in the northern Maya lowlands.

Third, Fox (1994) has used astronomical alignments to interpret Post-Classic Maya courts, regional settlement patterns, and even the actions of individuals and factions in terms of a complex set of cosmological principles. Archaeoastronomy is not new to the Maya area, but Fox's notion that K'iche'an political history is encoded in architectural plans and settlement patterns is unique.

Unfortunately, much of this analysis remains speculative. Site maps, often only crude plans, are not adequate for determining building functions. Detailed analyses of the artifact assemblages recovered from middens associated with different structures have not been used to infer building function, with the exception of Nance's (1998) recent study of ceramics from Iximche'. His conclusions, however, are tentative because Guillemín rarely kept adequate provenience data. Nevertheless, this work is exemplary of the kind of study archaeologists need to conduct in order to formulate more convincing narratives of the kinds of activities that took place in the royal courts of the Post-Classic highland Maya.

Ethnohistorical studies, rather than focusing on the interpretation of the architectural remains of Post-Classic highland royal courts, instead have concentrated on two anthropological issues: social structure and political organization. Several models of K'iche'an social structure have emphasized a hierarchical arrangement of greater and lesser lineages (e.g., Carmack 1981). Other researchers have considered the fundamental building-block of K'iche'an society to be the *chinamit*, a unit of territorial control similar to closed corporate communities and the Aztec *calpulli* (e.g., Hill 1984; Hill and Monaghan 1987). In this model, larger structures called *amaq'i'* were formed by alliances between *chinamita'*, and the major K'iche'an polities were confederations of *amaq'i'*. I see both idealizations as too rigidly organized and hierarchical, and I am not certain that all these terms referred to distinct kinds of social groups. In particular, I believe that there has been an overemphasis on the lineage concept and in interpreting K'iche'an society in terms of real, rather than metaphoric, kinship. There is no doubt that the building blocks of K'iche'an society "sound like lineages" (Tedlock 1989:498). But it seems more profitable to consider the K'iche' and their neighbors as house societies, particularly because the emic term for one kind of social unit means "great house." In other words, the social fabric of the Post-Classic Maya might have been determined as much by marriage and fictive kinship as by blood, and more by territory than by descent. Finally, I see factional competition as central to understanding the dynamics of large-scale social interaction.

Ethnohistorical studies of political organization have focused on the application of the segmentary state model and, by and large, have considered lineage structure as forming the basis of segmentation. Discourse concerning the political organization of ancient societies often becomes mired in attempts to pigeonhole them as either "chiefdoms" or "states," and the K'iche'an case is no exception. In our quest to patch Elman Service's worn-out classification scheme, we have looked too hard for categories that span the gap between these two types. Whether or not the Post-Classic highland Maya had crossed an illusory Rubicon between two ideal categories is irrelevant. It is more important to stress that in K'iche'an polities power was neither absolute nor organized in a simple hierarchical fashion. Principles of aristocracy, based on both ascribed and earned status, were used to determine the occupants of high-status roles. A complex balance was maintained between various groups whose membership fluctuated and was not determined solely by rules of kinship.

The complicated manner in which the titles of members of the K'iche'an royal courts were regulated by both kinship and merit is reminiscent of Polynesian aristocratic systems. In Samoa, primogeniture determined only the slight honor of *ulumatua*, or "first-born status." A first-born son inherited his father's rank as head of the household, but his father's higher public titles were conferred by the *fono*, or "village council" (Goldman 1970:252). Thus, rank in the *aiga*, or "extended family," was correlated rather than equated with titled status. In Tonga, the rule governing the inheritance of political titles was male primogeniture. This ideal was more exactly adhered to for more important titles, although the highest positions, *Tui Takalaua* and *Tui Kanokupolu*, often were greatly contested. Despite the strictness of the rule of primogeniture in Tongan society, in later times the *Tui Kanokupolu* was appointed by high-ranking chiefs in the Samoan manner (Goldman 1970:289). The K'iche'an case lies somewhere between the Samoan and Tongan rules for status inheritance. On a local level, the numerous councils of K'iche'an society may have elected the leaders of the *chinamita'*, albeit from important families with a history of leadership. Higher-status offices, particularly those of the titled aristocrats who dwelled in royal courts, may have been more firmly rooted in particular clans and descent lines.

Despite a long history of both ethnohistorical and archaeological research in the central Maya highlands, these two sources of data rarely have been used in a truly conjunctive manner. Few ethnohistorians find the questions asked by archaeologists relevant, and many have attempted to use archaeological data without a thorough understanding of regional culture history. The wealth of ethnohistorical data only serves to underline the critical need to conduct problem-oriented archaeological investigation at Post-Classic highland sites. The players of the royal courts are richly costumed, but the stage remains bare.

References

Arana X., Francisco Hernández, and Francisco Díaz X. 1573–1605. *Annals of the Cakchiquels*. Manuscript. Philadelphia: University of Pennsylvania Museum Library.

Arnauld, Marie-Charlotte. 1997. "Relaciones interregionales en el área maya durante el Postclásico en base de datos arquitectónicos." In Juan Pedro Laporte and Héctor L. Escobedo, eds., *X Simposio de Investigaciones Arqueológicas en Guatemala, 1996*, pp. 117–131. Guatemala: Museo Nacional de Arqueología y Etnología.

Braswell, Geoffrey E. 1993. "Ri Rusamäj Jilotepeke: investigaciones en una antigua zona productora de obsidiana (kanojkïl pa jun ojer xoral rub'anon richin chay)." In Juan Pedro Laporte, Héctor L. Escobedo, and Sandra Villagrán de Brady, eds., *VI Simposio de Investigaciones Arqueológicas en Guatemala, 1992*, pp. 479–498. Guatemala: Museo Nacional de Arqueología y Etnología.

_____. 1996. "A Maya Obsidian Source: The Geoarchaeology, Settlement History, and Prehistoric Economy of San Martín Jilotepeque, Guatemala." Ph.D. diss., Tulane University.

_____. 1998. "La arqueología de San Martín Jilotepeque, Guatemala." *Mesoamérica* 35: 117–154.

_____. 2001. "K'iche'an Origins, Symbolic Emulation, and Ethnogenesis in the Maya Highlands: A.D. 1400–1524." In Michael E. Smith and Francis Berdan, eds., *The Postclassic Mesoamerican World*. Salt Lake City: University of Utah Press. In Press.

Braswell, Geoffrey E., Joel D. Gunn, María del Rosario Domínguez C., William J. Folan, Laraine A. Fletcher, Abel Morales L., and Michael D. Glascock. 2001. "Defining the Terminal Classic at Calakmul, Campeche." In Don S. Rice, Prudence M. Rice, and Arthur A. Demarest, eds., *The Terminal Classic in the Maya Lowlands: Collapse, Transition, and Transformation*. Boulder: Westview Press. In press.

Breton, Alain, ed. 1993. *Representaciones del espacio político en las tierras altas de Guatemala*. Cuadernos de Estudios Guatemaltecos 2, Centro de Estudios Mexicanos y Centroamericanos. Guatemala: Editorial Piedra Santa.

Brown, Kenneth L. 1983. "Some Comments on Ethnohistory and Archaeology: Have We Attained (or Are We even Approaching) a Truly Conjunctive Approach?" *Reviews in Anthropology* 10(2): 53–71.

_____. 1985. "Postclassic Relationships between the Highland and Lowland Maya." In Arlen F. Chase and Prudence M. Rice, eds., *The Lowland Maya Postclassic*, pp. 270–281. University of Texas Press: Austin.

Brumfiel, Elizabeth M. 1994. "Factional Competition and Political Development in the New World: An Introduction." In Elizabeth M. Brumfiel and John W. Fox, eds., *Factional Competition and Political Development in the New World*, pp. 3–13. Cambridge: Cambridge University Press.

Carmack, Robert M. 1973. *Quichean Civilization*. Berkeley: University of California Press.

_____. 1977. "Ethnohistory of the Central Quiché: The Community of Utatlán." In Dwight T. Wallace and Robert M. Carmack, eds., *Archaeology and Ethnohistory of the Central Quiche*, pp. 1–19. Institute for MesoAmerican Studies Publication No. 1. Albany: State University of New York.

_____. 1979. "La verdadera identificación de Mixco Viejo." In Robert M. Carmack, ed., *Historia social de los quichés*, pp. 131–162. Guatemala: Editorial "José de Pineda Ibarra."

_____. 1981. *The Quiche Mayas of Utatlan*. Norman: University of Oklahoma Press.

Carmack, Robert M., and Dwight T. Wallace. 1977. "Overview." In Dwight T. Wallace and Robert M. Carmack, eds., *Archaeology and Ethnohistory of the Central Quiche*, pp. 98–109. Institute for MesoAmerican Studies Publication No. 1. Albany: State University of New York.

Carrasco, Pedro. 1964. "Los nombres de persona en la Guatemala antigua," *Estudios de Cultura Maya* 4: 323–334.

_____. 1967. "Don Juan Cortés, cacique de Santa Cruz Quiché." *Estudios de Cultura Maya* 6: 251–266.

Cortés, Hernán. 1961. *Cartas de relación de la conquista de México*. Mexico: Espasa-Calpe Mexicana.

Coto, Thomás de. 1983. *[Thesavrvs verborō]*. René Acuña, ed. Mexico: Universidad Autónoma de México.

Fauvet-Berthelot, Marie-France. 1986. *Ethnoprehistoire de la maison maya*. Collection Etudes Mésoaméricaines I–13. Centro de Estudios Mexicanos y Centroamericanos. Mexico: Praxis Editorial Gráfica.

Fauvet-Berthelot, Marie-France, Cecilia Rodríguez L. de March, and Gregory Pereira. 1996. "Costumbres funerarias de la elite de Mixco (Jilotepeque) Viejo." In Juan Pedro Laporte and Héctor L. Escobedo, eds., *IX Simposio de Investigaciones Arqueológicas en Guatemala, 1995*, pp. 513–535. Guatemala: Museo Nacional de Arqueología y Etnología.

Feldman, Lawrence H. 1985. *A Tumpline Economy: Production and Distribution Systems in Sixteenth-Century Eastern Guatemala*. Culver City, CA: Labyrinthos.

Fox, John W. 1975. "Centralism and Regionalism: Quiché Acculturation Processes in Settlement Patterning." Ph.D. diss., State University of New York at Albany.

_____. 1977. "Quiché Expansion Processes: Differential Ecological Growth Bases within an Archaic State." In Dwight T. Wallace and Robert M. Carmack, eds., *Archaeology and Ethnohistory of the Central Quiche*, pp. 82–97. Institute for MesoAmerican Studies Publication No. 1. Albany: State University of New York.

_____. 1981. "The Postclassic Eastern Frontier of Mesoamerica: Cultural Innovation Along the Periphery." *Current Anthropology* 22: 321–346.

_____. 1987. *Maya Postclassic State Formation*. Cambridge: Cambridge University Press.

_____. 1994. "Political Cosmology among the Quiché Maya." In Elizabeth M. Brumfiel and John W. Fox, eds., *Factional Competition and Political Development in the New World*, pp. 158–170. Cambridge: Cambridge University Press.

Fox, John W., and Garrett W. Cook. 1996. "Constructing Maya Communities: Ethnography for Archaeology." *Current Anthropology* 37: 811–821.

Fox, John W., Dwight T. Wallace, and Kenneth L. Brown. 1992. "The Emergence of the Quiche Elite: The Putun-Palenque Connection." In Diane Z. Chase and Arlen F. Chase, eds., *Mesoamerican Elites*, pp. 169–190. Norman: University of Oklahoma Press.

Fuentes y Guzmán, Francisco Antonio de. 1932–1933. *Recopilación Florida*. 3 volumes. Biblioteca "Goathemala," vols. 6–8. Guatemala: Sociedad de Geografía e Historia, Tipografía Nacional.

Gillespie, Susan D. 1995. "The Role of Ancestor Veneration in Maya Social Identity and Political Authority." Paper presented at the ninety-fourth annual meeting of the American Anthropological Association, Washington, DC.

Gillespie, Susan D., and Rosemary A. Joyce. 1997. "Gendered Goods: The Symbolism of Maya Hierarchical Exchange Relations." In Cheryl Claasen and Rosemary A. Joyce, eds., *Women in Prehistory: North America and Mesoamerica*, pp. 189–207. Philadelphia: University of Pennsylvania Press.

_____., eds. 2000. *Beyond Kinship: Social and Material Reproduction in House Societies*. Philadelphia: University of Pennsylvania Press.

Goldkind, Victor. 1965. "Social Stratification in the Peasant Community: Redfield's Chan Kom Reinterpreted." *American Anthropologist* 67: 863–884.

_____. 1966. "Class Conflict and Cacique in Chan Kom." *Southwestern Journal of Anthropology* 22: 325–345.

Goldman, Irving. 1970. *Ancient Polynesian Society*. Chicago: University of Chicago Press.

Goody, Jack. 1971. *Technology, Tradition, and the State in Africa*. New York: Oxford University Press.

Guillemín, Jorge F. 1959. "Iximché." *Antropología e Historia de Guatemala* 11(2): 22–64.

_____. 1964. "Excavaciones en Iximché. [Resumen]." *Actas y memorias del XXXV Congreso Internacional de Americanistas, México, D.F. 1962* 1: 365.

_____. 1965. *Iximché: capital del antiguo reino cakchiquel*. Guatemala: Publicaciones del Instituto de Antropología e Historia de Guatemala.

_____. 1968. "Notas sobre restauración y reconstrucción en los sitios Tikal y Iximché, Guatemala." *Verhandlungen des XXXVIII Internationalen Amerikanistenkongresses, München, 1969* 2: 119–123.

_____. 1967. "The Ancient Cakchiquel Capital of Iximché." *Expedition* 9: 22–35.

_____. 1969. "Exploración du Groupe C d'Iximché (Guatemala)." *Bulletin de la Société Suisse des Américanistes* 33: 23–33.

_____. 1977. "Urbanism and Hierarchy at Iximche." In Norman Hammond, ed., *Social Process in Maya Prehistory*, pp. 227–264. London: Academic Press.

Guillemín, Jorge F., and Ferdinand Anders. 1965. "Ausgrabungen in Iximche—Ein Beitrag zur Kunst der Cakchiquel-Maya." *Wiener Völkerkundliche Mitteilungen* 7: 73–83.

Hill, Robert M. II. 1984. "*Chinamit* and *Molab*: Late Postclassic Highland Maya Precursors of Closed Corporate Community." *Estudios de Cultura Maya* 15: 301–327.

_____. 1996. "East Chajoma (Cakchiquel) Political Geography: Ethnohistorical and Archaeological Contributions to the Study of a Late Postclassic Highland Maya Polity." *Ancient Mesoamerica* 7: 63–87.

Hill, Robert M. II, and John Monaghan. 1987. *Continuities in Highland Maya Social Organization: Ethnohistory in Sacapulas, Guatemala*. Philadelphia: University of Pennsylvania Press.

Ichon, Alain. 1979. *Rescate arqueológico en la cuenca del Río Chixoy 1: Informe Preliminar*. Guatemala: Editorial Piedra Santa.

Ichon, Alain, and Rita Grignon C. 1981. *Archéologie de sauvetage dans la vallée du Río Chixoy 3: El Jocote*. Guatemala: Editorial Piedra Santa.

_____. 1983. *Archéologie de sauvetage dans la vallée du Río Chixoy 5: les sites classiques de la vallée moyenne du Chixoy*. Guatemala: Editorial Piedra Santa.

_____. 1984. "Pratiques funéraires et stratification sociale dans les Hautes Terres Mayas. Las cimetières protohistoriques de La Campana à Mixco Viejo (Guatemala)." *Journal de la Société des Américanistes* 70: 89–117.

Ichon, Alain, and Marion Hatch. 1982. *Archéologie de sauvetage dans la vallée du Río Chixoy 4: Los Encuentros*. Guatemala: Editorial Piedra Santa.

Ichon, Alain, Marie-France Fauvet-Berthelot, Christine Plocieniak, Robert M. Hill II, Rebecca González L., and Marco-Antonio Bailey. 1980. *Archéologie de sauvetage dans la vallée du Río Chixoy 2: Cauinal*. Guatemala: Editorial Piedra Santa.

Ichon, Alain, Denise Douzant-Rosenfeld, and Pierre Usselmann. 1996. *La cuenca media del Río Chixoy (Guatemala)*. Cuadernos de Estudios Guatemaltecos 3, Centro de Estudios Mexicanos y Centroamericanos. Guatemala: Caudal.

Joyce, Rosemary A. 1996. "Social Dynamics of Exchange: Changing Patterns in the Honduran Archaeological Record." In Carl Henrik Langebaek and Felipe Cardenas-Arroyo, eds., *Chieftains, Power and Trade: Regional Interaction in the Intermediate Area of the Americas*, pp. 31–46. Bogotá: Departamento de Antropología, Universidad de los Andes.

_____. 1999a. "Social Dimensions of Pre-Classic Burials." In David C. Grove and Rosemary A. Joyce, eds., *Social Patterns in Pre-Classic Mesoamerica*, pp. 15–47. Washington, DC: Dumbarton Oaks Research Library and Collection.

_____. 1999b. *Gender and Power in Prehispanic Mesoamerica: Ambiguity and Difference*. Austin: University of Texas Press.

las Casas, Bartolomé de. 1909. *Apologética historia sumaria cuanto a las cualidades, disposición, descripción, cielo y suelo destas tierras . . .* Nueva Biblioteca de Autores Españoles, volumen 13. Madrid: Serrano y Ganz.

_____. 1957. *Historia de las Indias*. Madrid: Ediciones Atlas.

Lehmann, Henri. 1968. *Mixco Viejo: guía de las ruinas de la plaza fuerte Pokoman*. Guatemala: Tipografía Nacional.

Lévi-Strauss, Claude. 1983. *The Way of the Masks*. London: Jonathan Cape.

_____. 1987. *Anthropology and Myth: Lectures, 1951–1982*. Oxford: Basil Blackwell.

Lothrop, Samuel K. 1933. *Atitlán: An Archaeological Study of Archaeological Remains on the Borders of Lake Atitlán, Guatemala*. Carnegie Institution of Washington, Publication No. 444. Washington, DC.

———. 1936. *Zacualpa: A Study of Ancient Quiché Artifacts*. Carnegie Institution of Washington, Publication No. 472. Washington, DC.

Marcus, Joyce. 1993. "Ancient Maya Political Organization." In Jeremy A. Sabloff and John S. Henderson, eds., *Lowland Maya Civilization in the Eighth Century A.D.*, pp. 111–183. Washington, DC: Dumbarton Oaks Research Library and Collection.

———. 1998. "The Peaks and Valleys of Ancient States: An Extension of the Dynamic Model." In Gary M. Feinman and Joyce Marcus, eds., *Archaic States*, pp. 59–94. Santa Fe: School of American Research Press.

Marcus, Joyce, and Gary M. Feinman. 1998. "Introduction." In Gary M. Feinman and Joyce Marcus, eds., *Archaic States*, pp. 3–13. Santa Fe: School of American Research Press.

Miles, Suzanne W. 1957. "The Sixteenth-Century Pokom-Maya: A Documentary Analysis of Social Structure and Archaeological Setting." *Transactions of the American Philosophical Society* 47: 731–781.

Morán, Pedro. 1720. *Arte breve y compendioso de la lengua Pocomchí de la Provincia de la Verapaz*. Manuscript. Cambridge, Massachusetts: Peabody Museum Library, Harvard University.

Nance, C. Roger. 1998. "La cerámica y palacios de Iximché: examen preliminar de la colección Guillemín proveniente de la capital kaqchikel." *Mesoamérica* 35: 199–215.

Navarrete, Carlos. 1962. *La cerámica de Mixco Viejo*. Cuadernos de Antropología No. 1. Guatemala: Universidad de San Carlos Borromeo de Guatemala.

———. 1996. "Elementos arqueológicos de mexicanización en las tierras altas mayas." In Sonia Lombardo and Enrique Nalda, eds., *Temas mesoamericanos*, pp. 305–352. Colección Obra Diversa. Mexico, D.F.: Instituto Nacional de Antropología e Historia.

Recinos, Adrian. 1957. *Crónicas indígenas de Guatemala*. Guatemala: Imprenta Universitaria.

Robinson, Eugenia J. 1990. *Reconocimiento de los municipios de Alotenango y Sumpango, Sacatepéquez*. La Antigua, Guatemala: Centro de Investigaciones Regionales de Mesoamérica.

———. 1993. "Santa Rosa, un sitio defensivo de los altiplanos de Guatemala." In Juan Pedro Laporte, Héctor L. Escobedo, and Sandra Villagrán de Brady, eds., *VI Simposio de Investigaciones Arqueológicas en Guatemala, 1992*, pp. 409–428. Guatemala: Museo Nacional de Arqueología y Etnología.

———. 1997. "Protohistoric to Colonial Settlement Transition in the Antigua Valley, Guatemala." In Janine Gasco, Greg Charles Smith, and Patricia Fournier-García, eds., *Approaches to the Historical Archaeology of Mexico, Central, and South America*, pp. 59–70. Institute of Archaeology, Monograph 38. Los Angeles: University of California.

———. 1998. "Organización del estado kaqchikel: el centro regional de Chitak Tzak." *Mesoamérica* 35: 49–71.

Szeczy, Janos de. 1979. "Utatlán." *Boletín Bibliográfico de Antropología Americana* 41(50): 149–175.

Sharer, Robert J. 1994. *The Ancient Maya.* 5th ed. Stanford: Stanford University Press.

Southall, Aidan W. 1956. *Alur Society: A Study in Process and Types of Domination.* Cambridge: Heffer.

———. 1988. "The Segmentary State in Africa and Asia." *Comparative Studies in Society and History* 30: 52–82.

———. 1991. "The Segmentary State: From the Imaginary to the Material Means of Production." In Henri J. M. Claessen and P. van de Velde, eds., *Early State Economics*, pp. 75–96. New Brunswick, New Jersey: Transaction Publishers.

Tedlock, Barbara. 1989. Review of *Continuities in Highland Maya Social Organization: Ethnohistory in Sacapulas, Guatemala*, by Robert M. Hill II and John Monaghan. *American Anthropologist* 91: 498–499.

Thompson, J. Eric S. 1943. "A Trial Survey of the Southern Maya Area." *American Antiquity* 9: 106–134.

Vico, Domingo de. ca. 1550. *Vocabulario de la lengua Cakchiquel y Quiché.* Manuscript. Chicago: Newberry Library.

Wallace, Dwight T. 1977. "An Intra-Site Locational Analysis of Utatlán: The Structure of an Urban Site." In Dwight T. Wallace and Robert M. Carmack, eds., *Archaeology and Ethnohistory of the Central Quiche*, pp. 20–54. Institute for MesoAmerican Studies Publication No. 1. Albany: State University of New York.

Wauchope, Robert. 1947. "An Approach to the Maya Correlation Problem Through Guatemala Highland Archaeology and Native Annals." *American Antiquity* 13: 59–66.

———. 1948. "Utatlán, Iximché, and the Maya Correlation Problem." *Central States Archaeological Bulletin* 2: 19.

———. 1949. "Las edades de Utatlán and Iximché." *Antropología e Historia de Guatemala* 1(1): 10–22.

———. 1970. "Protohistoric Pottery of the Guatemalan Highlands." In William R. Bullard, ed., *Monographs and Papers in Maya Archaeology.* Papers of the Peabody Museum of Archaeology and Ethnology No. 61. Cambridge: Harvard University.

Webster, David. 1997. "City-States of the Maya." In Deborah L. Nichols and Thomas H. Charleton, eds., *The Archaeology of City-States: Cross Cultural Approaches*, pp. 135–154. Washington, DC: Smithsonian.

Weeks, John M. 1976. "Archaeology of Greater Utatlán. El Quiché, Guatemala: El Resguardo and Pakaman Excavations." Master's thesis, State University of New York at Albany.

———. 1977. "Evidence for Metalworking on the Periphery of Utatlán." In Dwight T. Wallace and Robert M. Carmack, eds., *Archaeology and Ethnohistory of the Central Quiche*, pp. 55–67. Institute for Mesoamerican Studies Publication No. 1. Albany: State University of New York.

———. 1980. "Dimensions of Social Differentiation at Chisalín, El Quiché, Guatemala: A.D. 1400–1524." Ph.D. diss., State University of New York at Albany.

———. 1983a. "Chisalín: una comunidad ilocab quiché del siglo XVI." In Robert M. Carmack and Francisco Morales S., eds., *Nuevas perspectivas sobre el Popol Vuh*, pp. 81–86. Guatemala: Editorial Piedra Santa.

———. 1983b. *Chisalín: A Late Postclassic Maya Settlement in Highland Guatemala.* BAR International Series No. 169. Oxford: British Archaeological Reports.

———. 1983c. "Locational Analysis and the Perception of Social Groups at Chisalín, El Quiché, Guatemala." *American Antiquity* 48: 139–141.

———. 1997. "Las ruinas de Utatlán: 150 años después de la publicación de *Incidents of Travel in Central America, Chiapas, and Yucatan* de John L. Stephens." *Apuntes Arqueológicos* 5(1): 7–25.

Whittington, Stephen L., and David M. Reed. 1998. "Evidencia de dieta y salud en los esqueletos de Iximché." *Mesoamérica* 35: 73–82.

Woodbury, Richard B., and Aubrey S. Trik. 1953. *The Ruins of Zaculeu*. 2 volumes. Richmond, Virginia: William Byrd Press.

Ximénez, Francisco de. 1929–1931. *Historia de la provincia de San Vicente de Chiapa y Guatemala de la Orden de Predicadores*. 3 volumes. Biblioteca "Goathemala," volumenes 1–3. Guatemala: Sociedad de Geografía e Historia, Tipografía Nacional.

Zúñiga, Dionysius. 1608. *Diccionario Pocomchí-Castellano y Castellano-Pocomchí de San Cristóbal Cahcoh*. Manuscript. Philadelphia: University of Pennsylvania Museum Library.

Notes

1. K'iche'an polities have been called "kingdoms" and their rulers "kings" since the sixteenth century. This convention is followed here, but is not meant to imply that K'iche'an polities were states.

2. Throughout this chapter, I endeavor to use the orthographic system proposed by the Academia de las Lenguas Mayas de Guatemala and approved by the Ministerio de Cultura y Deportes (Acuerdo Gubernativo 1046–87) and the Congreso de la República (Decreto Legislativo 65–90:Ley de las Lenguas Mayas de Guatemala) as the only legal way to represent the Mayan languages of Guatemala in Latin characters. More recently, many publications, particularly in K'iche', have used duplication to indicate long vowels (e.g., *K'ichee'* instead of *K'iche'*). I have not followed this convention.

3. Some Late Classic (A.D. 600–1000) carved stone monuments in the Guatemalan highlands do contain brief inscriptions (numbers and names), but they are written using the "Mexican"-like glyphs of Cotzumalguapan art (e.g., Robinson 1993).

4. Married K'iche'an men lived with their wives in a pattern of weak patrilocality. Because residential units included men and women from distinct lineages, the term "lineage precinct" seems incorrect.

5. Robinson (1997) writes of three settlement types in the Antigua valley: surface scatters, isolated mounds, and single-group sites. Iximche' and the other K'iche'an capitals are much larger than any of these sites, so on a regional level her site hierarchy would contain four levels. Applying the criteria used by the author (Braswell 1996:194–203) to the data from the Antigua Valley survey yields a site hierarchy with only two levels, or three for the entire central Maya highlands.

6. The list of *ajawa'* status positions extracted from the *Historia Quiché de don Juan de Torres* (Recinos 1957:48–56) and presented above contains several examples derived in part from Nahua. These include *Maku[p]il Tuch, Saqrij Kamachal*, and *Tz'aqi' Istayol*.

11

The People of the Patio: Ethnohistorical Evidence of Yucatec Maya Royal Courts

MATTHEW RESTALL*

The Spaniards and Nahuas who marched into Calkini one morning in spring 1541 must have been nervous. On and off for over a decade the region centered on the town had witnessed Spanish-Maya violence. The Spaniards now fired their guns three times, once outside the town, once at its periphery, and again near the center, as they slowly made their way toward the plaza, their central Mexican auxiliaries fanned around them as protection against a possible ambush. But apprehension must have turned to relief as they saw not the battle-ready warriors of the Canul and Canche lords but the ruling court of Calkini presented to them in a dazzling array of material and human abundance and appeasement. What no one could have foreseen was that this encounter would signal the end of the Calkini court as it had been for a century—what we might take as the symbolic final moment of the ruling court of the ancient Yucatec Maya. The Spaniards and Nahuas departed that same day in 1541, leaving the Maya court to react, adapt, and persist, as it always had. Yet it would never be the same again.

---

*I am grateful to Stephen Houston and Takeshi Inomata for their invitation to participate in this volume, for their patience and efficiency, and for their comments on chapter drafts; to Patricia McAnany, Matthew Rockmore, and reviewers for the press, for their comments; to Tsubasa Okoshi Harada and John Monaghan for commenting on conference-paper versions of portions of the work; to Sergio Quezada for inspiring (via Quezada 1997) many of my illustration selections; to Gregory Finnegan of the Tozzer Library and to Okoshi for use of some of the illustrations; and to the National Endowment for the Humanities and the Pennsylvania State University for financial support.

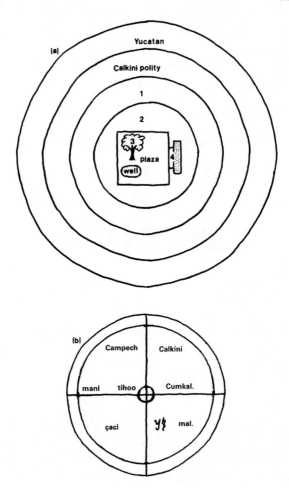

FIGURE 11.1 (a) Plaza and patio as courtly centers: the example of Calkini in 1541; (b) A Maya map of Yucatan, centered on Tiho (Merida) (drawing by the author from the original in the *Book of Chilam Balam of Chumayel*). Key to (a): (1) territorial Calkini *cah*; (2) residential Calkini *cah*; (3) the ceiba tree; (4) Napot Canche's patio. Sources: (a) based on text in TC: 11–17 (Restall 1998a:86–90); (b) facsimile in CBC (Edmonson 1986:195).

This encounter in Calkini was no great turning point in the decades-long Spanish invasion campaign; neither was the community of great importance in the peninsula—as we shall see, Calkini was but one of a dozen or so small Yucatec polities. But the incident is worth highlighting because, first, it is a rare case of a Conquest-era event that is well documented in the Maya language (the *Title of Calkini*, or TC);[1] and second, the details of the encounter contain all the key elements of the "royal" Maya court that is our topic of discussion—including a prefiguring of the court as it developed under Colonial rule.[2]

I shall discuss these elements below in two categories. The first is that of space and place, consisting of a conception of the court as a series of concentric spaces emanating from a center (Figure 11.1 is my visualization of the Calkini example and a complementary Maya rendering of the colony).[3] The force invading Calkini in 1541 traveled through those zones as they marched from the outer reaches of the peninsula ("Yucatan" in Figure 11.1) through the greater Calkini region or polity (discussed below), into the territory of the *cah* (municipal community) of Calkini, then into the *cah* proper, and finally into its center. The central space was the plaza, marked by its symbolic and sacred *yaxche* (ceiba tree, literally "principal tree"), the central community well, and the patio that fronted the house of the *cah* governor, Napot Canche. Having entered the plaza, the invaders proceeded to gather up the goods displayed for them beneath the ceiba tree—sacks of turkeys, corn, honey, and cotton.

In symbolically claiming their "right" to the produce of the land, these outsiders were forcing a shift in Maya conceptions of center and subject. Calkini, with its central elements of plaza, patio, tree, and well, would remain at the courtly core of a local world, as would be the case in all the *cahob* (Maya communities) of the peninsula. But Maya rulers of Colonial *cahob* would also be forced to recognize another structure of courts and centers leading all the way to Spain—a structure that was both parallel to the Maya world and rendered it subject and peripheral.

Although this discussion of place and space emphasizes cultural conception and social usage, the other category of courtly elements is a more directly human one—the court as rulers and retinue (i.e., members of the court). The people of Calkini's court of 1541, in presenting tribute, watching its seizure, and later recording it for posterity, were ritually communicating both their status as the rulers and principal men of the court as well as their acceptance of Spanish domination (at least for the time being). However, there was a further dimension to the ritual that the Mayas had not anticipated. Before leaving town, the Spaniards entered Napot Canche's patio, the space that lay between his house and the plaza; there they seized, bound, and carried off members of the court of the local Canul and Canche rulers. The written account of the event names eleven of these captives, including speakers (*ah canob*, i.e., councilors), priests, and a couple of courtly slaves (TC:12–17; Restall 1998a:86–90).

Yet both sides of the Maya perception of the ritual's meaning would remain intact. The subordination of the local elite to Colonial rule would become permanent (no doubt far more so than anyone, perhaps even the Spaniards, would have imagined in 1541). But the status of the local elite—their position as members of a ruling court—would from the onset be confirmed by the colonists, who relied upon the Maya elite to govern at the local level—to keep the tribute coming for three centuries. Symbolic of the continuity of the court despite the disruption of conquest is the fact that one of those seized on Napot Canche's patio was a grandson of his, Nachan Couoh, who would later become baptized and serve as *batab* (governor) of Calkini (TC:17–18; Restall 1998a:90–91). In the second half of this chapter I discuss the four methods used by the Maya ruling class to perpetuate this continuity of status.

First, a word on this chapter's sources and temporal focus. The sources are archival documents written alphabetically in the Colonial period in Yucatec Maya. I have primarily used the four extant Yucatec examples of the quasinotarial genre known as the "primordial title," namely the *Title of Acalan-Tixchel* (TAT), the *Title of Calkini* (TC), and the *Pech titles* (TCH; TY).[4] In addition I have drawn upon another quasinotarial genre, that of the *Books of Chilam Balam*,[5] as well as the extensive corpus of notarial documents in Maya, most notably petitions by Maya rulers to Spanish officials.[6]

My temporal focus is primarily the sixteenth century, as that is the period of most relevance to these ethnohistorical sources. However, the sources also illuminate two broader time periods that meet in the sixteenth century. The first of these I have dubbed the "Segmented Century," because in the hundred years between the collapse of the Mayapan arrangement in the 1440s and the founding of a Spanish colony centered on Merida in the 1540s, no dynasty or region dominated any significant portion of the peninsula and none came close to forcing any kind of regional hegemony comparable to those of Mayapan and Merida.

The second period under study ran from the pivotal decades of the Spanish invasion, the 1530s–1560s, through the seventeenth century. For Spaniards 1542—the date Merida was founded—was a watershed that marked the province's transition into the civilized world (Chamberlain 1948; Restall 1998a:4–23); for Mayas the transition to Colonial rule was more gradual, in some ways as long as the Colonial period itself. Indeed, although the Spanish (and modern scholars') perception of the Conquest as marking a sharp division between two time periods was borne out by the profound Spanish impact upon Maya life, the emphasis by Maya rulers upon continuity in the sixteenth century was also borne out by colonialism's consolidation of Maya geopolitical segmentation. In short, these centuries are not as cleanly separated by the Spanish Conquest as one might expect; continuity and change played equally important roles.[7]

The Court as Place and Space

In this section we will follow the 1541 Spanish-Nahua departure from Calkini—beginning beneath the ceiba tree in the plaza, moving to the well, crossing to the patio, then moving back across the plaza, out through the town, and into the surrounding region—with each element drawn from the Calkini story representing the broader Yucatec picture (see Figure 11.1).

Trees

According to Fray Diego de Landa, sixteenth-century chronicler, proselytizer, and bishop in Yucatan, contact-era Mayas believed that the heavenly afterlife was lived beneath the branches of a very cool and shady ceiba tree (*muy fresco y de gran sombra*; Landa 33).[8] Certainly trees played an important role in Maya economic, social, and cultural life. They provided construction materials and food, were frequently left to family members in wills, marked boundaries in place of walls or fences, and were used in various ritual, ceremonial, and ornamental ways (Marcus 1982; Patterson 1992; Restall 1997a:203–205). Trees also provided refuge of all kinds, ranging from the shade of the afterlife, to shade in the middle of the plaza, and the shelter offered to those living in or traveling through the forest.[9]

Among the many uses and meanings of trees, two are of particular relevance here. One is the tree-ruler association in Maya culture, a topic discussed in this chapter's second half. The other relevant image is that of the tree as the axis of the cosmos—the World Tree whose best-known example is an ornamented, stone-carved tree from Palenque (Schele and Freidel 1990:66–77). Another example is on a stela from Izapa (see Figure 11.2), an image that seems particularly apposite here because its depiction of a cayman-tree resembles a ceiba; it appears to be functioning as a World Tree stretching from sky to underground, and some sort of commercial activity is depicted beneath the tree (loosely evoking the tribute ceremony of many centuries later beneath Calkini's ceiba).[10]

In the decades after the Conquest a myth regarding such carved stone trees, which looked somewhat like foliated crosses, circulated in the Mani region and possibly throughout Yucatan, to the effect that these "green trees of the world" were placed in temples by Maya prophets in preparation for the coming of Christianity and its crosses (Gaspar Antonio Chi, in RHGY, I:69). Perhaps the notion of a tree as a universal pivot was important enough to the Maya worldview that it needed to be accommodated to the incoming iconography of Christianity. As the link between the underworld, the earth, and the heavens, the Maya World Tree needed to be reinterpreted as an anticipator of the new notion of what heaven was. Likewise, Calkini's ceiba could continue to be the axis that symbolically held together that community's world; through the image of the tree, Calkini was still a microcosm of the universe.

Wells

Calkini's ceiba was a symbol of life in Calkini because, like the community's inhabitants, it was sustained by the water beneath the plaza. The

FIGURE 11.2 The Ceiba at the Center of the World: Stela 5, Izapa, Chiapas (drawing by the author after Gareth Lowe in Lowe et al. 1982:30, 93, 298; and Pons 1997).

connection between wells and human settlement in Yucatan, a limestone peninsula virtually devoid of surface water, is too well known to be worth dwelling on here. It takes little more than a cursory glance at the various maps available from Mexico's Instituto Nacional de Estadistica Geografía e Informatica (known as INEGI) to see that ancient, Colonial, and modern settlements have tended to cluster around *cenotes* (as Yucatan's natural wells are called) and places where the water table can be accessed from the surface with relative ease. Every archaeological site features wells; the inherited well (*chen*) is ubiquitous in the written testaments of Colonial-era Mayas (Restall 1995; 1997a:Chapters 8, 9). Suffice it to observe here, then, as we walk past the well in Calkini's plaza to Napot Canche's patio, that no Maya court could exist without access to a well or *cenote*; indeed, as a recent study of Classic-period water management suggests (Scarborough 1998), one of the court's underpinnings was control over water.

Patios

The space that I have called a "patio" was somewhat more courtly than that English word suggests. The Maya term, *tancabal*, might literally be translated as "the space in the middle"; one possible gloss is thus "court(yard)" (Ringle and Bey, Chapter 9 in this volume). The *tancabal*, however, was not within a building or in the middle of a complex of structures but was at the entrance to the building that housed the ruler or the ruling council. There are four uses of the term *tancabal* in the Calkini manuscript (TC:12, 14, 16, 17; Restall 1998a:87, 88, 89, 90); in three, the patio in question is simply described as Napot Canche's, but in the other a different patio is indicated, defined as "the patio at the entrance to the town hall" (literally "the patio at the entrance to the home of the council houses"; *u tancabal tu chi yotoch tu popolnaob*). The *tancabal* was thus "in the middle" of, or between, the inner space of a building and the outer space of a public area.

Because the interior space of buildings before and after the Conquest tended to be small, the spaces in front of important buildings were crucial courtly spaces and the sites of significant community gatherings and ceremonies. At their most grand, patios might have been large areas featuring roofs supported by columns and steps leading into the plaza; at their most modest (and the Colonial-era restriction of monumental architecture to religious buildings meant Maya rulers lived in or governed from modest dwellings), patios were simply plaza-facing open front yards. A good example of how these ancient and Colonial traditions came together is the *palacio* of the Cocom dynasty in Sotuta (see Figure 11.3). Initially constructed in the sixteenth century on the site of its pre-Colonial predecessor, from which much of its stone was probably drawn, the building as it stands today is a dilapidated mixture of centuries of construction and alteration, some of it post-Colonial. Still, one can appreciate the form and function of the arched patio that fronted the residence and seat of Cocom rule in the region, a patio that in Colonial times probably sported steps from the columns directly down into Sotuta's plaza.[11]

The inner space of such buildings was also important to the court. If the building was the home of a ruling family or the community council, it was here that some courtly rituals took place—although, as shall be discussed in a moment, such events primarily took place outside, on the patio or in the plaza.[12] If the building was the town hall, it was here that one further material object crucial to the court was nurtured and maintained—the written text.

Texts

With respect to ancient times, the writing, maintenance, and use of texts varied from texts on perpetual display, such as Copan's Hieroglyphic

FIGURE 11.3   The patio of the Cocom Palace, Sotuta (photograph courtesy of Tsubasa Okoshi Harada).

Stairway and the Bonampak murals (Miller, Chapter 7 in this volume), to movable texts (on paper, wood, bone, ceramic, or small pieces of stone) usually generated in the neighborhood where prominent scribes lived (as in the Copan case; Fash 1991) and kept inside monumental structures near or at the community center.

With respect to ethnohistorical evidence, most mentions of texts not surprisingly appear to be partially self-referential—in other words, to alphabetic documents. Nevertheless, some references give us a sense of pre-Colonial patterns. For example, the *Book of Chilam Balam of Mani* talks of a "book of generations" (*acab libro*; CBM:70), a Colonial Maya phrase relevant in meaning to much pre-Colonial movable literature. The book consisted of "documents given to the priests to revere, to look at, to deduce the *katun* count" (*u hunil ab ti ah kinob lae u xocob u yilicob u hokol u ppicil u cuch katun*); "this great aid, the seven-generation book" (*noh anahte uuc acab libro*) was kept at Chuncaan in the center of Tiho, presumably in a building atop the Chuncaan mound structure (CBM:71). In another passage the Mani text states that "the seven-generation book shall be laid out on the great altar [or stone throne]" (*tiix bin chelan uuc acab libro ti noh temte*), so the priests (or rulers) could read it (CBM:68). The book was removed around the time that it recorded the displacement of the Maya deity Hunab Ku by "the holy virgin mother" (*suhuy kulbil na*; CBM:71), that is, when Merida was built over Tiho's center and Chuncaan ceased to be a locus of political and religious power and ritual (CBM:68–71; Restall 1998a:139). Tiho's *Book of Generations* was likely one of the sources of the *Book of Chilam Balam of Mani*, as the latter evolved through the Colonial period; in fact, all the books named after Chilam Balam might just as accurately be called "generation books."

Many pre-Colonial books were surely removed from their homes when those buildings were destroyed in the Conquest or ceased to be ritual centers due to Spanish campaigns of extirpation and persecution and to the gradual impact of conversion. Most infamously, Landa and his Franciscan colleagues "found a great number of books in their letters [hieroglyphs], and as they contained nothing but superstitions and falsehoods of the devil, we burned them all, which greatly amazed them [the Mayas] and caused them much pain" (Landa 41).[13] In the late sixteenth century both Chontal and Xiu rulers described how, in efforts to satisfy Spanish priests, their people went out and searched for "idols" to be gathered and burned;[14] it is possible that some books, after being copied out alphabetically, or instead of being hidden, were similarly destroyed.

The loss of such texts hardly ended Maya literary traditions. On the contrary, the importance of the written document survived and evolved with the Maya court. Hieroglyphic and semihieroglyphic books continued to be produced illicitly and were regularly destroyed by Spanish priests in extirpation campaigns (Chuchiak 2000:400–407). Meanwhile, Colonial circumstances ensured that notaries and their product would be more crucial to community culture and integrity than ever before. Although Colonial law determined the format and formula of many of these texts, Maya notaries still found ample room for individual community expression. Mayas viewed the notarial profession as a powerful and prestigious political office second only to the *batab* (community governor); notaries were usually among the few principal men in a community seen as eligible to be *batab* (see Figure 11.4 for examples of the signatures of Maya notaries, some of them *batabob*). Under Colonial rule, the written word became a vital weapon in the battle for the survival and promotion of community and dynasty in an era when warfare and regional political ambition were no longer viable options, and a higher authority could be petitioned and manipulated for local purposes.[15]

The records of such petitions, along with community land records, the testaments of the ancestors, the election records of the community council, and the histories of community and dynasty contained within the primordial titles and local versions of the Chilam Balam books—all this literature was maintained in a building or buildings located on the central plaza of the Colonial *cah*, behind the *tancabal* of the ruler or the council house (Restall 1997a:Chapters 5, 6, 18–21; 1997b). Documents were not simply kept where the court was located; these texts *were* the court, just as the basis of the court's legitimacy, its history, was kept *as* text. As one

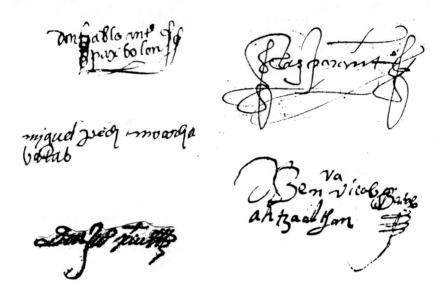

FIGURE 11.4 "Royal" hands: the signatures of don Pablo Paxbolon, *batab* of Tixchel, 1567; don Miguel Pech, *batab* of Mococha, 1567; Gaspar Antonio Chi, interpreter general, Merida, 1578 (onetime *batab* of Mani); don Juan Xiu, nobleman and petitioner, Yaxakumche/Oxkutzcab, 1640 (onetime *batab* of Oxkutzcab and Maxcanú); don Bentura Uicab, *batab* and notary, Citilcum, 1669. Sources: AGI-*México* 367:68r; AGI-*México* 367:71v; AGN-*Inquisición*, 69, 5:158; XC: 13; AGI-*Escribanía* 317c, 2:312.

scholar has said of the Bonampak murals (Miller, Chapter 7 in this volume), ancient Maya rulers not only had the wherewithal to tell the story—they owned the story. No less so in Colonial times, the story was the property of the rulers and their courtly retinues; it was of their creation and manipulation, and it served their purposes.

Plazas

One final Maya mention of an ancient book shall serve to draw our attention away from courtly buildings and across the patio to the plaza; the Mani text also calls the book of generations "the ceiba book" (*yaaxche libro*), the book made from ceiba paper (CBM:68). Indeed, it was probably in the plaza, perhaps beneath sacred trees such as the ceiba, that books were read by the literate elite in religious or political performance. Thus, the outer space on the public side of the patio was as important as the inner space of court structures. In the case of Napot Canche—or in that of another example, the patio of Nadzaycab Canul, ruler of Campeche when the Spaniards invaded (TCH:13/TY:7v; Restall 1998a:122)—this space faced the plaza, the two being a contiguous ritual site. In the fifteenth and sixteenth centuries these rituals may have involved reading the kind of material contained in the *Books of Chilam Balam*, such as prayers and incantations, calendrical information on farming cycles, and community myth-history.

With respect to the latter, the strong Maya tradition of the public presentation of dynastic "propaganda" (Marcus 1992), as well as architecture's potentially political function (Freidel and Suhler 1999; Houston 1998; Kowalksi and Dunning 1999), also continued well into the Colonial period. Don Pablo Paxbolon, governor of Tixchel and effective ruler of the Colonial Chontal Maya region of Acalan from 1566 to 1614, recorded how in 1612 he read aloud to the principal men of the community a history of Acalan and its ruling dynasty, so that "they hear of the origin, region, and people of the governor don Pablo Paxbolon" (*yubinob u thuntel u payolel u uincilel don pablo paxbolon gouernador*; TAT:70v; Restall 1998a:60). One imagines such a performance taking place on the Tixchel plaza. Ancient and Colonial plazas, like the patios that linked them to courtly buildings (see Figure 11.3), were central to political ceremony. Although the size and function of plazas at ancient sites appears to have varied greatly, the plaza's public role seems to be deeply rooted in Maya history (Folan et al. [Chapter 8 in this volume]; Reents-Budet [Chapter 7 in Volume 1]; Webster [Chapter 5 in Volume 1]; Houston 1998; Kowalski 1999). Spanish requirements after the Conquest forced Maya plazas to become somewhat more uniform, although they still varied in size and shape, seldom being mirrors of the model plaza that Merida represented, forming rectangular and *L*-shaped variations.

Regardless of architectural shifts, the plaza's ceremonial and symbolic importance to the local court was unaltered. The buildings that were of greatest political, social, and religious significance in the community—the temple/church, the council buildings, the residences of the ruler and other elite families—remained centrally located and almost always faced the plaza (cf. Ringle and Bey, Chapter 9 in this volume). Local and regional gatherings and ceremonies were also centered on the plaza and adjacent patios. In addition to the examples of the 1541 Calkini tribute ceremony and the 1612 Tixchel reading of dynastic history, there are records of other such meetings. A Pech/Cupul account describes how the lords of Izamal to the east and Mani to the south gathered at the Chuncaan mound in Tiho in 1542 to agree on offering up tribute to the Spaniards (TCH:9/TY:4v; Restall 1998a:117). The Xiu lords that held a 1561 Mani summit were severely punished by Colonial officials for excessive drunkenness (AGI-*Justicia* 248, 2; Quezada 1993:134). On other occasions rulers and their courtiers met to plan wars against rival dynasties and regions (see Table 11.1 for an example).

Most such summits, however, seem to have revolved around land, with territorial control and the promotion of dynastic power being the

TABLE 11.1 Courtly Meetings in Conquest Times: Some Examples of Maya Summits, circa 1530–1600

Year	Venue	Rulers/cahob represented	Summit agenda
1530s	Calkini	Nachan Canul, batab of Calkiní, and Napot Canche; Ah Tzab Euan, batab of Mopila, his son and 3 of his ah canob; followed by meetings with principal men of the Calkini-Mopila region	Land boundary treaty between the two cahob
1537	Mani	Ah Mochan Xiu and 12 principal men of Mani and subject cahob[a]	Plan Xiu revenge on the Cocom for the massacre at Otzmal
1545	Sotuta	47 governors & principal men of 9 cahob in Sotuta polity, including Sotuta governor Nachi (don Juan) Cocom[a]	Land boundaries of Sotuta polity; reaffirmation of Cocom power
1557	Mani	Don Francisco de Montejo Xiu and the rulers and courts of the cahob of the Maní and adjacent polities	Land boundaries of Mani polity; reaffirmation of Xiu power
1550s	Yaxkukul and Chicxulub	The Pech batabob and other Pech nobles of the cahob, principal men of some neighboring cahob, and some Spanish officials; parallel but separate summits	Land boundaries of Pech cahob; reaffirmation of Pech power
1600	Yaxcaba	Governors and principal men of 8 cahob in the Yaxcaba and northwest Sotuta regions (series of two summits)	Land boundaries of these regions; reaffirmation of power of Cocom, Cupul, and others

NOTE: [a] See Table 11.4 for the names of the court members at these summits.
SOURCES (in the above order): TC:20-23 [Restall 1998a:92-94]; CBC:53; DTS:424-427; XC (also see Roys 1943:173–94; Quezada and Okoshi 1999:2–13); TY:8 [Restall 1998a:125–127] and TCH:16–18 (also see Barrera Vásquez 1984; Restall 1998a:220n87); DTS:422, 426–431.

principal purposes of the meetings (again, see Table 11.1). These summits invite us to widen our perspective to include not only the role of the centers of these *cahob* but also the manner in which the meetings at their centers projected their importance onto their respective regions. Earlier I made passing mention of the maintenance of community land records at the Colonial court; the most important of these land documents—territorial border treaties or agreements forged and recorded on Maya patios and plazas—were the early-modern Maya equivalents of modern summits, complete with private discussions and public statements, private agendas of rivalry, and public agendas of peace.

Such meetings thus reaffirmed the political legitimacy of the rulers representing the region's communities—before each other, before their own subjects, and later before Colonial officials. They also served to ratify territorial boundaries so as to prevent possible future conflict or loss of land through Spanish intervention or acquisition. The demographic and political upheaval of the post-Mayapan and Conquest years—high mortality, internecine conflict, migration, invasion—made such agreements all the more necessary. The difference between the two time periods was that during the Segmented Century civil war was an omnipresent threat, whereas the late sixteenth century saw a series of Spanish attempts to impose new structures and methods of government; these efforts, combined with the persistent Spanish failure to understand (or disinterest in) Maya ways of doing things motivated Maya rulers to complete written agreements that presented Colonial officials with solutions—rather than riddles—to local political and territorial landscapes.

Such summits had deep roots in Maya history; one example is the summit portrayed in Piedras Negras's Panel 3 (Houston and Stuart, Chapter 3 in Volume 1). At the Piedras Negras event, prominent regional lords and relatives of the community ruler are gathered around, drinking what might have been chocolate and listening to the ruler speak. At a Calkini summit held shortly before the Spanish invasion, prominent members of the courts of Calkini and Mopila gathered at the home of Napot Canche (whose patio faced the plaza) and "drank much chocolate and wine while they were in discussion with the *batab* of the people of Calkini" (*ti yanix bakaal haaob y uciob tamuk u cana calob lay u Batab ah Calkiniob*) (see Table 11.1). Other summits involved tours or walks of territorial boundaries (such as Nachi Cocom's of 1545), processions that could take days before the protagonists would sit down in summit and draw up a written record of what they had seen and agreed upon.[16]

Town and Country

Tree and well, patio and plaza, the buildings around them, and the events that took place there made the center of the community the effective and symbolic seat of Maya political power. The empowering mantle of centrality was further strengthened if a community also dominated a region of affiliated or subject communities. This broader perspective was crudely suggested by Figure 11.1; it can be seen more specifically in Figure 11.5, which is one of the so-called Mani Maps, a late-sixteenth-century depiction of the Mani region and the position of that *noh cah* ("great community" or Maya "city") as its political center.[17]

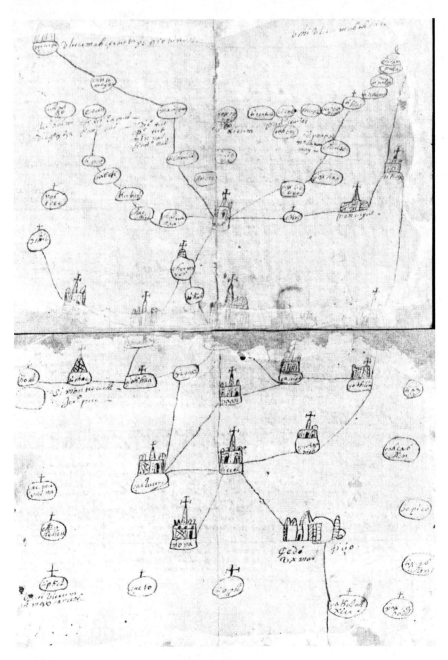

FIGURE 11.5 The Mani Map version in the Xiu papers, showing the Mani region in the late sixteenth century (from XC, courtesy of the Tozzer Library, Harvard University).

The degree to which central court power could be exercised on the periphery depended not only on what lay at the edge (such as the *cahob* depicted at the edge of the Mani map) but also in the way in which the periphery was tied to the center—if indeed it was. The ambiguity of Segmented Century geopolitical entities and the fluidity of regional hierarchies and intercommunity relationships, combined with Spanish disinterest in the pre-Conquest system and the invaders' emphasis on the imposition of an administrative structure that at least looked Spanish, have served to create a confused and confusing historiography on the topic.[18] In an attempt to avoid adding to this confusion, I would like to make three brief points on Maya geopolitics that suggest a simple paradigm of regional power and organization.

The first point is the nature and number of the Segmented Century polities. These were not "provinces," a term more appropriate to describe the Spanish colony of Yucatan (indeed, the Spaniards used it—*provincia*). Rather, pre-Conquest polities were loosely organized, with subject communities governed neither directly from the center nor by representatives sent from the center but surviving as self-governing entities whose subordination was expressed through tribute relations. There were multiple layers of subordination, and all were potentially open to negotiation (when Calkini offered tribute to the Spaniards in 1541, recognizing the new center in Campeche, Calkini's rulers were not surrendering their own dominance of Calkini's subjects—from whence the tribute came). The fluidity and ambiguity of such relationships makes it impossible to accurately calculate either the size of each polity (they varied greatly and boundaries were often ambiguous) or the total number of polities (there were probably about two dozen). In the north and west, the issue is academic by about 1570, when the administrative districts and parishes of the colony had become well established; beyond the colony, to the south and east, the loosely formed and constantly shifting polities of the Segmented Century persisted.[19]

The second point is the significance of the municipal community—the *cah*. Colonial-era sources reveal the *cah* to be the principal focus of Maya self-identity, loyalty, organization, and activity. The *cah* was a geographical entity, consisting of a residential core and outlying territorial lands (see Figure 11.1); a political entity, being the locus and focus of Maya gubernatorial autonomy; and the center of the social and cultural world of each Maya *cahnal*, or "*cah* member" (Restall 1997a:13–40). Although archaeological evidence suggests that Maya society became urbanized many centuries before the Spanish invasion (Houston 1998; Sabloff and Henderson 1993), it is not clear how far back this degree of *cah*-centrism goes. It would appear that the Mayapan arrangement of the thirteenth to fifteenth centuries was an attempt to recognize, represent, and contain the rivalry of dynasties whose status was rooted in their control of a home *cah* and its cluster of subordinate *cahob* (Restall 1998a:23–26; Ringle and Bey, Chapter 9 in this volume). It was the centrifugal pull of the *cahob* that helped destroy Mayapan and led to the localized politics of the Segmented Century. The remains of Maya regionalism—efforts by dynasties to tie *cahob* together or consolidate the dominance of one *cah* over lesser neighbors—were destroyed in the sixteenth century by the Spanish assertion of a monopoly on regional authority and the Colonial confirmation of the integrity and autonomy of the *cah*.

The third point relates to the role played by patronym groups, or *chibalob*, particularly the dynasties and other ruling families. This point offers a segue into the second half of the chapter, which is in large part a treatment of dynasty and *chibal*. Suffice it to remark here, then, that the *chibal* complemented the *cah* as the other fundamental unit of Maya society. At the intersection of *cah* and *chibal* lay the extended family, within which every Maya individual enjoyed meaningful and productive social existence (Restall 1998b).

If the family existed where lineage and locale met, so did regional organization. In short, Maya "provinces" were loosely conceived polities because they were forged by dynastic *chibalob* whose social, political, and economic vitality were rooted in the *cah* (either a single dominant *cah*, such as Calkini, Mani, or Sotuta; or a nexus of *cahob* ruled by members of one dynasty, such as the Pech or Cupul). The centrifugal forces of *cah*-centrism, having helped to destroy Mayapan, and having prevented the rough polities of the Segmented Century from developing into cohesive provinces or states, found full expression after the Conquest in a golden age of localized politics.[20]

The Court as Rulers and Retinue

The preceding discussion of the court as place and space began with the imagery of trees, and so it is with people—specifically rulers—as trees that this portion of the chapter will begin. The tree-ruler image has deep roots in Maya culture (see Lincoln 1991); Copan's past rulers were commemorated on "tree stones," and the rulers that preceded Pakal in Palenque were portrayed as trees in an ancestral orchard (Cortez 1995:117–139; Schele and Freidel 1990:71, 220). The purpose of promoting such imagery, it has been suggested, was to tap into potent themes of agrarian regeneration; furthermore, like the ceiba at Calkini's center, valued tree species appear to have been planted and maintained near site centers, especially adjacent to elite residential complexes (McAnany 1995:43, 76, 164).

The ruler-tree tradition was expressed in Colonial times in the language of petitionary and reverential discourse, typically through the imagery of protection. The arm (*kab*) of a ruler was seen as offering shelter the way the branch (also *kab*) of a great tree offered shade; one term for "protect," *boybes*, literally meant "to provide shade." Thus, one eighteenth-century Maya petition to the Spanish provincial governor asked him "to protect us beneath the shade of your arm" (*ca a boybeson yalan u boy a kab*; ANEY, 1736–37:c.400). Similarly, one term for "principal man" that was used in Colonial times (and presumably earlier), *nucteil*, literally meant "important tree" or "great tree" (Restall 1997a:253).

The notion of ancestors as trees, or at least as branches of a tree, is hardly alien to the culture of the West (Figure 11.7 is an example of the way in which we conventionally convey kin relations in arboreal diagrams); indeed, in one extraordinary Colonial Yucatec document the tree-ancestor iconographic traditions of both the West and the Mayas converge. This is the Xiu Family Tree, created about 1560 most likely by Gaspar Antonio Chi, with additions made to one branch by don Juan Xiu in about 1685 (see Figure 11.6). More shall be said about the Xiu dynasty later; for now, our concern is the Tree's relevance to the imagery of lineage, rulership, and the court.

The Xiu Tree is based in part upon two Christian tree images —the biblical Tree of Jesse and the Franciscan Tree of Life—but it also draws upon Maya tree-ancestor associations. The prominent Xiu nobles of the fifteenth and sixteenth centuries are the branches of the Tree, with their living progeny the flowers or fruit at the ends of the branches. At the base of the trunk is the eleventh-century dynastic founder, the original Tutul Xiu (the name became a title for subsequent Xiu patriarchs); his buttocks and thighs are the Tree's roots.

As a recent scholar of the Xiu Tree has observed (Cortez 1995:110–139), trees were frameworks for temporal references, linking ancestors to living lineage members, current rulers to ancient ones. Furthermore, present-day lineage heads were the living representations of the World Tree and, in death, would transubstantially become one with the Tree, as their ancestors were (hence the merging of Tutul Xiu's loins and the Xiu Tree's roots; the immobility of trees suggests that rulers were rooted to their roles and to the court; see Webster, Chapter 5 in Volume 1).

In addition, the World Tree was the recipient of sacrifice (also see Lincoln 1991); an offering of burning deer legs is made to the Xiu Tree. This association takes us back to the ceiba in Calkini; from this perspective, the produce laid out beneath that great tree in the town plaza was a sacrificial offering, ostensibly a tribute payment to the foreign invaders but also effectively a gift to the tree as representative and protector of the ancestors and living descendents of Calkini's lineages.

If the officers of a Maya court, ancient and Colonial, were an orchard of trees, the great Tree—be it the Xiu Family Tree, the Maya World Tree, or the ceiba in the *cah* plaza—represented simultaneously the founders, ancestors, and living rulers of the dynasty, the elite lineages, and, indeed, the community itself. The Maya court in the fifteenth to seventeenth centuries was thus both a locus of objects—a place of plazas and patios, of sacred trees and precious documents—and a human forest.

FIGURE 11.6 The Xiu Family Tree (ca. 1560 with ca. 1685 additions; from XC, courtesy of the Tozzer Library, Harvard University).

At the most elevated level, where courts came closest to being "royal," ruling families claimed and traced their regional dominance back hundreds of years. Before and after the Spanish invasion, the Maya elite worked to maintain their position through a "royal" ideology of superior status. This ideology rested on four supports: social differentiation; an oligarchical monopoly over political activity; group hereditary status; and the perpetuation of dynastic origin mythology.

Social Differentiation

On the surface, Maya society was divided with binary simplicity into nobles (*almehenob*) and commoners (*macehualob*). Beneath the surface, however, the determinants and levels of social differentiation were more complex. In a recent case study of the *cah* of Ixil in the 1760s, I identified eight loosely defined socioeconomic layers (Restall 1995, 1997a:92–97); this case offers a useful paradigm for discussing Maya social differentiation.

Ixil's bottom four layers were commoners, comprising three-quarters of the community's *chibalob* (patronym groups or extended families); the top four layers were the remaining quarter, comprising three layers of *almehenob* and a crème-de-la-crème layer of *almehenob* who were also *indios hidalgos*. As this was a small *cah* in the Pech region, only the Pech dynasty occupied that top layer. *Almehen* was a category of nobility recognized and given meaning within the Maya world; Spaniards were aware of the category but either confused it with *indio hidalgo* or were indifferent to it, as it afforded no special privileges from the colonists' perspective. However, *indio hidalgo*, literally "Indian nobleman," gave a Maya elite man (or woman—*india hidalga*) some of the privileges of nobles in Spain and Spaniards in the colonies, most notably exemption from tribute. From both Spanish and Maya viewpoints, then, *indio hidalgo* status meant something.

Of course, *indios hidalgos* existed only after the Spanish invasion; it was through collaboration with the invaders that Pech, Xiu, and other elite families acquired the status.[21] But we might reasonably assume that during the Segmented Century, too, Maya society was divided into multiple layers of commoners and nobles. Data from the sixteenth century enable us not only to identify an important criterion for differentiating between the upper crust and the lesser nobility—namely, the control of community *batabilob*, or governorships—but also to identify by name the ruling families that enjoyed regional and local authority (see Table 11.2). It is significant that the number of *chibalob* listed in this table as "ruling" represent about a quarter of the total number of *chibalob* in Colonial Yucatan, the same ratio as that of nobles to commoners in the case study from Ixil. In Late Colonial Ixil, one *chibal*, the Pech, filled the dynastic layer (i.e., 3 percent of the total); census data from the end of the Colonial period suggest that in other communities a similar percentage of inhabitants made up the upper social echelon (6 percent of Hunucma's Maya residents in 1815 were *indios hidalgos*, for example; AME:104). In sixteenth-century Yucatan, 4 percent of the *chibalob* were at this level (the dynastic dozen of Table 11.2).

Thus, despite changes in detail, the framework of Maya social rank from the fifteenth through eighteenth centuries, if not before and after, consisted of multiple socioeconomic layers topped by a dynastic elite

TABLE 11.2 Yucatan's Ruling Dynasties at the Time of the Spanish Conquest, circa 1520–70.

Chibalob[a]	Polities where *chibal* members held *batabilob*[b]	Number and percentage of *batabilob* held in that polity[c]	
First Tier: The Dynastic Dozen			
Caamal	n/a[d]	5	
Canul	Calkini	4*	44%
	Chancenote	1*	11%
	Sotuta	1	7%
	n/a	23	
Canche	Calkini	2*	22%
	Motul	2	7%
Chan	Chancenote	2*	22%
	Dzidzantun	3*	8%
	Mani	1	5%
	n/a	1	
Che	Mani	3*	15%
	Calkini	1	11%
	Hocaba	1	9%
	Motul	1	4%
	Dzidzantun	1	3%
Chel	Dzidzantun	5*	14%
Cochuah	Tihosuco	4	40%
Cocom	Sotuta	5*	36%
	n/a	3	
Cupul	Ekbalam	4*	80%
	Chichen Itza	2	50%
	Saci	4	57%
	Popola		(75%)[e]
	Tihosuco	1*	10%
	Dzidzantun	1	3%
	n/a	7	
Iuit	Hocaba	6*	55%
Pech	Motul	24	83%
	Dzidzantun	3*	8%
	Sotuta	2*	14%
	n/a	4	
Xiu	Mani	8	40%
	Calotmul	3	43%
	n/a	1	

(continues)

TABLE 11.2 (continued)

Chibalob[a]	Polities where chibal members held batabilob[b]	Number and percentage of batabilob held in that polity	
Second Tier: Other Ruling *Chibalob*			
Cauich	Tihosuco	1	10%
	Sotuta	1*	7%
	Dzidzantun	1*	3%
	n/a	1	
Ek	Mani	1*	5%
	Motul	1	4%
	Dzidzantun	1	3%
	n/a	1	
Euan	Calkini	1	11%
	Mani	1*	5%
	Dzidzantun	1	3%
	n/a	1	
Pot	Calotmul	1	14%
	Tihosuco	1	10%
	Hocaba	1	9%
	Dzidzantun	1	3%
	n/a	2	
Tun	Dzidzantun	2	5%
	Ekbalam	1	20%
	Hocaba	1	9%
	Sotuta	1	7%
	n/a	1	
Tzeh	Chancenote	4	44%
Uicab	Tihosuco	1	10%
	Dzidzantun	1	3%
	n/a	2*	
Third Tier: Other Ruling *Chibalob*			
Ake	Dzidzantun	1*	3%
Balam	Dzidzantun	1*	3%
Batun	Chichen Itza	1	25%
	Dzidzantun	1	3%
Can	Dzidzantun	1	3%
Canche	Dzidzantun	1	3%
	Cantun	n/a	2*

(*continues*)

TABLE 11.2 (continued)

Chibalob[a]	Polities where *chibal* members held *batabilob*[b]	Number and percentage of *batabilob* held in that polity	
Ceh	Calotmul	1	14%
	Tihosuco	1	10%
Cen	n/a	1	
Chin	Dzidzantun	1	3%
Chuc	n/a	1	
Chuil	Saci	1	14%
Ci	n/a	1	
Col	Calotmul	1*	14%
Couoh	Dzidzantun	1	3%
	n/a	1	
Cuy	n/a	1	
Dzib	Dzidzantun	1	3%
	n/a	2	
Dzul	Dzidzantun	1	3%
	n/a	1	
Huchim	Dzidzantun	1	3%
Ix	Sotuta	2	14%
Kauil	n/a	1	
Ku	Mani	1	5%
	Dzidzantun	1*	3%
Macun	n/a	1	
May	n/a	1	
Miz	Chichen Itza	1	25%
	n/a	2	
Mo	n/a	1	
Motul	Dzidzantun	2	5%
Na	n/a	2	
Namon	Hocaba	1*	9%
Naual	Sotuta	1	7%
Nauat	Mani	1	5%
Noh	n/a	1	
Oxte	Motul	1	4%
Pacab	Mani	1	5%
Pax	n/a	1	
Pol	Dzidzantun	1*	3%
	n/a	1	
Pola	n/a	1	
Puc	Chancenote	1	11%
	n/a	1	
Tayu	Calkini	1	11%

(continues)

TABLE 11.2 (continued)

Chibalob[a]	Polities where chibal members held batabilob[b]	Number and percentage of batabilob held in that polity	
Te	Calotmul	1	14%
Tuyu	Sotuta	1	7%
Tuyub	Chancenote	1	11%
Tzab	Hocaba	1	9%
Uc	Saci	1	14%
Ucan	Dzidzantun	2	5%
Uitz	Dzidzantun	1	3%
Uluac	Mani	2*	10%
Uz	Mani	1	5%
Xoc	n/a	2	
Xol	Saci	1	14%
Tihosuco		1	10%
Yam	n/a	1	

NOTES: [a]The patronym-group or extended family; see the text of the chapter (and Restall 1997a; 1998b) for discussion of chibal and cah.

[b]Governorships of cahob (Maya communities). There are a total of 213 cahob and their batabilob represented in this table, almost all the cahob in what was becoming the colonial province of Yucatan. Note that this excludes the Chontal Maya region, dominated by the Paxbolon dynasty (Scholes and Roys 1948; Restall 1998a:Chapter 3).

[c]These polities more or less correspond to the polities of the Segmented Century, although note that the sources are colonial and thus to some extent reflect post-Conquest Spanish administrative divisions. Only those communities whose batabob (governors) can be identified have been counted; the purpose of these percentages is thus to give an approximate sense of the degree to which certain chibalob functioned as dominant dynasties effectively ruling polities or clusters of communities.

[d]Not available or not applicable: some cahob were independent and the district affiliation of others is unclear.

[e]This figure is speculative; according to the relación of Popola, it was the center of a Cupul-controlled district of thirteen cahob, but it is only known for sure that a Cupul was batab of Popola itself (RGHY, II:216; Quezada 1993:166, 182).

*This indicates that one or two of the batabil counted here are from the same cah, due to the change in control of the position during the decades in question; otherwise, each cah/batabil has only been counted once. Where a batabil changed hands within a chibal, it was likewise only counted once. Obviously there were other changes in batabil control during this period for which we do not have records.

SOURCES: Quezada 1993:157–202, who cites seventy primary sources, the following of which I directly consulted: RHGY; Roys 1957; TC; TY.

comprising about 5 percent of the population and with the layers of lesser nobility making up roughly another 20 percent. I have refrained from terming these levels "classes" because that term carries baggage that is not necessarily relevant to the Maya, although "class" is certainly a more apt term than "caste," as Mayas were not strictly divided from each other by birth and occupation. In fact, the bases and mechanisms of social differentiation, combined with the political circumstances of the Segmented Century and the Spanish invasion, allowed for a certain degree of mobility. Furthermore, even though non-nobles were surely aware of their socioeconomic status—an awareness hinted at in *Chilam Balam* passages (CBC:20, 22; Restall 1998a:37, 134–138)—only the dynastic elite developed an ideology that approximated "class-consciousness."

These bases and mechanisms of differentiation, although closely intertwined, can be divided for analytical purposes into three categories (the sources for this analysis are Colonial-era; Restall 1997a:72–97, 110–120, 206–211). The first is social and can be subdivided into two: social rank as marked by the terminology of social differentiation (such as *almehen*); and *chibal* affiliations, both membership by birth and connection through alliances of marriage, economic enterprise, and political faction. The second is economic and can also be subdivided into two: ownership of land, both agrarian (*col* and *kax*) and urban (*solar*); and overall wealth. Thus far the categories pertained to women as well as men. The third category was relevant to men only, being that of politics: factional affiliation and career in political office.

As our primary concern here is with the "royal" court, let us look at this same structure again, but this time from a dynastic perspective. The characteristics of dynastic status were, in the social category, fourfold. These were: one, recognition in their *cah* (or in their region) as *almehen* and *don*;[22] two, connection by marriage and other forms of alliance to other local elite *chibalob* (the taboo on intra-*chibal* marriage was maintained throughout the Colonial period, with rare exceptions among the dynastic dozen); and three, connection to regional authority, meaning the region's dominant dynasty before the Conquest (if they were not members of that dynasty themselves), and the Colonial authorities after the Conquest—connected as *indios hidalgos*, as Maya conquistadors (see Restall 1998a), and as Spanish-sanctioned *cah* rulers, Colonial *batabob*. Finally, Maya dynasties maintained and promoted a mythology of origin, settlement, and legitimacy (discussed below).

In economic and political terms, the criteria of dynastic status were dominant landownership in the *cah*; distinguishing levels of overall wealth; and the domination of an oligarchical monopoly over regional and local political offices (after the Conquest, the *batabil* and senior *cabildo* positions in the *cah*). This monopoly was significant enough to be considered here as the second foundation of "royal" ideology.

Oligarchical Political Monopoly

The oligarchies that monopolized political activity and office in the *cahob* of Yucatan consisted of more than just the core of dynastic nobles; certainly the upper crust by definition exercised the greatest control over community politics, but retinues (subordinate court members) were just as important to the form and function of oligarchies as were rulers. Indeed, as much as any other vestige of status or expression of power, Maya courts in the Segmented Century and Colonial period were defined in terms of their broader membership (for this membership in the Classic period, see Houston and Stuart, Chapter 3 in Volume 1; Inomata, Chapter 2 in Volume 1). Although the size and nature of courts varied greatly over time and place, they tended to be large, usually including (in descending order of importance): previous rulers; relatives of the ruler eligible to succeed him; prominent members of allied or competing noble families; the rest of the general pool of principal men, including those with specific offices; representatives of commoner families holding lesser offices; and non–office-holding servants and dependents, including, in pre-Colonial times, slaves. The largest courts of pre-Colonial and Conquest times would have been those of regional rulers (*halach uinicob*), with membership running the full gamut of the social scale from the *batabob* of subordinate *cahob* to *pentacob* (male slaves).

Slaves are worth a brief digression (not least because, as Inomata and Houston observe [see Chapter 1, Volume 1], not all court members were necessarily elites). The ethnohistorical evidence on Maya slaveholding in and before the sixteenth century is effectively limited to one source, the *Title of Calkini*.[23] In this text there is one reference to a female slave (*munach*) and nine to male slaves (*pentac* or *ppentac*). This is a slim base for analysis, but some patterns can be observed. First, the gender balance of these examples suggests that male slaves may have been more common than female ones. Second, the two labor references in these examples indicate why this may have been the case: One is to cultivable land worked by slaves (*pentac kax*); the other is to the fishermen slaves who worked the fleet of Ah Kin Canul. Third, slaves seem to have been held in small numbers; in six of these examples slave numbers are given, the average being 2.5. Fourth, in more than half the examples slaves are named. The great importance of patronyms in pre-Colonial and Colonial Yucatan, the importance of matronyms in pre-Colonial times—and the concomitant heavy peppering of Maya historical documents with the names of ancestors and their friends and enemies, their relatives and retinues—suggest that slaves were often far more than just a source of labor. Indeed, nowhere in these ten examples are slaves both named and described as workers of any kind. Thus, some, perhaps most, slaves may have been prestigious members of (enemy or rival) courts by virtue of their

TABLE 11.3   The Officers of the Court: Political Offices in Yucatan, circa 1400–1800

Segmented Century	Colonial Period
Primary level (regional ruler)	
halach uinic, "supreme ruler (lit. true man)"	[Spanish provincial governor]
yax batab, "principal governor", *noh batab*, "great governor"	[*yax* and *noh batab* are used through the C16th but with decreasing relevance as Spanish officials assert their monopoly over regional-level offices]
Secondary level (municipal community [*cah*] ruler)	
batab, "governor"	*batab*, "governor" [survives into late-C19th but *gobernador* also used by Mayas]
Tertiary level (cah ruling council and extra-council principal men)[a]	
holpop, "headman"	*teniente*, "lieutenant"
ah dzib hun, "notary, scribe"	*escribano, ah dzib hun*, "notary, scribe"
ah can, "speaker"	*alcalde*, "judge, councilman"
ah cuch cab, "district deputy"	*regidor*, "councilman"
ah kul, "deputy", "officer"	
nacon, "captain"	[*capitán*, "captain", but exclusive to *batab* or former *batab*]
kul uinic, "officer", "principal man"	*kul uinic, nucil uinic, nucteil, principal*, "principal man"; offices of various rank, role, and origin, including *ah cuch cab* ("deputy"), *belnal* ("officer"), *chun than* ("speaker"), *procurador* ("counsel"), *mayordomo* ("steward"), *alguacil* ("executor"), *tupil* ("constable")
ah kin, "priest"	various religious officials, such as *sacristán, fiscal, cantor*, and *canan*, none of which were officially equated with priesthood

NOTE: [a]Note that while the ranking of colonial-era tertiary level offices is based on substantial documentation (Restall 1997a:51–83, 267–275), the ranking of Segmented-Century offices is tentative. Likewise the equivalencies of pre- and post-Conquest offices are suggestive only, as it is unlikely that there was any conventional or consistent Maya perception of office equivalencies except at short-term community levels.

SOURCES: TC (Restall 1998a:86–103); TY (Restall 1998a:107–128); Landa XXVII–XXIX; Okoshi Harada 1993:Chapter 2; Quezada 1993:38–58; Restall 1997a:70, 72.

patronym or *chibal* affiliation; probably war captives, they were symbols of political authority. Because men monopolized politics in Maya society, this would also help to explain the suggested gender imbalance among slaves.[24]

Some of the details of this court portrait are illustrated in Tables 11.3 and 11.4. These tables are also intended to highlight the continuities and contrasts between pre-Colonial and Colonial patterns. Table 11.3 identifies most of the offices of Maya courts before and after the Conquest, suggesting their relative ranking and some ways in which Mayas maintained continuity of function and meaning through the transition to new formats and titles. Two aspects of this process should be emphasized.

One, the Maya *cabildo* (municipal council) was not the same as the Spanish *cabildo*, despite its name and the use of Spanish office titles. It looked the same, as it was intended to; but in reality it was not a courtly system imposed from the outside. Rather, it was a mere framework adopted from external sources and quickly reshaped into a mechanism for the continued exercise of self-rule by community oligarchical courts. Within the court the titles of *cabildo* posts and other offices encoded the relative status of the members of the oligarchy and the progress of their political careers. Among a number of Spanish-Maya *cabildo* contrasts was the role of the *escribano* (notary), a relatively minor post *outside* the Spanish *cabildo* that was, as mentioned earlier, a prestigious office *within* the Maya *cabildo* and a potential stepping-stone to the *batabil* (governorship). In short, the *cabildo* was at the core of the Colonial Maya court.

Two—and this is an important expression of both the pattern of continuity from pre-Conquest times and the contrast between Spanish and Maya *cabildos*—the Maya *cabildo* was by definition a local body that varied in size and nature from community to community. Often on legal documents submitted to Colonial courts there is an effort to conform to the Spanish model, with *alcaldes* and *regidores* (usually Mayanized as *alcaldesob* and *regidoresob*) signing records in twos or fours (numbers that could have reflected Maya models anyway), but by and large the numbers of *cabildo* offices and officers varies greatly over time and between *cahob*. Furthermore, efforts to incorporate the full body of principal men into the *cabildo* were paralleled by the continued use of many pre-Colonial office titles. In other words, the Colonial Maya court included not only an extended localized *cabildo*, with a *batab* above it, but also an extended retinue of extra-*cabildo* officers below it (Restall 1997a:Chapters 5, 6, 20).

Table 11.4 is a necessarily anecdotal attempt to personalize these patterns. The examples chosen are two fully pre-Conquest courts, with names and titles all pre-Hispanic; two on the cusp of the Conquest, in which names and titles are mixed in origin, including the names of the

TABLE 11.4   Some Examples of Maya Courtly Retinues, circa 1440–1700

The court of Canul rulers that left Mayapan for Calkini, 1440s

... the *batabob* were Ah Dzuum Canul, who came from this [the Canche] *chibal*; Ah Iztam Kauat; and those of the Canul, who were Itza settlers when they departed at that time from Mayapan—Ah Tzab Canul; Ah Kin Canul; Ah Paal Canul; Ah Sulim Canul; Ah Chacah Canul; Ix Co Pacab Canul, and Nabich Canul; these *batabob* that I have listed are the nine of them.[a]

The first-tier retinue and one of the sub-retinues of Paxbolonacha, Chontal ruler of Acalan, 1527

To assist Paxbolonacha in his realm [*y ahaulel*] were his principal men, who were the lords Mututzin; Kintzucti; Padzayato; and Tamalyaxun, as they were named ... one lord, named Lord Palocem went [to meet Cortés] with some principal men named Patzinchiciua; Tamalbinyan; Paxuanapuk; and Paxhochacchan, companions of the ruler Palocem.[b]

The court of Ah Mochan Xiu as it met in summit in Mani, 1537

... when the noblemen gathered together in conference at Mani ... these were their names: Ah Moochan Xiu; Nahau Ez; Ah Dzun Chinab; Napoot Cupul; Napot Che; Nabatun Itza; Ah Kin [priest] Euan, who came from Cocel [Caucel]; Nachan Uc, who came from Dzibilkal; Ah Kin Ucan, who came from Ekob; Nachi Uc; Ah Kul [deputy] Koh; Nachan Motul; Nahau Coyi.

The courtly retinue of Nachi Cocom, aka don Juan Cocom, during his tour of the Sotuta polity's territorial boundaries, 1545

Naitza Cocom; Naium Pech; Francisco Dzay; Pedro Dzul, who brought as porters [*tameneb*] Francisco Canul, *alguacil*, and the carpenter Jorge Cauich; Francisco Uc, also called Ah Kin [priest] Uc; and Blas Puc; Juan Dzay and Francisco Oy, *ah cuch cab* of Sotuta; Napuc Us of Yaxcabá; Ah Kul [deputy] Tep of Titanus; Ah Kul Balam; Ah Kul Noh; Holpop [headman] Hau of Tikom; Ah Kul Tzotz; Ah Kul Euan; Holpop Cach of Pomonot; Ah Kul Ueuet; Ah Kul Chi of Homulna; Nacamal Us; Ah Kin Be; Ah Kul Cetz; Ah Kul Cauich; Nachan Tzek; Ah Kul Can; Ah Kul Coyi; Ah Kul Cab; Nachan Tzek of Tikuch; Ah Kul Coyi; Ah Kul Can; Ah Kul Cal [Cab?]; Napot Canche[c]; Holpop Tun; Ah Kul Hau of Cisteel [Cisteil?]; Ah Kul Euan; Ah Kul Cab; Napot Couoh; Ah Kul Hoil of Chanonot; Nacamal Chi; Ah Kul Chi; Ah Kul Chuc; Nahau Chable; Ah Nabatun Mo of Huntulchac; Ah Kul Puc; Napuc Tuyu of Tikom; Ah Kul Ucan: principal men.

The retinue of Ah Macan Pech, aka don Pedro Pech, ruler of Yaxkukul, extended through collaborative conquest and resettlement, ca. 1542–1553

... Kul Chuc was captured there in Cupul by Ah Ceh Pech ... he was then given to don Pedro Pech, to Ah Macan Pech, by don Francisco de Montejo, the *adelantado* ... and brought here to the *cah* with Ah Kin [priest] Pech, Macan Pech, the first conquistador, and the servants [*u palil*] and officers [*u nacomob*] of Macan

(continues)

TABLE 11.4 (*continued*)

Pech, here to Yaxkukul . . . [where there were don Pedro's] sons, don Alonso Pech, don Miguel Pech, don Lucas Pech, and don Francisco Pech. There was also Ursula Pech, who was called Cakuk Pech; she gave chocolate to the *adelantado* . . . she was elder sister of Ixkil Itzam Pech and the daughter of Tunal Pech, conqueror of Motul . . . the councillors and officers included Kom Pech and his son Nakuk Pech of the principal *chibal* [of the region] . . . among those who came down here to this land, this principal *cah*, from Cupul were the captains Chan, Cen, and Xuluc; the warriors Nacom [officer] Kuob, Nacom Xuluc, Nacom Poot, Nacom May, Nacom Ek, and Kul Chuc—the Kul Chuc who was the servant of Macan Pech and Nacom Poot; and the deputies; the rest of the principal men, sons, and sons-in-law . . . and the deputies who accompanied the captains were named Ah Kul [deputy] Matu, Ah Kul Chel, Kul Kiix, and Kul Che; and the priests were Ah Kin Cocom and Ah Kin Tacu.

The court under don Juan Dzib, governor of Tekanto, as elected in December 1690 for 1691[d]

These, then, are the members of the royal court [*audiençia Real*] in the center of the *cah*; their names are written here below: Antonio Caamal, Gaspar Oy, *alcaldesob*; Pasqual Balam, *alcalde meson*; Feliciano Dzib, Joseph Hau, Gregorio Dzib, Agustin Pech, *regidoresob*; Mateo Batun, *procurador*; Agustin Couoh, *aluasil [alguacil] mayor*; Pedro Kantun, *mayoldomo [mayordomo]*; Juan Ake, Andres Canul, Pedro Canul, Pedro Chan, Francisco Dzib, Francisco Hau, *aluasilesob [alguaciles]*; Josef Cab, Agustin Chable, *madamiento [mandamiento] meson*. Salaried: The salary of Mateo Couoh, notary, is 7 pesos, 12 loads of corn; the salary of Juan May, *maestro*, is 7 pesos, 12 loads of corn; Francisco Hau, *tupil dotrina madamientas [doctrina mandamiento]*.

NOTES: [a] In one of its chronicle sections, the Book of Chilam Balam of Mani names "seven men of Mayapan"; CBM:135–136 (Restall 1998a:141).

[b] The pattern here of retinues of four is mythically rooted in the Chontal text in the retinue of four of Auxaual, the founding patriarch of six generations before Paxbolonacha (TAT:69v [Restall 1998a:58]); the don Pablo Paxbolon mentioned elsewhere in the present chapter was Paxbolonacha's son.

[c] Although Calkini was not subject to Sotuta, it is possible that this was the Napot Canche who was governor of Calkini at this time and mentioned elsewhere in this chapter (e.g. see Figure 11.7).

[d] For the complete Maya text and English translation of this record, and for a discussion of it and other documents in the genre, see Restall 1997a:267–275, 324–326.

SOURCES (in the above order, with language of original text indicated): TC:13–14 [Restall 1998a:88] (Maya); TAT:71v–72r [Restall 1998a:62] (Chontal Maya); CBC:53 (Maya); DTS:424–425 (Spanish with some Maya terms and orthography); TY:5v–6r [Restall 1998a:119–120] (Maya); AGEY-A, 1, 1 [see note c above] (Maya).

rulers, both of which are given in the full texts; and one Colonial Maya court as recorded in a Spanish-approved election document.

It is worth making an additional comment about numbers, as this is often a topic of scholarly interest (Ringle and Bey, Chapter 9 in this volume). Although the source in Table 11.4 on the Colonial *cabildo*, an election document, is almost certainly a complete record of the Maya court at that time and place (Tekanto, 1691), the sources on earlier courts are different in genre and cannot be taken as complete listings. Nevertheless, the variety in numbers is probably a faithful representation of the pre-Colonial pattern—one that continued, as stated above, in the localization of *cabildos* and courts by Colonial *cahob*. Although four, seven, and nine appear with greatest frequency in quasinotarial sources, none of these magic numbers appears more significant than the rest (see Table 11.4); notarial sources show officers in pairs of fours more often than other numbers, but this could in part be Spanish influence. Tekanto consistently elected twenty-one officers in the late seventeenth century and Cacalchen, in the same region, elected twenty-eight (LC:47). However, evidence from both ends of the Colonial period suggests that courts at their broadest definition (including, for example, religious offices, be they pre-Christian or church choir posts) numbered more like fifty people; Nachi Cocom's 1545 summit retinue was close to fifty, and an 1821 Maya election document details more than fifty *cah* offices (Table 11.4; MT:65; Restall 1997a:268–269).

Transcending these details—and the tension between change and continuity from the fifteenth to seventeenth centuries—is the consistent application of a simple principle: No one man, or even one family, ruled a Maya community or polity alone; the members of the court, to degrees depending on rank, participated in rulership. This principle, increasingly referred to by scholars as *multepal*, may go back as far as the Classic period and has recently been identified in pre-Conquest seventeenth-century Peten.[25] It certainly survived into the Colonial period and, indeed, helps explain the quick adoption, easy adaptation, and long-term success of the *cabildo* system by post-Conquest Mayas.

Hereditary Status

Thus far the elite as a group has been defined in terms of social "class" and in terms of the political offices and bodies of the *cah*; in other words, the argument that the ideology and perpetuation of Maya elite status embodied a principal of corporate heredity has largely been made above. Ubiquitous in this analysis has been the *chibal*, or patronym group, and a number of *chibalob* have been frequently cited, particularly those I have called the "dynastic dozen." The taboo on intra-*chibal* marriage encouraged elite *chibalob* to form marital alliances with one another (Restall 1997a:87–97, 110–140; 1998b), thereby consolidating and domesticating the intra-elite ties that nurtured social differentiation, underpinned the "royal" court, and produced the oligarchical system of rule.

The dynastic dozen were the Caamal, Canul, Canche, Chan, Che, Chel, Cochuah, Cocom, Cupul, Iuit, Pech, Xiu (see Table 11.2), whose dominance of clusters of *cahob* gave them a regional authority that marked them as the upper crust. Of these dozen, the most important were probably the Canul, Chel, Cupul, Cocom, Pech, and Xiu, due to the size and location of the regions they dominated. This in turn determined the significance of the role they played in the Conquest, which in turn determined how well they survived that period. There is evidence that the status and regional power of the Cocom, Xiu, Chel, and possibly others in the dynastic dozen went back to before the Segmented Century, perhaps into Classic times, and most of these dynasties maintained considerable status through the Colonial period; however, the sixteenth century was the crucial test of the strength of the foundations of dynastic status and the adaptability of elite *chibalob*.

From the dynastic dozen's viewpoint, one of the most serious ramifications of the Conquest was the Spanish claim to a monopoly over regional authority, with Maya political power restricted to the level of the *cah*. This transition was not as drastic as it might appear; as discussed above, the integrity of Maya regional polities during the Segmented Century was based not on centralized government but on the control of *cah* governorships (*batabilob*) by members of the dominant dynasty or their allied kin. Certainly the position of *halach uinic,* the regional supreme ruler, as held by a Maya lord, would not survive the sixteenth century (for most of the Colonial period, the title is accorded by Mayas to the Spanish provincial governor in Merida). But Spanish confirmation of dynastic dozen nobles in governorships throughout the colony promoted dynastic continuity and helped these *chibalob* maintain their legitimacy with their own subjects at local as well as regional levels. Due in part to the deep-rooted centrality of *cah* identity in Maya culture, the Spanish were eventually able to restrict Maya political authority to the *cah* level (producing the above-mentioned golden age of localized politics; Quezada 1993; Restall 1997a). But the demise of Maya regional power was slow and gradual, and the regional cooperation of *batabob* in the 1761 uprising (AGI-*México* 3050; Patch 1998) and during the so-called Caste War (Dumond 1997; Rugeley 1996) suggests that it went dormant rather than died.

This is not to say that the Conquest period was characterized solely by continuities in dynastic status. The inevitable rise and fall of *chibal* fortunes were accelerated by the Spanish invasion, which brought issues of legitimacy to the fore, providing opportunities for some and endangering the political fortunes of others. The Canche, for example, were a dynastic dozen *chibal* by virtue of their *batabilob* (governorships) in both the Motul and Calkini regions, where they enjoyed alliances with the Pech

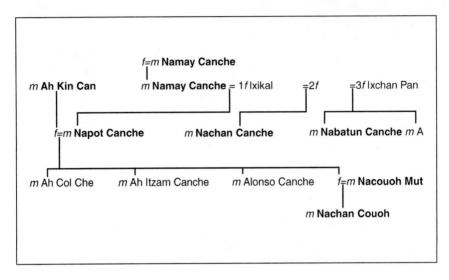

FIGURE 11.7 A Family of rulers: the Canche of sixteenth-century Calkini. Note: The names in bold served as *batab* (governor) of Calkini or another *cah* in the region; the elder Namay was part of the departure from Mayapan in the 1440s and a member of the Canul court; the younger Namay won through warfare the *batabil* (governorship) of Dzitbalche; he died before the Spanish invasion; his son Napot was confirmed as *batab* of Calkini in 1541, when Spanish officials also confirmed the eligibility (and possibly gubernatorial positions in the region) of two of his brothers and his son-in-law; a grandson of Napot, Nachan Couoh, was *batab* of Calkini in the late-sixteenth century; Alonso Canche served as *alcalde* (see Table 11.1) in Calkini in the 1570s and was still alive in 1595. Source: TC: 13–18 (Restall 1998: 88–91).

and the Canul respectively. Figure 11.7 illustrates their survival in Conquest times as a ruling *chibal* in and around Calkini. Although marital alliances with several other *chibalob* are shown in this genealogy, the Canul are conspicuously absent. This reflects efforts by the Canche to alter the balance of power between themselves and the Canul in this region, efforts that may have gone back into the Segmented Century but that certainly met with some success in the Colonial period—as reflected in the *Title of Calkini* (the source for Figure 11.7), a community history that shows signs of having been reworked in Colonial times to promote the Canche (Okoshi Harada 1993; Restall 1998a:Chapter 5).

The Xiu seem also to have maneuvered well during the Conquest decades, but they lost political ground in the late sixteenth and seventeenth centuries. A brief history of the dynasty, highlighting events in the 1530s and 1560s, illustrates both points emphasized in this section: the persistence of group hereditary status; and the simultaneous systemic changes that came in the wake of the Conquest.

FIGURE 11.8 The memorial to the massacre at Otzmal (drawing by the author after the seventeenth-century etching in Cogolludo 1867–68, 3:VI).

In the early years of the Spanish invasion, the senior lord of the dynasty was Nappol Chuuah Xiu, whose grandfather had established or consolidated Xiu authority in Mani after Mayapan's collapse. In 1536 Nappol and his son and heir Ah Ziyah Xiu were both killed by a rival Maya dynasty in the massacre at Otzmal (see Figure 11.8), an event that helped determine the Xiu policy of appeasement toward the Spanish invaders.[26]

By 1548 the senior lordship had passed to a great-nephew of Nappol's, Ah Kukum Xiu—baptized don Francisco de Montejo Xiu in the presence of his godfather, don Francisco de Montejo (the younger).[27] Montejo Xiu ruled for two decades. He presided over the great Mani summit of 1557, when the Xiu and neighboring dynastic lords such as the Cocom and the Canul surveyed and agreed upon their territorial borders (Figure 11.5 is one of the maps drawn to accompany the treaty; also see Table 11.1). The summit represented the apex of Montejo Xiu's rule; it promoted and celebrated his status as *halach uinic* and, by extension, the regional authority of the Xiu dynasty. The summit also represented the flourishing of the "royal" Maya court and its underlying ideology in spite of the Conquest—indeed, in a sense because of it, as the new colony provided the impetus behind the treaty (XC:12–13; Quezada and Okoshi 2001).

However, the events of the 1560s sapped some of the strength of the Maya court as a regional authority. In 1561–1565 Crown official don Diego Quijada was able to undermine Maya courts and restrict the authority and privileges of dynastic and regional lords. Symbolic of this assault on dynastic dignity, and marking a dramatic contrast with the triumph of 1557, was don Francisco de Montejo Xiu's prosecution by Quijada for drunkenness during a 1561 Xiu summit in Mani.[28] The following summer brought even greater ritual humiliation, as Landa's torture-driven inquisition into "idolatrous" practices culminated in the whipping of hundreds of Maya "penitents" and the burning of religious statues and other objects at the Mani *auto da fe* (Clendinnen 1987:72–82; Scholes and Adams 1938).

In 1567, the year of his death, Montejo Xiu was the principal author and signator of a letter to the king of Spain from a group of Xiu and Pacab rulers denouncing Landa, his fellow Franciscan "torturers," Quijada, and other Spanish officials. "May our descendents to the fourth generation be recompensed the great persecution that came to us," wrote the Xiu lords, but one wonders how much faith they really had in the likelihood of compensation (Restall 1998a:165–168).

The 1560s marked a turning point in the evolution of the Maya court and, probably, in the Maya evaluation of the status of dynastic authority. After the 1560s dynastic persistence relied increasingly upon three strategies, albeit ones with deep pre-Conquest roots and that continued to be supported by the elite ideology of superior status: working the Spanish legal system through petitions (an old Maya tradition) and lawsuits; consolidating local power on a *cah*-by-*cah* basis; and redefining dynastic corporatism to permit new alliances with "lesser" *chibalob*. Symbolic of this shift in the Xiu world was the fact the *batabil* of Mani passed to Gaspar Antonio Chi in 1571 and to a Francisco Be in 1575.[29] Meanwhile, the direct line of Xiu lordship shifted to the less prominent Xiu *cah* of Oxkutzcab and, by the late seventeenth century, to the tiny *cah* of Yaxakumche (XC; see Table 11.5). The Xiu dynasty survived, but its authority became increasingly localized.

Don Francisco de Montejo Xiu's name was rich in symbolism, representing the status of the Xiu dynasty as Maya conquistadors—as equals, within their own domain, to the Spanish dynasty that headed the new dominant court at Mani. But his Christian name also marked the Xiu ruler as subordinate to his Spanish godfather; as a representative not only of the Xiu dynasty and its ancestors but also of the Montejos and the colony they had founded; as not only the head of the court at Mani but also a subordinate member of the new Colonial court at Merida. The Xiu world, centered on Mani, persisted, but it was now part of a larger world of concentric spaces centered on Merida, Mexico City, and Madrid.

Montejo Xiu's christening was paralleled by that of the head of the Pech dynasty, Ah Naum. As don Francisco de Montejo Pech, Ah Naum was confirmed in office in the 1540s as *batab* of Motul, the most important *cah* in the Pech region. But like his namesake in Mani, the Pech lord thereby confirmed the Spanish establishment of a colony in Yucatan. This is efficiently illustrated by the depiction in the *Title of Motul* of Ah Naum

FIGURE 11.5 The Yaxakumche Branch of the Xiu Lineage

Time	Line of descent by primogeniture	Source
C11th	Hun Uitzil Chac Tutul Xiu	The ca.1560 portion
C15th	Ah Tzun Xiu	of the Xiu Family
C15th	Ah Op Xiu	Tree (by Gaspar
d.1536	Nappol Chuuah Xiu	Antonio Chi) (from
d.1536	Ah Ziyah Xiu	XC)
c.1522–1548	Don Melchor Xiu	
c.1547–1624	Don Francisco Xiu	The ca.1685 portion
C16th–17th	Don Pedro Xiu	of the Xiu Family
d.c.1630	Don Alonso Xiu	Tree (by don Juan
c.1620–ca.1690	Don Juan Xiu	Xiu)
b.1661	Don Juan Antonio Xiu	The papers of the
1697–1759+	Don Salvador Xiu	Xiu Chronicle
C18th	Don Lorenzo Xiu	(C17th to early-19th)
C18th	Don Pablo Xiu	(XC)
C18th–19th	Don Pedro Xiu	
C18th–19th	Don Antonio Xiu	
b.1788	Don Andrés Xiu	Gates 1937:125
b.1814	Don Bentura Xiu	
1839–1911	Don Bernabé Xiu	
1861–1911	Don Ildefonso Xiu	
b.1887	Don Nemensio Xiu	
b.1915	Don Dionisio Xiu	

Pech as a prophet-ruler, who entreats his people to welcome the Spaniards with food and drink "so that Christianity may enter the *cah*" (*yoklal ocol cah ti cristianoil*; TY:7r; TCH:12; Restall 1998a:121). The lordship of don Francisco de Montejo Pech, and his descendents, survived beyond the Conquest, but Pech history would later be written to project the impact of Spanish colonization back into the pre-Conquest mind of Ah Naum himself.

The Pech seem to have maneuvered better than the rest of the dynastic dozen through the upheaval of the Spanish invasion to consolidate much of their regional authority. The *batabil* of Motul was passed by don Francisco de Montejo Pech to his son don Melchor in the 1550s and on through his branch of the Pech dynasty into the next century. The persecution of the 1560s little affected the Pech region, as reflected in the fact that the Pech continued to promote themselves as the Spaniards' chief allies; in 1567 two dozen Pech rulers of *cahob* in the Motul-Conkal region, headed by don Melchor Pech, wrote a letter to the king of Spain on the same topic as the Xiu letter of that year, only the Pech heaped praise on Landa and pleaded for more like him (AGI-*México* 367:62, 70; Restall 1998a:156–158).

Thus by allying themselves to Spanish Colonial authority, Pech and Xiu nobles survived the Spanish invasion and even consolidated their local power, the Pech being particularly successful at holding onto *batabilob* in their region.[30] Other nobles preserved their courts in similar ways. Don Pablo Paxbolon, the Chontal ruler of Acalan-Tixchel, extended his regional power by acting as a Colonial agent and Maya conquistador; his campaign against noncolonized Maya groups lasted into the seventeenth century (Restall 1998a:Chapter 3; Scholes and Roys 1948). Ah Kul Caamal of Sisal learned that resisting Spanish demands resulted in imprisonment and the loss of his rulership; his subsequent cooperation and baptism as don Juan de la Cruz Caamal led to his confirmation as governor of Saci-Sisal (upon which Valladolid was founded), where "he was *batab* a long time before he died" (*ont kinac u batabil cat cimi lay*; TY:5r; TCH:9–10; Restall 1998a:117–118). Don Fernando Uz rose to prominence as a senior Maya official who, like his elder contemporary Gaspar Antonio Chi, also served the colony as an interpreter and notary and lived partly in the Spanish world; although he held a number of *batabilob* during his career, he also kept a house in Merida (AGI-*Escribanía* 305a; Farriss 1984:98–99).

There was a price to be paid, however, for redefining legitimacy through association with the Spanish authorities. First of all, Spanish concern with political stability and the provision of tribute took precedence over loyalty to a particular dynasty or fidelity to a particular alliance—as the Xiu history above illustrates. Second, the subject Maya population remained an important audience that needed to be reassured and convinced of the legitimacy of the local rulers. Negotiation and persuasion played as much of a role in internal Maya relations as it did in relations between the Spanish and Maya courts. The *Books of Chilam Balam* contain several references to the poor quality of rulership during troubled times, including the Conquest period (CBT:63, 67–68; CBC:20; CBM:70–72; Restall 1998a:133–135, 138–140). In one notable incident of 1610, the Xiu *batab* of Tekax was almost murdered by his rioting subjects, who were incited by a gubernatorial rival, the above-mentioned don Fernando Uz (AGI-*Escribanía* 305a; Farriss 1984:98–99, 193–195, 246). The near escape of the Xiu lord and the subsequent imprisonment of Uz showed that the traditional basis of legitimacy—the quadripartite ideology that underpinned the Maya court—remained just as important in Colonial times as the newer tactic of association with the Spaniards.

Dynastic Origin Mythology

The fourth and final support for the Maya elite's ideology of superior status was a mythology that claimed external origins.[31] This mythology—taken by most Mayanists since Landa to be based on a historical migration from central Mexico—is, I suggest, without historical foundation, being a metahistorical construct serving particular cultural purposes.

TABLE 11.6 Maya Origin Myth References in the Ethnohistorical Sources

Source	Places of origin	Ancestors of origin
Title of Acalan-Tixchel (1567/1612)	"Cozumel"	"Auxaual", four other Chontal Maya nobles (Chacbalam, Huncha, Paxmulu, & Paxoc)
Title of Calkini (1595/1821)	"the Itza region", "the east", "West Zuyua"	"those people of West Zuyua", "those of the Canul name"
Book of Chilam Balam of Chumayel	"Cartabona", "Viroa Chacunescab"	"the chibal of the Tutul Xiu"
Book of Chilam Balam of Mani	"the land and home of Nonoual", "West Zuyua", "Tulapan"	"the Tutul Xiu"
ªProbanza of don Juan Kauil (1618)	"the kingdom of Mexico"	"a Cocom", "a relative of Moctezuma named Tumispolchicbul", "Cuhuikakcamalcacal-puc", "Ixnahaucupul" and "Kukumcupul"
ªGaspar Antonio Chi (1579)		"the Tutul Xiu" as "foreigners"
ªLanda's Relación (1566)	"the west"; "the south," "Chiapas"	"Kukulcan", "the Itzas"; "the Tutul Xiu"

NOTE: ªSpanish-language document.
SOURCES: TAT, 69v (Restall 1998a:58); TC, 36 (Restall 1998a:101); CBC, 21 (Restall 1998a:135–136); CBM, 134 (Restall 1998a:140); Brinton 1882:114–118 and Quezada 1997:214–216; RHGY, I:319 (Restall 1998a:149); Landa VI; XIII; IX.

Ethnohistorical sources such as the *Books of Chilam Balam* and the primordial titles contain a number of examples of the myth (see Table 11.6). Paxbolon's dynasty originated with founding ancestor Auxaual, who "in the beginning came from Cozumel to conquer the territories here" along with four of "his principal men" (*u na cahibal auxaual tali cuçumil tali u chuci cabil cabob uij . . . yithoc u nucalob*; TAT:69v; Restall 1998a:58). The myth-histories of both the Canul and Xiu lineages claim origins in a place called "West Zuyua." The principal men of Calkini state that "we know how we came from the east, we Maya men, and that we come from those people of West Zuyua . . . Travelling along the road, they [sic] came to rest in the Itza region, which is where those of the Canul name came from" (*c oheliix hibiciix teil talon ti lakine coon ah maya uinice tiix u talob lae ah chikin suyuaob . . . lay u bel beob lubob tal ti peten ytza ulci ah canul ukabaob lae*; TC:36; Restall 1998a:101). The Chilam Balam text from Mani asserts that "the Tutul Xiu were at West Zuyua for four eras; the land they came from was Tulapan . . . the land and home of Nonoual" (*can te anilo tutul xiu ti chikin zuiua u lumil u talelob tulapan . . . ti cab ti yotoch nonoual*; CBM:134; Restall 1998a:140). According to Gaspar Antonio Chi (a Xiu on his mother's side), one dimension of the rivalry between the noble lineages of the Cocom and the Xiu was that the Cocom claimed that "they were native lords and the Tutul Xiu foreigners" (RHGY, I:319; Restall 1998a:149); accordingly, Chi's Xiu Family Tree (Figure 11.6) features some central Mexican iconographic elements.

Even this brief summary reveals the contradictions and ambiguities in the sources; they are internal and intertextual and concern geography and nomenclature. For example, the Chontal myth names Auxaual as the founding ancestor of the ruling dynasty; Auxaual is possibly a name of Nahuatl origins, and there is a similarly named site to the west of the Chontal region; however, Auxaual is described as coming from Cozumel, which is far to the east. The Calkini text claims that the Canul lineage came from West Zuyua to the Itza region and then to Calkini, which has been taken to suggest a migration from central Mexico through the Chontal region and into Yucatan; however, the Calkini text also states that this place of origin was in the east—again, the opposite direction—and the Itza region referred to here is probably the area around Chichen Itza.[32]

Zuyua is also mentioned in the *Book of Chilam Balam of Chumayel*, usually in association with rulership. It has been interpreted variously by scholars (Burns 1991:35; Edmonson 1986:168; Marcus 1992:78–79; Roys 1933:88–98; Sigal 2000:233–240), but Zuyua itself is almost universally assumed to be a Nahuatl-derived toponym and located in central Mexico.[33] Yet, as one linguist has pointed out, there is "no convincing evidence that Zuyua has anything to do with Nahuatl place names, the Nahuatl language, or central Mexico" (Karttunen 1985:6). Indeed, the word's possible components (*zuy* and *ha'*, for example) are very plausible Yucatec toponymic elements. Nevertheless, no place in Yucatan has been identified as a possible historical site for Zuyua. Equally unidentifiable are other place-names given as dynastic provenances in the origin-myth sources, such as Nonoual, Cartabona, and Viroa Chacunescab.[34]

A 1618 source records a claim that the Cocom and other local nobles were descended from lords "who came from Mexico," one of whom was related to Moctezuma.[35] Although knowledge of one or both the Moctezumas may have circulated in pre-Conquest Yucatan, it seems more likely that tales of him arrived with the Spaniards and/or their Nahua auxiliaries. Besides, the Cocom name has been identified in Chichen Itza hieroglyphs dated long before the Moctezumas ruled in Mexico (Ringle 1990; Stuart 1993:346–347). Furthermore, another source claims that it was the Xiu who were widely perceived as foreign, usually central Mexican, and the Cocom as locally rooted (see Chi in Table 11.6). In fact, the names cited in the Valladolid document as those of ancestral migrants are Maya, not Nahuatl. Likewise, the patronyms featured in other versions of the origin myth—such as Canul, Caamal, and Cupul—are as Yucatec Maya as is Cocom. The name "Xiu" is usually assumed to be Nahuatl-derived, but this, too, is a dubious assumption.[36] Even if *xiu* were to be viewed as a loan-word from Nahuatl, that would hardly prove that the lineage or *chibal* named Xiu came from central Mexico.[37]

Not only have scholars been quick to take literally and uncritically the vague and contradictory origin mythology of dynastic dozen chibalob such as Canul, Caamal, Cocom, Cupul, and Xiu; they have added Pech to the list. By misreading statements in the Pech primordial titles, one historian argued that the Pech nobles arrived in the region north of Merida not only after the fifteenth-century fall of Mayapan but "in conquest times" (Roys 1957:41). In fact, the assertion by Pech nobles that they were "the first noble conquistadors here in this land" (*yax hidalgo concixtador uay ti lum*; TY:2v; TCH:1; Restall 1998a:109) is a reference to the acquisition of prestigious Spanish titles, not the initial arrival of the Pech in the region; it relates to elite Maya reactions to foreign invasion, not to their own putative foreignness (Restall 1998a:44–45, 104–128). But the erroneous interpretation was used by another historian to characterize the Pech as "parvenu 'adventurers'" (Farriss 1984:245), thus grafting onto Maya mythology a historiographical myth.[38]

If the myth of Maya elite origins was not rooted in historical fact—that is, none of the dynastic dozen were descended from central Mexicans—what purpose did the myth serve the Mayas who perpetuated it?

Put simply, such mythology made the elite who they were. Put metaphorically, it was the crucial agent that prevented the mortar used to construct the Maya court from eroding and crumbling. Tales of foreign origins were used by the Maya elite to ideologically underpin socioeconomic differences and help perpetuate the dominance of their *chibalob*. As discussed above, Maya social differentiation was marked and maintained in a variety of ways. But in times of political and economic crisis—as in the fifteenth century, when the Mayapan arrangement collapsed, or in the sixteenth century, when the Spaniards invaded—the elite needed a foundation to their status that transcended the material and the mundane. This need was fulfilled by the assertion of a sacred and celestial connection to distant places and ancestors. The exclusivity of this connection was of the utmost importance; its monopoly imbued it with meaning.

David Henige (1982:90–96) has argued that "there seem to be few important differences between the styles of origin theories" from thousands of societies, both oral and literate, with external origins proving again and again to be "uncannily attractive . . . perhaps because it often seems desirable to distinguish the ruling classes from the rest of the population." Similarly, in a series of studies (e.g., 1993, 1994, 1998), Mary Helms has proposed that "in human cosmologies geographical distance corresponds with supernatural distance" (1998:xi) and that status is gained through knowledge of—and claimed ancestral links to—distant places. Most societies "recognize two ideological centers—one at the heartland of the polity and the other . . . located geographically 'out there'" and viewed as a place of cultural and ancestral origin (1994:361, 363).[39]

Zuyua and the other places cited in Maya texts precisely fit this mythological category of the temporally and geographically ambiguous homes of founding ancestors. Such toponyms are not easily identified because their meaning to the Maya was rooted in their remoteness and otherness—in the fact that they were not supposed to be readily identifiable, geographically, temporally, or linguistically.

The sacred element commonly found in origin mythology elsewhere is also present in the Maya case. Cozumel was probably significant to the Chontals because it had for many centuries been a pilgrimage site, usually associated with the Itzas. Indeed, "Itza" or the Itzas—possibly the name that Yucatec Mayas gave to Chontals during Chichen Itza's heyday—are frequently cited in Maya texts in connection with elite origin mythology and usually with sacred associations.[40]

Thus, the otherness of names and places allowed them to function as spatial metaphors for the sacred and the exotic, allowing rulers—in accordance with deep-rooted Maya tradition—to transcend their earthly roles and assert connections to the supernatural.[41] But at the same time it was important to maintain the deeply rooted local connections that served to legitimate the material basis of social and political status—to nourish Helms's "ideological center . . . at the heartland of the polity." The dynastic dozen thus laid claim to "the logically awkward but not unfamilar claim to a double legitimacy" (Clendinnen 1987:150). Long into the Colonial period Maya elites asserted this paradoxical dual legitimacy deriving both from their mythical external origins and their long-term occupation and rule of the region they dominated.

Origin mythology enabled Maya dynasties to appropriate the vestiges of prestige and power resulting from encounters with the peoples and/or cultures of central and southern Mexico in pre-Conquest times—all with a view to reinforcing a nativist claim to local rule. This ideological principle was reinforced by the Spanish Conquest and the attempt by some elite *chibalob* to assert status as "noble Maya conquistadors"—Xiu, Pech, and other elites attempted to distance themselves from the Maya masses and to appropriate the Conquest as a way of inverting defeat and maintaining status.

Elite origin mythology and the Yucatec historical experience therefore fed off each other, with the perpetuation of the origin myth being one legacy of centuries of multiple contacts and exchanges between Yucatan and the outside world. Colonial-period Maya references to the foreign origin of certain elite lineages do not reflect a historical migration or invasion; rather, they reflect the complexity of the Maya social structure, the sophistication of the Maya reaction to the Spanish invasion, and the tenacity of the rulers of the Maya court.

Colonial Epilogue

The story of the Maya court in the sixteenth century thus features at its heart a dialectic between change and continuity. There are many similarities between the court of 1450 and that of 1650, and yet the court was never static at any point during those centuries. Ruling dynasties, noble families, and courtly retinues had to adapt continually to changing political and social circumstances prompted in particular by the post-Mayapan wars, by the Spanish invasion, and by the imposition and evolution of colonialism in the peninsula.

In fact, the Colonial period witnessed competing campaigns of adaptation between Maya courts and Spanish colonists, both of whom attempted to make Colonial Yucatan look and function as much as possible to their way of perceiving and doing things. The Maya elite had the advantages of being native, being in the majority, and being permitted to govern themselves at the local level; but the political and economic advantages of the colonists were greater in the long run. In using the Colonial courts (the Spanish legal and administrative system) to perpetuate themselves, Maya courts gradually undermined their own political and cultural independence.

In short, the Maya court survived the Conquest, but in order to do so it had to allow itself to become partially colonized. To return to the metaphor of concentric spaces introduced at the start of this chapter: Two Colonial developments altered the positioning of the Maya court within this spatial metaphor.

One was the gradual insertion of Spaniards and Spanish concepts of the built environment into the center. Initially the Maya elite achieved continuity around the plaza by amalgamating Spanish and Maya perceptions of the prestige of stone (rather than wattle-and-daub) houses and the prestige of living on the plaza; the Pech history of Chicxulub describes three buildings constructed around the plaza—the new church; the *cah* government building; and the stone house of the *batab*.[42] But the patio of Spanish-style houses was inside the building, not in front of it; it was an inner courtyard rather than a spatial link between building and plaza. The church that replaced the "pyramid" and temple, as much as it was valued and nurtured as a symbol of *cah* status and integrity, was likewise an internal space.

Furthermore, the most significant rituals performed in the church were the monopoly of Spanish priests, just as, in time and in the most important *cahob*, the house-plots on the plaza became monopolized by Spaniards.[43] Some Maya rulers embraced Spanish concepts of space and status to the extent of creating and partially residing on Spanish-style *estancias* (agricultural estates)—a notable example is the Chontal ruler don Pablo Paxbolon, who lived on his *estancia* outside Tixchel (TAT:n.f.; Restall 1998a:73)—but this, too, had the effect of partially removing the court from its traditional center. Eventually, one way or another, Mayas were pushed into the outer concentric spaces as the Spanish presence in the plaza, so temporary that day in Calkini in 1541, became permanent.

The other Colonial development that altered the metaphorical positioning of the Maya court was the evolution of new centers of power. I have argued above that elite origin mythology was perpetuated to promote the sacred "otherness" of dynastic *chibalob*; viewed through the model of concentric spaces, this mythology allowed rulers to be both at the physical center of their domain and transcend it metaphysically, occupying alone a three-dimensional space outside the flat model.

However, in the Colonial period, Maya rulers lost their monopoly on the "otherness" of rulership. Increasingly that space came to be co-occupied also by the remote higher powers of Spanish Colonial rule—the governor in Merida, the viceroy in Mexico City, and the king in Spain. These Spanish rulers were at the centers of a vast interlocking set of concentric zones that served to peripheralize Maya courts. The *cahob* and their courts remained at the center of their own worlds, but Maya courtly members were increasingly aware of their subordinate status within a larger world centered far away (Hanks 1996:287; Restall 1998a:155).

By the Late Colonial period, the titles of *ajaw* ("lord") and *halach uinic* (regional ruler), so important to the pre-Conquest Maya,[44] became applied only to the Spanish governor, viceroy, or king—two of whom, or even all three, were often conflated by Maya *cabildos* into a single, remote, kingly personage. In an effort to hold on to their position at the center, Mayas recast their own rulers as Spanish-style conquistadors (Restall 1998a) and Spanish-style kings (see Figures 11.6, 11.8, and 11.9). In doing so, Mayas conceded the colonization of their "royal" courts.

Abbreviations

AGEY   Archivo General del Estado de Yucatán, Merida
AGI   Archivo General de las Indias, Seville
AGN   Archivo General de la Nación, Mexico City
AME   Archivo de la Mitra Emeritense [cited numbers are page numbers in Dumond and Dumond 1982]

FIGURE 11.9 Imagining kings: Colonial Maya depictions of Maya rulers (drawings by the author after originals in *The Book of Chilam Balam of Chumayel*). Source: CBC (drawings in Roys 1933:150, 153, 158, 161; facsimiles in Edmonson 1986:128, 150, 218, 66).

ANEY   Archivo Notarial del Estado de Yucatán, Merida
CBC   *Book of Chilam Balam of Chumayel* [cited numbers are page numbers in Roys' 1933 edition; also cited with each reference, where applicable, is the translation in Restall 1998a]
CBM   *Book of Chilam Balam of Mani* [cited numbers are page numbers in the Codex Pérez manuscript, photostat in Tozzer Library, Harvard University; also cited with each reference, where applicable, is the translation in Restall 1998a]
CBT   *Book of Chilam Balam of Tizimin* [cited numbers are page numbers in Edmonson's 1982 edition; also cited with each reference is the translation in Restall 1998a]
CCA   Colección Carrillo y Ancona, in the Centro de Apoyo a la Investigación Histórica de Yucatán, Merida
DTS   Documentos de Tierras de Sotuta [cited numbers are page numbers in Roys 1939]
LC   Libro de Cacalchen [cited numbers are folio numbers in the photostated manuscript in Latin American Library, Tulane University]

MT Montes de Tsek [cited numbers are folio numbers in the photostated manuscript in Latin American Library, Tulane University]
RHGY *Relaciones histórico-geográficas de la gobernación de Yucatán* [cited numbers are page numbers in Garza 1983]
TAT *Title of Acalan-Tixchel* [cited numbers are folios of original manuscript in the Archivo General de las Indias, Seville; facsimiles are in Scholes and Roys 1948; also cited with each reference is the translation in Restall 1998a]
TC *Title of Calkini*, a/k/a *Códice, Codex,* or *Chronicle of Calkini* [cited numbers are pages of original manuscript, photostat in Tozzer Library, Harvard University; also cited with each reference is the translation in Restall 1998a]
TCH *Title of Chicxulub*, a/k/a *Chronicle of Chicxulub*, a/k/a *Crónica de Chac-Xulub-Chen,* a/k/a *Códice de Nakuk-Pech* [cited page numbers are photostat pages of nineteenth-century Regil manuscript in Tozzer Library, Harvard University and in Latin American Library, Tulane University; also cited with each reference is the translation in Restall 1998a]
TY *Title of Yaxkukul,* a/k/a *Crónica de Yaxkukul* [cited numbers are folios of 1769 manuscript, Latin American Library, Tulane University; also cited with each reference is the translation in Restall 1998a]
XC *The Xiu Chronicle,* a/k/a the Xiu Papers [original manuscript in Tozzer Library, Harvard University]

References

Barrera Vásquez, Alfredo. 1984. *Documento No.1 del Deslinde de las Tierras en Yaxkukul, Yucatán.* Mexico, D.F.: Instituto Nacional de Antropología e Historia.

Bracamonte, Pedro. 1994. *La memoria enclaustrada: Historia indígena de Yucatán, 1750–1915.* Series on the *Historia de los pueblos indígenas de México.* Mexico, D.F.: Centro de Investigaciones y Estudios Superiores en Antropología Social.

Brinton, Daniel G. 1882. *The Maya Chronicles.* Philadelphia: Library of Aboriginal Research.

Brown, Denise Fay. 1993. "Yucatec Maya Settling, Settlement, and Spatiality." Ph.D. diss., University of California–Riverside.

Burns, Allan F. 1991. "The Language of Zuyua: Yucatec Maya Riddles and Their Interpretation." In Mary H. Preuss, ed., *Past, Present, and Future: Selected Papers on Latin American Indian Literatures,* pp. 35–40. Lancaster, CA: Labyrinthos.

Calderón, Héctor M. 1982. *Manuscrito de Chan Cah.* Mexico, D.F.: Grupo Dzibil.

Carmack, Robert. 1981. *The Quiché Mayas of Utatlán: The Evolution of a Highland Guatemalan Kingdom.* Norman: University of Oklahoma Press.

Chamberlain, Robert S. 1948. *The Conquest and Colonization of Yucatan.* Washington, DC: Carnegie Institution.

Chatterjee, Kumkum. 1998. "History as Self-Representation: The Recasting of a Political Tradition in Late Eighteenth-Century Eastern India." *Modern Asian Studies* 32(4): 913–948.

Christensen, Alexander F. 1999. "History, Myth, and Migration in Mesoamerica." Manuscript.

Chuchiak, John F. IV. 2000. "The Indian Inquisition and the Extirpation of Idolatry: The Process of Punishment in the Provisorato de Indios of the Diocese of Yucatan, 1563–1812." Ph.D. diss., Tulane University.

Clendinnen, Inga. 1987. *Ambivalent Conquests: Maya and Spaniard in Yucatan, 1517–1570*. Cambridge: Cambridge University Press.

Coe, Michael D. 1993. *The Maya*. 5th ed. New York: Thames and Hudson.

Cogolludo, Diego López de. 1867–1868. *Los tres siglos de la dominación española en Yucatán o sea Historia de Esta Provincia* [ca. 1654]. 2 vols. Mérida: Manuel Aldana Rivas.

Cortés, Hernán. 1986. *Letters from Mexico*. Anthony Pagden, ed. and trans. New Haven: Yale University Press.

Cortez, Constance. 1995. "Gaspar Antonio Chi and the Xiu Family Tree." Ph.D. diss., University of California–Los Angeles.

Craine, Eugene R., and Reginald C. Reindorp, eds. 1979. *The Codex Pérez and the Book of Chilam Balam of Maní*. Norman: University of Oklahoma Press.

Dumond, Carol Steichen, and Don E. Dumond, eds. 1982. *Demography and Parish Affairs in Yucatan, 1797–1897: Documents from the Archivo de la Mitra Emeritense Selected by Joaquín de Arrigunaga Peón*. Anthropological Papers No. 27. Eugene: University of Oregon.

Dumond, Don E. 1997. *The Machete and the Cross: Campesino Rebellion in Yucatan*. Lincoln: University of Nebraska Press.

Edmonson, Munro S. 1982. *The Ancient Future of the Itzá: The Book of Chilam Balam of Tizimin*. Austin: University of Texas Press.

_____. 1986. *Heaven Born Mérida and its Destiny: The Book of Chilam Balam of Chumayel*. Austin: University of Texas Press.

Farriss, Nancy M. 1984. *Maya Society Under Colonial Rule: The Collective Enterprise of Survival*. Princeton: Princeton University Press.

Fash, William L. 1991. *Scribes, Warriors, and Kings: The City of Copán and the Ancient Maya*. London: Thames and Hudson.

Freidel, David, and Charles Suhler. 1999. "The Path of Life: Toward a Functional Analysis of Ancient Maya Architecture." In Jeff Karl Kowalski, ed., *Mesoamerican Architecture as a Cultural Symbol*. New York: Oxford University Press.

de la Garza, Mercedes, et al. 1983. *Relaciones Histórico-Geográficas de la Gobernación de Yucatán*. 2 vols. Mexico, D.F.: Universidad Nacional Autónoma de México.

Gates, William. 1937. *Diego de Landa: Yucatan Before and After the Conquest*. Baltimore: Maya Society. Reprinted by Dover, 1978.

Gillespie, Susan D. 1989. *The Aztec Kings: The Construction of Rulership in Mexica History*. Tucson: University of Arizona Press.

Gruzinski, Serge. 1993. *The Conquest of Mexico: The Incorporation of Indian Societies into the Western World, 16th–18th Centuries*. Cambridge: Polity Press.

Hanks, William F. 1990. *Referential Practice: Language and Lived Space Among the Maya*. Chicago: University of Chicago Press.

_____. 1996. *Language and Communicative Practices*. Boulder: Westview Press.

Helms, Mary W. 1993. *Craft and the Kingly Ideal: Art, Trade, and Power*. Austin: University of Texas Press.

———. 1994. "Essays on Objects: Interpretations of distance made tangible," in Stuart B. Schwartz, ed., *Implicit Understandings*, pp. 355–377. Cambridge: Cambridge University Press.

———. 1998. *Access to Origins: Affines, Ancestors, and Aristocrats*. Austin: University of Texas Press.

Henige, David. 1982. *Oral Historiography*. London: Longman.

Hill, Robert M. II. 1992. "The Social Uses of Writing among the Colonial Cakchiquel Maya: Nativism, Resistance, and Innovation." In David H. Thomas, ed., *Columbian Consequences*, vol. 3, pp. 283–299. Washington, DC: Smithsonian Institution Press.

Houston, Stephen. 1994. "Literacy among the Pre-Columbian Maya: A Comparative Perspective." In Elizabeth Hill Boone and Walter D. Mignolo, eds., *Writing Without Words: Alternative Literacies in Mesoamerica and the Andes*, pp. 27–49. Durham: Duke University Press.

———. 1997. "The Shifting Now: Aspect, Deixis, and Narrative in Classic Maya Texts." *American Anthropologist* 99: 291–305.

———., ed. 1998. *Function and Meaning in Classic Maya Architecture*. Washington, DC: Dumbarton Oaks Research Library and Collection.

Houston, Stephen, and David Stuart. 1996. "Of Gods, Glyphs, and Kings: Divinity and Rulership Among the Classic Maya." *Antiquity* 70: 289–312.

Jones, Grant. 1989. *Maya Resistance to Spanish Rule: Time and History on a Colonial Frontier*. Albuquerque: University of New Mexico Press.

———. 1998. *The Conquest of the Last Maya Kingdom*. Stanford: Stanford University Press.

Jones, Lindsay. 1995. *Twin City Tales: A Hermeneutical Reassessment of Tula and Chichén Itzá*. Niwot: University Press of Colorado.

———. 1997. "Conquests of the Imagination: Maya-Mexican Polarity and the Story of Chichén Itzá." *American Anthropologist* 99: 275–90.

Karttunen, Frances. 1985. *Nahuatl and Maya in Contact with Spanish*. Austin: University of Texas, Department of Linguistics and Center for Cognitive Science.

Kowalski, Jeff Karl. 1999. *Mesoamerican Architecture as a Cultural Symbol*. New York: Oxford University Press.

Kowalski, Jeff Karl, and Nicholas P. Dunning. 1999. "The Architecture of Uxmal: The Symbolics of Statemaking at a Puuc Maya Regional Capital." In Jeff Karl Kowalski, ed., *Mesoamerican Architecture as a Cultural Symbol*. New York: Oxford University Press.

Landa, Fray Diego de. 1959. *Relación de las cosas de Yucatán* (1566). Mexico, D.F.: Editorial Porrua.

Lincoln, Charles E. 1991. "Ethnicity and Social Organization at Chichén Itzá, Yucatán, Mexico." Ph.D. diss., Harvard University.

Lockhart, James. 1992. *The Nahuas after the Conquest: A Social and Cultural History of the Indians of Central Mexico, Sixteenth through Eighteenth Centuries*. Stanford: Stanford University Press.

Lowe, Gareth W., Thomas A. Lee Jr., and Eduardo Martínez Espinosa. 1982. *Izapa: An Introduction to the Ruins and Monuments*. New World Archaeological Foundation Papers, No. 31. Provo: Brigham Young University.

Marcus, Joyce. 1982. "The Plant World of the Sixteenth- and Seventeenth-Century Lowland Maya." In Kent V. Flannery, ed., *Maya Subsistence*, pp. 239–273. New York: Academic Press.

_____. 1992. *Mesoamerican Writing Systems: Propaganda, Myth, and History in Four Ancient Civilizations*. Princeton: Princeton University Press.

_____. 1993. "Ancient Maya Political Organization." In Jeremy A. Sabloff and John S. Henderson, eds., *Lowland Maya Civilization in the Eighth Century A.D.*, pp. 111–183. Washington, DC: Dumbarton Oaks Research Library and Collection.

McAnany, Patricia A. 1995. *Living With the Ancestors: Kinship and Kingship in Ancient Maya Society*. Austin: University of Texas Press.

Morley, Sylvanus. 1946. *The Ancient Maya*. Stanford: Stanford University Press.

Morley, Sylvanus, and Ralph L. Roys. 1941. *The Xiu Chronicle*. Unpublished manuscript in Tozzer Library, Harvard University.

Okoshi Harada, Tsubasa. 1993. "Los Canules: analisis etnohistorico del Codice de Calkiní." Ph.D. diss., Universidad Nacional Autónoma de México.

Ouellet, Pierre. 1998. "Le lieu et le non-lieu: La structuration spatiale des images de soi et de l'autre dans les contextes interculturels." In Laurier Turgeon, ed., *Les Entre-Lieux de la Culture*, pp. 357–371. Quebec: Les Presses de L'Université Laval.

Patch, Robert W. 1993. *Maya and Spaniard in Yucatan, 1648–1812*. Stanford: Stanford University Press.

_____. 1998. "Culture, Community, and 'Rebellion' in the Yucatec Maya Uprising of 1761." In Susan Schroeder, ed., *Native Resistance and the Pax Colonial in New Spain*, pp. 67–83. Lincoln: University of Nebraska Press.

Patterson, Steven. 1992. "In Search of a Mesoamerican Floricultural Tradition: Ceremonial and Ornamental Plants Among the Yucatecan Maya." Ph.D. diss., University of California, Los Angeles.

Quezada, Sergio. 1993. *Pueblos y Caciques Yucatecos, 1550–1580*. Mexico City: El Colegio de México.

_____. 1997. *Los pies de la república: Los indios peninsulares, 1550–1750*. Series on the *Historia de los pueblos indígenas de México*. Mexico D.F.: Centro de Investigaciones y Estudios Superiores en Antropología Social.

Quezada, Sergio, and Tsubasa Okoshi Harada. 2001. *Papeles de los Xiu de Yaxá*. Mexico City: Universidad Nacional Autónoma de México, Centro de Estudios Mayas.

Recinos, Adrián. 1984. *Cronicas Indígenas de Guatemala* (1957). Guatemala City: Academia de Geografía e Historia de Guatemala.

Restall, Matthew. 1995. *Life and Death in a Maya Community: The Ixil Testaments of the 1760s*. Lancaster, CA: Labyrinthos.

_____. 1997a. *The Maya World: Yucatec Culture and Society, 1550–1850*. Stanford: Stanford University Press.

_____. 1997b. "Heirs to the Hieroglyphs: Indigenous Writing in Colonial Mesoamerica." *The Americas* 54(2): 239–267.

_____. 1998a. *Maya Conquistador*. Boston: Beacon Press.

_____. 1998b. "The Ties That Bind: Social Cohesion and the Yucatec Maya Family." *Journal of Family History* 23(4): 355–381.

_____. 2001. "Origin and Myth: Ethnicity, Class, and *Chibal* in Post-Classic and Colonial Yucatán." In Tsubasa Okoshi Harada and Lorraine Williams-Beck, eds., *Interrelación entre los linajes y la organización político-territorial en la península de Yucatán desde el clásico hasta la colonia*. Mexico, D.F.: Universidad Nacional Autónoma de México, Universidad Autónoma de Campeche, and the Foundation for the Advancement of Mesoamerican Studies.

Restall, Matthew, and John F. Chuchiak. N.d. "The Friar and the Maya: The Definitive English Edition of Fray Diego de Landa's Relacion de las cosas de Yucatan." Unpublished manuscript.

Ringle, William M. 1990. "Who Was Who in Ninth-Century Chichén Itzá?" *Ancient Mesoamerica* 1: 233–243.

Roys, Ralph L. 1933. *The Book of Chilam Balam of Chumayel*. Washington, DC: Carnegie Institution.

_____. 1939. *The Titles of Ebtun*. Washington, DC: Carnegie Institution.

_____. 1943. *The Indian Background to Colonial Yucatán*. Washington, DC: Carnegie Institution.

_____. 1957. *The Political Geography of the Yucatan Maya*. Washington, DC: Carnegie Institution.

_____. 1962. "Literary Sources for the History of Mayapan," in H.E.D. Pollock, Ralph L. Roys, T. Proskouriakoff, and A. Ledyard Smith, eds., *Mayapan, Yucatan, Mexico*, pp. 25–86. Washington, DC: Carnegie Institution.

Rugeley, Terry. 1996. *Yucatán's Maya Peasantry and the Origins of the Caste War*. Austin: University of Texas Press.

Sabloff, Jeremy A., and E.W. Andrews V., eds. 1986. *Late Lowland Maya Civilization: Classic to Post-Classic*. Albuquerque: University of New Mexico Press.

Sabloff, Jeremy A., and John S. Henderson, eds. 1993. *Lowland Maya Civilization in the Eighth Century A.D.* Washington, DC: Dumbarton Oaks Research Library and Collection.

Sahlins, Marshall D. 1981. *Historical Metaphors and Mythic Realities: Structure in the Early History of the Sandwich Islands Kingdom*. Ann Arbor: University of Michigan Press.

Scarborough, Vernon L. 1998. "Ecology and Ritual: Water Management and the Maya." *Latin American Antiquity* 9(2): 135–159.

Schele, Linda, and David A. Freidel. 1990. *A Forest of Kings: The Untold Story of the Ancient Maya*. New York: Morrow.

Scholes, France V., and Eleanor B. Adams, eds. 1938. *Don Diego Quijada, Alcalde Mayor de Yucatán, 1561–1565*. 2 vols. Mexico City: Editorial Porrua.

Scholes, France V., and Ralph L. Roys. 1948. *The Maya Chontal Indians of Acalan-Tixchel*. Washington, DC: Carnegie Institution. Reprinted by University of Oklahoma Press, 1968.

Sharer, Robert J. 1994. *The Ancient Maya*. 5th ed. Stanford: Stanford University Press.

Sigal, Pete. 2000. *From Moon Goddesses to Virgins: The Colonization of Yucatecan Maya Sexual Desire*. Austin: University of Texas Press.

Stuart, David. 1993. "Historical Inscriptions and the Maya Collapse." In Jeremy A. Sabloff and John S. Henderson, eds., *Lowland Maya Civilization in the Eighth Century A.D.*, pp. 321–354. Washington, DC: Dumbarton Oaks Research Library and Collection.

Thompson, J. Eric S. 1956. *The Rise and Fall of Maya Civilization*. London: Gollancz; Norman: University of Oklahoma Press.

_____. 1970. *Maya History and Religion*. Norman: University of Oklahoma Press.

Thompson, Philip C. 1978. "Tekanto in the Eighteenth Century." Ph.D. diss., Tulane University.

Tozzer, Alfred M. 1957. *Chichén Itzá and Its Cenote of Sacrifice: A Comparative Study of Contemporaneous Maya and Toltec*. Memoirs of the Peabody Museum, 11–12. Cambridge: Harvard University.

Notes

1. The relevant passage from the Calkini text, with my translation, is as follows (note that here and throughout this chapter I have used Colonial Maya orthography): *Cimenili ah tzab canul ti uli kul uinicob lae lay tun Naapot canche ti kamiob ti patan ca ti uliob tu tancabale ti tacan u Batabob tumen lay nachanchee canule lay napot canche tu an uba tutan kul uinicob tanlah ti yan u pentac lay ah cot mas u kaba y ix ix cahum kuk u uinic ti tun ti alabi Batabil tumenel dzul y u haan ti nacouoh mut y y in ti nachan canche ylix nabatun canche u canan uinic u mehen yalic he napot canche lae lay cuchmail cah uay Calkiní lae tu tancabal ti uch u kubul patan ti monxo cap.* ca ti uliob uay Calkiníe y u holcanob tu pach he ca hulob tal sacnicteel cħene paybe ulci u kekenob y u culuaob ti gonsalo u cap." culuaob lae hetun ca huliob u dzulilob tune hun chup kin tu chun caan cu sastal ti likin ca uliob he ca tali u kuchulob tu hol cah uay Calkiní lae ca oniob tu hunten he tun ca kuchiob tu uol chakane tiix oniob xani hunten hi catun kuchiob ti yotoch tun tix oniob tu yoxten xani bay tun u cibahob lae ti hunmol ah Calkiníob u pakteob u ocol yulel u patan hunhuntzuc ti cabe catun u kubahob ti cap." lae chuyub pix kin ti hatzcabe he patan u kubahob lae hokal yiximal ti molcab hex yulumale hokali xan lahuyoxkal u pulil cab hunkal xuxac pi u bal cuyub occi bay ix u sac kuchil xan lay u patannob tu kamah mondejo yalan yaxche ti ix halim lae catun ti hopi u thoxicob yxim tu batanbaob tumen u tupilob ti ah tacan tupil yalabale ma ohelan u kabae maix u tanciob yulmal xan baix toxci yulmal xan baix thoxci u pi il xan heix u kuchile hun banhal u cibah catun hopi u bakti thot chotun ca thani u capitanob ca yalah aex chaex tulacalex ci yalabalob catun u pah ubaob yokolob ca u holmektahob tu huntucob yan yab u cħah yan ma yab u cħaah tu than huntul tulacalob cħuplal y xiblalob batun cu caluacticob lae lay u chun tu tancabal napot canche lae hex almehen cabob ah otochnal laobi lae lay u batabob nachan canul u cuchma yilah yuchul buucah lae te tacan tu nii yotoche ti yan tucan ti yotoch Naapot canche lae lay u tabtahob tumen ul lay u cħayah u naal lae namay tayu y nachan y ah kul couoh y yah canob laobi lae tzlante tu chune lay yah kin lae ah kinob kin may y ah kul uh nabatu uc kalo namay tayu huntuli ah dza ti ya huntul xani ah cħauil huntul xani ah dzuun che u pentac ah cħauil lae ah chuen chay u catul u pentac.* Translation: As Ah Tzab Canul had already died when the officers [i.e., Spaniards] arrived, Napot Canche received them with tribute—when they arrived on his patio where Nachanche Canul had gathered the *batabob* together. Napot Canche presented himself before the officers, so that the men might be served by slaves of his named Ah Cot Mas and Ix Cahum Kuk. He was then appointed to the *batabil* by the foreigners, along with his son-in-law Nacouoh Mut and his younger brothers Nachan Canche and Nabatun Canche, to whom he was guardian. This Napot Canche held the *cah* governorship here in Calkini; it was on his patio that the tribute was delivered to the captain Montejo, when he and his soldiers arrived here in Calkini, when they arrived near the well at Sacnicte. Their swine and their Culhuas arrived first; the captain of the Culhuas was Gonzalo. When the foreigners arrived, there was on the horizon a sliver of the sun as it dawned in the east. When they reached the entrance to this *cah* of Calkini, they fired their guns once; when they arrived where the savannas begin, they also fired their guns once; and

when they arrived at the houses, they then fired their guns a third time. The people of Calkini then gathered together to discuss the completion of the bringing of tribute from each district, which they then delivered to the breast-plated Captain. That morning they delivered this tribute: one hundred loads of corn all in all; one hundred turkeys also; fifty jars of honey; twenty large baskets of ginned cotton; the sisal breast-armor was brought in; also the white cotton yarn. These were the tribute items received by Montejo under the ceiba of Halim. Then the constables began to distribute the corn among themselves—the names of the assembled constables are not known—distributing not just half of the turkeys, but all of them, as they did the cotton and the yarn. Then, having become gluttonous, they began to break the line and form a tightening circle. And the Captain said: "Give it up!" "Take all of it!" they replied. Then they began to be suspicious of each other, holding piles of things tightly in their arms; some were able to grab a great deal, others grabbed a little; one and all, women and men alike. And thus they did it in haste. Then the following began to occur on Napot Canche's patio: the district nobles, the residents, and their *batab* Nachan Canul, who were not responsible for watching this splitting up of spoils that took place, were hidden at the back of their homes; but those in front of Napot Canche's home were tied up by the foreigners. They took all who were there: Namay Tayu, and Nachan and Ah Kul Couoh; and the speakers, the priests, those who interpret the cause of things; the priests Kin May and Ah Kul Uh; Nabatun Uc. One who was there was Namay Tayu; Ah Dza Tiya was another one; Ah Chauil was one more—Ah Dzuun Che was Ah Chauil's slave, and his second slave was Ah Chuen Chay (TC:16–17; Restall 1998a:89–90).

2. In the fifteenth century and after there were no Maya rulers who could usefully be called "kings"; neither could any Maya dynasties be taken as "royal" in the sense that such a term is customarily defined—that is, a single ruling family governed by principles of heredity and (modern royalty aside) represented by a king or queen enjoying permanent and absolute rule, perhaps by divine right. However, "royal" is pertinent to the Classic period (see especially Chapter 1 by Inomata and Houston in Volume 1 and Chapter 3 by Harrison in this volume) and retains a certain relevance in the Post-Classic and Colonial periods (see the second half of this chapter).

3. For similar Maya models and maps see the drawing in the *Book of Chilam Balam of Chan Cah* (Calderon 1982:123), the circular version of the Mani Map (reproduced widely; e.g., Marcus 1993:127; Roys 1943; Sharer 1994:505; the noncircular version is presented below as Figure 11.5), and the citations and discussions in Restall (1997a:200–201) and Marcus (1993:125–128). For an analysis of the conception of geopolitical space by the independent Itza Maya of the seventeenth century, a conception that fits well the models in Figure 11.1 (from the plaza and concentric residential spaces of the Itza capital to the territorial center around it to the four outlying territories), see Jones (1998:60–107). On present-day Maya conceptions of space, see Brown (1993) and Hanks (1990).

4. "Quasinotarial" means that the documents were only partially (or in some secondary sense) generated by Spanish-approved notaries for a Spanish audience according to Colonial legal guidelines and formats; on Maya quasinotarial material, see Restall (1997a:Chapter 21). Primordial titles were written in various Colonial Mesoamerican languages; most extant examples are in Nahuatl (see Gruzin-

ski 1993:Chapter 3; Lockhart 1992:376–392; Restall 1997a:Chapter 21; 1997b [which contains extensive references to the relevant literature, in particular articles by Robert Haskett and Stephanie Wood], 1998a:Chapters 2, 3, 5, 6). The Acalan-Tixchel document is in Chontal Maya (a Yucatecan language, despite its frequent classification as Cholan). The Pech titles are a pair of near-identical texts, the Chicxulub (or Chacxulubchen) and the Yaxkukul, which contain within them shorter, subsumed titles that I have named after Motul and Saci-Sisal. All the Yucatec titles are published in English in Restall (1998a).

5. The literature on the *Books of Chilam Balam* is too large to cite here, but for examples see Edmonson (1982, 1986); for an introduction, short excerpts, and further references, see Restall (1998a:Chapter 7).

6. Restall (1997a) is a study of the notarial material in Maya; see also Roys (1939); Thompson (1978); Quezada (1997); Restall (1997b; 1998a).

7. There are three book-length studies of the conquest of Yucatan: Chamberlain (1948); Clendinnen (1987); Restall (1998a), which offer varying emphases on questions of change and continuity.

8. Citations of Landa are by chapter to facilitate the reader in finding passages in any edition. The standard Spanish-language edition is Landa (1959); my translations are drawn from Restall and Chuchiak n.d.

9. Living "beneath the branches, beneath the foliage" was a Maya metaphor for homelessness; traveling "beneath the trees, beneath the branches" was a metaphor for a long journey through a region without towns; Mayas who lived outside the colony were called by Colonial Mayas *ah tepp cheob*, "those covered by trees" (e.g., TCH:13/TY:7v; CBM:135; XC:35; Restall 1998a:122, 141, 177).

10. The cayman-tree is the caimito, *ek ya*, *Chrysophyllum cainito* (Stephen Houston and D.J.B. Restall, personal communications). For other ancient Maya images of trees see the illustrations to Cortez (1995); for an illustrated introduction to the role of the ceiba in Maya culture, see Pons (1997).

11. Also see the description of Maya palaces and patios by Cortés in his first letter to the Spanish king (1986:30–35).

12. It is possible that there were thrones of some kind in rulers' residences or in council buildings, although the small size of polities and the concomitant lack of monumental architectural construction in the Segmented Century make it unlikely that such thrones were very grand or in special throne rooms (as in Tikal, for example; see Harrison, Chapter 3 in this volume). I have translated a phrase in the Chontal primordial title as "seated on his throne" (*chumul tu tepeual*), being reported speech by Cortés and referring to the king in Castile (TAT:72r; Restall 1998a:63); as tempting as it is to comment on a possible Colonial Maya view of royal thrones as exclusive to Spaniards, I now believe that "established in his reign" is a more accurate gloss. There is no other reference to a throne in the Maya primordial titles or any in the Maya notarial record of which I am aware. There are two terms used in the *Books of Chilam Balam* that could be glossed as "throne," *am* and *kanche*, but neither are very common, and the latter, which the Tizimin text uses more often than the former, means "wooden chair or bench" when removed from a courtly context (Edmonson 1982, 1986; Restall 1997a:106, 365; Roys 1933 on the noncourtly *kanche*).

13. *Hallámosles gran número de libros de estas sus letras, y porque no tenían cosa en que no hubiese superstición y falsedades del demonio, se los quemamos todos, lo cual sin-*

tieron a maravilla y les dio mucha pena. On the spiritual conquest of Yucatan see Farriss (1984:Chapters 10, 11); Clendinnen (1987); Restall (1997a:Chapter 12; 1998a:Chapter 9); and Chuchiak (2000).

14. TAT:74v (Restall 1998a:67); AHN, caja III; Restall (1998a:167). For Spanish testimony that substantiates the Xiu claim with respect to various parts of the colony in 1562, see Scholes and Adams (1938, I:37, 68, 220, cited and summarized in Clendinnen 1987:83).

15. The larger point may be that legitimacy and authority were tied to a monopoly on knowledge, be it maintained through the keeping of texts or the memory of oral tradition (Stephen Houston, personal communication). The *Title of Calkini*, for example, illustrates the importance of both the written record and the memory of "those who are in the know" (TC:26–28; Restall 1998a:96–97). On the relevance of orality to Maya literacy pre- and post-Conquest, see Houston (1994, 1997) Restall (1997b).

16. The circumstances of Conquest that necessitated a proliferation of these courtly gatherings in the sixteenth century were repeated in a different form in the final century of Colonial rule, when population growth increased demand for land among both Spaniards and Maya communities. As a result, land summits reappeared in significant number. For example, a walk and summit agreement in the area just north of Merida in 1786 involved eight Spaniards and the *cabildo* officers of four *cahob* and took five days (CCA, Chichi papers, III); among the last such multicourt rituals to be recorded in the Colonial period were major border walks and summits in the Mani region and in the Uman region south of Merida, both in 1815 (ANEY 1826ii:34–36; AGN-*Tierras*, 1419, 2:55–56; Restall 1997a:193–200, 218–255; see Hill 1992 for highland Guatemala parallels).

17. Each copy of the 1557 Mani Land Treaty was accompanied by a variant copy of this map; this version was the one maintained by the Yaxakumche branch of the Xiu dynasty (see Table 11.5).

18. See Ringle and Bey's able navigation through these waters (Chapter 9 in this volume), as well as Roys (1957:3); Farriss (1984:147–148); Marcus (1993); Quezada (1993:32–58); and Restall (1997a:39–40, 169–177).

19. On the administrative evolution of the colony, see Farriss (1984:Chapters 3, 5); Patch (1993:Chapters 2–3); Quezada (1993:Chapters 2–4; 1997:Chapter 6); Bracamonte (1994:Chapter 1); and Restall (1997a:Chapters 3, 5, 13). On the survival of extra-Colonial independent Maya communities and their struggle to stay independent in the face of Spanish and Colonial-Maya hostility, see Scholes and Roys (1948:Chapter 11); and Jones (1989; 1998).

20. For a complementary model presented in far greater detail and representing a sophisticated attempt to reconcile Classic-period and Conquest-period evidence, see Marcus (1993).

21. Nahua elites who lead the native auxiliaries of invading Spaniards from central Mexico, primarily from the Montejo *encomienda* of Azcapotzalco, also received *indio hidalgo* status, but they were absorbed into Spanish/mestizo society, not the Maya world.

22. *Don* was an appropriated Spanish title applied by the Maya to *indios hidalgos*, to *batabob*, and to former *batabob*; there are various examples throughout this chapter and in Ringle and Bey (Chapter 9 in this volume); also see Restall (1997a:46, 91–94).

23. TC:13, 16, 17, 18, 20, 30, 31, 32, 38; Restall (1998a:87, 88, 89, 90, 91, 92, 98, 102). There are references to slavery in the *Books of Chilam Balam*, but the term used, *munal*, is somewhat ambiguous, and the contexts are that of bondage in a general rather than a specific or detailed sense. The *Tizimin* uses *u munal* five times and the *Chumayel* uses *u munal*, *u munnal*, and *ah mun* once each; in all eight instances Edmonson glosses the term as "slavery" or "slaves" (1982:38, 62, 99, 104; 1986:247, 98, 240), but Roys glosses the *Chumayel* variants as "tender boy" or "young maize plant," "slaves," and "tender green shoot" respectively (1933:115, 76, 112). As *munal* does not appear as such in the Colonial dictionaries, Roys' uncertainty is understandable, although Edmonson's consistent use of "slave" is more helpful. A clumsy but more accurate translation would be "tender, young man or boy, subordinated or possibly enslaved." All of this may help to illuminate the *Chilam Balam* passages in question, but it does not tell us much about the role of slavery in Maya society. I can find no *Chilam Balam* use of the less ambiguous terms used in the Calkini text.

24. There is slave reference in another ethnohistorical source, the *Title of Acalan-Tixchel*, but it comes in a passage for which we have only the Spanish translation (Restall 1998a:70), and I suspect the term in the lost Maya page was one of the terms that appears elsewhere in this text, such as *chanbel uinicob*, "subject people." Nevertheless, the context of the reference is relevant, being the raiding of uncolonized Maya communities by the semicolonized Chontal Mayas under don Pablo Paxbolon in the late sixteenth century; the captives kept fleeing back to their original homes, "because they were [i.e., had been made] slaves of the ruler and the other principal men." Even if the Maya term that the Spanish notary glossed as "slaves" was in fact "subjects," this kind of low-grade warfare between communities was probably the way in which notable opponents were enslaved in other parts of Yucatan during the Segmented Century.

25. Schele and Freidel (1990:360–61, 370) asserted that the term was used in Chichen Itza, but this reading has since been re-evaluated (Stephen Houston, personal communication). On Peten, see Jones (1998:104–105). *Multepal* is usually translated as "joint rule" or "joint government" (e.g., Brinton 1882:103; Craine and Reindorp 1979:139; Marcus 1993; Roys 1962:72, 74, 76), but Edmonson has glossed it as "crowd rule" (1982:10; 1986:54), and I have suggested "factional rule" (1998a:141). The rare incidence of the term in ethnohistorical sources (as far as I can find, one each in the *Books of Chilam Balam of Chumayel*, *Mani*, and *Tizimin*; source just cited) means it should be used with caution. The term may effectively describe a long-lasting principle in Maya court/government culture, but it does not necessarily convey the full picture of the governmental system. A relevant and illuminating parallel can be found in the Maya's own terminology of inheritance, encapsulated in the terms *cetil* and *multial*, "even distribution" and "joint ownership"; the application of both principles of inheritance represented Maya attempts to recognize both the rights of individual family members to inherit property and the importance of group inclusion and integrity (Restall 1997a:110–120). With respect to government, *multepal* reflected the latter, with the group being the courtly nexus of dynastic and elite family members; the sibling principle (and here the analogy is loosely drawn) was the right of individual elites, especially the dominant men of a dynasty, to inherit status and office.

26. Some forty Xiu and other court members were slaughtered in Cocom territory while en route to perform a rain-bringing ceremony at Chichen Itza. The massacre was rooted in a Xiu-Cocom feud going back to the fall of Mayapan and renewed by a 1533 Xiu alliance with invading Spaniards; it sparked several years of warfare in the Mani-Sotuta region. The drawing reproduced in Figure 11.8 is a seventeenth-century etching printed in Cogolludo (1867–1868, 3:VI) and probably based on a lost sixteenth-century commemorative drawing. Maya accounts of the Otzmal massacre are in two *Chilam Balam* books (CBM:136; Craine and Reindorp 1979:187–188; Roys 1933:138), in the *Annals of Oxkutzcab* (XC:154), and in one of the *relaciones* contributions by Gaspar Antonio Chi (whose father was among the Otzmal victims; RHGY, I:318). Spanish accounts include Cogolludo (3, VI) and Landa (XIV). See also Restall (1998a:40, 81, 144, 149).

27. On the Xiu succession up to 1548, see Morley and Roys (1941:120–148); Cortez (1995:237–242); also Figure 11.6 and Table 11.5 in this chapter.

28. Both *halach uinic* Montejo Xiu and another Xiu *batab* (don Juan of Hunacti) were removed from office for six months, fined twenty pesos, and given fifty lashes (AGI-*Justicia* 248, 2; Scholes and Adams 1938; Quezada 1993:134, 150).

29. Chi was a Xiu noble by maternal descent and a staunch defender of the dynasty, but he was raised and pursued a career largely in the orbit of Landa and the colonists (Restall 1998a:Chapter 8); Be's term of office (Quezada 1993:196) marked the first time since the fall of Mayapan that Mani had been ruled by a non-Xiu.

30. On evidence of Pech court continuities, some from the fall of Mayapan through the eighteenth century, see Quezada (1993:187–191); Restall (1997a:92–97, 281–292; 1998a:Chapter 6); and Ringle and Bey, Chapter 9 in this volume, Figure 9.1.

31. A fuller version of the argument presented in this section is in Restall (2001).

32. Okoshi Harada suggests this (1993:14–18). There is similar directional confusion in the Landa version (see Table 11.6).

33. Brinton (1882:110); Roys (1933:88; 1943:59, 151); Thompson (1970:23); Edmonson (1982:38); Coe (1993:171); Sharer (1994:406). Variations on the theme have Zuyua in the Tabasco region (Carmack 1981:46; Okoshi Harada 1993:5) and the Peten Itza region (Jones 1998:7). Zuyua's central Mexican location could be inferred from the claim in Cakchiquel Maya sources that lineage ancestors came from "Tulan, Zuyua"; however, such sources also claim that local elites were descended from Abraham and the ancient Israelites (see, e.g., the Xpantzay primordial titles from Tecpan); Recinos (1984:120–121, 168–169).

34. Nonoual might be derived from Nonohual, the name of a mountain adjacent to Tula, although Brinton (1882:109–124), Carmack (1981:46), and Okoshi Harada (1993:4) argue that Nonoual is the Chontal area. Cartabona appears to be an altered Spanish place-name, possibly based on Cartagena (Edmonson 1986:101 proposes Constantinople). Viroa Chacunescab is also obscure; Edmonson (1986:103) proposes that Viroa is a Maya reduction of Babylonia, whereas Roys (1933:80) opts for Chacunescab as the name of a member of the Tutul Xiu *chibal*.

35. Statement made in Maya in Valladolid, written down in Spanish; reproduced in Brinton (1882:114–118); Quezada (1997:214–216); quoted at length in

Roys (1962:66 and erroneously dated 1718). The Maya witness cites local Kauil and Caamal noblemen as sources.

36. The supposed source of the Maya patronym is the Nahuatl word *xihuitl*, which means both "grass" and "year." There is a Maya term, *xiu*, meaning "plant," but arguably, as Karttunen suggests, "one would expect the Maya form of such a loan to be *xiuit*, and in fact *xiuit* appears as a common noun in the Chilam Balam of Tizimin apparently meaning 'year'" (1985:10). It is therefore just as likely that *xiu* and *xihuitl* are derived from a common Mesoamerican origin. The only personal name in Maya origin mythology that could be Nahuatl is Auxaual, but the four principal men who are named as his cosettlers have distinctly Yucatec and Chontal Maya names (see Table 11.1).

37. The evidence relating to patronyms has both linguistic and ethnic implications; the lack of non-Maya patronyms in Yucatan, especially among the allegedly foreign elite *chibalob*, reflects the fact that Yucatec Maya contains a very modest quantity of words derived from Nahuatl—and some of those are either derived from common Mesoamerican origins or entered the language under post-Conquest Spanish mediation (Karttunen 1985; Restall 1997a:Chapter 22). Linguistic evidence, in fact, "strongly supports indirect and mediated contact" between Yucatan and central Mexico before the Spanish invasion, not "direct and sustained contact" (Karttunen 1985:14). Likewise there is no evidence, either from the Colonial or modern periods, of ethnic differences between the Maya *chibalob* of alleged foreign origins and the peninsula's other *chibalob*—although the issue has yet to be studied using biological methods.

38. An important additional component to the development and perpetuation of the myth, and the perception of its historicity, is the longtime hegemony of the Toltec invasion paradigm in which "two radically different pre-Columbian people" (Jones 1997:285) clashed, producing a new Mexican-Maya elite (Clendinnen 1987:149; Coe 1993:155; Gillespie 1989:201–207; Morley 1946:211–212; Thompson 1956:99–105; Tozzer 1957:128–129) whose origins even inspired them to capitulate early to the Spaniards (Farriss 1984:245; Roys 1933:192–199; 1957:41). Of relevance here is the suggestion by Jones (1997) that the binary global politics of World War II and the Cold War provided a cultural context that nurtured this vision of ancient Yucatan; also relevant may be a broader Western perception, rooted in Colonial times, of a cultural and material dichotomy between central Mexico and the Maya area. The Toltec invasion interpretation has, of course, been well undermined by recent archaeological scholarship (Gillespie 1989:207; Jones 1995, 1998:7–16; Ringle 1990; Sabloff and Andrews 1986; Sabloff and Henderson 1993; Sharer 1994:338–408).

39. For other examples, both from Mesoamerica and from other cultures, see Sahlins (1981); Lincoln (1991); Chatterjee (1998); and Christensen (1999).

40. The Pech texts refer to local pagan priests as "the Itza priests" (*ytza u yah kinob*; TY:6r; Restall 1998a:121), whereas the *Books of Chilam Balam* make various references to Itza priests and Itza migration mythology (e.g., CBC:20; Restall 1998a:134). Similarly the Canul ancestors of the Calkini myth were imbued with sacredness by passing through Itza territory. This passage is quoted above; in the original Calkini text a Maya/Christian cross (all four arms of equal length) is drawn in by the word *ytza* (TC:36). Although the Itzas are also called foreigners in the *Chilam Balam* literature, there are no specific references to their place of origin;

if anything, the Itzas are associated with places within Yucatan rather than outside it (CBC:20, 22; CBM:135–136; Restall 1998a:134, 136, 141). Itza "otherness" is thus primarily achieved through associations of sacredness (although in other *Chilam Balam* passages there is an equation made between the Itzas and the Spaniards as bringers of warfare and related disasters; Restall 1998a:41–43). For a discussion of the connection of the term "Itza" to sacredness and shamanism, see Jones (1998:428–429).

41. For a discussion of spatial metaphors in contexts of cultural interaction and "otherness," see Ouellet (1998). Henige (1982:90) calls origin tales "the major metaphors." On the pre-Conquest tradition of the transcendency of rulers, see Houston and Stuart (1996); Inomata and Houston (2001, Chapter 1 in Volume 1 of this series).

42. TCH:15; Restall (1998a:124). "I also built my home, a house of stone, to the north of the church. The Maya people [i.e., the commoners] may not say one day that it belongs to them; this is why I make it clear that I did not build it for them" (*Bay xan licix in betic in uotoch pakil na tu xaman iglesia ma u yalic maya uinicob ua utialtob tu kinil lay tumen ci chicil besic hebix in mentah ma ilobe*).

43. A forthcoming doctoral dissertation by Christopher Nichols of Tulane University details this change in Tekax in the late eighteenth and early nineteenth centuries.

44. *Ajaw* goes back at least as far as the Classic period (Houston and Stuart, Chapter 3 in Volume 1), but *halach uinic* seems to be a Post-Classic development.

Contributors

Joseph W. Ball is Professor of Anthropology at San Diego State University, where he has been a faculty member since 1975. He holds Ph.D. and M.A. degrees in anthropology from the University of Wisconsin–Madison. Ball is Project Co-Director and Ceramic Analyst for the SDSU Mopan-Macal Triangle Archaeology Project, a position he has held since 1983. His research interests include behavioral reconstructions based on contextual analysis; the use of ceramics in sociocultural analysis and socioprocessual reconstructions; the functional analysis of chipped-stone implements; and the archaeology of the early Milling-stone cultures of Southern California. Ball currently is copreparing an extensive set of final papers and monographs on the 1984–1992 SDSU Mopan-Macal Triangle Project.

George J. Bey III is associate professor of anthropology at Millsaps College. He was educated at the University of the Americas, University of New Mexico (B.A., 1977) and Tulane University (M.A., 1984; Ph.D., 1986). His research interests are the development of complex societies in Mesoamerica and ceramic analysis. He has directed an archaeological project at Tula, Hidalgo, and between 1984 and 1999 has served as codirector of the Ek Balam Archaeological Project in northeastern Yucatan. He is presently co-director of the Kiuic Archaeological Project in the southern Puuc region of Yucatan. His publications include the introductory chapter to *Ceramic Production and Distribution: An Integrated Approach*, edited by G. Bey and C. Pool (Boulder: Westview Press, 1992); "Classic to Post-Classic at Ek Balam, Yucatan: Architectural and Ceramic Evidence for Defining the Transition" (with C. Hanson and W. Ringle) (*Latin American Antiquity* 8(3) [1997]); and "The Ceramic Chronology of Ek Balam, Yucatan, Mexico" (with T. Bond et al.) (*Ancient Mesoamerica* 9(1) [1998]).

Geoffrey E. Braswell (Ph.D., Tulane, 1996) is Assistant Professor in the Department of Anthropology at State University of New York at Buffalo and has previously served as Profesor Titular Visitante at the Universidad Autónoma de Yucatán and as Catedrático Fulbright at the Universidad del Valle de Guatemala. He has conducted field and laboratory research at Chichen Itza, Copan, and numerous sites in the Guatemalan highlands, including Kaminaljuyu. His interests include prehistoric exchange in the Maya region and lower Central America, lithic analysis, geoarchaeology, obsidian hydration dating, and Maya ethnohistory and linguistics.

Arlen F. Chase is Professor of Anthropology at the University of Central Florida. He received his B.A. from the University of Pennsylvania in 1975 and his Ph.D. from the same institution in 1983 ("A Contextual Consideration of the Tayasal-Paxcaman Zone, El Peten, Guatemala"). His research interests focus on archaeological method and theory in the Maya area with particular emphasis on urbanism and ethnicity, hieroglyphic interpretation, settlement patterns, and ceramic and contextual analysis. After working in Mexico and Guatemala, he began archaeological research in Belize in 1978; since 1985 he has codirected research at the Classic-period site of Caracol in the country on an annual basis. He has published numerous articles and a half-dozen monographs and books, many with Diane Z. Chase, to whom he has been married for twenty-five years. He is currently working on a book, being coauthored with D.Z. Chase, called *Maya Archaeology*.

Diane Z. Chase is Professor of Anthropology at the University of Central Florida. She received her B.A. from the University of Pennsylvania in 1975 and her Ph.D. from the same institution in 1982 ("Spatial and Temporal Variability in Postclassic Northern Belize"). Her research interests focus on archaeological method and theory in the Maya area with particular emphasis on complex societies and hermeneutics, ethnohistory, and ceramic and mortuary analysis. For the last seventeen years, she has codirected excavations at Caracol, Belize; before that she directed a seven-year project at Santa Rita Corozal in the same country. She has authored scores of articles, as well as *Investigations at the Classic Maya City of Caracol, Belize* (1987, with A.F. Chase), *A Postclassic Perspective* (1988; with A.F. Chase), *Mesoamerican Elites: An Archaeological Assessment* (1992; 1994; edited with A.F. Chase), and *Studies in the Archaeology of Caracol, Belize* (1994; with A.F. Chase).

John Clark is Professor of Anthropology at Brigham Young University and director of the New World Archaeological Foundation. His research interests include ancient technologies, political economy, social evolution, and political thought.

Joel D. Gunn studies global change as it influences regional cultures and how they are reflected in material remains. His research has focused on the apparent inverse relationship between florescence in the Maya lowlands and Western Europe as case studies on the opposite sides of the Bermuda-Azores high. The analysis of stone tools provides important insights into the Maya collapse, a possible local manifestation of global change. Gunn is an adjunct faculty member of the Department of Anthropology, University of North Carolina, and an archaeological research consultant.

Richard D. Hansen is an Assistant Research Scientist with the Institute of Geophysics and Planetary Physics at UCLA. He also is the director of the Foundation for Anthropological Research and Environmental Studies (FARES). He received a Ph.D. in archaeology from UCLA in 1992, and previously received B.S. degrees in Spanish and archaeology (1978) and an M.S. in anthropology (1984) from Brigham Young University. At UCLA he was National Graduate Fellow (1987–1988), a Jacob Javits Fellow (1988–92), the UCLA Distinguished Scholar (1988), a Fulbright Scholar (1990), and UCLA Outstanding Graduate Student (1991). He has conducted archaeological research in Israel, the U.S. Great Basin, the U.S. Southwest, and Central America. Hansen is currently the director of the Regional Archaeological Investigation of the North Peten, Guatemala (RAINPEG), project in the Mirador Basin of the northern Peten. His research interests include the origin and development of complex societies, ancient subsistence strategies, environmental adaptations, archaeological method and theory, and Maya sculpture and architecture.

Peter D. Harrison received his Ph.D. from the University of Pennsylvania in 1970. His fieldwork in the Maya area included fifty months at Tikal, Guatemala; four seasons of survey in Quintana Roo, Mexico; and two seasons investigating ancient agriculture at Pulltrouser Swamp in Belize. Besides ancient economy, Harrison's major interests are in architectural form and function and the uses of space in Maya architecture. Current affiliations include Research Associate, MARI (Tulane); Research Associate, American Division, University of Pennsylvania Museum; and Research Professor, Maxwell Museum of Anthropology, University of New Mexico.

William J. Folan is the Director and Research Professor of the Centro de Investigaciones Históricas y Sociales of the Universidad Autónoma de Campeche, Mexico. He received his Ph.D. in anthropology from Southern Illinois University (1972). His research interests include anthropology in general, archaeology, paleoclimatology, paleohydrology, ethnobotany, and ecology in Mexico and the Northwest coast of Canada. He has 220 publications. He has presented papers and organized symposia in various countries. He is currently the director of el Peten Campechano: Su Pasado, Presente y Futuro project.

Stephen D. Houston is an archaeologist who serves as Jesse Knight University Professor at Brigham Young University. His research focuses on Maya glyphic decipherment, monumental architecture, Classic Maya religion, and sacred kingship. Most of his archaeological fieldwork has taken place in Guatemala, where he has codirected the Piedras Negras Project, an interdisciplinary study of urban genesis and collapse in a tropical zone. His publications include *History and Hieroglyphs at Dos Pilas*, *Classic Maya Place Names* (with David Stuart), and an edited volume entitled *Function and Meaning in Classic Maya Architecture*. He is now at work on a book, *Ancient Maya Writing*, to be coauthored with D. Stuart, and a joint effort with Takeshi Inomata on Classic Maya civilization.

Takeshi Inomata is Assistant Professor of Anthropology at the University of Arizona. He received his M.A. from the University of Tokyo in 1988 and completed his Ph.D. at Vanderbilt University in 1995. He conducted field research at the Classic Maya center of Aguateca, Guatemala, from 1990 to 1999, focusing on the excavation of artifact-rich burned structures. He has also worked in Honduras, Peru, and Japan. His research interests include the development of complex societies, warfare and social change, spatial analysis, and household archaeology.

Mary Miller currently directs the Bonampak Documentation Project. She is the author of the recent *Art and Architecture of the Maya* (1999), as well as *The Art of Mesoamerica* (1986; 1996) and *The Murals of Bonampak* (1986), and coauthor (with Karl Taube) of *The Gods and Symbols of Ancient Mexico and the Maya: A Dictionary of Mesoamerican Religion* (1993) and (with Linda Schele) *The Blood of Kings* (1986). In 1998 she was named Vincent Scully Professor of the History of Art at Yale University, where she is also Master of Saybrook College.

Matthew Restall was educated at Oxford University and UCLA and is now Associate Professor of Colonial Latin American History at Pennsylvania State University. His publications include *Life and Death in a Maya Community: The Ixil Testaments of the 1760s* (1995), *The Maya World: Yucatec Culture and Society, 1550–1850* (1997), and *Maya Conquistador* (1998). He is currently writing a book on

Africans in colonial Yucatan while working on various projects having to do with Maya history.

William Ringle, Professor of Anthropology at Davidson College, Davidson, received his Ph.D. in 1985 from Tulane University. His fieldwork has focused on the northern Maya lowlands, where he currently codirects the Kivic project. Previous fieldwork includes settlement work at Komchen, El Mirador, Ek Balam and Labna. In addition to interests in political and community organization, he also maintains a strong interest in the pre- and post-Columbian historical records.

María del Rosario Domínguez Carrasco is a Research Professor at El Centro de Investigaciones Históricas y Sociales of the Universidad Autónoma de Campeche, Mexico, and also serves as a member of El Facultad de Derecho and Humanidades at the same university. She received her *licenciatura* in archaeology from La Escuela Nacional de Antropología e Historia, Mexico (1993). Her research interests include the analysis of ceramics and lithics. She has 28 publications and has presented papers in Mexico, the United States, and Guatemala. She is currently participating in the Peten Campechano: Su Pasado, Presente y Futuro project.

Jennifer T. Taschek is Adjunct Professor of Anthropology at San Diego State University. She holds Ph.D. and M.A. degrees in anthropology from the University of Wisconsin–Madison and a B.A. in the same discipline from Bryn Mawr College. Taschek is project codirector and field director of the SDSU Mopan-Macal Triangle Archaeology Project, a position she has held since 1983. Her research interests include architectural and spatial analyses of cultural behavior; the use of space in sociocultural analysis and reconstruction; and the use of architectural-artifactual associations in sociocultural analysis and reconstruction. Taschek currently is copreparing an extensive set of final papers and monographs on the 1984–1992 SDSU Mopan-Macal Triangle Project.

Loa Traxler is Assistant Curator of Pre-Columbian Studies at Dumbarton Oaks, Washington, D.C. She will receive her doctorate from the University of Pennsylvania based on her research with the University of Pennsylvania Museum excavations at the Acropolis of Copan, Honduras. Her interests focus on the architectural evolution of Maya centers and the nature of sociopolitical organization of these societies. As an archaeologist and surveyor Traxler has worked on other projects in the U.S. Southwest and the Near East.

Juan Antonio Valdés is Professor at the Universidad de San Carlos de Guatemala. He received his doctorate in archaeology from the Sorbonne in 1983, and served as the General Director of El Patrimonio Cultural de Guatemala and as the Director of El Instituto de Antropología e Historia de Guatemala. His research interests include architecture and the use of space. He has participated in various archaeological projects in the Maya area as director and investigator, including Tikal, Copan, Uaxactun, Petexbatun, and Kaminaljuyu. Valdés has published six books and numerous articles on Maya civilization. His most recent book is *Reyes, Tumbas y Palacios: La Historia Dinástica de Uaxactun* (1999).

Index

Abaj Takalik, 153
Acropolis, 14, 138
  at Buenavista del Cayo, 175
  Calakmul and its architectural
    components, 229–244
  and Caracol, 108, 118–120
  and Copan, 54–68
  and MFC pattern, 30
  thrones and throne structures of Tikal,
    74–101
  and Tikal, 146
Adams, R.E.W., 228
Adoratorios, 235, 278, 279
Agricultural past, invoking of by rulers, 203
Agrinier, Pierre, 9–11
Aguateca
  exterior throne at, 156–158, 157(fig.),
    158(fig.)
  palaces of, 151–152, 152(fig.)
Ajaw (ajawa')
  as a class in Maya Highlands, 311–312,
    324
  and Bonampak mural, 210, 211(fig.)
  as Divine component in middle of triad,
    254
Ajpop, 312–313
Ajtz'ib' (scribe or painter), 311
Akhenaten, 185
Alvarado, Pedro de, 308, 325
Amaq', 320–321, 326
American Anthropological Association
  symposium, 165
Andrews, E. Wyllys V, 235
Andrews, George, 229
Annals of the Cakchiquels, 309, 310, 318, 322,
  324
Archaeoastronomy, 190, 199–200, 230, 231,
  316, 326
Archaeology
  and Copan, 68, 69
  of Guatemalan highlands and issues up
    to 1970s, 313–314
  in highlands, 313–318
  and interpretation of data, 104–105
  and the people of Caracol's royal court,
    128–130
Architecture
  and architectonic complexes and
    political and social organization,
    316–317, 326
  and the Calakmul Acropolis, 229–244
  and Caracol, 107–124
  and Colonial restriction of monumental
    to religious buildings, 341
  court, 275–287
  developed by Ruler 2 of Copan, 62–65
  during late Early Classic period, 149
  and Early Classic court at Copan, 53–55
  of early kingship, 1–45
  and east-west versus north-south site
    arrangement, 18
  and innovations in San José Mogote, 13
  and palace groupings at Tikal, 76
  and Palenque palace, 202–204
  and personal attire, 204
  and politics at Copan, 66–68
  and "radial pyramid-temple complex"
    of western central highland, 318
  and royal compound of K'inich Yax
    K'uk' Mo', 55–58
  and royal court and household, 48–49
  and segmental components of site
    centers, 280–281, 284, 287
  and tandem-traverse room pattern, 89
  and transition from royal compounds to
    palaces at Chiapa de Corzo, 25–26
  triadic temple, 17, 22, 34, 253, 254–255,
    256–257
  and unification with sculpture and
    painting, 140

395

and vaulted multiroomed structures and Late Pre-Classic, 139
See also "E-group" architectural arrangement; Later Pre-Classic and Protoclassic architectural patterns; Middle Formative Chiapas (MFC) architectural pattern; Middle Pre-Classic royal compounds
Arnaud, Marie-Charlotte, 317–318, 326
Artisans, 310
Astronomy, 190, 199–200, 230, 231
and Q'umarkaj as cosmogram, 316, 326
Attire, 204, 206(fig.)
Audiencia, 191, 191(fig.), 200(n19)
Auxaual, 371–372
Avila Chi, Rubentino, 227
Awe, Jaimie, 186
Aztecs
and comparison of *chinamit* and *calpulli*, 319, 326
and duty of stone, 204
and *huehuetl* drum, 214
and influence on Late Post-Classic Guatemalan sites, 314
and invoking of past of nomadic hunters and gatherers, 203
and jade and quetzal feathers, 219

Balam Na temple, 247, 248–249
Ball, Joseph, 165–200
Ballcourt Marker of Tikal, 149
Ballcourts
and association with temples, 280
at Cahal Pech and Buenavista, 180–185, 182(fig.), 183(fig.), 184(fig.)
and center-point cache, North Ballcourt, Buenavista, 183(fig.), 184, 184(fig.), 198(n8)
Batabil, 269
Baudez, Claude-François, 54
Be, Francisco, 368
Belize
and connection with Tikal, 19, 192
Valley region, 171
and Xuanantunich as Late Classic zonal focus of royal ancestral veneration, 188, 196–197(n3), 199(n15), 200nn 20, 21
See also Buenavista; Cahal Pech; Caracol royal court
Benches, 77–79
associated with Bonampak murals, 204
and Caracol, 108–110
during the Late Classic period, 150
and Tikal, 86–89

Berlin, Heinrich, 224, 229, 255
Betanzos, Pedro de, 312–313
Bey, George, 266–307
Binford, Lewis and Sally, 235
Bishop, Ronald, 127, 179, 240, 245
Blanton, Richard, 13
Bonampak, architecture of, 202, 204
Bonampak murals, 51, 342
battle scene, 215–219
and Chan Murwan, 208, 213, 217, 218(fig.), 219
and depiction of emotion, 210
and idealization of actual life, 207–208, 221
and jade and quetzal feathers, 219
life at court depicted in murals of, 201–221
and lords paying tribute (Room 1), 210, 211(fig.), 212(fig.)
and lords preparing for celebration, 210–211, 212(fig.)
and the Maize God, 215
and music, 213–215, 214(fig.)
and northeast corner of Room 1, 215, 216(fig.)
and parasols, 215
and ritual of dancing, 213–214
Room 1, 206(fig.), 210–215, 220
Room 2, 215–219, 216(fig.), 218(fig.)
Room 3, 214, 217, 219–221, 219(fig.), 220(fig.)
and singing, 215
and Structure 1 that holds, 204, 205(fig.), 207, 207(fig)
and Uaxactun murals, 209–210, 209(fig.)
visually narrative quality of, 213
"Book of generations," 342–343
Books. *See* Texts
Books of Chilam Balam, 338, 342, 343, 370
and dynastic origins myth, 371–372, 389–390(n40)
and references to slaves, 387(n23)
ritual reading of, 345
and socioeconomic status, 358
and Zuyua, 372
Borrowing or diffusion and Pre-Classic Maya, 32–35
Braswell, Geoffrey, 255, 308–334
Bricker, Victoria, 268
Brown, Kenneth, 315, 321
Budet, Dorie, 179
Buenavista-Cahal Pech royal court, 165–200
and alternatives to identity argument, 186–187

and argument of two independent centers, 186, 198–199(n11)
and ballcourts, 180–185, 182(fig.), 183(fig.)
and Buenavista as regal-ritual center, 172–174, 187, 199(n14)
and Buenavista as "winter palace," 190
and Buenavista "palace school" style of ceramics, 174–175, 174(fig.)
and Cahal Pech as regal-residential center, 172–174, 186–187, 199(n14)
and Cahal Pech as three season palace, 190
and configurations and dimensions of courtyards and surrounding rooms, 176–178, 177(fig.), 197(n6)
and "court mobility" definition, 166
and definition of "court," 168
and distinction between "holding court" and conducting business, 166–167
and identity of the courts, 176–186, 188–193, 197(n5)
and identity or difference of pottery vessels and assemblages, 179–180
and map and description of Buenavista del Cayo, 171–172, 172(fig.), 175, 188–190, 189(fig.)
and map and description of Cahal Pech, 171–172, 171(fig.), 175, 188–190, 189(fig.)
and map and description of overall area, 170–171, 171(fig.)
and North Plaza Group as *audiencia*, 191, 191(fig.)
and "palace" definition, 165, 168
and palace of Buenavista and community-oriented activities, 175–176
and palace of Cahal Pech and personal activities of regal residence, 175
and reasons for palaces in dual locations, 187–192
and regnal burial comparisons, 180, 181(fig.), 185, 197–198(n7)
and seasonal cycle between locations, 166–167
and shifting of dynastic seat between locations, 167–168, 180–181
and social-political grade or rank, 176
and spatial proximity and its implications, 187–188
and topographic separation and climatic "distance," 188–192, 189(fig.)
and travel time between, 188, 199(n16)
and viewing of the solstice, 190, 199–200(n18)
See also Ballcourts; Ceramics; Xuanantunich
Buenavista del Cayo, 165–200
Buikstra, Jane, 57, 58, 60
Burials
and Calakmul, 239–240, 256
and Caracol, 117, 118, 119, 123, 127–130, 128(fig.), 129(fig.), 133
and funerary complex of Yax Pasah, 153
and K'iche', 317
and K'inich Yax K'uk' Mo', 57, 58, 61
and Later Pre-Classic and Protoclassic patterns, 18
of local and nonlocal personages, 57–58
of possible wife of K'inich Yax K'uk' Mo', 60
regnal, comparisons between Cahal Pech and Buenavista, 175, 180, 181(fig.), 185
and royal compound at Copan, 57–58, 69
of royal personages at Chiapa de Corzo, 7, 31

Caamal, Au Kul, 370
Caana Palace, 110–116, 110(fig.)
main court, 113–115
midrange palace, 111–113, 111(fig.)
and stone axe found in, 112(fig.), 113
temple, 226
Cabildo (municipal council), 361
Cah, 349–350
Cahal Pech, 19, 22, 165–200
See also Buenavista-Cahal Pech royal court
Calakmul Biosphere Reserve, 228
Calakmul royal court complex, 139, 223–265
and abandonment following drought around A.D. 900, 229, 244
Acropolis of and architectural components in Classic period, 230–234, 231(fig.), 232(fig.), 233(fig.)
Acropolis of and architectural components in Pre-Classic period, 229–230, 230(fig.)
and activity areas of Structure II, 236–237, 237(fig.), 240–244, 241(fig.), 242(fig.), 243(fig.), 246, 247(fig.)
and activity areas of Structure III, 235–236, 236(fig.), 246, 248(fig.)
and architecture in Early Classic period, 143–144

and Building II-B palace, 251–252, 252(fig.), 255–256
and ceramics, 227, 238–239, 245, 252
"Chronological Sequence of Calakmul, Compeche, Mexico," 226, 226(table)
and comparison with Noh Cah Santa Cruz society, 247–253, 256
cultural setting of, 227–229
demographic analysis of, 227
and detailed artifact recording, 235–236
and Divine King, 251
and ethnohistory and ethnology, 244–253
and figurines, 239, 245–246, 247(fig.), 248(fig.)
and human skeletal material, 240, 241(fig.)
and Late-Classic carried forward into Terminal Classic, 257
and links with highland Mexico during Terminal Classic, 238
and lithics, 236, 252, 254
and musical instruments, 245, 246, 247(fig.), 248(fig.)
and *ox-té-tun* symbolism, 223, 254, 256
and paucity of trade with centers outside Yucatan, 240
physical description and maps of, 223, 224(fig.), 227, 228(fig.)
and pyramidal usage as architectural metaphor of hierarchical society, 252–253, 254
and regal burials, 239–240
sociopolitical and economic organization of, 225
and symbolic center of summit of Structure II, 253
and symbolism of Structure III., 254–255
and tool kits, 242–244, 243(fig.)
and triadic design and social cosmology, 220, 253, 254–255, 256–257
and triadic Temple VII, 229, 230(fig.)
Calkini, 245, 255
and Canche family, 365–366, 366(fig.)
and Spanish and Nahua visit to court of in 1541, 335–336, 383–384(n1)
Campbell, Mark, 186
Campeche, 228, 344, 349
See also Calakmul royal court complex
Canche, Napot, 337, 347
patio of, 341
plaza of, 344
Canche dynastic family, 365–366, 366(fig.)
Candelaria River, 229
Cannon, Aubrey, 254
Canul, Nadzaycab, 344

Canul dynastic family and purported origin in West Zuyua, 371–372
Capitals, regional, 31–32
observations of, 14–15
Caracol royal court, 47, 102–134, 257
archaeological fieldwork in, 107
and archaeology and people, 128–130
and burials, 117, 118, 119, 123, 128–130, 128(fig.), 129(fig.), 133
and dietary analysis, 127, 128–130
and economics, administration, and infrastructure, 130–132, 134
and graffiti of person being carried on palanquin, 115, 127(fig.)
and history and epigraphy, 125–126, 125(fig.)
and iconography, 126–128, 127(fig.), 128(fig.)
map of central portion of, 105(fig.)
palaces of, 107–124, 133
Barrio, 120–122, 121(fig.), 132
Caana, 110–116, 110fig., 111(fig.), 112(fig.)
the Caracol Palace Sample, 107–110
and Central Acropolis, 118–119, 118(fig.)
C Group, 122–123, 123(fig.)
different kinds of, 107–108
and South Acropolis, 119–120, 119(fig.)
and special palace compound entryways, 108, 109(fig.)
and Structures B4, B5, and B6, 116–118, 117(fig.)
people in court of, 124–132
and portraits of sovereigns, 105–106
temples in, 107, 110, 114, 117
and use of epicentral buildings for royal court, 105–107
variability in benches of, 108–110
See also Burials, and Caracol; Caana
Carbon-14 dating. See radiocarbon dating
Carmack, Robert, 310, 317
and *chinamita'* as a feudal estate, 319
and inherited priestly roles, 312
and leadership roles among K'iche', 313
and Mayan books, 311
and *nimja* council houses, 317
Carnegie Institution
and Copan, 53, 55
and excavation at Uaxactun, 21
and project at Mayapan, 286
Carramiñana, 231
Carrasco, Domínguez, 223–265
Carsten, Janet, 287, 297
Caste War, 365

Ceh Peh courts, 272
Ceiba tree. *See* Trees
Ceramics
  and break between Late and Terminal Classic period, 244–245
  and Buenavista del Cayo "palace school" style, 174–175, 174(fig.)
  at Calakmul, 227, 238–239, 245, 252
  and depiction of tamales, 203
  evidence from Mayapan, 277
  from Iximché, 315, 326
  and linkage of Buenavista and Cahal Pech Late Classic and Terminal palaces, 179
Cerrito de la Campana, 239
Cerros and Str. 5C–2a, 139, 142, 146
Chajoma'
  burial patterns of, 317
  capitals of, 323
  royal court of, 322
Chanel Balam of Tamarindito, 152
Chan Murwan, 208, 213, 217, 218(fig.), 219
Chase, Arlen and Diane, 102–137, 225–226
Cheek, Charles, 54, 55
Chel dynastic family, 365
Chi, Gaspar Antonio, 368, 370, 388(nn 26, 29)
  and dynastic origin rivalries, 372
  and former homes of nobles, 286
  and Xiu Family Tree, 351
Chiapa de Corzo, 3, 6(fig.), 12, 24–30
  and burials of royal personages, 7, 31
  and Early Middle Pre-Classic period, 6–8
  and early palace and its destruction, 25–30, 26(fig.), 27(fig.), 44–45(n8)
  and Later Pre-Classic and Postclassic patterns, 24–30
  and La Venta, 6, 7, 8, 14–15
  as oldest continuously occupied city in Western Hemisphere, 6
  and Olmec influence, 7, 24
  and periodic relocation of royal residence, 17
  and pottery assemblage, 29(fig.)
  and shifts in royal compounds and architecture during Late Pre-Classic, 34
  site plan of ceremonial center of Protoclassic, 25(fig.)
Chiapas, 1, 3, 4, 6, 11, 32
Chichen Itza, 158, 235, 318
  and antiquity of name Cocom, 372
  and continuation of sacred functioning of, 226–227

  and Court of the Thousand Columns, 278, 279, 296, 297
  ethnohistoric use of plazas as court settings, 277–278, 277(fig.)
  and hieroglyphic inscriptions and "house society" theory, 292–294, 293fig.)
  and house "dedication" texts, 292–294, 293(fig.)
  and joint rule, 273
  locations of chacmools and benches and thrones, 277–278, 277(fig.)
  and military iconography, 296
  and ritual dancing, 213
  and rule of Three Brothers, 250, 273
  serpent temple of, 280
  and similarities to Mayapan and Uxmal, 284
Chicxulub, 225, 249, 375
  and triadic design, 255, 257
Chilam Balam of Tizimin, 268, 270, 271
  and *mul tepal*, 273
  and references to slavery, 387(n23)
Chinamit, 319–320, 321, 323, 326
Chontals, 374
Chronicle of Calkini, 268, 271, 272, 280, 294, 305(n19)
  and bilateral names, 290
  and Canul origin in West Zuyua, 372
  and court architecture, 275
  and term *ch'ibal*, 288, 290
  and use of *naal* matronym, 291
Chronicle of Chacxulub Chen, 268, 271
  and term *ch'ibal*, 288–289
Chumayel, 268, 273, 387(n23)
Cigars, 215
Clark, John E., 1–45, 239, 242
  and dating of architecture, 32–33
  and "E-Group" and MFC pattern, 23
  and La Venta as a Zogue city, 3
  and Mayan king's connections to western frontier, 35
Classic period (A.D. 250–900)
  and Calakmul, 230–234
  Maya palace of, 103
  and royal court at Caracol, 103
  royal court during, 46–47
  See also Early Classic period; Late Classic period; Terminal Classic
Coba, continuation of sacred functioning of, 227
Cocom, Nachi, 273, 347
Cocom dynastic family, 273, 274, 286
  and *palacio* of Sotuta, 341, 342(fig.)
Cogolludo, López de, 268, 273–274

Colonial
  dictionaries as source of data, 319
  histories as source of data, 308–309
Cook, Garrett, 320
Copan Acropolis Archaeological Project, 47, 54–55, 73(n2)
Copan and its royal court, 46–69
  and architecture and politics, 66–68
  architecture of the Early Classic court at, 53–55
  and carved monuments, 50, 73(n2)
  and Cult of the Founder, 68
  and ECAP plan of initial masonry palace structures, 63(fig.), 64
  and ECAP plan of masonry palace groups, 64, 65(fig.)
  and ECAP plan of Witik Platform and contemporary structures, 59(fig.), 60
  and ECAP plan of Yule Platform and contemporary structures, 55, 56(fig.)
  excavation of, 235
  and Hieroglyphic Stairway, 341–342
  and Hunal, 55–56, 58
  and information from inscriptions, 49–51, 68
  plan of Main Group at site of, 54, 54(fig.)
  representations of the court of, 51–53
  royal compound of K'inich Yax K'uk' Mo', 55–58
  royal household of K'inich Yax K'uk' Mo', 58–62
  and Str. 10L–18! funerary complex, 153, 154(fig.)
  and thrones decorated with sky-band, 78–79, 100
  and ties with Peten, 58
  and Yehnal, 60
Copan Archaeological Project (PAC), 54
Copan Mosaics Project, 73(n3)
Cortés, Hernán, 308, 311, 385(n11)
Cotaguana, Honduras, 245
Cotecpan, 305(n16)
Coto, Thomás de, 312, 320
  and dictionary term for slave, 309–310
Council houses (nimja), 317–318, 319, 321, 323
Couoh, Nachan, 337–338
Court of the Thousand Columns, Chichen, 278, 279, 296, 297
Courts. See Royal court
Cozumel oracle, 255
Cuchcabal, 269, 303(nn 3, 4)
Cuchteel, 269

Cu-Ix, 51, 64, 69
Cuzco, royal court of, 76

Dancers and dancing, 158–159
  ritual of and Bonampak murals, 213–214, 220
Demarest, Arthur, 78, 159, 229
Denison, J.H., 230
Dental inlays, 15
De Palacio,, 311
Dietary analysis of Caracol residents, 127, 128–130, 129(fig.), 131(fig.)
Diffusion or borrowing and Pre-Classic Maya, 32–35
Domínguez Carrasco, Ma. del Rosario, 238, 256
Dos Pilas, 159
Dressing, ritual of, 211–213, 212(fig.)
Dumond, Don, 246, 250
Dunbarton Oaks symposium, 165
Dunning, Nicholas, 280, 281
Dynastic origin mythology, 370–375, 389(n38)
Dzibilchaltun, Yucatan, 225, 239, 280

Early Classic period
  architectural innovations of Late, 149, 149fig.)
  architectural of nobles and royalty during, 140
  building explosion in, 144
  and complex symbolism in Calakmul, 223–224
  court politics of, 66–68, 69
  and fixed thrones, 140
  and materials used for thrones, 80, 81, 83
  palaces of, 143–149
  and representational art, 52–53
  and royal compound of K'inich Yax K'uk' Mo', 55
Early Copan Acropolis Program (ECAP), 54–55
  and plan of initial masonry palace structures, 63(fig.), 64
  and plan of masonry palace groups, 64, 65(fig.)
  and plan of Witik Platform and contemporary structures, 59(fig.), 60
  and plan of Yune Platform and contemporary structures, 55, 56(fig.)
Early Copan Acropolis Program, 47
Edmonson, Munro,, 270
"E-Group" architectural arrangement, 4, 12, 16, 32, 43(n6), 43–44(n7)
  and MFC pattern, 18–19

and Nakbe, Wakna, and El Mirador, 16
  origin of, 43(n5)
  at Pre-Classic Calakmul, 230
  and stereotypic arrangement of royal
    compounds, 17
  and Tikal, 19, 20, 21
  and Uaxactun, 21, 22, 23, 24, 44(n7)
Ek Balam
  distribution of temple assemblages and
    plazas, 279–280, 279(fig.), 286
  founding of, 305(n22)
  and independent quadrangle, 297
  and military iconography, 296
  and palaces, 295
  and segmentary organization, 284
El Laberinto Bajo, 245
El Mirador, 3, 16, 26, 257
  and activities of royal courts, 17–18
  and competition for prominence, 139
  and shifts in courtly life during Late Pre-
    Classic, 34–35
Entertainment, 158–160
Environment, outstripping of by Mayans,
  207–208
Epigraphy
  and Buenavista and Cahal Pech, 176
  and Caracol's royal court, 124
  and definition of *mul tepal*, 275
  and royal palaces of Caracol, 106
  of thrones, 79
Escobedo, Héctor, 229
Ethnohistory
  and approaches to social and political
    structure of Mayan highlands of Post-
    Classic period, 318–321, 326–328
  and ethnology of Calakmul, 244–253
  and use of plazas of Chichen Itza as
    court settings, 277–278, 277(fig.)
  and Yucatec Maya royal courts, 335–390

Farfán, Juan, 158–159
Farriss, Nancy, 268, 306(n31)
Fash, William, 47, 67
Fialko, Vilma, 43(n7), 229
Figurines, 239, 245–246, 247(fig.), 248(fig.)
Flannery, Kent, 13, 227, 234
Fletcher, Larraine, 227
Folan, William, 223–265
  and Dzibilchaltun, 255
Fox, John, 245, 316, 320, 326
Freidel, David, 291, 292
Fuentes y Guzmán, Francico Antonio de, 311

Gallegos Gómara, Miriam Judith, 256
Gann, James, 227

Glyphic texts. *See* Hieroglyphic inscriptions
Goldkind, Victor, 319
Goody, Jack, 288, 291
Great Jaguar Claw (Toh Chak Ich'ak), 87,
  88(fig.), 146–147
Grove, David, 7
Grube, Nikolai, 275, 292, 294
Guatemala
  Post-Classic Maya courts of highlands
    of, 308–344
  and trade with La Libertad, 11
  and trade with Nakbe, 15
Guillemín, Jorge, 315, 326
Gunn, Joel, 223–229
  and study of Calakmul drought of 800s,
    228, 229
Guzmán, Ruíz, 225, 245

Hall, Jay, 67
Hansen, Richard D., 1–45
  and autochthonous origin of kings in
    Mirador basin, 35
  and Olmec or Zoque influence on Maya,
    33
Harrison, Peter D., 74–100, 103, 109, 146
Hasaw Chan K'awil, 81, 85, 89, 96
  depictions of, 91, 93
  residence of, 90, 95
  thrones of, 92
Hauck, F.R., 227
Haviland, William, 236, 237, 246
Hayden, Brian, 254
Helms, Mary, 374
Henige, David, 373–374
Heredity status. *See* Lineages, noble
Hero Twins, 215
Herrera,, 273, 274
Hieroglyphic inscriptions
  at Caracol, 125–126, 125(fig.)
  at Copan, 49–51, 68
  from Guatemalan highlands, 311
  and house society concept, 292–294,
    293(fig.)
  from Late Classic period in Guatemalan
    highlands, 334(n3)
  and texts, 341–344
Highlands Maya, Late Post-Classic royal
  courts of, 308–334
  and *ajawa'* or noble class, 311–312
  and archaeological research, 313–318
  and architectonic complexes as key to
    political and social organization,
    316–317, 326
  and *chinamit* and other units of social
    integration, 319–321, 323, 326, 328

as conglomerations of great houses, 324
and ethnohistorical approach to social and political structure, 318–321, 326–328
and function of buildings posited from form, 325
and kings not necessarily absolute monarch, 312
and slaves, 309–310
sources of information for ethnohistorians of, 318
and vassals, 309, 310
Hill, Robert, 290, 312
and archaeology in Guatemalan Highlands, 314
and *chinamit*, 319, 320
and long structures and *chinamit*, 317
Historia Quiché de don Juan de Torres, 311
Hodell, David, 229
Holpop, 271, 272
Household, royal, 47–48
House society, 287, 290–296
and archaeological evidence, 294–296
and *chinamit* as kin group, 319–320, 327
glyphic evidence relative to, 292–294, 293(fig.)
linguistic evidence relative to, 291–292
medieval European, 291
versus lineage organization, 297–298
Houston, Stephen, 74, 79, 307(n39)
and royal personal presence and political stability, 169, 196(n2)
Huamango, 239
Hugh-Jones, Stephen, 287, 297
Human skeletal remains and Calakmul, 240, 241(fig.)
Hunab Ku, 342
Hunal, 55–56, 58–59, 62

Iconography
and conception of court as houses, 294–296
military, 296
of peasant agriculture, 203
and royal court at Caracol, 126–128, 127(fig.), 128(fig.)
and royal installation, 210
of rulership at Palenque, 202–203
Indio hidalgo (Indian nobleman), 353, 386(n21)
Inomata, Takeshi, 74, 287
Inscriptions. *See* Hieroglyphic inscriptions
Instituto Nacional de Estadistic Geografía e Informatica (INEGI), 340

Itza and elite origin mythology, 374, 389–390(n40)
Itzam Balam, 220
Ixil and case study of social differentiation in, 353
Iximche', 315, 322, 326
Izamal, 274
Izapa, world-tree stela from, 339

Jade, 219
Jaguar Paw, 232
Jayavarman VII, 169
Jones, Grant, 268, 305(n18)
Jones, Lindsay, 389(n38)

Kaminaljuyu
and architectural comparison with Copan, 58
earliest thrones at, 153
K'an II, 113
Kaqchikel, 308
and ambassadors, 311
burial patterns of, 317
and conflict with Tuquche', 312, 320, 321
and priests of, 312
and "radial pyramid-temple complex," 318
rulership of, 315
and titles for nobles, 311
See also Highlands Maya, Late Post-Classic royal courts of
Kelley, David, 292
Kerr, Justin, 77, 85, 86
K'iche'
and the *amaq'*, 320–321, 326
and architectonic patterns and political and ideological geography, 316–317, 326
as a segmentary society, 321–322, 327
and burial patterns, 317
and *chinamit*, 319–320, 321, 323, 326, 328
and emergence of kingdoms through emulation or autochthonous development, 325
and factional competition, 319, 327
and formation of semistates, 324–325
and house society model, 319–320, 324, 327
and kingdoms, 334(n1)
and organization as one or more states, 322–323
palaces of, 324
political organization of, 321–325, 327–328

Index 403

and "radial pyramid-temple complex," 318
and religious hierarchy, 312
rulership of, 312–313
social structure of, 319–321, 326–327
and titles, 311
See also Highlands Maya, Late Post-Classic royal courts of
Kings
as a cultural borrowing by the Maya, 33, 34, 35–36
as a Divine figure, 142, 313
and the court, 168, 266
as highest lords of *ajawa* class, 312
as mediators between heavens and earth, 31
not necessarily absolute monarchs, 312
and palaces as exclusive "sacred residences" during Late Pre-Classic, 142
political system strengthened and centralized under, 138
as priest-kings, 30
rulership of K'iche'an, 322
status of after fifteenth century, 384(n2)
and visits to other cities, 161
K'inich Kan K'awil, 159
K'inich Popol, 69
K'inich Yax K'uk' Mo, 49–50, 52, 53
architectural group associated with, 53
architectural program of and politics, 66–67, 68–69
burial chamber of, 57, 58
court of, 60–62
injuries indicated from physical remains of, 58–60
royal compound of, 55–58
royal household of, 58–60
Kom, Chan, 319
Kowalski, Jeff, 283
Krochock, Ruth, 292
K'uk' Mo, 149
Kuri, Rosas, 245
Kurjack, Edward, 280, 295

Labna, 281, 283, 283(fig.), 295, 296, 307(41)
Lacandon, 239, 242, 245
Laguna Chichancanab, 229
Lake Peten Itza, 268
La Libertad, 3, 11–12, 11(fig.), 14, 24, 31
Lamanai, 139
Landa, Diego de, 31, 255, 268, 273
and activities of sixteenth-century Mayans, 225
and burning of hieroglyphic books, 343
and draughts and famine, 245
and dynastic origin mythology, 370
and heaven under ceiba tree, 339
and inquisition of "idolatrous" practices, 368
and lineage, 287
and Mayapan, 274, 284, 286
and presentation of theater pieces, 158
and ritual of dancing, 213
Laporte, Juan Pedro, 81
Las Casas, Bartolomé de, 311, 312, 322
Late Classic period (A.D. 650–900), 77
architectural developments in, 140
and Barrio palace, 122
and Bonampak murals, 51
and break with Terminal Classic period, 244–245
and Buenavista-Cahal relationship, 185
and Calakmul, 234
and distribution of thrones, 153–154
and fixed thrones, 140
and materials used for thrones, 80–81, 83
and palace function and court life, 166
palaces of, 150–153
and palace use in Caracol, 106, 134
and royal court at Caracol, 103
Late-Post Classic period, political structure of, 268–271
Late Pre-Classic period
and architectural advances during, 140–142, 160
and palaces with vaulted edifices, 142–143
and vaulted structures, 140–142
Later Pre-Classic and Protoclassic architectural patterns (600 B.C.-A.D. 100), 15–30
and beginning of vaulted multiroomed structures, 139
and Calakmul, 229–230
Chiapa de Corzo, 24–30
Nakbe, 15–19
Tikal, 19–21
Uaxactun, 21–24
See also Middle Pre-Classic royal compounds
La Venta, 3–5, 4(fig.), 13, 24, 33, 42(n2)
acropolis at, 14
and Chiapa de Corzo, 6, 7, 8, 14–15
and Clark's bias for early dating of, 41–42(n1)
and Middle Formative Chiapas pattern, 42–43(n3)

Lehmann, Henri, 314–315
LePlongeon, 278
Lévi-Strauss, Claude and house society, 287, 290, 298
Limestone and limestone plaster, 13, 140
Limestone scale architectural model, 139, 139(fig. 139)
Lineages, noble, 287–290, 297–298
  and archaeological evidence relative to house society concept, 294–296
  and bilateral or ambilateral descent, 290
  as fundamental element of Maya society, 350
  and glyphic text evidence relative to house society concept, 292–294, 293(fig.)
  Goody's weaker interpretation of, 288
  and hereditary status, 364–370
  and K'iche' society, 327
  and linguistic evidence relative to house society concept, 291–292
  and Polynesia, 327
  and Roys, 287–288, 289–290, 306(n31)
  and scarcity of marriages between individuals of the same patronym, 307(n36)
  and term *tzucub*, 270, 287
  See also "House Society"
Lithics, 236, 252, 254
Long-Lipped Jawbone, 246
Longyear, John, 54
López, Morales, 230
Louis XIV of France, 76
Lowe, Gareth, 12, 27–28, 44–45(n8)
Lundell Palace, 233–234, 233(fig.)

Magaloni, Diana, 219
Maize God, 203
  and Bonampak murals, 215, 221
Maler, Teobert, 82
  See also Palace of the Great Stone Benches
Mam, 318
Mani Maps, 347, 348(fig.), 349
Manos, 243, 243(fig.), 244
Marcus, Joyce, 13, 227, 234, 246, 321, 324–325
Masks, 286
Masonry specialists and Nakbe, 16
Mathews, Peter, 278
Maya, Northern, and Late Post-Classic
  political structure of, 268–271, 296–297
  major primary sources of, 268
  and *mul tepal*, 273–275

  and segmentary political or social organization, 280–281
  studies of, 268
  and types of courts, 271–273
Maya lowlands, palaces and thrones tied to royal courts of, 138–161
"Maya Origin Myth References in the Ethnohistorical Sources," 371(table)
Mayapan, 318
  and Basic Ceremonial Group (BCG), 284–286, 285(fig.)
  collapse of, 268
  and issue of *mul tepal*, 273–274
  physical description of in primary text materials, 276–277
  plan of main group of ruins, 285(fig.)
  and rivalry of dynasties, 349–350
  and segmentary organization, 284
  and Serpent Temple Group (STG), 284–286, 285(fig.)
  and similarities to Uxmal and Chichen Itza, 284
  and Temple Assemblage (TA), 284–285, 285(fig.)
  temple assemblages at, 280
Maya Vase Book (Kerr), 77, 85, 86
Medel, López, 317
Merida
  built over Tiho's center, 342–343
  plaza at, 345
  Spanish founding of, 338
Mesoamerican peoples and invoking of past to affirm authority, 203
Metates, 243, 243(fig.)
Mexico
  and influence at Post-Classic Guatemalan sites, 314
  and war for independence by Maya polity, 246
MFC pattern. *See* Middle Formative Chiapas (MFC) architectural pattern
Middle Formative Chiapas (MFC) architectural pattern, 4, 14, 33
  definition of, 42–43(n3)
  and E-Group, 17–18
  and La Libertad, 11–12
  and Nakbe, 18
  and royal compound as centralizing institution, 30
Middle Pre-Classic royal compounds, early (850–600 B.C.), 3–15
  and Calakmul, 229–230
  Chiapa de Corzo, 6–8
  La Libertad, 11–12
  La Venta, 3–5

map of centers and sites, 2(fig.)
Mirador, 9–11
Monte Alban, 12–14
San José Mogote, 12–14
See also Later Pre-Classic and Protoclassic architectural patterns; Middle Formative Chiapas (MFC) architectural pattern
Military service, 310
Miller, Donald, 12
Miller, Mary, 51, 52, 201–222
Mirador Basin, 1, 3, 13, 33
and Mirador, 9–11, 9(fig.)
and Nakbe, 15
origins of original kings of, 35
and Tikal, 19
Moctezumas, 372
Moholy-Nagy, Hattula, 235, 236, 246, 254
Monaghan, John, 290
Monjas, Las, Uxmal, 278, 281, 283, 283(fig.), 284, 292, 294, 297
and glyphic texts, 292, 293(fig.)
Monte Alban, 12–14
Mopan-Macal drainage zone, 171(fig.), 189(fig.)
See also Buenavista-Cahal Pech royal court
Moseley, Michael, 106
Motmot Marker, 50, 50(fig.)
Mul tepal, 273–275, 305(n18), 364, 387(n25)
Murals, Bonampak. *See* Bonampak murals
Music, 213–215, 214(fig.), 220, 310
Musical instruments, 245, 246, 247(fig.), 248(fig.)

Nahua
titles borrowed from, 325, 334(n6)
and visit to Calkini court with Spanish in 1541, 335–336, 383–384(n1)
and Zuyua, 372
Nakbe, 14, 15–19, 16(fig.), 35, 240
and competition for prominence, 138
dating of in comparison with La Venta, 41–42(n1)
and east-west site arrangement, 18
E-group at, 44(n7), 45(n9)
and formalized architectural programs, 33
possible royal compound, 17(fig.)
and radiocarbon dating, 43(n4)
Nance, Roger, 315, 326
Navarrete, Carlos, 315
Nimja (council house), 317–318, 319, 321, 323
9.0.0.0.0, 49–50, 66

Noh Cah Santa Cruz Maya, 225, 246–251
and Balam Na temple, 247, 248–249
continued functioning of court and plaza of, 227
map of, 249(fig.)
and retaining of pre-Hispanic Mayan elements, 248–251
and similarity to Calakmul, 247–253, 256
and Talking Cross, 247, 248, 250, 257
and *tatich* (head priest), 249, 250
and triadic design, 257
Notaries, 343, 344(fig.)

Oaxaca, 1, 12–13
"Officers of the Court, The: Political Offices in Yucatan, circa 2400–1800," 360(table), 361
Okoshi Harada, Tsubasa, 268, 272, 280, 306(n30)
and definition of political structure, 269, 270, 303–304(n7)
Olmec
influence and Chiapa de Corzo, 7, 24
and influence on Middle Pre-Classic Maya, 1, 3, 33, 34, 35–36
and MFC siteplans and royal compounds, 33
Oratory, 271, 276–277
Otzmal, massacre at, 367, 367(fig.), 388(n26)
Oval Tablet depiction of throne, 154, 201, 202
Oxpemul, 227
Ox-té-tun symbolism, 223, 254, 256

Pakal, 154
Palace of the Great Stone Benches, 82–83, 98, 98(fig.), 99(fig.)
Palaces, 48–49, 75, 103
administrative, 150–151
appearance and elaboration during Late Classic period, 295
and Buenavista and Cahal Pech, 175–176
in Calakmul, 226, 251
in Central Acropolis of Tikal, 86
compounds of at Caracol, 106–124
and consolidation of power, 295
and Copan Acropolis masonry structures, 63–64
definition of, 103, 165, 168
during the Late Pre-Classic period, 142–143
of Early Classic Period, 143–149
K'iche'an, 324
of Late Classic period, 150–153
Lundell, 233–234, 233(fig.)

and Maya courts as based in, 102–103
and necessity of multiple for mobile courts, 170
Palenque, 202–204, 202(fig.)
at Puuc, Yucatan, 281–283
as "sacred residences," 142
"scenic" or "presentation," 151–152, 159
variation amongst Classic, 165
of *xanil nah* type, 146–147
See also Caracol royal court, palaces of
Palanquins, 84–85, 115, 126
Palenque, 79, 80
 and architecture of Cross Group, 224, 229
 and Caracol, 108
 and Cross-like world tree, 257, 339
 and House E of palace, 202, 202(fig.)
 and non-patrilineal inheritance, 291
 and Oval Tablet depiction of throne, 154, 201, 202
 palace of, 202–204, 202(fig.)
Papagayo, 50–51, 64
Parasols, 215
Patio. *See* Plazas and patios
Paxbolon, Pablo, 345, 370, 376, 387(n24)
Paxbolon papers, 268, 305(n19)
Peabody Museum and Copan, 53
Pech, Ah Kom, 289, 304(n13)
Pech, Ah Macan, 271–272, 289, 304, 304(n13)
Pech, Franciso de Montejo (Ah Naum), 368–369
Pech, Nakuk, 271–272, 304(n13)
Pech family
 and alliance with Spanish Colonial authority, 370
 and dynastic origin myths, 373
 as dynastic rulers in late Colonial Ixil, 353
 genealogy, 271–272, 272(fig.), 289
Pech titles, 338
Peten, 1
 and *multepal*, 364
 and Nakbe, 15
 and reminiscences of old power system in Post-Classic period, 161
 and ties with Copan, 58
 and Tikal, 19
Peter the Great, 190–191, 198(n9)
Petexbatun region, rapid abandonment of, 229
Petexbatun Regional Archaeological Project, 150
Petitions, 343–344
Philip II of Spain, 192, 198(n9)
Piedras Negras
 and availability of stone for thrones, 80

and dancing, 213
and developments in Late Classic period, 150
and panel portraying summit meeting, 347
and thrones, 79, 159–160, 201
Piercing, 220–221
Piña Chan, Román, 257
Plazas and patios, 225, 281
 archaeological attention to, 276
 as a ritual space, 344–347
 as field about which buildings were built, 278–279
 and patio as space or place, 341, 342(fig.), 345
 and quadrangles, 281, 283–284, 297, 298
 and summit meetings, 345–347, 346(table)
 and targeting for future study, 298
 use of as court settings, 277–278, 277(fig.)
 and variation in access, 297
 and Verapaz plazas, 317–318, 326
Political structure of Late-Classic period, 268–271
 batabil, 269
 cuchcabal, 269, 303(nn 3, 4)
 cuchteel, 269
 governing units, 268–270
 officials of, 270–271
 provincia, 268–270, 296
 tzucub, 269–270
Ponoma, 204
Popol Wuj, 309, 318, 320, 324
Poqomchi, 318
Post-Classic and Terminal Classic courts of the Northern Maya Lowlands, 266–307
Post-Classic period, 161
 and archaeology at sites in Guatemalan highlands, 313–318
 palaces of, 103
Pre-Classic Maya. *See* Later Pre-Classic; Middle Pre-Classic
Proskuriokoff, Tatiana, 229, 276, 280, 284
Provincia, 268–270, 296, 349
Proyecto Arqueológico del Àrea Kaqchikel excavations, 314
Puuc, Yucatan
 and quadrangles, 283, 283(fig.)
 and segmentary organization of site plans, 280–281, 281(fig.)

Q'eq'chi', 318
Quadrangles, 281, 283–284, 283(fig.), 297, 298
 See also Plazas and patios

Index 407

Quetzalcotal, shrine centers of cult of, 284
Quetzal feathers, 219
Quezada, Sergio, 268, 271
    and definitions of governing units,
        269–270
    and term *tzucub*, 270, 287, 303(n6)
Quiché Project of State University of New
        York-Albany, 315–316
Quijada, Diego, 367–368
Quintana Roo, 229
    as continuing Maya state until 1974, 227,
        246
    See also Noh Cah Santa Cruz
Quirigua, 48, 49
Q'umarkaj, 315–316, 322
    as a cosmogram, 316–317
    and architectonic patterns and political
        and ideological geography, 316–317,
        326

Rabinal Achi', 318
Radiocarbon dating, 41–42(n1), 43(n4), 59,
        60
    and isotope analysis of diet, 128–130,
        129(fig.), 131(fig.)
Real, Ciudad, 268, 274
Reception
    scene from burial 116 (Hasaw Chan
        K'awil), 81, 82(fig.)
    of tribute goods (vessel painting), 77,
        78(fig.)
Reed, David, 315
Reents-Budet, Dorie, 240
Reilly, F. Kent, 5
Relaciones as source of data, 308–309
Relaciones de Cansahcab, 274
Relaciones de Yucatán, 268, 271, 273
Relaciones Históico-Geográficas (Farfan),
        158–159
Relación of Ek Balam, 305(n22)
Religion. *See* Ritual and ceremonial
    functions
Religious buildings and question of
    domestic residence in, 225–226
Religious hierarchy of K'iche', 312
Representations of the court of Copan,
    51–53
Residential court compounds, 1, 2, 48
    at Buenavista and Cahal Pech, 175–176
    and Caana palace in Caracol, 110–116
    in Central Acropolis at Tikal and
        distribution of benches, 86–89, 95
    during the Late Pre-Classic period,
        142–143
    early Middle Pre-Classic, 3–15

and Nakbe, 16–17
and origins of Mayan kingship, 35–36
and ready access to sacred space, 14–15
and royal compound of K'inich Yax
    K'uk' Mo', 55–58
and royal palace, 48–49
and Ruler 2 of Copan, 62–64, 68
and serving God and mammon, 30–32
spatial dimension of, 30–32
and tandem-traverse room pattern, 89
and transition to palaces, 25–26
See also Middle Pre-Classic Royal
    Compounds; Palaces
Restall, Matthew, 268, 306(n31), 335–390
Ricketson, Oliver G., 21, 44(n7)
Ringle, William, 266–307
Ri Rusamäj Jilotepeke survey and excavation
    project, 314
Ritual and ceremonial functions
    and cigars, 215
    and dancing, 213–214
    and dressing, 211–213, 212(fig.)
    and involvement of those living in
        acropolis in, 14–15
    and kings as priest-kings, 30
    at La Venta, 5
    monopolized by Spanish priests after
        Conquest, 376
    and music, 213–215, 214(fig.), 220
    relating to trajectory of the sun and the
        king, 142, 146
    sacrificial, 312
    and singing, 215
    standardization of, 210
    and use of plaza and patio, 344–347
    and use of small figurines, 245–246
Robinson, Eugenia, 334(n5)
Rosario, María Del, 223–265
Royal court, 224, 266–268
    and architecture of Northern Maya
        lowlands, 275–287
    of Calakmul, 223–257
    of Caracol and its palaces and people,
        102–134
    and characteristics of dynastic status,
        358
    and cross-cultural mobility, 166, 167,
        169–170
    and distinction between "holding court"
        and conducting business, 166
    ethnohistorical evidence of Yucatec,
        335–390
    functions of, 77, 168
    inferring of past activities of, 17–18
    influence of, 48

of Kaqchikel and K'iche', 311
of K'inich Yax K'uk' Mo', 60–62
and Maya highlands of Late Post-
   Classic, 309–334
and mobility and usage in Buenavista-
   Cahal Pech, 166–193
and mythology of origin, 37–75, 358,
   389(n38)
not confined by architecture, 267
and oligarchical political monopoly in
   Yucatan, 359–364
as palace-based, 102–103
and pomp and festivities, 267
Post-Classic and Terminal Classic of the
   Northern Maya lowlands, 266–307
and royal household, 47–49
of Ruler 2 at Copan, 65–66
size of, 47, 364
and social differentiation in Yucatan,
   353–358
and Temple Assemblage, 279–280,
   279(fig.), 284–285, 285(fig.), 296
throne and throne structures in Central
   Acropolis of Tikal as an expression of,
   74–101
types of, 271–275
Roys, Ralph, 268, 275, 387(n23)
   interpretive problems presented in
      documentation amassed by, 273
   and Late-Classic political structure,
      268–271
   and Mayan lineages, 287–288, 289–290,
      306(n31)
   and Mayapan, 276, 286
Ruler 2 of Copan, 50–51, 57, 62
   architecture of and politics, 67–68, 69
   court architecture of, 62–64
   court of, 65–66
   and Xukpi stone, 60
Ruppert, Karl, 208, 230
Ruz, Mario Humberto, 158

Sacbeob (causeways), 280
Sahagún, Bernardino de, 158, 287
Sanders, William, 54, 234
San José Mogote, 12–14, 16, 22
San Lorenzo, 1, 5, 13
Sayil, 234, 281, 283, 295
Schele, Linda, 52, 278, 291, 292
Schmidt, Peter, 180
Scholes, France, 268
Sculpture
   and chacmools, 278
   Man of Tikal, 149
   of sovereign found at Uaxactun, 143

and tradition of Yaxchilan, 211
and unification with architecture and
   painting, 140
Sedat, David, 55, 56
Sellato, 298
Service, Elman, 327
SGmoa, 327
Sharer, Robert, 47, 58, 66
Shrines, raised, 276–277
Singing, 215
   See also Music
Slaves, 309–310, 359, 361, 387(nn 23, 24)
Smith, Ledyard, 148
Smoke Monkey, 52
Society for American Archaeology, 165
Solstice
   architecture incorporating viewing of,
      190, 199–200, 230
   and architecture of Q'umarkaj, 316–317
"Some Examples of Maya Courtly Retinue,
   circa 1440–1700," 361, 362–363(table),
   364
Sotuta palacio, 341, 342(fig.)
Southall, Aiden, 321
Spanish
   documents and interpretations of Post-
      Classic highland Maya courts, 318
   domination of indigenous peoples, 308
Stela 63, 50–51
Stephens, John, 278
Stone, Andrea, 203
Stone roofs, 140–141
Strömsvik, Gustav, 53
Stuart, David, 53, 307(n39)
Summit meetings, 345–347, 346(table)
Sundial concept, 230

Talking Cross (Noh Cah Santa Cruz), 247,
   248, 250, 255
Tamarindito, 150–151, 152
   and vase depicting royal court, 153(fig.)
Tancab, 275–276
Taschek, Jennifer, 165–200
Tatich (head priest), 249, 250
Taylor, Walter, 257
Te:m, 79
Tedlock, Dennis, 321
Temple Assemblage, 279–280, 279(fig.),
   284–285, 285(fig.), 296
Temple of Tojil, 316
Teopantecuanitlan, 13
Teotihuacan, 90
Terminal Classic period, 113, 244–245
   and Barrio palace, 122
   burials of, 123

and Cahal Pech and Buenavista, 166, 185
in Calakmul, 244–245, 257
and Calakmul Structure II, 232–233
and functioning society at Calakmul, 235
and use of Classic molds in ceramics, 245
Texts, 341–344
books, 311
burning of by Landa, 343
and extirpation campaigns of Spanish, 343
and notaries, 343, 344(fig.)
and petitions, 343–344
Thrones and throne structures
and benches during Late Classic period, 150
discovered at Aguateca, 156–158, 157(fig.), 158(fig.)
fixed stone, 140
function and significance of, 153–161
and jaguar throne at Chichen, 277–278
made of wood, 154
and murals at Bonampak, 201
Oval Tablet depiction of, 154, 201, 202
at Piedras Negras, 159–160, 201
at Tikal, 74–101, 148
and benches in lowlands compared to Tikal, 77–79
and decorations accompanying, 78(fig.), 81, 82(fig.), 83–85, 83(fig.), 84(fig.), 86, 87(fig.)
depictions of on painted vessels, 77, 85, 86
and distribution of benches in residential structures in Central Acropolis, 86–89
epigraphy of, 79
and Lost World Group throne, 154–156, 155(fig.), 156(fig.)
material for making of and time variables, 80–81
materials for, 83
painted scene on vessel showing presentation of jaguar skin, 78(fig.), 81, 86
portable, 00, 83–85, 83(fig.), 84(fig.), 100
and reception scene illustrating throne type, 81, 82(fig.)
and separate throne structures, 89–97
and sources of knowledge for decoration, 81–83
and throne rooms in buildings, 97–100
throne structure 5D-59, 89–92, 90(fig.), 91(fig.), 100

throne structure 5D-61 addition, 96–97, 96(fig.)
throne structure 5D-118, 90(fig.), 94–96, 94(fig.)
throne structure 5D-123, 90(fig.), 92–94, 93(fig.)
at Uaxactun, first known stone, 147–148
at Uxmal placed in plaza, 278
and variability of benches at Caracol, 108–110
and wedge-legged throne of Usumacinta, 208
in Yucatan, 385(n12)
Ticul, 246
Tiesler, Vera, 240
Tikal, 19–21, 33, 257
and architectural inventions during Early Classic period, 144
architectural style of and Copan, 58
and *Ballcourt Marker of Tikal*, 149
and Caracol, 108, 109
and ceramics, 19, 20
and competition for prominence, 138
detail of ceremonial center of, 75, 76(fig.)
early "E-group" at, 20(fig.)
as example of Late Classic architectural transformation, 140
and Gran Plaza, 254
and interruption of patrilineal succession, 291
and limestone scale model discovered in, 139, 139(fig.)
and limestone use during Late Pre-Classic, 140
Lost World complex at, 76, 139, 154–156
map of Central, 75(fig.)
and material for making thrones, 80–81, 83
and materials excavated at Calakmul, 235
and palace of Toh Chak Ich'ak, 146–147, 147(fig.), 148
royal court at, 47
and source materials available for making of thrones, 80–81
and throne found in Lost World Group, 154–156, 155(fig.)
and thrones and thrones structures in Central Acropolis, 74–101
and thrones of simplest styles, 78, 79
and Toh Chak Ich'ak (Great Jaguar Claw) and his palace, 87, 88(fig.), 146–147, 147(fig.)
See also Thrones and throne structures, at Tikal

Tintal, 139
Title of Acalan-Tixchel, 338, 387(n24)
Title of Calkini, 336, 338, 359, 366, 386(n15)
Title of Motul, 368–369
Tixchel, 345
Tlapacoya, 13
Toh Chak Ich'ak (Great Jaguar Claw), 87, 88(fig.), 146–147
Toltecs, 314, 389(n38)
Tonga, 327
Tool kits, 242–244, 243(fig.)
Topoxte and benches, 161
Tourtellot, Gair, 234, 246
Traxler, Loa P., 46–73
Trees, 339, 385(nn 9, 10)
 or branches and ancestors, 351, 352(fig.)
 and carved cross as prophetic of coming of Christianity, 339
 and ceiba tree at Calkini, 337, 339, 340(fig.), 344, 351
 as rulers, 339
 sacrifices made to, 351
 and tree-ruler image, 350–352, 352(fig.)
 and "tree stones," 350
 world, 257, 270, 339, 340(fig.)
Triadic
 character of Mayan culture, 229
 design, 254–255
 temple architecture, 17, 22, 34, 253, 254–255, 256–257
Tzucub, 269–270, 287
Tz'utujil, 313, 318

Uaxactun, 21–24, 23(fig.), 33, 255, 257
 and A–18 palace, 147–148, 148(fig.)
 and architectural inventions during first half of Early Classic period, 144
 and Caracol, 108
 and competition for prominence, 138
 "Dimensions of Palace H-Sub 2 of Uaxactun," 143(table)
 "Dimensions of Palace H-Sub 5," 144(table)
 "E-Group" at, 44(n7), 230
 and Late Pre-Classic Group H acropolis with vaulted edifices, 140–141, 141(fig.), 146, 149
 and multiple functions in single palaces in Early Classical period, 146
 murals of, and comparison with Bonampak, 209–210, 209(fig.)
 and new architecture of vaulted multiroomed structures, 139

 and royal palace of Sub–2C or beginning Early Classic period, 145–146, 145(fig.)
 and stone roofs, 140–141
 and triadic character of Mayan, 229
Usumacinta, 208
Uxmal
 and architectural evidence of political functioning, 284
 and conception of court as houses, 294, 295
 internal organization of, 281–283, 282(fig.)
 and Las Monjas, 278, 281, 283, 283(fig.), 284, 292, 293(fig.), 294, 297
 and military iconography, 296
 and similarities to Mayapan and Chichen Itza, 284
 temple assemblages at, 280
 and use of plazas as court settings, 277, 278
 and Uxmal jaguar thrones, 278
Uz, Fernando, 370

Valdes, Juan Antonio, 138–164
Vargas, Leticia, 295, 296
Vásquez, Barrera, 275
Vaulted architectural structures, 139, 140–142
Verapaz plazas, 317–318, 326
Viel, Rene, 67
Voorhies, Barbara, 240

Wakna, 16, 18, 138
Wallace, Dwight, 316, 326
Wauchope, Robert, 316
Way of the Masks, The (Lévi-Strauss), 290
Webster, David, 324
Wells, 339–340
Whittington, Stephen, 315
Women and Bonampak murals, 220–221
World tree. See Trees

Ximénez, Francisco, 316
Xiu, Ah Xupan, 274
Xiu, Francisco de Montejo (Ah Kumkum), 367
Xiu, Gaspar, 273, 274
Xiu, Juan, 351
Xiu, Tutul, 274, 351, 352(fig.)
Xiu dynastic family, 286, 303(n3), 365
 brief history of dynasty of, 366–370
 and family tree, 351, 352(fig.)

and lordship reverting to Yaxakumche *cah*, 368, 369(fig.)
and origin myths, 371–372
and origin of name "xiu," 373, 389(n36)
Xiu province, political organization of, 272, 303(n3)
Xuanantunich, 170, 172, 192, 200(nn 20, 21)
as "ancestor-mountain" of Mayan Moan-Macal triangle, 188, 196–197(n3), 199(n15)
Xukpi stone, 50, 60

Yax Ain II, 95, 147
Yaxchilan
and ritual of dancing, 213
royal family of, 210
Yax Pasah, 51, 52
Yazakumche, 368, 369(fig.)
Yehnal, 60, 62
Yik'in Chan K'awil, 80, 85, 92, 95
Yucatan Peninsula, as independent Maya state as late as first year of twentieth century, 246
"Yucatan's Ruling Dynasties at Time of the Spanish Conquest, circa 1520–70," 354–357(table)
Yucatec royal courts, 335–390
and *cabildo* adapted to continued Mayan self-rule, 361
and characteristics of dynastic status, 358
and conception of court as series of concentric places and spaces emanating from center, 336(fig.), 337, 338–350
and dynastic origin mythology, 358, 370–375, 389(n38)
and dynasties and other ruling families, 350, 365
and giving of power to Spanish by Late Colonial period, 376
and hereditary status, 364–370
and internalizing of outdoor spaces by Spanish, 375–376
and land summits, 347, 386(n16)
"Maya Origin Myth References in the Ethnohistorical Sources," 371, 371(table)
and multiple socioeconomic layers topped by dynastic elite, 353, 358
and municipal community or *cah*, 349–350
and numbers of individuals comprising courts, 364
"Officers of the Court, The: Political Offices in Yucatan, circa 1400–1800'", 360(table), 361
and oligarchical political monopoly, 359–364
and patios, 341
and plazas, 344–347
and pre-Conquest polities as loosely organized, 349
and retinues, 359
and Segmented Century, 338, 347, 349
and slaves, 359, 361, 387(nn 23, 24)
and social differentiation, 353–358
"Some Examples of Maya Courtly Retinues, circa 1440–1700," 361, 362–363(table), 364
and Spanish and Nahua visit to court of Calkini in 1541, 335–337, 383–384(n1)
and summit meetings, 345–347, 346(table)
and survival of Conquest by allowing partial colonization, 337, 375
and texts, 341–344, 386(n15)
and town and country, 347–350
and trees, 339, 350–352, 352(fig.)
and wells, 339–340
and Xiu family dynasty history, 366–370
"Yucatan's Ruling Dynasties at Time of the Spanish Conquest, circa 1520–70," 354–357(table)

Zapotec culture, 1, 13
Zoques
and Chiapa de Corzo, 25
and influence on Middle Pre-Classic Maya, 1, 3, 33, 35–36
and La Venta, 3
Zuyua
location of in central Mexico, 372, 388(n33)
as place of mythic origins, 371–372, 374, 388(n33)